FRONTIERS OF SOCIAL THEORY
The New Syntheses

FRONTIERS OF SOCIAL THEORY

The New Syntheses

❀

George Ritzer, Editor

COLUMBIA UNIVERSITY PRESS
New York

Columbia University Press
New York   Oxford
Copyright © 1990 Columbia University Press
All rights reserved

Library of Congress Cataloging-in-Publication Data

Frontiers of social theory : the new syntheses /
George Ritzer, editor.
p.   cm.
Includes bibliographical references.
Based on a conference held at the University of Maryland,
College Park, Md., March 11, 1988;
sponsored by the College of Behavioral and Social Sciences,
the Graduate School, and the Department of Sociology
at the University of Maryland.
ISBN 0-231-07078-0 (alk. paper)
1. Sociology—Methodology—Congresses.
2. Sociology—United States—Congresses.
I. Ritzer, George.   II. University of Maryland, College Park.
College of Behavioral and Social Sciences.
III. University of Maryland (System). Graduate School.
IV. University of Maryland, College Park. Dept. of Sociology.
HM13.F76   1990   301'.01—dc20   90-1407
                                        CIP

Casebound editions of Columbia University Press books are Smyth-sewn
and printed on permanent and durable acid-free paper

Printed in the United States of America

c 10 9 8 7 6 5 4 3 2 1

CONTENTS

Preface   vii

1. The Current Status of Sociological Theory:
   The New Syntheses   1
   GEORGE RITZER

PART I. NEW LIFE IN SOME TRADITIONAL SOCIAL
AND SOCIOLOGICAL THEORIES

2. Neofunctionalism Today: Reconstructing a
   Theoretical Tradition   33
   JEFFREY C. ALEXANDER AND PAUL COLOMY
3. Conflict Theory and the Advance of Macro-Historical
   Sociology   68
   RANDALL COLLINS
4. The Decline of the Grand Narrative of Emancipatory
   Modernity: Crisis or Renewal in Neo-Marxian Theory?   88
   ROBERT J. ANTONIO
5. Symbolic Interactionism in the Post-Blumerian Age   117
   GARY ALAN FINE
6. Exchange Theory: A Blueprint for Structure and Process   158
   KAREN S. COOK, JODI O'BRIEN, AND PETER KOLLOCK

PART II. LIVELINESS OF MORE RECENT SOCIAL
AND SOCIOLOGICAL THEORIES

7. The World as It Happens: Ethnomethodology and
   Conversation Analysis   185
   DEIRDRE BODEN

8. The Comparative Advantages of Rational Choice Theory   214
   DEBRA FRIEDMAN AND MICHAEL HECHTER
9. The Uses of French Structuralisms in Sociology   230
   CHARLES C. LEMERT
10. The Postmodern Turn: Positions, Problems, and Prospects 255
   DOUGLAS KELLNER
11. Betwixt and Between: Recent Cultural Sociology in Europe
   and the United States   287
   MICHELE LAMONT AND ROBERT WUTHNOW
12. Feminist Sociological Theory: The Near-Future Prospects   316
   PATRICIA M. LENGERMANN AND JILL NIEBRUGGE-BRANTLEY

PART III. OVERVIEWS OF SOCIAL AND SOCIOLOGICAL THEORY

13. Micro-Macro Linkage in Sociological Theory:
   Applying a Metatheoretical Tool   347
   GEORGE RITZER
14. The Past, Present, and Future of Theory in American
   Sociology   371
   JONATHAN TURNER
15. The History and Politics of Recent Sociological Theory   392
   NORBERT WILEY

Name Index   417
Subject Index   429

PREFACE

This book grew out of a conference titled "Sociological Theory: Current Status, Near-Term Prospects" that was held at the University of Maryland, College Park, Maryland on March 11, 1988. The conference was sponsored by the College of Behavioral and Social Sciences, the Graduate School, and the Department of Sociology at the University of Maryland. It was also supported by a Problems of the Discipline grant from the American Sociological Association. Among those who I would like to thank for their help in gaining the needed support are Murray Polakoff, Stuart Edelstein, Jacob Goldhaber, Bill Falk, and Bill D'Antonio.

The conference centered around ten presentations, nine of which have been transformed into papers included in this volume. The nine original presenters were Jeffrey Alexander, Robert Antonio, Karen Cook, Gary Fine, Charles Lemert, Patricia Lengermann and Jill Niebrugge-Brantley, George Ritzer, Jonathan Turner, and Norbert Wiley. In two cases (Alexander and Cook) co-authors have been added for the writing of the papers that appear here. In order to give a fuller representation to important developments in contemporary theory, several other people were invited to contribute papers to this volume. The additions include works by Deirdre Boden, Randall Collins, Debra Friedman and Michael Hechter, Michelle Lamont and Robert Wuthnow, Douglas Kellner, as well as my own substantive essay.

The idea behind the conference was to bring together the younger generation of leaders of social and sociological theory to assess theory's current status and short-term prospects. While the essays in this volume certainly do that, a central, but unanticipated, theme has emerged from them. Most of them in one way or another deal with a range of new synthesizing developments within social theory. There is clearly a move away from adherence to a given theory and a focus on a single level of social reality and toward synthesizing theories and analyzing the interrelations among various levels of analysis. To me, this is the dominant theme of the book and, I believe, the dominant theme of sociological theory as it moves into the 1990s.

I should say something about the use of "social" and "sociological" theory throughout this volume. While at one time there was a clear difference between more general (social) theory and theory (sociological) specific to the field, the line between the two types of theory has grown increasingly blurred in recent years. While this book focuses on sociological theory, many of the essays deal with or reflect the influence of an array of social theories (e.g., feminist theories, post-structuralism, post-modernism, cultural theory, etc.). Thus, social theory and sociological theory are used interchangeably throughout this book.

In addition to those mentioned above, I would like to thank Cass O'Toole, Debbi Griffith, Pam Gindoff, and especially Terri LeMoyne for their help in arranging the conference and, in the latter case, in editing this book as well. I would also like to thank Louise Waller at Columbia University Press for believing in this project and helping to bring it to fruition. Most of all I would like to thank my wife, Sue, for being who she is.

George Ritzer
January 1990

FRONTIERS OF SOCIAL THEORY
The New Syntheses

1

The Current Status of Sociological Theory: The New Syntheses

❁

GEORGE RITZER
University of Maryland

There is a powerful love-hate relationship between sociologists and their theories and theorists. On the one hand, national and international conferences such as the one on which this volume is based, as well as theory sessions at national and regional sociology meetings, are always extremely popular and well-attended. On the other hand, sociologists, especially sociological theorists, love to attack sociological theories. For example, in a recent essay in *Theory and Society* (no less!), Hirsch, Michaels, and Friedman (1987, 332) argue that "grand theorist" is a derisive term and the best works of grand theorists "provide fodder for graduate courses and other grand theorists, but in practice are ignored by most sociologists."

Along the same lines, I found particularly interesting Arthur Stinchcombe's (1986) attack on sociological theory in a talk given at the 1983 Thomas and Znaniecki Memorial Conference on Social Theory at the University of Chicago. Stinchcombe excoriated sociological theory for being divorced from the real world. In his usual clever way Stinchcombe (1986, 45–46) attacked theory by arguing that the "higher the prestige of a piece of sociological work, the fewer people in it are sweaty, laughing, ugly or pretty, dull at parties, or have warts on their noses . . . it is the theories that are most divorced from blood, sweat, and tears that have the highest prestige."

There are many problems in sociological theory, but there also is, as I think this volume will show, abundant vitality and promise for the future in sociological theory. I like the comments of Robert Merton (1986, 61), also at the Thomas and Znaniecki conference, since Merton, unlike some others, has achieved the status and maturity that allow

I would like to thank Ken Kammeyer and, especially, Bob Antonio for helpful comments on this chapter.

1

him to take a more generous, and in my opinion more accurate, view of sociological theory: "Pessimism results from the growing pains of a rapidly differentiating discipline in which the differentiation has multiplied so fast that we haven't the human resources to develop each sphere of inquiry in sufficient degree. The sociological enterprise requires a sense of tolerance rather than of battle, consolidating a mutual awareness of various theoretical orientations with a reasonable confidence that their mutual theoretical connections will be progressively defined." I think that Merton's confidence in the fact that we will see more theoretical synthesis is borne out in this volume.

In fact, the essays in this volume will demonstrate that the most widespread and important development in sociological theory as we enter the 1990s is the move away from theoretical dogmatism and in the direction of theoretical synthesis.[1] The old, reified labels that have dominated sociological theory for many decades ("structural functionalism," "symbolic interactionism") seem increasingly less meaningful and important. As a younger generation of sociological theorists takes center stage, older theoretical and conceptual (e.g., micro-macro) boundaries and divisions are breaking down and some younger theorists are even taking an active role in trying to shatter those borders. Contemporary supporters are much less interested in defending traditional interpretations of theories and far more interested in reaching out to other theoretical traditions in an effort to develop new, more synthetic theories. In addition, more recent theories are less likely to focus on a single level of social analysis and more apt to be interested in the interrelationship of multiple levels. While there is great interest in synthesis, there seems to be a recognition that earlier efforts to create a single, overarching synthetic theory were misguided. Several papers in this volume (Antonio, Kellner, Lemert) discuss intellectual developments (e.g., neo-Marxian theory, postmodernism, post-structuralism) that involve an attack on the idea of such a grand synthesis (grand or master narrative).[2] Rather, contemporary efforts at synthesis are more limited and circumscribed. Thus, we can think of the "new syntheses" rather than a "new synthesis." *This move toward theoretical syntheses is, in my view, the overriding theme of this essay, of the papers in this volume, and of contemporary sociological theory.*

As welcome as the growth of theoretical syntheses is,[3] it is far from the only reason to believe that this is a particularly auspicious era in the history of sociological theory:

> The (relatively) new journal *Sociological Theory* sponsored by the American Sociological Association is well-established and joins *Theory and Society* and other more general journals (e.g., *Ameri-*

can Journal Of Sociology) as outlets for a substantial quantity and significant diversity of sociological theory.

There is a steady infusion of new (or revived) theories from Europe including Giddens' (1984) "structuration" theory, Bourdieu's (1977) work focusing on "habitus," Foucault's "archaeology of knowledge" and "genealogy of power" (*see* the Foucault memorial issue in *Human Studies* 1987), Elias' "figurational" sociology (*Theory, Culture and Society* published a special issue in 1987 entitled "Norbert Elias and Figurational Sociology"), and the work of a number of postmodern theorists like Baudrillard and Lyotard (Kellner 1988, this volume; Denzin 1986).

The works of the classical theorists continue to be mined and those efforts persist in paying dividends. Significant recent examples included Collins' (1989) analysis of Mead, Camic's (1987) reexamination of the methods of the early Parsons, Marske's (1987) look at Durkheim's "cult of the individual," Hilbert's (1987) subjectivistic interpretation of Weber's views on bureaucracy, and Elster's (1985) micro-interpretation of Marx.

Most traditional theoretical perspectives (e.g., structural functionalism and conflict theory) continue to be viable with some even experiencing at least mini-booms in interest.

There is no overwhelmingly dominant theory like structural functionalism in the 1940s and 1950s to retard or prevent the development of newer theoretical perspectives.

There is less dogmatic refusal to listen to other theoretical approaches with the result that there appears to be at least a small audience for a wide range of theories.

The older generation of theorists is passing into retirement (e.g., Merton, Coser), and while their work continues to be influential, members of a younger generation are taking over the leadership positions within sociological theory.

And there is an array of startling new developments in sociological theory such as the explosion of interest in cultural sociology, postmodernism, feminist sociological theory, and the micro-macro and agency-structure linkages.

Relatedly, sociological theorists have grown increasingly introspective and are more likely to examine metatheoretically (Ritzer 1988a, 1990) where the field stands and where it seems to be heading.

I should note at this point that while I see much merit in contemporary theory, others, such as Jonathan Turner in his essay in this volume, take a very different position. From Turner's point of view, theory is bankrupt because it has lost sight of its positivistic roots. While this may be true from the point of view of a positivist, it is not a perspective shared by most theorists who, as Turner recognizes, do not adopt a positivistic orientation.

Part I of this book looks at the current state and near-term prospects of some theoretical perspectives that have been with us for some time and continue, even as they are undergoing significant change, to attract the attention of sociological theorists. In this category are Jeffrey Alexander and Paul Colomy's look at structural functionalism, or as they now call it, neofunctionalism, Randall Collins' essay on conflict theory, Robert Antonio's piece on neo-Marxian theory, Gary Fine's examination of symbolic interactionism, and Karen Cook, Jodi O'Brien, and Peter Kollock's analysis of exchange theory. Part II deals with theories of more recent vintage, at least in sociology, including works on ethnomethodology and conversation analysis by Deirdre Boden, rational choice theory by Debra Freidman and Michael Hechter, structuralism and post-structuralism by Charles Lemert, postmodern social theory by Douglas Kellner, cultural sociological theory by Michelle Lamont and Robert Wuthnow, and feminist theory by Patricia Lengermann and Jill Niebrugge-Brantley. Part III includes a set of more general essays including my own on micro-macro synthesis in sociological theory, an overview of the state of sociological theory by Jonathan Turner and Norbert Wiley's comments on all of the essays in this volume.

Before turning to a general overview of contemporary sociological theory, and of the movement toward theoretical syntheses more specifically (and thereby much of what is covered in this volume), it would be useful to examine what is omitted. Clearly, no volume of this type can hope to cover everything taking place in sociological theory. For one thing, this book focuses primarily on what is occurring in American sociological theory and to a slightly lesser degree developments in Europe, especially France. Furthermore, it does not cover theoretical developments in other parts of the world. Another limitation is that it is unlikely that all of the major developments in American and European sociological theory will be treated in this volume. This is true of some aspects of each of the theories that are discussed, but of greater importance are the theories that are not singled out for separate treatment. Great effort has been made to concentrate on theories that demonstrate a high level of current interest and are likely to continue to attract attention in the foreseeable future.[4] However, some notable theories have been excluded because a judgment was made that they are not now as lively and not likely to grow substantially in the near future. For example, action theory, in spite of its classic roots in the work of Weber and Parsons, as well as a recent revival in the works of

Coleman (1986a) and others, is not deemed worthy of full-scale, chapter-length treatment.

In the next section as well as the one that follows I discuss the most important theories in contemporary sociology. In doing so, I will use conventional labels (e.g., structural functionalism, symbolic interactionism). However, as I will be pointing out, the movement toward syntheses makes these labels progressively less meaningful.

NEW LIFE IN SOME TRADITIONAL THEORIES

It was only a little more than a decade ago that Wilbert Moore (1978) saw structural functionalism as a near "embarrassment" and Turner and Maryanski (1979) argued that structural functionalism was dead as an explanatory theory and urged its abandonment. This seemed to be linked to intellectual and social changes (e.g., the loss by America of its position of world hegemony) during the late 1960s and early 1970s (Huaco 1986). But today there seems to be more than a flicker of life in what is now called neofunctionalism (Alexander 1985a, 1985b). Colomy (1986, 139) has recently responded to the critics: "Functionalism is not dead. To the contrary, there are signs that the functionalist tradition is being revitalized." The resuscitation of functionalism is closely linked to the so-called "Parsons revival" (Sciulli and Gerstein 1985), being spearheaded by Alexander in the United States, but certainly not restricted to him (Sciulli, Camic) nor to the United States (Munch, Luhmann). Furthermore, the Parsons revival is not limited to the predictable scholars as is shown by the attention to Parsonsian theory by the contemporary neo-Marxist, Jürgen Habermas (1987). Structural functionalism appears to have a whole new generation of adherents and that group is being added to the holdovers from the heyday of functionalism in the 1950s. In fact, many non-theorists were unaware of structural functionalism's near-demise in the 1970s so they will not be surprised by its current strength, nor will they need to be lured back to a fold they never left.

The adoption of the label "neofunctionalism" is clearly designed to show continuity with structural functionalism,[5] but also to indicate that the new perspective seeks to overcome some of the problems associated with structural functionalism as well as to extend that perspective. Alexander (1985a, 10) has enumerated the problems associated with structural functionalism that neofunctionalism will need to surmount, including "anti-individualism," "antagonism to change," "conservatism," "idealism," and an "anti-empirical bias." Efforts are being made to overcome these problems programmatically (Alexander

1985a) and at more specific theoretical levels, for example Colomy's (1986) attempt to refine differentiation theory, but even Alexander (1985a, 16) has had to admit that "neofunctionalism is a tendency rather than a developed theory."

In their paper in this volume, Alexander and Colomy stake out a very ambitious claim for neofunctionalism. They do not see it as, in their terms, a more modest "elaboration," or "revision," of structural functionalism, but rather a "reconstruction" of it in which differences with the founder (Parsons) are clearly acknowledged and explicit openings are made to other theories (e.g., conflict, interactionism).[6] In other words, and consistent with the basic theme of this essay, Alexander and Colomy are endeavoring to synthesize structural functionalism with a number of other theoretical traditions. Such reconstruction can both revive structural functionalism and provide the base for the development of a new theoretical tradition. Alexander and Colomy clearly have such ambitious objectives for neofunctionalism. We will have to wait and see whether neofunctionalism achieves such goals, or even whether it attains the more modest goal of merely reviving structural functionalism. While a wide range of thinkers are rediscovering the strengths of Parsonian theory (which, by the way, Alexander and Colomy seem, erroneously in my view, to equate with structural functionalism), many theorists remain dubious about any form of structural functionalism, whether it be elaborated, revised, or reconstructed.

It has been difficult to see much life in conflict theory. Conflict theory enjoyed a small boom in the 1960s as the macro-level alternative to structural functionalism. However, except for Collins' (1975) *Conflict Sociology,* and that book was much more micro-oriented than the conflict theory of Dahrendorf and others, there have been few notable contributions to this theoretical perspective.

That situation has been rectified, at least in part, by Collins' contribution to this volume. After devoting more than a decade to other concerns, especially interaction ritual chains, Collins has returned to his interest in conflict theory. In Collins' view, conflict theory has not been moribund for the last decade, but has been developing quietly under a variety of different guises in a number of areas within sociology. For one thing, Collins believes that conflict theory has become the dominant perspective in a number of sub-areas within sociology. Although he does not go into it in detail, one example of what he has in mind is the emergence of the "power approach" as the dominant orientation in the sociological study of the professions (Ritzer and Walczak 1986). Collins' main concern is to show how conflict theory lies at the heart of much of historical/comparative research, especially the work of Michael Mann (1986). Collins sees Mann doing a kind of network theory and Collins seeks to synthesize Mann's approach with mainstream work in network theory. Whether or not conflict theory moves in this particular direction, it seems clear that Collins' effort will help to revive interest in conflict theory and contribute to the movement toward theoretical integration.

A related effort worth undertaking, but not underscored by Collins, would be a review of the array of specific conflict theories that have developed within various sub-areas in sociology, with the objective of putting this disparate body of work together into a broader conflict theory of society in general. The fact is that conflict theory is a well-established label that is woefully lacking in substance. If conflict theory is to become a renewed force in sociological theory, it is going to need to flesh out what has been heretofore little more than a theoretical skeleton.

If conflict theory has seemed weak, neo-Marxian theory has grown dramatically, albeit unevenly, since its emergence in American sociology in the late 1960s. Bottomore (1984) asserts correctly that "Marxism has now established itself as one of the major paradigms in sociology."[7] Much of the strength of neo-Marxian theory has been in critical theory, but Bottomore (1984) has claimed that "the Frankfurt School, in its original form, and as a school of Marxism or sociology, is dead." That assertion seems far too strong, especially in light of the widespread interest in the work of the contemporary inheritor of the critical school tradition—Jürgen Habermas—and a revival of interest in the work of original members of the Frankfurt School such as Adorno and Benjamin. While it is hard to agree with Bottomore on the death of critical theory, it is far easier to accept Benton's (1984) view that structural Marxism, as in the work of Althusser and Poulantzas, is in decline.

While some varieties of neo-Marxian theories may be weakening, others are rising to take their place. Many of those who at one time were attracted to critical theory and structural Marxism have now moved in the direction of a variety of perspectives soon to be discussed: post-structuralism, postmodernism, and newer varieties of neo-Marxism. Then there is much interest in game-theoretic, or rational-choice, Marxism in the work of Roemer (1982, 1986) and Elster (1985). Game-theoretic Marxism continues the effort, found in critical theory and its turn toward Freud, to give Marxian theory a micro base, this time in assumptions about a rational actor derived from economics. But game-theoretic Marxism goes further and poses a largely micro-level theory that stands in stark contrast to the macro-level orientation of virtually all other Marxian theories. Activity within this domain, as well as the attacks it is likely to elicit from macro-oriented Marxists,[8] are likely to breathe considerable life into Marxian theory. Other lively areas of interest in neo-Marxian theory are world-system theory (Wallerstein 1980, 1988; Boswell and Bergesen 1987); neo-Marxian economic sociology (*Theory and Society* 1986); "post-Marxist" (building on the Marxian tradition, but rejecting the "primacy of class and economic dynamics" [Wright 1987, 749]) theory (e.g., Bowles and Gintis 1986), as well as empirically oriented research done from a Marxian perspective (Wright and Martin 1987).

Antonio seeks to review much of the history of neo-Marxian theory from the point of view of its relationship to one of Marx's totalistic perspectives, his materialist emancipatory modernism. In Antonio's view, Marx from this perspective offered a grand view of society moving toward its teleological end (communism) impelled by the collective subject, the proletariat. For a time, this view shaped (and distorted) Marxian theory, but later an array of neo-Marxian theorists sought in a variety of ways to distance themselves from this grand narrative. In some cases, however, they merely replaced Marx's materialist emancipatory modernism with other equally problematic grand narratives. More recently, an array of decentered neo-Marxian theories have emerged. While they have served to overcome the excesses of Marx's materialist emancipatory modernism, they threaten to offer an excessively pluralistic image of society. Antonio suggests that neo-Marxians build on Marx's "historical holism" rather than his emancipatory modernism.[9] Historical holism is a global theory of capitalism without the excesses (e.g., teleology) of materialist emancipatory modernism. Whether or not neo-Marxian theory moves in that direction, Antonio has succeeded in using the idea of totality to both give an overview of the history of and to point to a future direction for neo-Marxian theory.

Symbolic interactionism is another traditional sociological theory that seems to have defied the doomsayers by enjoying something of a renaissance. In the 1970s it appeared as if symbolic interactionism was about to lose its traditional turf to a number of much more exotic theories of consciousness, action and interaction, especially phenomenological sociology, ethnomethodology, existential sociology, hermeneutical sociology and the like (Ritzer 1985). While the latter theories have, in the main, grown in importance, that growth has not been at the expense of symbolic interactionism. Symbolic interactionism has its association (Society for the Study of Symbolic Interaction), its journal (*Symbolic Interaction*), significant re-analyses of the classic works of Mead (Collins 1989) and Blumer (*Symbolic Interaction* 1988), major new program statements (Perinbanayagam 1985), and a number of new theorists (e.g., Fine 1986; Shalin, 1986, 1988) who are continuing to work with the perspective while refining it in a variety of ways. Also aiding symbolic interactionism is the growing recognition that Erving

Goffman was a first-rank theorist (Collins 1986) and that his ideas will continue to be of utility in dealing with a variety of theoretical and empirical issues (Rawls 1987). Although there is considerable disagreement over whether Goffman should be considered a symbolic interactionist (Gonos 1977, 1980), many do view his work in that way and the likelihood of a continued mining of his ideas is apt to contribute to substantial interest in symbolic interactionism. In recent years a number of works employing a significant aspect of Goffman's symbolic interactionism, his dramaturgical approach, have appeared (Haas and Shaffir 1982; Snow, Zurcher, and Peters, 1984; Zurcher 1985; Kitahara 1986).

In his essay in this volume, Gary Fine argues that symbolic interactionism has entered a new, "post-Blumerian" age (*see also* the special issue of *Symbolic Interaction* [1988] devoted to Herbert Blumer). This new symbolic interactionism "has cobbled a new theory from the shards of other theoretical approaches." Symbolic interactionism now combines indigenous insights with those from other micro theories like exchange theory, ethnomethodology, and phenomenology. More surprising is the integration of ideas from macro theories (e.g., structural functionalism) as well as the ideas of macro theorists like Parsons, Simmel, Weber, and Marx. Post-Blumerian symbolic interactionism is a much more synthetic perspective than it was in Blumer's heyday.

Even action theory, long a weak component of the contemporary theoretical scene, is showing some faint signs of life. Coleman (1986a, 1987) has sought to revive action theory by returning to its roots in Parsons' (1937) *The Structure of Social Action*. He is trying to undo Parsons' mistake of abandoning action theory in favor of structural functionalism. Thus Coleman is seeking to move action theory away from the system level and back toward the actor who for Coleman, as for Parsons, can be "either persons or corporate actors" (1986a, 1312). In other words, Coleman is seeking the development of a broader action theory which synthesizes interests in actors and systems. Another work of this genre is Sciulli's (1986) effort to clarify the meaning of voluntaristic action and to link it to work in legal theory.

Exchange theory, while as strong or even stronger than ever, is clearly a theory in transition. Its modern founder, George Homans (1974), seems more of a historical forerunner than an active participant in ongoing work in exchange theory. Peter Blau (1964), who helped pioneer exchange theory and extend it to the macro levels, has made it abundantly clear that he has abandoned exchange theory for structural theory (Blau, 1987a). Furthermore, he has moved from the traditional micro-level concerns of exchange theory, and the more integrative micro-macro foci of his own exchange theory, to a focus on the macrostructural level. It is Richard Emerson and his disciples, especially Karen Cook (1987a, 1987b), who seem to have moved to the center of ongoing work in exchange theory. While starting with the traditional micro-level concerns of exchange theory, this group is seeking to build toward the macro level and develop a more synthetic exchange theory.

Indeed, in their essay in this volume, Cook, O'Brien, and Kollock define exchange theory in inherently integrative terms as being concerned with exchanges at various levels of analysis, including among individuals, corporations, and nation states. They identify two strands of work in the history of exchange: one at the micro level focusing on social behavior as exchange, and the other at the more macro level of social structure as exchange. Cook et al. identify three contemporary trends, all of which point toward a more integrative exchange theory. The first is the increasing use of field research focusing on more macroscopic issues, which can complement the traditional use of the laboratory experiment to study microscopic issues. Second, they note a shift in substantive work away from a focus on dyads and toward larger networks of exchange. Third, and most important, is the ongoing effort to synthesize exchange theory and structural sociologies, especially network theory. Along the way, Cook et al. discuss the gains to be made from integrating insights from rational choice and decision theory as well as symbolic interactionism. Most generally, they see their synthetic version of exchange theory as being well-equipped to deal with the centrally important issue of the micro-macro relationship.

THE LIVELINESS OF SOME MORE RECENT THEORIES

While the theories discussed in the preceding section can be traced back in sociology for many decades, the theories to be discussed in this section are generally of more recent vintage, or at least have come to be accepted by large numbers of theorists only in recent years.

Ethnomethodology (and the related conversation analysis), while it has certainly not swept across the sociological domain, has succeeded in moving beyond its southern California enclave and has created a number of beachheads throughout the United States as well as some notable centers on the British Isles (Sharrock and Anderson 1986). Intellectually, ethnomethodology has retained its core interests in everyday interaction and conversation analysis (see the special 1986 issue of *Human Studies* devoted to "Interaction and Language Use"; Heritage and Atkinson 1984), but it also now seems to be expanding into domains that appear more in line with mainstream sociology. A good example is Heritage and Greatbatch's (1986) analysis of British political speeches and the methods used to generate applause from audiences. The typology of devices developed by them seems little different from the kinds of typologies employed by various other types of sociological theorists.

Boden (this volume) makes a strong, albeit somewhat self-conscious, case for ethnomethodology and conversation analysis. It is certainly true that ethnomethodology has widened and deepened its support in sociology. However, one wonders whether it, or any sociological theory for that matter, is, as Boden contends, "here to stay." In any case, such an argument contradicts the basic theme of this volume, which is that theoretical boundaries are weakening and new synthetic perspectives are emerging. It may be that ethnomethodology is still too new and too insecure to consider an erosion of its boundaries.

Nevertheless, much of Boden's essay deals with synthetic efforts within ethnomethodology, especially in terms of dealing with the relationship between agency and structure, the embeddedness of action, and fleeting events within the course of history. More directly, Boden deals with the extent to which European and American theorists have begun to integrate ethnomethodology and conversation analysis into their orientations. Unfortunately, what is lacking is a discussion of the degree to which ethnomethodologists are integrating the ideas of other sociological theories into their perspective. Ethnomethodologists seem quite willing for other theorists to integrate ethnomethodological perspectives, but they are far less eager to reciprocate.

Phenomenology, too, remains viable with its own association (Society for Phenomenology and the Human Sciences), newsletter *(Phenomenology and Social Science)*, and a journal *(Human Studies)* that is a major outlet for work of this genre (e.g., Rehorick 1986), as well as that of ethnomethodologists. But while there seem to be major new works and directions in ethnomethodology, the same does not seem to be the case in phenomenology. Phenomenology does not appear to have gone far beyond the work of Husserl, Schutz, and the derivative work of Berger and Luckmann (1967).

While not nearly as institutionalized as phenomenology, existential sociology seems to be in a similar state intellectually. While work of this type continues to appear (e.g., Kotarba and Fontana 1984; Fontana 1984), existentialism, too, seems tied to the work of its masters, like Sartre. Both phenomenological sociology and existentialism will need to show some important advances in the next few years, or they will face the likelihood of declining significance in the field.

While theories with a micro base such as phenomenology and existential sociology seem to be foundering, another theory of this genre, rational choice theory (and other perspectives derived primarily from economics), is booming (as indicated by the recent founding of a new journal devoted to the issue of rationality). Some notable examples of this include the work in game-theoretic Marxism mentioned above and more mainstream sociological work by Hechter (1983a, 1983b, 1987) and Coleman (1986a). This work is unified in its methodological individualism and seeks to base sociological theory on a philosophical anthropology (homo economicus) of rational, maximizing, self-interested actors making correct, most efficient choices of means to ends on the basis of information available to them. It was just such a philosophical anthropology that was rejected by many of the early sociological theorists who sought to develop a more realistic, i.e., less rational, view of the actor as driven by values, beliefs, etc. However, in recent years, the success of economics has lured some sociologists back to the model of the rational actor with the promise of clean, simple, and elegant theories.

However, it seems to me unlikely that rational choice theory will attract as wide a number of adherents in sociology for many of the same reasons that it was rejected by the early theorists. Among other things, it ignores or downplays values and beliefs, has an unrealistic view of the actor, ignores the reality of the empirical world, and tends toward micro determinism. Furthermore, movement in the direction of rational choice will put sociologists in the position of being second-rate economists. In addition, a variety of economists are themselves questioning the utility of rational choice theory within economics.[10] As Hirsch, Michaels, and Friedman (1987; see also Swedberg, Himmelstrand, and Brulin 1987) conclude, sociology would be well-advised to continue working with its traditional "dirty hands" than being seduced by the "clean models" of economic rational choice theory. While it might be impossible for sociology as a whole to adopt rational choice theory, that is not to say that there are not gains to be made by some sociologists working in this tradition.

In their essay in this volume, Friedman and Hechter (*see also* Friedman and Hechter 1988) offer a spirited defense of rational choice theory by enumerating twenty of its most important insights. Furthermore, they recognize some of the limitations discussed above and point future theorists in the directions needed to overcome these limitations. Among other things, they urge more work on the rationality of individual actors and its internal limits, on the origin of preferences within actors, on how to aggregate from individual actions to macrosocial outcomes, and on how rational egoists produce institutions. To put it simply, Friedman and Hechter are urging a fuller sense of the actor and greater concern with various facets of the micro-macro linkage. In emphasizing this linkage, Friedman and Hechter are urging a more synthetic type of rational choice theory than is usually found in the literature. They make this perfectly clear in their earlier essay: "Why, then, prefer rational choice? Perhaps the most compelling reason is that it is explicitly concerned with linking micro and macro levels of analysis rather than asserting the analytical supremacy of one or the other" (1988, 212).

Structuralisms of various types are demonstrating considerable liveliness in contemporary sociology. One example is the tendency to interpret Goffman as a structuralist and to use his basic concepts in that way (e.g., Snow 1986). While Kurzweil (1980, 2) may have been right when referring to French structuralism, she argued that "in Paris, the structuralist age is nearly over," it is the case that post-structuralism or neostructuralism (Rose 1984; Wuthnow et al. 1984) is with us, particularly in the work of Michel Foucault (1965, 1975, 1979, 1980). A large number of books and articles have been written about Foucault and his work and Foucaldian scholarship promises to expand in the future. Foucault created an extraordinary body of work that has the depth, sophistication, ambiguities, and changes over time that can occupy interpreters and new theorists in the future. A number of theoretical inputs can be found in Foucault's work in addition to structuralism, including Marxian theory, Weberian iron-cage imagery, phenomenology, and Nietzsche's concern with the linkage between power and knowledge. There is a strong element of structuralism in Foucault's early work and his archaeology of knowledge, but that tended to be supplanted later by a genealogy of power in which Foucault is primarily absorbed in the study of the power-knowledge linkage. I suspect that many sociologists (as well as thinkers from a number of other fields) will continue to find much of value in Foucault's work and derive from it a variety of perspectives that will find their way into various aspects of sociology.

In his essay on structuralism and post-structuralism in this volume, Charles Lemert makes a strong case for the integration of such an orientation into mainstream sociology. In spite of the barriers to such integration, Lemert feels that post-structuralism has much to offer to sociological analysis. Part of the problem is the dense and elusive language of the French structuralists. More important is the threat posed by structuralism to mainstream sociology because of its focus on discourse and texts rather than the "real world." Lemert counters the latter criticism by using post-structuralism to focus on discourse and texts associated with the Vietnam War. This case study allows him to show the utility of such a focus and to ask, rhetorically, whether there is now anything (or whether there was ever anything) else to study but texts. Lemert concludes by excoriating sociology (and political science) for ignoring such political phenomena as the Vietnam War and argues that post-structuralism could hardly do less in this area.

In a related paper, Kellner examines postmodernism (Lemert also touches on this and Kellner touches on structuralism), particularly as it is manifest in the contemporary works of Baudrillard, Lyotard, and Jameson. It is clear the postmodernism had its roots in structuralism and post-structuralism, but has now developed into a distinctive perspective. In addition to defining postmodernism, examining it through the ideas of its major proponents, critiquing it, and offering his own ideas on postmodernism, Kellner also relates postmodernism to the issue of the new syntheses.

One of the key aspects of postmodernism is its tendency to "subvert" and "explode" boundaries between disciplines and to create a multidisciplinary, multidimensional perspective that synthesizes ideas from a range of fields (e.g., philosophy, political economy, cultural theory, history, anthropology, and sociology). Postmodernism proclaims the end of an era in social and intellectual life and the search for "new social theories, methods of research, paradigms of knowledge, and political practice." Such new theories will involve new concatenations of Marxism, critical theory, feminism, postmodern social theory, and other currents of critical social theory to solve the theoretical and political problems which confront us today. In his own ideas on "techno-capitalism" Kellner seeks to rescue viable aspects of Marxian theory and to synthesize them with the ideas of the postmodernists. In this sense Kellner, like Antonio, comes down on the side of the need for a new holistic perspective while, at the same time, accepting the need for a wide range of synthetic efforts.

In a third paper drawing heavily on French intellectual life, Lamont and Wuthnow point to a boom in interest in cultural sociology in both Europe and the United States. Interestingly, the theorists (and empiricists) who produced this body of knowledge came from a wide array of traditional theoretical approaches, but their collective body of work is now coalescing into a new and distinctive approach to the social world. Lamont and Wuthnow focus on the similarities and differences in the study of symbolic codes and culture-mediated power relations in Europe and the United States. In the course of their review they touch on the work of many of the most notable contemporary theorists in Europe (e.g., Lévi-Strauss, Foucault, Bourdieu, Habermas, Douglas) and America (Goffman, Parsons, Berger, Alexander). While not all of their work falls under the heading of cultural sociology, enough of it does, and there is sufficient coherence in it as a set, to give the continued development of cultural sociology a powerful theoretical base.

One of the most striking developments in recent years has been the rise of feminist sociological theory. As Lengermann and Niebrugge-Brantley (1988, this volume) make clear, feminist theory is woman-centered in that it takes women as the central subject, looks at the world from the point of view of women, and seeks a better world for women. The closest analogy in sociological theory to feminist theory is the various branches of neo-Marxian theory; the parallel to the woman-centeredness of feminist theory is the proletariat-centeredness of neo-Marxian theory. As Lengermann and Niebrugge-Brantley (1988) point out, feminist sociological theory is inherently synthetic since it has been formed out of the intersection of three broad inputs: theories of gender differences including biological, institutional, and social psychological theories of gender; theories of gender inequality including liberal feminism and Marxian feminism; and theories of gender oppression including psychoanalytic, radical feminist, and socialist feminist theories. Some of these idea systems are indigenous to sociology while others feed into sociology from a variety of external sources. The confluence of these internal and external forces is leading to the development of a distinctive feminist sociological theory. While that theory is in its early, formative stages, it seems clear that such a theory (or theories) will undergo expansion and consolidation in the coming years.

In spite of continuing barriers to its acceptance (e.g., the differences in the languages of extant sociological theory and feminist sociological theory), the institutional structure needed for the development of feminist sociological theory is already in place. The organization Sociologists for Women in Society offers a natural constituency for the development and dissemination of feminist sociological theory. In existence are a number of journals that serve as outlets for works in feminist sociological theory, including *Signs, Feminist Studies,* and *Gender and Society.* And there are a number of works, already published, that are theoretical, or at least have a strong theoretical component (Rich 1976; Chodorow 1978; Chafetz 1984, 1988; Smith 1979; Hartsock 1983; Farganis 1986). Finally, there are a number of sociological theorists who are agitated over the exclusion of women from many sociological theories and eager to rectify this omission by developing women-centered sociological theories.

In addition to the acceptance of feminist sociological theory in the next few years, Lengermann and Niebrugge-Brantley point to four other areas of future development. First, they see additional work on the issue of *difference,* feminist theory's fundamental concern in the study of social organization. Central to the issue of difference is social production, an expansion of the Marxian category of the production of goods to the production of social life in general. Second, additional work is needed on a feminist epistemology, especially giving those being researched an important voice and developing an intimate relationship between researcher and subject. Third, feminist sociologists are likely to continue to critically analyze sociology's penchant for dualistic rhetoric and attempt to develop more integrated conceptions of the social world. Finally, considerable attention will be devoted to the issue of power, redefined as the ability to set and execute projects. In sum, Lengermann and Niebrugge-Brantley see feminist sociological theory engaged in nothing less than a reworking of sociological theory's most fundamental characteristics: its model of social structure (to a focus on difference), its epistemology, its fundamental (dualistic) concepts and rhetoric, and its conception of power. Furthermore, they seek to move sociological theory in general in a more activistic direction.

Accomplishment of all, or even some, of these goals will be a daunting task. Furthermore, one wonders whether the emerging feminist sociological theory can sustain itself as a woman-centered theory. In my view, this may be an important starting point, but it is doubtful that feminist sociological theory will or should remain a woman-centered theory. To go back to the analogy with Marxian and neo-Marxian theories, while those theories began as proletarian-centered, a number of the modern versions have developed a much broader base. Feminist sociological theory will likely need to broaden its base in order to solidify its position as a legitimate sociological theory. Such a broadened base is made more likely, in my view, by the fact that many of feminist sociological theory's basic orientations (e.g., anti-positivism, rejection of dualistic rhetoric, concern for power) are in line with a number of other recent developments in sociological theory. In other words, feminist sociological theory may be critical of traditional sociological theories, but it is in fundamental accord with many of the most recent theoretical developments.

Returning to more structural theories, indigenous versions of contemporary theories with a structural orientation are Blau's structural theory as well as network theory. Blau (1977a, 1977b) has been active not only in creating a structural theoretical perspective, but also serving as a cheerleader for it (Blau 1987a, 1987b). In contrast to the invisible structures of concern to structuralists, Blau (1977a, 2) argues that the structures of concern to him are visible phenomena, "observable aspects of social life." While a number of recent works have appeared utilizing this theory, most of them have been authored by Blau and/or his close supporters (e.g., Blum 1984, 1985; Blau, Beeker, and Fitzpatrick 1984; Messner 1986) and it is not yet clear whether Blau's approach will have significant influence outside of this limited ambit.

Much more promising is network theory, which has already demonstrated more widespread acceptance. Like Blau's structural theory, network theory is more indigenous to sociology than other structuralisms and highly attuned to integrating theory with research that is methodologically rigorous. The focus of network theory is on social structure, the pattern of ties linking individual (Granovetter 1973, 1983, 1985) and collective (Clawson, Neustadtl, and Bearden 1986; Mizruchi and Koenig 1986) members of society. While these may be seen as deep structures, that is structures that lie below the surface (Wellman 1983), they are closer to traditional sociology's sense of social structure than to the structures of concern to, for example, French structuralists. While there is a substantial amount of work being done in network theory, and it even has its own journal, *Social Networks*, the fact is that it is still a rather loosely defined body of work (Burt 1982, 20).

Of interest here are the emerging ties between network theory and exchange theory (and, as we have noted, between network theory and conflict theory; *see* Collins, this volume). Network theory appears to offer exchange theory a highly compatible macro theory that complements exchange theory's micro orientation. For example, network theorists, like exchange theorists, are little interested in individual motives. The network theorists' interest in objective ties meshes nicely with the exchange theorists' interest in objective patterns of behavior. To put it in negative terms, network theory would not fit as well with the sociological theories that are primarily interested in consciousness (symbolic interactionism, phenomenology, ethnomethodology, existentialism). On the other side, exchange theory would not tie in well with the (macro) subjectivistic orientation of other macro theories such as structural functionalism and critical theory.

It is Emerson's social structural brand of exchange theory that is particularly appropriate for linkage to network theory. Instead of focusing on actors or interaction, Emerson is concerned with structures, corporate groups, and networks. The focus on corporate groups leads to a concern for interorganizational exchange while the latter leads to exchange relations among positions in networks. In fact, Cook and her colleagues (1983, 277; *see also* Cook 1987b) in discussing "exchange networks," or social structures made up of two or more connected exchange relations (sets of exchange opportunities that are historically developed and used) between actors, make the point that this concept "has the theoretical advantage of allowing the extension and application of already well developed dyadic concepts of exchange . . . to more macro . . . levels of analysis." Some worry, however, that this move to the macro level and to structurally mandated exchange involves a loss of the traditional micro focus and strength of exchange theory (Mc-Mahon 1984).

THE NEW SYNTHESES:
A METATHEORETICAL ANALYSIS

As was made clear at the beginning of this essay, and throughout the discussion, the dominant theme in contemporary sociological theory is the various moves toward theoretical syntheses. In this section, we want to return to this theme through the lens of another dramatic development in contemporary sociological theory: the rise of meta-theory (Ritzer 1988a, 1990). The objective in this section is to delineate the basic character of metatheorizing and then to relate it to the movement toward theoretical syntheses.

Metatheorizing may be defined very broadly as the systematic study of the underlying structure of sociological theory. We can differentiate between three broad types of metatheorizing: metatheorizing as a prelude to the development of sociological theory (M_P); metatheorizing in order to achieve a deeper understanding of sociological theory (M_U); and metatheorizing in order to create an overarching theoretical perspective (M_O). Virtually all of the papers in this volume involve the first type of metatheorizing. We will return to that type later in this section,[11] but first let us deal with M_U since even though we have seen an efflorescence of work of that type in sociology, not as much of it appears explicitly in this volume as M_P.

There are four basic types of M_U, but all of them involve the formal or informal study of sociological theory in order to attain a deeper understanding of it. The first sub-type focuses on intellectual or cognitive issues internal to sociology. The largest body of work of this type is derived from Thomas Kuhn's (1962, 1970) philosophy of science (as well as that of others) and attempts to identify the major cognitive paradigm(s) in sociology (Ritzer 1975). Efforts to map the cognitive structure of sociological theory are not restricted to those inspired by Kuhn. Examples of non-Kuhnian efforts include Wagner and Berger's (1985) distinction among theoretical contexts—orienting strategies, unit theories, and theoretical research programs; the "schools of thought approach" (Tiryakian 1979); and more dynamic views of the underlying structure of sociological theory (Wiley 1979; Harvey 1982, 1987).

A variant of this first, internal-intellectual approach involves the development of general metatheoretical tool(s) with which to analyze existing sociological theories and to develop new theories. Included here would be Gouldner's (1970) use of concepts like "background assumptions" and "domain assumptions" to analyze the underlying structure of sociological theory, Alexander's (1982) study of sociological theorists from the point of view of action and order, efforts to deal with "levels" of analysis within sociological theory (Edel 1959; Wiley 1988; Ritzer 1989), and more specific attempts to analyze "micro-macro" linkages (Alexander et al. 1987; Ritzer, this volume) in sociology.

The second sub-type of M_U (internal-social) also looks within sociology, but focuses on social rather than cognitive factors. The main approach here emphasizes the communal aspects of various sociological theories. Of utmost importance are the approaches that have sought to identify the major "schools" in the history of sociology (Tiryakian 1979, 1986; Bulmer 1984, 1985) as well as the more formal, network approach to the study of the ties among groups of sociologists (Mullins 1973, 1983) to identify the major "theory groups" in sociology. Another internal-social approach involves turning to the sociological theorists themselves and examining, among other things, their training, their institutional affiliations, their career patterns, their positions within the field of sociology, and so on. (Gouldner 1970).

The third variant of M_U (external-intellectual) involves turning to other academic disciplines for ideas, tools, concepts, theories, and the like that can be used in the analysis of sociological theory. Paradigm analyses in sociology obviously owe a great debt to philosophy and the ideas of Kuhn, Lakatos, and others. Currently, a great deal of theoretical work is being done in sociology using economics as a model (e.g., Coleman 1987; Gerstein 1987). One other example of this is found in the efforts to look at sociological theories as forms of discourse and to analyze them using an array of linguistic tools (Brown 1987).

Finally, the external-social approach involves shifting to the more macro level to look at the larger society and the nature of its impact on sociological theorizing. For example, Tiryakian (1979) suggests that we look at the national setting (Vidich and Lyman 1985), the sociohistorical setting (Shalin 1988), the relationship between sociology and various institutions, the relationship between sociology and its funding agencies, sociology as an institution and the process of institutionalization (Shils 1970), as well as sociology as a profession.

This volume offers some examples of metatheoretical efforts of the sub-types described above. For example, in their analysis of neofunctionalism, Alexander and Colomy use a variant of the internal-intellectual type to develop and deploy a whole range of metatheoretical tools. They offer a three-phase approach to the post–World War II history of sociological theory; a view of social science as discourse and research program; and a theory of change and growth in social science involving elaboration, revision and reconstruction, conflict and competition between theoretical traditions, and shifts in theoretical sensibilities. They then use these metatheoretical tools to analyze the recent history of structural functionalism and to show how neofunctionalism represents a new theoretical development. I use the micro-macro tool to analyze recent developments in sociological theory. Turner also primarily uses an internal-intellectual metatheory in his examination of the history of theoretical ideas in the United States and in detailing the loss of a positivistic orientation. He also utilizes the external-social approach in linking some of these intellectual changes to social changes within the larger society. Lengermann and Niebrugge-Brantley do both an internal- and external-intellectual analysis of developments in feminist theories in general and their relationship to the emerging feminist sociological theory. Lamont and Wuthnow employ all four types of M_U in their analysis of the differences between American and European sociologies of culture-internal-intellectual (positivism vs. hermeneutics, differential focus on religion), internal-social (differences in the immediate settings in which scholars work), external-social (status and influence of intellectuals in the larger society, presence or absence of research funding), and external-intellectual (cross-national differences in how people experience power). Finally, this paper may also be considered an example of internal-intellectual M_U since the goal is to understand the current status of sociological theory through an examination of the essays in this volume as well as the larger body of contemporary sociological theory. It is this analysis that leads to the conclusion that we are witnessing new syntheses within contemporary sociological theory.

We can also extend M_U analysis to better understand the movement toward theoretical syntheses in the context of the recent history of sociological theory. For example, in a series of internal-intellectual M_U analyses over the last two decades I have sequentially described recent sociological theory as moving through four major epochs: multi-paradigmatic status in the 1960s (Ritzer 1975),[12] the rise of micro-sociological theory in the 1970s (Ritzer 1985), the explosion of interest in micro-macro integration in the 1980s (Ritzer 1988c, this volume), and now the movement toward a broader array of theoretical syntheses as we enter the 1990s. Or we could suggest an external-social type of analysis in linking changes in theory to changes in the larger society. We can think of the current moment in history as one characterized by a breakdown of many things (e.g., liberalism, communism around the world) that shaped sociological theory for many years. The current period of transition facilitates pluralistic thinking as well as diverse attempts at linking various theories. A more settled epoch (such as

America in the 1950s) would encourage more dogmatic thinking (e.g., the dominance of structural functionalism in the 1950s).[13]

However, most of the metatheorizing in this book, and in sociology in general, is not M_U, but is rather metatheorizing as a prelude to the development of sociological theory (M_P). The fact is that most important classic and contemporary theorists developed their theories, at least in part, on the basis of a careful (metatheoretical) study of, and reaction to, the work of other theorists. The examples here are legion, but let me just mention a few of the most important: Karl Marx's theory of capitalism developed out of a systematic engagement with Hegelian philosophy as well as that of the Young Hegelians, political economy, utopian socialism, etc.; Parsons' action theory developed out of a systematic study of the work of Durkheim, Weber, Pareto, and Marshall; Alexander's multidimensional, neofunctional theory based on a detailed study of the work of Marx, Weber, Durkheim, and Parsons; and Habermas' critical theory based on his examination of the work of first-generation critical theorists Marx, Weber, Parsons, Mead, Durkheim, etc. These theorists, and many others, have developed their theories on the basis of a metatheoretical engagement with the ideas of their predecessors.[14]

While theorists have always used M_P, I have a sense that contemporary theorists are much more likely to do this than their predecessors. Major contemporary theorists like Habermas, Giddens, and Alexander have devoted enormous portions of their work to such metatheorizing. While I see much merit in metatheorizing, it is possible that it can be overdone and that theory can completely lose touch with the real world.

Virtually all of the papers in this volume utilize M_P. To take just a few examples, Collins reviews the work of comparative/historical sociologists and network theorists in order to begin developing a new orientation to conflict theory. Fine deals with a number of macro theorists in order to help symbolic interactionism move toward a more integrated conception of the social world. Antonio critically reviews the history of Marxian theory from the point of view of Marx's grand narrative of emancipatory modernism in order to argue that Marxian theory can build upon Marx's historical holism and thereby avoid becoming overly pluralistic. Lengermann and Niebrugge-Brantley (1988) have previously reviewed feminist theory and in this volume utilize that review to develop an agenda for feminist sociological theory. Kellner reviews the work of postmodernist theorists and integrates their ideas with Marxian perspectives to produce a distinctive approach to the postmodern condition. Thus, M_U and M_P occupy a prominent place in this volume as well as in sociology in general.

Both M_U and M_P works have contributed to the movement toward theoretical synthesis. Studies of the M_U type have allowed us to understand better our history of theoretical extremism as well as the current movement toward integration. Many M_P works, including a number in this volume, have proven useful in actually beginning the work of creating more synthetic theories.

CONCLUSION

As mentioned above, the 1980s were in my view defined by the movement in sociological theory toward micro-macro synthesis (Ritzer 1988c, this volume).[15] Explicit attention to the micro-macro issue is clear in a number of places in this volume. However, there are works, including essays in this volume, that show an inadequate sensitivity to this issue and the need for greater attention to it. For example, in his essay Turner generally fails to recognize that "mentalism" can be analyzed at the micro (e.g., consciousness) and macro (e.g., cultural norms and values) levels. Turner persistently assumes that a concern for mentalism must lead in a micro (social psychological) direction.

Many of the essays in this volume deal with micro-macro integration, but only as one of a broad array of synthetic efforts. Alexander and Colomy declare neofunctionalism open to insights from micro theories of contingencies and macro theories of conflict, among others. Collins makes a strong case for the integration of conflict theory and network theory. Fine declares post-Blumerian symbolic interactionism available to insights from an array of micro and macro theories and theorists. Cook et al. argue for a synthesis of exchange theory and structural theories such as network theory (as well as with a number of other theories), and for an image of exchange theory that offers an integrated micro-macro approach to the social world. Boden seeks to show what other theories can gain from ethnomethodology and to link micro and macro levels in the discussion of, among other things, the relationship between agency and structure. Friedman and Hechter present rational choice theory as offering an integrated, micro-macro conception of the social world. Kellner describes postmodernism as inherently multidisciplinary and he explicitly seeks to integrate it with Marxian theory. Lamont and Wuthnow discuss the growing interpenetration of European and American cultural sociology. What these essays demonstrate collectively is that micro-macro integration is now but one part of the broader movement toward theoretical syntheses.

Many sociological theories now seem to be borrowing heavily from one another and cutting across multiple levels of social analysis with the result that the traditionally clear borders between theories are growing increasingly blurred and porous. How this will sort out is not yet clear. It may be that in the near-term we will see a dramatically different, less differentiated, more synthetic theoretical landscape in sociology. Or it may be that old theoretical allegiances will be revived, thereby maintaining the separate and warring fiefdoms that have characterized sociological theory for the last several decades. Many of the authors in this volume (Cook, O'Brien, and Kollock; Lamont and Wuthnow; Ritzer) worry explicitly about a renewal of such fiefdoms, and the interminable political infighting that inevitably accompanies them. One indicator in this volume of this possibility is Boden's citation of a recent statement by Garfinkel that ethnomethodology is an "incommensurably alternate sociology." This coupled with the absence of much indication in Boden's essay of a willingness on the part of ethnomethodology to adopt the ideas of other theories indicates a high probability of continued conflict between ethnomethodology and other theoretical perspectives. While we need to continue to be concerned about this problem, this volume allows us to luxuriate for the moment in the glow of the new movement toward syntheses within sociological theory.

NOTES

1. I am certainly not the first to recognize this development. Among others, Smelser (1988) has described this trend and in this volume Alexander and Colomy deal with it as a backdrop to their focal concern with synthetic efforts in neofunctionalism.

2. Antonio attacks the idea of Marx's grand narrative while Kellner is critical of the idea of a master narrative. In spite of these attacks, both see a crucial role for some sort of holistic thought, without the liabilities of the above narratives, in social theory.

3. There is a negative side to pluralism and pluralistic efforts at synthesis that will not be discussed in this paper. However, it should be noted that theoretical specialization, specialized efforts at integration, professional allegiances, and specialized vocabularies and the resulting inability to communicate can all impede the development of any kind of holistic thinking.

4. One especially unfortunate omission is network theory which is touched on by Collins and dealt with in more depth by Cook, O'Brien, and Kollock, but is not the subject of a separate essay because Ronald Burt, who attended the conference on which this book is based, was unable to provide a paper for the book. This omission is critical because network theory is one of those theories that many different types of theorists seem eager to integrate into their perspectives. Another notable omission, although it too is touched on in various places, is structuration theory.

5. Turner and Maryanski (1988) have recently challenged neofunctionalism by arguing that it is not really functional in its orientation; it has abandoned many of the basic tenets of structural functionalism.

6. This seems to be in accord, at least partially, with Turner and Maryanski's

(1988) claim that neofunctionalism has little in common with structural functionalism.

7. Although I agree with the spirit of Bottomore's position, unlike Bottomore I do not consider Marxian theory a "paradigm."

8. For example, Weldes and Duvall (1987, 899) have labeled this "Marxism without Marx."

9. For a similar view, see Kellner (this volume).

10. And they have joined some sociologists (e.g., Etzioni 1988) in a new society of socio-economics.

11. We will not deal with M_O because little of it appears in this volume.

12. This, in turn, succeeded the previous period (1940s and 1950s) in which structural functionalism was preeminent.

13. I would like to thank Bob Antonio for suggesting this last line of analysis.

14. It is not only important to understand that metatheory can be a prelude to theorizing, but also to underscore what makes for good and bad metatheorizing. For one thing, such metatheorizing ought to be as systematic as possible. Too often, haphazard metatheorizing is used as a basis for theory development. For another, metatheorizing ought to be done explicitly. Frequently such metatheorizing is only implicit (e.g., the way Weber deals with Marx) and the reader is unable to understand fully the metatheoretical roots of a theory. Finally, while metatheory can be an important source of theory, an exclusive reliance on it can cause theorists to lose sight of the real world that their theories are supposed to deal with.

15. This is clearly evidenced by the fact that two sessions at the 1988 American Sociological Association meetings were devoted to this theme and, most importantly, micro-macro integration was *the* theme of the 1989 ASA meetings.

REFERENCES

Alexander, Jeffrey C. 1982. *Theoretical Logic in Sociology, Volume I, Positivism, Presuppositions, and Current Controversies.* Berkeley: University of California Press.

Alexander, Jeffrey C. 1985a. "The 'Individualist Dilemma' in Phenomenology and Interactionism." In Eisenstadt and Helle, eds., *Macro-Sociological Theory.*

Alexander, Jeffrey C., ed. 1985b. *Neofunctionalism.* Beverly Hills, Cal.: Sage.

Alexander, Jeffrey C. 1987. "Action and Its Environments." In Alexander et al., eds., *The Micro-Macro Link.*

Alexander, Jeffrey C. et al., eds. 1987. *The Micro-Macro Link.* Berkeley: University of California Press.

Benton, Ted. 1984. *The Rise and Fall of Structural Marxism: Althusser and His Influence.* New York: St. Martin's.

Berger, Peter, and Thomas Luckman. 1967. *The Social Construction of Reality.* Garden City, N.Y.: Anchor.

Blau, Peter. 1964. *Exchange and Power in Social Life.* New York: Wiley.

Blau, Peter. 1977a. *Inequality and Heterogeneity: A Primitive Theory of Social Structure.* New York: Free Press.

Blau, Peter. 1977b. "A Macrosociological Theory of Social Structure." *American Sociological Review* 83:26–54.

Blau, Peter. 1987a. "Contrasting Theoretical Perspectives." In Alexander et al., eds., *The Micro-Macro Link.*

Blau, Peter. 1987b. "Microprocess and Macrostructure." In Cook, ed., *Social Exchange Theory.*

Blau, Peter, Caroline Beeker, and Kevin Fitzpatrick. 1984. "Crosscutting Social Circles and Intermarriage." *Social Forces* 62:585–606.

Blum, Terry C. 1984. "Racial Inequality and Salience: An Explanation of Blau's Theory of Social Structure." *Social Forces* 62:607–617.

Blum, Terry C. 1985. "Structural Constraints on Interpersonal Relations: A Test of Blau's Macro-Sociological Theory." *American Journal of Sociology* 91:511–521.

Boswell, Terry, and Albert Bergesen, eds. 1987. *America's Changing Role in the World-System*. New York: Praeger.

Bottomore, Tom. 1984. *The Frankfurt School*. Chichester, Eng.: Ellis Harwood.

Bourdieu, Pierre. 1977. *Outline of a Theory of Practice*. Cambridge: Cambridge University Press.

Bowles, Samuel, and Herbert Gintis. 1986. *Democracy and Capitalism: Property, Community, and the Contradictions of Modern Social Thought*. New York: Basic Books.

Brown, Richard. 1987. *Society As Text: Essays on Rhetoric, Reason and Reality*. Chicago: University of Chicago Press.

Bulmer, Martin. 1984. *The Chicago School of Sociology: Institutionalization, Diversity, and the Rise of Sociological Research*. Chicago: University of Chicago Press.

Bulmer, Martin. 1985. "The Chicago School of Sociology: What Made it a School?" *The History of Sociology: An International Review* 5:61–77.

Burt, Ronald. 1982. *Toward a Structural Theory of Action: Network Models of Social Structure*. New York: Academic Press.

Camic, Charles. 1987. "The Making of a Model: A Historical Reinterpretation of the Early Parsons." *American Sociological Review* 52:421–439.

Chafetz, Janet Saltzman. 1984. *Sex and Advantage*. Totowa, N.J.: Rowman and Allanheld.

Chafetz, Janet Saltzman. 1988. *Feminist Sociology: An Overview of Contemporary Theories*. Itasca, Ill.: Peacock.

Chodorow, Nancy. 1978. *The Reproduction of Mothering: Psychoanalysis and the Sociology of Gender*. Berkeley: University of California Press.

Clawson, Dan, Alan Neustadtl, and James Bearden. 1986. "The Logic of Business Unity: Corporate Contributions to the 1980 Congressional Elections." *American Sociological Review* 51:797–811.

Coleman, James. 1986a. "Social Theory, Social Research, and a Theory of Action." *American Journal of Sociology* 91:1309–1335.

Coleman, James. 1986b. *Individual Interests and Collective Action: Selected Essays*. Cambridge: Cambridge University Press.

Coleman, James. 1987. "Microfoundations and Macrosocial Behavior." In Alexander et al., eds., *The Micro-Macro Link*.

Collins, Randall. 1975. *Conflict Sociology: Toward an Explanatory Science*. New York: Academic Press.

Collins, Randall. 1981. "On the Microfoundations of Macrosociology." *American Journal of Sociology* 86:984–1014.

Collins, Randall. 1985. *Weberian Sociological Theory*. Cambridge: Cambridge University Press.

Collins, Randall. 1986. "Is 1980s Sociology in the Doldrums?" *American Journal of Sociology* 91:1336–1355.

Collins, Randall. 1987a. "Interaction Ritual Chains, Power and Property: The Micro-Macro Connection as an Empirically Based Theoretical Problem." In Alexander et al., eds., *The Micro-Macro Link*.

Collins, Randall. 1987b. "A Micro-Macro Theory of Intellectual Creativity: The Case of German Idealistic Philosophy." *Sociological Theory* 5:47–69.

Collins, Randall. 1988. "The Micro Contribution to Macro Sociology." *Sociological Theory* 6:242–253.

Collins, Randall. 1989. "Toward a Neo-Meadian Sociology of Mind." *Symbolic Interaction* 12:1–32.

Colomy, Paul. 1986. "Recent Developments in the Functionalist Approach to Change." *Sociological Focus* 19:139–158.

Cook, Karen, ed. 1987a. *Social Exchange Theory*. Beverly Hills, Cal.: Sage.

Cook, Karen. 1987b. "Emerson's Contributions to Social Exchange Theory." In Cook, ed., *Social Exchange Theory*.

Cook, Karen S., Richard M. Emerson, Mary R. Gillmore, and Toshio Yamagishi. 1983. "The Distribution of Power in Exchange Networks: Theory and Experimental Results." *American Journal of Sociology* 89:275–305.

Denzin, Norman. 1986. "Postmodern Social Theory." *Sociological Theory* 4:194–204.

Edel, Abraham. 1959. "The Concept of Levels in Sociological Theory." In L. Gross, ed., *Symposium on Sociological Theory*. Evanston, Ill.: Row Peterson.

Eisenstadt, S. N., and H. J. Helle, 1985. "General Introduction to Perspectives on Sociological Theory." In S. N. Eisenstadt and H. J. Helle, eds., *Macro-Sociological Theory*. London: Sage.

Elster, Jon. 1985. *Making Sense of Marx*. Cambridge: Cambridge University Press.

Emerson, Richard. 1981. "Social Exchange Theory." In Morris Rosenberg and Ralph H. Turner, eds., *Social Psychology: Sociological Perspectives*. New York: Basic Books.

Etzioni, Amitai. 1988. *The Moral Dimension: Toward a New Economics*. New York: Free Press.

Farganis, Sondra. 1986. *The Social Construction of the Feminine Character*. Totowa, N.J.: Rowman and Littlefield.

Fine, Gary. 1986. "Interpreting the Sociological Classics: Can There Be a 'True' Meaning of Mead?" *Symbolic Interaction* 9:129–146.

Fontana, Andrea. 1984. "Introduction: Existential Sociology and the Self." In Kotarba and Fontana, eds., *The Existential Self in Society*.

Foucault, Michel. 1965. *Madness and Civilization: A History of Insanity in the Age of Reason*. New York: Vintage.

Foucault, Michel. 1975. *The Birth of the Clinic: An Archaeology of Medical Perception*. New York: Vintage.

Foucault, Michel. 1979. *Discipline and Punish: The Birth of the Prison*. New York: Vintage.

Foucault, Michel. 1980. *The History of Sexuality. Vol. 1: An Introduction*. New York: Vintage.

Freidman, Debra, and Michael Hechter. 1988. "The Contribution of Rational Choice Theory to Macrosociological Research." *Sociological Theory* 6:201–218.

Gerstein, Dean. 1987. "To Unpack Micro and Macro: Link Small with Large and Part with Whole." In Alexander et al., eds., *The Micro-Macro Link*.

Giddens, Anthony. 1984. *The Constitution of Society: Outline of the Theory of Structuration*. Berkeley: University of California Press.

Gonos, George. 1977. " 'Situation' Versus 'Frame': The 'Interactionist' and the 'Structuralist' Analyses of Everyday Life." *American Sociological Review* 42:854–867.

Gonos, George. 1980. "The Class Position of Goffman's Sociology: Social Origins of an American Structuralism." In J. Ditton, ed., *The View from Goffman*. New York: St. Martin's.

Gouldner, Alvin. 1970. *The Coming Crisis of Western Sociology*. New York: Basic Books.

Granovetter, Mark. 1973. "The Strength of Weak Ties." *American Journal of Sociology* 78:1360–1380.

Granovetter, Mark. 1983. "The Strength of Weak Ties: A Network Theory Revisited." In Randall Collins, ed., *Sociological Theory—1983*. San Francisco: Jossey-Bass.

Granovetter, Mark. 1985. "Economic Action and Social Structure: The Problem of Embeddedness." *American Journal of Sociology* 91:484–510.

Haas, Jack, and William Shaffir. 1982. "Taking on the Role of Doctor: A Dramaturgic Analysis of Professionalization." *Symbolic Interaction* 5:187–203.

Habermas, Jürgen. 1984. *The Theory of Communicative Action, Vol. 1, Reason and the Rationalization of Society*. Boston: Beacon Press.

Habermas, Jürgen. 1987. *The Theory of Communicative Action, Vol. 2, Lifeworld and System: A Critique of Functionalist Reason*. Boston: Beacon Press.

Hartsock, Nancy. 1983. *Money, Sex and Power: Towards a Feminist Historical Materialism*. New York: Longman.

Harvey, Lee. 1982. "The Use and Abuse of Kuhnian Paradigms in the Sociology of Knowledge." *British Journal of Sociology* 16:85–101.

Harvey, Lee. 1987. "The Nature of 'Schools' in the Sociology of Knowledge: The Case of the 'Chicago School.' " *Sociological Review* 35:245–278.

Hechter, Michael. 1983a. "Introduction." In Michael Hechter, ed., *The Microfoundations of Macrosociology*. Philadelphia: Temple University Press.

Hechter, Michael. 1983b. "A Theory of Group Solidarity." In Michael Hechter, ed., *The Microfoundations of Macrosociology*. Philadelphia: Temple University Press.

Hechter, Michael. 1987. *Principles of Group Solidarity*. Berkeley: University of California Press.

Heritage, John, and J. Maxwell Atkinson. 1984. "Introduction." In J. Maxwell Atkinson and John Heritage, eds., *Structures of Social Actions*. Cambridge: Cambridge University Press.

Heritage, John, and David Greatbatch. 1986. "Generating Applause: A Study of Rhetoric and Response in Party Political Conferences." *American Journal of Sociology* 92:110–157.

Hilbert, Richard A. 1986. "Anomie and Moral Regulation of Reality: The Durkheimian Tradition in Modern Relief." *Sociological Theory* 4:1–19.

Hilbert, Richard A. 1987. "Bureaucracy as Belief, Rationalization as Repair: Max Weber in a Post-Functionalist Age." *Sociological Theory* 5:70–86.

Hirsch, Paul, Stuart Michaels, and Ray Friedman. 1987. " 'Dirty Hands' versus 'Clean Models': Is Sociology in Danger of Being Seduced by Economics?" *Theory and Society* 16:317–336.

Homans, George. 1974. *Social Behavior: Its Elementary Forms*. New York: Harcourt Brace Jovanovich.

Huaco, George. 1986. "Ideology and General Theory: The Case of Sociological Functionalism." *Comparative Studies in Society and History* 28:34–54.

Human Studies. 1986. "Interaction and Language Use." Special Issue 9.

Human Studies. 1987. "Foucault Memorial Issue." Special Issue 10.

Kellner, Douglas. 1988. "Postmodernism as Social Theory: Some Challenges and Problems." *Theory, Culture and Society* 5:239–269.

Kemeny, Jim. 1976. "Perspectives on the Micro-Macro Distinction." *Sociological Review* 24:731–752.

Kitahara, Michio. 1986. "Commodore Perry and the Japanese: A Study in the Dramaturgy of Power." *Symbolic Interaction* 9:53–65.

Kotarba, Joseph A., and Andrea Fontana, eds. 1984. *The Existential Self in Society*. Chicago: University of Chicago Press.

Kuhn, Thomas. 1962. *The Structure of Scientific Revolutions*. Chicago: University of Chicago Press.

Kuhn, Thomas. 1970. *The Structure of Scientific Revolutions*. 2d ed. Chicago: University of Chicago Press.

Kurzweil, Edith. 1980. *The Age of Structuralism: Lévi-Strauss to Foucault.* New York: Columbia University Press.

Kurzweil, Edith. 1987. "Psychoanalysis as the Macro-Micro Link." In Alexander et al., eds., *The Micro-Macro Link.*

Lengermann, Patricia Madoo, and Jill Niebrugge-Brantley. 1988. "Contemporary Feminist Theory." In Ritzer, *Sociological Theory.* 2d ed.

Luhmann, Niklas. 1987. "The Evolutionary Differentiation between Society and Interaction." In Alexander et al., eds., *The Micro-Macro Link.*

McMahon, A. M. 1984. "The Two Social Psychologies: Postcrises Directions." In Ralph H. Turner and James F. Short, eds., *Annual Review of Sociology.* Vol. 10. Palo Alto: Annual Reviews.

Mann, Michael. 1986. *The Sources of Social Power* Vol. 1. New York: Cambridge University Press.

Marske, Charles E. 1987. "Durkheim's 'Cult of the Individual' and the Moral Reconstitution of Society." *Sociological Theory* 5:1–14.

Merton, Robert. 1986. "Comments." In Siegwart Lindenberg, James S. Coleman, and Stefan Nowak, eds., *Approaches to Social Theory.* New York: Russell Sage Foundation.

Messner, Steven F. 1986. "Modernization, Structural Characteristics, and Societal Rates of Crime: An Application of Blau's Macrosociological Theory." *The Sociological Quarterly* 27:27–41.

Mizruchi, Mark S., and Thomas Koenig. 1986. "Economic Sources of Corporate Political Consensus: An Examination of Interindustry Relations." *American Sociological Review* 51:482–491.

Moore, Wilbert. 1978. "Functionalism." In Tom Bottomore and Robert Nisbet, eds., *A History of Sociological Analysis.* New York: Basic Books.

Monk, Richard, ed. 1986. *Structures of Knowing.* Lanham, Md.: University Press of America.

Mullins, Nicholas. 1973. *Theories and Theory Groups in Contemporary American Sociology.* New York: Harper and Row.

Mullins, Nicholas. 1983. "Theories and Theory Groups Revisited." In Randall Collins, ed., *Sociological Theory—1983.* San Francisco: Jossey-Bass.

Munch, Richard, and Neil Smelser. 1987. "Relating the Micro and Macro." In Alexander et al., eds., *The Micro-Macro Link.*

Parsons, Talcott. 1937. *The Structure of Social Action.* New York: McGraw-Hill.

Perinbanayagam, Robert S. 1985. *Signifying Acts: Structure and Meaning in Everyday Life.* Carbondale: Southern Illinois University Press.

Rawls, Ann Warfield. 1987. "The Interaction Order Sui Generis: Goffman's Contribution to Social Theory." *Sociological Theory* 5:136–149.

Rehorick, David Allan. 1986. "Shaking the Foundations of Lifeworld: A Phenomenological Account of an Earthquake Experience." *Human Studies* 9:379–391.

Rich, Adrienne. 1976. *Of Woman Born: Motherhood as Experience and Institution.* New York: Bantam.

Ritzer, George. 1975. *Sociology: A Multiple Paradigm Science.* Boston: Allyn and Bacon.

Ritzer, George. 1985. "The Rise of Micro-Sociological Theory." *Sociological Theory* 3:88–98.

Ritzer, George. 1988a. "Sociological Metatheory: A Defense of a Subfield by a Delineation of Its Parameters." *Sociological Theory* 6:187–200.

Ritzer, George. 1988b. "The Micro-Macro Link: Problems and Prospects." *Contemporary Sociology* 17:703–706.

Ritzer, George. 1988c. *Sociological Theory.* 2d ed. New York: Knopf.

Ritzer, George. 1989. "Of Levels and 'Intellectual Amnesia.'" *Sociological Theory,* forthcoming.

Ritzer, George, ed. 1990. Special Mini-Issue on Metatheory. *Sociological Forum*, forthcoming.

Ritzer, George, and David Walczak. 1986. *Working: Conflict and Change.* 3d ed. Englewood Cliffs, N.J.: Prentice-Hall.

Roemer, John. 1982. "Methodological Individualism and Deductive Marxism." *Theory and Society* 11:513–520.

Roemer, John. 1986. *Analytical Marxism.* Cambridge: Cambridge University Press.

Rose, Gillian. 1984. *Dialectic of Nihilism: Post-Structuralism and Law.* New York: Basil Blackwell.

Schegloff, Emanuel. 1987. "Between Marco and Micro: Contexts and Other Connections." In Alexander et al., eds., *The Micro-Macro Link.*

Sciulli, David. 1986. "Voluntaristic Action as a Distinct Concept: Theoretical Foundations of Societal Constitutionalism." *American Sociological Review* 51:743–766.

Sciulli, David, and Dean Gerstein. 1985. "Social Theory and Talcott Parsons in the 1980s." *Annual Review of Sociology* 11:369–387.

Shalin, Dimitri. 1986. "Pragmatism and Social Interactionism." *American Sociological Review* 51:9–29. .

Shalin, Dmitri. 1988. "G. H. Mead, Socialism, and the Progressive Agenda." *American Journal of Sociology* 93:913–951.

Sharrock, Wes, and Bob Anderson. 1986. *The Ethnomethodologists.* Chichester, Eng.: Ellis Horwood.

Shils, Edward. 1970. "Tradition, Ecology, and Institution in the History of Sociology." *Daedalus* 99:760–825.

Smelser, Neil. 1987. "Depth Psychology and the Social Order." In Alexander et al., eds., *The Micro-Macro Link.*

Smelser, Neil. 1988. "Sociological Theory: Looking Forward." *Perspectives: The Theory Section Newsletter* 11:1–3.

Smith, Dorothy. 1979. "A Sociology for Women." In Julia A. Sherman and Evelyn Torton Beck, eds., *The Prism of Sex: Essays in the Sociology of Knowledge.* Madison: University of Wisconsin Press.

Snow, David A. 1986. "Frame Alignment Processes, Micromobilization, and Movement Participation." *American Sociological Review* 51:464–481.

Snow, David, Louis A. Zurcher, and Robert Peters. 1984. "Victory Celebrations as Theatre: A Dramaturgical Approach to Crowd Behavior." *Symbolic Interaction* 8:21–42.

Stinchcombe, Arthur. 1986. "The Development of Scholasticism." In Siegwàrt Lindenberg, James S. Coleman, and Stefan Nowak, eds., *Approaches to Social Theory.* New York: Russell Sage Foundation.

Swedberg, Richard, Ulf Himmelstrand, and Goran Brulin. 1987. "The Paradigm of Economic Sociology: Premises and Promises." *Theory and Society* 16:169–213.

Symbolic Interaction. 1988. "Herbert Blumer's Legacy." 11:1–143.

Theory, Culture and Society. 1987. "Norbert Elias and Figurational Sociology." Special issue.

Theory and Society. 1986. "Structures of Capital." Special Issue.

Tiryakian, Edward A. 1979. "The Significance of Schools in the Development of Sociology." In William Snizek, Ellsworth Fuhrman, and Michael Miller, eds., *Contemporary Issues in Theory and Research.* Westport, Conn.: Greenwood Press.

Tiryakian, Edward A. 1986. "Hegemonic Schools and the Development of Sociology: Rethinking the History of the Discipline." In Richard G. Monk, ed., *Structure of Knowing.* Lanham, Md.: University Press of America.

Turner, Jonathan, and Alexandra Maryanski. 1979. *Functionalism.* Menlo Park, Cal.: Benjamin/Cummings.

30 *George Ritzer*

Turner, Jonathan H., and Alexandra R. Maryanski. 1988. "Is 'Neofunctionalism' Really Functional?" *Sociological Theory* 6:110–121.

Vidich, Arthur J., and Stanford M. Lyman. 1985. *American Sociology: Worldly Rejections of Religion and Their Directions*. New Haven: Yale University Press.

Wagner, David, and Joseph Berger. 1985. "Do Sociological Theories Grow?" *American Journal of Sociology* 90:697–728.

Wagner, Helmut. 1964. "Displacement of Scope: A Problem of the Relationship between Small Scale and Large Scale Sociological Theories." *American Journal of Sociology* 69:571–584.

Wallace, Walter. 1969. "Overview of Contemporary Sociological Theory." In Walter Wallace, *Sociological Theory*. Chicago: University of Chicago Press.

Wallerstein, Immanuel. 1980. *The Modern World-System II: Mercantilism and the Consolidation of the European World-Economy, 1600–1750*. New York: Academic Press.

Wallerstein, Immanuel. 1988. *The Modern World-System III: The Second Era of Great Expansion of the Capitalist World Economy, 1730–1840s*. New York: Academic Press.

Weldes, Jutta, and Raymond D. Duvall. 1987. "Marxism without Marx." *Contemporary Sociology* 16:897–899.

Wellman, Barry. 1983. "Network Analysis: Some Basic Principles." In Randall Collins, ed., *Sociological Theory—1983*. San Francisco: Jossey-Bass.

Wiley, Norbert. 1979. "The Rise and Fall of Dominating Theories in American Sociology." In William Snizek, Ellsworth Fuhrman, and Michael Miller, eds., *Contemporary Issues in Theory and Research*. Westport, Conn.: Greenwood Press.

Wiley, Norbert. 1988. "The Micro-Macro Problem in Social Theory." *Sociological Theory* 6:254–261.

Wright, Erik Olin. 1987. "Towards a Post-Marxist Radical Social Theory." *Contemporary Sociology* 16:748–753.

Wright, Erik Olin, and Bill Martin. 1987. "The Transformation of the American Class Structure, 1960–1980." *American Journal of Sociology* 93:1–29.

Wuthnow, Robert et al., eds. 1984. *Cultural Analysis*. Boston: Routledge and Kegan Paul.

Zurcher, Louis A. 1985. "The War Game: Organizational Scripting and the Expression of Emotion." *Symbolic Interaction* 8:191–206.

I
NEW LIFE IN
SOME TRADITIONAL
SOCIAL AND
SOCIOLOGICAL THEORIES
❋

2

Neofunctionalism Today: Reconstructing a Theoretical Tradition

❁

JEFFREY C. ALEXANDER
University of California, Los Angeles

PAUL COLOMY
University of Denver

In 1979, Alexander acknowledged that "despite Parsons' enduring impression on the sociological tradition, it is too early to determine the ultimate fate of his theoretical legacy." There seemed a real possibility that "the Parsonian synthesis will break down completely." It was also possible, however, that in time a "more loosely-defined, less sectarian version of functionalist theory" might appear (Alexander 1979a, 355). In this essay we will try to demonstrate that it is the latter, not the former, of these possibilities that actually has come to pass.

When the initial volumes of *Theoretical Logic in Sociology* began to appear in 1982 (Alexander 1982a, 1982b, 1983a, 1983b), they were not greeted with unanimous approval. Incredulity, dismay, even indignation were prominently displayed. Marxist, humanist, constructivist, and positivist theorists, and even one older Parsonian, wrote negative reviews, warning the profession away from what they considered a retrograde development. The one thing about which these critics agreed was that the Parsonian foundation of *Theoretical Logic* represented a holdover from the past, rather than a new development in contemporary sociological thought.

These initial responses emerged from self-understandings of theoretical orientations that had been formed in a struggle against structural-functional thought. Positivism, conflict theory, Marxism, exchange theory, symbolic interactionism, phenomenology—all had once been obstreperous challengers to the Parsonian edifice. By 1980, it might be said, with only some exaggeration, that they were triumphant, not challengers but the dominant theories in a new, if internally divided, establishment. Surely, if sociological progress was to have any meaning at all, the Parsonian approach could not be revived. The very *raisons d'etre* of these positions demanded that such an alternative not be raised.

In the January 1988 issue of *Contemporary Sociology*, Marco Orru describes the works he has under review as sharing an "enthusiastic reappraisal of Parsonian sociology." He develops a perspective within which to view them by pointing precisely to the doubt their existence casts on linear conceptions of social scientific development.

> As social scientists, we wish for theories about the social world to build on each other in some linear fashion but more often than not we observe, instead, a cyclical pattern by which different schools of thought replace each other in commanding our attention over time. Leading figures in the various theoretical traditions follow this same pattern. (Orru 1988, 115)

Only after suggesting the validity of a more cyclical pattern can Orru conclude by suggesting that "the revival of Parsonian thought is one of the distinguishing features of 1980s sociology."

If Orru is right about the conspicuous importance of the Parsonian revival, and we think he is, there has been a sea change in sociology in the last half dozen years. In retrospect, at least, it seems clear that *Theoretical Logic* was not the final aftershock in response to the anti-Parsonian quake. As we will suggest later in this essay, it was not, in fact, an effort to revive earlier, orthodox Parsonian theory at all. It was, rather, a challenge to central tenets of the Parsonian orientation, an effort to revise it in a radical, post-Parsonian way. As such, it might better be seen as a preshock, a premonition of things to come. It has become evident in retrospect that *Theoretical Logic* was not anomalous. The previous year, indeed, Habermas had pointedly demanded the relegitimation of Parsonian theory in a not dissimilar way, as had Richard Munch in a powerful double set of articles in the *American Journal of Sociology*.[1]

When Alexander (1985a) subsequently introduced the term "neo-functionalism," it was in order to emphasize the double element of continuity and internal critique. This emphasis is revealed in his analogy to neo-Marxism. Current sociology a la Parsonian is to the earlier orthodoxy as neo-Marxism is to its orthodox earlier variant. Neo-Marxism has tried to overcome the mechanistic rigidities of Marx by incorporating the most important advances of twentieth-century social thought. The relation of neofunctionalism to the traditions that challenged early Parsonian theory, it was suggested, is much the same.

This public assertion of the continuing vitality of the Parsonian tradition drew, once again, a decidedly mixed response. In *Footnotes*, an elder statesman (Page 1985) wrote an open letter to warn his colleagues about the dangers of revivifying functionalism. A younger theorist, Charles Camic (1986), in his review of *Neofunctionalism*, reassured his readers that the revivalists had learned nothing from the criticisms of Parsons and that in their theorizing one could find nothing new. Another contemporary, George Ritzer (1985), reinforced this skepticism, while offering that he was willing to wait and see.

Today, while fundamental doubts about the validity and desirability of neofunctionalism have not disappeared, the disciplinary community is gradually coming to terms with the fact that something new has appeared on the sociological scene. Orru's observation attests to this recognition. So does Giddens and Turner's (1987, 3) reference to the recent "considerable revival" of Parsonian thought in their introduction to *Social Theory Today*. Contemporary textbooks in sociological theory (e.g., Ritzer 1988; Collins 1988a) are being revised to reflect this shift in the theoretical map.[2]

In the course of the twentieth century, critics and sympathizers of neo-Marxism have often asked, "What is Marxist about it?" In so doing, they have indicated the extent of the critical departure from the original form. In Jonathan Turner and Alexandra Maryanski's (1988) "What is Functionalist about Neofunctionalism?" the same doubt is raised about recent neofunctionalist work. There is no doubting that in certain respects Turner and Maryanski have grounds for complaint. Neofunctionalism differs from orthodox Parsonian thought in decisive and often radical ways. Even while it disputes the discipline's evaluation of earlier functionalism, it does not itself accept some of the central tendencies of that earlier thought. Even while it sustains fundamental links with Parsons' earlier work, therefore, it does not conceive of itself as an attempt to resuscitate an older orthodoxy. Whether its originality is undermined by its continuing roots in Parsonian thought is, of course, a matter of debate. The claim can be made, however, that neofunctionalism is the only new theoretical movement to have emerged in Western sociology in the 1980s.[3]

One of our ambitions in this paper is to indicate the substance of this new theoretical movement in sociology—its general discursive structure, its interpretations of the classics, the scope of its research programs, and its relation to other theoretical discourse and research programs in the field. This will involve a critical look at the wide variety of work that is currently underway. We would like to begin, however, by exploring some of the reasons why this unexpected revival has come about. In this regard, to point to the intrinsic interest of current neofunctionalist works is besides the point. Their very appearance has been a response to underlying developments in sociology. Neofunctionalism, we will argue, is only one indication of a deep groundshift in the entire sociological field. To understand its relevance on the contemporary scene one must understand the new and different theoretical situation that is emerging today.

THE EMERGING THIRD PHASE OF POSTWAR SOCIOLOGY

Since World War II, Western sociology has passed through two periods, and it is entering a third. In the first phase, which lasted into the 1960s, structural-functionalism, in its Parsonian and Mertonian form, could be said to be the dominant force. Whatever its ideological weaknesses, its anti-empirical stance, its naive confidence in equilibrium—and we will talk about all these below—that functionalism was committed to the syntheses of what Parsons called the "warring schools" of sociological thought seems impossible to deny. This orientation toward theoretical integration and synthesis was one casualty of the rebellion against functionalism that began in the 1960s and continued triumphantly into the early 1980s.

Two major battle lines were drawn. On the one side, microsociology set contingent action against social structure in the name of creativity and individual freedom. On the other side, conflict sociology argued that social change could be explained only by emphasizing material rather than ideal forces. These propositions denied the central tenets of Parsons' work. Thus, as Goffman, Homans, and Garfinkel gained increasing authority, interest in socialization and personality structure correspondingly declined. As Rex, Lockwood, and Dahrendorf became central figures, with Collins, Giddens, Wright, and Skocpol following in their stead, macrosociological interest in culture and symbolic legitimacy dramatically declined.

Yet even as these brilliant challengers became the new establishment, even as the "multiparadigmatic" character of sociology passed from daring prophecy (e.g., Friedrichs 1970) to conventional wisdom (e.g., Ritzer 1975), the vital and creative phase of these theoretical movements was coming to an end. Stimulated by the premature theoretical closure of the micro and macro traditions, a new phase is beginning. It is marked by an effort to relink theorizing about action and order, conflict and stability, structure and culture. Such efforts have been made from within each of the newly dominant theoretical traditions, from both sides of the great micro/macro divide. They are also the most clearly distinguishing characteristics of the new directions in general theory. The old lines of confrontation are being discredited. There is a movement back to synthesis once again. We believe that it is this development that marks the third phase of postwar sociology.

In symbolic interaction, a whole spate of work has challenged the emphasis on individualistic contingency that, under Blumer's leadership, marked this tradition's earlier development. Goffman's writing (1974) on frame analysis and Becker's (1982) on the social organization of art can be seen as marked departures from earlier, much more negotiation-oriented work. Stryker (1980) has called for a reintegration of interactionism with systems theory, Lewis and Smith (1980) have argued that Mead was a collectivist, and Fine (1984, 1988) has moved forcefully into the area of cultural and organizational studies.

In the exchange tradition, leading theorists (e.g., Coleman 1986a, 1986b, 1987; Wippler and Lindenberg 1987) increasingly reject the notion that the individual/structure relation can be seen as a causal relation between discrete empirical events. Because there is empirical simultaneity, the linkage between micro and macro must be seen as an analytical one sustained by larger systemic processes. This analytical linkage is achieved by the application of what are called "transformation rules," such as voting procedures, to individual actions. In the work of theorists like Goode, Blau, and Coleman, structural explanations—about the rules of constitutions (e.g., Coleman 1987), the dynamics of organizations and intergroup relations (Blau 1977), and the system of prestige allocation (Goode 1978)—have begun to replace utility arguments.

Within ethnomethodology, one can point to similar developments in the work of Cicourel, who has recently pushed for a linkage with macrosociological work (Knorr-Cetina and Cicourel 1981). Recent work by Molotch (Molotch and Boden 1985) and Schegloff (1987) demonstrates how discursive practices are structured by organizational context and the distribution of power, even while their analytical autonomy is maintained. Heritage and Greatbatch's (1986) research on political conventions makes a similar effort to establish micro-macro links.

When one examines the structural or conflict position, one finds similar efforts to overcome the splits of the second phase. Moore (1978) has turned from objective to subjective injustice, Skocpol and Finegold (1982) have raised the possibility that religion may be an independent cause of social policy and political change. Sewell (1980, 1985), once a devoted Tilly student, and Darnton (1982), once a leading *Annaliste*, are now developing cultural approaches to social change and history. Calhoun (1982) and Prager (1986) have published polemically antistructural works of historical sociology. Meyer and Scott (1983) link organizations to cultural structures rather than technical ones. This cultural turn in macrosociology is responsible, we believe, for the emergence of a new disciplinary specialty, cultural sociology, which has just become the newest American Sociological Association section. It is instructive that theorists who associate themselves with this specialty argue that culture cannot be understood in terms of what we have called the dichotomies of the second phase. Wuthnow (1988) argues that culture need not be understood individualistically or even subjectively, Swidler (1986) for culture's opening to contingency, Archer (1988) for its sensitivity to change, Eisenstadt (1986) for its link to material force and institutional life.

Within general theory there is an equally strong movement away from the one-sided polemics of earlier theoretical work. Where Giddens' earlier work (1971) was part of conflict and neo-Marxist theorizing, in the last decade he (1984) has sought to interweave contingency, material structure, and normative rules. Collins' (1975) earlier work was paradigmatic of conflict sociology; in recent years, by contrast, he has embraced microsociology (1981), the later Durkheimian emphasis on rituals (1987, 1988b), and even the framing concept of multidimensionality (1988a). Habermas, too, began his career with a typical Frankfurt school emphasis on the destructively capitalist features of modern life; more recently, he (1984) has theorized about the normative and micro processes that underline and often oppose the macrostructure of capitalist societies, making these cultural forces "equal but separate" subsystems.[4]

We earlier pointed to premature theoretical closure as the intellectual reason for the denouement of phase two. One-sided theories are effective polemical means; they are decidedly less successful when they must function as sources of theoretical cohesion, if not disciplinary integration, in their own right. Social and institutional factors, however, are also involved. One certain factor is the changing political climate in the United States and Europe. Revolutionary social movements have faded away; because of developments like Solidarity and revelations about the Chinese Cultural Revolution, in the eyes of many critical intellectuals Marxism itself has been morally delegitimated.

The ideological thrust that fueled post-Parsonian discourse in its micro and macro form and that justified Marxist structuralism on the Continent is largely spent. There is a new realism, even pessimism, about the possibilities for social change, which has manifest itself in two very different ways. On the one hand, there is the resignation, even fatalism of so much postmodern thought, with its nostalgic return to localism (Lyotard 1984) and its abandonment of the possibility of a more rational social life (Foucault 1984). On the other hand, there is the search for less apocalyptic ways of institutionalizing rationality, approaches which concentrate on the difficulties of preserving political democracy rather than on the unlikely, and perhaps undesirable, possibility of some socialist transformation (Lefort 1986; Alexander 1988a).

PARSONS' NEW RELEVANCE IN THE CONTEMPORARY PHASE

Is it any wonder that neofunctionalism has flourished in this changing social and disciplinary environment? Parsons' original work contained within it a wide and contradictory range of theoretical ideas. There are central areas in his corpus, however, that complement this third phase. Developing in a period of reaction against the limits of the second phase, neofunctionalists have interpreted the "natural concerns" of Parsons' thought in just this way. They have argued that it provides critical theoretical resources for addressing the concerns of this new period in postwar sociological work.

More than anything else, perhaps, neofunctionalism has presented itself as a prototypically synthetic form of theorizing. After all, it was Parsons' original and flawed effort at theoretical integration—and what were seen as its attendant weaknesses—that provoked micro and macro theorists to launch the one-sided theories that themselves have recently come under increasing doubt. It is not surprising, therefore, that as contemporary theorists have returned to the project of synthesis, they have often returned to some core element in Parsons' earlier thought. It is striking that this return is manifest in the work of theorists who have never had any previous association with Parsonian thought. The motive is theoretical logic, not personal desire.

No more clear example of this theoretical pressure can be found than Habermas' *Legitimation Crisis* (1975). Departing from the safe harbor of critical theory, Habermas wanted to incorporate into his model of economic contradictions factors like personality strain, the universalist potential of value commitments, and the latently anticapitalist pressures that emanate from the formal equality of political and legal institutions. What he ends up employing, de facto if not de jure, is Parsons' AGIL model and also his division between culture, personality, and social system. Similar examples can be found in a wide range of recent theoretical work. When Schluchter (1979, 1981) wants to present a newly integrated view of Weber's civilizational work, he makes use of the evolutionary and developmental language of Parsons' differentiation theory. When Collins (1988b) pushes to expand his "conflict-Durkheimian" theory of social rituals into the realm of democratic politics, he is forced to acknowledge the importance Parsons' multidimensional theory of political support. In Holton's (1986) effort to transcend both market and Marxist approaches to political economy, he turns with relief to the rich conceptual legacy of Parsons and Smelser's model of the economy-society relation. To reaffirm the delicate but distinctive pluralism of Western social systems, Turner (1986a, 1986b, 1987) extends the concepts of inclusion, citizenship, and value generalization from Parsons' theory of social change. In our own efforts (Alexander and Giesen 1987; Alexander 1987a; Colomy and Rhoades 1988) to construct a model of the micro-macro link—efforts that challenge orthodox functionalism in fundamental ways—we have found that Parsons' analytic model provides the only viable foundation for a new synthesis.

This new relevance of Parsonian thought can also be seen in the renewed theorizing about culture and society. It is not accidental, in this regard, that it has been the former students and coworkers of Parsons who have assumed a central role in the revival of macro-cultural studies. Geertz (1973) initiated this "cultural revolution" with his essays in the 1960s, which stood firmly upon Parsons' insistence on the analytical autonomy of the cultural realm. Bellah's (1970, 1973) argument for the relationship between symbolic realism and democratic social integration can also be traced back to key themes in Parsons' normative work. When Eisenstadt criticizes contemporary structuralist approaches to historical and contemporary sociology for their "ontological" rather than analytical approach to culture and society relations (1986), he is drawing from Parsons' theory of the institutionalization of values. Archer's (1985, 1988) ambitious metatheory of culture begins from the Parsonian distinction between culture, action, and social system. Robertson's (1987) work on global culture issues in critical respects (Robertson 1982; cf. Robertson 1988) from Parsons' concepts of value generalization and societal community. In Alexander's (1982b, 211–296; 1984, 1988b) own effort to construct a model of cultural structures and processes, he, too, begins with the analytic differentiation of symbolic patterns from the exigencies of social and personality systems.

We have indicated here the convergence between the interests that mark the current, third phase of sociological thought and some of the earlier concerns of Parsonian work. We have demonstrated this coincidence in terms of the desire for theoretical synthesis and the new attempt to theorize culture. The third element of this third phase—the clearly changing ideological environment of sociology—will be taken up below, in the context of a more systematic discussion of neofunctionalist work. Up until this point, we have noted the convergence between developments in neofunctionalism and more general movements in the theoretical field, but we have not looked at specific arguments or tried to construct the details of a new disciplinary map.

Before taking up these tasks, we need a framework within which to consider issues of disciplinary conflict and change.

SOCIAL SCIENCE AS DISCOURSE AND RESEARCH PROGRAM [5]

To understand correctly the issues involved in the emergence and decline of theoretical orientations, we must see that social science is neither the fact-bound nor middle-level enterprise that empiricists describe. Social science is organized by traditions, and traditions, whatever their aspirations for rationality, are founded by charismatic figures. At the beginnings of a discipline, powerful intellectual figures are regarded as classical founders (Alexander 1987b); at later points, they are accorded quasi-classical status and treated as founders of powerful schools. Social reality, then, is never confronted in and of itself. Because perception is mediated by the discursive commitments of traditions, social scientific formulations are channeled within relatively standardized, paradigmatic forms. The matrix social scientists inhabit need not be drawn from a single tradition or be wholly of a piece, but inhabit it they must, aware of it or not.

While traditionalism implies habitual behavior, it need not imply stasis or lack of change. In social science, this openness to change is intensified by the universalism of institutionalized standards that mandate impersonal rationality and push against the particularism of a traditional first response. Social science traditions define themselves by staking out theoretical cores that are highly resistant to change. The substantial areas surrounding these nuclei, however, are subject to continuous variation. In ideal-typical terms, changes in the peripheral areas of traditions can be conceived as proceeding along two lines, "elaboration" and "revision." While both lines of development present themselves as loyally carrying out traditional commitments, they differ in the creativeness with which they pursue this task. Because elaborative sociological work proceeds from the assumption that the original tradition is internally consistent and relatively complete, it aims primarily at refinement and expansion of scope. In revisionist work, by contrast, there is a greater sense of the vulnerabilities of the established tradition; in the guise of loyal specification, an often implicit effort is made to address these strains and offer formulations that can resolve them (see, e.g., Alexander 1979a; Colomy 1986).

Elaboration and revision are lines of specification that recur periodically in a tradition's history, not only in the period of routinization that immediately follows the charismatic founding but in the wake of the powerful reformulations that must emerge if a tradition is to remain intact.[6] It is this latter possibility that points to a third ideal-typical form of theoretical change. Insofar as cores themselves undergo substantial shifts—without abandoning their association with the overarching tradition—there occurs the theoretical activity we will call "reconstruction." Reconstruction differs from elaboration and revision in that differences with the founder of the tradition are clearly acknowledged and openings to other traditions are explicitly made. Reconstruction can revive a theoretical tradition, even while it creates the opportunity for the kind of development out of which new traditions are born.[7] Finally, of course, traditions can be destroyed. This does not happen because core and peripheral commitments are falsified, but because they have become delegitimated in the eyes of the scientific community. Even in this situation, however, traditions do not so much disappear as become latent; the possibility always remains that they may be picked up once again.[8]

According to this model, then, social science does not grow simply because of the compulsion to understand empirical reality; nor can its growth be measured merely in relation to the expansion of empirical knowledge or conceptual scope. The primary motor of social scientific growth is conflict and competition between traditions. The primary reference points for measuring scientific growth are established by the relations between traditions and by signposts internal to a given tradition itself. Instead of speaking about theoretical or empirical progress per se, one must speak of relative explanatory and theoretical success vis-à-vis one's own tradition or competing ones.[9]

Elaboration, revision, and reconstruction are concepts that describe the closeness of fit between subsequent theoretical work and original tradition. They do not describe the degree of real advance. Elaboration, for example, may be thin or thick, to redeploy Geertz's ethnographic standards. Traditions may be enriched and elevated by these processes of theoretical change; they may also be impoverished and simplified, robbed of their sophistication and denuded of some of their most powerful intellectual sustenance.[10] If social science change can be progressive, therefore, it can be reactionary as well. It is rare, moreover, for these modes of theoretical development to proceed in either an entirely progressive or reactionary way.

A disciplinary community's switch from one theoretical position to another is determined neither by the theoretical effectiveness and sophistication of the respective positions nor by their objective empirical scope. It is usually motivated, rather, by broad shifts in what might be called the disciplinary community's "scientific sensibility."[11] Shifts in disciplinary sensibility put different questions on the floor. They place a premium on the development of different modes of discourse. Indeed, it is often only after new discursive commitments are made to an approach that increased theoretical sophistication and empirical scope emerge. It is in this sense that one can speak less of social scientific "development" than of social scientific "movements." Disciplines should not be understood as being organized primarily by specialties defined by their empirical objects of investigation, into Mertonian middle-range subfields like deviance, stratification, or political sociology. The deep structure of a discipline consists of the networks and literatures that are produced by the contact between empirical objects, ongoing traditions, and new disciplinary movements.

By this route we can return to the topic of neofunctionalism. In the phase of routinization that followed the emergence of Parsons' founding work, functionalism was presented as a consistent and increasingly completed theory, and elaboration and revision were the order of the day. In the second phase of postwar sociology, shifts in the disciplinary sensibility delegitimated these efforts and functionalism as a vital tradition came near to extinction. In the emerging third phase, scientific sensibility has shifted once again. In an altered theoretical and historical climate, new questions are being asked. These questions represent opportunities for dramatic disciplinary shift. In response, the functionalist tradition has entered a phase of reconstruction. Neofunctionalism is the result.

To fully elaborate the changes that have occurred within the functionalist tradition would be a complex and detailed task, for one would have to examine developments at every level of the scientific continuum. The discussion can be simplified by examining the process in terms of two basic genres, generalized discourse and research programs. By generalized discourse, we refer to discussions that argue about presuppositions, about ontology and epistemology, about the ideological and metaphysical implications of sociological argument, and about its broad historical grounding. Within the context of research programs, by contrast, such generalized issues are assumed to be relatively unproblematic. What becomes problematic, what propels this mode of scientific activity, is the need to provide interpretations or explanations of specific empirical structures and processes.

The discourse/research program distinction must not be confused with the distinctions introduced above. It is not isomorphic, for example, with core and peripheral concerns. The specific commitments that are pursued by research programs may be considered vital to the core of a tradition. Generalized discourse, for its part, is often directed to peripheral elements. Thus, in twentieth-century Marxism, in contrast to that of the nineteenth century, presuppositions about materialism and idealism have been considered part of the core; shifts toward idealism are not conceived of as threatening the "Marxist" character of theorizing. As for our model of scientific development, the processes we have identified as elaboration, revision, and reconstruction can occur through both discourse and research programs alike. In practice, it is usually discourse about more general issues that announces and introduces a reconstructive phase, for it is generalized issues that provide a framework within which more specific explanatory concerns can be conceived.[12] Indeed, in our consideration of neofunctionalism, we will focus primarily on the new kind of generalized discourse that has challenged the core. Following that discussion, we will present a brief overview of the research programs that have followed in its wake.

THE GENERALIZED DISCOURSE OF NEOFUNCTIONALISM

Generalized discourse occurs in both interpretive and expository modes. Via interpretation, theorists treat the work of the founder and other major figures in the tradition as difficult and problematic texts. Interpretive challenges are also mounted against the primary and secondary texts of other classical traditions and against the secondary literature that has developed within the home tradition as well. In the expository mode, by contrast, discourse is conducted on its own terms, general principles are set out and comparative frameworks established. While these modes of generalized discourse can be carried out by different theorists or at different points in the same discussion by a single person, they are connected to one another in an intimate way. No matter how apparently scholastic an interpretive discussion, the broader context of disciplinary struggle ensures that texts will never be considered simply for their own sake. Arguments about the meaning and validity of various texts represent one alternative, and sometimes the most effective one (Alexander 1987b) for engaging in substantive theoretical debate.

Generalized discourse makes arguments within the framework of, and in reference to, presuppositions, models, metamethodological commitments, and *Weltanschauung*, or world views. While it is possible to argue that Parsons took definite positions on each of these elements, we would argue, as neofunctionalists, that on each of these levels Parsons' orientation was ambiguous (Alexander 1983b). In terms of the problem of action, Parsons committed himself to a synthesis of material and idealist presuppositions; yet he consistently deviated from this professed aim in an idealist way. In terms of order, he aimed at linking individual actions and social structures, but from within his collectivist position he never theorized contingent effort. In terms of Parsons' theoretical model, functional and systems terminology are employed to describe a society of interrelated yet relatively independent parts. None of these are conceptualized as dominant, and equilibrium is considered an analytic reference point for evaluating social systems, not an empirical description of them. When Parsons' converted this model into a cybernetic system, however, he tilted toward one set of social system parts, the normative, raising it to a vertical position over another set, the material. He had great difficulty, moreover, in maintaining the analytic status of his model, often conflating the conceptualized ideal of equilibrium with the condition of an empirical society. Finally, there are extremely significant ambiguities in Parsons' ideology or *Weltanschauung*. Over the course of his long career, his ideological outlook shifted from critical to quiescent liberalism. What was a hopeful pessimism in the 1930s and 1940s became full-throated optimism in the 1950s and 1960s as a dedicated social scientist who aimed at constructing general covering laws, Parsons denied the connection of facts and values. Yet his growing confidence in modern, and particularly American, society made his work significantly less sensitive to the darker sides of modernity, to a wide range of depressing but undeniable facts about contemporary life.

What is perhaps most distinctive about the initial phases in the elaboration and revision of a sociological tradition is that they typically do not occur in a discursive mode. If we examine the three or four decades of Parsons' students' works, most of it, whether elaborative or revisionist, takes place within the school's research program. One need only think here of Bellah's *Tokugawa Religion* and *Beyond Belief*, Smelser's *Social Change in the Industrial Revolution* and *Theory of Collective Behavior*, and Eisenstadt's *The Political Systems of Empires*. In each of these works there is a powerful challenge to an element in the tradition's ambiguous core (Alexander 1979a, 1983b), but it is expressed in the mode of an implicit revision of explanatory apparatus, not in the framework of general discourse.[13]

When generalized discourse does emerge in this initial period, it is almost entirely affirmative, its aim being to explain the intricacies of a difficult text to students or outsiders. Good illustrations of such occasional discursive references are the Devereaux (1961) and Williams (1961) contributions to the Max Black volume on Parsons, various sections in Harry Johnson's (1960) once popular introductory textbook, and the initial chapters to the seminal books by Parsons' students we have listed above. Only in the waning days of functionalism's initial period, when Parsons came under increasing attack, did consistent exercises in generalized discourse appear. Victor Lidz's (1970, 1972) rejoinders to Albert Syzmanski's (1970a, 1970b, 1972) attacks on the value-laden character of Parsonian theory are a case in point. For the first time, Lidz raised the metamethodological underpinnings of Parsons' work in an explicit way. His rejoinders were brilliant elaborations and generalized defenses of Parsons' value-neutral stance, strictly from within the confines of the technical theory. The editors' introductions to the various sections of the two-volume Free Press festschrift for Parsons can be read in much the same way, as the last attempts by the last generation of "real Parsonians" to develop a general discourse that could affirm, elaborate, and revise the founder's work (Loubser et al. 1976).

Neofunctionalism can be distinguished from functionalism by its effort to reconstruct the core of the Parsonian tradition. Elaborative and revisionist efforts remain; indeed, the emergence of reconstructive efforts have relegitimated these more moderate, internalist lines of development. It is reconstruction, however, that has established the framework for a "neo" functionalism in the contemporary phase. Among those loosely associated with this movement, there is virtually no effort to return to the research program or discourse of the earlier period. A surprisingly large portion of earlier peripheral criticism has been accepted, just as the core itself is being reshaped in a responsive way. From this perspective, neofunctionalism is post-Parsonian. Its aim is to go beyond both the first and second phase of postwar sociology and to construct a new synthesis on the basis of the contributions of each.

It should not be surprising, then, that in contrast to the earlier phase of functionalist theorizing, generalized discourse has been central in the development of neofunctionalist work. Primarily, this has been in the service of reconstructive arguments about the core, but it has appeared also in the more affirmative practices of revisionism and even elaboration. Alexander's (1983b) work has explicitly attacked the idealist tendencies in Parsons' approach to action and argued that this reduction was responsible for many defects in Parsons' work, such as its tendency to see change in teleological terms and its relative slighting of economic rewards and political coercion. In a series of articles and working papers, Gould also sought to reemphasize material factors, in order similarly to reconstruct a more truly multidimensional tradition. His explicit challenge to Parsons remained reserved for his more specific and explanatory work (Gould 1987); in this more generalized domain, he chose revisionism (Gould, 1976), arguing that Parsons had issued an "urgent warning" against neglecting the material domain (Gould 1981).

In the initial period of neofunctionalism, the order issue seemed less salient. Here too, however, explicitly reconstructive discourse has strongly emerged. Recently, Alexander (1988c) has sharply criticized Parsons for his failure to bring contingency back into his theorizing of collective order. In response to this "black box" of individual action, Alexander has suggested formulations that are modeled on theories of individual exchange, interpretation, and pragmatic experience. In complementary efforts, Colomy (1982, 1985, 1990a, 1990b) has argued against the lack of attention to open-ended group processes in the functionalist understanding of change; in a series of theoretical and historical papers, he has developed systematic theories integrating work on collective behavior with structural approaches to social differentiation. Motivated by a similar interest to bring the individual back into functionalist work, Sciulli (1986, 1988) has argued that the early and the later Parsons himself understood voluntarism in a manner that emphasized its protean and individualistic qualities. Strongly criticizing Parsons' emphasis on socialization in his middle period work, Sciulli has argued for a convergence between Blumer's understanding of public negotiation and a neofunctionalist theory of public political life. Finally, though Munch's (1981, 1982) early articles on Parsons' neo-Kantian core were couched in the language of affirmative revision rather than reconstruction,[14] they, too, can be seen as a powerful attempt to bring effort and individual will back into the center of functionalist work.

There has also been an efflorescence of general and often polemical discussions about the model level of functional theory. Alexander (1983b) made a series of criticisms about the reification of functionalist and systems reasoning in Parsons' work. He also criticized the conflation between the AGIL divisions in the model and the empirical differentiation of contemporary society. Because these problematic applications of the model made it difficult to avoid the identification of functionalism with stasis and conflation, Alexander called for a return to the more concrete, group-oriented, early-middle phase of Parsons' work, in which the institutional content of a particular social system was clearly differentiated from its abstract mechanisms.

While in Germany it is actually the functionalized Weberianism of Schluchter and the Parsonian Marxism of Habermas that comes closest to this ideal, the German neofunctionalists have also altered Parsons' model in a revealing way.[15] Luhmann (1982), too, has criticized Parsons for reducing the dynamism of systems analysis by reifying it as a fourfold table; with his insistence on the tension between the internal and external environments of systems, he has developed a more supple and dynamic model.[16] Munch (1987a, 1988) has also changed the model forcefully, renaming the four subsystems in a manner that emphasizes contingency and the ideological and cultural imperative of rational communication.

Powerful and complementary challenges to Parsons' systems model have come from Gould and Colomy. In an ambitious challenge to Parsons, Gould (1985) has argued that functional models, drawn from systems or organicist theories, are necessary but limited. Developmental models must also be employed: abstract sketches of phases through which particular historical societies must pass if specified levels of development are to be achieved. Finally, in an argument that parallels Alexander's criticism of conflation, Gould insists that neither of these models should be confused with the actual structure of historical societies. This is provided by a "structural" model of particular institutional and group relations in a given period. For his part, Colomy (1985) has directed his efforts at altering Parsons' differentiation theory in a neofunctionalist way. He has argued that differentiation should be treated as a sharply delimited model; it is a "master trend" rather than an actual empirical description, much less an explanation for change. Within this altered framework, Colomy has offered a series of specific models of the structure and process of social change.

In the realm of ideology, the most radical break with orthodox funtionalism has simply been to make the ideological dimension of this tradition explicit. While arguing for the generally progressive and humanistic thrust of Parsons' work, Alexander has agreed with many of Parsons' critics about some of its conservative features. He himself has sought to politicize functionalism and tie it to the normative issues of the day. In his eulogy for Parsons in *The New Republic*, Alexander (1979b) described Parsons as providing "a sociology for liberals," stressing the normative and critical potential of Parsons' concepts of inclusion, differentiation, and value-generalization. Since that time he has tried to push neofunctionalism in a left-leaning but not radical direction. In an independent contribution to this effort, Colomy (1990c) has discussed this neofunctionalist orientation under the rubric of "critical modernism." Mayhew's (1982, 1984, 1990) work on the centrality of the public in democratic polities elaborates a similar normative-cum-empirical claim, as does Robertson's (1988) developing theory of globalization, which argues simultaneously for a new worldwide cosmopolitanism and for an increased tolerance for national variance, which, he suggests, Parsons' own modernization theory overlooked.

Sciulli and Gould have staked out more radical ideological claims. Operating in the space provided by his voluntaristic interpretation of

Parsons' macrosociology, Sciulli (1989a) has developed empirical criteria for evaluating democratization in his theory of "societal constitutionalism." Arguing that modern industrial societies are threatened by
political and economic oligarchies, on the one hand, and by a pacified
citizenry on the other, he finds a countervailing force in Parsons' understanding of the increasing importance of collegial, self-governing communities. Gould (1987, 1985) embraces an even more restrictive and
critical conception of capitalist political economy, and he has reconstructed a model of contemporary societies whose strains can be alle-
viated only through the transformation of property relations.

The most ambitious effort to transform disciplinary understandings
of the functionalist *Weltanschauung* can be found in Holton and Turner's (1986) work. Describing Parsons as the only major theorist rooted
in a society that did not experience the damaging transition from feudalism to capitalism, they argue that he has been the only theorist to
conceptualize the positive possibilities of a progressive and stable modernity. Compared to Marx, Weber, and Durkheim, Parsons escapes
from nostalgia because he sees the moral and pluralistic possibilities of
Gesellschaft.

> An alternative option is to consider the possibility that *Gesellschaft*
> permits authentic expressions of values, rather than the "false," or "fe-
> tished" forms of consciousness as diagnosed by exponents of the Frank-
> furt school. In addition, value-pluralism under *Gesellschaft* need be con-
> sidered neither as a series of narcissistic worlds, in retreat from the public
> domain, nor as an irreducible battle of Nietzschian wills. Rather it can be
> conceived as generating a normative basis for the orderly resolution of
> pluralism and diversity. (Holton and Turner 1986, 215–216)

In the second phase discourse of postwar work, Parsons was a conservative because he was not a radical. Arguing against the picture or Parsons
as "an apologist for that kind of crass economic individualism that is
often taken to underlie the capitalist economy," Holton and Turner
portray Parsons' optimism, to the contrary, as reflecting "a profoundly
moral and political identification with liberal democratic values" (216–
217). In their view, it is Parsons, not his second phase critics, who now
must be seen as occupying the higher moral ground.

> Parsons emerges from most confrontations with his critics as both mor-
> ally engaged and politically committed, not as an apologist for capitalism,
> but as an anti-elitist and anti-Utopian social theorist. This standpoint
> moves us beyond the ambivalence of the classical sociologists toward
> modernity. . . . In all these respects Parsons' social theory announces the
> end of the classical phase of sociological thought. (218)

Earlier in this paper we spoke of the significance of the new ideological and political environment in generating the contemporary, third phase of sociological work. For neofunctionalism, the effect of this altered environment has been most powerfully crystallized by Holton and Turner; indeed, they present an argument that simply could not have been made at any earlier point. While offered as an affirmative elaboration and revision of the original rather than its reconstruction, their argument can take this position only because it is neofunctionalism, not orthodoxy, that now provides the framework for discourse in the Parsonian mode.[17] The powerfully reconstructive effects of their Parsons' portrait helps to renew the kind of critical modernism that is necessary to reform and sustain a liberal and democratic society.

The interpretive mode of generalized discourse is intimately tied to the expository mode we have just discussed. We have earlier pointed to the affirmative quality of the orthodox Parsonians' elaborations and revisions of their founder's texts. More interesting, perhaps, was this group's approach to classical texts outside the home tradition. Parsons (1937) had set the tone in *The Structure of Social Action*, when he stressed convergence within the work of his "group of recent European writers." That Parsons had himself constructed this convergence through powerful interpretation was never acknowledged, nor was the crucial fact that what they converged with was Parsons' emergent social theory rather than their own. Parsons often "revisited" Durkheim, Weber, and Freud, as his theory continually evolved. He needed to incorporate new elements from their work, but he could do so only by presenting these elements as if they converge with the new elements in his own. Between those theorists admitted to the classical canon of sociology there could be no fundamental strains, nor could there be any unresolvable strains between these theories and Parsons' own. This affirmative approach to interpretation—its expression as elaboration and revision— reached its apogee in Parsons and his collaborators' *Theories of Societies* (1961). In its depiction of the convergence of the entire history of social thought with action theory, this work was either extraordinarily naive or disingenuous.

Still, interpretive discourse did not flourish in the orthodox phase of functionalism any more than did discourse in the expository mode. When Parsonians engaged in interpretation, moreover, they modeled their discussions on Parsons' convergence model. Bellah's (1959) penetrating early article on Durkheim as a differentiation theorist is a case in point. Smelser's (1973) edition of Marx, Eisenstadt's (1971) of Weber, and the Lidz brothers' (1976) treatment of Piaget are similarly powerful examples.

Interpretation in the contemporary phase has, by contrast, been much more central and aggressively reconstructive. We have indicated above how Parsons' own work has been the object of several neofunctionalist critiques. In discussing classical works outside the home tradition, neofunctionalists have adopted a decidedly un-Parsonian line. They have stressed divergence rather than convergence, for they have need of theoretical resources beyond the home tradition itself.

We will take up the neofunctionalist dialogue with the classics of macrosociology first. Where Parsons not only neglected but in effect tried to repress Marx, Alexander (1982b) makes Marx paradigmatic of the material and instrumental theorizing that he criticizes Parsons for trying to ignore. He (1983a) sets Weber against Parsons in much the same way, arguing that Parsons underplayed the objectification that for Weber was the necessary underside of individuation. In a similar vein, Alexander (1988b) has stressed the symbolic and culturalistic elements in Durkheim, playing them off against the culturally reductionist tendencies in the orthodox functionalist concentration on "value." Gould (1987) has treated Marx, Hegel, Keynes, and Piaget in much the same way, stressing their distance from Parsons in the first instance, and the need to incorporate their "antifunctionalism" in the second. His theory of revolution and radical collective behavior has emerged from this reconstructed mix. For Sciulli (1985), the absence that interpretation must overcome is Habermas. While stressing in a revisionist mode the areas of convergence between Parsons and Habermas, he has also interpreted Habermas in a manner that exposes the self-limitations of Parsons' orthodox work. He has interpreted the legal theorist Lon Fuller in the same reconstructive way. Both Habermas and Fuller (Sciulli, 1989, 1990) provide critical resources for Sciulli's neofunctionalist theory of societal constitutionalism.

There has also emerged within neofunctionalist interpretation a significant dialogue with the central texts of the microsociological tradition. Because Parsons did not recognize the problem of contingent action, it is not surprising that his relation to these traditions never went beyond ceremonial remarks on their convergence with his own. For neofunctionalism, by contrast, it has become important to understand the divergence between microsociology and the orthodox tradition, in order to develop theoretical resources for opening neofunctionalism up to contingency in the ways we have discussed above.

Alexander (1985b, 1987c, 195–280) has emphasized, for example, a collective thrust in Mead, Peirce, and Goffman, and also in the phenomenological theory of Husserl, Schutz, and the early Garfinkel, arguing that such theoretical resources have been largely ignored by these traditions' contemporary interpreters. While Munch (1986, 1987b) and Sciulli (1988), by contrast, do not refer to this thrust in their interpretations of interactionist theory, all three theorists agree that neofunctionalism must draw upon these traditions in order to incorporate considerations of contingency and voluntarism. These theoretical appropriations are openly presented as remedies to the acknowledged shortcomings of orthodoxy, and defended as a means by which the more original, creative, and synthesizing project of neofunctionalists can be advanced.

Within the new environments of the third postwar phase, and in response to the opportunities and provocations provided by the new generalized discourse, there has been an outpouring of neofunctionalist research that, if this term is taken in its broad rather than restricted sense, can be called a research program. Earlier functionalist research was guided by a reaffirmative strategy, envisioning a single, all-embracing conceptual scheme that tied areas of specialized research into a tightly wrought package. What neofunctionalist empirical work points to, by contrast, is a package loosely organized around a general logic and possessing a number of rather autonomous "proliferations" and "variations" at different levels and in different empirical domains (Wagner 1984; Wagner and Berger 1985).

A NOTE ON RESEARCH PROGRAMS IN NEOFUNCTIONALISM

In the preceding sections we have described the emergence of neofunctionalism, treating it as a central feature of the third phase of postwar sociology and identifying the intellectual and socio-political grounds for its resurgence. Neofunctionalism's discursive elements—its presuppositions, ontology, epistemology, and ideological implications—have been outlined. But neofunctionalism is more than generalized discourse. It also seeks to explain particular facets of the social world.

The most developed neofunctionalist research programs have emerged in the areas of social change, cultural sociology, political sociology, mass communications, feminist studies, the professions, and economic sociology. While a detailed examination of these programs cannot be presented here, an overview highlighting the most prominent contours of this work is in order.[18]

Much of neofunctionalist research has charted a decidedly revisionist course. Studies of structural differentiation, for instance, revise orthodox functionalism's approach to change in four ways: 1) they supplement descriptions of the "master trend" toward increasingly specialized institutions by developing models of patterned departures from that trend (e.g., Alexander 1981; Lechner 1984, 1985, 1990; Tiry-akian 1985, 1990; Champagne 1990; Colomy 1982, 1985, 1990a, 1990b; Hondrich 1990; Surace 1982; Smelser 1985, 1990; Colomy and Tausig 1988); 2) they move beyond purely systemic and evolutionary explana-tions of differentiation toward accounts that stress contingency, con-crete groups, conflict, and social movements and collective behavior (e.g., Eisenstadt 1980; Colomy 1985, 1990a, 1990b; Colomy and Rhoades 1988; Colomy and Tausig 1988; Rhoades 1990; Mayhew 1990; Alexan-der 1980; Smelser 1985); 3) they recognize that the orthodox emphasis on adaptive upgrading, inclusion, and value generalization represent but one configuration among a much broader array of the possible outcomes of social differentiation (e.g., Luhmann 1982, 1990a, 1990b; Alexander 1978, 1983b, 1984; Eder 1990; Rhoades 1990; Munch 1981, 1982, 1983, 1987a, 1988, 1990a, 1990b; Sciulli 1985, 1990b; Mayhew 1984, 1990); 4) they replace a complacent liberal optimism concerning the process and consequences of differentiation with a critical modern-ism that is more attuned to the dark sides that are ineluctably related to it (e.g., Sciulli 1990a, 1990b; Mayhew 1984, 1990; Munch 1987a, 1988; Colomy 1990c).[19]

Conventional functionalist research into the culture-society relation has also been critiqued and revised. The orthodox approach posited a cultural system neatly institutionalized in the social system through values that the personality internalized via socialization. Archer (1985, 1988) argues that this model is guilty of "downward conflation," for it holds that an integrated cultural system engulfs the social and person-ality systems. Alexander (1984) suggests that this conventional ap-proach to institutionalization, which he calls the cultural specification model, represents only one form culture-society relations can assume. He proposes two additional modes. In cultural refraction, conflicting social groups and functions produce antagonistic subcultures that con-tinue to draw upon a value system that is integrated at the cultural level. In cultural columnization, by contrast, there are fundamental antagonisms in both the social and cultural systems, interest groupings have no significant common beliefs, and genuinely antagonistic politi-cal cultural groupings emerge.[20]

In their effort to develop a broadly neofunctionalist feminist sociol-ogy, Miriam Johnson and her colleagues (Johnson 1975, 1977, 1981, 1982, 1988a, 1988b; Johnson et al. 1975, 1981; Gill et al. 1987; Stockard and Johnson 1979) reappropriate and revise elements of the Parsonian legacy others have left behind. They reconceptualize the traditional distinction between instrumentality and expressiveness, the structural differentiation model of the family, socialization, and Parsons' particu-lar application of his culture, society and personality model to account for the origins and reproduction of gender inequality. When considered in isolation, each of their reconceptualizations can be accurately characterized as revisionist. Taken together, however, it is readily apparent that this research program is animated by a reconstructionist thrust. It aims not at describing how the family "produces" human personalities capable of assuming adult roles in a complex, differentiated society— the orthodox Parsonian issue—but at explaining the radically different question of how a cultural and social system subordinates and distorts a particular class of personalities.

Johnson and her colleagues not only revise and reconstruct Parsons, they also wed their reconfiguration of orthodox functionalism to other intellectual traditions, especially psychoanalysis and feminist scholarship. Jeffrey Prager (1986) has extended and revised the functionalist treatment of political sociology in an analogous way. He draws on Parsons' discussion of a differentiated societal community to devise a neofunctionalist conception of the public sphere. He ties that structural concept to the more concrete and processual symbolic interactionist approach that emphasizes the content, dynamics and effects of actual public discourse. With the aid of this powerful theoretical link between functionalism and interactionism, Prager's investigation of Ireland's movement toward democracy demonstrates not only how democratic institutions operate, but also how they are created in the first place.

In addition to its reconstructionist and revisionist thrust, neofunctionalist research also contains an elaborationist current. For instance, Robertson's (1985, 1986, 1987, 1990; Robertson and Chirico 1985; Robertson and Lechner 1985) analyses of the relationship between globalization and cultural change carries the Parsonian theme of value generalization to the level of the world system. At the same time, because he is sensitive to the wide diversity of cultural responses engendered by globalization, Robertson revises Parsons by eschewing the notion that these changes amount merely to a global version of cultural specification and normative integration.

More recently, such elaborative research has occurred less against the backdrop of earlier orthodox functionalism, but in relation to the rapidly developing body of neofunctionalist theory itself. Rothenbuhler (1986a, 1986b, 1987, 1988a, 1988b, 1988c, 1988d, n.d.; Peters and Rothenbuhler 1988) draws on general statements of the neofunctionalist position as well as on neofunctionalist treatments of culture to fashion an impressive research program in mass communications. Drawing upon highly abstract neofunctionalist discussions of the micro-macro link, Colomy and Rhoades (1988) develop a series of ideal-typical models and causal hypotheses to explain educational change in the late nineteenth century United States. In a similar way, Lehman (1988) uses Alexander's analysis of presuppositions about action and order to generate a new and more complex empirical research program on political power and the state. Rambo's (1988) work in economic sociology elaborates neofunctionalist treatments of culture, while Edles (1988) draws on the same neofunctionalist literature to analyze Spain's civil religion and its recent transition to democracy.

In sum, while a central part of neofunctionalism has been carried out at the level of general theory, there is a complementary, and rapidly growing, body of more empirically oriented work. This work supplements the reconstructionist thrust of neofunctionalist metatheory with several significant revisions of orthodox functionalism and has even begun to elaborate neofunctionalist general theory itself.

CONCLUSION

Our task in this paper has been to demonstrate that neofunctionalism is delivering on its promissory notes. Today, neofunctionalism is much more than a promise; it has become a field of intense theoretical discourse and growing empirical investigation. We have conducted this demonstration within the framework of a nascent model of social scientific knowledge. Because sociological knowledge is generated by traditions, the most compelling criteria for evaluating scientific progress is comparative, in terms of different phases in the life of a particular tradition and in terms of the relations between competing traditions. By making such comparisons we can measure social scientific progress, although, to be sure, this is progress in a postpositivist sense.

In this paper, we assessed neofunctionalism's advances primarily by comparing them to the older orthodoxy. Toward that end several terms —reconstruction, expropriation, revision, and elaboration—have been employed. Our thesis has been that, at both discursive and more empirical levels, neofunctionalism has produced significant advances relative to earlier renditions of the tradition. We have tried to show that the reconstructions, revisions, and elaborations that compose neofunctionalism have been directed precisely at those areas of the orthodox tradition that critics, both internal and external, earlier identified as theoretically or empirically suspect. If neofunctionalism represents theoretical progress—and we think it does—this reflects its ability to produce satisfactory reconstructions and revisions in response to critiques that once threatened to destroy the functionalist tradition altogether.

Of course, theoretical progress cannot be judged on internal grounds alone. Comparisons must also be made with competing traditions. Certainly the "critics of functionalism" will respond with new kinds of ripostes. Some will try to ignore the vast changes that neofunctionalism has wrought. Others will recognize that fundamental shifts have occurred and will reformulate the nature of their critiques. We eagerly await these reformulations. The conventional debates have become stale and dry. We are in the midst of a sea change in sociological theory. Old alignments are dissolving; new configurations are being born. "Neofunctionalism" cannot be stuffed back into the old box.

NOTES

1. Now that the second volume of Habermas' *Theory of Communicative Action* has been translated into English (Habermas 1987), the seriousness of his encounter with Parsons will clearly be seen. We would argue, in fact, that the framework Habermas employs in both volumes of this work can be seen as a neo-Marxist revision of Parsonian concepts.

2. But not revised enough, from our point of view. Ritzer, for example, simply places "neofunctionalism" as the concluding section to "functionalism," following it with sections on conflict theory and so forth. We will argue below that the vitality of neofunctionalism casts doubt on this conventional division of theory texts. Neofunctionalism has taken as its project to open itself up to social conflict and contingent interaction. Insofar as it does so, then certainly "conflict theory" and "ethnomethodology" cannot be presented as responses to contemporary functionalist work. These reified divisions were never theoretically accurate ones (Alexander 1982a), but they did represent at least the historical self-consciousness of the profession in what we will below call the second phase of postwar sociology. At this point, we believe, they do not even do that. Sociology is embarked upon a third phase of postwar development which is in the process of making these textbook divisions obsolete.

3. After making this claim, we want immediately to stress that neofunctionalism, while a genuine intellectual movement, is not an integrated theory. There is much disagreement between those who we would classify under this rubric, and some, in fact, do not welcome the general designation as such. We will talk more openly about this unformed and emergent character below.

4. We have limited our discussion only to developments within what American sociologist consider to be the matrix of their discipline. Outside of it, of course, there are also extremely important illustrations of this third phase. In France, for example, we would point to the poststructuralist movement, where cultural structures—discursive formations (Foucault 1984), cultural capital (Bourdieu), and political narratives (Lyotard 1984)—have replaced material ones.

5. We are drawing here from a work on sociological theory in preparation for the Prentice-Hall *Foundations of Sociology* series.

6. After Marx, there are the elaborations and revisions of writers like Engels, Kautsky, Otto Bauer, Labriola, and others. These specifications were interrupted, however, by the more radical reconstructionist efforts of the World War I generation, theorists like Lenin, Gramsci, Lukacs, Korsch, and others. Subsequent specification of Marxism often occurred within these reformulated Marxian traditions of Lenin-Marx, Gramsci-Marx, Lukacs-Marx, etc., whether or not the reconstruction was

explicitly recognized. Later in the history of the Marxian tradition, thinkers like Sartre, Althusser, E. P. Thompson, and those associated with the Frankfurt School introduced a new round of more radical reformulation.

7. Thus, theorists who created new traditions were at an earlier point usually important reconstructors of the traditions out of which their new theories were formed. Marx is a case in point. In the early 1840s he was a "Young Hegelian," which was a radical, quasi-religious movement of Hegel's last students to reopen the master's theory to critical strands of the Enlightenment and even to socialist thought. When Marx encountered political economy, he felt compelled to leave the Hegelian fold and created historical materialism. Interesting parallels can be drawn for Parsons. For the first ten years of his scholarly life, through the very publication of *The Structure of Social Action*, he seemed devoted to reconstructing the classical sociological traditions. He became more ambitious only at a later point in his career. One should be careful not to see the ideal-typical sequences—elaboration-revision-reconstruction-tradition creation—as a scale of theoretical contribution. Most of the greatest minds in social science, for example, never make the transition from reconstruction to tradition creation, and many who have made the transition were much the worse for it. The works of Von Wiese are long forgotten, but the writings of Gramsci, Lukacs, Mannheim, and Mauss continue to be intently pursued.

8. Vico's work represents just such an example from classical traditions, Spencer's from the sociological.

9. For an excellent discussion from a very similar point, see the detailed critiques Bryan Turner makes of the efforts at theoretical cumulation that comprise the collection of ASA miniconference papers Jonathan Turner (1989) has collected in *Theory Building in Sociology*. Bryan Turner (1989, 132) concludes: "In sociology, we appear to have more dispersal and fragmentation of approaches than cumulation and organized growth, and these theoretical fragmentations are products of institutional fragmentation and competition between intellectuals for audience and patronage. . . . Analytical rupture rather than theory cumulation is the decisive aspect of sociology's history in the twentieth century."

10. Think here of vulgar Marxism, which actually encompasses most of what has been accepted as legitimate Marxist work, or of the reductionistic and mechanistic applications of Durkheim and Weber, which have been offered by some of their most devoted followers. It need hardly be said that Parsonian functionalism had its own large share of simplifiers.

11. For a discussion that highlights the concept of "sensibility" in the investigation of the shifting commitments of a major contemporary theorist, *see* Alexander (1986).

12. This is by no means always true, however. Bernstein's empirical challenge to the reigning Marxist proposition about the falling rate of profit—an issue of research program rather than generalized discourse—struck at the core of the tradition and initiated the reconstruction that came to be called the "social democratic" tendency in Marxism. This tendency was accompanied, however, by a great deal of generalized discourse.

13. Bellah's essays for "symbolic realism" would have to be read as an exception in this regard, they were discursive, generalized arguments. Yet they remained revisionist. Rather than critically confronting Parsons' cultural theory, Bellah argued symbolic realism was one clear implication of it.

14. In this regard, Munch's articles of this period, and some of his later work as well, resemble Alexander's (1978) own earlier discursive defense of Parsons. Though clearly engaging in revision, Alexander did not choose to confront Parsons' theory in a reconstructive way. In the late 1970s, the second phase of postwar theorizing was still a vigorous rising tide, and those sympathetic to Parsons' tradition confronted

his critics in the polemical spirit of the time. It may have been Parsons' death in 1979 as well as the changing theoretical and political climate that allowed a less defensive and more reconstructive posture to be assumed.

15. It might be useful, in fact, to introduce the concept "expropriation" to refer to the incorporation by one tradition of key elements of an opposing tradition in order to elaborate, revise, and reconstruct the home tradition itself. Thus, while Schluchter and Habermas express a sharp antipathy to functionalism, in this third phase of theorizing they have expropriated Parsons' theory in creative and quite thorough-going ways. Expropriation is one sign of the expansionary phase of a tradition.

16. The problem for Luhmann is quite different: he has not developed a theory of institutions, groups, and concrete interaction. The differences between Luhmann's and Munch's work, on the one hand, and the American and English neofunctionalists', on the other, is a topic which must soon be taken up. The differences stem less from differences in national traditions, perhaps, than from the contrasts in the disciplinary environments within each emerged. In Germany, neither conflict nor micro sociology ever became as strongly institutionalized.

17. "Since the death of Talcott Parsons in Munich in 1979, it has become clear that a significant re-appraisal of Parsons' sociology and his impact on modern sociology is well underway. . . . This volume . . . may appropriately be regarded as part of this new wave of re-evaluation" (Holton and Turner 1986, 1). The movement beyond affirmative revision is demonstrated by the fact that in his review of Holton and Turner's book in the *American Journal of Sociology*, Lechner (1988)—himself an active theorist in the reconstructionist movement—offers the criticism that it is "too positive" about Parsons!

18. For a detailed discussion of these research programs, *see* Alexander and Colomy (forthcoming).

19. For a much more detailed analysis of recent developments in differentiation theory, *see* Colomy (1986, 1990c). For discussions that situate the emergence and development of differentiation theory in a broader historical and theoretical context *see* Giesen (1988, 1990) and Alexander (1988d).

20. Our discussion here has focused only on the primordial issue of culture-society boundary relations. Once the possible attenuation of this boundary relation has been acknowledged, however, a more internalist and less socially circumscribed understanding of the cultural system can begin to be developed. In his efforts to incorporate semiotic and hermeneutic models, and to elaborate the "late Durkheimian" approach to cultural studies, Alexander's research has recently moved in this direction (1988b). *See also* Edles (1988) and Rambo and Chan (1988).

REFERENCES

Alexander, Jeffrey C. 1978. "Formal and Substantive Voluntarism in the Work of Talcott Parsons: A Theoretical and Ideological Reinterpretation." *American Sociological Review* 43:177–198.

Alexander, Jeffrey C. 1979a. "Paradigm Revision and 'Parsonianism.' " *Canadian Journal of Sociology* 4:343–357.

Alexander, Jeffrey C. 1979b. "Sociology for Liberals." *The New Republic* (June 2):10–12.

Alexander, Jeffrey C. 1980. "Core Solidarity, Ethnic Outgroups, and Social Differentiation: A Multi-Dimensional Model of Inclusion in Modern Societies." In Jacques

Dofny and Akinsola Akiwowo, eds., *National and Ethnic Movements*. Beverly Hills: Sage.

Alexander, Jeffrey C. 1981. "The Mass Media in Systemic, Historical and Comparative Perspective." In Elihu Katz and Thomas Szeckso, eds., *Mass Media and Social Change*. Beverly Hills: Sage.

Alexander, Jeffrey C. 1982a. *Theoretical Logic in Sociology. Volume 1: Positivism, Presuppositions, and Current Controversies*. Berkeley: University of California Press.

Alexander, Jeffrey C. 1982b. *Theoretical Logic in Sociology. Volume 2: The Antinomies of Classical Thought: Marx and Durkheim*. Berkeley: University of California Press.

Alexander, Jeffrey C. 1983a. *Theoretical Logic in Sociology. Volume 3: The Classical Attempt at Theoretical Synthesis: Max Weber*. Berkeley: University of California Press.

Alexander, Jeffrey C. 1983b. *Theoretical Logic in Sociology. Volume 4: The Modern Reconstruction of Classical Thought: Talcott Parsons*. Berkeley: University of California Press.

Alexander, Jeffrey C. 1984. "Three Models of Culture and Society Relations: Toward an Analysis of Watergate." *Sociological Theory* 2:290–314.

Alexander, Jeffrey C. 1985a. "Introduction." In J. Alexander, ed., *Neofunctionalism*. Beverly Hills: Sage.

Alexander, Jeffrey C. 1985b. "The Individualist Dilemma in Phenomenology and Interactionism: Toward a Synthesis with the Classical Tradition." In S. N. Eisenstadt and H. J. Helle, eds., *Perspectives on Sociological Theory*. Vol. 1. Beverly Hills: Sage.

Alexander, Jeffrey C. 1986. "Science, Sense, and Sensibility." *Theory and Society* 15:443–463.

Alexander, Jeffrey C. 1987a. "Action and Its Environments." In Jeffrey C. Alexander, Bernhard Giesen, Richard Munch, and Neil J. Smelser, eds., *The Micro-Macro Link*. Berkeley: University of California Press.

Alexander, Jeffrey C. 1987b. "On the Centrality of the Classics." In Anthony Giddens and Jonathan Turner, eds. *Social Theory Today*. London: Polity Press.

Alexander, Jeffrey C. 1987c. *Twenty Lectures*. New York: Columbia University Press.

Alexander, Jeffrey C. 1988a. "Between Progress and Apocalypse: Social Theory and the Dream of Reason in the Twentieth Century." Paper presented at the conference, "Social Progress and Sociological Theory: Movements, Forces, and Ideas at the End of the Twentieth Century." Krakow, Poland.

Alexander, Jeffrey C. 1988b. "Culture and Political Crisis: Watergate and Durkheimian Sociology." In Jeffrey C. Alexander, ed., *Durkheimian Sociology: Cultural Studies*. New York: Columbia University Press.

Alexander, Jeffrey C. 1988c. *Action and Its Environments*. New York: Columbia University Press.

Alexander, Jeffrey C. 1988d. "Durkheim's Problem and Differentiation Theory Today." In Jeffrey C. Alexander, *Action and Its Environments*. New York: Columbia University Press.

Alexander, Jeffrey C., and Paul Colomy. 1985. "Toward Neofunctionalism: Eisenstadt's Change Theory and Symbolic Interactionism." *Sociological Theory* 2:11–23.

Alexander, Jeffrey C., and Bernhard Giesen. 1987. "From Reduction to Linkage: The Long View of the Micro-Macro Debate." In Jeffrey C. Alexander, Bernhard Giesen, Richard Munch, and Neil J. Smelser, eds., *The Micro-Macro Link*. Berkeley: University of California Press.

Archer, Margaret S. 1985. "The Myth of Cultural Integration." *British Journal of Sociology* 36:333–353.

Archer, Margaret S. 1988. *Culture and Agency: The Place of Culture in Social Theory.* Cambridge: Cambridge University Press.

Becker, Howard. 1982. *Art Worlds.* Berkeley: University of California Press.

Bellah, Robert N. 1957. *Tokugawa Religion: The Values of Pre-Industrial Japan.* Glencoe, Ill.: Free Press.

Bellah, Robert N. 1959. "Durkheim and History." *American Sociological Review* 24:447–461.

Bellah, Robert N. 1970. *Beyond Belief.* New York: Harper and Row.

Bellah, Robert N. 1973. "Introduction." In Robert N. Bellah, ed., *Emile Durkheim: On Morality and Society.* Chicago: University of Chicago Press.

Blau, Peter M. 1977. *Inequality and Heterogeneity: A Primitive Theory of Social Structure.* New York: Free Press.

Calhoun, Craig. 1982. *The Question of Class Struggle: Social Foundations of Popular Radicalism during the Industrial Revolution.* Chicago: University of Chicago Press.

Camic, Charles. 1986. "The Return of the Functionalists." *Contemporary Sociology* 15:692–695.

Champagne, Duane. 1990. "Culture, Differentiation, and Environment: Social Change in Tlingit Society." In Jeffrey C. Alexander and Paul Colomy, eds., *Differentiation Theory and Social Change: Historical and Comparative Perspectives.* New York: Columbia University Press.

Coleman, James S. 1986a. "Social Theory, Social Research, and a Theory of Action." *American Journal of Sociology* 91:1309–1335.

Coleman, James S. 1986b. *Individual Interests and Collective Action: Selected Essays.* New York: Cambridge University Press.

Coleman, James S. 1987. "Microfoundations and Macrosocial Behavior." In Jeffrey C. Alexander, Bernhard Giesen, Richard Munch, and Neil J. Smelser, eds., *The Micro-Macro Link.* Berkeley: University of California Press.

Collins, Randall. 1975. *Conflict Sociology: Toward an Explanatory Science.* New York: Academic Press.

Collins, Randall. 1981. "On the Micro-Foundations of Macro-Sociology." *American Journal of Sociology* 86:984–1014.

Collins, Randall. 1987. "Interaction Ritual Chains, Power and Property: The Micro-Macro Connection as an Empirically Based Theoretical Problem." In Jeffrey C. Alexander, Bernhard Giesen, Richard Munch, and Neil J. Smelser, eds., *The Micro-Macro Link.* Berkeley: University of California Press.

Collins, Randall. 1988a. *Theoretical Sociology.* San Diego: Harcourt Brace Jovanovich.

Collins, Randall. 1988b. "The Durkheimian Tradition in Conflict Sociology." In Jeffrey C. Alexander, ed., *Durkheimian Sociology: Cultural Studies.* New York: Cambridge University Press.

Colomy, Paul. 1985. "Uneven Structural Differentiation: Toward a Comparative Approach." In Jeffrey C. Alexander, ed., *Neofunctionalism.* Beverly Hills: Sage.

Colomy, Paul. 1986. "Recent Developments in the Functionalist Approach to Change." *Sociological Focus* 19:139–158.

Colomy, Paul. 1990a. "Uneven Differentiation and Incomplete Institutionalization: Political Change and Continuity in the Early American Nation." In Jeffrey C. Alexander and Paul Colomy, eds., *Differentiation Theory and Social Change: Comparative and Historical Perspectives.* New York: Columbia University Press.

Colomy, Paul. 1990b. "Strategic Groups and Political Differentiation in the Antebellum United States." In Jeffrey C. Alexander and Paul Colomy, eds., *Differentia-*

tion Theory and Social Change: Comparative and Historical Perspectives. New York: Columbia University Press.

Colomy, Paul. 1990c. "Revisions and Progress in Differentiation Theory." In Jeffrey C. Alexander and Paul Colomy, eds., *Differentiation Theory and Social Change: Comparative and Historical Perspectives.* New York: Columbia University Press.

Colomy, Paul and Gary Rhoades. 1988. "Specifying the Micro-Macro Link: An Application of General Theory to the Study of Structural Differentiation." Paper presented at the Annual Meetings of the American Sociological Association, Atlanta, Ga.

Colomy, Paul and Mark Tausig. 1988. "The Differentiation of Applied Sociology: Prospects and Problems." Manuscript.

Coser, Lewis A. 1956. *The Functions of Social Conflict.* New York: Free Press.

Darnton, Robert. 1982. *The Literary Underground of the Old Regime.* Cambridge, Mass.: Harvard University Press.

Devereux, Edward C., Jr. 1961. "Parsons' Sociological Theory." In Max Black, ed., *The Social Theories of Talcott Parsons.* Carbondale and Edwardsville: Southern Illinois University Press.

Eder, Klaus. 1990. "Contradictions and Social Evolution." In Hans Haferkamp and Neil J. Smelser, eds., *Social Change and Modernity.* Berkeley: University of California Press.

Edles, Laura D. 1988. "Political Culture and the Transition to Democracy in Spain." Ph.D. dissertation, University of California, Los Angeles.

Eisenstadt, S. N. 1963. *The Political Systems of Empires.* New York: Free Press.

Eisenstadt, S. N. 1971. "Introduction." In S. N. Eisenstadt, ed., *Weber on Charisma and Institution Building.* Chicago: University of Chicago Press.

Eisenstadt, S. N. 1980. "Cultural Orientations, Institutional Entrepreneurs, and Social Change: Comparative Analyses of Traditional Civilizations." *American Journal of Sociology* 85:840–869.

Eisenstadt, S. N. 1986. "Culture and Social Structure Revisited." *International Sociology* 1:297–320.

Fine, Gary Alan. 1984. "Negotiated Orders and Organizational Cultures." *Annual Review of Sociology* 10:239–262.

Fine, Gary Alan. 1988. "Symbolic Interactionism in the Post-Blumerian Age." Paper presented at the Maryland Theory Conference.

Foucault, Michel. 1984. *The Foucault Reader.* Edited by Paul Rabinow. New York: Pantheon.

Friedrichs, Robert. 1970. *A Sociology of Sociology.* New York: Free Press.

Geertz, Clifford. 1973. *The Interpretation of Cultures.* New York: Basic Books.

Giddens, Anthony. 1971. *Capitalism and Modern Social Theory.* Cambridge: Cambridge University Press.

Giddens, Anthony. 1984. *The Constitution of Society.* Berkeley: University of California Press.

Giddens, Anthony, and Jonathan Turner, eds. 1987. *Social Theory Today.* London: Polity Press.

Giesen, Bernhard. 1987. "Media and Markets." In M. Schmid and F. M. Wuketits, eds., *Evolutionary Theory in Social Science.* West Germany: Reidel.

Giesen, Bernhard. 1988. "The Autonomy of Social Change." *International Review of Sociology,* forthcoming.

Giesen, Bernhard. 1990. "The Change in 'Change': An Evolution Theoretical View on the History of the Concept." In Hans Haferkamp and Neil J. Smelser, eds., *Social Change and Modernity.* Berkeley: University of California Press.

Gill, Sandra, Jean Stockard, Miriam Johnson, and Suzanne Williams. 1987. "Measuring Gender Differences: The Expressive Dimension and Critique of Androgyny Scales." *Sex Roles* 17:375–400.

Goffman, Erving. 1974. *Frame Analysis*. New York: Harper and Row.

Goode, William. 1978. *The Celebration of Heroes: Prestige as a Social Control System*. Berkeley: University of California Press.

Gould, Mark. 1981. "Parsons versus Marx: An Earnest Warning." *Sociological Inquiry* 51:197–218.

Gould, Mark. 1985. "Prolegomena to Any Future Theory of Societal Crisis." In Jeffrey C. Alexander, ed., *Neofunctionalism*. Beverly Hills: Sage.

Gould, Mark. 1987. *Revolution in the Development of Capitalism*. Berkeley: University of California Press.

Habermas, Jürgen. 1975. *Legitimation Crisis*. Translated by Thomas McCarthy. Boston: Beacon Press.

Habermas, Jürgen. 1984. *The Theory of Communicative Action, Volume 1: Reason and Rationalization of Society*. Translated by Thomas McCarthy. Boston: Beacon Press.

Habermas, Jürgen. 1987. *The Theory of Communicative Action, Volume 2: Lifeworld and System: A Critique of Functionalist Reason*. Translated by Thomas McCarthy. Boston: Beacon Press.

Heritage, John, and David Greatbatch. 1986. "Generating Applause: A Study of Rhetoric and Response at Party Political Conferences." *American Journal of Sociology* 92:110–157.

Holton, Robert J. 1986. "Talcott Parsons and the Theory of Economy and Society." In Robert J. Holton and Bryan S. Turner, *Talcott Parsons: On Economy and Society*. London: Routledge and Kegan Paul.

Holton, Robert J., and Bryan S. Turner. 1986. *Talcott Parsons: On Economy and Society*. London: Routledge and Kegan Paul.

Hondrich, Karl Otto. 1990. "World Society versus Niche Societies: Paradoxes of Undirectional Evolution." In Hans Haferkamp and Neil J. Smelser, eds., *Social Change and Modernity*. Berkeley: University of California Press.

Johnson, Harry M. 1960. *Sociology: A Systematic Introduction*. New York: Harcourt, Brace.

Johnson, Miriam M. 1963. "Sex Role Learning in the Nuclear Family." *Child Development* 34:319–333.

Johnson, Miriam M. 1975. "Fathers, Mothers, and Sex Typing." *Sociological Inquiry* 45:15–26.

Johnson, Miriam M. 1977. "Androgyny and the Maternal Principle." *School Review* 86:50–69.

Johnson, Miriam M. 1981. "Heterosexuality, Male Dominance, and the Father Image." *Sociological Inquiry* 51:129–139.

Johnson, Miriam M. 1982. "Fathers and Femininity in Daughters: A Review of the Research." *Sociology and Social Research* 67:1–17.

Johnson, Miriam M. 1988a. *Strong Mothers, Weak Wives: The Search for Gender Equality*. Berkeley: University of California Press.

Johnson, Miriam M. 1988b. "Feminism and the Theories of Talcott Parsons." Paper presented at the American Sociological Association meetings, Atlanta, Ga.

Johnson, Miriam M., Jean Stockard, Joan Acker, and Claudeen Naffziger. 1975. "Expressiveness Reevaluated." *School Review* 83:617–644.

Johnson, Miriam M., Jean Stockard, Mary K. Rothbart, and Lisa Friedman. 1981. "Sexual Preference, Feminism, and Women's Perceptions of Their Parents." *Sex Roles* 7:1–18.

Knorr-Cetina, K., and Aaron V. Cicourel, eds. 1981. *Advances in Social Theory and Methodology: Toward an Integration of Micro- and Macro- Sociologies*. Boston: Routledge and Kegan Paul.

Lechner, Frank. 1984. "Ethnicity and Revitalization in the Modern World System." *Sociological Focus* 17:243–256.

Lechner, Frank. 1985. "Modernity and Its Discontents." In Jeffrey C. Alexander, ed., *Neofunctionalism*. Beverly Hills: Sage.

Lechner, Frank. 1990. "Fundamentalism as Path Away from Differentiation." In Jeffrey C. Alexander and Paul Colomy, eds., *Differentiation Theory and Social Change: Comparative and Historical Perspectives*. New York: Columbia University Press.

Lefort, Claude. 1986. *The Political Forms of Modern Society: Bureaucracy, Democracy, Totalitarianism*. Edited and with an introduction by John B. Thompson. Cambridge, Mass.: MIT Press.

Lehman, Edward W. 1988. "The Theory of the State versus the State of Theory." *American Sociological Review* 53:807–823.

Lewis, David J., and Robert L. Smith. 1980. *American Sociology and Pragmatism: Mead, Chicago Sociology, and Symbolic Interaction*. Chicago: University of Chicago Press.

Lidz, Charles W., and Victor M. Lidz. 1976. "Piaget's Psychology of Intelligence and the Theory of Action." In J. Loubser et al., eds., *Explorations in General Theory in Social Science*. New York: Free Press.

Lidz, Victor. 1970. "Values in Sociology: A Critique of Szymanski." *Sociological Inquiry* 40:13–20.

Lidz, Victor. 1972. "On the Construction of Objective Theory: Rejoinder to Syzmanski." *Sociological Inquiry* 42:51–64.

Loubser, J. J., R. C. Baum, A. Effrat, and V. M. Lidz, eds. 1976. *Explorations in General Theory in Social Science*. Vols. 1 and 2. New York: Free Press.

Luhmann, Niklas. 1982. *The Differentiation of Society*. Translated by Stephen Holmes and Charles Larmore. New York: Columbia University Press.

Luhmann, Niklas. 1990a. "The Paradox of System Differentiation and the Evolution of Society." In Jeffrey C. Alexander and Paul Colomy, eds., *Differentiation Theory and Social Change: Comparative and Historical Perspectives*. New York: Columbia University Press.

Luhmann, Niklas. 1990b. "The Direction of Evolution." In Hans Haferkamp and Neil J. Smelser, eds., *Social Change and Modernity*, Berkeley: University of California Press.

Lyotard, Jean Francois. 1984. *The Postmodern Condition: A Report on Knowledge*. Translated by Geoff Bennington and Brian Massumi. Minneapolis: University of Minnesota Press.

Mayhew, Leon, ed. 1982. *Talcott Parsons: On Institutions and Social Evolution*. Chicago: University of Chicago Press.

Mayhew, Leon. 1984. "In Defense of Modernity: Talcott Parsons and The Utilitarian Tradition." *American Journal of Sociology* 89:1273–1305.

Mayhew, Leon. 1990. "The Differentiation of the Solidary Public." In Jeffrey C. Alexander and Paul Colomy, eds., *Differentiation Theory and Social Change: Comparative and Historical Perspectives*. New York: Columbia University Press.

Meyer, John W., and W. Richard Scott. 1983. *Organizational Environments: Ritual and Rationality*. Beverly Hills: Sage.

Molotch, Harvey L., and Deirdre Boden. 1985. "Talking Social Structure: Discourse, Domination and the Watergate Hearings." *American Sociological Review* 50:273–288.

Moore, Barrington, Jr. 1978. *Injustice: The Social Bases of Obedience and Revolt*. New York: Pantheon.

Munch, Richard. 1981. "Talcott Parsons and the Theory of Action I: The Structure of Kantian Lore." *American Journal of Sociology* 86:709–739.

Munch, Richard. 1982. "Talcott Parsons and the Theory of Action II: The Continuity of Development." *American Journal of Sociology* 87:771–826.

Munch, Richard. 1983. "Modern Science and Technology: Differentiation or

Interpenetration?" *International Journal of Comparative Sociology* 24:157–175.

Munch, Richard. 1986. "The American Creed in Sociological Theory." *Sociology Theory* 4:41–60.

Munch, Richard. 1987a. *Theory of Action*. London: Routledge and Kegan Paul.

Munch, Richard. 1987b. "The Interpenetration of Microinteraction and Macrostructures in a Complex and Contingent Institutional Order." In Jeffrey C. Alexander, Bernhard Giesen, Richard Munch, and Neil J. Smelser, eds., *The Micro-Macro Link*. Berkeley: University of California Press.

Munch, Richard. 1988. *Understanding Modernity*. London: Routledge and Keagan Paul.

Munch, Richard. 1990a. "Social Change and Modernity in America: The System of Equality and Inequality." In Hans Haferkamp and Neil J. Smelser, eds., *Social Change and Modernity*. Berkeley: University of California Press.

Munch, Richard. 1990b. "Differentiation and Rationalization of Society: Recent German Debates." In Jeffrey C. Alexander and Paul Colomy, eds., *Differentiation Theory and Social Change: Comparative and Historical Perspectives*. New York: Columbia University Press.

Orru, Marco. 1988. "Review of *Talcott Parsons: On Economy and Society* (by Robert J. Holton and Bryan S. Turner) and *The Integration of Economic and Sociological Theory* (The Marshall Lectures, University of Cambridge, 1953)." *Contemporary Sociology* 17:115–117.

Page, Charles H. 1985. "On Neofunctionalism." *Footnotes* 13:10.

Parsons, Talcott. 1937. *The Structure of Social Action*. New York: Free Press.

Parsons, Talcott, Edward Shils, Kaspar D. Naegele, and Jesse R. Pitts, eds. 1961. *Theories of Society*. New York: Free Press.

Peters, John D., and Eric W. Rothenbuhler. 1988. "The Reality of Construction." In H. Simons, ed., *Perspectives on the Rhetoric of the Human Sciences*. London: Sage.

Prager, Jeffrey. 1986. *Building Democracy in Ireland: Political Order and Cultural Integration in a Newly Independent Nation*. Cambridge: Cambridge University Press.

Rambo, Eric. 1988. "Economic Culture." Ph.D. dissertation, University of California, Los Angeles.

Rhoades, Gary. 1990. "Differentation in Four Higher Educational Systems." In Jeffrey C. Alexander and Paul Colomy, eds., *Differentiation Theory and Social Change: Comparative and Historical Perspectives*. New York: Columbia University Press.

Ritzer, George. 1975. *Sociology: A Multiple Paradigm Science*. Boston: Allyn and Bacon.

Ritzer, George. 1985. "The Rise of Micro-Sociological Theory." *Sociological Theory* 3:88–98.

Ritzer, George. 1988. *Sociological Theory*. 2d ed. New York: Knopf.

Robertson, Roland. 1982. "Parsons on the Evolutionary Significance of American Religion." *Sociological Analysis* 43:307–326.

Robertson, Roland. 1985. "The Sacred and the World-System." In Phillip Hammond, ed., *The Sacred in a Post-Secular Age*. Berkeley: University of California Press.

Robertson, Roland. 1986. "Sociological Theory and Images of World Order: A Working Paper." Paper presented at the American Sociological Association and German Sociological Association Conference on Development and Change, Berkeley, California.

Robertson, Roland. 1987. "Globalization Theory and Civilizational Analysis." *Comparative Civilizations Review* 17:20–30.

Robertson, Roland. 1988. "The Sociological Significance of Culture: Some General Considerations." *Theory Culture and Society* 5:3–23.

Robertson, Roland. 1990. "Globality, Global Culture and Images of World Order." In Hans Haferkamp and Neil Smelser, eds., *Social Change and Modernity*. Berkeley: University of California Press.

Robertson, Roland, and JoAnn Chirico. 1985. "Humanity, Globalization and Worldwide Religious Resurgence." *Sociological Analysis* 46:219–242.

Robertson, Roland, and Frank Lechner. 1985. "Modernization, Globalization and the Problem of Culture in World-Systems Theory." *Theory, Culture and Society* 2:103–118.

Rothenbuhler, Eric W. 1986a. "A Cross-National Analysis of Communication in Social Conflict." Paper presented to the Annual Convention of the American Association for Public Opinion Research, St. Petersburg Beach, Florida.

Rothenbuhler, Eric W. 1986b. "Media Events and Social Solidarity: An Updated Report on the Living Room Celebration of the Olympic Games." Paper presented to the Annual Convention of the International Communication Association, Chicago.

Rothenbuhler, Eric W. 1987. "Neofunctionalism for Mass Communication." In M. Gurevitch and M. R. Levy, eds., *Mass Communication Review Yearbook*. Volume 6. Newbury Park, Cal.: Sage.

Rothenbuhler, Eric W. 1988a. "Live Broadcasting, Media Events, Telecommunication, and Social Form." In David R. Maines and Carl Couch, eds., *Information, Communication, and Social Structure*. Springfield, IL.: Charles C. Thomas.

Rothenbuhler, Eric W. 1988b. "The Liminal Flight: Mass Strikes as Ritual and Interpretation." In Jeffrey C. Alexander, ed., *Durkheimian Sociology*. New York: Columbia University Press.

Rothenbuhler, Eric W. 1988c. "The Living Room Celebration of the Olympic Games." Manuscript.

Rothenbuhler, Eric W. 1988d. "Values and Symbols in Public Orientations to the Olympic Media Event." Manuscript.

Rothenbuhler, Eric W. n.d. "Collective Action and Communication." Paper, Department of Communication Studies, University of Iowa.

Schegloff, Emanuel A. 1987. "Between Macro and Micro: Context and Other Connections." In Jeffrey C. Alexander, Bernard Giesen, Richard Munch, and Neil J. Smelser, eds., *The Micro-Macro Link*. Berkeley: University of California Press.

Schluchter, Wolfgang. 1979. "The Paradox of Rationalization." In Guenther Roth and Wolfgang Schluchter, *Max Weber's Vision of History*. Berkeley: University of California Press.

Schluchter, Wolfgang. 1981. *The Rise of Western Rationalism: Max Weber's Developmental History*. Translated by Guenther Roth. Berkeley: University of California Press.

Sciulli, David. 1984. "Talcott Parsons' Analytic Critique of Marxism's Concept of Alienation." *American Journal of Sociology* 90:514–540.

Sciulli, David. 1985. "The Practical Groundwork of Critical Theory: Bringing Parsons to Habermas (and Vice Versa)." In J. Alexander, ed., *Neofunctionalism*. Beverly Hills: Sage.

Sciulli, David. 1986. "Voluntaristic Action." *American Sociological Review* 51:743–767.

Sciulli, David. 1988. "Reconsidering Interactionism's Corrective Against the Excesses of Functionalism." *Symbolic Interaction* 11:69–84.

Sciulli, David. 1989. "Theory of Societal Constitutionalism: Foundations of a Non-Marxist Critical Theory." Manuscript.

Sciulli, David. 1990. "Differentiation and Collegial Formations: Implications of Societal Constitutionalism." In Jeffrey C. Alexander and Paul Colomy, eds., *Differ-

entiation Theory and Social Change: Comparative and Historical Perspectives. New York: Columbia University Press.

Sewell, William, Jr. 1980. *Work and Revolution in France: The Language of Labor From the Old Regime to 1848.* Cambridge: Cambridge University Press.

Sewell, William, Jr. 1985. *Structure and Mobility: The Men and Women of Marseille, 1820–1870.* Cambridge: Cambridge University Press.

Skocpol, Theda, and Kenneth Finegold. 1982. "State Capacity and Economic Intervention in the Early New Deal." *Political Science Quarterly* 97:255–278.

Smelser, Neil J. 1959. *Social Change in the Industrial Revolution.* Chicago: University of Chicago Press.

Smelser, Neil J. 1962. *Theory of Collective Behavior.* New York: Free Press.

Smelser, Neil J., ed. 1973. *Karl Marx: On Society and Societal Change.* Chicago: University of Chicago Press.

Smelser, Neil J. 1985. "Evaluating the Model of Structural Differentiation in Relation to Educational Change in the Nineteenth Century." In Jeffrey C. Alexander, ed., *Neofunctionalism.* Beverly Hills: Sage.

Smelser, Neil J. 1990. "The Contest Between Family and Schooling in Nineteenth Century Britain." In Jeffrey C. Alexander and Paul Colomy, eds., *Differentiation Theory and Social Change: Comparative and Historical Perspectives.* New York: Columbia University Press.

Stockard, Jean, and Miriam M. Johnson. 1979. "The Social Origins of Male Dominance." *Sex Roles* 5:199–218.

Stryker, Sheldon. 1980. *Symbolic Interactionism: A Social Structural Version.* Menlo Park, Cal.: Benjamin Cummings.

Surace, Samuel. 1982. "Incomplete Differentiation." Manuscript.

Swidler, Ann. 1986. "Culture in Action." *American Sociological Review* 51:273–286.

Syzmanski, Albert. 1970a. "Toward a Radical Sociology." *Sociological Inquiry* 40:3–13.

Syzmanski, Albert. 1970b. "The Value of Sociology: An Answer to Lidz. *Sociological Inquiry* 40:21–25.

Syzmanski, Albert. 1972. "Dialectical Functionalism: A Further Answer to Lidz." *Sociological Inquiry* 42:145–153.

Tiryakian, Edward A. 1985. "On the Significance of Dedifferentiation." In S. N. Eisenstadt and H. J. Helle, eds., *Macro-Sociological Theory: Perspectives on Sociological Theory.* Volume 1, Beverly Hills: Sage.

Tiryakian, Edward A. 1990. "Reenchantment and Dedifferentiation as Counter Processes of Modernity." In Hans Haferkamp and Neil J. Smelser, eds., *Social Change and Modernity.* Berkeley: University of California Press.

Turner, Bryan S. 1986a. *Citizenship and Capitalism.* London: Allen and Unwin.

Turner, Bryan S. 1986b. "Personhood and Citizenship." *Theory, Culture, and Society* 3:1–16.

Turner, Bryan S. 1987. "Marx, Weber, and the Coherence of Capitalism." In Norbert Wiley, ed., *The Marx-Weber Debate.* Beverly Hills: Sage.

Turner, Bryan S. 1989. "Commentary: Some Reflections on Cumulative Theorizing in Sociology." In Turner, ed., *Theory Building in Sociology.*

Turner, Jonathan H., ed. 1989. *Theory Building in Sociology.* Beverly Hills: Sage.

Turner, Jonathan H., and Alexandra Maryanski. 1988. "Is 'Neofunctionalism' Really Functional?" *Sociological Theory* 6:110–121.

Wagner, David G. 1984. *The Growth of Sociological Theories.* Beverly Hills: Sage.

Wagner, David G., and Joseph Berger. 1985. "Do Sociological Theories Grow?" *American Journal of Sociology* 90:697–728.

Williams, Robin M., Jr. 1961. "The Sociological Theory of Talcott Parsons." In

Max Black, ed., *The Social Theories of Talcott Parsons*. Carbondale and Edwardsville: Southern Illinois University Press.

Wippler, Reinhard, and Siegwart Lindenberg. 1987. "Collective Phenomena and Rational Choice." In Jeffrey C. Alexander, Bernhard Giesen, Richard Munch, and Neil J. Smelser, eds., *The Micro-Macro Link*. Berkeley: University of California Press.

Wuthnow, Robert. 1988. *Meaning and Moral Order: Explorations in Cultural Analysis*. Berkeley: University of California Press.

3

Conflict Theory and the Advance of Macro-Historical Sociology

❁

RANDALL COLLINS
University of California, Riverside

Conflict theory has been implicit in historiography and social thought since at least the time of Thucydides. Its basic themes are the following: 1) The central feature of social organization is stratification, the kind and degree of inequality among groups and individuals and their domination over one another. 2) The causes of what happens in society are to be sought in the interests of groups and individuals; above all, their interests in maintaining their positions of domination or evading domination by others. 3) Who wins what in these struggles depends on the resources controlled by the different factions, including material resources for violence and for economic exchange, but also resources for social organization and for shaping emotions and ideas. 4) Social change is driven especially by conflict; hence long periods of relatively stable domination are punctuated by intense and dramatic episodes of group mobilization.

It can be easily seen that these principles are an abstraction from more specific theoretical positions expressed by Marx and Engels; a little less obviously, these principles are also specified in a somewhat different form by Weber. In addition, there are a number of other classic statements of one or another principle, by Michels, Pareto, Mosca, and others. It is fair to say that modern conflict theory emerged as an effort to produce a nonideological version of Marxism, with a multidimensional emphasis that might be called "left Weberian." Since Marxism has continued as a vigorous school (or rather set of schools), it is worth pointing to its major differences from conflict theory.

Conflict theory per se has no commitment to socialism; nor for that matter is it committed to capitalism (though Weber was, unenthusiastically). A number of thinkers in conflict theory are sympathetic to the anarchist tradition (as I am personally) but conflict theory is concerned most fundamentally to make the most realistic analysis possible of society, leaving political commitments to personal choice. Since it does not regard movement towards socialism as an inevitable goal or even a central feature of history, conflict theory is better able than Marxism to analyze the multiple trajectories and turnings of history as driven by a wide variety of conflicts. The category of social class, although an important focus for the analysis of interests and resources, both material and ideological, does not assume a privileged position; power and status structures are perhaps even more important locations for domination and conflict.

For this very reason, conflict theory is in a better position than Marxism to understand socialism. It is not at all anomalous for conflict theory that power conflicts exist within socialist forms of organization —or even that pseudo-property conditions should reemerge there. As a historical note, I might add that as the socialist states in the late twentieth century appear to be turning back towards market economies, conflict theory is in a much better position than Marxism itself to explain this transformation. This is not to say conflict theory would expect the triumph of smoothly functioning capitalism. On the contrary, capitalism is especially riddled with conflicts, since private property makes for a relatively wide distribution of the material conditions which mobilize groups for conflict, as well as constituting an additional arena in which conflict can take place. Conflict theory envisions a future in which a variety of conflicts—military, organizational, economic, ideological—will continue according to their own rhythms, without end.

I do want to stress, however, that conflict theory has quite a lot in common with Marxism, and that it willingly incorporates whatever explanatory discoveries Marxism makes. Although economic contradictions and crises are not necessarily the central feature of analysis, they are frequently important. Such Marxian analyses as Perry Anderson (1974) on the crises within slave and feudal structures, Wallerstein (1974, 1980) on world system dynamics, and O'Connor's (1973) model of the fiscal crisis of the state contain many useful points for a general conflict theory of macro-historical change. The tendency to syncretism already exists on the Marxian side; Anderson explicitly amalgamates Marxian and Weberian theories of the crisis of ancient slavery, while Wallerstein's world system puts capitalism into the framework of geopolitics, a central focus of Weberian conflict theory. The most creative efforts in contemporary macro-historical Marxism thus have moved in a neo-Weberian direction.

A major difference remains, in that another version of current Marxism puts its emphasis on the Hegelian tradition, even verging on a full-blown revival of German idealism. This is the humanistic neo-Marxism which insists on the notion of species being, and the alienation of humans from their essence by the objectifying conditions of capitalism. Thus the classical schemas of Marxian economics continue to receive attention, not because they are of much use in explaining the actual historical dynamics of capitalism, but because they are a device for passing a metaphysical judgment on modern society. Conflict theory typically regards this kind of analysis as a sideshow, a diversion from understanding how domination and conflict take place. This is not to say that one might not also wish to add a condemnation onto one's analysis of society, but Hegelian metaphysics does not do the work of an explanatory analysis. For that purpose, a deeper intellectual commitment is needed to theorize the empirical evidence, irrespective of philosophical partisanship.

THE SCOPE OF CONFLICT THEORY

In one sense, the term "conflict theory" is somewhat of a misnomer. It is not simply a theory about conflict. As indicated, it is a theory about the organization of society, the behavior of people and groups, it explains why structures take the forms that they do at various historical times as well as in local situations, and how and what kinds of changes occur. Thus "conflict theory" is a good deal broader than specific theories about conflict itself. A narrower version was the now classic line of theory put forward by Simmel (1908) and developed by Coser (1956), which is concerned largely with the consequences of conflict within a social system, conceived in a functionalist manner. Other such theories have viewed conflict as a matter of structural strain, periods of transition among equilibrating systems, or of individual undersocialization or deviance. Such theories about conflict are not necessarily "conflict theories" in the larger sense.

Conflict theory is a general approach to the entire field of sociology. The phenomenon of conflict is only a dramatic emblem of the approach, for conflict itself is patterned by the structure of stratification, by the intensity of domination, by the resources that enable groups to organize and mobilize (or prevent them from it). Overt conflict is relatively rare; even military combat, as close analysis shows (Collins 1989), is more of a matter of maneuvering to break down organizational bonds than actual physical destruction. Conflict theory does not exclude a theory of social solidarity, even of social ideals, moral sentiments, and altruism. It is mainly because of the distribution of material and organizational conditions producing such ideals and sentiments that individuals are able to dominate hierarchies, or groups are able to form to engage in concerted conflict. The crucial point is that conflict theory does not take ideals and morals as analytically sacrosanct, as givens outside of sociological analysis. Instead, conflict theorists show the conditions under which ideas and ideals are generated, how and when they produce solidarity, when they aid domination by giving it legitimacy, and when these processes are structured so as to generate antagonisms and even overt conflict. Marx and Engels (1848) paved the way for such an analysis with their conception of the material means of intellectual production, this has been broadened, not only into an analysis of all the organizational conditions which produce ideas, but also into an analysis of what might be called the "means of emotional production."

Conflict theory to a large extent has developed by explicitly theorizing and codifying principles that have turned up recurrently in empirical research. The classic versions of conflict theory are mainly macro-historical. Marx, Weber, Pareto, and others, reflecting on the large-scale patterns of history, have been driven to focus upon the changing shapes of stratification, on political factions and conflicts, on ideological contentions as well as on periods of the domination in doctrines and morals. Most historians are implictly conflict theorists, for the simple reason that the dramatic materials of history which they write about consist of struggles, factions, and disagreements. Conflict theory took more definitive shape within sociology as research on stratification was carried out, and as it became apparent that a comprehensive picture of stratification cuts right across society, into every institution and affecting virtually every aspect of behavior.

It is not surprising that organizational analysis should also come to play a major role in the development of conflict theory, since organizations are both the sites of conflict, and the major weapons of domination and of revolt. Thus Weber took an analytical step beyond Marx in beginning a theory of the forms of organization (ideal-typically, bureaucratic, and patrimonial) as components of the structure of domination within any state, economy, or church. Weber's contemporary, Robert Michels, by analyzing domination within labor unions and political parties, opened another important wing, the way in which such structures themselves create a division of interests and hence at least latent struggles for control. When conflict theory was explicitly formulated as such, in the late 1950s, by Ralf Dahrendorf (1959), it was based on a generalization of this model of organizational conflict. Other theorists of that time, who more or less explicitly put forward conflict theory as a general paradigm (such as C. Wright Mills, Lockwood, and Rex) seized on the centrality of stratification and of hierarchic organization as keys for explaining all the phenomena of sociology.

My own main contribution to conflict theory (Collins 1975) was to add a micro level to these macro-level theories. I especially tried to show that stratification and organization are grounded in the interactions of everyday life. The two most important phenomena that need grounding are the patterns of antagonism, domination, and conflict on one hand—roughly speaking, what one might call the micro-level of "class conflict," seen in a multidimensional fashion—and on the other hand, the patterns of solidarity that tie groups together. Both kinds of phenomena, I argued, are understandable by a development of Goffman's model of interaction rituals: on the one hand, there are the opposing types of motivation and consciousness produced by front-stages and backstages in the performance of order-giving and order-taking in everyday life; on the other hand, the solidarity that is generated by ritual sociability among equals, involving a flow of emotions and of conversational exchange. I further attempted to demonstrate that empirically known patterns of variation among different types of organizational structures follow from the constraints of struggles over micro-control when certain kinds of activities are attempted and certain material resources are present. And since organizations are the building blocks of capitalist enterprises, parties, states, armies, churches, and virtually everything else, a conflict explanation can be consistently built throughout the empirical realms of sociology.

For these reasons, conflict theory has broader scope than most other current lines of sociological theory. The various micro theories, such as symbolic interactionism, ethnomethodology, and exchange theory, are intrinsically too narrow to be an explanation of the entire range of sociology; the same is true for cultural-interpretive positions, which let culture be an arbitrary vantagepoint on society, not itself amenable to explanation. Conflict theory, on the other hand, engages freely in what might be called intellectual piracy: it is quite willing to incorporate those elements (for instance, of micro-sociologies) which provide a good grounding for a comprehensive model of human cognition, emotion, and behavior. Its only criterion is that these borrowings must be capable of sustaining a model of social structure in which power and property, domination and struggle are central features.

The other way in which conflict theory departs from other theoretical positions is that it is especially oriented towards empirical research. As I have indicated, conflict theory arose in the first place from reflections on historical patterns, and from research on stratification and organizations. My own contributions to conflict theory came by way of building on the empirical contributions of Goffman, Garfinkel, Sacks, and Schegloff. The advances of historical sociology, insofar as these can be theorized beyond particularistic accounts of certain periods and events, constitute an ongoing input into conflict theory. I will focus below on these recent developments.

A major point of difference between conflict theory and other current theories is that, because of its closer connection to empirical sociology, conflict theory is much less wedded to metatheoretical reflection on the nature of theory per se. Although at one time in the past (around the 1960s) conflict theory engaged in high-level debates with functionalism over the general merits of approaches, conflict theory has gone on developing as an empirical enterprise, without a great deal of self-consciousness. Given the growing alienation between theorists and empiricists in sociology (based on an institutionalization in different specialties, professional organizations, networks, and journals), conflict theory is of all of today's theoretical camps most at home on the empirical side of the field. Recall the basic thrusts of conflict theory which I listed at the outset: a focus on domination, interests, resources for control and for mobilization, and the episodic and conflictual nature of change. These themes are particularly strong in a number of areas of research: they dominate political sociology, including its recent turn towards the analysis of geopolitics; social movement theory, in which the focus on resource mobilization, social movement organizations, and interests/ideologies continues the classic themes of conflict theory; the sociology of professions, in which revisionist theory since the 1970s is essentially conflict theory; much of the sociology of education; a major position in criminology; as well as the study of stratification, and of social change. The premises of conflict theory have become the "normal science" of numerous fields of empirical research. By virtue of this connection, the substantive content of conflict theory continues to grow, carried along on the accumulation of research findings.

For the remainder of this paper, I will concentrate on these recent advances in the area of macro-historical sociology, which has always been the core area for conflict theory.

MACRO-HISTORICAL SOCIOLOGY: MANN'S FOUR-NETWORK MODEL

A comprehensive framework for all aspects of macro-sociology is provided in Michael Mann's *The Sources of Social Power* (1986). This is a work of historical interpretation, the first of three projected volumes. It also includes a general analytical model which is useful for capturing the relationships among different areas of macro-historical conflict theory. Mann proposes that there are four dimensions of power: military/ geopolitical; political; economic; and cultural/ideological. These are Weber's familiar three dimensions (class, status, power) but with the power dimension subdivided into two components: the military as external and coercive force, and the political state apparatus with its parties or factions. Mann points out (1986, 11) that although the two dimensions of Weber's category of "party" or "power" may coincide (ideal-typically, in the modern state), historically military groups have also existed independently of the state, and the military can also be in opposition to a state, as in the dynamics of a military coup d'etat.

What is most significant about Mann's schema is not so much the number of categories but the way they are conceptualized. Each of the dimensions of power refers to actual organizations; they are all equally configurations of material resources. More specifically, each of them is a social network. Thus, although some of these networks may produce ideas, emotions, and feelings of legitimation, these are not simply descriptive or analytical categories; there is an underlying causal basis for whatever is produced and organized in each type of network. The organizations of fighting forces, with their weapons, communications, and logistics is what makes up the military network; the organizations of persons struggling to control the state, and those acting to administer a territory and extract its resources in the form of taxation, comprise the political network; the organization of the factors of production and the means of distribution and consumption make up the economic network; the organizations which produce ideas and emotions, whether structured as religious movements or churches, schools, channels of local culture, or of the mass media make up the ideological network.

The way these four kinds of networks are structured is what makes up the actual organization of social life at any given time and place. The networks themselves are subject to variation in *extensiveness* and *intensiveness*. In other words, power can vary in the range of territory it covers (extensiveness), but it can also vary in how much control it actually exerts over people in any spot (intensiveness). Geopolitical power, for example, in the case of nomadic raiders, could sometimes be extremely extensive, but was episodic and hence minimally intensive. To describe the extensiveness and intensiveness of each of the four kinds of networks would be to give us a comprehensive description of any historical social situation. Even more significantly, we can go beyond historicist description by concentrating on a theory of the causes and consequences of different degrees of extensiveness and intensiveness of each type of network.

Mann further stresses that the four kinds of network are overlapping and noncoinciding, not only analytically, but often factually. We escape from the straitjacket of the notion of a "society" as unit, making its own way through time, and thus from the simplifications of linear evolutionary (or for that matter cyclical) models of change. Mann's perspective bears a kinship to Wallersteinian world-system analysis, but extends its logic further. All the dimensions of social power are "world-system"-like, not merely in modern capitalism and geopolitics. But the extent to which military, political, economic, and cultural networks spread out across space is not constant across history; nor is there a single leap from local to world-system levels of organization.

Historical change is precisely the uneven spread of the different kinds of networks. This does not mean that history is a chaos without form; we are not left at the mercy of pure historicists, describing parochial details and giving up hope of any generalizations. The general principles are in the dynamics of each type of the four networks, and in their relationships. Since there are innumerable possible configurations of concrete combinations among the different conditions of the four networks, such a scheme can generate as much concrete complexity as one might desire. But the complexity itself is produced by a much more compact and determinate set of processes, much in the way that the table of chemical elements can combine to produce a huge variety of molecules that make up the history of the inorganic and organic universe.

Mann suggests two major principles regarding the overlap among the four networks. One is that the non-overlap itself is what drives historical change. It is when the geopolitical network, for instance, is much wider in scope than the other networks, that there will be militarily driven social change. Analogously, ideological networks (such as the spread of Christianity or other world religions beyond the boundaries of existing states and economies) can sometimes become the most extensive network and the leading edge of social change. Under yet other circumstances, the economic network may be the most extensive one (particular circumstances which were overgeneralized by the nineteenth-century European model of change). A related principle is that there will be different leading sectors in social change at various times; one or another form of power will come to the fore at different points in history.

The basic point here is that each type of network is a form of power, because it organizes people. Extrapolating from the general themes of conflict theory, one can say that where a kind of resource becomes available it will further the interests of some actors, who will use it to develop a form of stratification. Networks, in other words, are power resources for human actors. As forms of organization, they automatically structure people into groups. Some persons in those structures turn out to be those who are most favored by resources and hence most attached to the organization, and who become motivated to maneuver to maintain their domination of those resources. The same structural distributions make other persons disadvantaged or subordinated by that organization of resources, and hence disaffected. As Mann points out, the extension of power networks throughout history is a kind of entrapment of the human population. As long as there are opportunities to escape geographically, people flee from the net (as Mann points out in a highly original chapter entitled "How Prehistorical Peoples Evaded Power"). But as structures become ecologically closed, local networks cannot avoid impinging upon one another; escape from power of one sort now means finding resources to build some kind of counter-network but that in turn creates yet another form of power. The dialectic goes on.

THE SIGNIFICANCE OF NETWORK ANALYSIS

The fact that Mann describes the organizational structures of power as networks gives an opportunity for further theory-building. Network sociology has developed considerably as a research area in recent decades. For some time, however, the field was somewhat of "a method in search of a theory," a means of mathematical description of the shape of networks and of the place of individuals within them. It involves measures of such features as centrality, connectivity, holes in networks, and multiplexity of ties. Although the data typically used for network analysis have been of a more modest scope, these concepts could be applied to Mann's four dimensions to give greater precision to the picture of just how the military, political, economic, and ideological connections have been structured across historical situations.

The important step is to theorize, to be able to state conditions for causes and consequences of different network structures. A good deal of the research in macro-conflict theory makes contributions to explaining the dynamics of one or more of the four types of networks identified by Mann. In addition, a number of these theories point out ways in which one type of network is influenced by another. For instance, geopolitical networks affect political networks, while economic networks provide one of the inputs affecting geopolitical structures. This historical research constitutes one side of a theoretical convergence. On the side of network analysis, there have been some theoretical developments relevant to these same topics.

Geopolitical Networks

Geopolitics is an area that was largely neglected by sociologists until quite recently. Now steps have been made toward formulating some of the basic principles of geopolitics, which include the following. Resource advantage: military conflicts are usually won by the larger and richer state (Kennedy 1987). This principle is cumulative over time, as victorious states absorb the resources of the losers (Collins 1981a). Geopositional advantage: states with enemies in fewer directions have a military advantage over states with multiple enemies; thus, "marchland" (exterior) states tend to grow, middle states to become fragmented over time (Collins 1981a). Overextension: military efforts beyond certain geographical limits tend to strain resources and result in crises and often in rapid collapse of power (Kennedy 1987; Luttwak 1987; Collins 1981a, 1986, 167–209). The combination of such principles, worked out in greater detail, helps explain how and when states expand and contract (see also Gilpin 1981).

Geopolitical processes have a structural autonomy. This is true both because they are cumulative in themselves, and because the external line-up of states at any given time will affect what can happen to any particular state. It is in this sense that geopolitics can have an autonomously structuring effect upon economics. This is implicit (although not sharply theorized) in Wallerstein's world system theory, where hegemony in the world system is the key to the ability of core states to benefit economically by controlling the periphery. This is a causal link, then, from the geopolitical to the economic network. There is also a link in the opposite direction, insofar as economic resources are one of the inputs which make for geopolitical power. To say that geopolitics and economics both determine each other, however, does not reduce the theory to vacuousness. This is because there is a determinate flow from geopolitics to economics (e.g., via economic returns of world-system position), and vice versa (investment in military strength); on each side (economic and geopolitical) there are other factors which can be theoretically specified; and the time periods over which these effects happen are not equal. Thus there is a given time within which a state can benefit economically from geopolitical strength (usually rather long-run), while geopolitical processes themselves are much more volatile and subject to rapid turning points.[1]

Much attention has been given recently to the effects of geopolitics upon politics. Skocpol's theory of revolutions (1979) places emphasis on geopolitical crises bringing about fiscal strain and intra-elite conflict, and thus setting the stage for revolts. Her theory has a geopolitical component, but also a domestic component, since the nature of class relations determines which of the mobilized actors actually struggle over state power. Goldstone (1987, 1990) generalizes this logic into a model of "state breakdowns," which include not only revolutions, but also breakdowns with non-revolutionary consequences (such as those which happened in the Ming dynasty in China and in the Ottoman empire). Goldstone further widens the theory on the causal side, by showing how military strains intertwine with population growth, tax collecting capacities, and monetary inflation to produce a situation of state breakdown. Other work in this area (Downing 1988) attempts to demonstrate the effects of geopolitics, via military mobilization levels, upon the democratic or authoritarian structure of the state.

It is also possible to put together the various pieces of geopolitical theory with a predictive model of domestic politics. Geopolitical principles (outlined above) tell us when a state's international power will be expanding or contracting, and especially when crises can be expected to arise due to overextension and resource strain. If one adds the Weberian premise that the legitimacy of domestic rulers fluctuates with the power-prestige of the state, it follows that the rise and fall of political factions will depend on the coincidence of their tenure in political office with geopolitical events (Collins 1986, 145–66). This is of course only a partial theory of political dynamics, insofar as there are also domestic processes (largely in the area of class and status conflicts) which also affect political mobilization of various factions. But major geopolitical events, especially wars, dramatic incidents involving national prestige, and above all defeats, have an impact that overrides virtually all domestic events. Even severe economic breakdown, or a severe cultural crisis (highly mobilized religious conflict being the most likely) has an overriding influence on politics only in the absence of geopolitical crisis of even moderately comparable strength. Thus the prominence of events in one or another sector is the underlying structure affecting the flow of political power.

Political Networks

Network theory has generally theorized power as resource dependence: those network positions upon which other positions depend for scarce resources have power over the others (Cook et al. 1983). This is one form of power, and it is visible not only in experimental situations but in bargaining among political factions and within political coalitions. Much of the empirical work outside the laboratory has concentrated on descriptive questions regarding power structures in communities, and now at the level of the national state. Its most significant theoretical point has been to show that organizations rather than individuals are the prime actors in large-scale political arenas, and that the sheer numbers and density of organizations determine what issues will become part of the political agenda, and how rapidly they will be the subject of political action (Laumann and Knoke 1987). Although this work is couched as an analysis of specific policy domains in the U.S. government during the 1980s, its theoretical structure is potentially generalizable to politics in any arena of a sufficient scale.

An important—indeed the most important—form of political power is not captured by resource dependence. The missing feature is coercive power, in which some individuals are forced to comply with the demands of others, irrespective of scarce or non-scarce rewards they may obtain. Coercive power is a network phenomenon of a special kind. For violence and the use of weapons are episodic, and coercive structures operate primarily by threat; the first-line wielders of armed force discipline each other by mutual threat, channeled through a structure of command. Thus coercion must be based on what I call an "enforcement coalition" (Collins 1988, 436–442; the basic conception comes from Schelling 1963). Who will dominate an enforcement coalition; what shape such coalitions have; and how much stability, conflict, and change they exhibit; these are questions to be answered by an organizational/network theory of power. We know some of this from laboratory experiments which study how subjects react to (typically rather mild) coercive power (Willer 1987); other aspects are revealed by studies of armies in battle (Collins 1989). A crucial question is how coercive power is established in the first place, and what brings about its transformation into noncoercive forms of power.

A well-established research tradition deals in a more limited way with the conditions that mobilize conflict groups into action. Resource moblization theory (McCarthy and Zald 1977; Tilly 1978; Oliver and Marwell 1988) is a rather direct extension of the themes of conflict theory concerning interests and resources, with a stress on organizational conditions, incentives, and costs. Although this has not been brought directly into connection with network analysis, the links are not far to seek. It can be shown, for instance, that radical protest movements in early industrialism were generated above all by exposure to the mobilizing effects of the market itself; for this reason, traditional craft workers were more militantly anti-capitalist than factory workers, since the latter were insulated from direct contact with the national market, and channeled their struggles in the local power structure of the factory (Calhoun 1982). In another almost explicit application of network themes, Traugott (1985) showed that members of the working class could be mobilized either in revolutionary or counterrevolutionary forces, depending on whether their networks tied them into the working class community or isolated then as a military guard. The general principle appears strong: it is the structures themselves that mobilize people into political action which are most important in shaping their immediate sense of interests, and hence which side they will struggle for in a political conflict.

Economic Networks

Network analysis has been especially successful in broadening our understanding of economic structures. On the macro level, network analysis has begun to develop sophisticated theories of markets and of power. From a network point of view, a market in the classical sense is a limiting case: structurally, it is a network in which every node (every actor or organization) has links with every other node. This is of course an idealization; it is almost never true that everyone is a potential buyer or seller in relation to everyone else. Thus network analysis gives a more realistic picture of how markets operate, by showing what patterns of linkages actually exist. This does not mean that processes of supply and demand do not operate, but instead of there necessarily being equilibrium prices which clear a market, there is a differentiated structure in which only some buyers or sellers constitute these market relations. Thus prices and profits are variable, precisely because of how the particular network of economic exchange is structured.

This notion has become familiar in the conception of split labor markets: high-priced labor exists in a restricted network, whereas open networks with intense market competition drive down the price of labor. I have applied this model to the effects of educational credentials in stratifying occupations (Collins 1979); Parkin has applied it (1979) to exclusionary strategies directed downwards and usurpatory strategies directed upwards in labor markets. Murphy (1988) develops this into a full-fledged theory of social closure through monopolization and exclusion. Murphy's work builds a comprehensive theory of stratification, applying not only to the formation of classes based on private property, but also to closure based on political structures (such as the Communist party in bureaucratic socialist regimes) and on cultural traits (including education, ethnicity, and gender). All these, in effect, are variations in the shape of social networks.

We are now pulling together the pieces of a theory of capitalism, in which these social structures, rather than the market per se, are crucial. The theory goes back to a little-noticed portion of Weber ([1922] 1968,

144–150, 341–343, 638–639) in which he analyzes the dynamics of capitalism as a struggle over the appropriation of opportunities in the market. Accordingly, the dynamics of capitalism are a process of successive monopolizations, which build upon and also eventually undermine each other. Thus the monopolization of land as private property not only was a step towards feudalism, as was the monopolization of the rights to hold government office, but it also was a step towards creating a market in which land (and government sinecures too) could be traded and subjected to market forces (Collins 1986, 117–142). Appropriation on one level makes possible the creation of a super-organization in which bargaining takes place over the instruments of appropriation; financial markets could emerge upon commodity or land markets; educational credential markets could emerge upon the appropriation of fixed positions in organizations. It is for this reason that Braudel (1977, 51–53, 62; 1979, 2:329–405) conceives of capitalism as a series of layers, markets of different extensiveness, with the more long-range markets capable of manipulating the local ones. In the late twentieth century, meta-financial markets involving financial leveraging have emerged as an arena for struggle over control of corporate finance itself. This fits with the general conflict theory vision of endless creation of new structures of conflict built upon older structures.

Network analysis has explicitly dealt only with some components of stratification within markets. On the level of business organizations, it has been demostrated (Burt 1983) that profit goes to those organizations which occupy the most favorable positions of control in relation to their own suppliers and consumers. White (1981) proposes a general network theory of markets, in which capitalists are organized into networks of mutually monitoring producers; these circles are not engaged in exchange among themselves so much as they monitor each other's market success in order to find noncompetitive niches. One may also add, following Schumpeter's ([1911] 1961, 210) conception of banks as "the headquarters of the capitalist system," that financial organizations do the most important monitoring of structures in order to maximize noncompetitive niches (Collins 1986, 117–142). Thus stratification among capitalists has several layers: those who are most subject to the equilibrium prices of the open market; those who have established noncompetitive niches; and at the top, those in the meta-organizations of the financial sector which direct the flow of investments.

The picture of capitalism that emerges is, so to speak, an organizational politics of networks, rather than an open competitive market. There always remains an element of competition; in fact, this is one of the variables that network analysis could pin down for us more precisely. But it makes a crucial difference just how many competitors there are, and what organizational structures set them off from a general competition with everyone. There exist two different kinds of relationships in economic networks: networks of economic exchange —in which the network brings together buyers and sellers and thus sets prices in an autonomously coercive fashion, above the wishes of individuals—and networks of information, the mutually monitoring cliques in Harrison White's model whose contacts consist above all in avoiding situations of competition over material exchange. Not everyone of course is equally successful at avoiding competition and securing a profitable niche; and competitive conditions may break open a niche after a period of protection. The financial market, too, as a market for the meta-resources of investment capital, tends to unify different markets and to introduce indirect competition even into protected niches. For these reasons, there is a continuing dynamic of forming and breaking down restricted zones within an economic network.

Culture/Ideological Networks

To see culture as produced by social organizations enables us to state some conditions under which particular kinds of ideas and beliefs will be propagated. This type of analysis has been done for some time in narrower fields such as the sociology of science. Its larger structural importance has been mapped out in organizational analyses of the causes and effects of the educational expansion. Schools are organizations, based upon material inputs, but producing ideas and emotions. For the most part these are embodied in actual human beings, although one should not overlook the volume of material production which goes along with this, in the form of papers, books, and other cultural artifacts. But even immaterial culture can be used as a commodity; it has a structural position in networks of social exchange which is similar to money in commercial markets. It is on this conception that Bourdieu and his colleagues (Bourdieu 1977, 1984; Bourdieu and Passeron 1977) have built a theory of the production and distribution of cultural capital. In general, this is a conflict theory too, focusing upon stratification, struggle of interest groups, and the possession of material and ideal resources.

There are a number of different positions regarding the dynamics of change within culture-production systems. Bourdieu tends to emphasize a cyclical reproduction of the system, in which cultural capital is convertible into stratification in all dimensions including property, and those resources in turn are convertible again into culture. Although there are flows of this sort on a very general level of abstraction, this still leaves open the question of how such a system changes over time, including the conditions that start it in the first place, and those which might bring about a crisis within it. My version of the theory (Collins 1979) is that decentralized governmental structures potentially allow a competitive market of culture producers; this potential is realized to the extent that there is a multi-ethnic situation, or other circumstances moblizing diverse groups to compete over elite status credentials.[2] The result is an inflationary dynamic, the expansion of mass educational credentials of generally declining value; thus cultural inflation itself motivates still further efforts at raising levels of cultural credentials.

Logically, this dynamic could not continue indefinitely, both because it tends to delegitimate the existing culture by instrumentalizing and relativizing it, and also because the material expense of the culture-production system itself at some point escalates beyond what the economy can invest in it. The result has been periods of cultural crisis and deflation of the value of a given culture-producing system (for instance, the Protestant Reformation at the end of a long period of expansion of religious movements and educational organizations during the High Middle Ages; *see* Collins 1981b). There is not only a "fiscal crisis of the state," generated especially by geopolitical overexpansion, but there can also be a "fiscal crisis of culture-producing organizations." In both cases, there is a structure of competition or conflict—in one case, over military hegemony, in the other, over status hegemony within a domestic network of stratification. Conflict has its own autonomous dynamic, feeding upon itself and hence driving structures to new levels. But conflict of either kind, military or cultural, always depends on some material resource inputs, and those resources set a limit to how far a conflict can go. Beyond those limits, the organizational structures built up by conflict, whether they be military, educational, or religious, strain the resources available, and result in a crisis and collapse. This is a conflict model of the historical dynamics of religion as well as of secular culture-producing organizations.

But no single crisis is ever the end. The collapse of one form of stratification means the opportunity for its enemies, those who were oppressed by it, to seize the means of mobilization and of organization for themselves. New structures of domination are built over time, subject to the same kinds of underlying structural vicissitudes as before. Conflict theory is the vision of Heraclitus. However we might wish it otherwise, the processes of organization and reorganization through conflict are endless.

THE FUTURE OF CONFLICT THEORY

There are a number of empirical areas, listed above, in which conflict theory has been a major perspective and in which it will doubtless continue to develop. My own near-term efforts are in one such area, the sociology of science. My aim is to build a full-scale conflict theory of the social production of ideas by intellectual communities. The guiding theme is the competitive appropriation and elaboration of accumulated intellectual capital among the number of factions which the structure of supporting resources makes possible at a given time. Intellectual history is thus a conflict process, driven by divergent factions within the world of intellectual production. These factions make intellectual property out of ideas that have been produced in the past, and generate new ideas in opposition to the ideas of their rivals. Strikingly new positions are produced especially by the negation of pre-existing positions, along the lines of greatest political rivalry.

The high road of conflict theory, though, is likely to remain in the arena of macro-historical sociology. This is where the grand visions have been put forward of human societies as networks of privilege and domination, moving through long slow shifts in resources and in sudden dramatic outbursts of conflict. This kind of sociology has been in a golden age during the last few decades; the period has included both neo-Marxian work (like that of Barrington Moore, Perry Anderson, and Immanuel Wallerstein) which has pushed closer to multi-dimensional conflict premises, as well as ideologically free-floating work like that of Tilly, Skocpol, and Mann. There is every indication the creativity of macro-historical conflict sociology will continue in the years ahead. There are multi-volume works still in progress: Mann has produced but one of his three promised volumes, bringing his analytical story only down to 1760; it is his third volume that is to provide the full theoretical payoff. Wallerstein's parallel neo-Marxian project, now up to its third volume and reaching as yet only to the French Revolution, still has ahead of it the challenge of the nineteenth-century imperialisms as well as the shifting capitalist world system of the late twentieth century.

These kinds of works, I would stress, provide not just historical insight, but carry forward the general analysis of the modes of domination and conflict. Thus Jack Goldstone's work opens up the theoretical connections among demographic revolutions and slumps, monetary inflation, and the fiscal crisis of the state. Though he has concentrated on the great seventeenth-century breakdowns, Goldstone's model has obvious potential for generalizing to other epochs and other crises. It is a safe bet that these implications will be picked up by a new generation of researchers. Another multi-volume work in progress, Orlando Patterson's study of the world patterns of slavery, promises to recast our vision of the whole sweep of human history comprising the pre-industrial states; in doing so, we can expect that we will build up new understandings of the modes of property and politics, dehumanization and its dialectics. Geopolitics is another topic, recently opened up for vigorous comparative and historical study, that is becoming extensively cultivated. With it has come a theoretical challenge: the dynamics of military expansion and decline, of threat and domestic political response, loom increasingly at the center of our theoretical picture of both conflict and social order.

Conflict theory is not only about the patterns of conflict. It is about both social change, and the shaping of all the dimensions of social privilege, and therefore of social structure. The empirical advances that build up conflict theory thus promise to increase our understanding across the entire range of sociology.

NOTES

1. In addition, as Mann points out, the very existence of an effective army depends upon its ability to maintain an organizational network across space; hence the army depends on its material provision, its logistics and communications structure. Historically, the great empire-building armies were organizations which constructed their material infrastructure as they went along. It is for this reason that Mann (1986, 272–295) describes Rome as an army-based process of development, in which the army itself built the roads, laid down the structure of material provisioning, and thus rather literally paved the way for political, economic, and cultural networks to follow (not always very close behind).

2. A related version, put forward by Ramirez and Boli-Bennett (1982) points out that in the last century, educational systems have become an emblem of status within the international arena. Analogous to Weber's conception of the power-prestige of states dramatized by their military strength, there has developed a conception of what a culturally modern state is, including the possession of a mass educational system. Thus the international political network drives a status competition in the realm of cultural production.

REFERENCES

Anderson, Perry. 1974. *Passages from Antiquity to Feudalism*. London: New Left Books.

Bourdieu, Pierre. 1977. *Outline of a Theory of Practice*. Cambridge: Cambridge University Press.

Bourdieu, Pierre. 1984. *Distinction: A Social Critique of the Judgement of Taste*. Cambridge, Mass.: Harvard University Press.

Bourdieu, Pierre, and Jean-Claude Passeron. 1977. *Reproduction: in Education, Society, and Culture.* Beverly Hills: Sage.

Braudel, Fernand. 1977. *Afterthoughts on Material Civilization and Capitalism.* Baltimore: Johns Hopkins University Press.

Braudel, Fernand. 1979–1981. *Civilization and Capitalism, 1400–1800.* 3 vols. London: Collins.

Burt, Ronald S. 1983. *Corporate Profits and Cooperation: Networks of Market Constraints and Directorate Ties in the American Economy.* New York: Academic Press.

Calhoun, Craig. 1982. *The Question of Class Struggle.* Chicago: University of Chicago Press.

Collins, Randall. 1975. *Conflict Sociology: Toward an Explanatory Science.* New York: Academic Press.

Collins, Randall. 1979. *The Credential Society: An Historical Sociology of Education and Stratification.* New York: Academic Press.

Collins, Randall. 1981a. "Long-Term Social Change and the Territorial Power of States." In Randall Collins, *Sociology Since Midcentury: Essays in Theory Cumulation.* New York: Academic Press.

Collins, Randall. 1981b. "Crises and Declines in Credential Systems." In Randall Collins, *Sociology Since Midcentury: Essays in Theory Cumulation.* New York: Academic Press.

Collins, Randall. 1986. *Weberian Sociological Theory.* Cambridge and New York: Cambridge University Press.

Collins, Randall. 1988. *Theoretical Sociology.* San Diego: Harcourt Brace Jovanovich.

Collins, Randall. 1989. "Sociological Theory, Disaster Research, and War." In Gary Kreps, ed., *Social Structure and Disaster: Conception and Measurement.* Newark, Del.: University of Delaware Press.

Cook, Karen S., Richard M. Emerson, Mary R. Gillmore, and Toshio Yamagishi. 1983. "The Distribution of Power in Exchange Networks." *American Journal of Sociology* 89:275–305.

Coser, Lewis A. 1956. *The Functions of Social Conflict.* New York: Free Press.

Dahrendorf, Ralf. 1959. *Class and Class Conflict in Industrial Society.* Stanford: Stanford University Press.

Downing, Brian. 1988. "Constitutionalism, Warfare, and Political Change in Early Modern Europe." *Theory and Society* 17:7–56.

Gilpin, Robert. 1981. *War and Change in World Politics.* Cambridge and New York: Cambridge University Press.

Goldstone, Jack A. 1987. "Cultural Orthodoxy, Risk and Innovation: The Divergence of East and West in the Early Modern World." *Sociological Theory* 5:119–135.

Goldstone, Jack A. 1990. *State Breakdown in the Early Modern World.* Berkeley: University of California Press.

Kennedy, Paul. 1987. *The Rise and Fall of the Great Powers: Economic Change and Military Conflict from 1500 to 2000.* New York: Random House.

Laumann, Edward O., and David Knoke. 1987. *The Organizational State.* Madison: University of Wisconsin Press.

Luttwak, Edward N. 1987. *Strategy: The Logic of War and Peace.* Cambridge, Mass.: Belknap Press.

McCarthy, John D., and Mayer Zald. 1977. "Resource Mobilization in Social Movements: A Partial Theory." *American Journal of Sociology* 82:1212–1239.

Mann, Michael. 1986. *The Sources of Social Power.* Vol. 1. New York: Cambridge University Press.

Marx, Karl, and Friedrich Engels. [1846] 1947. *The German Ideology.* Reprint. New York: International Publishers.

Murphy, Raymond. 1988. *Social Closure: The Theory of Monopolization and Exclusion.* Oxford: Clarendon Press.

O'Connor, James. 1973. *The Fiscal Crisis of the State.* New York: St. Martin's.

Oliver, Pamela, and Gerald Marwell. 1988. "The Paradox of Group Size in Collective Action: A Theory of the Critical Mass." *American Journal of Sociology* 91:522–556.

Parkin, Frank. 1979. *Marxism and Class Theory: A Bourgeois Critique.* London: Routledge.

Ramirez, Francisco O., and John Boli-Bennett. 1982. "Global Patterns of Educational Institutionalization." In Philip Altbach, Robert Arnove, and Gail Kelley, eds., *Comparative Education.* New York: Macmillan.

Schelling, Thomas C. 1963. *The Strategy of Conflict.* Cambridge, Mass.: Harvard University Press.

Schumpeter, Joseph A. [1911] 1961. *The Theory of Economic Development.* Reprint. New York: Oxford University Press.

Simmel, Georg. [1908] 1955. *Conflict and the Web of Group-Affiliations.* Reprint. New York: Free Press.

Skocpol, Theda. 1979. *States and Social Revolutions.* New York: Cambridge University Press.

Tilly, Charles. 1978. *From Mobilization to Revolution.* Reading, Mass.: Addison-Wesley.

Traugott, Mark. 1985. *Armies of the Poor: Determinants of Working-Class Participation in the Parisian Insurrection of June 1848.* Princeton: Princeton University Press.

Wallerstein, Immanuel. 1974–1989. *The Modern World System.* Vols. 1–3. New York: Academic Press.

Weber, Max. [1922] 1968. *Economy and Society.* Reprint. Edited by Guenter Roth and Klaus Wittich. New York: Bedminster Press.

White, Harrison C. 1981. "Where Do Markets Come From?" *American Journal of Sociology* 87:517–547.

Willer, David. 1987. *Theory and the Experimental Investigation of Social Structures.* New York: Gordon and Breach.

4

The Decline of the Grand Narrative of Emancipatory Modernity: Crisis or Renewal in Neo-Marxian Theory?

❀

ROBERT J. ANTONIO
University of Kansas

The history of Marxist theory has been punctuated by frequent pronouncements about impending bankruptcy, but each time the death sentence is passed a revitalized version reappears phoenix-like on the scene. This remarkable capacity for self-renewal in the face of apparently irresolvable antinomies has given Marxism more than nine lives. In the 1970s and 1980s, a flourishing academic Marxist subculture, emphasizing empirical, historical, and interpretive research (and middle-range theorizing) on class, culture, extraction, power, revolution, ideology, and alienation, gained a strong foothold in the social sciences and humanities, especially in the English-speaking countries (Anderson 1983, 9–31). This pluralistic subculture employs diverse methods and approaches, and is integrated only by some overlapping research interests, a few basic concepts, and an underlying commitment to egalitarian values (which are themselves open to widely different interpretations). During the same period, global Marxist theory fell on hard times, and its political project seemed moribund (*see* Anderson 1983; Aronowitz 1981). A neo-Marxist describes the pessimistic mood,

> For many of its critics Marxism is not quite a god that failed, source of profound disillusion and betrayal, but rather an old-fashioned and simplistic outlook which, over time, has grown outmoded much like the Ptolemaic system, requiring too many epicyles upon epicyles to "save the phenomena." Simpler then to become frankly pluralist, or to look for

I have benefitted substantially from criticism by Steven Best, Douglas Kellner, and George Ritzer. This research was supported by University of Kansas General Research grant allocation 3627-X0-0038.

other keys and watchwords—"power" and "domination," for example. (Aronson 1985, 75)

The same pluralistic tendencies associated with the success of academic Marxism ran counter to the materialist grand narrative that had long centered Marxist theoretical discourse around a controversial conception of emancipatory modernity.

A most scathing attack on Marxist theory has come from postmodernists who contend it cannot address the complex linkages between new types of culture, knowledge, and power. They also argue that its holistic conceptions of labor, class, emancipation, and socialism legitimate bureaucratic centralism and cultural homogenization. Although Jean-François Lyotard, like other postmodern theorists, is broadly critical of Enlightenment reason, he had Marxism especially in mind when he sounded the battle cry: "Let us wage a war on totality" (Lyotard 1984, 82). However, this broadside against theoretical holism and consequent "decentering" also have gone on *within* Marxist theory, refashioning the familiar materialist concepts into highly generalized ideas of pluralism, discourse, and democracy. The changes have blurred the boundaries between scientific and critical Marxism and, more significantly, between Marxism and "post-Marxism." My focus concerns the issue of whether these recent trends amount to a terminal crisis or if yet another revitalized form of Marxist theory is rising from the ashes.

EMANCIPATORY TOTALITY: MARX'S MATERIALIST GRAND NARRATIVE OF MODERNITY

The main target of decentering efforts has been the emancipatory totality first expressed in Karl Marx's materialist grand narrative of modernity.[1] It is characterized by a *productivist* equation of material and social progress, naive optimism about *centralized* authority, uncritical *rationalism*, homogeneous *collective subject*, and a teleological *terminus to history*. The materialist locomotive of modernity carries seeds of a free, equal, and abundant society that sprout after capitalist development creates the transitional institutional structures and sets off the class struggles that lead inevitably to the emancipatory track. However, this grand narrative is entwined with other narratives in Marx's texts, and, in particular, with what I call historical holism.[2] This competing vision of history appears throughout the same works, suggesting a nonlinear and nondeterministic pattern of development. Even Engels

([1890–1894] 1959, 395–412) conceded that the claims of the grand narrative were too bold, admitting that Marx and he had rhetorically overplayed them in their polemical battles with critics. Engels argued that their real method was a nonmechanistic, multicausal, *historical* materialism, and declared the fundamentalist regurgitations of the grand narrative by younger "Marxists" to be "the most amazing rubbish." But the textual center of Marx's thought is beside the point; the grand narrative must be considered because it provided normative justification for Marx's politics (the raison d'être of his theory), it served as the prime eschatology of the communist movement, and it furnished the problematic that shaped many of the most important twentieth-century debates over Marxism (Gouldner 1980, 3–63, 289–323; Jay 1984, 1–20; Antonio 1983).

"Scientific Marxists" embraced Marx's economic writings, materialist epistemology, and class analysis, whereas "critical Marxists" preferred his theory of alienation, ideology critique, and revolutionary politics. Although both subtraditions deviated substantially from the grand narrative, their revisions tended to prop up emancipatory hopes in the face of historical conditions that contradicted its linear vision of history. The point is that the grand narrative set the agenda for Western Marxist theoretical discourse. And contrary to their claims about making a complete break, the exaggerated antirationalism and antiholism of radical postmodernists together constitute a negative phase of the despised totality that does not escape the problematic of the grand narrative.

At the heart of the grand narrative is the idea that capitalism's highly differentiated and interdependent division of labor constitutes a fundamental and progressive overcoming of the constraints of feudalism and of all preexisting (traditional) societies. Marx viewed the decline of independent production as a decisive emancipatory step because he believed that its simple productive process resulted in self-perpetuating material backwardness, social isolation, and narrowness of vision. His socialist ideal of a "society of associated producers" could not emerge as a collective project until after specialized wage labor and complex economic interdependence replaced peasant and artisan production. The revolutionary feature of capitalist development is a quantitative and qualitative expansion of needs, foreshadowing an even richer *social* individuality that rationally harnesses the untapped creative powers of "species-being." For Marx, capitalism marked the beginning of the end of human prehistory (Marx [1852] 1963, 122–135; Marx [1857–1858] 1973, 471–515, 526–528; Marx [1887] 1967, 333–335, 713–716).

Capitalism's "tendency towards an absolute development of the productive forces" was, in Marx's view, the ultimate determinant of the movement toward socialism (Marx [1894] 1967, 257). The separation of ownership and workers, and consequent institution of wage labor (controlled by impersonal authorities with extractive interests) ignited the logic of capitalist accumulation and the spiral of material progress. To survive the market version of Darwinian struggle, capitalists organized workers into complex "modes of cooperation," rationalized and mechanized the labor process, and coordinated private ownership and the anarchic market relations outside the firm. Marx promised that, in the long run, the firm's progressive *social* organization of production would prevail over the "irrational" system of extraction, producing an emancipatory *societal-wide rationalization* (Marx [1887] 1967, 444–447; Marx [1983] 1967, 34–36; Marx [1857–1858] 1973, 586–589; Engels [1880] 1982, 54–75).

Concentration and centralization greatly accelerate the movement toward socialism. Marx even spoke of the huge stock companies and monopoly capitalism as "the abolition of the capitalist mode of production within the capitalist mode of production" (Marx [1894] 1967, 438, 436–441; Marx [1887] 1967, 626–628). He held that the transfer of effective control to professional managers marks a higher stage of socialization in which ownership is purely extractive and vestigial, and thus becomes a highly vulnerable target of expropriation. Moreover, managerial planning stimulates socialization *outside* as well as inside the firm; the big state arises in response to new forms of societal interdependence that accompany "big industry's" corporate bureaucracies, monopolistic combinations, and networks of interfirm collusion. Finally, the expansionary capitalist "world market" destroys the "natural exclusiveness of separate nations," creates "everywhere the same relations between the classes," and eradicates "the peculiar individuality of the various nationalities" (Marx and Engels [1845–1846] 1964, 75–76; Marx and Engels [1894] 1967, 438).

According to Marx, capitalism produces an international proletariat "which in all nations has the same interest" (Marx and Engels [1845–1846] 1964, 76). The collective experience of the new forms of exploitation and socialization is so powerful that it overrides all other differences. Marx viewed the social distinctions of capitalist civil society as either atavistic throwbacks to precapitalist religious affiliations and status orders or as alienated products of newly emerged class divisions. Bourgeois law and public institutions are similarly tainted. Marx affirmed capitalism's corrosive effect on association (outside the productive sphere) and public life because it supposedly opened the way for proletarian class consciousness and solidarity. Authentic human differences develop only under emancipated conditions where individual capacities are freely formed. Therefore, the social fabric of postcapitalism must be created anew on the basis of the concrete conditions of freedom (new needs and rich individuality) that Marx hoped would arise among associated producers (Marx [1843] 1967, [1875] 1959).

As the "social brain" of modernity, science is a central player in the grand narrative.[3] Marx thought that the final stage of capitalist development would be dominated by an *"automatic system of machinery"* based almost entirely upon "general scientific labor" and "technological application of natural sciences." Although initially drawn into action by capital, science ultimately creates the material conditions for emancipation by causing profits to fall, by generating new conditions of accumulation (no longer governed strictly by the capitalist "laws of motion"), and by diminishing the need for living labor (Marx [1857–1858] 1973, 692, 700). Like other capitalist productive forces, science is still ensnared in relations of exploitation and domination that "fetter" its development. But after the full socialization of productive property, autonomous science, in the form of socialist planning, gears production to social needs, transforming "the government of persons" into the pacific "administration of things" and unleashing the full creative potentialities of species-being (Engels [1880] 1982, 70.)

Invisible during the long evolutionary march through the ascendant stages of production (Marx and Engels [1845–1846] 1964, 23–95; Marx and Engels [1859] 1970, 19–22), emancipatory modernity finally appears when the "immanent laws" of capitalism, "with iron necessity," culminate in their "inevitable results" (Marx [1887] 1967, 7–11, 763–764). According to the grand narrative outlined above, an emancipatory telos inherent in capitalist *productivism, centralism,* and *rationalism* is appropriated consciously, for the first time, by a *collective subject* (both product and agent of these conditions) who, through labor and struggle, realizes the communist ideal in a *historical terminus* of freedom and abundance. Marxists later appealed to this emancipatory vision to validate their authority to speak in behalf of the whole of humanity and with certainty that their own plans for global social reconstruction would yield only emancipatory results (Gouldner 1980, 3–8; Jay 1984, 12–14). Critics, on the other hand, contended that the grand narrative was a chiliastic fantasy with affinity for authoritarian rule.

STUBBORN HISTORY: SEGMENTED SOCIETY VS. HOMOGENEOUS THEORY

By the 1930s, the Soviet Communist Party (CPSU) adopted a particularly crude version of the grand narrative as its official ideology (Marcuse 1971, 114–132; Jacoby 1971). To correct the "errors" of early critical Marxists (Lukács, Gramsci, and Korsch) and to command absolute obedience to the Stalinist dictatorship, the CPSU fashioned a completely scientistic and deterministic materialism that diminished the agency of the proletariat and sanctified the Party's "leading" role. Perfect grasp of the laws of history granted the Party political infallibility and justified its totalitarian powers. Raphael Samuel's (1987, 66) autobiographical account of British communism of the 1930s and 1940s exemplifies the gushy optimism about communist modernity.

> As against "dying culture," Communism represented what was "new," what was "developing." Industrially it stood on the side of electrification, ideologically of science, educationally of experiment, politically of internationalism—those modernizing tendencies which, in the world crisis of the 1930s, could still be represented as an unproblematic good. It championed progress against reaction, reason against revelation, the future against the past. Communism was the "youth of the world."

The idiom of the grand narrative pervaded everyday thought and communication within the Party (*see* Samuel 1985, 1986, 1987). Party members "dealt in absolutes and totalities, ultimates and finalities, universals and organic wholes," and spoke assuredly of "laws of social development" that serve as "an infallible guide to progress" and that guarantee "the liberation of mankind" (Samuel 1985, 40). Classes were "living, sentient beings" with "instincts," "distinct personality traits," and "interests." And the "military virtues" (i.e., the "readiness to sacrifice themselves") of the proletariat insured that, under the Party's guidance, modernity would be carried to its emancipatory conclusion (Samuel 1987, 64–65). The grand narrative was an apodictic truth that left no opening for challenging Party unity, discipline, or ideology. Although its exact role in Marx's thought is a matter of debate, the centrality of the grand narrative to communist ideology cannot be disputed.

But CPSU politics still made very significant concessions to history; its central policies of "socialism in one country" (making the defense of the USSR first priority) and "popular front" (the World War II antifascist alliance with noncommunist forces) deviated from the grant narrative. The retreat from internationalism reflected the Party's understanding that the working class, in the advanced capitalist countries, was not yet ready to accept its "historical role" (the revolution of 1917 itself did not spring from the actions of a class-conscious proletariat). The grand narrative had contended that that the spread of worldwide capitalism would quickly transform humanity into an undifferentiated mass of semi-skilled operatives. But this position was an erroneous extrapolation of homogenizing trends that began during early capitalism's simple transformation of independent producers into wage workers and that accelerated during the early stages of capitalist mechanization. Although he was prescient about some of its features, Marx did not live to see corporate capitalism. His claims about the ever increasing homogenization of the proletariat presumed continuing material and cultural leveling driven by relentless automation. On the contrary, twentieth-century capitalism brought vastly increased segmentation of production, labor markets, class structure, and status orders, making proletarian class politics even more problematic than it was in Marx's time (see Gordon, Edwards, and Reich 1982; Johnston 1986).[4] Moreover, international differences were far greater than those within national borders because world economic development was highly uneven. Since the logic of capital did not follow the grand design of emancipatory modernity, Western Marxists had to reformulate their ideas about the revolutionary subject.

After World War II, the authoritarian Soviet model was imposed widely in Eastern Europe and in the Third World but many Western European communists leaned in a divergent direction toward separate national strategies and parliamentary democracy. Despite the suppression of the Hungarian revolt in 1956, Khrushchev's de-Stalinization stirred hope for a broader democratization of state socialism. But this dream ended with Brezhnev's 1968 invasion of Czechoslovakia and the cruel "normalization" that hardened the totalitarian regime. Southern European communist parties broke with Moscow, adjusting their policies to attract broader domestic political support and to express increasingly divergent national aspirations. The ideal of proletarian universalism languished in the climate of postwar abundance and segmented class factions. Even if a revolutionary class bloc could have been formed, an assault on the bourgeoisie would have meant a despotic end to democracy rather than the dawn of socialism. Therefore, Eurocommunists settled for democratic institutions, coalitions with bourgeois parties, and progressive reforms that someday might forge cross-class alliances anchored in the working class. They hoped that these policies would build a democratic consensus for socialism, while preserving the desirable structural features and pluralistic character of bourgeois society (Mandel 1978a, 188–220; Carrillo 1978). Hence the demiurgic teleology and apocalyptic revolutionism of the grand narrative were supplanted by quiet reformism and practical politics.

Besides economic and class segmentation, Western Marxists had to contend with new forms of social differentiation. The countercultural ideals of the New Left contradicted the grand narrative's emphases on cultural homogenization and emancipatory abundance. Radical French students led a national mobilization and general strike in 1968 that verged on revolution, and in the same year, protests by American students against the Vietnam War culminated in nationally televised street battles at the Chicago Democratic National Convention. Although they had specific political goals, both movements expressed a new cultural politics that was highly critical of modernity (attacking technocracy, bureaucracy, discipline, rationalism, consumerism, and workaday existence) (*see* Hirsh 1981, 139–56, 208–235; Hodgson 1978, 263–411). After 1968, the leading edge of popular protest (e.g., the feminist, antinuclear, gay, and environmental movements) in the advanced capitalist societies addressed differentiated forms of domination, and expressed divergent cultural and political interests aiming at mostly nonmaterialist goals.[5] Although the new social movements could not be identified with a precise social location, they tended to be anchored in the middle strata rather than in the working class and the labor movement. Moreover, they lacked party organization, discipline, and doctrine; participants usually shared certain cultural and political affinities against a much broader background of contrasting characteristics and conflicting commitments. The pluralistic, loosely organized, and spontaneous nature of the new social movements made unity, and even identity, of "the Left" a highly problematic matter. Under these conditions, the grand narrative's automatic consensus (reflecting the homogeneous proletariat's "objective" class interests) was exposed as a complete fiction. The waning hopes for class politics now rested upon the uncertain process of democratic discourse, negotiation, compromise, and coalition building.

NEGATIVE TOTALITY
VS. SUBJECTLESS STRUCTURES

Political divisions on the left over the 1968 revolt in France manifested an emergent split between the new social movements and the Eurocommunists. The critical left (e.g., Sartre, Lefebvre, Castoriadis, Lefort, and Gorz) backed the Movement, while the French Communist Party (PCF) was opposed (Hirsh 1981, 139–56). PCF officials and intellectuals rejected the New Left because their politics invalidated the Party's centralized organization, discipline, and class politics. On the other hand, the French New Left, stressing self-management, spontaneous mass actions, and pluralistic coalitions, considered the PCF to be bureaucratic, authoritarian, and lifeless. This divide was elaborated theoretically throughout the West in resurgent forms of critical and scientific Marxism that pitted cultural politics against class politics.[6]

Although the Frankfurt School initially retained much of the grand narrative, during their "dialectic of Enlightenment" phase, they appropriated Max Weber's theories of rationalization and bureaucratization, and wove them into a one-sided, highly pessimistic broadside against Marxist holism and, in particular, against its fusion of rationality and emancipation. In contrast to Weber's ambivalent approach to modernity (which affirmed the civilizing features of science and bourgeois institutions), critical theorists treated rationalization as a cultural logic of total domination.[7] Capitalist productive forces were viewed almost exclusively as instruments of reification and commodity fetishism, serving an overarching system of cultural control that Marx never imagined. Critical theorists argued that the new domination system had deep cultural roots that preceded capitalism, ultimately reflecting the repressive character of Western reason. They considered the grand narrative's scientism, productivism, and collectivism to express a totalitarian variant of this tradition that subordinated the individual to authoritarian bureaucracy. By the start of the postwar era, the Frankfurt School substituted the negative totality of "total administration" for emancipatory modernity (Dubiel 1985; Benhabib 1986; Held 1980; Wolin 1987).

According to Herbert Marcuse (1964), consumer society neutralizes dissent by "delivering the goods" and realizing *bourgeois* democracy, freedom, and abundance. Rampant euphoric alienation and possessive individualism integrate workers into the system, and put an end to class politics. "One-dimensional" society wipes out the immanent contradiction between legitimations and social reality, destroying the historical grounds for Marxian ideology critique. But despite his deeply pessimistic vision of society "without opposition," Marcuse, in contrast to many of his Frankfurt School colleagues, never abandoned Marxism or emancipatory politics. And by the late 1960s, he spoke of a "new sensibility" that signaled the rise of an alternative revolutionary subject. Marcuse contended that anticapitalist needs and values, expressed in New Left cultural politics, were evidence that important segments of the populace were *not* integrated into the system. The increasing numbers of youthful "drop-outs" threatened capitalist reproduction by cutting the supply of highly trained technical and professional workers. Revolts by minorities and Third World peoples were further evidence of deep system instabilities. Although he did not see revolution on the near horizon, Marcuse believed that the growing wave of cultural and political radicalism contained seeds of a long-term emancipatory social transformation (Marcuse 1969, 1970, 83–108; Marcuse 1972; Kellner 1984, 276–319).

Besides Marcuse's thought, the New Left turned to the young Marx, early Western Marxist theory, and the Frankfurt School. Fresh critical Marxist works and translations appeared en masse during the late 1960s and early 1970s.[8] Fragments from these diverse theories were woven together haphazardly with other divergent approaches (e.g., Maoism). Even though strong anti-intellectual currents discouraged systematic theorizing, New Left thinkers hinted at an alternative to the grand narrative. They implied a revolutionary subject who is *not* the product of a single class location, who does *not* have the worker-bee discipline of the proletariat, and who does *not* need the guidance of a party. This stand-in for the proletariat is the subject of a cultural revolution stressing new types of valuation, new modes of understanding, and new capacities that dialectically transcend Western reason and *homo faber*. The New Left dwelled on Marx's critique of alienation and reification, and substituted utopian cultural radicalism for emancipatory modernity. Although the New Left was defunct by the mid-1970s, its intellectually inclined refugees became the core of the academic Marxist enclave that still thrives today.

Building on the work of thinkers (e.g., Claude Lévi-Strauss) who earlier opposed existentialist "subjectivism" (i.e., of Jean-Paul Sarte), Marxist structuralists defended Eurocommunism against the New Left's "humanism," "historicism," and "voluntarism." Their leading thinker, Louis Althusser, argued that Marx's "pre-Marxist" early writings should be put aside in favor of his later "scientific" theorizing about the capitalist mode of production and subjectless structures.[9] Regardless of the earnest-sounding defense of Marxist orthodoxy, structuralists broke decisively with the grand narrative. Althusser refashioned its vision of unsegmented class structure and linear development into a "decentered" totality with disjunctive layers of structure and process. Depending on the particular conditions of the specific setting, politics or ideology, as well as economics, could be the primary societal structuring principle (Althusser 1970, 200–218). Althusser's " 'pluralist' conception of history" dispensed with Marxist "monism," "economism," and evolutionary "historicism" (1970, 99–100, 163, 201, 213). "Revolutionary ruptures" originate from "a vast accumulation" of "heterogeneous" contradictions that depend on divergent sets of contingent circumstances. Development is so discontinuous and uneven that emphasis shifts from the historical long-term, and even from the historical conjuncture to the "current situation" (Althusser 1970, 179).

Structuralism's reduction of materialism to a "last instance" determinant of the "structure in dominance," and its contentions about the " 'relative autonomy' of superstructure" and independence of "theoretical practices" overthrow the grand narrative's economically based conceptions of crisis and transformation (Althusser 1970, 110–111, 164–175; Althusser 1971, 134–136). Rejection of crude determinism meant that the state was much more than a passive reflection of forces and social relations of production and that it was no longer viewed as the arbitrary instrument of the bourgeoisie. Because of its central role in reproducing the material infrastructure and in regulating productive activities, the state actively shapes the mode of production and is reciprocally shaped by it. Moreover, factional splits over the state's diverse functions and responsibilities divide hegemonic power-holding coalitions, creating opportunities for new alliances and power blocs that favor the working class (Poulantzas 1973). The affinity between Marxist structuralism and Eurocommunism is easy to detect; structuralism's scientistic and antivoluntaristic themes affirm the leading role of the Party, whereas the revisionist emphases on multicausality and relative autonomy uphold the new coalition politics. Both structuralism and Eurocommunism lost favor in the late 1970s, but their major departures from the grand narrative set the stage for a much more radical decentering.

PLURALISM, DISCOURSE, AND DEMOCRACY: NEO-MARXISM AND "POSTMODERNITY"

Regardless of the thriving new social movements, party politics turned sharply right in the late 1970s. In the United States, New Left hopes about a unified radical opposition withered with the student movement, and the laissez-faire rhetoric accompanying the defeated Humphrey-Hawkins Bill foreshadowed the return of the free market. Reaganism and Thatcherism were on the rise, while the post-1968, Prague winter sent a chill throughout the Soviet bloc. And China, in the wake of Mao's cultural revolution, which proved to be a brutal fraud, befriended the United States and reactionary Third World regimes. Resounding electoral defeats of the Latin Eurocommunists and strong setbacks for the northern European social democrats raised fears that even the modest postwar political gains might be in danger. Marcuse (1979, 23) sensed the increasingly defensive posture of the left.

> To conclude: The tendency is to the Right. It meets an enlarged opposition, qualitatively weakened by internal division, and by the lack of an organization adapted to the conditions of corporate capitalism. At the same time, the global conflicts between the capitalist powers, and with the Third World tend to weaken the stabilization of the system, without, however, posing a serious threat. The life-and-death question for the Left is: can the transformation of the corporate State into a neo-fascist State be prevented?

In response to the pessimistic political climate and to the demoralized state of global Marxist theory (after the demise of both New Left and structuralist theory), the leading critical theorist, Jürgen Habermas, executed a sweeping reconstruction of Marx's emancipatory totality based on a partial appropriation and revisionist reading of G. H. Mead's theory of communicative democracy and Max Weber's rationalization theory (Habermas 1979, 1981, 1982, 1983, 1984, 1987a, 1987b; Jay 1984, 462–509; Antonio 1989). But his reshaping of Marx's concepts to fit a socially differentiated and culturally fragmented era culminates in a radically decentered totality. Habermas abandons the grand narrative's productivist vision of materially driven social progress, and substitutes *labor* and *interaction* for base/superstructure in order to separate production (and bureaucracy) from communication (and consensual integration). He contends that labor's logic of "purposive-rationalization" tends to expand the domain of power and money into the interactive sphere, and this "colonization" substitutes technocratic control for democratic process. Habermas agrees with the view of dialectic Enlightenment critical theorists and postmodernists that bourgeois values (i.e., democracy, freedom, and abundance) are in eclipse and that social differentiation and cultural fragmentation have destroyed the historical bases of Marxian social criticism. Since there are no widely held progressive values that can be turned against the structure of power and be translated into a rhetoric of emancipatory solidarity, ideology critique is obsolete. In contrast to these other theorists, however, Habermas sought a new normative foundation to reconstruct Marxism.

"Communicative rationality," manifested in the taken-for-granted properties of interaction, supposedly provides an implicit standard for distinguishing normatively right actions from instrumental ones (based on power/money) and for giving direction to critical theory. Habermas claims that Marx and Weber both had this normative foundation in mind but left it undeveloped because of their preoccupation with the course of "purposive-rationalization" (i.e., capitalist development). Habermas' core idea is that competent speakers understand the difference between true and false statements and that true statements can be reached only in uncoerced dialogue. This means that a "counterfactual" ideal of voluntaristic social relations and procedural democracy is implicit in all "normal" interaction. In any linguistic community this ideal potentially can be activated to help resolve disputes when interaction breaks down. However, Habermas contends that the secularization of Protestant values qualitatively enhances the individual's capacity to tap this implicit normative content and favors communicatively rational institutional development (e.g., legal protection of human rights) (Habermas 1979, 1–94; Habermas 1984; Benhabib 1986, 279–353; Geuss 1981, 65).

Habermas reformulates the grand narrative into a quasi-Weberian theory of progressive cultural rationalization. Social differentiation and disenchantment diminish the intolerant moralism of traditional society and increase the possibility of coming to voluntaristic understandings. Communicative rationalization runs alongside purposive rationalization, acting as a counterforce against colonization. Although he affirms the global tradition of Marxian critical theory, Habermas' reconstructions of rationality, emancipation, and modernity break sharply with Marx's historical holism as well as the grand narrative. His effort to establish nondeterministic and nonmaterialist grounds for critical theory eliminates many of classical Marxism's most indefensible features (e.g., the homogeneous collective subject), but at the same time generates new metatheoretical problems (i.e., concerning the validity of his quasi-foundationalism and evolutionism), abandons the utopian features of Marxian revolutionism, and gives up the historical concreteness of Marx's political economy. Still Habermas' partial fusion of American pragmatism (i.e., G. H. Mead) and Weberian theory with Marxism has initiated a discourse that potentially could lead to a new theoretical synthesis and a new emancipatory theory based on historical holism. However, the outline of such an approach cannot begin to emerge until Habermasian theorists confront fully the ethical historicism of the pragmatists and the sociological historicism of Weber. And this requires a much more radical decentering that destroys all traces of foundationalism and evolutionism.

In contrast to Habermas, "analytic Marxists" attempted to defend the materialist theory of history. But they also radically decentered the grand narrative. Analytic Marxists replace the labor theory of value with a broader theory of exploitation that can be applied to socialism as well as capitalism. This effort to increase the approach's scope, however, eliminates the theoretical basis for Marxist crisis theory and severes the grand narrative's explicit link between material development and emancipatory politics. Although analytic Marxists defend class analysis, their pluralistic conception of power recognizes important noneconomic spheres of domination, exploitation, and conflict. Most important, they contend that the state has a much more determinate influence than productive forces in shaping the pattern of social development. Rather than paving a single road to socialism, material determination is reduced to a highly generalized process that sets broad boundaries on societal development and that, in interaction with noneconomic forces, opens divergent socio-political possibilities (Cohen 1978; Elster 1985, 1986a, 1986b; Roemer 1982, 1986a, 1986b; Carling 1986).

Analytic Marxists alter the methodology of historical materialism as significantly as the substance. They borrow rational choice models, game theory, general equilibrium theory, and mathematical modeling techniques from neoclassical economics in an attempt to elaborate the "microfoundations" of macroscopic processes. Their adoption of techniques that follow the precepts of methodological individualism has the explicit intent of ridding Marxism of its teleological and functionalist features. But the new idiom and method breaks with Marx's historical holism as well as with the objectionable features of the grand narrative (Roemer 1981, 7–10; 1986a; Elster 1986b; Hindess 1984).[10]

Decentering is most evident in analytic Marxist discussions of class politics. According to Erik Olin Wright, workers still constitute the largest class. However, modern class structure is highly differentiated, containing "contradictory class locations" with occupants (e.g., managers and bureaucrats) who are at the same time both exploitees and exploiters. Because their numbers are large and because they may side with either the property-holding or the working class, the shifting commitments of persons in contradictory locations have decisive impact on shaping class alliances. But the patterns of individual decisions that create such alliances reflect a broad range of particular historical circumstances, cultural experiences, and needs, and cannot be predicted exclusively on the basis of economic interest. Wright argues that efforts to forge emancipatory cross-class alliances must appeal on grounds *other than* material interest and that socialism requires, first, the creation of "radical democracy" (Wright 1985, 283–291; 1986). Wright's analytic colleague, Adam Przeworski agrees, arguing that, in the capitalist democracies, material improvement of the working class has not been translated into socialist electoral victories and cannot be the motor of a general emancipation. He concludes that Marxists must refashion their politics along nonmaterialist lines into a cultural project

(Przeworski 1986, 235–248). Here, socialism blends with the new social movements, blurring the differences with Habermasian theory and eroding the borders between scientific and critical Marxism.

The prominent, "post-Marxist" American political economists, Samuel Bowles and Herbert Gintis (1986) also argue that Marxist theory should turn away from economically driven conceptions of crisis. They contend that the *social conflict* between personal rights (e.g., welfare and civil rights) and property rights has been the primary societal contradiction of post-WWII capitalism. The costs of expanded personal rights contributed heavily to the profit squeeze and economic contraction of the mid-1970s and to a mobilization of the right that regained lost territory for capital. By stressing this state-mediated social dynamic and dropping the labor theory of value, Bowles and Gintis break sharply with Marx's crisis theory and grand narrative. But they still argue that the economy is the main site where personal and property rights clash, and therefore should be transformed from a private to a public sphere. This means democratic economic planning, public controls regulating the use and disposition of private productive property, and under some conditions, nationalization.

Bowles and Gintis retain central elements of Marx's emancipatory project but without the grand narrative's rosy optimism. They argue that the concepts of class and class politics are too narrow to express modernity's heterogeneous sites of hegemony (e.g., the state, patriarchal family) and differentiated forms of emancipatory opposition. Moreover, because it ignores democracy and human rights, Marxist theory neither comes to terms with the new social movements nor with America's primary societal contradiction. On the contrary, liberalism has provided an emancipatory idiom for the most important movements of our time. Yet by treating the economy as a private sphere, liberals have shielded economic matters from critique. Bowles and Gintis call for a new theoretical discourse that combines features of liberalism with Marxism and that aims at "postliberal democracy."

Post-Marxists ("without apologies") Ernesto Laclau and Chantel Mouffe draw on structuralist themes of overdetermination, ideology, and discourse, and on Gramscian "hegemony" divested of all taints of Marxian materialism and class politics. In their view, no necessary relation exists between emancipatory values and class location. The new cultural and social dynamics between the fragmented and shrunken working class, marginalized underclass, and postmaterialist new social movements require a complete rewriting of emancipatory theory. In place of class struggle and emancipatory subjectivity, Laclau and Mouffe speak of a *"field of discursivity"* with incomplete, open, and negotiable "discursive totalities" and "ambiguous, incomplete and polysemical" subjects (Laclau and Mouffe 1985, 111, 121). In this "detotalized" discursive world, emancipatory efforts leave party politics behind, and instead aim at forging radical democratic power blocs (crossing class, status, and other subgroup lines) and "a much wider and unstable system of democratic institutions" (Laclau 1987, 32). Since they fail to articulate the substantive features of "radical democracy" and the historical conditions that favor its creation, Laclau and Mouffe do not explain why their coalition politics is likely to succeed where the structuralists' class-centered coalitions failed. Similar to Althusserian (i.e., on "the current situation") and postmodernist presentism,[11] Laclau and Mouffe's one-sided emphasis on discourse and pluralism neglects the historical reckoning of organizational and material constraints and possibilities needed to make concrete estimations about the prospects for deeper democratization. Despite their critical decentering of the grand narrative, Laclau and Mouffe's highly generalized discussion of discursive democracy is a poor substitute for Marx's effort, however flawed, to theorize historically specific structural conditions and determinate emancipatory possibilities (Laclau and Mouffe 1985, 1987; Laclau 1987; Geras 1987, 1988; Mouzelis 1988).

But orthodox Marxist theory is not dead. Ellen Meiksins Wood (1986) argues that the theoretical innovations of the structuralists (i.e., especially the "relative autonomy" of superstructure) began a decentering process that culminated in the independence of discourse from class and, for that matter, from any external social base. She considers the "post-Marxism" of Laclau and Mouffe and of Bowles and Gintis to exemplify the contemporary "retreat from class" and the substitution of liberalism for Marxism (Wood 1986, 47–75, 140–145). Although her critique has some merit, Wood's own position pivots on the grand narrative's identification of the working class with universal emancipatory interests. Accordingly, socialist politics must be anchored in class, and could never emerge from a "radical democratic coalition." The underlying class divisions and contradictory class interests would never permit authentic democracy (Wood 1986, 167–200).

Wood's scathing denunciation of the so-called utopianism of contemporary left theorists (i.e., "the new true socialists") constitutes a polemical last stand of the old class politics without historical grounds. Her defense of the grand narrative fails to confront the historical conditions (i.e., the segmentation, differentiation, and fragmentation of the empirical proletariat) that caused other theorists to change course. Even in Marx's time the grand narrative was a questionable proposition with deep theoretical problems. Yet Marx's historical holism provided contestable historical arguments for emancipatory modernity. Because the grand narrative was interwoven with his historical analysis of capitalist development and contained defensible projections about capitalism's apparent tendencies, this totality, when Marx posed it, suggested an objectively possible course of events. Indeed, the grand narrative served as a sort of moral rhetoric designed to stir the proletariat into action to realize what Marx estimated to be concrete emancipatory possibilities. Conversely, Wood's argument lacks the support of such historical grounds, and for that reason her rendition of the grand narrative breaks down into the type of idealism that Marx himself castigated.

"Postmodernism" has been described as having "shifted from awkward neologism to derelict cliché without ever attaining . . . the dignity of a concept" (Hassan 1985, 119). But the term still connotes a distinctive type of theorizing (e.g., of Baudrillard, Deleuze, DeMan, Derrida, Foucault, Guattari, Kroker and Cook, Lacan, Lyotard) that has been highly influential across disciplinary borders (e.g., in social and political theory, philosophy, literary and artistic criticism, architecture, popular culture). Generally speaking, postmodern theory developed out of French structuralism (and poststructuralism), occupied space left by the collapse of Marxist structuralism, and gained wide popularity among English-speaking theorists (especially American literary critics) (Anderson 1983, 32–55; Dews 1987, xi–xvii).[12] Postmodernists reject the grand narrative's global philosophy of the subject and teleological vision of historical progress. However, their critique extends far beyond the emancipatory totality to the more modest concepts of rationality, representation, and the subject [13] implied in Marx's historical holism. They adopt instead a radical perspectivalism that links truth to power, deriving from Nietzsche's ([1887] 1967, 15–163) genealogical critique of Western reason. Postmodernists reject the core assumption of modern scientific epistemology (i.e., that knowledge can be judged according to how well it depicts empirical reality) as well as that of classical rationalism (i.e., that knowledge can be ranked according to intuitive truth standards). Instead of being accounts of external reality (privileged by compliance with analytic methods that follow consensual truth standards), postmodernists treat portrayals of the social world as narratives tied to specific forms of empowerment. For this reason, pluralism and discourse reign among the postmodernists.

Postmodern theory is not merely a critique of epistemology but is also a genealogy of the ever more effective methods of social control accompanying Western reason's imperialistic march. For example, Michel Foucault argues that modern views of madness, criminality, illness, and sexuality increased domination to heretofore unimaginable levels. The forms of power manifested in the practices of the new "helping" professions and total institutions depended increasingly on the conception of a rational subject governed by internal controls. Social regulation thus becomes more pervasive and oppressive when self-regulation (based on internalized notions of rationality and normalcy) replaces the physical constraints of incarceration and "treatments." Western reason's ideal of truth and "well-intended" institutional embodiments (e.g., the welfare state and socialism) mask connections between knowledge and power, and consequently increase their joint dominion (Foucault 1967, 1973, 1975, 1979, 1980a, 1980b; Callinicos 1985).

Jean Baudrillard also depicts a historical movement toward control based on knowledge but dwells on the cultural effects of the postmodern information explosion. According to Baudrillard, contemporary life is governed by a terroristic sign system; a counterfeit process of "simulation," hardly distinguishable from TV, masquerades as reality. Sign power obliterates history, leaving only the immediacy of ongoing, disjunctive events. The epistemological rules, normative understandings, and intersubjective structures of consciousness that produced distance between subject and object are washed away in the flux of divergent messages, information, and images; borders between different spheres of life lose meaning and are easily transgressed; and the social disappears in superficial, immediate, and flat experience. Hyperconformity rules in this vortex; even "criticism" and "rebellion" are reduced to robotic simulations that merely reproduce existing images and add to the overwhelming state of ennui (Baudrillard 1975, 1981, 1983; Kroker 1985; Chen 1987; Kellner 1987). Postmodernism rejects the rule of rationality, and at the same time heralds the beginning of its self-disintegration.

Although they are by no means identical, postmodern theory resembles critical theory's "dialectic of Enlightenment" (*see* Raulet 1983, 200; Jay 1984, 525–529; Dews 1986, 1987, 220–242; Ingram 1986). Both launch Nietzschean attacks on Western rationalism and theoretical holism that treat the ideal of emancipation as an instrument of power, oppression, and culture homogenization. And although they still participate in the Enlightenment critique of domination, both approaches forbid emancipatory moral rhetorics and collective political strategies. Finally, their extremely pessimistic negative totalities (i.e., one-dimensional society and postmodernity) were each responses to grim sociopolitical contexts where emancipatory modernity appeared to be in eclipse (Aronowitz 1987–1988; Anderson 1983, 32–84; Callinicos 1985; Kellner 1988; Wolin 1987).

The doyen of Marxist literary criticism, Fredric Jameson (1981, 1984a, 1984b, 1988; Stephanson 1987), begins a synthesis of postmodernism and Marxist theory. Jameson speaks of chaotic "postmodern hyperspace" undermining cognitive organization of the environment and destroying critical distance (1984a, 65, 83–92). In his view, Marxists must confront theoretically the cacophony of narratives, the "multidimensional set of radically discontinuous realities," and the "fragmented and schizophrenic" subject (Jameson 1988, 351). However, the new theory must break with Marxian ideology critique and with Habermasian critical theory because any type of moralizing criticism is defunct under these postmodern cultural conditions. Jameson calls on theorists instead to build "cognitive maps" ("spatial picture models") and to forge a new "cultural politics."

Jameson's thought has clear Marxist threads: he argues that class and capital accumulation are still the prime movers in postmodern societies; that a holistic defense of the socialist project should be mounted; and that postmodernism is the "cultural logic of late capitalism." He rejects contentions about the autonomy of culture, instead equating postmodernism with hypercommodification. Jameson borrows Ernest Mandel's (1978a) notion of late capitalism, which retains much of the economic baggage of orthodox Marxism with slight modification (e.g., the labor theory of value), to express the macroscopic socioeconomic structures that shape postmodern cultural life. But Jameson does not make determinate connections between the cultural formation, political economy, and emancipatory possibilities. Marx, on the other hand, grounded his political hopes in the characteristics and tendencies of capitalism that he believed would generate the cultural space for proletarian revolution. Whatever the historical deficits of his theorizing, he systematically linked political economy with specific possibilities for emancipation. On the contrary, Jameson provides neither the historical nor normative grounds to support his claims about the continued relevance of class politics and socialism.

By incorporating postmodern cultural themes within Marxist holism, Jameson begins a fundamental refocusing of Marxist theory. However, he does not get far, because he retains enough postmodernist antirationalism to negate the clear and explicit elaboration of the linkages between culture, political economy, and politics demanded by Marxist holism. The problem is made worse by Jameson's uncritical appropriation of Mandel and ambivalence about Marx's grand narrative. Because he is not sufficiently critical of either postmodernism or Marxism, Jameson juxtaposes the two approaches rather than completing the critical fusion that he began.

ECLIPSE OF THE GRAND NARRATIVE: HISTORICAL HOLISM AND NEW THEORETICAL SYNTHESES

The defensive posture and highly generalized conceptions of pluralism, discourse, and democracy, characteristic of many recent forms of Marxist and post-Marxist theory, may be short-lived responses to the right turn and transitional social conditions of the 1980s. More specific theories probably will have to await the new forms of political and economic organization that someday will arise in response to the breakdown of the postwar accommodation between labor and capital, the erosion of the structure of accumulation, the increased internalization of the economy, the mounting social and environmental costs, and the emergent forms of organizational and cultural life. A sharp economic downturn and consequent social conflicts might ignite these new discourses. On the other hand, the achievement of a substantive democratization and modernization in the USSR and Eastern Europe would propel Mikhail Gorbachev's "restructuring" to the heart of neo-Marxist theoretical debates and possibly stimulate a recentering of emancipatory theory around new substantive and conceptual poles. It is still unclear whether the sudden, sweeping socio-political changes in the East will result in the extension of capitalism, the emergence of new mixed political economies, the development of democratic socialism, or even the restoration of communism. However, the changes have falsified cold-war claims that state socialist regimes cannot change from within. In the past, major political and economic transitions have initiated sharp turnabouts in Marxist theory. But present trends do not favor a reemergence of the grand narrative; its deterministic productivism, naive centralism, uncritical rationalism, homogeneous collective subject, and teleological terminus cannot come to terms with the new forms of social differentiation and cultural fragmentation or with the consequent new needs, aspirations, and potentialities for change.

Historical holism should not be scrapped with the grand narrative (*see* Wolff and Cullenberg 1986). Marx conceptualized capitalism as a determinate social totality with specific forms of production, property, political organization, association, and legitimation, and as a historical conjuncture in a long-term developmental path. This holistic approach addressed the organizational sites that determine the macroscopic patterns of misery and well-being among the populace, and provided systematic analyses of the current tendencies, major sources of conflict, normative aspirations, and objective possibilities for change on this level. Certain substantive features of his theory have been attacked deservedly, especially his mechanistic vision of proletarian class consciousness, which woefully underplayed the problematic issues of coming to intersubjective understandings and of developing bonds of solidarity. But Marx's analysis of capitalism still towers above other global theories of his day. That it has been the center of scientific and political debate for over a century attests to its power.

Marx built on a long tradition of holistic thought, stretching from Aristotle to early nineteenth-century social theory. These approaches, at least implicitly, theorized the social order from the point of view of particular (superordinate) social strata. Although these theories facilitated critical discourse about the state of society, their universalistic claims and absolutist eschatologies veiled underlying social and material interests and undermined the type of unconstrained critical thought that opens all interests to discussion and possible alteration. By developing a historically periodized theory of society that systematically conceptualized the linkages between the material, social, and normative levels, with the intent of putting an end to class society, Marx created a new variant of holistic thought—*emancipatory theory*. Yet Marx's historical holism, on account of its links to the grand narrative's *evolutionary dogmatism*, did not shake off completely the absolutism of its eschatological precursors, and consequently retained an authoritarian thread that prevented full realization of its radically historicist and radically democratic core.

The postmodernist attack on Western reason scuttles, along with the teleological baggage of the grand narrative, the necessary holistic tools for addressing increasingly "global" (regional, national, and international) social interdependencies. Perhaps Marx's greatest achievement was his compelling argument that modernity's growing networks of interdependence (linking huge social circles) have sweeping significance for human suffering and welfare and therefore ought not to be ignored. These networks cry out for holistic expression because they are obscured by increasing social differentiation and cultural fragmentation and by the demagogic manipulation of information about socioeconomic inequalities and impositions of power. Marxian historical holism provides a language to express these interdependencies and to expose their costs and consequences when they either go unnoticed or are mistakenly attributed to microscopic forces.

Two aspects of contemporary Marxist theory favor the reappropriation and reconstruction of historical holism. The growing body of empirical-historical data and middle-range theories from Marxian social science has already contributed significantly to improving the historical adequacy of Marxist theory. Most important, the pluralist and empirical thrust of this research provides a counterweight to the strong normative aspirations of emancipatory theory and improves the chances of keeping the approach concrete and undogmatic. Second, theoretical infusions from non-Marxist approaches presage a richer historical holism that transcends Marx's original version. Despite its partial and problematic character, Habermas' synthesis of Marxism with Weberian and pragmatist theories is a promising development. Weber's historical-comparative sociology and the pragmatists' theory of communication together provide means for spelling out methodological grounds for historical holism that Marx left vague and for ridding the approach of the remains of Hegelian teleology. Moreover, the synthesis hints at the development of a *via media* that steers between one-sided individualism and one-sided collectivism (*see* Kloppenberg 1986), and that deepens Marxist sensitivity to the democratic hopes and possibilities of late modernity. Jameson's effort to incorporate postmodernism within Marxist holism also has potentially important implications for future theoretical developments. He rejects the extreme antirationalism of radical postmodernism that evaporates the epistemological bases (i.e., representation and holism) needed to privilege its own sweeping claims about "postmodernity" over competing accounts. The broader synthesis that Jameson points toward, but has hardly begun, aims at a new Marxism cognizant of the limits of rationalism and capable of addressing contemporary cultural conditions. As both Habermas and Jameson have argued, these conditions require a rethinking of Marxian theory and emancipation.

Throughout this paper I have explained how Marxist theory has changed and fragmented in response to the disjunctive pattern of social and political change. The eclipse of the grand narrative and the rise of the current pluralistic, discursive, and open-ended Marxism is likely to accentuate this tendency. But even the decentered conception of emancipation in contemporary Marxism still contains traces of a utopian desire to transcend history, and as long as these remain, another return of the grand narrative cannot be ruled out. Although it provides no guarantees, historical holism counters this tendency to seek refuge in fixed totalities and insists on the continuing renewal of the historical meaning of its own emancipatory project.

NOTES

1. As will become apparent below, I am not suggesting that the grand narrative is the most important or the most central theme in Marx's thought. Indeed, it is absent from many pages of his texts, and contradicts the concrete and historical side of his work.

2. I use "historical holism" to refer to Marx's historical method of analyzing and criticizing the capitalism of his day. It is roughly consistent with the features that Engels attributed to "historical materialism" but its exact outline is unclear because Marx left this method mostly implicit and incompletely developed. Still historical holism is analytically separable from the materialist grand narrative (see Antonio 1989). More will be said below about historical holism.

3. Marx treated science as a productive force, distinguishing it from ideological forms of knowledge (see Cohen 1978, 45–47).

4. Despite the grand narrative's linear and deterministic logic, Marx was aware that the road to socialism would be rocky. In his historical commentaries he mentioned frequently how class fragmentation and factional alliances with superordinate strata damaged the proletariat's emancipatory prospects (e.g., Marx [1852] 1963). On the other hand, Marx did not imagine the levels of class differentiation and fragmentation that have accompanied the development of twentieth-century capitalism.

5. The feminist movement has raised fundamental questions about the grand narrative and, in particular, about its inability to come to terms with noneconomic forms of exploitation and domination (e.g., see Fisk 1982; Nicholson 1985).

6. For an example of the polemics between scientific and critical Marxists, see Goren Therborn (1970) and Russell Jacoby (1980). See Alvin Gouldner (1980) for a comprehensive analysis of this split.

7. The Frankfurt School's appropriation was heavily influenced by Georg Lukàcs' earlier reading of Weber (Lukàcs [1923] 1971; Kellner 1985; Benhabib 1986, 182–85).

8. For a small sample of the many new interpretations, reconstructions, and translations in English, see: on alienation—Meszaros (1970), Ollman (1971), Israel (1971); Western Marxist theory—Lukàcs ([1923] 1971), Korsch ([1923–1930] 1970), Gramsci ([1929–1935] 1971), Schaff (1970), Markovic (1974), Kosik (1976); critical theory—Horkheimer and Adorno ([1944] 1969), Horkheimer ([1932–1941] 1972, [1947] 1974, [1967] 1974), Adorno ([1966] 1973), Habermas (1970, 1971), Jay (1973), Schroyer (1975), Wellmer (1974). During this era, important new critical Marxist journals also appeared in English (e.g., *Telos, New German Critique*).

9. Note that most of the citations in my earlier discussion of the grand narrative are drawn from Marx's *mature* economic writings. Since this narrative contains throughout strong taints of Hegelianism, my argument contradicts Althusser's contentions about the two Marxes. I believe that the contrasting narrative themes, implied by Althusser, are intertwined uncomfortably throughout Marx's mature thought.

10. Certain analytic Marxists are critical of methodological individualism (e.g., Levine, Sober, and Wright 1987).

11. As will be explained below, the radical postmodernist vision of collapsed borders between different spheres of life, the erosion of all types of standards, and the loss of distance imply a mode of experience that reduces life to an ongoing, disjunctive spectacle completely devoid of historical consciousness. The search for determinants of and constraints to action is futile under such conditions.

12. See Douglas Kellner's essay in this volume for a detailed account of the origins and development of postmodern theory, and Antonio and Kellner (1990) for a discussion of its limits. For some other attempts to define, explain, and criticize postmodernism: see Aronowitz (1987–1988), Bauman (1988), Bell (1976), Berman (1982), Bernstein (1987), Callinicos (1985), Denzin (1988), Dews (1987), Eagleton (1985), Friedman (1988), Hassan (1985), Huyssen (1986), Kellner (1988), Kroker and Cook (1986), Lyotard (1984), Merquior (1986), Moi (1988), and Wolin (1984–1985).

13. For example, Gilles Deleuze states: "For us, the intellectual has ceased to be a subject, a representing or representative consciousness. Those who act and struggle have stopped being represented either by a party or by a trade union which in turn

abrogates the right to be their consciousness. Who speaks and who acts? Always a multiplicity, even in the person who speaks or who acts. We are all a complex of different, miniature groups. There is no longer representation, but only action, the action of theory, and the action of practice in relation to relays and networks." (Foucault and Deleuze 1973, 103). For other examples of this type of radical decentering, *see* Deleuze and Guattari (1977), Derrida (1981), and Lotringer and Baudrillard (1986).

REFERENCES

Adorno, Theodor W. [1966] 1973. *Negative Dialectics.* Reprint. New York: Seabury Press.

Althusser, Louis. 1970. *For Marx.* New York: Vintage.

Althusser, Louis. 1971. *Lenin and Philosophy and Other Essays.* New York: Monthly Review Press.

Anderson, Perry. 1983. *In the Tracks of Historical Materialism.* London: Verso.

Antonio, Robert J. 1983. "The Origin, Development, and Contemporary Status of Critical Theory." *The Sociological Quarterly* 24:325–351.

Antonio, Robert J. 1989. "The Problem of Normative Foundations in Emancipatory Theory: Evolutionary versus Pragmatic Perspectives." *American Journal of Sociology* 94:721–748.

Antonio, Robert J., and Douglas Kellner. 1990. "The Limits of Postmodern Thought." In David Dickens and Andrea Fontana, eds., *Postmodernism and Social Inquiry.* Chicago: University of Chicago Press.

Aronowitz, Stanley. 1981. *The Crisis in Historical Materialism: Class, Politics, and Culture in Marxist Theory.* New York: J. F. Bergin.

Aronowitz, Stanley. 1987–1988. "Postmodernism and Politics." *Social Text* 18:99–115.

Aronson, Ronald. 1985. "Historical Materialism, Answer to Marxism's Crisis." *New Left Review* 152:74–94.

Baudrillard, Jean. 1975. *The Mirror of Production.* St. Louis: Telos Press.

Baudrillard, Jean. 1981. *For a Critique of the Political Economy of the Sign.* St. Louis: Telos Press.

Baudrillard, Jean. 1983. *Simulations.* New York: Semiotext(e).

Bauman, Zygmunt. 1988. "Is There a Postmodern Sociology?" *Theory, Culture and Society* 5:217–237.

Bell, Daniel. 1976. *The Cultural Contradictions of Capitalism.* New York: Basic Books.

Benhabib, Seyla. 1986. *Critique, Norm, and Utopia.* New York: Columbia University Press.

Berman, Marshall. 1982. *All That is Solid Melts Into Air.* New York: Simon and Schuster.

Bernstein, Charles. 1987. "Centering the Postmodern." *Socialist Review* 96:45–56.

Bowles, Samuel, and Herbert Gintis. 1986. *Democracy and Capitalism.* New York: Basic Books.

Callinicos, Alex. 1985. "Postmodernism, Post-Structuralism, Post-Marxism?" *Theory, Culture and Society* 2:85–101.

Carling, Alan. 1986. "Rational Choice Marxism." *New Left Review* 160:24–62.

Carrillo, Santiago. 1978. *Eurocommunism and the State.* Westport, Conn.: Lawrence Hill.

112 Robert J. Antonio

Chen, Kuan-Hsing. 1987. "The Masses and the Media: Baudrillard's Implosive Postmodernism." *Theory, Culture and Society* 4:71–88.

Cohen, G. A. 1978. *Karl Marx's Theory of History: A Defence.* Princeton: Princeton University Press.

Deleuze, Gilles, and Felix Guattari, 1977. *Anti-Oedipus.* New York: Viking.

Denzin, Norman K. "*Blue Velvet:* Postmodern Contradictions." *Theory, Culture and Society* 5:461–473.

Derrida, Jacques. 1981. *Positions.* Chicago: University of Chicago Press.

Dews, Peter. 1986. "Adorno, Post-Structuralism and the Critique of Identity." *New Left Review* 157:28–44.

Dews, Peter. 1987. *Logics of Disintegration.* London: Verso.

Dubiel, Helmut. 1985. *Theory and Politics.* Cambridge, Mass.: MIT Press.

Eagleton, Terry. 1985. "Capitalism, Modernism, and Postmodernism." *New Left Review* 152:60–73.

Elster, Jon. 1985. *Making Sense of Marx.* New York: Cambridge University Press.

Elster, Jon. 1986a. "Three Challenges to Class." In John Roemer, ed., *Analytic Marxism.* New York: Cambridge University Press.

Elster, Jon. 1986b. "Further Thoughts on Marxism, Functionalism and Game Theory." In John Roemer, ed., *Analytic Marxism.* New York: Cambridge University Press.

Engels, Frederick. [1880] 1982. *Socialism: Utopian and Scientific.* Reprint. New York: International Publishers.

Engels, Frederick. [1890–1894] 1959. "Letters on Historical Materialism." In *Marx and Engels: Basic Writings on Politics and Philosophy.* Edited by Lewis S. Feuer. Garden City, N.Y.: Anchor.

Fisk, Milton. 1982. "Feminism, Socialism, and Historical Materialism." *Praxis International* 2:117–140.

Foucault, Michel. 1967. *Madness and Civilization.* New York: Mentor.

Foucault, Michel. 1973. *The Order of Things.* New York: Vintage.

Foucault, Michel. 1975. *The Birth of the Clinic.* New York: Vintage.

Foucault, Michel. 1979. *Discipline and Punish.* New York: Vintage.

Foucault, Michel. 1980a. *Power/Knowledge.* New York: Pantheon.

Foucault, Michel. 1980b. *The History of Sexuality.* Vol. 1. New York: Vintage.

Foucault, Michel, and Gilles Deleuze. 1973. "The Intellectuals and Power: A Discussion between Michel Foucault and Gilles Deleuze." *Telos* 16:103–109.

Freidman, Jonathan. 1988. "Cultural Logics of the Global System: A Sketch." *Theory, Culture and Society* 5:447–460.

Geras, Norman. 1987. "Post-Marxism?" *New Left Review* 163:40–82.

Geras, Norman. 1988. "Ex-Marxism Without Substance: Being a Real Reply to Laclau and Mouffe." *New Left Review* 169:34–61.

Geuss, Raymond. 1981. *The Idea of a Critical Theory.* New York: Cambridge University Press.

Gordon, David M., Richard Edwards, and Michael Reich. 1982. *Segmented Work, Divided Workers.* New York: Cambridge University Press.

Gouldner, Alvin W. 1980. *The Two Marxisms.* New York: Oxford University Press.

Gramsci, Antonio [1929–1935] 1971. *Selections from the Prison Notebooks.* Edited by Quintin Hoare and Geoffrey Nowell Smith. New York: International Publishers.

Habermas, Jürgen. 1970. *Toward a Rational Society.* Boston: Beacon Press.

Habermas, Jürgen. 1971. *Knowledge and Human Interests.* Boston: Beacon Press.

Habermas, Jürgen, 1979. *Communication and the Evolution of Society.* Boston: Beacon Press.

Habermas, Jürgen, 1981. "Modernity versus Postmodernity." *New German Critique.* 22:3–14.

Habermas, Jürgen, 1982. *"The Entwinement of Myth and Enlightenment: Re-Reading* Dialectic of Enlightenment." *New German Critique* 26:13–30.

Habermas, Jürgen, 1983. "Neoconservative Cultural Criticism in the United States and West Germany: An Intellectual Movement in Two Political Cultures." *Telos* 56:75–89.

Habermas, Jürgen, 1984. *The Theory of Communicative Action.* Vol. 1. Boston: Beacon Press.

Habermas, Jürgen, 1987a. *The Theory of Communicative Action.* Vol 2. Boston: Beacon Press.

Habermas, Jürgen, 1987b. *The Philosophical Discourse of Modernity.* Cambridge: MIT Press.

Hassan, Ihab. 1985. "The Culture of Postmodernism." *Theory, Culture and Society.* 2:119–131.

Held, David. 1980. *Introduction to Critical Theory.* Berkeley: University of California Press.

Hindess, Barry. 1984. "Rational Choice Theory and the Analysis of Political Action." *Economy and Society* 13:255–277.

Hirsh, Arthur. 1981. *The French New Left: An Intellectual History from Sartre to Gorz.* Boston: South End Press.

Hodgson, Godfrey. 1978. *America in Our Time.* New York: Vintage.

Horkheimer, Max. [1932–1941] 1972. *Critical Theory.* Reprint. New York: Herder and Herder.

Horkheimer, Max. [1947] 1974. *Eclipse of Reason.* Reprint. New York: Seabury Press.

Horkheimer, Max. [1967] 1974. *Critique of Instrumental Reason.* Reprint. New York: Seabury Press.

Horkheimer, Max, and Theodor W. Adorno. [1944] 1969. *Dialectic of Enlightenment.* Reprint. New York: Seabury Press.

Huyssen, Andreas. 1986. *After the Great Divide.* Bloomington: Indiana University Press.

Ingram, David. 1986. "Foucault and the Frankfurt School." *Praxis International* 6:312–327.

Israel, Joachim. 1971. *Alienation: From Marx to Modern Sociology.* Boston: Allyn and Bacon.

Jacoby, Russell. 1971. "Towards a Critique of Automatic Marxism: The Politics of Philosophy from Lukács to the Frankfurt School." *Telos* 10:119–146.

Jacoby, Russell. 1980. "What is Conformist Marxism?" *Telos* 45:19–43.

Jameson, Fredric. 1981. *The Political Unconscious.* Ithaca, N.Y.: Cornell University Press.

Jameson, Frederic. 1984a. "Postmodernism, or The Cultural Logic of Late Capitalism." *New Left Review* 146:53–92.

Jameson, Fredric. 1984b. "Periodizing the 60s." In Sohnya Sayres, Anders Stephanson, Stanley Aronowitz, and Frederic Jameson, eds., *The 60s Without Apology.* Minneapolis: University of Minnesota Press.

Jameson, Fredric. 1988."Cognitive Mapping." In Cary Nelson and Lawrence Grossberg, eds., *Marxism and the Interpretation of Culture.* Urbana: University of Illinois Press.

Jay, Martin. 1973. *The Dialectical Imagination.* Boston: Little, Brown.

Jay, Martin. 1984. *Marxism and Totality.* Berkeley: University of California Press.

Johnston, Lew. 1986. *Marxism, Class Analysis and Socialist Pluralism.* London: Allen and Unwin.

Kellner, Douglas. 1984. *Herbert Marcuse and the Crisis of Marxism.* Berkeley: University of California Press.

Kellner, Douglas. 1985. "Critical Theory, Max Weber, and the Dialectics of Domination." In Robert J. Antonio and Ronald M. Glassman, eds., *A Weber-Marx Dialogue.* Lawrence: University Press of Kansas.

Kellner, Douglas. 1987. "Baudrillard, Semiurgy and Death." *Theory, Culture and Society* 4:125–146.

Kellner, Douglas. 1988. "Postmodernism as Social Theory: Some Challenges and Problems." *Theory, Culture and Society* 5:239–269.

Kloppenberg, James T. 1986. *Uncertain Victory.* New York: Oxford University Press.

Kosik, Karel. 1976. *Dialectics of the Concrete.* Boston: D. Reidel.

Korsch, Karl. [1923–1930] 1970. *Marxism and Philosophy.* Reprint. New York: Modern Reader.

Kroker, Arthur. 1985. "Baudrillard's Marx." *Theory, Culture and Society* 2:69–83.

Kroker, Arthur, and David Cook. 1986. *The Postmodern Scene.* New York: St. Martin's.

Laclau, Ernesto. 1987. "Class War and After." *Marxism Today* 31:30–33.

Laclau, Ernesto, and Chantal Mouffe. 1985. *Hegemony and Socialist Strategy.* London: Verso.

Laclau, Ernesto, and Chantal Mouffe. 1987. "Post-Marxism without Apologies." *New Left Review* 166:79–106.

Levine, Andrew, Elliott Sober, and Erik Olin Wright. 1987. "Marxism and Methodological Individualism." *New Left Review* 162:67–84.

Lotringer, Sylvere, and Jean Baudrillard. 1986. "Forgetting Baudrillard." *Social Text* 15:140–144.

Lukàcs, Georg. [1923] 1971. *History and Class Consciousness.* Reprint. Cambridge, Mass.: MIT Press.

Lyotard, Jean-François. 1984. *The Postmodern Condition: A Report on Knowledge.* Minneapolis: University of Minnesota Press.

Mandel, Ernest. 1978a. *From Stalinism to Eurocommunism.* London: New Left Books.

Mandel, Ernest 1978b. *Late Capitalism.* London: Verso.

Marcuse, Herbert. 1964. *One-Dimensional Man.* Boston: Beacon Press.

Marcuse, Herbert. 1969. *An Essay on Liberation.* Boston: Beacon Press.

Marcuse, Herbert. 1970. *Five Lectures.* Boston: Beacon Press.

Marcuse, Herbert. 1971. *Soviet Marxism.* Middlesex, England: Penguin.

Marcuse, Herbert. 1972. *Counterrevolution and Revolt.* Boston: Beacon Press.

Marcuse, Herbert. 1979. "The Reification of the Proletariat." *Canadian Journal of Political and Social Theory* 3:20–23.

Markovic̀, Mihailo. 1974. *From Affluence to Praxis.* Ann Arbor: University of Michigan Press.

Marx, Karl. [1843] 1967. "On the Jewish Question." In *Writings of the Young Marx on Philosophy and Society.* Edited by Lloyd D. Easton and Kurt H. Guddat. Garden City, N.Y.: Doubleday.

Marx, Karl. [1852] 1963. *The Eighteenth Brumaire of Louis Bonaparte.* Reprint. New York: International Publishers.

Marx, Karl. [1857–1858] 1973. *Grundrisse.* Reprint. New York: Vintage.

Marx, Karl. [1859] 1970. *A Contribution to the Critique of Political Economy.* Reprint. Moscow: Progress Publishers.

Marx, Karl. [1875] 1959. "Critique of the Gotha Program." In *Marx and Engels:*

Basic Writings on Politics and Philosophy. Edited by Lewis Feuer. Garden City, N.Y.: Anchor.

Marx, Karl. [1887] 1967. *Capital.* Vol. 1. Reprint. New York: International Publishers.

Marx, Karl. [1893] 1967. *Capital.* Vol. 2. Reprint. New York: International Publishers.

Marx, Karl. [1894] 1967. *Capital.* Vol. 3. Reprint. New York: International Publishers.

Marx, Karl, and Frederick Engels. [1845–1846] 1964. *The German Ideology.* Reprint. Moscow: Progress Publishers.

Merquior, J. G. 1986. *From Prague to Paris.* London: Verso.

Meszaros, Istvan. 1970. *Marx's Theory of Alienation.* New York: Harper.

Mouzelis, Nicos. 1988. "Marxism or Post-Marxism." *New Left Review* 167:107–123.

Nicholson, Linda. 1985. "Feminism and Marx: Integrating Kinship with the Economic." *Praxis International* 5:367–380.

Nietzsche, Friedrich. [1887] 1967. *On the Genealogy of Morals and Ecce Homo.* Reprint. New York: Vintage.

Ollman, Bertell. 1971. *Alienation: Marx's Conception of Man in Capitalist Society.* New York: Cambridge University Press.

Poulantzas, Nicos. 1973. *Political Power and Social Classes.* London: New Left Books.

Przeworski, Adam. 1986. *Capitalism and Social Democracy.* New York: Cambridge University Press.

Raulet, Gérard. 1983. "Structuralism and Post-Structuralism: An Interview with Michel Foucault." *Telos* 55:195–211.

Roemer, John E. 1981. *Analytical Foundations of Marxian Economic Theory.* New York: Cambridge University Press.

Roemer, John E. 1982. *A General Theory of Exploitation and Class.* Cambridge: Harvard University Press.

Roemer, John E. 1986a. " 'Rational Choice' Marxism: Some Issues of Method and Substance." In John Roemer, ed., *Analytic Marxism.* New York: Cambridge University Press.

Roemer, John E. 1986b. "New Directions in the Marxian Theory of Exploitation and Class." In John Roemer, ed., *Analytic Marxism.* New York: Cambridge University Press.

Samuel, Raphael. 1985. "The Lost World of British Communism." *New Left Review* 154:3–53.

Samuel, Raphael. 1986. "Staying Power: The Lost World of British Communism, Part Two." *New Left Review* 156:63–113.

Samuel, Raphael. 1987. "Class Politics: The Lost World of British Communism, Part Three." *New Left Review* 165:52–91.

Schaff, Adam. 1970. *Marxism and the Human Individual.* New York: McGraw-Hill.

Schroyer, Trent. 1975. *The Critique of Domination.* Boston: Beacon Press.

Stephanson, Anders. 1987. "Regarding Postmodernism—A Conversation with Fredric Jameson." *Social Text* 17:29–54.

Therborn, Goren. 1970. "The Frankfurt School." *New Left Review* 63:65–96.

Wellmer, Albrecht. 1974. *Critical Theory of Society.* New York: Seabury Press.

Wolff, Richard D., and Stephen Cullenberg. 1986. "Marxism and Post-Marxism." *Social Text* 15:126–35.

Wolin, Richard. 1984–1985. "Modernism vs. Postmodernism." *Telos* 62:9–29.

Wolin, Richard. 1987. "Critical Theory and the Dialectic of Rationalism." *New German Critique* 41:23–52.

Wood, Ellen Meiksins. 1986. *The Retreat from Class*. London: Verso.

Wright, Erik Olin. 1985. *Classes*. London: Verso.

Wright, Erik Olin. 1986. "What is Middle About the Middle Class?" In John Roemer, ed., *Analytic Marxism*. New York: Cambridge University Press.

5

Symbolic Interactionism in the Post-Blumerian Age

❧

GARY ALAN FINE
University of Minnesota

Those who wrap themselves in the mantle of prognostication wear the "emperor's new clothes." Fortunately, as was true for that legendary emperor, few observers remark on the naked arrogance. Before commenting on the present and future of symbolic interaction (SI) and donning my transparent vestments, I shall cloak myself briefly in the robes of the tradition's past.

The "true" beginnings of any intellectual tradition are enveloped by mists, but first published use of the label "symbolic interaction" is known. The label was coined by Herbert Blumer in 1937 in a chapter of Emerson Schmidt's *Man and Society*, a social science textbook. Blumer distinguished three approaches to social psychology: one grounded in instinctualism and Darwinian evolutionism; the second emphasizing the importance of reflexes, as found in the writing of behaviorists, such as John Watson; and the third was a new synthesis, which Blumer claimed was based on the work of one of his teachers and colleagues at the University of Chicago, George Herbert Mead.[1] Blumer labeled this approach "symbolic interactionism." For this reason Mead is often taken to be the "founder" of the symbolic interactionist approach, even though Blumer's analysis, published six years after Mead's death, is a synthesis of the writings of other theorists as well, and critics claim that it differs from Mead's writing in important areas.

There was a little gall in Blumer's tripartite division in that Mead himself was heavily influenced by both Darwin and Watson (see Mead 1934).[2] It began what became common in Blumer's writing: the separation of Mead from those methodological and theoretical currents in which Mead was most interested. The justice of Blumer's claims has been enormously controversial (e.g., Bales 1966; McPhail and Rexroat 1979; Lewis and Smith 1980; Joas 1985), and the controversy has not been entirely helpful (Fine and Kleinman 1986). Rather than seeing Blumer as the interpreter of the works of Mead, I prefer to see Blumer as a theorist in his own right who was responding to the writings of Mead, as well as to those of others.

Interactionism has deep roots in Western thought. For example, the dramaturgical metaphor, made popular by Erving Goffman, resounds through philosophical writing from Plato on. Pragmatism had antecedents in the Romantic movement and in the writings of British empiricists (*see* Stryker 1980; Shalin 1984, 1986) before coming to fruition in the writings of Royce, Peirce, James, and Dewey. No great and good idea is ever truly new. It only seems new when renamed or tagged with a catchy slogan.

Symbolic interactionism as a distinctively named approach to sociology has been around for over half a century—a remarkable achievement when one considers the fickleness of academic fashion. Marxism holds the record for longevity, and behaviorism has endured, but symbolic interactionism differs from both in that it is an academic, theoretical approach, with little in the way of an applied or political dimension (Gouldner 1970; Huber 1973).[3] Most symbolic interactionists do not consider SI to be a "theory," because "theory" generally presumes a set of assumptions from which can be logically deduced a set of hypothetical propositions, and interactionists typically emphasize that they are "inductive," rather than "deductive," working from the data up (Glaser and Strauss 1967; Strauss 1987). We speak of the "interactionist perspective," rather than "interactionist theory."

Like any perspective with some measure of longevity, popularity, and intellectual vigor, practitioners of SI have argued over theoretical interpretations, differed as to what constitutes an appropriate topic, and developed distinctive intellectual styles.[4] One might wonder: Is there a core to the approach? While this intellectual tradition is held together organizationally and through Wittgensteinian family resemblances, there are some areas of common agreement. Central to the perspective are Blumer's three premises of symbolic interaction:

> The first premise is that human beings act toward things on the basis of the meanings that the things have for them. . . . The second premise is that the meaning of such things is derived from, or arises out of, the social interaction that one has with one's fellows. The third premise is that these meanings are handled in, and modified through, an interpretative process used by the person in dealing with the things he encounters. (Blumer 1969b, 2)

Even given these premises, interactionists disagree on how to interpret them properly. Some emphasize that all meaning is ultimately negotiated, whereas others (myself included) accept the existence of real, structural, and physical constraints. Blumer's passage can be read to support either view. Beyond the implications of this passage, there is heated debate on what presuppositions are implied by the interactionist approach to self, identity, interaction, organization, collective action, and the like.

An underlying legitimation for this paper is that whatever one might think of the history of interactionism, contemporary sociology would have a very different texture without symbolic interactionism, notably in the areas of deviance (labeling theory), social psychology (self and identity theory), the sociology of mental illness (impression management), the sociology of culture (artistic conventions), organizational theory (negotiated order), and collective behavior (emergent norm theory).

Examined globally, interactionism has had two main streams of research and theory. I do not refer to the differences between the Chicago school and the Iowa school that so many textbooks emphasize. Rather, some interactionists study the "self" and others focus on the "situation." These two groups have different lineages: the former drawing insights from Mead and Cooley; the latter from Park and Thomas. While for socio-political reasons interactionists have huddled under the umbrella of Mead, the umbrella does not protect all equally. A stream of theorists gaze inward toward ways of measuring and conceptualizing the self (Kuhn and McPartland 1954; Stryker 1957; Rosenberg 1979; Zurcher 1977). Others look outward to the world which bodies inhabit, often with little interest in how people might feel about these worlds (Goffman 1959; Unruh 1979). The first approach is distinctly "social psychological" with a heavy overlay of cognitive imagery, and is most clearly grounded on the central concerns of Mead; the latter is "microsociological" but *not* social psychological, with strong ties to social and cultural antrhopology and a focus on "behavior," not "cognition." While both have been conceptualized as symbolic interaction, the two have coexisted somewhat uneasily. Traditionally the Iowa school focused on understanding the self-concept, while the Chicago school, growing out of the works of Park, through the teaching of Hughes, focused on settings and situations. This is no longer the case (and never was much the case), not just because interactionism is not much present at either Chicago or Iowa, but also because those trained as Chicago interactionists deal with self-concept (e.g., Turner 1976, 1978) and those associated with the Iowa school have become more interested in the structure of situations (e.g., Couch et al. 1986).

In his update of *Theories and Theory Groups in Contemporary American Sociology*, Nicholas Mullins (1983, 329) recognized that in the previous decade symbolic interaction had revitalized itself organizationally by the founding of the Society for the Study of Symbolic Interaction, but he did not recant his earlier expression that symbolic interaction was "a dead tradition" which has "not yet gone beyond a rehearsal of the faith and its application to some new ground." Similarly, Ritzer (1985) has written of the "decline of symbolic interactionism." The attempt to take theoretical vital signs is surely an act of hubris which the examiner does at his or her risk. I shall not attempt to raise the dead, but will assume only that what acts alive, is so.

However symbolic interaction might be evaluated, it is in a post-Blumerian age. Symbolic interactionists are not duplicating Blumer's arguments, and certainly not the sloganized Blumer depicted in the textbooks (Flaherty 1987; Maines 1988). Blumer hasn't been ignored, but he has been reconstructed. In a recent special issue of *Symbolic Interaction*, prominent interactionists elaborated Blumer's intellectual contributions. Several essays—notably the contributions of Maines (1988), Wellman (1988), and Tucker (1988)—attempt to reconstruct Blumer as having a greater concern with social structure and macro-sociological issues than he has been generally recognized as having. These interactionists are doing for Blumer (or *to* Blumer) what neofunctionalists have done for Parsons. The reconstruction of theorists is a useful exercise, *provided* we do not convince ourselves that our reconstruction is the only "real" meaning (Fine and Kleinman 1986).

Contemporary interactionism addresses traditional sociological questions, but provides answers grounded in interactionist themes, such as meaning, interaction, experience, and identity. Interactionists deal with macro-structural issues.[5] A common thread in interactionist writings is the belief that interactionism is capable of addressing macro-sociological themes—and according to some (e.g., Maines 1988) always has been. Whether this is a defensive posture, claiming the right to be "where the action is," I leave for others.

Although interactionism once had the somewhat deserved reputation of parochialism, today interactionists are almost promiscuous in their willingness to thrash in any theoretical bedding they can find: there are Durkheimian interactionists (Barry Schwartz, Erving Goffman), Simmelian interactionists (Eviatar Zerubavel, Jules Wanderer), Weberian interactionists (the late Hans Haferkamp, Marcello Truzzi), Marxist interactionists (Charlotte Wolf, David Ashley), postmodernist interactionists (Norman Denzin, Gisela Hinkle), phenomenological interactionists (Arthur Frank, Eugene Rochberg-Halton), radical feminist interactionists (Patricia Clough), semiotic interactionists (Peter Manning, Heinz-Günter Vester), and behaviorist interactionists (John Bald-

win). Indeed, contemporary interactionism might be faulted for its easy willingness to forget the traditional problems of the perspective.

How did the diversity of interactionisms arise? One explanation is the dissipation of the institutional centers of interactionist training— particularly Iowa and Chicago. By the 1960s, interactionists were being trained everywhere. Interactionists have degrees from Harvard, Yale, Princeton, Columbia, Duke, North Carolina, UCLA, Santa Barbara, San Diego, Illinois, Minnesota, Indiana, Northwestern—a cross-section of major American graduate programs. Many sociology departments had one or several interactionists on staff, training students; even when no interactionists were on staff, students read Mead, Blumer, Becker, and Goffman and could decide that this was the perspective that they found most appealing. The diversity of origins eliminated a single font of wisdom or subcultural consensus. This produced an array of dialects.

Given this, do we still have a single perspective? Are the theorists who label themselves, or are labeled, interactionists, *truly* members of the same group? This question reverberates around many theories: Marxism, feminism, functionalism, and structuralism. One response is to agree that if a sufficient number of individuals are willing to refer to themselves by a particular theoretical label or join a particular organization (such as the Society for the Study of Symbolic Interaction), then such a theoretical perspective exists. This does not answer all questions, as some (even some central individuals) do not label themselves in such a way. Erving Goffman never, to my knowledge, labeled himself a symbolic interactionist, but if we exclude him, we exclude our soul. Definitions are not made only by the individuals themselves, as labeling theorists have emphasized. However, to accede ultimate power to theory textbook authors to set theoretical boundaries gives them too much. The placement of boundaries involves a complex negotiation among practitioners, interested outsiders, and organizations and journals. Whatever its future, interactionism as a perspective, semi-coherent as it may be, continues to exist.

In ascertaining the current status of interactionism I shall examine six major areas in which interactionists have contributed to sociology over the past two decades:[6] 1) self and identity theory; 2) dramaturgy, accounts, and presentation of self; 3) collective behavior and collective action; 4) culture and art; 5) sociolinguistic approaches; and 6) social problems theory. Following this I shall address three areas that have begun to emerge over the past decade, and which hold considerable promise for the future: 1) new approaches to ethnography; 2) symbolic interactionist approaches to emotion; and 3) interactionist analyses of organizations. To conclude I shall address the current theoretical infrastructure of symbolic interaction, and examine some possible future scenarios for the perspective.

SELF, ROLE, AND IDENTITY THEORY

The question of the social self has had a long history in pragmatist philosophy and in interactionist sociology. "What is the self?" echoes throughout the writings of James, Cooley, and Mead. It would not be much of an overstatement to claim that the most significant contribution of these theorists is their claim that an individual's self is responsive to and shaped by social forces. The belief that the self is not present at birth nor a natural consequence of intellectual development, but is a consequence of the responses of others is a cornerstone of interactionism and sociological social psychology (see Cooley [1902] 1964; Mead 1934; James 1890s), and may have been in part the crucial insight necessary for distinguishing a sociological social psychology from the approach that is more common in psychology.

The idea of the self (as mediated through the socially situated concepts of role and identity) has always been crucial for an interactionist view of the person, and has raised profound questions about the way in which individuals connect themselves to social situations. Most of the images of the self used by interactionists concern how individuals fit themselves into social worlds, and as a result symbolic interactionists have created or expanded concepts such as the looking-glass self (Cooley [1902] 1964), the generalized other (Mead 1934), role-taking (Mead 1934), role-playing (Coutu 1951), role-making (Hewitt 1976), identity salience (Stryker 1968), the impulsive self (Turner 1976; Zurcher 1986), the self-concept (Gecas 1982), role merging (Turner 1978), or altercasting (Weinstein and Deutschberger 1963).

The methodologies for examining this model of the self are diverse. Unlike studies of situations, these methodologies typically do not involve participant observation. More typically, they are grounded in armchair theorizing, in-depth interviews, open-ended questionnaires, experimental studies, or large-scale survey research. Methodologically this research tradition was and remains less distinctively "interpretive" and "qualitative" than studies of situations and interactions. Although the theoretical arguments differ from positivist social science, recognizing the mutability of self, the methodologies are not radically dissimilar. Indeed, self theorists such as Morris Rosenberg (1981) or Sheldon Stryker (1980), who can be legitimately included as symbolic interactionists, are scorned by some interactionists who claim that they reify the self's social reality by virtue of their attempts to specify that reality. Theorists like Stryker and Rosenberg, sometimes called "structural symbolic interactionists," recognize the existence of role making and changes in self-image, but they assume that the process by which these changes occur can be specified, and occurs in a predictable fashion. To these theorists changes that affect the self are more gradual and less dramatic than many interactionists claim.

Closer to the symbolic interactionist mainstream are the works of Ralph Turner, Viktor Gecas, and Louis Zurcher, who examine fluidity of role-constructs for individuals, even while admitting that these "mutable selves" (Zurcher 1977) have spatial, institutional, and temporal stability. In contrast to "structural" symbolic interactionists, these writers do not propose predictive hypotheses of the social forces that lead selves to be conceptualized in various ways. They focus more directly on the symbolic (and cultural) meaning of selves (Turner 1976, 1978; Zurcher 1986). The self is not an object that has meaning, but is a construct that is given meaning through the relationships in which it is embedded.

Self theory remains a central focus of interactionist writers, but it is the area that is the subject of the most acrimonious debate by those who disagree about the level of stability and reification of identity and selfhood. Further, self theory has been hobbled by never fully developing a standardized terminology that permits consensus on what is meant by "self," "identity," and "role." While some have attempted to distinguish these concepts (e.g., Rosenberg 1981), the terms are often used loosely and in contradictory ways.

In the next decade self theory may incorporate insights developed from studies of the emotions, demonstrating that the self is not merely a cognitive self, as is sometimes implied in much of self theory (most particularly in Mead). Second, the interest in organizational sociology shown by interactionists should be better incorporated into self theory. Selves are channeled by the organizations and institutions in which they are embedded—including the family, school, church, and workplace. We are not dealing merely with abstracted selves and identities; these selves and identities are inevitably lodged in institutional settings. Goffman recognized this point in his analysis of "total institutions" (Goffman 1961a), but it has only recently been incorporated into the core of self theory (*see* Zurcher 1986). Like the rest of symbolic interaction, self theory will move away from being considered a purely social psychological perspective, as it addresses the domains of macrosociology.

DRAMATURGY AND ACCOUNTS

Without question the "symbolic interactionist" whose works have been most widely accepted as "privileged texts" in the sociological canon is Erving Goffman. It does the richness and multivocal character of his writings a disservice to call Goffman a "symbolic interactionist." Although influenced by Blumer, Mead, Cooley, and Hughes, Goffman also draws on Durkheim, Simmel, and Schutz. His approach, like all classic theories, is "bricolage" rather than mimicry. The recognition of the importance of Goffman's writings by Collins (1981) and Giddens (1984) provides testimony to the generic impact of his arguments on sociology (*see* Ditton 1980).

Whatever Goffman might have called himself, his impact on interactionism was at least as significant as on the rest of sociology. Yet, the approach that Goffman pioneered in *The Presentation of Self in Everyday Life* was not his alone. To see social life as a drama, and a person as an actor has been used by thinkers over the past 2500 years, including Plato, Thomas Hobbes, Adam Smith, Denis Diderot, and Jean Jacques Rousseau. Goffman's contribution was to add sociological content to the casual use of the metaphor. The metaphor implies a highly conscious, manipulative individual. While Goffman wanted not to be chained to all of the implications of his metaphor (*see* Goffman 1959, 254), the assumption is that people behave *as if* they are scripting their own roles.

The publication of *Presentation of Self*, first in 1956, had considerable impact on interpretive sociologists, who looked for, and found, masks (Strauss 1959), performances (Messenger et al. 1962), and strategies (Scott and Lyman 1968; Hewitt and Stokes 1975). By the late 1980s many of Goffman's theories have been unconsciously incorporated into the doing of sociology, and are rarely topics in and of themselves.[7] However, the sociology of "rhetorical strategies," derived from Goffman's concerns with impression management and signs given and given off, remains productive, and has spread from a concern with smoothing out interpersonal interaction into more macro-sociological areas. Most notable in this regard is the image of "accounts" presented by Scott and Lyman (1968). This approach derives from C. Wright Mills (1940) and his notion of "vocabularies of motives" and from Kenneth Burke's (1969) rhetorical dramaturgy, as well as from Goffman, who was influenced by Burke and Mills. The "vocabulary of motive," or an "account," is a technique for understanding the process by which people manage the impressions that others have of them. Throughout our interaction we find ourselves trapped in various "delicts," intentionally or not, and we need exits, keeping our pride and reputation intact (see Gross and Stone 1964). By proposing an explanation after the fact—an excuse or a justification—or a disclaimer prior to the untoward event, some negative implications of the action can be mitigated. At least the actor can demonstrate that he or she is conscious of the opinions of others and the moral legitimacy of those opinions.

Much of the empirical work based on this approach has attempted to apply the accounts and disclaimer framework to substantive areas: murder (Ray and Simons 1987), school life (Kalab 1987), rape (Scully and Marolla 1984), or forgery (Fine 1983a).[8] Some sociologists have recognized that the accounts framework applies not only to individuals, but to social problems arenas (e.g., Gusfield's [1981] analysis of drunk driving research). In Gusfield's view, actors attempt to shape the views that others have of this social concern. The focus of analysis is no longer the *situation*, in which a speaker speaks for himself, but the *condition* in which a speaker speaks for a class of others—generalizability is built into the analysis. Accounts are socially sedimented; once given, an account can be used with increasing ease, and eventually becomes how members of a social group understand their world.

Although researchers will continue to analyze individual accounts, disclaimers, and other aligning actions, the understanding of alignment by larger, more consequential social units is becoming increasingly significant. The accounts (and self-presentation) framework can uncover the role of actors who speak in the name of collectivities. Once interactionists recognize that representatives regularly negotiate with other representatives the idiosyncratic, personalized quality of accounts can be overcome, as they are seen as being in large measure institutionally based, historically grounded, and economically shaped.

COLLECTIVE BEHAVIOR AND COLLECTIVE ACTION

The sociological study of collective behavior, although not originating in symbolic interaction, has been closely associated with the perspective. Blumer's macro-sociology emphasized collective behavior, which he analyzed through the establishment of lines of collective action (*see* Blumer 1962). He transmitted this focus to his students, notably Ralph Turner, Tamotsu Shibutani, and John Lofland. Once sociologists began examining instances of collective behavior in detail, it became evident that the creation of symbolic meaning was of profound importance. The seemingly irrational behavior that is characteristic of collective action is not easily analyzed through a rational actor model. An approach, such as symbolic interaction, that emphasizes that behavior is grounded in the dynamics of consensual symbolic meaning is well-equipped to deal with behaviors that appear to violate the assumptions of individual economic rationality.

Many of the leading theories of collective behavior analysis—emergent norm theory (Turner and Killian 1972), frame analysis (Snow et al. 1986; Gamson, Fireman, and Rytina 1982), and convergence theory (McPhail and Miller 1973)—rely on symbolic interactionist premises of the dynamics of interaction and the construction and negotiation of meanings. In related areas such as rumor the symbolic interactionist perspective, emphasizing meaning construction, is dominant (*see* Fine 1985b; Shibutani 1966; Paine 1968; Szwed 1966), although a strong case can also be made for seeing rumor as an economic transaction (*see* Rosnow and Fine 1976; Gluckman 1963).

The emphasis on collective behavior among symbolic interactionists, especially Blumer (1939), demonstrates that interactionism is not antithetical to macro-sociology. Blumer relies on the concept of the fitting together of lines of action to argue that behaviors are not merely functions of individual determinations or "local" negotiations; in contrast, actors necessarily take into account the actual and expected behaviors of others in determining their behavior. In the stereotypical "crowd" scene, participants do not have the time or the interaction opportunities to determine "thoughtfully" how to respond to particular symbolic actions. They respond immediately, consequentially, viscerally, and in ways that define the trajectory for future actions. Individual choice may be tightly bounded, and crowd behavior is not the sum of individual choices individually made.

As in any area in which one research tradition is dominant, interactionism must fight complacency. One of the most intriguing approaches to collective behavior are the studies by David Snow and his colleagues on how collective behavior is organized as a consequence of frames of understanding. In other words, how the type of situation and the expectations for comprehension affect probable outcomes. The keying of meaning into frames that actors use—codes that are collectively held—permit an understanding of whether, for example, violence is likely or protest is possible. Although *Frame Analysis* has not had a massive impact on much of sociology, within the study of collective behavior the impact has been noticeable. Meanings are generated through the class of interpretations social actors have in common. The study of fabrications may explain demagogic imagery. Indeed, Goffman's emphasis on the vulnerability of experience allows us to address the question that troubled LeBon: how can reasonable people do such things?

CULTURE AND ART

Sociological perspectives that emphasize the importance of symbolic and implicit meaning—such as semiotics, French structuralism, ethnomethodology, and symbolic interactionism—have an advantage in understanding symbolic productions. Of course, such a perspective is not necessary. Marxist sociology has a well-developed sociology of art (Goldmann 1975; Fischer 1959), but Marxists generally see art as a material product, growing out of material relations of production. Art has no special place as a symbol system, but is, in effect, a mode of production, and the challenge for an understanding of art from a critical theory perspective is to take seriously the symbolic meaning of art in its own terms (e.g., Wolff 1981).

It is significant, if not widely known, that Blumer's first major empirical investigation was a study of the movies, produced under the auspices of the Payne Fund (Blumer 1933; Blumer and Hauser 1933). As Clough (1988) points out, Blumer's decision to study cinematic reality permitted him to understand the process of symbolic socialization. Film represents a reality that is quintessentially symbolic interaction. Blumer's later work on fashion (1969a) reflects the same recognition of the importance of the social organization of the symbolic world.

Unquestionably the most significant contemporary voice in the symbolic interactionist study of culture and art is that of Howard Becker. Becker's writings (1974a, 1976, 1978), culminating in his book, *Art Worlds* (1982), reenergized the area in sociology, and especially in symbolic interactionism. Becker argued that segments of the "art world" could be viewed as social worlds. Although an interactionist, Becker focused on "structural" characteristics of the art world that led to the production of forms of art. In order to organize behavior (to guide negotiations), social actors rely upon "conventions," modes of doing things. Becker does not argue that these conventions are unchangeable or unbreakable, but rather that there are consequences for violating them. One needs a support network in order to make these "deviant," convention-breaking decisions artistically significant.

Within the sociology of art, the dominant theoretical approach is the "production of culture" perspective, which suggests that the art world should be analyzed like any industry that produces a product. This perspective really involves two related views. Both examine the "production" of culture, but do so in different ways. The first is structural, attempting to understand the organizational constraints in the production of culture (Hirsch 1972; DiMaggio 1977; Peterson 1979). The second, more relevant, approach analyzes how culture is produced on the interactional/relational/interpersonal level (e.g., Faulkner 1983). Becker's empirical focus is the conventions and interpersonal structure of the world of photography (Becker 1974b; *see also* Rosenblum 1978); his colleagues and students have described rock musicians (Bennett 1980; Kealy 1982), classical musicians (Gilmore 1987), film makers (Mukerji 1976, 1977), and actors (Lyon 1974).

Perhaps the most consequential weakness of the "production of culture" approach is the reluctance to examine aesthetics. This stems from the relativist belief that one cannot distinguish productions in terms of aesthetic value. But aesthetics do matter—to producers and to clients. The issue is not efficiency, as this literature implies, but the sensory qualities of the outcomes. In my research with restaurants and trade school cooking programs (*see* Fine 1985a, 1987c), I claim that students and workers are socialized to aesthetic appreciation, and that their desire to create aesthetically satisfying objects is limited by the structural conditions of work.

During the past decade, the sociology of culture has emerged as an important and vigorous area of the discipline, and it is likely to remain so, particularly if the connections between the humanities and the social sciences broaden and deepen. Symbolic interactionists must refine the connection between the two components of their name: how are symbols a function of interaction, and how is interaction a consequence of symbolic display? Addressing the meaning and experienced form of cultural objects (their aesthetic content) will become central to the interactionist study of culture.

SOCIOLINGUISTIC CONTRIBUTIONS

Any approach that emphasizes the existence of symbols in social order must examine that most obvious and important symbol system: language. Language was central to Mead, although it was routinely ignored by the next generation of interactionists, notably Blumer and Hughes. The rejuvenation of the sociological study of language must be attributed to ethnomethodologists and anthropological linguists, rather than to symbolic interactionists. Ethnomethodological conversation analysis (particularly that group that developed around Harvey Sacks and Emmanuel Schegloff) attempted to delineate the patterns in language use, on the most detailed (read: micro) level possible. Turn-taking, laughter, and error correction follow patterns that, even though "locally generated," are not random. These rules are capable of being specified (Sacks 1974; Sacks, Schegloff, and Jefferson 1974); the approach of the conversation analysts seems very Simmelian with its search for elegant formal properties of talk. The other sociolinguistic approach developed primarily from linguistic anthropology, particularly the writings of Sapir (1949) and Whorf (1956). Their assumption is that language and perception are intimately related. Social and environmental needs affect linguistic elaboration, and the available linguistic terms shape what members of that group are able to perceive. Language is centrally implicated in the social construction of meaning.

Symbolic interactionists typically avoid data as fine-grained as bits of conversations and as comparative as talk from other cultures. Still, interactionists recognize that language is a primary shaper of meaning, and with the increasing prominence of the study of language, symbolic interactionists have been drawn to the topic. Conversation analysis has been integrated into symbolic interaction by the research of members of the "Santa Barbara school," an approach with ties to both ethnomethodology and symbolic interaction. While interested in the structure of talk, Zimmerman abjures the level of burps and groans, focusing on the structure of interruptions and sentences. He asks how power and authority affect language use. Zimmerman and West find that conversational interruptions are affected by the gender and social position of the speakers (e.g., Zimmerman and West 1975; West 1984). Likewise, claims of authority direct the structure of talk, as in the Watergate hearings (e.g., Molotch and Boden 1985).

The more anthropological tradition (and in particular the writings of William Labov [1972a, 1972b] heavily influenced Goffman's (1974, 1981) later writings. Goffman (influenced by the conversation analysts, as well) was interested in how talk is used by interactants to structure meanings; he examines, for instance, the interactional remedies available to persons who commit some form of linguistic delict (Goffman 1981). This situational focus on talk is also reflected in studies of the social dynamics of children's language usage (Corsaro 1985; Fine 1986) —the role of talk in building a sense of community. Children use talk to reaffirm their social structure. Talk, not behavior, is typically how actors learn what others expect of them. Without talk the world is opaque.

The future of sociolinguistics research involves attempts to address the macro-micro link. Deirdre Boden (1988) argues that talk structures social organization. Business works through the regular and expected conversing of employees. It is not merely the content of the talk that is significant, but the placement of that talk in a time-space continuum. This model lays the groundwork for the interactionist examination of talk as the mortar of social structure and institutional analysis.

SOCIAL PROBLEMS THEORY

Interactionists were deeply involved with the founding of the Society for the Study of Social Problems, and interactionists have always maintained a visible presence in the organization and in the journal, *Social Problems*. Howard S. Becker's (1963) exposition of labeling theory revolutionized the sociological analysis of social problems, recognizing that the public is (at least) as responsible for the creation of deviants as are the perpetrators. Labeling theory is in some respects a micro version of Durkheim's (1933) emphasis on the need of the society to create a class of deviants and unacceptable behavior to maintain the sanctity of communities and norms (*see* Erikson 1963). However, recognizing that labeling affects individuals provided a way of analyzing the creation of particular forms of behavior that we term "social problems," rather than the general assertion that some unspecified boundaries of behavior are necessary. Although it was never without its critics (Gove 1975; Gouldner 1970), the labeling perspective had an enormous impact on the study of social problems in the 1960s and early 1970s, affecting topics as diverse as mental illness, crime, and sexual deviance. Over the last decade the approach has lost some of its vitality, and has generally been integrated into the commonsense assumptions that sociologists bring to their subject matter.

More recently, interactionists interested in social problems have attempted to address a more macro formulation of social problems. Why do certain "dysfunctional" behaviors become social problems at certain points while other "dysfunctional" behaviors are ignored? In the felicitous phrase of Malcom Spector and John Kitsuse (1977), how are social problems *constructed?* This image has become the most important contemporary interactionist approach to social problems theory. The "social constructivist" approach has permitted interactionists to examine long-term trends that affect the social system, such as "the medicalization of deviance" (Conrad and Schneider 1980).

In social problems theory one can most visibly see the connection between interactionism and the rhetorical theory of Kenneth Burke. The world can only be known through the metaphorical construction that we make of it, and the identifications that derive from this construction. Academics (Gusfield 1976; Manning 1979) and social movement entrepreneurs (Gusfield 1981; Loseke 1987) use rhetorical strategies to build consensus that action needs to be taken to constrain the behaviors of others. As both labeling theory and social constructionism suggest that "social problems" are fundamentally epiphenomenal, they imply either a "libertarian" (Fine 1985c) or "anarchist" (Lofland 1988) political stance. Why should one group of social actors restrain the freedom of any other group?

Social problems theory has witnessed the most complete integration of macro-sociological questions into interaction theory. This emphasis is likely to continue, with more attention being paid to big business, labor, and government as social actors. Interactionists have not addressed economic social problems frequently, but this should be a high priority for interactionist researchers, who need to explain why "structural poverty," the underclass, unemployment, and military expenditures exist and are seen as problems. Further, interactionists should examine social problems as sedimented into historical periods, recognizing that often the solution of one social problem will lead to the development of another, as a latent consequence. The "chaining of social problems" underlines the recognition that social problems are temporally and contextually bound.

THE FUTURE

Predicting the future is more difficult to do well than unearthing the past or describing the present. Most analyses of the future are mere extrapolations of the present. I, too, shall be guilty of extrapolation in my discussion of several recent topics of interactionist research, and possibilities for future development.

New Approaches to Ethnography

Although this book devotes itself to "theory," we must never forget that methodological choices are theoretical choices (Lieberson 1985). The "standard" methodology of symbolic interactionism had been ethnography.[9] Ethnography has changed over the past decade, and this change is becoming more self-consciously recognized. Two changes have significant reverberations in contemporary ethnographies: a greater significance of theory in directing ethnographies and a greater self-consciousness of the role of the researcher as author and witness (*see* Clifford and Marcus 1986).

Traditionally ethnography was a technique to gather descriptive material—to find out what was *really* happening in a previously unexplored social setting. As a result, there arose the somewhat unjust, if understandable, claim that participant observation was little more than glorified journalism. This emphasis on carefully describing a very different cultural milieu was important for compiling evidence, but led to dissatisfaction with the lack of theoretical development.

In both anthropology and sociology styles of ethnographic investigation have changed markedly over the past decade. Among anthropologists this can be seen in the attempts to write reflexive and theoretically developed ethnography (see Rabinow 1977; Clifford and Marcus 1986). Sociologists have generally been less concerned with reflexivity (but see Johnson 1975; Douglas 1976; Van Maanen 1988), but they have emphasized the theoretical grounding of ethnography. In 1978 on becoming editor of *Urban Life,*[10] the leading sociological journal of ethnography, Peter Manning announced that he wanted to recruit "more systematically theoretically grounded papers" (Manning 1978, 283). Whether as a result of the editor's bully pulpit, or the fact that the announcement was timely, such articles flowered.

This theoretical emphasis is clear in Arlie Hochschild's (1983) admirable ethnography, *The Managed Heart,* a study of how airline attendants are trained to use emotion in a commercialized occupation. The work fails as standard ethnography in that the reader learns very little about the work life of flight attendants. It is not an occupational study; rather Hochschild has written a focused ethnography. Material extraneous to the argument of seeing emotion as a form of impression management, structured through industrial demands, has been excised. Unlike many descriptive ethnographies, Hochschild brings in material from other sources that addresses her theoretical issue.

Sherryl Kleinman's purpose in her estimable study of seminary students, *Equals Before God* (1984), is to examine the rhetorical devices that emerge in a deprofessionalizing occupation—e.g., the liberal Protestant ministry. How can values such as equality and community alter personal identity? As a study of clerical socialization, it fails. Kleinman is not a sociologist of religion; she is an interactionist theorist, following Burke, Blumer, and Stone.

Even more "traditional" studies that present a descriptive ethnographic account have become more self-consciously theoretical. In *Shared Fantasy: Role-Playing Games as Social Worlds* I attempted to expand Goffman's model of frame analysis through a detailed examination of the social world of fantasy gaming (Fine 1983b). I asked how "self" is constructed when individuals must operate within several social frames simultaneously (character, player, and person). In *With the Boys: Little League Baseball and Preadolescent Culture* I attempted to build an approach to small group culture, based on instrumental and expressive activities of preadolescents (Fine 1987b). In current research projects I am presenting a sociological analysis of aesthetics based on the experience of restaurant cooks, given the occupational and aesthetic constraints under which they must work (Fine 1988). In a study of amateur mushroom collectors I attempt to examine how individuals think about and act toward nature (Fine 1987a).

Contemporary ethnographers believe that they can build general theory from any set of data (see Glaser and Strauss 1967); under this model theory is emergent from data. Theory is to be inductive, rather than deductive. One can enter a field setting because it is convenient or because one has a personal interest, and emerge with a new concept, important substantive approach, or contribution to grand theory (the situation, self, social order).

A traditional issue in ethnographic research is the role of the observer, both in drawing conclusions (i.e., should it be the investigator's theory ["etic"] or the theory of the informants ["emic"]) and in describing the situation. Social scientists have moved away from secret (or "covert") observation, which had characterized some ethnography (e.g., Lofland 1966; Erikson 1967). Secret observation was designed to gain access to settings that an outsider could not have penetrated (e.g., the Unification Church or Alcoholics Anonymous), but it was also an attempt to see the group from the inside freed from the biases created when actors know they are being observed. Researchers now are more likely to admit their roles, but still use their own "lived reality" to understand feelings of actors. In analyzing fantasy games, I recorded my experiences as a player and a referee: my boredom, exhaustion, and reactions to aggressive and sexual game content. I didn't claim that I was a typical player, but that my reactions were *real*, and captured something about the game.

More radically, Ellis (1986) has taken extensive notes of the lengthy death of her significant other in order to understand how persons (starting with herself) cope with grief and illness. This "introspective ethnography" is controversial because she has only studied herself and has no "external" measures, subjective as they may be. Are her feelings relevant to those of any other actor? Ellis implies that we must rediscover the introspectionism of early twentieth-century psychologists, a tradition eclipsed by the inexorable rise of behaviorism. Unlike those such as Geertz who rely upon their own reading of a scene, or those who want to get the perspective of others, contemporary interactionist ethnographies desire a mix—the social scientist's reading and theorizing must be informed by the understandings of the members of the group.

Emotion

In the late 1970s sociology, and particularly symbolic interaction, discovered emotions. Previously emotions had been almost exclusively a topic of interest to psychologists (but *see* Foote 1953; Cooley [1902] 1964). In the division of human activity into cognition, behavior, and affect, symbolic interactionists had focused on the first two, ignoring the third. In 1979 two articles appeared nearly simultaneously in the *American Journal of Sociology* that erased this neglect by attempting to analyze emotions from an interactionist perspective (Shott 1979; Hochschild 1979).[11] Gordon (1981) underlined several topics that he considered central to the study of emotions, each relating to symbolic interactionist theory: the socially created differentiation of emotions, the socialization of emotions (how a cultural vocabulary becomes an interpretive resource), and the social management of emotions.

The sociological study of emotion draws heavily on the dramaturgical approach, suggesting that emotions are clues given by social actors, and that social actors are socialized in their use. Emotional display can be (and is) learned. This view owes a debt to William James (and to Adam Smith and Niccolo Machiavelli), and later to Schachter and Singer (1962). Schachter and Singer argue that emotion is excitation that is made meaningful by the existence of an interpretive context. Joy or anger are known by context. This view, which I have oversimplified, has been disputed by those who suggest that primary emotions have real and distinct physiological properties (*see* Kemper 1987). Still, the secondary emotions—those not grounded in physiological response— are not known only by their "feeling," but through their context. Emotions are not uncontrollable; rather there exist "feeling rules" that determine when emotions will be shown. Emotional display constitutes a symbolic transaction. Different countries have different feeling rules, as do different occupations (Hochschild 1983), ages (Cahill 1987), genders (Clark 1987), and historical periods (Stearns 1987).

With the special issue of *Symbolic Interaction* on emotions in 1985, and two years later with the establishment of the Sociology of Emotions section of the American Sociological Association, led largely by interactionists, the study of emotions is on the cutting edge of interactionism. It permits a bridging of the traditional interactionist concerns with self and situation. Emotion has become emblematic of the symbolic interactionist approach to social psychology. Being in a relatively new field, emotions researchers can expect more theoretical and conceptual innovations, such as "sympathy margins" (Clark 1987) and methodological approaches, such as introspectionism (Ellis 1986).

Eventually "normal science" problems will emerge, such as the scripting of particular emotions and the role of emotions in limited situations. At that point new approaches to emotion will be needed. One approach will surely be to describe how emotions are handled within organizations and social institutions [12]—another linkage of micro and macro themes.

Organizations

It appears that *everyone* has discovered the micro-macro link. I shall discuss this below as it relates to interactionist theory. For now, I note that the study of organizations and actors within organizations has become increasingly prominent in symbolic interaction. This emphasis can be traced to the survey article by David Maines (1977) in the *Annual Review of Sociology*, "Social Organization and Social Structure in Symbolic Interactionist Thought." This article reminded symbolic interactionists that contrary to the claims of some critics, interactionists *do* have constructs that permit the analysis of large-scale social units: collective action, negotiated order, commitment to organizations (*see also* Kleinman and Fine 1979; Maines 1982). Simultaneously, within organization research, scholars recognized the negotiated and symbolic character of organizations (e.g., Pfeffer 1981). Writers suggested that organizations are characterized by "loose-coupling" (Weick 1976), are fundamentally anarchic (Cohen, March, and Olsen 1972), and have recognizable cultures (Kamens 1977; Mitroff and Kilmann 1976; Pettigrew 1979). The culture metaphor, in particular, became dominant during the early 1980s (*see* Fine 1984; Ouchi and Wilkins 1985).

The classic interactionist study of organization is Melville Dalton's *Men Who Manage* (1959; *see also* Roy 1959–1960, 1952, 1954; Strauss et al. 1963, 1964). By the late 1970s organizations became a popular field site for interactionist ethnographers who wanted to understand structural negotiations. Studies of psychiatric clinics (Kahne and Schwartz 1978), art worlds (Faulkner 1983), restaurants (Fine 1987c), used car dealers (Farberman 1975), liquor distributors (Denzin 1977), health care clinics (Peyrot 1982), and social service agencies (Miller 1983) reflect the range of organizations studied. The core concepts of negotiated order, constraint, and symbolic meaning provide an entre to the interactionist study of organization. That actors are "corporate" in that they represent positions or agencies does not mean that the interactionist perspective on social action is irrelevant. That these are "symbolic" actors makes the dramaturgical and interpretive perspective more powerful, if it admits that these actors are constrained by structures.

Given that this is an area with which I have been associated, I have great hope for continued progress. Interactionists started examining social organizations by studying those that were least "organizational" — those that were least connected to models of economic rationality, such as social service agencies. Increasingly, interactionists examine "real" organizations, most noticeably businesses. Economic realities are incorporated in analyzing the determinants of action. The work of such Marxist "interactionists"[13] as Michael Burawoy (1979) and Victoria Smith (1987) is particularly stimulating, even aside from the fact that they utilize classical qualitative methodologies. Burawoy demonstrates how the negotiation of work on a factory shop floor is responsive to the political economy and in turn shapes efficient organizational production. Even actions that seem counterproductive to the maximization of profit support management objectives in that they keep the workforce satisfied and docile, and preserve the stability of production. Smith's analysis of a large bank demonstrates that upper and middle management have different economic interests, which need not be congruent. Turning middle managers into entrepreneurs, a commonplace technique of contemporary management philosophy, places them in a situation in which they must, in effect, become shop floor stewards, despite the rhetoric in which they are ostensibly given greater authority. These studies, which take the economic realities of management and labor into account as they are played out in *the doing of work*, serve as models for organizational research in their recognition of the emergent qualities of economic organization, authority, and bureaucracy.

THE THEORETICAL INFRASTRUCTURE OF SYMBOLIC INTERACTION

Having analyzed prominent areas of substantive theory and empirical investigation, I turn to the theoretical infrastructure of symbolic interaction. As a rule interactions are less tolerant of "pure" theory than other approaches, given the pragmatist belief that all knowledge should be grounded in empirical particulars and should reveal itself in practice. Interactionists sense that grand theory is secondary to substantive theory. Still, some theoretical concerns transcend the particulars of circumstance. I shall address these theoretical concerns, particularly as they have developed over the past decade, and as they may be developed in the post-Blumerian decade to come.

No theory stands alone. Post-Blumerian interactionism has cobbled a new theory from the shards of other theoretical approaches. Admittedly the shape of what is cobbled depends to a large degree on the cobbler. I am expressing my own beliefs and goals in arguing that symbolic interactionism has incorporated many other social theories to enrich its own. Some colleagues are happy to have others borrow from us, but hesitate to use "positivist" theory. Still others, seeing themselves as an oppositional intellectual movement (*see* Mullins 1973), are deeply suspicious of flow in either direction. My claim that we can and will borrow fruitfully from the classical macro theorists (Durkheim, Weber, particularly Simmel, and even Parsons and the neo-Marxists) should be seen as personal, not necessarily predictive, and not entirely descriptive.

Perhaps the most extreme example revolves around the connections between Blumer and Parsons. These arguments are not often recognized by interactionists, but more often by neofunctionalists (Faia 1987; Alexander 1987; Alexander and Colomy 1984; Sciulli 1988). Turner (1974) made an early attempt to merge these approaches, alleging that Parsons' theory is congruent with Blumerian interactionism—a claim to which both men objected (Blumer 1975; Parsons 1975). Talcott Parsons, unfairly I think, is a straw man in interactionism. He reigns as a demonic figure for such diverse groups as exchange theorists, Marxists, and most critical theorists. By attacking Parsons, interactionists join the contemporary mainstream. As Sciulli suggests, Parsons (and Blumer) is easy to attack particularly if one does not read his varied and tough texts.

Parsons and Blumer both presented theories based on the assumption of voluntarism and a cultural basis of action (whether that be "situated meaning" or Parsonian normative structure) (*see* Sciulli 1988). One would be foolish to claim that no significant divergences separate the theories, particularly as Blumer emphasized micro interaction, while Parsons typically stressed macro concerns. Still, both address how "order" is possible in a nonauthoritarian social structure. Could Parsons provide the macro-sociology that some interactionists are looking for? Perhaps not, but techniques for translating pattern variables into the sedimentation of structure do exist in Parsons' writings.

Parsons is only the most extreme example of the attempt to meld interactionism with other theoretical approaches. The attempt is most conventionally made with the other micro theories such as exchange theory, phenomenology, and ethnomethodology. These theories take relationships and individual actors as the primary units of analysis, and in the process empower the actor's judgment. In each, external constraints affect the sense the individual can make of the world. Conversation analysis is, perhaps, most formal, claiming that the constraints, although they are "local," have considerable potency in structuring interaction. Conversation analysis emphasizes the form of interaction, downplaying the substance. In contrast, interactionism allows a lot more "slop" in the system—more of the meaningful context affects how talk is structured. To compare the work of conversation analysts closer to interactionism (such as Corsaro [1977], West [1984], Molotch and Boden [1985]) with those who are more closely aligned with Garfinkel's approach to ethnomethodology (e.g., Psathas 1979) is to compare theorists who argue that the *meaning* of the talk and the situation affects the form of talk with those who focus on the construction of the form of talk without regard to speaker characteristics or content. The form of talk is important, and interactionists who incorporate "formal sociology" with their recognition of the effects of meaningful action enrich interactionist theory.

Collins (1986) has argued plausibly that there has been no great sociological theory without an affiliated economic theory. He cites Marxism, and the connection of Weber with Schumpeter. Interactionism and exchange theory share a connection with the writings of Adam Smith. Both theories rely implicitly on Adam Smith's laissez-faire economics, with its emphasis on individual action, freedom, and in the importance of images of value. The world, like the market, is a social construction. Supply and demand are not objective features of the world, but are based on decisions grounded in role-taking. The connection between exchange theory and Smith is self-evident; with interactionism it is less directly clear, but is reflected in the struggles of Charles Horton Cooley to come to terms with Smith (*see* Creelan 1987). Both used the metaphor of the "looking-glass self."

The image of actors coping with others socially and economically reverberates throughout Smith's writings and later in the writings of Homans and Goffman. Yet there are differences. For example, exchange theory takes the propositional form that interactionists have traditionally rejected (but *see* Stryker 1981).

The thin elegance of exchange theory contrasts to the fat richness of interactionism. If exchange theory includes too little, interactionism may incorporate too much, i.e., more than is necessary to express general propositions. In other words, where exchange theory is underdetermined (e.g., Turner 1987), interactionism is overdetermined. Yet the attempts by Stryker and his colleagues to examine how self and identity are constructed owes much to both the theoretical and methodological injunctions of the exchange framework. Stryker believes, in a much more precise way than do most interactionists, that actors attempt to *maximize* their satisfactions through role-taking and identity formulations. This permits him to develop propositions that specify the situations in which such alterations in identity become likely (e.g., Stryker 1981, 24: "the more congruent the role expectations of those to whom one is committed by virtue of an identity, the higher that identity will be in the salience hierarchy"). While Stryker leaves room in his model for meaning and negotiation, the model is premised on an emotional marketplace—a marketplace that is only distantly recognizable in Goffman's writing. Stryker's research has underlined that interactionism is not by its nature inimical to the propositional theorizing of exchange theory. Some interactionists claim Stryker misundertands classic interactionism (and therefore is acceptable to positivists), but I think his approach can be read as emphasizing that situations can be formulated with greater or lesser formality and precision, remaining true to the pragmatic bases of interactionism.

Of the three micro-sociologies, phenomenology (and the phenomenological side of ethnomethodology) has been the most recognized as akin to interactionism—so similar that debates over boundaries are common and not theoretically productive (e.g., Gallant and Kleinman 1983; Rawls 1985; Denzin 1970; Perinbanayagam 1974; Zimmerman 1978). Part of the problem is that although the substantive outcomes are similar and there are common "enemies," the theoretical bases of the two approaches are dissimilar. Whereas interactionism traces its lineage to pragmatism and Romanticism, phenomenology is grounded in the writings of Husserl, Wittgenstein, and Heidegger. The interactionist perspective is *at its core* social and relational, whereas the phenomenological approach emphasizes the individual construction of the world, a world of discrete and separate actors. As a result, interactionists feel uncomfortable with the writings of Schutz whose concept of relations is attenuated, compared to those of Mead and other interactionists. Interactionism and phenomenology are lands separated by a river of "the social"—only occasionally are bridges built.[14] The most notable bridge is Peter Berger and Thomas Luckmann's *The Social Construction of Reality* (1966), a work that transcends parochial divisions and is claimed and referred to by both groups. Berger and Luckmann manage to emphasize the social construction of reality, while underlining the cognitive and personal process that such a construction entails. Borrowing through sociological bricolage has been productive, and will undoubtedly continue. Yet interactionists must pay the same close attention to the roots of phenomenology as they pay to the exegesis of Mead. For example, interactionists should examine how Wittgenstein's language games are congruent with the motive or accounts framework described in interactionist writing or how the social conditions in which Husserl's and Schutz's bracketing occurs operates in social interaction (e.g., Goffman 1974, 3–7).

The Challenge of Classic Theorists

SIMMEL

If challenged to name the single greatest change in orientation toward classical social theorists over the past decade among interactionists, I would cite the increasing attention to the writings of Georg Simmel. It is not that Simmel was totally ignored previously (his essay "On Visual Interaction" is included in Stone and Farberman 1970, 300–303). Interactionists are impressed by the pseudo-ethnography implicit in Simmel's accounts of the Stranger and the Secret Society (see Simmel 1950). The recognition that Park was a student of Simmel meant that Simmelian sociology was incorporated into Chicago sociology at the outset. Indeed, Helle (1985, 9–10) raises the intriguing possibility that Mead may have been well aware of Simmel during Mead's stay at the University of Berlin, perhaps attending some of Simmel's lectures.

As Arthur Frank (1987) notes, deep theoretical connections exist between the sociology of Simmel and traditional concerns of symbolic interactionists; Simmel may help in an interactionist understanding of modernity. Rock notes, in emphasizing the importance of Simmel for interactionist theory,[15] "The first works of symbolic interaction thus married the local, the particular and the evanescent with the logic of Simmelian sociology" (1979, 53). The similarity is perhaps most evident in the writings of Everett Hughes (1971) on "dirty work" or Goffman's studies of "stigma" (1963) or "role distance" (1961b).

Interactionists find it difficult to "handle" Simmel because of his formal sociology. His lack of interest in ethnographic particulars and social psychology make him a stranger. Yet as Zerubavel (1980) notes in his influential article on the relevance of a Simmelian methodology for interactionism, Simmel and Blumer share a belief in the importance of "sensitizing concepts," concepts that are analytically derived, but set apart from the particulars of the setting in which they were noted. Such analytical induction (*see* Glaser and Strauss 1967) is the basis for theoretical generalization.

As symbolic interactionists have attempted to develop sensitizing concepts and, more recently, formal analysis, they have drawn on Simmel—as in analyses of adventure (Vester 1987; Wanderer 1987), confidence (Fine 1987a), time (Zerubavel 1979, 1987; Molseed 1987), and sexuality (Davis 1983). Studies of this type will continue contributing to the "new ethnography." The continuing reading of Simmel's extensive written corpus, much still untranslated, suggests that there is much yet to be learned from Simmel. Of all the classic European sociologists, Simmel's soul is closest to the interactionist tradition.

WEBER

The second classical European theorist who has a notable place in interactionism is Max Weber. Ritzer (1975, 1985), examining sociological paradigms, placed symbolic interactionism under the "social definition" paradigm—a view for which he claims Max Weber is the exemplar. Yet despite this claim, more than is true for Simmel, Weber is a problem. In part, this is because Weber wrote different things at different points in his career (*see* Collins 1986). Still, Weber is perhaps the single most *central* sociological theorist if only because of his writings abut every major sociological perspective: phenomenology, Marxism, functionalism, structuralism, and, of course, interactionism. This centrality is as much of a curse as a blessing, particularly for those who wish to know what Weber really meant.

The two shells in Weber's theoretical arsenal that have the most impact on symbolic interactionism are his concerns with "verstehen" and his belief in "action theory." "Verstehen" with its emphasis on attempting to understand the world (from the meaningful character of events to individuals) from the inside is immediately appealing to interactionists, whose methodological preferences are seemingly supported by the concept of verstehen. Discovering the world from the perspective of the social actors is congruent with Weber's methodological imperative. Yet the meaning of "verstehen" is by no means clear (e.g., Truzzi 1974), and whatever Weber's own preferences in this matter, his own macro-comparative-historical research would not recognizably reflect a *"verstehende Soziologie."* Still, Weber provides a rhetorical grounding for a qualitative methodology.

Weber's action theory has been less utilized by American interactionists, although it seems to be a driving force behind the emergence of German interactionism (*see* Haferkamp 1987b). Whereas Americans tether Mead to Simmel, Germans link Mead to Weber. Action theory, with its emphasis on social action within the reality of structure, economy, and organization, provides a means by which interactionism can address macro-sociological problems. The attempt of Haferkamp (1987a) to address the problems of oligarchy through a merging of Mead and Weber (and Michels) addresses power and order while still doing justice to the experienced and negotiated understandings of members. Attempts to connect Weber's action theory to Mead's interactionism have begun to bear fruit. Despite Haferkamp's sudden death, such a productive marriage will continue through the explicit attention to traditional macro-sociological issues by micro-sociologists and the discovery of the riches of Mead by critical theorists (e.g., Habermas and Collins).

DURKHEIM

Interactionists must feel a certain frustration that the struggle between Emile Durkheim and Gabriel Tarde in fin-de-siécle France was won by the former. Interactionist sympathies naturally lie with Tarde. Tarde is the micro-sociologist, while Durkheim's concerns with "social facts" and "external realities" seem to run counter to interpretist sociology. Tarde's theory of imitation recognizes the possibility of individuals determining their own action in a way that Durkheim's analysis excludes. Yet Tarde's theories (admittedly a vague precursor to interactionism) have had little impact.

Interactionists have occasionally attempted to suggest that Durkheim was "really" on "some level" or at "some time" an interactionist, yet these arguments (e.g., Stone and Farberman 1967) are a presentist fantasy (Jones 1977). Durkheim was not an interactionist, and would have been aghast to learn that he was thought of in such a way.

Still, there is one area in which interactionists and Durkheim share a common ground: collective symbols and ritual action. This emphasis is notably evident in the early work of Erving Goffman who was explicitly exploring Durkheimian issues (see Creelan 1987; Collins 1980, 178–191). Goffman's early essays are attempts to understand the profoundly Durkheimian question of how social order is possible in the face of individual action. The answer is that collective symbols channel behavior, and this symbolism becomes "taken-for-granted" (see Fine 1988). The negotiation of symbols is not truly an issue, although in Goffman's later writings it comes to be seen as more central (Goffman 1974). Goffman's (1983) last essay, "The Interaction Order," can be read as an attempt to return to the Durkheimian questions of his early career: the recognition that order and structure are not merely epiphenomenal but provide a cocoon around action; a cocoon which is slowly affected by that action.

Much of the recent interest among symbolic interactionists in exploring historical evidence is a return to questions of the power of symbolization, particularly the writings of Barry Schwartz and Eviatar Zerubavel (Schwartz 1983, 1987; Zerubavel 1981; Schwartz, Zerubavel, and Barnett 1986). These scholars bracket interaction in favor of examining the structural use and negotiation of symbols. Symbols are unselfconsciously meaningful and referential, and these "interactional

Durkheimians" are more concerned with the contextualization and embeddedness of symbols that Durkheim was, but the theoretical impulse is identical: to examine the stability and reality of social order through culture. As interactionists bracket the local production of meaning in focusing upon the macro-construction of symbolism, Durkheim's writing will gain in centrality—not because he was an interactionist, but because his concerns can be utilized in theory building.

MARX

Fourth among the European quadrumvirate is Karl Marx. The classical reading of Marx presents a scholar whose structural views are opposed to interactionism. Marx's dismissal of agency in favor of structure in his most central writings is clear, although other parts of his writing seem more sympathetic (*see* Ashley 1985; Goff 1980). Certainly the writings of some of Marx's more social psychological followers are relevant to interactionism. I noted above the value of the research of Burawoy and Smith to an interactionist understanding of organization. Other interactionists have attempted to explicate such Marxist concepts as oppression (Wolf 1986), although in this case Marx is mediated through Habermas' emphasis on communicative structures as the bases of legitimation.

Interactionists deal with Marx through the works of his interpreters rather than from his own work. Habermas (1984, 1987) provides a particularly accessible transformation of Marx, because of his recent interest in Mead and his emphasis on the communication (symbolic) order as the basis for social order (*see* Tejera 1986; Ashley 1982). Although it is not quite accurate to suggest that Habermas is a Marxist, that label may have as little descriptive credibility as that of symbolic interactionist.

The New Mead

Each generation needs to reinvent the theorists of the past (Fine and Kleinman 1986). "We" revise Shakespeare, Freud, DaVinci, and the other cultural heroes of our privileged canon. So it is on a smaller scale with Mead. For some fifty years Blumer covered himself with the mantle of Mead. While there were doubters (Bales 1966; Miller 1973; Natanson 1973; Cottrell 1980), for many interactionists, and for most of the rest of the discipline, Blumer's interpretations were dominant. Over the past decade, the critiques of Blumer's description of Mead grew stronger and more vociferous (McPhail and Rexroat 1979; Baldwin

1986; Lewis and Smith 1980; Stewart 1981; Stryker 1988); Mead was a more richly textured and contradictory theorist than Blumer gave him credit for being. Further, new intellectual histories made Mead's intellectual roots seem more varied than had been previously depicted (*see* Deegan and Burger 1978; Burger and Deegan 1981; Shalin 1986, 1987; Collins 1989; Joas 1985; Cook 1977). Mead was transformed from a uniquely American social theorist into a theorist more attuned to Continental events. This produced a more complex reading of Mead, or perhaps more properly it led to several sometimes mutually incomprehensible Meads: a critical Mead, an objectivist Mead, a political Mead, and a phenomenological Mead (Fine and Kleinman 1986).

Losing sight of the "real" Mead injected new theoretical vigor into interactionism. No longer did interactionists take their founders for granted.[16] Rather than being a somewhat isolated figure outside of the mainstream of classic sociological theorists—a theorist with an idiosyncratic, individualistic agenda—as Blumer underlined, Mead is now understood as addressing the same kinds of issues as Simmel, Marx, Weber, and even Durkheim. I do not mean to conflate theories excessively; their answers still differ, but the questions (of voluntarism, self and society, social order, and power) seem more similar under the revised readings. The interpretation of Mead has become problematic and intellectually central to sociology.

Along with the revisionist understanding of George Herbert Mead, interactionists are exploring the writings of other pragmatic philosophers. Rochberg-Halton (1987) has argued that there is much of value in the writings of Dewey and Peirce, and he calls for additional investigation of these figures, especially in light of their possible connections with European social philosophy. Others, such as Johnson and Picou (1985), have argued that William James provides a grounding for an improved interactionist social psychology. Lewis and Smith (1980), in underlining a connection between Mead and Peirce, suggest that interactionists can discover their theoretical roots within the writings of Peirce. Whichever pragmatist turns out to have the most insight for our current problems, we are witnessing an increased appreciation of these thinkers, who previously were unread figures, secondary intellectual colleagues of George Herbert Mead.

The Age of the Post

As we near a new fin de siécle with political threats (legitimized struggles of an interdependent world), military threats (nuclear war), biological threats (AIDS), environmental threats (depletion of the ozone level), and technological threats (nuclear power), we live in an age in which the future is defined by our having left the past behind: we face postmodernism, poststructuralism, and post-feminism. These intellectual approaches share with interactionism an emphasis on interpretation and a deep suspicion of positivism and scientism. These new theoretical developments are exciting for their attempts to provide new metaphors (in that they abjure truths) by which we might examine social worlds. Each approach suggests that we must examine our assumptions about the reading of the world — that the world is a decentered, socially constructed place, and that meaning does not adhere in objects but in relations, for example between readers and texts. In this, despite differences in jargon, style, and topic, post-structuralism (and associated perspectives) are discovering what interactionists have claimed all along: the contingent nature of meaning, and, hence, of reality.

Among interactionists the writing of Norman Denzin (1986, 1987), Richard Brown (1987), and Patricia Clough (1988, 1989) are particularly influential in their attempt to connect postmodernism and radical feminism to interactionist concerns. By their writing they demonstrate convincingly that, despite differences in emphasis and tone, the approaches are theoretically congruent and contact is mutually rewarding. Interactionism, with its emphasis on careful observation, curbs some of the carelessness of deconstructionism, while deconstructionism connects interactionism to themes of the humanities. While interactionism is not as self-consciously political and "ideological" as these "deconstructive" approaches, the undermining of the positivistic assumptions of texts, data, and role are common to both. Although poststructuralism may be "where the action is," that action can also be found in interactionism. The wheel was rediscovered in post-industrial France. Post-structuralism is still being developed and an anti-codified credo is developing. Interactionists should, I believe, participate more explicitly in that debate — a debate which makes Mead and Burke equal partners with Habermas, Gadamer, Kristeva, and Derrida. The work of interactionists who are attuned to postmodern thought (e.g., Denzin 1987) indicates that interactionism with its tradition of blending theoretically sophisticated analysis with rich empirical research is a source of stability ("a decentered center") for post-structural thought, while postmodernism provides the ideological breadth that interactionism has sometimes seemed to lack.

A HAZY FUTURE

I return to the dangers of prediction. This essay may read as more of a wish list than a realistic evaluation of the current state and future trends of symbolic interactionism. I do believe that by the year 2001 interactionism will be an active partner in the theoretical integration of sociology and not merely the loyal opposition (Mullins 1973) (a memorable phrase that really sticks in the symbolic interactionist's craw—whether because they doubt they are an opposition or they deny they are loyal). Interactionists will unself-consciously address the standard issues of sociology: agency, structure, contingencies, status mobility, resources, political economy, and the like. For "mainstream sociology," interactionist issues will be mainstream—constraint, negotiation, self-presentation, collective activity, conventions, temporality (e.g., Hall 1987).

Yet it is well to remember that change is endemic, fashion is fickle, process is unending. I predict that by the year 2037—symbolic interactionism's centenary—symbolic interaction will not exist as an active, ongoing theoretical perspective. Whatever sociology will be like at that time, there will be other oppositional groups, and other theoretical perspectives will have made their way into the mainstream. Mead will have entered the sociological pantheon. Parsons, Homans, and Blumer will be enshrined as the three leading theorists of mid-twentieth-century sociology. Goffman, Becker, Turner, and Strauss will be given due for rejuvenating sociology from its functionalist doldrums, and some of today's young Turks will be the old guard whose images need to be overthrown. I believe that sociology will still be with us in 2037 —if only because of the resistance of academic bureaucracies to change. Still, whatever our organizational status, I am confident that sociologists will face all coming crises with both hope and dread.

NOTES

1. Although Blumer's debt to Mead cannot be denied, it is clear that other scholars such as Robert Park, Everett Hughes, Frederick Teggart, W. I. Thomas, Charles Horton Cooley, and Florian Znaniecki influenced his theoretical vision as well (e.g., Fisher and Strauss 1978; Lyman 1988).

2. Blumer admitted that the reflex approach and the symbolic interactionist approach were not necessarily in conflict, but only that they emphasize different attributes of the individual (1937, 153). This first statement of the interactionist position was considerably more open and flexible than the image that came across in Blumer's later writings (*see* Blumer 1969b).

3. Recall Goffman's (1974, 14) sardonic comment on this matter: "I can only

suggest that he who would combat false consciousness and awaken people to their true interests has much to do, because the sleep is very deep. And I do not intend here to provide a lullaby but merely to sneak in and watch the way the people snore."

4. I shall choose to be inclusive in my discussion of writers within the "symbolic interactionist" tradition. In doing so I include several who might object to such inclusion. My only justification for such a stance—other than the desire to gain credit for the perspective by virtue of the eminence of those I include—is that these writers are used by interactionists and are seen as making contributions that fall within the perspective. I use "interactionism" as a shorthand synonym for symbolic interactionism.

5. A few areas have remained unexplored, such as world-systems theory, although the writing of Mukerji (1983) suggests that global information transfer can be a focus for symbolic analysis.

6. It is not my intention to claim that these are the only six areas that might be chosen, but in their diversity they demonstrate the theoretical richness of interactionism.

7. Interestingly, Goffman's magnum opus, *Frame Analysis* (1974), is among his least influential. While there has been some use of the concepts of *Frame Analysis* (*see* Fine 1983b; Gonos 1977), the perspective as such has had nothing like the impact of his earlier work. Unlike the theatrical metaphor, the images of *Frame Analysis* are less accessible and require a phenomenological belief in the existence of multiple planes of reality.

8. There is a tradition of examining reactions to errors in ethnomethodology as well. While there is some overlap between the two approaches, interactionists tend to focus on the content and placement of accounts, whereas ethnomethodologists examine the micro-construction of conversational repair (e.g., Schegloff, Jefferson, and Sacks 1977).

9. By this I don't mean that it has been the only methodology, the most effective, or even the most common. However, it has been the approach that has been most closely associated with the perspective, although many of the earliest influential ethnographies have had little direct connection to interactionist theory (e.g., Whyte 1943; West 1945; Vidich and Bensman 1968; Liebow 1967; Gans 1962).

10. In 1987 the journal changed its name to *Journal of Contemporary Ethnography*. Although there were several justifications for this change, one was that *Urban Life* seemed too descriptive in focus.

11. For a non-interactionist perspective on emotion from this same period see Kemper 1978.

12. Gross (1986) attempts this by showing the way in which historical ceremonies (e.g., coronations and pageants) attempt to script emotional reactions for states and communities.

13. I should emphasize that this is my characterization, not theirs.

14. This division can be seen organizationally in sociology departments in which there are considerable numbers of symbolic interactionists and ethnomethodologists. Rather than working in harmony, the two groups may reveal as much hostility as that expected between quantitative and qualitative sociologists.

15. Rock essentially gives Simmel equal status with the pragmatists as a root of interactionist thought (1979, 59).

16. A similar process is occurring in the case of Blumer, as the richness of his writings are being discovered (e.g., Wellman 1988; Clough 1988; Sciulli 1988; Maines 1988; Tucker 1988).

148 *Gary Alan Fine*

REFERENCES

Alexander, Jeffrey. 1987. *Twenty Lectures: Sociological Theory Since World War II*. New York: Columbia University Press.

Alexander, Jeffrey, and Paul Colomy. 1984. "'Institutionalization' and 'Collective Behavior': Points of Contact Between Eisenstadt's Functionalism and Symbolic Interactionism." In Erik Cohen et al., eds., *Social Dynamics: Essays in Honor of S. N. Eisenstadt*. Boulder, Colo.: Westview.

Ashley, David. 1982. "Jürgen Habermas and the Rationalization of Communicative Norms." *Symbolic Interaction* 5:79–96.

Ashley, David. 1985. "Marx and the Category of 'Individuality' in Communist Society." *Symbolic Interaction* 8:63–83.

Baldwin, John. 1986. *George Herbert Mead*. Beverly Hills: Sage.

Bales, Robert Freed. 1966. "Comment on Herbert Blumer's Paper." *American Journal of Sociology* 71:545–547.

Becker, Howard S. 1963. *Outsiders*. New York: Free Press.

Becker, Howard S. 1974a. "Art as Collective Action." *American Sociological Review* 39:767–776.

Becker, Howard S. 1974b. "Photography and Sociology." *Studies in Visual Communication* 1:3–26.

Becker, Howard S. 1976. "Art Worlds and Social Types." *American Behavioral Scientist* 19:703–718.

Becker, Howard S. 1978. "Arts and Crafts." *American Journal of Sociology* 83:862–889.

Becker, Howard S. 1982. *Art Worlds*. Berkeley: University of California Press.

Bennett, H. Stith. 1980. *Becoming a Rock Musician*. Amherst: University of Massachusetts Press.

Berger, Peter, and Thomas Luckmann. 1966. *The Social Construction of Reality*. Garden City, N.Y.: Doubleday.

Blumer, Herbert. 1933. *Movies and Conduct*. New York: Macmillan.

Blumer, Herbert. 1937. "Social Psychology." in Emerson Schmidt, ed., *Man and Society*. New York: Prentice-Hall.

Blumer, Herbert. 1939. "Collective Behavior." In Robert E. Park, ed., *An Outline of the Principles of Sociology*. New York: Barnes and Noble.

Blumer, Herbert. 1962. "Society as Symbolic Interaction."in A. M. Rose, ed., *Human Behavior and Social Processes*. Boston: Houghton Mifflin.

Blumer, Herbert. 1969a. "Fashion: From Class Differentiation to Collective Selection." *The Sociological Quarterly* 10:275–291.

Blumer, Herbert. 1969b. *Symbolic Interactionism*. Englewood Cliffs, N.J.: Prentice-Hall.

Blumer, Herbert. 1975. "Comment" [on Turner and Parsons]. *Sociological Inquiry* 45:59–62, 68.

Blumer, Herbert and Philip M. Hauser. 1933. *Movies, Delinquency, and Crime*. New York: Macmillan.

Boden, Deirdre. 1988. "People are Talking: Conversation Analysis and Symbolic Interaction." Paper presented to the Stone Symposium of the Society for the Study of Symbolic Interaction, Chicago.

Brown, Richard. 1987. *Society as Text*. Chicago: University of Chicago Press.

Burawoy, Michael. 1979. *Manufacturing Consent*. Chicago: University of Chicago Press.

Burger, John S., and Mary Jo Deegan. 1981. "George Herbert Mead on Internationalism, War, and Democracy." *The Wisconsin Sociologist* 18:72–84.

Burke, Kenneth. 1969. *A Grammar of Motives.* Berkeley: University of California Press.

Cahill, Spencer. 1987. "Children and Civility: Ceremonial Deviance and the Acquisition of Ritual Competence." *Social Psychology Quarterly* 50:312–321.

Clark, Candace. 1987. "Sympathy Biography and Sympathy Margin." *American Journal of Sociology* 93:290–321.

Clifford, James, and George E. Marcus. 1986. *Writing Culture.* Berkeley: University of California Press.

Clough, Patricia. 1988. "The Movies and Social Observation: Reading Blumer's *Movies and Conduct.*" *Symbolic Interaction* 11:85–97.

Clough, Patricia. 1989. "Letters from Pamela: Reading Howard S. Becker's *Writing(s) for Social Scientists.*" *Symbolic Interaction* 12:159–170.

Cohen, M. D., J. G. March, and J. P. Olsen. 1972. "A Garbage Can Model of Organizational Choice." *Administrative Science Quarterly* 17:1–25.

Collins, Randall. 1980. "Erving Goffman and the Development of Modern Social Theory." In Jason Ditton, ed., *The View from Goffman.* New York: St. Martin's.

Collins, Randall. 1981. "The Microfoundations of Macrosociology." *American Journal of Sociology* 86:984–1014.

Collins, Randall. 1986. *Weberian Sociological Theory.* Cambridge: Cambridge University Press.

Collins, Randall. 1989. "Toward a Neo-Meadian Sociology of Mind." *Symbolic Interaction* 12:1–32.

Conrad, Peter, and Joseph W. Schneider. 1980. *Deviance and Medicalization: From Badness to Sickness.* St. Louis: Mosby.

Cook, Gary A. 1977. "G. H. Mead's Social Behaviorism." *Journal of the History of the Behavioral Sciences* 13:307–316.

Cooley, Charles Horton. [1902] 1964. *Human Nature and the Social Order.* New York: Scribner's.

Corsaro, William. 1977. "The Clarification Request as a Feature of Adult Interactive Styles with Young Children." *Language in Society* 6:183–207.

Corsaro, William. 1985. *Friendship and Peer Culture in the Early Years.* Norwood, N.J.: Ablex.

Cottrell, Leonard. 1980. "George Herbert Mead: The Legacy of Social Behaviorism." In Robert K. Merton and Matilda White Riley, eds., *Sociological Traditions from Generation to Generation.* Norwood, N.J.: Ablex.

Couch, Carl J., Stanley L. Saxton, and Michael A. Katovich, eds. 1986. *Studies in Symbolic Interaction: The Iowa School.* 2 vols. Greenwich, Conn.: JAI Press.

Coutu, Walter. 1951. "Role-Playing Versus Role-Taking: An Appeal for Clarification." *American Sociological Review* 16:180–187.

Creelan, Paul. 1987. "The Degradation of the Sacred: Approaches of Cooley and Goffman." *Symbolic Interaction* 10:29–56.

Dalton, Melville. 1959. *Men Who Manage.* New York: Wiley.

Davis, Murray. 1983. *Smut.* Chicago: University of Chicago Press.

Deegan, Mary Jo, and John S. Burger. 1978. "George Herbert Mead and Social Reform." *Journal of the History of the Behavioral Sciences* 14:362–373.

Denzin, Norman K. 1970. *The Research Act.* Chicago: Aldine.

Denzin, Norman K. 1977. "Notes on the Criminogenic Hypothesis: A Case Study of the American Liquor Industry." *American Sociological Review* 42:905–920.

Denzin, Norman. 1986. "Postmodern Social Theory." *Sociological Theory* 4:194–204.

Denzin, Norman. 1987. "On Semiotics and Symbolic Interactionism." *Symbolic Interaction* 10:1–19.

DiMaggio, Paul. 1977. "Market Structure, the Creative Process, and Popular Culture." *Journal of Popular Culture* 11:436–452.

Ditton, Jason, ed. 1980. *The View from Goffman.* New York: St. Martin's.

Douglas, Jack. 1976. *Investigative Social Research.* Beverly Hills: Sage.

Durkheim, Emile. 1933. *The Division of Labor in Society.* New York: Macmillan.

Ellis, Carolyn. 1986. "Studying Dying and Grief Through Systematic Sociological Introspection or 'Sociology from the Heart.'" Manuscript.

Erikson, Kai. 1963. *Wayward Puritans.* New York: Wiley.

Erikson, Kai. 1967. "A Comment on Disguised Observation in Sociology." *Social Problems* 12:366–373.

Faia, Michael A. 1987. *Dynamic Functionalism.* Cambridge: Cambridge University Press.

Farberman, Harvey. 1975. "A Criminogenic Market Structure: The Automobile Industry." *The Sociological Quarterly* 16: 207–218.

Faulkner, Robert R. 1983. *Music on Demand.* New Brunswick, N.J.: Transaction Books.

Fine, Gary Alan. 1983a. "Cheating History: Rhetorics and Art Forgery." *Empirical Studies in the Arts* 1:75–93.

Fine, Gary Alan. 1983b. *Shared Fantasy: Role-Playing Games as Social Worlds.* Chicago: University of Chicago Press.

Fine, Gary Alan. 1984. "Negotiated Orders and Organizational Cultures." *Annual Review of Sociology* 10:239–262.

Fine, Gary Alan. 1985a. "Occupational Aesthetics: How Trade School Students Learn to Cook." *Urban Life* 14:3–32.

Fine, Gary Alan. 1985b. "Rumors and Gossiping." In Teun van Dijk, ed., *Handbook of Discourse Analysis.* Vol. 3. London: Academic Press.

Fine, Gary Alan. 1985c. *Talking Sociology.* Boston: Allyn and Bacon.

Fine, Gary Alan. 1986. "Adolescent Gossip as Social Interaction." In Jenny Cook-Gumperz, William A. Corsaro, and Jürgen Streeck, eds., *Children's Worlds and Children's Language.* Berlin: Mouton de Gruyter.

Fine, Gary Alan. 1987a. "Trivial Pursuits: Mushroom Collecting and the Culture of Nature." Paper presented at the Qualitative Research Conference, Hamilton, Ontario.

Fine, Gary Alan. 1987b. *With the Boys: Little League Baseball and Preadolescent Culture.* Chicago: University of Chicago Press.

Fine, Gary Alan. 1987c. "Working Cooks: The Dynamics of Professional Kitchens." In Helena Z. Lopata, ed., *Current Research on Occupations and Professions.* Greenwich, Conn.: JAI Press.

Fine, Gary Alan. 1988. "The Proof of the Pudding: The Production of Aesthetics in Restaurant Kitchens." Manuscript.

Fine, Gary Alan. 1989. "The Process of Tradition: Cultural Models of Change and Content." In Craig Calhoun, ed., *Studies in Comparative Historical Sociology.* Greenwich, Conn.: JAI Press.

Fine, Gary Alan, and Sherryl Kleinman. 1986. "Interpreting the Sociological Classics: Can There be a 'True' Meaning of Mead?" *Symbolic Interaction* 9:129–146.

Fischer, Ernst. 1959. *The Necessity of Art.* Hammondsworth: Penguin.

Fisher, Berenice, and Anselm Strauss. 1978. "The Chicago Tradition and Social Change: Thomas, Park and Their Successors." *Symbolic Interaction* 1:5–23.

Flaherty, Michael. 1987. "The Depiction of Symbolic Interactionism in Theory Textbooks." Paper presented at the SSSI/Stone Symposium, Urbana, Ill.

Foote, Nelson N. 1953. "Love." *Psychiatry* 16:245–251.

Frank, Arthur. 1987. "Review Essay." *Symbolic Interaction* 10:295–306.

Gallant, Mary, and Sherryl Kleinman. 1983. "Symbolic Interactionism vs. Ethnomethodology." *Symbolic Interaction* 6:1–18.

Gamson, William, Bruce Fireman, and Steven Rytina. 1982. *Encounters with Unjust Authority.* Homewood, Ill.: Dorsey.

Gans, Herbert J. 1962. *The Urban Villagers.* Glencoe, Ill.: Free Press.

Gecas, Viktor. 1982. "The Self-Concept." *Annual Review of Sociology* 8:1–33.

Giddens, Anthony. 1984. *The Constitution of Society.* Berkeley: University of California Press.

Gilmore, Samuel. 1987. "Coordination and Convention: The Organization of the Concert World." *Symbolic Interaction* 10:209–227.

Glaser, Barney, and Anselm Strauss. 1967. *The Discovery of Grounded Theory.* Chicago: Aldine.

Gluckman, Max. 1963. "Gossip and Scandal." *Current Anthropology* 4:307–316.

Goff, Tom W. 1980. *Marx and Mead: Contributions to a Sociology of Knowledge.* London: Routledge and Kegan Paul.

Goffman, Erving. 1959. *The Presentation of Self in Everyday Life.* Garden City, N.Y.:Anchor.

Goffman, Erving. 1961a. *Asylums.* New York: Anchor.

Goffman, Erving. 1961b. *Encounters.* Indianapolis: Bobbs-Merrill.

Goffman, Erving. 1963. *Stigma.* Englewood Cliffs, N.J.: Prentice-Hall.

Goffman, Erving. 1974. *Frame Analysis.* Cambridge, Mass.: Harvard University Press.

Goffman, Erving. 1981. *Forms of Talk.* Philadelphia: University of Pennsylvania Press.

Goffman, Erving. 1983. "The Interaction Order." *American Sociological Review* 48:1–17.

Goldmann, Lucien. 1975. *Towards a Sociology of the Novel.* London: Tavistock.

Gonos, George. 1977. " 'Situation' vs. 'Frame,' the Interactionist and the 'Structuralist' Analysis of Everyday Life." *American Sociological Review* 42:854–868.

Gordon, Steven. 1981. "The Sociology of Sentiments and Emotion." In Morris Rosenberg and Ralph H. Turner, eds., *Social Psychology: Sociological Perspectives.* New York: Basic Books.

Gouldner, Alvin. 1970. *The Coming Crisis of Western Sociology.* New York: Basic.

Gove, Walter, ed. 1975. *The Labelling of Deviance.* New York: Wiley.

Gross, Edward. 1986. "The Social Construction of Historical Events Through Public Dramas." *Symbolic Interaction* 9:179–200.

Gross, Edward, and Gregory Stone. 1964. "Embarrassment and the Analysis of Role Requirements." *American Journal of Sociology* 70:1–15.

Gusfield, Joseph. 1976. "The Literary Rhetoric of Science: Comedy and Pathos in Drinking Driver Research." *American Sociological Review* 41:16–33.

Gusfield, Joseph. 1981. *The Culture of Public Problems.* Chicago: University of Chicago Press.

Habermas, Jürgen. 1984. *The Theory of Communicative Action.* Vol. I. Boston: Beacon Press.

Habermas, Jürgen. 1987. *The Theory of Communicative Action.* Vol. II. Boston: Beacon Press.

Haferkamp, Hans. 1987a. "Beyond the Iron Cage of Modernity? Achievement, Negotiations and Changes in the Power Structure." *Theory, Culture and Society* 4:31–54.

Haferkamp, Hans. 1987b. "Interactionist Theory in the Federal Republic of Germany." *Symbolic Interaction* 10:143–165.

Hall, Peter. 1987. "Interactionism and the Study of Social Organization." *The Sociological Quarterly* 28:1–22.

Helle, Horst J. 1985. "The Classic Foundations of Micro-Sociological Paradigms."

In H. J. Helle and S. N. Eisenstadt, eds., *Micro-Sociological Theory*. Beverly Hills: Sage.

Hewitt, John. 1976. *Self and Society*. Boston: Allyn and Bacon.

Hewitt, John, and Randall Stokes. 1975. "Disclaimers." *American Sociological Review* 40:1–11.

Hirsch, Paul M. 1972. "Processing Fads and Fashions: An Organization-Set Analysis of Cultural Industry Systems." *American Journal of Sociology* 77:639–659.

Hochschild, Arlie. 1979. "Emotion Work, Feeling Rules, and Social Structure." *American Journal of Sociology* 35:551–573.

Hochschild, Arlie. 1983. *The Managed Heart*. Berkeley: University of California Press.

Huber, Joan. 1973. "Symbolic Interaction as a Pragmatic Perspective: The Bias of Emergent Theory." *American Sociological Review* 38:278–284.

Hughes, Everett. 1971. *The Sociological Eye*. Chicago: Aldine.

James, William. 1890. *The Principles of Psychology*. New York: Holt.

Joas, Hans. 1985. *G. H. Mead*. Cambridge: MIT Press.

Johnson, G. David, and J. Steven Picou. 1985. "The Foundations of Symbolic Interactionism Reconsidered." In H. J. Helle and S. N. Eisenstadt, eds., *Micro-Sociological Theory*. Beverly Hills: Sage.

Johnson, John. 1975. *Doing Field Research*. New York: Free Press.

Jones, Robert Alun. 1977. "On Understanding a Sociological Classic." *American Journal of Sociology* 83:279–319.

Kahne, M. J., and C. G. Schwartz. 1978. "Negotiating Trouble: The Social Construction and Management of Trouble in a College Psychiatric Context." *Social Problems* 25:461–475.

Kalab, Kathleen A. 1987. "Student Vocabularies of Motive: Accounts for Absence." *Symbolic Interaction* 10:71–83.

Kamens, David H. 1977. "Legitimating Myth and Educational Organization: The Relationship Between Organizational Ideology and Formal Structure." *American Sociological Review* 42:208–219.

Kealy, Edward. 1982. "Conventions and the Production of Popular Culture." *Journal of Popular Culture* 16:100–115.

Kemper, Theodore. 1978. *A Social Interactional Theory of Emotions*. New York: Wiley.

Kemper, Theodore. 1987. "How Many Emotions Are There? Wedding the Social and the Autonomic Components." *American Journal of Sociology* 93:263–289.

Kleinman, Sherryl. 1984. *Equals Before God*. Chicago: University of Chicago Press.

Kleinman, Sherryl, and Gary Alan Fine. 1979. "Rhetorics and Action in Moral Organization: Social Control of Little Leaguers and Ministry Students." *Urban Life* 8:275–294.

Kuhn, Manfred H., and Thomas S. McPartland. 1954. "An Empirical Investigation of Self-Attitudes." *American Sociological Review* 19:68–77.

Labov, William. 1972a. *Language in the Inner City*. Philadelphia: University of Pennsylvania Press.

Labov, William. 1972b. *Sociolinguistic Patterns*. Philadelphia: University of Pennsylvania Press.

Lewis, J. David, and Richard L. Smith. 1980. *American Sociology and Pragmatism*. Chicago: University of Chicago Press.

Lieberson, Stanley. 1985. *Making It Count*. Berkeley: University of California Press.

Liebow, Elliott. 1967. *Tally's Corner*. Boston: Little, Brown.

Lofland, John. 1966. *Doomsday Cult*. Englewood Cliffs, N.J.: Prentice-Hall.

Lofland, John. 1988. "Interaction as Anarchism." *SSSI Notes* 14:5–6.

Loseke, Donileen. 1987. "Lived Realities and the Construction of Social Problems: The Case of Wife Abuse." *Symbolic Interaction* 10:229–243.

Lyman, Stanford M. 1988. "Le Conte, Royce, Teggart, Blumer: A Berkeley Dialogue on Sociology, Social Change, and Symbolic Interaction." *Symbolic Interaction* 11:125–143.

Lyon, Eleanor. 1974. "Work and Play: Resource Constraints in a Small Theatre." *Urban Life* 3:71–97.

McPhail, Clark, and David Miller. 1973. ""The Assembling Process: A Theoretical and Empirical Examination." *American Sociological Review* 38:721–735.

McPhail, Clark, and Cynthia Rexroat. 1979. "Mead vs. Blumer: The Divergent Perspectives of Social Behaviorism and Symbolic Interactionism." *American Sociological Review* 44:449–467.

Maines, David R. 1977. "Social Organization and Social Structure in Symbolic Interactionist Thought." *Annual Review of Sociology* 3:235–259.

Maines, David. 1982. "In Search of Mesostructure: Studies in the Negotiated Order." *Urban Life* 11:267–279.

Maines, David. 1988. "Myth, Text, and Interactionist Complicity in the Neglect of Blumer's Macrosociology." *Symbolic Interaction* 11:43–57.

Manning. P. K. 1978. "Editor's Remarks." *Urban Life* 7:283–284.

Manning, P. K. 1979. "Metaphors of the Field: Varieties of Organizational Discourse." *Administrative Science Quarterly* 24:660–671.

Mead, George. 1934. *Mind, Self and Society.* Chicago: University of Chicago Press.

Messenger, Sheldon E., Harold Sampson, and Robert D. Towne. 1962. "Life as Theater: Some Notes on the Dramaturgic Approach to Social Reality." *Sociometry* 25:98–110.

Miller, David. 1973. *George Herbert Mead: Self, Language and the World.* Austin: University of Texas Press.

Miller, Gale. 1983. "Holding Clients Accountable: The Micro-Politics of Trouble in a Work Incentive Program." *Social Problems* 31:139–151.

Mills, C. Wright. 1940. "Situated Actions and Vocabularies of Motive." *American Sociological Review* 5:904–913.

Mitroff, Ian, and Ralph Kilmann. 1976. "On Organizational Stories: An Approach to the Design and Analysis of Organizations Through Myths and Stories." In Ralph H. Kilmann and D. P. Slevin, eds., *The Management of Organizational Design.* New York: Elsevier.

Molotch, Harvey, and Deirdre Boden. 1985. "Talking Social Structure: Discourse, Domination, and the Watergate Hearings." *American Sociological Review* 50:173–88.

Molseed, Mari J. 1987. "The Problem of Temporality in the Work of Georg Simmel." *Sociological Quarterly* 28:357–366.

Mukerji, Chandra. 1976. "Having the Authority to Know: Decision-Making on Student Film Crews." *Sociology of Work and Occupations* 3:63–87.

Mukerji, Chandra. 1977. "Film Games." *Symbolic Interaction* 1:20–31.

Mukerji, Chandra. 1983. *From Graven Images: Patterns of Modern Materialism.* New York: Columbia University Press.

Mullins, Nicholas. 1973. *Theories and Theory Groups in Contemporary American Sociology.* New York: Harper and Row.

Mullins, Nicholas. 1983. "Theories and Theory Groups Revisited." In Randall Collins, ed., *Sociological Theory 1983.* San Francisco: Jossey-Bass.

Natanson, Maurice. 1973. *The Social Dynamics of George H. Mead.* The Hague: Martinus Nijhoff.

Ouchi, William G., and Alan L. Wilkins. 1985. "Organizational Culture." *Annual Review of Sociology* 11:457–483.

154 *Gary Alan Fine*

Paine, Robert. 1968. "Gossip and Transaction." *Man* 3:305–308.
Parsons, Talcott. 1975. "Comment" [on Turner and Blumer]. *Sociological Inquiry* 45:62–65.
Perinbanayagam, Robert. 1974. "The Definition of the Situation: An Analysis of the Dramaturgical and Ethnomethodological View." *The Sociological Quarterly* 15:521–541.
Peterson, Richard A. 1979. "Revitalizing the Culture Concept." *Annual Review of Sociology* 5:137–166.
Pettigrew, Andrew M. 1979. "On Studying Organizational Culture." *Administrative Science Quarterly* 24:570–581.
Peyrot, Mark. 1982. "Caseload Management: Choosing Suitable Clients in a Community Health Clinic Agency." *Social Problems* 30:157–167.
Pfeffer, Jeffrey. 1981. "Management as Symbolic Action: The Creation and Maintenance of Organizational Paradigms." In L. L. Cummings and B. M. Staw, eds., *Research in Organizational Behavior*. Vol. 3. Greenwich, Conn.: JAI Press.
Psathas, George. 1979. *Everyday Language*. New York: Irvington.
Rabinow, Paul. 1977. *Reflections on Fieldwork in Morocco*. Berkeley: University of California Press.
Rawls, Anne W. 1985. "Reply to Gallant and Kleinman on Symbolic Interactionism vs. Ethnomethodology." *Symbolic Interaction* 8:121–140.
Ray, Melvin C., and Ronald L. Simons. 1987. "Convicted Murderers' Accounts of Their Crimes: A Study of Homicide in Small Communities." *Symbolic Interaction* 10:57–70.
Ritzer, George. 1975. *Sociology: A Multiple Paradigm Science*. Boston: Allyn and Bacon.
Ritzer, George. 1985. "The Rise of Micro-Sociological Theory." *Sociological Theory* 3:88–98.
Rochberg-Halton, Eugene. 1987. *Meaning and Modernity*. Chicago: University of Chicago Press.
Rock, Paul. 1979. *The Making of Symbolic Interaction*. London: Macmillan.
Rosenberg, Morris. 1979. *Conceiving the Self*. New York: Basic Books.
Rosenberg, Morris. 1981. "The Self-Concept: Social Product and Social Force." In Morris Rosenberg and Ralph H. Turner, eds., *Social Psychology: Sociological Perspectives*. New York: Basic Books.
Rosenblum, Barbara. 1978. *Photographers at Work*. New York: Holmes and Meier.
Rosnow, Ralph, and Gary Alan Fine. 1976. *Rumor and Gossip: The Social Psychology of Hearsay*. New York: Elsevier.
Roy, Donald. 1952. "Quota Restriction and Goldbricking in a Machine Shop." *American Journal of Sociology* 57:427–442.
Roy, Donald. 1954. "Efficiency and the Fix: Informal Intergroup Relations in a Piecework Machine Shop." *American Journal of Sociology* 60:255–266.
Roy, Donald. 1959–1960. "Banana Time: Job Satisfaction and Informal Interaction." *Human Organization* 18:156–168.
Sacks, Harvey. 1974. "An Analysis of the Course of a Joke's Telling in Conversation." In R. Bauman and J. Sherzer, eds., *Explorations in the Ethnography of Speaking*. Cambridge: Cambridge University Press.
Sacks, Harvey, Emmanuel Schegloff, and Gail Jefferson. 1974. "A Simplest Systematics for the Organization of Turn-Taking for Conversation." *Language* 50:696–735.
Sapir, Edward. 1949. *Selected Writings in Language, Culture, and Personality*. Berkeley: University of California Press.
Schachter, Stanley, and Jerome Singer. 1962. "Cognitive, Social and Physiological Determinants of Emotional States." *Psychological Review* 69:379–399.

Schwartz, Barry. 1983. "George Washington and the Whig Conception of Heroic Leadership." *American Sociological Review* 48:18–33.

Schwartz, Barry. 1987. *George Washington: The Making of an American Symbol.* New York: Free Press.

Schwartz, Barry, Yael Zerubavel, and Bernice Barnett. 1986. "The Recovery of Masada: A Study in Collective Memory." *Sociological Quarterly* 27:147–164.

Sciulli, David. 1988. "Reconsidering Blumer's Corrective Against the Excesses of Functionalism." *Symbolic Interaction* 11:69–84.

Scott, Marvin, and Stanford Lyman. 1968. "Accounts." *American Sociological Review* 33:46–62.

Scully, Diana, and Joseph Marolla. 1984. "Convicted Rapists' Vocabulary of Motive: Excuses and Justifications." *Social Problems* 31:530–544.

Shalin, Dmitri N. 1984. "The Romantic Antecedents of Meadian Social Psychology." *Symbolic Interaction* 7:43–65.

Shalin, Dmitri. 1986. "Pragmatism and Social Interactionism." *American Sociological Review* 51:9–29.

Shalin, Dmitri. 1987. "Socialism, Democracy and Reform: A Letter and an Article by George H. Mead." *Symbolic Interaction* 10:267–278.

Shibutani, Tamotsu. 1966. *Improvised News.* Indianapolis: Bobbs-Merrill.

Shott, Susan. 1979. "Emotion and Social Life: A Symbolic Interactionist Analysis." *American Journal of Sociology* 84:1317–1334.

Simmel, Georg. 1950. *The Sociology of Georg Simmel.* New York: Free Press.

Smith, Victoria. 1987. "Corporate Culture or Corporate Control: The Politics of Managing Corporate Reorganization." Paper presented to the American Sociological Association, Chicago.

Snow, David A., E. Burke Rochford, Jr., Steven K. Worden, and Robert D. Benford. 1986. "Frame Alignment Processes, Micromobilization and Movement Participation." *American Sociological Review.* 51:464–481.

Spector, Malcolm, and John I. Kitsuse. 1977. *Constructing Social Problems.* New York: Aldine.

Stearns, Peter N. 1987. "The Problem of Change in Emotions Research: New Standards for Anger in Twentieth-Century American Childrearing." *Symbolic Interaction* 10:85–99.

Stewart, Robert L. 1981. "What George Mead Should Have Said: Exploration of a Problem of Interpretation." *Symbolic Interaction* 4:157–166.

Stone, Gregory, and Harvey Farberman. 1967. "On the Edge of Rapprochement: Was Durkheim Moving Toward the Perspective of Symbolic Interaction?" *Sociological Quarterly* 8:149–164.

Stone, Gregory, and Harvey Farberman. 1970. *Social Psychology Through Symbolic Interaction.* Waltham, Mass.: Ginn-Blaisdell.

Strauss, Anselm. 1959. *Mirrors and Masks.* Glencoe, Ill.: Free Press.

Strauss, Anselm. 1987. *Qualitative Analysis for Social Scientists.* New York: Cambridge University Press.

Strauss, Anselm, L. Schatzman, D. Ehrlich, R. Bucher, and M. Sabshin. 1963. "The Hospital and its Negotiated Order. In E. Friedson, ed., *The Hospital in Modern Society.* New York: Free Press.

Strauss, Anselm, Leonard Schatzman, Rue Bucher, D. Erlich, and M. Sabshin. 1964. *Psychiatric Ideologies and Institutions.* Glencoe, Ill.: Free Press.

Stryker, Sheldon. 1957. "Role-Taking Accuracy and Adjustment." *Sociometry* 20:286–296.

Stryker, Sheldon. 1968. "Identity, Salience and Role Performance: The Relevance of Symbolic Interaction Theory for Family Research." *Journal of Marriage and the Family* 30:558–564.

Stryker, Sheldon. 1980. *Symbolic Interactionism: A Social Structural Version.* Reading, Mass.: Cummings.

Stryker, Sheldon. 1981. "Symbolic Interactionism: Themes and Variations." In Morris Rosenberg and Ralph H. Turner, eds., *Social Psychology: Sociological Perspectives.* New York: Basic.

Stryker, Sheldon. 1988. "Substance and Style: An Appraisal of the Sociological Legacy of Herbert Blumer." *Symbolic Interaction* 11:33–42.

Szwed, John F. 1966. "Gossip, Drinking, and Social Control: Consensus and Communication in a Newfoundland Parish." *Ethnology* 5:434–441.

Tejera, V. 1986. "Community, Communication, and Meanings: Theories of Buchler and Habermas." *Symbolic Interaction* 9:83–104.

Truzzi, Marcello. 1974. *Verstehen: Subjective Understanding in the Social Sciences.* Reading, Mass.: Addison-Wesley.

Tucker, Charles. 1988. "Herbert Blumer: A Pilgrimage with Pragmatism." *Symbolic Interaction* 11:99–124.

Turner, Jonathan H. 1974. "Parsons as a Symbolic Interactionist: A Comparison of Action and Interaction Theory." *Sociological Inquiry* 44:283–294.

Turner, Ralph. 1976. "The Real Self: From Institution to Impulse." *American Journal of Sociology* 81:989–1016.

Turner, Ralph. 1978. "Role and the Person." *American Journal of Sociology* 84:1–23.

Turner, Ralph, and Lewis Killian. 1972. *Collective Behavior.* Englewood Cliffs, N.J.: Prentice-Hall.

Turner, Stephen. 1987. "Underdetermination and the Promise of Statistical Sociology." *Sociological Theory* 5:172–184.

Unruh, David. 1979. "Characteristics and Types of Participation in Social Worlds." *Symbolic Interaction* 2:115–129.

Van Maanen, John. 1988. *Tales From the Field.* Chicago: University of Chicago Press.

Vester, Heinz-Günther. 1987. "Adventure as a Form of Leisure." *Leisure Research* 6:237–249.

Vidich, Arthur J., and Joseph Bensman. 1968. *Small Town in Mass Society.* Rev. ed. Princeton: Princeton University Press.

Wanderer, Jules. 1987. "Simmel's Forms of Experiencing: The Adventure as Symbolic Work." *Symbolic Interaction* 10:21–28.

Weick, Karl. 1976. "Educational Organizations as Loosely Coupled Systems." *Administrative Science Quarterly* 21:1–19.

Weinstein, Eugene A., and Paul Deutschberger. 1963. "Some Dimensions of Altercasting." *Sociometry* 26:454–466.

Wellman, David. 1988. "The Politics of Herbert Blumer's Sociological Method." *Symbolic Interaction* 11:59–68.

West, Candace. 1984. *Routine Complications.* Bloomington: Indiana University Press.

West, James. 1945. *Plainville, U.S.A.* New York: Columbia University Press.

Whorf, Benjamin. 1956. *Language, Thought and Reality.* Cambridge: MIT Press.

Whyte, William Foote. 1943. *Street Corner Society.* Chicago: University of Chicago Press.

Wolf, Charlotte. 1986. "Legitimation of Oppression: Response and Reflexivity." *Symbolic Interaction* 9:217–234.

Wolff, Janet. 1981. *The Social Production of Art.* New York: St. Martin's.

Zerubavel, Eviatar. 1979. *Patterns of Time in Hospital Life.* Chicago: University of Chicago Press.

Zerubavel, Eviatar. 1980. "If Simmel Were a Fieldworker: On Formal Sociological Theory and Analytical Field Research." *Symbolic Interaction* 3:25–33.

Zerubavel, Eviatar. 1981. *Hidden Rhythms.* Chicago: University of Chicago Press.

Zerubavel, Eviatar. 1987. "The Language of Time: Toward a Semiotics of Temporality." *Sociological Quarterly* 28:343–356.

Zimmerman, Don. 1978. "Ethnomethodology." *American Sociologist* 13:6–15.

Zimmerman, Don, and Candace West. 1975. "Sex Roles, Interruptions, and Silences in Conversation." In Barrie Thorne and Nancy Henley, eds., *Language and Sex: Differences and Dominance.* Rowley, Mass.: Newbury House.

Zurcher, Louis. 1977. *The Mutable Self.* Beverly Hills: Sage.

Zurcher, Louis A. 1986. "The Bureaucratizing of Impulse: Self-Conception in the 1980s." *Symbolic Interaction* 9:169–178.

6

Exchange Theory: A Blueprint for Structure and Process

❀

KAREN S. COOK, JODI O'BRIEN, AND PETER KOLLOCK
University of Washington

EXCHANGE THEORY AS A CONCEPTUAL FRAMEWORK

Exchange theory is a well-established approach to the study of social processes and structures in the social sciences. The intellectual history of the theory is a long one and incorporates several diverse traditions. As Turner (1986, 215) notes: "I find current exchange theories to be a curious and unspecified mixture of utilitarian economics, functional anthropology, conflict sociology, and behavioral psychology." While there are numerous ways to distinguish each of these traditions, we wish to direct our attention to the commonalities between them in setting forth exchange theory as a unique conceptual approach to the study of social phenomena.

A central feature of exchange theory is the observation that exchange processes are ubiquitous. For example, the anthropologist Malinowski (1922) describes a circle of exchange relations among the Trobriand Islanders known as the Kula ring. This form of symbolic exchange served to reaffirm and support the complex network of trade existing between the islands according to Malinowski's explanation. Utilitarian economists, beginning with Adam Smith, view all interactions between actors as transactions in which each party seeks to meet its needs through exchange with some other party. The work of the economist Gary Becker (1976, 1981) on such topics as racial prejudice, crime, and the family demonstrates the utility of this approach in

Work on this paper was supported by a National Science Foundation grant (SES 85-11117).

arenas commonly assumed to be beyond the scope of economic analysis. At the global level, world systems theories in sociology conceive of international relations as exchanges between interdependent countries. At the individual level, social psychologists have analyzed intimate relationships profitably by focusing on each partner's transactions with the other as a means of meeting their personal needs (e.g., Kelley 1979, 1986; Kelley et al. 1983).

Whether it be a husband and wife negotiating who will fix dinner, two business partners negotiating a new contract, or two nations engaged in the exchange of hostages for arms, exchange relations are an integral part of the social phenomena that we as social scientists are interested in explaining. Exchange theory focuses attention on the relationships *between* interconnected actors, be they individuals, corporations or nation-states, rather than represent actors as isolated entities. Embedded in these relations are other social processes of interest to exchange theorists—processes like the exercise of power and influence, the potential for coalition formation and other power-gaining strategies, the normative aspects of exchange, especially conceptions of fairness and unfairness, inequalities in the distribution of resources and perceptions of the legitimacy of power.

As our examples indicate, the exchange framework has been used at various levels of analysis in different fields of inquiry which cross disciplinary boundaries. Fields of inquiry include dyadic relations, families, small groups, organizations, interorganizational relations, political-economic relations, economic relations, and international trade relations, among others. Levels of analysis include dyads, groups, networks, corporate actors, firms, markets, and nation-states. There are many names associated with the development of exchange theory. Anthropologists, as noted above, have made major contributions to this theoretical framework. They include, most prominently, Malinowski, Mauss, and Levi-Strauss.[1] In sociology, the models of exchange discussed in texts and readers most commonly reference three key theorists: Homans, Blau, and Emerson. While there are other important contributors, these three theorists in particular are credited with the development and articulation of the model. Homans, Blau, and Emerson each offer distinctive versions of the theory. The focus for this chapter, however, will be on their shared conception of social phenomena as a product of exchange relations.[2]

Coleman (1986a, 1987a) argues that to have a complete picture of social reality a theory needs to address three central problems: individual action; how actions aggregate to produce social structures; and how these structures in turn impact future actions. Exchange theory addresses each of these points. The applicability of exchange theory is not limited to relations between two actors (be they individuals or corporate entities). These dyadic relations are embedded in larger networks of relations which have significant implications for all of these social processes. Structure is conceived, according to exchange theory, as the interconnection of various positions in an exchange network. Framed this way, exchange theory can illuminate not only the behavior of actors, but the structures that emerge as the result of these exchange relations. Furthermore, by focusing on a given structure or social institution, exchange theory provides an explanation both for the behavior of actors within the structure and for changes in the structure itself.

Within sociology, exchange theory has developed along these two somewhat distinct lines: one tradition focuses on social behavior, the other on social structure. In the remainder of this section, we will emphasize these two distinct traditions in a brief outline of the basic elements of exchange theory. The second section will discuss current trends in the development of exchange theory, future directions, and the implications of each of these trends. In addition, general theoretical concerns that have arisen from this work will be addressed. One significant aspect of the exchange perspective is its potential contribution to the ongoing dialogue concerning how to link micro and macro levels of inquiry. This issue is the focus of the third section. We conclude with a brief discussion of the future of exchange theory.

Social Behavior as Exchange

The ubiquity of exchange processes points to the importance of incorporating these concepts into the analysis of both social behavior and structure. The theoretical tradition that treats social behavior and social interaction as exchange is most commonly associated with Homans' early work. For Homans (1958, 1961), interacting individuals are the building blocks, the "sub-institutional" level that must be understood before we can arrive at a complete understanding of society and the structure of social relations at the organizational and institutional levels. Homans conceives behavior in its most elementary form as an attempt to gain rewards while avoiding costs and punishment. People enter into interactions that are rewarding while avoiding punishing interactions. Society is then conceived as a product of these exchange interactions, or "sub-institutional" building blocks.

Homans emphasizes behavioral psychology as the basis for exchange behavior. Emerson adopts this framework in his early work (1969, 1972a, 1972b). Blau (1964) and Coleman (1972) from the beginning adopt a rational-choice model of behavior, which is also apparent in

Homans' revised edition (1974) and the later work of Emerson in conjunction with Cook (Emerson 1976, 1981). The key differences in these formulations have to do with the underlying psychology of the process, not their models of interaction, on which they tend to agree.[3] The model of interaction developed by each of these theorists views social interaction as a process involving the exchange or directed flow of valued resources over time in social relations. The primary unit of analysis is not the actor, but the social relations between actors.

This perspective has been applied to a large number of substantive areas. For example, in social and personal relationships, Kelley and Thibaut (1978; Kelley 1979) have constructed a powerful and elegant model that details the patterns of interdependence between two actors and the various dimensions that underlie those patterns. Kelley (1986, 15) has even argued that such seemingly psychological attributes as interpersonal traits are actually the result of patterns of interdependence within the relationship and the problems of exchange that flow from those patterns: "Theoretical analysis of the patterns of interdependence reveals the major features of interpersonal disposition. Were there not conflicts of interest, unequal dependence, exchange and coordination problems, there would be no need for the domain of interpersonal dispositions to ever come into existence. In a world of high but bland interdependence (interdependence without problems), love, dominance, competitiveness would have no meaning." Similarly, Berscheid (1983, 1985) has used the patterns of interdependence and exchange between two partners to explain the emotional tenor of their relationship.

The extensive research by Hatfield and her colleagues (Hatfield et al. 1979, 1985; Hatfield and Traupmann 1981) has demonstrated that intimate couples are very concerned with the rates of exchange in their relationship and whether or not those rates are equitable. Couples who perceive their relationship as equitable are significantly more satisfied and their relationship is likely to be more stable. Deutsch (1975) and Clark and Mills (1979; Clark 1985; Mills and Clark 1982) have shown that the rules actors use to evaluate the fairness of rates of exchange will differ depending on the type of relationship. Within a family, for example, the distribution of valued resources is more likely to be based on individual need rather than the amount one has contributed to the production of the resources. Personal relationships are also likely to have looser "accounting systems" which allow actors the luxury of not immediately repaying their partners when they become indebted. Along these lines, Murstein et al. (1977) and O'Connell (1984) have researched the character and benefits of looser and more generalized systems of exchange.

In each case the focus of attention has been on the *relationship* between two actors. Patterns of interdependence or rates of exchange are properties of relationships, not actors. Indeed, this line of research, i.e., exchange theory, turns an old tradition on its head: rather than try to explain the nature of a relationship as the result of qualities within the actors, this research explains the qualities of the actors by exploring the nature of the relationship.

Social Structure as Exchange

The second major focus of work in exchange theory is on social structure and sources of structural change. Not only is social interaction viewed as an exchange process, but these interactions are asserted in exchange theory to be the fundamental basis for social structure. It is the repetitive aspect of exchange which results in patterned social interactions that become institutionalized over time (e.g., as friendship relations, marriage relations, informal and formal relations within organizational settings, political alliances or coalitions, international trade relations, etc.).

Anthropologists are credited with being the first to conceive of exchange as the basis for structure and order. As early as 1919, Sir James Frazer applied an exchange framework to the understanding of marriage and political practices in primitive societies (Turner 1986). Through subsequent decades anthropologists have debated the extent to which social structure is the result of exchange relations based on individual utility versus the social solidarity produced by exchange relations. For example, Sahlins (1972) and Barth (1966) both offer models of social organization based on utilitarian exchange. Alternately, Mauss (1966) and Malinowski (1922) view social structure as a product of the solidarity produced through symbolic exchange.[4] Despite these differences, there is nonetheless a long-standing agreement that exchange plays an integral role in the understanding of societies and cultures. As Macneil (1986) points out, the relationship between systems of generalized exchange (e.g., symbolic exchange and gift giving) and exchange based on individual utility is symbiotic; both are necessary for understanding social structure.

Sociologists have taken up the theme of exchange in explanations of social structure and change, some more explicitly than others. Several have recognized the need to focus on the strategic interactions of intentional actors in studying the formation of institutional structures and norms (e.g., Coleman 1986a, 1986b, 1988; Hechter 1983, 1987; Shapiro 1987; Wippler and Lindenberg 1987). The task is how to represent the relationship between actor and social structure and to conceptualize structure in a dynamic way that can account for individual action in accordance with existing structural constraints. Exchange theory provides a theoretical model of action. More importantly, because exchange theory focuses on the relations between actors, structure can be conceived in terms of extended links between interconnected parties. This allows for a dynamic view of structure conceived in terms of actors' connections vis-à-vis one another and the flow of resources between them, including symbolic resources such as status and information. This implies, for example, that a given structure can change with the addition or deletion of one or more exchange partners, or a change in the amount or flow of resources. These changes then have subsequent effects on both the structure and the actors.

Coleman, in both his theoretical work on social structure and norms (e.g., 1986a, 1986b, 1987a, 1988) and his research on collective action (e.g., 1973) acknowledges the role of exchange theory. Many researchers studying the maintenance and change of institutions and organizations apply exchange theoretic concepts without explicitly referencing the theory. This includes the work of Stinchcombe (1986) on organizations as information processing systems. Williamson (1981), Ben-Porath (1980), and Ouchi (1980) all address the structures that emerge as exchange partners deal with transaction costs. Shapiro (1987) focuses on the formation of trust in the exchange relationship between principals and agents in market settings. This line of research is not unique to economic institutions, and includes the study of symbolic and social institutions as well (e.g., Becker 1981; O'Brien 1988). Meeker (1971) addresses the issue of types of decision rules (e.g., reciprocity, altruism, or competition) in exchange relations. She constructs a theory to explain how these exchange rules operate as institutionalized norms. The analysis of social institutions, such as kinship structures, polities, and religion, is especially strong in the work by anthropologists on generalized exchange.[5]

Many concepts borrowed from the study of generalized exchange creep into sociological analyses of households, the family, and political institutions. Heath (1976), for example, argues that Merton's analysis of the latent and manifest functions of local politics conceives the political machine in terms of an exchange between the wants and needs of local voters and political entrepreneurs who agree to meet these needs when other legitimate institutions are unable to do so. Gouldner (cited in Heath 1976) notes that while Merton can point to the demand for the political machine's services, he fails to provide an account of "the feedback through which the groups whose needs are satisfied by the political machine in turn 'reciprocate' and repay the machine for the services received from it" (102). Gouldner (1960) grapples with this problem in his work on the norm of reciprocity. Heath (1976) concludes that Gouldner also falls short of the mark because he fails to specify why each party to the exchange (in this case local voters and political institutions) sees it as the best alternative. A transaction analysis of social structure was not Gouldner's intent, however. Had it been, he might indeed have focused on the need to specify alternatives in determining the reasons for each party's involvement in the exchange relations that result in one type of social structure as opposed to others.

Many sociologists, in their attempts to construct rigorous models of social action and order (including both Gouldner and Merton) appear, as Heath points out, to hold an implicit conception of society in terms of social exchange. The dynamics of the social world are viewed in terms of reciprocity between individuals and institutions. However, and this is precisely the point, because they lack a theory of action, these structural theories of social institutions remain static; they fail to provide a complete explanation of the mechanisms involved. To extend Coleman's (1987b) metaphor, these theories provide a chassis but no engine. A major strength of exchange theory is that in making explicit the reciprocal nature of social interaction it provides a theoretical engine of action to power the chassis that is our understanding of social structure.

Central to the study of social exchange and structure are the concepts of power and dependence. The differentiation of social systems in terms of privilege and power and differential access to resources are topics of central concern to most exchange theorists. In *Exchange and Power in Social Life* (1964), Blau's focus is on institutionalized exchange networks in macrostructures as a basis for explaining social order. Blau's primary objective was to build a theory of social organization on the basis of social exchange relations. Blau later abandoned this pursuit with the conclusion that exchange theory cannot adequately cope with the properties of populations and collectivities (Blau, referenced in Turner 1987). Others, including Turner, disagree with Blau's premature dismissal of exchange theory in favor of the more static structural concepts advanced in his book *Inequality and Heterogeneity* (1977). In Turner's (1987, 229) words:

> Questions of centrality, social circles, social classes, brokerage activity, density, and other topics in exchange-network analysis are more than merely "complementary" to Blau's view of macrostructural analysis in terms of parameters, inequality, and heterogeneity. Indeed, exchange-network analysis can offer a more precise specification of the *actual*

structure of inequality and heterogeneity. . . . It can inform us about the operative dynamics of the parameter itself, and the structure and dynamics of these parameters can be analyzed in terms of resources, exchange, dependence, power, and balancing.

Emerson's later work focuses almost entirely on power and dependence in exchange relations. Power is conceived in terms of structure, i.e., it emerges from the patterns of exchange relations or the way actors are linked to one another through access to resources. Social structure, then, is conceived as a series of interconnected positions in an exchange network. We will have more to say about the marriage of exchange theory and network analysis in sections two and three.

Among sociologists in general there is great interest in the transmission and maintenance of institutions of inequality, income distribution, status attainment, and discrimination. Exchange analysis provides a theoretical framework for understanding why power and resources accrue to some and not to others. In doing so the theory can account for both existing structures and individual actions. In addition, it has the potential for predicting change within these structures (e.g., Stolte and Emerson 1977; Stolte 1983; Cook et al. 1988). It can also explain how perceptions of equity and justice either support and maintain social institutions or lead to attempts to instigate social change (Della Fave 1980). Investigations of the mechanisms of social change include work on coalition formation (e.g., Cook and Gillmore 1984) and collective action (e.g., Coleman 1973; Olson 1965; Stroebe and Frey 1982; Yamagishi 1986). For a general review of the work on justice and equity processes from an exchange perspective, see Cook and Hegtvedt (1983).

With respect to exchange theory and social structure, it is important to emphasize that exchange theory focuses on the link between social relations and the strategic interdependent actions that form the basis for institutions and the changes in these institutions over time. Embedded in the theory is the idea that these structures are maintained for strategic and power-related reasons and not simply because they are enshrined in norms.[6] The theoretical orientation of exchange theory offers two main points of consideration in the analysis of social structure: the conception of social structure in terms of network relations paves the way for the formulation of more dynamic explanations of structure and change; in conjunction with this, exchange theory provides the basis for a theory of action, thus bringing social process back into explanations of structure. The unique conceptual grid that forms the basis of exchange theory offers new perspectives on the study of social behavior and structure. New research directions can be charted using conceptual and theoretical tools that have proven their utility throughout decades of research across the social sciences.

THE FUTURE OF EXCHANGE THEORY

Current Trends and Future Implications

Cook (1987) has argued that there are at least three distinct trends in current theory and research on exchange theory that are significant and likely to be the focus of activity in the next few years. One trend concerns methodological changes. Experimental laboratory studies have been the dominant research strategy for the past two decades (House 1977). Still the most productive methodology for exchange theorists, researchers are now developing more sophisticated experimental settings and procedures for examining exchange processes. Complementing the formal laboratory studies, more field research is being conducted on exchange processes in natural settings. This research is going on particularly in family, organizational, and community contexts, as well as more recently at the macro-political level (e.g., Galaskiewicz 1979; Fischer 1982; Marin 1987).

It is interesting to note the groundwork that forms the bulk of early exchange theory is the result of anthropological field studies. These studies in turn generated many of the theoretical propositions that have been evaluated in the laboratory over the past two decades. These laboratory advances are now directing attention back to the field for further empirical grounding. In addition to returning to the detailed studies of anthropologists, exchange theorists are beginning to recognize the potential contribution of contemporary field research and historical studies. This methodological trend represents a movement back and forth between the tightly controlled, if somewhat "sterile," atmosphere of the laboratory and the intractable richness of the field. Each method must build upon the other if theoretical advances are to be made along the way. The methodological history of exchange theory is a testament to this point.

An additional trend is the shift in substantive work away from the focus on dyadic analysis to the investigation of larger networks of exchange. Though there remain enormous opportunities for the further application of power-dependence/exchange principles in fundamentally dyadic situations (e.g., physician-patient interactions, where information transfer and control is a key issue and a recent topic of inquiry), much of the earlier work in exchange theory has been criticized as being applicable primarily to dyads. Current work on dyadic exchange, however, no longer focuses on these relations in isolation from larger exchange networks. Recent empirical research on exchange networks by Cook et al. (1983) and by others (e.g., Cook and Emerson 1978; Willer and Anderson 1981) moves beyond dyads to examine the structural properties of networks as determinants of exchange processes. For example, one set of experimental investigations in this tradition examines the nature of the relationship between centrality and the distribution of power in the network (e.g., Cook et al. 1983; Markovsky et al. 1988). This work provides an explicit theoretical interpretation of the link between structural centrality and power as well as a framework within which collective action (or coalition formation) can be understood in terms of the dynamics of structural change based on power-dependence reasoning. This work also demonstrates empirically the importance of investigating structural constraints on social interaction (i.e., the impact of the embeddedness of dyadic relations in larger network structures). Related to this trend is the renewed emphasis upon corporate actors as key actors in networks rather than natural persons (e.g., Laumann and Pappi 1976; Marin 1987; Coleman 1974). A complementary focus is the work of Molm (1981, 1985) on the differences between reward power and punishment power in exchange.

Third, and most significant from our perspective, is the explicit attempt to link exchange theory and research to recent developments in "structural sociology" more broadly. One of the most important efforts along these lines is the work linking exchange theory with current research on social networks, both network methods for representing social structure and empirical work investigating the impact of various properties of social networks. As Turner (1987, 237) puts it, "The continued merger of exchange and network analysis will be highly beneficial in making network analysis more theoretical and exchange theory more structural."

Yamagishi (1987) and Marsden (1987) both demonstrate ways in which this merger of exchange theory and network analysis provides new insights into social exchange processes. Yamagishi (1987), for example, clarifies important differences among the various conceptions of network position and discusses their theoretical implications. The residual network approach, he argues, is more consistent with the substantive theory of social exchange and suffers from fewer inconsistencies than the more standard relational approaches (e.g., Burt 1976) developed by network theorists. Marsden (1987) provides the general outlines of a synthesis between social exchange theory as applied to the analysis of collective decision making and social network analysis as a method. Marsden's (1987) work also suggests ways in which Emerson's (1972a, 1972b) notions of power and dependence link to Coleman's (1973) mathematical model of a system of action.

Exchange network concepts and principles focus attention on the structure of social relations (its causes and consequences). Unlike much of the social network research, however, this work is based on a coherent body of theory that gives substantive content to the nodes, edges paths, and semi-cycles that comprise these networks. The Kula ring, friendship relations, employee-employer contracts, spousal relations, and consumer-dealer transactions can all be represented as exchange relations within different types of network structures. Blau (1987, 86) states that exchange theory has great appeal precisely because "its basic ideas are widely applicable and give new meaning to everyday observations." Further development of exchange network theory will depend in part on the success of these efforts to integrate exchange notions with network structural principles.

Further Issues for Consideration

While there have been substantial advances, there are two key areas that require further elaboration for the continued development of exchange theory. First, a more complete model of the actor that addresses the cognitive complexities of decision making is required. Second is the question of value: what is it that actors want and how is value determined in exchange.

In our discussion of a more complete model of the actor we begin with a focus on decision theory. Exchange theory has an interest in decision theory, which also has interdisciplinary roots. This interest stems from the recognition that exchange models require a better understanding of the way actors make choices relevant to transactions. Traditionally, exchange theorists have relied on a rational choice model of decision making as elaborated in neoclassical economics. However, current work in decision theory and cognitive psychology, particularly by such researchers as Kahneman and Tversky (1982, 1984), Machina (1987), and others suggests that there are considerable limitations to this model. For example, Kahneman and Tversky (1984) demonstrate in a series of empirical studies that, while actors may desire to make rational decisions, it is often not possible for them to do so unless the choice is framed in a way that makes the most rational alternative easily discernible. In other words, it is sometimes cognitively too difficult for actors to figure out what is the most rational choice.

Whether or not actors do make conscious, calculated decisions continues to be a point of debate. The decisions and subsequent behavior of Homans' actor, in accordance with the propositions of operant conditioning, are nonconscious responses to reinforcers present in the environment. Such an actor is rooted completely in the past: "If an unbiased coin has come up heads on one trial, Homans' [actor] is apt to believe it will come up heads on the subsequent trial too" (Heath 1976, 14). In contrast, the rational actor found in the work of Blau and Coleman makes conscious deliberations about the best means to obtain specific goals. Emerson (1987) recognized that actors behave in response to both nonconscious reinforcers and the calculated weighing of alternatives. His last work was, in large part, an attempt to specify the choice domains to which rational decision theory applies and those to which it does not.

Given these issues, the task of integrating important new advances in rational choice and decision theories is a challenge to exchange theory (cf. Cook and O'Brien 1990). One area to which attention may be fruitfully directed is cognitive science. Advances in decision theory, cognitive anthropology, and artificial intelligence shed more light on the way in which actors perceive, process, and retrieve information (for examples of the application of recent concepts and techniques from cognitive science to sociological issues, see Fararo and Skvoretz 1984; Carley 1986; Kollock 1988; Majeski 1990). This information is necessary for exchange theorists in developing a more complete model of why people make the choices they do in exchange transactions.

Connected to the question of how people make choices is the question of what they value. Exchange theory, or at least much of the empirical work derived from it, has focused too narrowly on specific classes of resources (typically those with monetary value). This is more than a measurement issue. The exchange model cannot tell us what people value; to say that they value what they exchange and exchange what they value is a tautology, hence independent knowledge of value is required. What it is that is exchanged in social relations is a question that must be addressed for every transaction. The type of resources exchanged in social relations include the transmission of information and symbolic resources as well as material resources.

There are two possible approaches to this question. One requires that a separate set of auxiliary assumptions regarding what it is that actors value be specified, independent of the exchange analysis. In other words, if we were to fruitfully analyze the Kwakiutl from an exchange perspective, it would be necessary to have separate information regarding their cultural valuation of status as an exchange resource. A second approach involves the attempt to arrive at a sociologically relevant theory of value. Emerson (1987) took up this task but did not complete it before his death. According to Emerson, "[Exchange] analysis is either hampered or rendered meaningless without some attention to the interpersonal comparison of benefits from exchange. Such comparison requires a concept of subjective value or utility possessing a nonarbitrary origin and unit of measure" (Emerson 1987, 12). The development of a general, deductive theory of value is an ambitious task, but one that Emerson felt would greatly enhance the overall applicability of exchange theory. Notions of exchange domain and need as a determinant of resource value are important in field investigations in which the researcher must first tackle the problem of determining what the relevant resources are in the exchange relations or system under examination.[7]

In addition to addressing the issues of decision making and value, exchange theory could be further enhanced through a dialogue with current developments in symbolic interactionism. For example, exchange theory is found wanting in its consideration of transaction costs in general and information costs in particular. An actor may, for example, choose to remain in a long-standing exchange relationship when better alternatives appear to exist. Commitment as a rational strategy is addressed both in economic and exchange theories (e.g., Ben-Porath 1980; Cook and Emerson 1978, 1984). However, these theories cannot explain fully how it is that actors signal their intentions to one another. This is particularly important in understanding how it is that trust and commitment become significant aspects of exchange relations. Exchange theory does not adequately address this question despite the common occurrence of this situation in everyday life (for an extended example, *see* Macaulay 1963). Given the inability of actors to assess directly the character and likely exchange strategies of potential transaction partners, symbolic interactionism provides crucial information concerning how actors signal one another as to their intentions. This knowledge rounds out the model of why parties to an exchange choose the partners they do and why they become committed to long-term exchange relations.

A final and highly significant trend concerns the theoretical contribution of exchange theory to the recent dialogue concerning what has been labeled "the link" between microprocesses and macrostructure. This is the focus of the last section of this paper.

THE MICRO-MACRO QUESTION

Coleman (1987a, 154) states that "a central intellectual problem in the discipline is the movement from the individual level, where observations are made, to the systemic level. . . . This has been called the 'micro-to-macro problem' and it is a problem that is pervasive in the social sciences generally." The question for Coleman and many other social theorists interested in the relations between microprocesses and macrostructures is, in part, a question of transformation: how is individual level social behavior transformed into collective phenomena. Coleman (1987a, 157), by way of example, summarizes the problems involved in several explanations of collective outcomes such as revolutions: "A simple aggregation of individual level aggression [is] somehow to magically produce a social product. Yet this bypasses important social processes: A revolution involves organization and the interplay of actions on the part of a number of actors."

Simple aggregation procedures have long been demonstrated to produce failures in prediction at the collective level (e.g., the case of arriving at collective decisions through voting procedures). Different decision-rules in these contexts produce different kinds of "collective irrationalities," Coleman (1987a) points out. The lesson to be learned for those concerned with micro-to-macro transitions is that simple aggregation procedures based on individual preferences (i.e., expressed as votes) and particular decision rules (e.g., majority rules or some other political "institution") do not provide adequate explanation of the macro-level outcome.

An additional debate concerns the issue of reductionism, the central argument being that macrostructures are not reducible to micro-level components. However, as Alexander and Giesen (1987) point out, the question of reductionism is a byproduct of early dialogues in sociological theory which focused on arguments concerning the ontological primacy of either individuals or social structures. These "conflated dichotomies" were misleading, and resulted in an overemphasis on the question of "whether social order was negotiated between individuals or imposed by collective, or emergent, forces" (Alexander and Giesen 1987, 2). The relationship between individuals and society is a reciprocal one. To continue to debate the ontological primacy between them is no longer productive: "The conflict over reduction is replaced by the search for linkage" (3).

The theme of micro-macro linkages has gained momentum recently in sociology. It is precisely the reemergence of this theme that we believe will continue to fuel interest in exchange theory and research. There are two primary reasons. First, the effort to link levels of analysis (treated in the past decade basically as a methodological issue, e.g., problems of aggregation and disaggregation, contextual effects and so forth) is fundamentally a theoretical problem—one that cannot be resolved at the level of methods and data analysis techniques alone.

Second, exchange theory is one of a limited number of theoretical orientations in the social sciences that explicitly conceptualize purposeful actors in relation to structures. According to Collins (1988, 412):

> [Exchange network models] picture individuals as both free and constrained. Human beings have the capacity to create or negotiate . . . but they always act in a structured situation, so that the consequences and conditions of their creativity and negotiations are nevertheless patterned by larger relationships beyond their control. The perspective avoids not only the reification of the macro structure but also a disembodied view of micro interactions by showing structures as patterns among individuals.

The potential for exchange network theory to bridge levels of analysis is described by Turner (personal communication to Emerson, cited in Cook 1987):

> You seem to have resolved the nagging problem of levels of analysis by viewing what Simmel recognized (and modern social scientists forgot) as the basic unit of sociological analysis: social relations. The problem with other exchange models is that they must build new kinds of actors as they move from micro to macro levels. In your analysis, new theorems or principles are added to account for the increased complexity of the networks, regardless of the nature of the actor.

In contrast, Blau (1987) is less than sanguine regarding the potential of exchange theory to bridge the micro-macro gap. He argues that exchange theory, which he once embraced as the basis for macrosociological theory, is a microsociological theory and as such is not capable of explaining macrostructures and events. He concludes, "the two theories require different, if not complementary, perspectives and approaches (Blau 1987, 24)." A major reason he cites for this incompatibility is that the "two involve incommensurate conceptual schemes." He gives the following examples:

> Basic concepts of microanalysis, such as reciprocity, obligation, network density, or multiplexity, are not relevant for macroanalysis, because it does not dissect social interaction and role relations between individuals. At the same time, basic concepts of macroanalysis, such as heterogeneity, inequality, and the degree to which various social differences are related, are emergent properties of collectivities that cannot refer to individuals and thus are not appropriate for the study of role relations between individuals.

Turner (1987), as we noted earlier in this chapter, disagrees with Blau's assessment and goes so far as to argue that Blau's macrostructural conceptions are entirely compatible with the concepts of exchange network theory.

Our own approach (and that of other contemporary exchange theorists) differs in some important respects from Blau's earlier efforts in ways which make exchange theory more capable of providing at least a partial solution to the problem of bridging levels of analysis, and possibly even as Turner (1987) suggests, incorporating Blau's recent macro conceptual scheme. The key contribution (*see* Emerson 1972a, 1972b, 1976, 1981) was the explicit introduction of exchange network concepts and propositions linking structure and process within the exchange framework. In addition, the theory was defined as applicable to corporate actors (as well as individuals), a second key element in the attempt to bridge levels of analysis. Coleman (1987a) provides examples of analyses of labor markets, marriage markets, and other phenomena he claims are amenable to a modified, more social exchange market analysis.

Here Coleman's work comes into direct contact with recent work on exchange networks (e.g., Cook et al. 1983; Yamagishi et al. 1988; Marsden 1983; Markovsky et al. 1988) since labor markets and marriage markets have been demonstrated to function more like complex social networks rather than "pure" markets. The work on exchange theory (including some of Coleman's own earlier work) represents, through its emphasis upon networks and corporate groups, one class of theoretical attempts to specify processes which link individual-level exchange behavior to larger structures and processes (e.g., the distribution of power in network structures). A major component of these theories, as noted above, is the explicit acknowledgment of the embeddedness of these processes in larger structures. Thus dyadic exchange relations, once viewed by exchange theorists to a large extent as relatively isolated, are now commonly viewed in the context of a larger network of relations (sometimes referred to in the literature in a much more limited way as social support networks). This acknowledgment is significant in that it also brings exchange network theory into contact with recent developments in organizational theory and institutional economics (*see also* Winship and Rosen in the recent special issue of the *American Journal of Sociology* [1988, vol. 94] on sociology and economics, titled "Organizations and Institutions").

The theoretical strategy adopted by exchange network theorists is to specify the implications of exchange processes for the emergence of particular social structures (including, but not limited to, market structures) and for processes of structural change (e.g., through coalition formation or some other form of collective action, or other processes resulting in structural change at the network-structural level). In this sense Emerson's version of the theory (and extensions by Cook et al. 1983; Yamagishi et al. 1988; Markovsky et al. 1988) actually represent what Markovsky (1987) refers to as "multi-level" theories. This is one avenue of theoretical development in sociology that has not been fully explored in terms of its potential contributions to the problem of bridging levels of analysis. In addition, exchange network theorists attempt to specify the nature of the effects of particular exchange structures for processes occurring in those structures (e.g., the exercise of power and influence, the formation of coalitions, collective action, etc.). For a good example of work in this genre see the work of Molm (1981, 1985, 1987) on the use of power in power-balanced and imbalanced network structures, the work of Gillmore (1987) on the effect of different types of exchange structures on rates of coalition formation, and the work of Cook and Yamagishi (1988) on exchange structures which generate trust. What is central to all of this research is the awareness of what Marsden (1982) refers to as the embeddedness of exchange processes in larger social and political structures and institutions.

Recent theoretical efforts begin to explore the specific ways in which networks as social structures affect exchange transactions that occur within these structures. Certainly they determine the nature of the distribution of exchange opportunities and thus structurally determine dependence and power. Markovsky (1987) has begun to investigate the interaction between what he calls structure and actor conditions (e.g., strategies, etc.). This is another attempt to bridge levels of analysis within the exchange network framework. Different types of network connections and configurations create different structural conditions which affect the exchange processes engaged in by the actors who occupy the various positions in such structures. However, exchange is not the only social process going on within these networks, thus a next step is to investigate the link between exchange processes and other important social processes occurring in these networks. Some of this exploration has been accomplished by exchange theorists interested in the exercise of power and influence, in coalition formation and collective action, and in the role of equity processes in the distribution or allocation of exchange benefits.

Exchange networks are represented as sets of connected exchange relations. Events occurring in one location of the network often have predictable consequences for events occurring in other network locations (Cook and Emerson 1978). This framework has been demonstrated to be a powerful theoretical tool in understanding and predicting microprocesses. While exchange network theory has much promise, there are potential pitfalls in any attempt to extend a well-developed micro-level framework to apply to more macro levels. Exchange theory will need a more explicit specification of the processes at the macro-level it seeks to explain and some vision of the nature of these macro-level processes in relation to other existing structures and events (e.g., an explicit acknowledgment of the historical, political, and institutional context in which the events of interest are likely to occur.)

The micro-macro problem is, to a large extent, one of determining how to represent the relationship between levels of analysis. As framed by Münch and Smelser (1987, 385):

> Both microscopic processes that constitute the web of interactions in society and the macroscopic frameworks that result from and condition those processes are essential levels for understanding and explaining social life. Moreover, those who have argued polemically that one level is more fundamental than the other (in some kind of zero-sum way), or who have argued for the complete independence of the two levels, must be regarded as in error.

This is precisely the strength of exchange theory: it includes in a single theoretical framework propositions that apply to individual actors as well as to the macro-level (or systemic level) and it attempts to formulate explicitly the consequences of changes at one level for other levels of analysis.

CONCLUSIONS

In the preface to their 1945 book on twentieth-century sociology, Gurvitch and Moore write:

> Nineteenth century sociology was characterized by a limited number of problems more or less dogmatically accepted and differently resolved in conflicting "schools." . . . The field was marked by eternal discussion between the defenders of the "individual" or of "Society," contrasted with each other as isolated entities; between the promoters of psychology against sociology, and vice versa; and among the proponents of a "predominating factor" in social life, such as the . . . biological, . . . demography, technological, and so on. . . . These conflicts threatened to compromise the scientific character of early sociological research. The practice of seeking and formulating "sociological laws" on which different sociologists could never agree complemented the rather dismal picture of sociology in the first century of its birth. (1)

As we stand on the precipice of the twenty-first century more than four decades since this statement was written, let us hope that we have not come full circle. There have been significant advances in sociology, both methodologically and theoretically, in a wide number of subfields.

It will be unfortunate, however, if these gains are lost as the result of an overconcentration of resources on the building and maintenance of these separate "sociological fiefdoms," rather than creating new energy behind more synthetic and integrative efforts.

A central strength of the exchange theoretic approach is its broad applicability across substantive areas and its ability to cross-cut levels of analysis. This is due in large measure to its level of abstraction. As we have demonstrated, exchange concepts are found in sociological analyses of a wide range of topics. We project that as exchange theory is further developed its application throughout the social sciences will increase. Exchange theory, primarily because of its unique representation of social interaction, institutions, and structures, offers a dynamic conceptual scheme for understanding the relationship between individuals and society—a blueprint, as it were, for understanding the mechanisms of integration between structure and process. This blueprint, which traces patterned relationships between actors, directs researchers to be more explicit about the mechanisms of action and process, the structures in which exchange relations are embedded, and how these structures constrain and influence action. This theoretical approach offers a more complete representation of social behavior and social institutions with the promise of a more thorough understanding of both structure and process.

NOTES

1. The most frequently referenced work of these authors is Levi-Strauss (1969), Malinowski (1922), and Mauss (1966).

2. For further elaboration of the history of exchange theory and a comparison of the work of Blau, Emerson, and Homans, *see* Turner (1986).

3. Homans' psychology of the individual posits behavior in terms of operant conditioning. Blau and Coleman view behavior as the result of decisions made in accordance with the basic tenets of rational choice theory. Emerson adopts Homans' operant psychology in his early treatment of exchange theory. He later attempts to combine this theory with the rational choice model in trying to formulate a more accurate theory of decision behavior. (*See* Heath [1976] and Turner [1986] for an elaboration of this distinction.)

4. For an extended discussion of the debate concerning the collective and individual utilities of exchange theory, *see* Ekeh (1974).

5. A similar type of institutional analysis in sociology is the recent trend referred to as the new institutional economics. For an overview and analysis of this enterprise, *see* Zald (1987).

6. Exchange theory is not antithetical to the notion that these institutions become embedded in the culture and thus are transmitted across "generations" through socialization and other mechanisms which result in the transmission of institutionalized elements of the culture. It simply does not fully address this aspect of institutionalized exchange systems in any explicit fashion.

7. There is one other possible way out of this problem: by positing universal needs that are assumed to exist in any interaction in any historical or cultural setting (a strategy followed, for example, by sociobiologists). In economic analyses the universal value of material incentives is often taken for granted. However, while it may in fact be the case that monetary incentives are highly valued, this remains an auxiliary assumption to the application of rational choice theory in market analysis (cf. Brennan 1990).

REFERENCES

Alexander, Jeffrey C., and Bernhard Giesen. 1987. "From Reduction to Linkage: The Long View of the Micro-Macro Link." In J. C. Alexander, B. Giesen, R. Münch, and N. J. Smelser, eds., *The Micro-Macro Link*. Berkeley: University of California Press.

Barth, F. 1966. "The Analytical Importance of Transaction." In *Models of Social Organization*, Royal Anthropological Institute Occasional Paper No. 23. Glasgow: Royal Anthropological Institute.

Becker, Gary S. 1976. *The Economic Approach to Human Behavior*. Chicago: University of Chicago Press.

Becker, Gary S. 1981. *A Treatise on the Family*. Cambridge, Mass.: Harvard University Press.

Ben-Porath, Y. 1980. "The F-connection: Families, Friends, and Firms and the Organization of Exchange." *Population and Development Review* 6:1–30.

Berscheid, E. 1983. "Emotion." In H. H. Kelley, E. Berscheid, A. Christensen, J. H. Harvey, T. L. Huston et al., eds., *Close Relationships*. New York: Freeman.

Berscheid, E. 1985. "Compatibility, Interdependence, and Emotion." In W. Ickes, ed., *Compatible and Incompatible Relationships*. New York: Springer-Verlag.

Blau, Peter M. 1964. *Exchange and Power in Social Life*. New York: Wiley.

Blau, Peter M. 1977. *Inequality and Heterogeneity: A Primitive Theory of Social Structure*. New York: Free Press.

Blau, Peter M. 1987. "Microprocesses and Macrostructure." In K. S. Cook, ed., *Social Exchange Theory*. Newbury Park, Cal.: Sage.

Brennan, Geoffrey. 1990. "What Rationality Might Fail to Do: A Comment on Elster's Diagnosis." In Karen Cook and Margaret Levi, eds., *The Limits of Rationality*. Chicago: University of Chicago Press.

Burt, R. S. 1976. "Positions in Networks." *Social Forces* 55:93–122.

Carley, K. M. 1986. "An Approach for Relating Social Structure to Cognitive Structure." *Journal of Mathematical Sociology* 12:137–189.

Clark, M. S. 1985. "Implications of Relationship Type for Understanding Compatibility." In W. Ickes, ed., *Compatible and Incompatible Relationships*. New York: Springer-Verlag.

Clark, M. S. and J. Mills. 1979. "Interpersonal Attraction in Exchange and Communal Relationships." *Journal of Personality and Social Psychology* 37:12–24.

Coleman, James S. 1972. "Systems of Social Exchange." *Journal of Mathematical Sociology* 2:145–163.

Coleman, James S. 1973. *The Mathematics of Collective Action*. Chicago: Aldine.

Coleman, James S. 1974. *Power and the Structure of Society*. New York: Norton.

Coleman, James S. 1986a. "Social Theory, Social Research, and a Theory of Action." *American Journal of Sociology* 91:1309–1335.

Coleman, James S. 1986b. *Individual Interests and Collective Action*. Cambridge: Cambridge University Press.

Coleman, James S. 1987a. "Microfoundations and Macrosocial Behavior." In J. C. Alexander, B. Giesen, R. Münch, and N. J. Smelser, eds., *The Micro-Macro Link.* Berkeley: University of California Press.

Coleman, James S. 1987b. "Free Riders and Zealots." In K. S. Cook, ed., *Social Exchange Theory.* Newbury Park, Cal.: Sage.

Coleman, James S. 1988. "Social Capital in the Creation of Human Capital." *American Journal of Sociology* 94 (Supplement):S95–S120.

Collins, Randall. 1988. *Theoretical Sociology.* New York: Harcourt Brace Jovanovich.

Cook, Karen S. 1987. "Emerson's Contributions to Social Exchange Theory." In K. S. Cook, ed., *Social Exchange Theory.* Newbury Park, Cal.: Sage.

Cook, Karen S., and Richard M. Emerson. 1978. "Power, Equity, and Commitment in Exchange Networks." *American Sociological Review* 43:721–739.

Cook, Karen S., and Richard M. Emerson. 1984. "Exchange Networks and the Analysis of Complex Organizations." *Research in the Sociology of Organizations* 3:1–30.

Cook, Karen S., Richard M. Emerson, Mary R. Gillmore, and Toshio Yamagishi. 1983. "The Distribution of Power in Exchange Networks: Theory and Experimental Results." *American Journal of Sociology* 89:275–305.

Cook, Karen S., and Mary R. Gillmore. 1984. "Power, Dependence, and Coalitions." *Advances in Group Processes* 1:27–58.

Cook, Karen S., and Karen Hegtvedt. 1983. "Distributive Justice, Equity, and Equality." *Annual Review of Sociology* 9:217–241.

Cook, Karen S., Karen Hegtvedt, and Toshio Yamagishi. 1988. "Structural Inequality, Legitimation, and Reactions to Inequity in Exchange Networks." In M. Webster and M. Foschi, eds., *Status Generalization: New Theory and Research.* Stanford, Cal.: Stanford University Press.

Cook, Karen S., and Jodi O'Brien. 1990. "Rational Choices, Rational Behavior." In Karen Cook and Margaret Levi, eds., *The Limits of Rationality.* Chicago: University of Chicago Press.

Cook, Karen S., and Toshio Yamagishi. 1988. "Generalized Exchange, Networks, and the Problem of Collective Action." Paper presented at the International Social Networks Conference.

Della Fave, L. Richard. 1980. "The Meek Shall Not Inherit the Earth: Self-Evaluation and the Legitimacy of Stratification." *American Sociological Review* 45:955–971.

Deutsch, M. 1975. "Equity, Equality, and Need: What Determines Which Value Will Be Used as the Basis of Distributive Justice?" *Journal of Social Issues* 31:137–150.

Ekeh, P. P. 1974. *Social Exchange Theory: The Two Traditions.* Cambridge, Mass.: Harvard University Press.

Emerson, Richard M. 1969. "Operant Psychology and Exchange Theory." In R. Burgess and D. Bushell, eds., *Behavioral Sociology.* New York: Columbia University Press.

Emerson, Richard M. 1972a. "Exchange Theory, Part I: A Psychological Basis for Social Exchange." In J. Berger, M. Zelditch, and B. Anderson, eds., *Sociological Theories in Progress.* Vol. 2. Boston: Houghton-Mifflin.

Emerson, Richard M. 1972b. "Exchange Theory, Part II: Exchange Relations and Networks." In J. Berger, M. Zelditch, and B. Anderson, eds., *Sociological Theories in Progress.* Vol. 2. Boston: Houghton-Mifflin.

Emerson, Richard M. 1976. "Social Exchange Theory." *Annual Review of Sociology* 2:335–362.

Emerson, Richard M. 1981. "Social Exchange Theory." In M. Rosenberg and R. H. Turner, eds., *Social Psychology: Sociological Perspectives.* New York: Basic.

Emerson, Richard M. 1987. "Toward a Theory of Value in Social Exchange." In K. S. Cook, ed., *Social Exchange Theory*. Newbury Park, Cal.: Sage.

Fararo, Thomas J., and John Skvoretz. 1984. "Institutions as Production Systems." *Journal of Mathematical Sociology* 10:117–182.

Fisher, C. S. 1982. *To Dwell Among Friends: Personal Networks in Town and City*. Chicago: University of Chicago Press.

Frazer, Sir James G. 1919. *Folklore in the Old Testament* Vol. 2. New York: Macmillan.

Galaskiewicz, J. 1979. *Exchange Networks and Community Politics*. Beverly Hills, Cal.: Sage.

Gillmore, Mary Rogers. 1987. "Implications of Generalized Versus Restricted Exchange." In K. S. Cook, ed., *Social Exchange Theory*. Newbury Park, Cal.: Sage.

Gouldner, A. W. 1960. "The Norm of Reciprocity: A Preliminary Statement." *American Sociological Review* 25:161–178.

Gurvitch, G., and W. E. Moore. 1945. *Twentieth Century Sociology*. New York: Philosophical Library.

Hatfield, E., and J. Traupmann. 1981. "Intimate Relationships: A Perspective from Equity Theory." In S. Duck and R. Gilmour, eds., *Personal Relationships. Vol. 1: Studying Personal Relationships*. New York: Academic.

Hatfield, E., J. Traupmann, S. Sprecher, M. Utne, and J. Hay. 1985. "Equity and Intimate Relationships: Recent Research." In W. Ickes, ed., *Compatible and Incompatible Relationships*. New York: Springer-Verlag.

Hatfield E., M. Utne, and J. Traupmann. 1979. "Equity Theory and Intimate Relationships." In R. L. Burgess and T. L. Huston, eds., *Social Exchange in Developing Relationships*. New York: Academic.

Heath, Anthony. 1976. *Rational Choice and Social Exchange*. Cambridge: Cambridge University Press.

Hechter, Michael. 1983. *Microfoundations of Macrosociology*. Philadelphia: Temple University Press.

Hechter, Michael. 1987. *Principles of Group Solidarity*. Berkeley: University of California Press.

Homans, George C. 1958. "Social Behavior as Exchange." *American Journal of Sociology* 63:597–606.

Homans, George C. 1961. *Social Behavior: Its Elementary Forms*. New York: Harcourt Brace Jovanovich.

Homans, George C. 1974. *Social Behavior: Its Elementary Forms*. 2d ed. New York: Harcourt Brace Jovanovich.

House, James. 1977. "The Three Faces of Social Psychology." *Sociometry* 40:161–177.

Kahneman, D., and A. Tversky. 1982. "The Psychology of Preferences." *Scientific American* 246:160–174.

Kahneman, D., 1984. "Choices, Values, and Frames." *American Psychologist* 39:341–350.

Kelley, H. H. 1979. *Personal Relationships: Their Structures and Processes*. Hillside, N. J.: Erlbaum.

Kelley, H. H. 1986. "Personal Relationships: Their Nature and Significance." In R. Gilmour and S. Duck, eds., *The Emerging Field of Personal Relationships*. Hillsdale, N. J.: Erlbaum.

Kelley, H. H., E. Berscheid, A. Christensen, J. H. Harvey, T. L. Huston et al. 1983. *Close Relationships*. New York: Freeman.

Kelley, H. H. and J. W. Thibaut. 1978. *Interpersonal Relations: A Theory of Interdependence*. New York: Wiley.

Kollock, Peter. 1988. "The Economics of Thinking: Cognitive Science and Models of Social Action and Order." Paper presented at the Annual Meeting of the American Sociological Association, Atlanta.

Laumann, Edward O., and Franz U. Pappi. 1976. *Networks of Collective Action.* New York: Academic.

Lévi-Strauss, C. 1969. *The Elementary Structures of Kinship.* Rev. ed. Boston: Beacon.

Macaulay, Stewart. 1963. "Non-contractual Relations in Business: A Preliminary Study." *American Sociological Review* 28:55–67.

Machina, Mark J. 1987. "Choice Under Uncertainty: Problems Solved and Unresolved." *Journal of Economic Perspectives* 1:121–154.

Macneil, Ian R. 1986. "Exchange Revisited: Individual Utility and Social Solidarity." *Ethics* 96:567–593.

Majeski, Stephen J. 1990. "Comment on James Coleman's 'Norm Generating Structures.'" In Karen Cook and Margaret Levi, eds., *The Limits of Rationality.* Chicago: University of Chicago Press.

Malinowski, B. (1922). *Argonauts of the Western Pacific.* London: Routledge and Kegan Paul.

Markovsky, Barry. 1987. "Toward Multilevel Sociological Theories: Simulations of Actor and Network Effects." *Sociological Theory* 5:101–117.

Markovsky, Barry, David Willer, and Travis Patton. 1988. "Power Relations in Exchange Networks." *American Sociological Review* 53:220–236.

Marin, B. 1987. "Generalized Political Exchange." In A. Pizzorno and B. Marin, eds., *Generalized Political Exchange.* Fiesole, Italy: European University Institute.

Marsden, Peter. 1982. "Brokerage Behavior in Restricted Exchange Networks." In N. Lin and P. Marsden, eds., *Social Structure and Network Analysis.* Beverly Hills, Cal.: Sage.

Marsden, Peter. 1983. "Restricted Access in Networks and Models of Power." *American Journal of Sociology* 88:686–717.

Marsden, Peter. 1987. "Elements of Interactor Dependence." In K. S. Cook, ed., *Social Exchange Theory.* Newbury Park, Cal.: Sage.

Mauss, M. 1966. *The Gift: Forms and Functions of Exchange in Archaic Societies.* London: Cohen and West.

Meeker, B. F. 1971. "Decisions and Exchange." *American Sociological Review* 36:485–495.

Mills, J. and M. S. Clark. 1982. "Exchange and Communal Relationships." *Review of Personality and Social Psychology* 3:121–144.

Molm, Linda D. 1981. "The Conversion of Power Imbalance to Power Use." *Social Psychology Quarterly* 44:151–163.

Molm, Linda D. 1985. "Relative Effects of Individual Dependencies: Further Tests of the Relation Between Power Imbalance and Power Use." *Social Forces* 63:810–837.

Molm, Linda D. 1987. "Linking Power Structure and Power Use." In K. S. Cook, ed., *Social Exchange Theory.* Newbury Park, Cal.: Sage.

Münch, Richard and Neil J. Smelser. 1987. "Relating the Micro and Macro." In J. C. Alexander, B. Giesen, R. Münch, and N. J. Smelser, eds., *The Micro-Macro Link.* Berkeley: University of California Press.

Murstein, B. I., M. Cerreto, and M. G. MacDonald. 1977. "A Theory and Investigation of the Effect of Exchange Orientation on Marriage and Friendship." *Journal of Marriage and the Family* 39:543–548.

O'Brien, Jodi. 1988. "The Mormon Ethic and the Spirit of Altruism: A Rational-Choice Explanation of Voluntary Cooperation." Paper presented at the Annual Meeting of the Pacific Sociological Association, Las Vegas.

O'Connell, L. 1984. "An Exploration of Exchange in Three Social Relationships:

Kinship, Friendship, and the Marketplace." *Journal of Social and Personal Relationships* 1:333–345.

Olson, Mancur. 1965. *The Logic of Collective Action: Public Goods and the Theory of Groups.* Cambridge, Mass.: Harvard University Press.

Ouchi, W. G. 1980. "Markets, Bureaucracies, and Clans." *Administrative Science Quarterly* 25:129–141.

Sahlins, M. 1972. *Stone Age Economics.* New York: Aldine-Atherton.

Shapiro. S. P. 1987. "The Social Control of Impersonal Trust." *American Journal of Sociology* 93:623–658.

Stinchcombe, Arthur. 1986. "Organizations as Information Processing Systems." Manuscript.

Stolte, John. 1983. "The Legitimation of Structural Inequality: Reformulation and Test of the Self-Evaluation Argument." *American Sociological Review* 48:331–342.

Stolte, John, and Richard M. Emerson. 1977. "Structural Inequality: Position and Power in Network Structures." In R. Hamblin and J. Kunkel, eds., *Behavioral Theory in Sociology.* New Brunswick, N. J.: Transaction.

Stroebe, W., and B. Frey. 1982. "Self-Interest and Collective Action: The Economics and Psychology of Public Goods." *British Journal of Social Psychology* 21:121–137.

Turner, J. H. 1986. *The Structure of Sociological Theory.* 4th ed. Chicago: Dorsey.

Turner, J. H. 1987. "Social Exchange Theory: Future Directions." In K. S. Cook, ed., *Social Exchange Theory.* Newbury Park, Cal.: Sage.

Willer, D., and B. Anderson. 1981. *Networks, Exchange and Coercion: The Elementary Theory and Its Applications.* New York: Elsevier.

Williamson, O. E. 1981. "The Economics of Organization: The Transaction Cost Approach." *American Journal of Sociology* 87:548–577.

Winship, Christopher, and Sherwin Rosen, ed. 1988. "Organizations and Institutions: Sociological and Economic Approaches to the Analysis of Social Structure." *American Journal of Sociology* 94, supplement.

Wippler, Reinhard, and Siegwart Lindenberg. 1987. "Collective Phenomena and Rational Choice." In J. C. Alexander, B. Giesen, R. Münch, and N. J. Smelser, eds., *The Micro-Macro Link.* Berkeley: University of California Press.

Yamagishi, Toshio. 1986. "Structural Goal-Expectation Theory of Cooperation in Social Dilemmas." *Advances in Group Processes* 3:51–87.

Yamagishi, Toshio. 1987. "An Exchange Theoretical Approach to Network Positions." In K. S. Cook, ed., *Social Exchange Theory.* Newbury Park, Cal.: Sage.

Yamagishi, Toshio, Mary Gillmore, and Karen S. Cook. 1988. "Network Connections and the Distribution of Power in Exchange Networks." *American Journal of Sociology* 93:833–851.

Zald, M. N. 1987. "Review Essay: The New Institutional Economics." *American Journal of Sociology* 93:701–708.

II

LIVELINESS OF MORE RECENT SOCIAL AND SOCIOLOGICAL THEORIES

❊

7

The World as It Happens:
Ethnomethodology and Conversation Analysis

❀

DEIRDRE BODEN
Washington University

Ethnomethodology is here to stay. It has, as Mullins (1973) long ago pointed out, not only come "in from the cold," but become a permanent if feisty feature of the American sociological landscape. Indeed, with several generations of practicing ethnomethodologists established at institutions across the country and training clusters of future scholars, it is well along the path proposed by Mullins for the development of theory groups in American sociology. More importantly, the joint fields of ethnomethodology and conversation analysis are also well established in Europe; early in England where important strains of research have long been conducted, more recently in France, Holland, Germany, and Switzerland. Indeed, there are now practicing groups of ethnomethodologists as far afield as Poland, Japan, and Australia.

Yet, in a haunting sort of way, the scope and depth of Garfinkel's seminal ideas have also been simultaneously underestimated and misunderstood to a surprising degree. What follows is thus mildly pedagogic and consciously programmatic. My purpose in this chapter is to briefly sketch[1] early ethnomethodological developments and to expose several rich, recent veins of research both in ethnomethodology and conversation analysis. I shall conclude by offering some speculative comments on current trends and future trajectories for this research. I shall be rather insistent that the core concepts of ethnomethodology have serious and quite pressing relevance within the main currents of

I appreciate helpful comments from Anthony Giddens, Charles Lemert, Douglas W. Maynard, Hugh Mehan, George Ritzer, and Thomas P. Wilson, as well as an insightful exchange with Harold Garfinkel who helped me disentangle my own ideas on "local logic" and rational action. An earlier version of the section on local logic was presented in the Ethnography of Communication Seminar at Indiana University in fall 1987; thanks especially to Allen Grimshaw, Donna Eder, William Corsaro, David Braine, John Flood, and David Heise. The current paper, of course, reflects my own affections for, and affectations about, the slippery topic called "ethnomethodology" (cf. Garfinkel 1974).

social theory and research today, both in the United States and elsewhere.

RADICAL CHIC: GARFINKEL AND ETHNOMETHODOLOGY

Despite trenchant resistance within what Giddens calls the "orthodox consensus" of American sociology, a provocative and tendentious creativity has made Garfinkel one of the major social thinkers of his era and something of a legend in his own times. In near-canonical Kuhnian manner, he has pushed the limits of contemporary social paradigms (Kuhn 1970; cf. Ritzer 1980), redefining both the orientation and outcome of social research. One of the most cited of contemporary sociologists, Garfinkel's ideas have sparked interest and drawn debate across the social sciences and beyond. Yet ethnomethodology is one of the least genuinely understood areas of American sociology.

Much of this problem can be attributed to three basic factors. In the first place, ethnomethodology is, to use a current expression of Garfinkel's (1988, 108), an "incommensurably alternate sociology," which is to say that it is radical in an intellectual sense and irreducibly distinct. It cannot be subsumed as simply phenomenological sociology because its roots, as Heritage has been particularly effective in underlining (1984a, 10–36), lie at the very center of Parsonian social theory (*see also* Garfinkel 1988; Alexander 1988). More centrally, it should never be confused with the constructionist approach with which it has often, yet incorrectly, been associated (cf. Mehan 1990). Ethnomethodology does *not* propose that the world is merely a momentary social construct, though there are important affinities to the purely phenomenological approach (cf. Heap and Roth 1973; Pollner 1987). Furthermore, it does not bear, in any direct theoretical sense, on either the work of symbolic interactionists or Goffmanian approaches to the so-called micro level of social analysis (cf. Zimmerman and Wieder 1970), although there is assuredly shared empirical ground (e.g., Boden 1990b).

In the second place, early studies in ethnomethodology were almost intractably presented in dense and often technical style. Garfinkel's highly original formulations about the nature of the social world are coupled with a considerable concern for precision in terminology and a deep distrust of sociologists' ability to respect the inherent indexicality of language itself. These preoccupations resulted in rather impenetrable prose and frequent misreadings (e.g., Attewell 1974; Coser 1975). It is a mistake, however, to think of such literary technique as part of the cult quality alluded to by Gellner (1975) and others. Since the complexity of human behavior cannot be captured in summary equations,[2] Garfinkel and others have been forced to filter a necessarily alternate set of ideas through the fragmenting lens of everyday language. The result has been decidedly opaque, yet there is a precise and exacting quality that defies both facile summary and simple adoption. More consequential generally is the fact that few American sociologists will admit how little of the field they have actually read and fewer still recognize the pervasive ethnomethodological influence on their own work.[3] Major European social theorists have instead used it, and the findings of sociolinguists and American micro analysts generally, to tremendous effect and thereby moved the center of theoretical creativity and innovation in sociology firmly back to its home ground in England, France, and Germany (e.g., Giddens, Bourdieu, Habermas).

Third, and following from the first two points, the large volume of research and writing by second and third generation ethnomethodologists, many of whom are conversation analysts "by trade," is often absorbed into the sociological mainstream of the substantive areas in which they work.[4] Despite over sixty monographs and collections, as well as hundreds of published articles in the past ten years, most general citations to ethnomethodological or even conversation analytic literature stop at about 1974. Giddens (1976, 1984, 1987a) and Collins (1981, 1987, 1988b) have, however, been most effective in incorporating main writings into their own theoretical advances (*see also* Alexander 1988). The consequence of this borrowing, however acknowledged, has led to a diffusion of ethnomethodological concepts within the main body of sociological work, combined with a level of considerable acceptance, albeit unconscious, of fundamentally ethnomethodological findings. Thus, as I suggested above, ethnomethodology is well and truly abroad in the sociological landscape. The problem becomes one of, on the one hand, demystifying the basic concepts of the field and, on the other, making them more fully available as useful, innovative, and fundamentally sociological concepts.

BEYOND THE FRINGE: ETHNOMETHODOLOGY AS SOCIAL MOVEMENT

It would take several volumes to address and redress the many misreadings of the early writings of Garfinkel and Cicourel and the first generation of ethnomethodological research.[5] The image of a southern California cult grew quickly and satisfyingly so that by the mid-1970s usually urbane scholars such as Gellner (1975) and Coser (1975) were hurling harsh accusations across public settings while potentially sympathetic reviewers were offering their own rather self-serving versions (e.g., Gouldner 1970, 1975; Denzin, 1970). If social movements, as Gusfield suggests, take on the character of "an explicit and conscious indictment" of some or all of the social order, with a distinctly *"ideological* component" (1968, 445, emphasis in original), then early ethnomethodology would seem to fit well into such a description. Levels of commitment among ethnomethodologists were (and are) high, and exclusionary practices were common in those formative years, as was a strong indictment of conventional analytic sociology. Reactions to early experiences continue to shape the solidarity among succeeding generations of scholarship. "The Company" (as Garfinkel likes to call it) is now large, very international, and experiencing the routinization and institutionalization common to later stages of innovative movements (*see also* Dingwall 1981).

The movement that Garfinkel founded has, at the same time, persisted in engaging in what Gouldner termed "intellectual deviance" (1965, 205), namely a deviant and radical stance that resists dilution in the currents of conventional social science. The force of Garfinkel's own creativity, as noted, has carried him across a variety of intellectual traditions. This boundary transgression has involved, as do many innovative intellectual shifts, a persistent critique "of the established paradigms of normal science and scholarship" (Gouldner 1965, 204–205). It is important to note, however, that in neither early (e.g., Garfinkel [1967] 1984) nor recent time (Garfinkel 1988; Garfinkel et al. n.d.) has Garfinkel argued that the ethnomethodological position precludes or excludes conventional sociology (*see also* Heritage 1984a, 136). Even Cicourel's pathbreaking critique of conventional research methodology (1964) and more recent (1981) concerns with interview techniques do not reject the sociological enterprise. Instead, ethnomethodologists have simply insisted that the sociologist is in no exclusive or superior position vis-à-vis the phenomenon of social order.[6] That the sociologist is inextricably part of the world under study is taken to be both the challenge and strength of the sociological enterprise, as Giddens and others have more recently reiterated (e.g., Gouldner 1970; Giddens 1976, 1984; Cohen, 1988, 1989).[7]

A Theory by Any Other Name

The fundamental twist of ethnomethodology was and is to turn Parsons' problem of order upside down. The "problem" of order is not one of understanding how the so-called larger social order is internalized by actors who then act out those norms and values, but rather how order is produced as the local achievement of those same actors (Heritage, 1984a, 75–84; Zimmerman and Boden, 1990).[8] Order is thus transformed into *structure-in-action*. Garfinkel, as Heritage notes, "rejected the view that normative rules—no matter how detailed and specific or deeply internalized—could in any way be determinative of conduct" (Heritage 1984a, 34). Having respecified the problem of order, Garfinkel went on to reject the even more fundamental sociological conceit that actors' views of their social worlds are somehow flawed or marginal to a full understanding of social phenomena (*see also* Cicourel 1964).

We may note a theme familiar in recent years, and deriving in large part from ethnomethodology, namely that human actors are knowledgeable agents, not cultural dopes, and that the meaning they attribute to their joint actions both shapes and renews those understandings in consequential ways. Note that authors as diverse as Giddens (1976, 1981, 1984), Bourdieu (1982), Bhaskar (1979), Collins (1981), Abrams (1982), Sahlins (1985), Callinicos (1988), and Alexander (1988) have all been much preoccupied with just this reflective capacity of human actors. It is a preoccupation that is central to ethnomethodology and conversation analysis. Indeed, it may be argued that each and every ethnomethodological principle hinges on an insistence on a *member's* (as opposed to analyst's) perspective on action, a perspective or position that is necessarily local and locally practical in that it guides actions that are at once temporal and sequential.

Put simply, people do what they do, right there and then, to be reasonable and effective and they do so for pervasively practical reasons and under unavoidably local conditions of knowledge, action, and material resources. Here the influence of Schutz (1962) is particularly important as it is in Garfinkel's examination of rationality that the Hobbesian problem of order is radically respecified—not as some external yet internalized control but as the practical and lived production of members of society.[9] Social structure, for ethnomethodologists, does not work behind the backs of actors, but is instantiated in and constituted through their actions (*see also* Giddens 1981, 1984).

It is, oddly enough, this insistence on members' methods and members' practices that seems most alarming to many sociologists—with their models, their instruments, their measuring devices, and their urge to abstract away from concrete behavior. The alarm seems rooted in the notion that if indeed everything is local, detailed, contingent, and situation-specific, then the predictive needs of science will never be met (Cicourel 1974). Taken to its apparent extreme, not only would social science be impossible but everyday life would be a nightmare—

chaos, in fact. Yet, just as chaos theory in the natural sciences is pointing to the unpredictability of discrete events in the face of totally deterministic systems, ethnomethodology argues quite simply that structure coheres in the apparently idiosyncratic moments of daily life. The basic position is that social structures, conventionally defined as patterned social relationships, become visible and viable only as practical features of concrete moments of human existence. As actors collaborate to achieve *local* details of action, they are also collaborating in sustaining, shifting, or totally altering those arrangements of action, that is to say, the social structure (*see also* Wilson 1990).

The World as It Happens

The conviction that the firmest ground of sociological investigation is the concrete yet momentary events of actual people in everyday situations has led ethnomethodologists, and with them conversation analysts, to study what I call the-world-as-it-happens (cf. Zimmerman and Pollner 1970; Sacks 1984). A companion traveller, conversation analysis, started with a shared interest in the *details of action* and the detailed production of order, and has both drawn its theoretical framework from ethnomethodology while contributing in turn innovation, a more rigorous methodology, and an ever-widening group of practitioners. Animated by a desire to *directly* observe the social world, with none of the mediating and filtering effects of the whole range of social science research methodologies, Harvey Sacks turned to audiotape recordings in the early 1960s. His interest was, as a sociologist, not in language nor in linguistic structure. Instead here were data of the social world of human actors that could be observed, analyzed, and reanalyzed, over and over again. The talk "caught" forever on the magnetic base was assuredly not *all* that "happened" but at least we know *that* it happened (Sacks 1984). Sacks' initial insight that everyday conversation would give a direct handle on the essential social and organization features of order has paid off dramatically (*see* especially Sacks 1989).[10] For Sacks and his early colleagues, Gail Jefferson and Emanuel Schegloff, the greatest innovation of all has been to isolate and model properties of conversational turn-taking that are the linchpin of all verbal interaction and, I suspect, a far wider range of social intercourse (Sacks et al. 1974). The organizational mechanisms detailed in their now-classic paper on turn-taking hold across *all* languages and cultures studied (e.g., Moerman 1977; Boden 1983; *but see* Besnier 1989) and in ways that illuminate long-standing interest in the origins of language and basic considerations of social integration and sociability. And, in the past ten years especially, conversation analysis has been largely responsible for a truly impressive outpouring of scholarship.[11]

With foundational research in both fields proceeding in tandem, Garfinkel's innovative ideas joined Sacks' remarkable sensibility for interactional data. A shared concern with the *details* of action also required firm bracketing of all conventional sociological theorizing and an insistence on what Garfinkel and Sacks (1970) termed "ethnomethodological indifference." Far from abandoning systematic method, ethnomethodological indifference is actually central to scientific enquiry. By bracketing a priori assumptions about social phenomena, relationships, and even outcomes, the investigator can go and look at the world and observe what is happening in a rigorously empirical manner. Ethnomethodological indifference therefore recommends one rather basic assumption, namely that there is order in the world. By extension, this means that in the social world there is an order that is the *production* of social actors, observable to them (and to the analyst), recognizable, shared as familiar (and thereby historical and historically located), and, in its familiarity, patterned, recognizably and reproducibly so. It is not, however, characterized as patterned in some abstract, general, or generic sense, as sociologists typically want, but rather consists of typifications that have, in situ, particular relevance in a stream of experience that is simultaneously historical and unique. The shared, collaborative, contingent, and accomplished nature of social action collapses history into the moment for what Garfinkel calls "another next first time" (Garfinkel et al. n.d.). In the real-time details of real lives we may, as sociologists, lose the satisfying abstraction of aggregates but the gains —according to the ethnomethodologists—are considerable. Through the microscope, one can see glimpses of the fine structure of the social universe.[12]

The essence of ethnomethodological theorizing and research remains deeply sociological, as we shall see, and it is a mistake, as Collins (1988b) has noted, to treat "human-size" findings as merely "micro" and having little to do with history, social change, and structures of power. One of the tasks of ethnomethodologists has been "stripping away the innumerable theoretical and methodological barriers which imperceptibly interpose themselves between observers and the organizationally significant features of social activity" (Heritage 1984a, 311). The challenge for future generations of ethnomethodologists will be to throw more bright light on the activities that actually shape those structures and outcomes most sociologists choose to study as proxies for the real thing. The issue is, I believe, quite critical at this conjuncture of sociological theorizing and research (cf. Lieberson 1985; Ritzer 1985; Collins 1986; Alexander et al. 1987; Wiley 1988).

BACK TO THE FUTURE: ETHNOMETHODOLOGY AND SOCIAL THEORY TODAY

We live, as the Chinese saying goes, in interesting, which is to say in troubled, times. American social scientists of various persuasions have now trained several generations of graduate students almost exclusively in statistical analysis and computer methodology (cf. Collins 1984). All too often the result is a kind of "statisticism" (Duncan 1984, 226) in which social data are "sliced, chopped, beaten, molded, baked and finally artificially colored until the researcher is able to serve us proudly with a plateful of mock experiment" (Lieberson 1985, 4). The need to operationalize variables to, almost literally, fit into computer models has meant that several decades of innovative quantitative sociological research in the United States has proceeded with little parallel progress in theoretical formulations. This collection thus comes at an important point in our intellectual development. Without attempts to centralize and synthesize American theoretical positions, our conceptual horizons may continue to be severely limited.

In this section, I shall briefly trace a few major debates in sociology today and attempt to show how long-standing approaches within ethnomethodology and conversation analysis illuminate these issues. My purpose will not be to argue or offer ethnomethodology as a *solution* to these problems; even less will I be inclined to propose ethnomethodology as a theoretical alternative, though theory it is, and alternate to be sure. Rather I shall want to trace out major elements in ethnomethodological thinking that seem largely lost or decidedly misunderstood in the general literature. It is my hope that this exposition will guide the reader's own assessment of available insights and approaches in the ethnomethodological literature itself. These themes are of a piece in that they weave one into another: 1) the return of the agent in social theory; 2) the essential embeddedness or reflexivity of action; 3) the role of rationality; and 4) the current vogue in temporal and spatial analysis of action and structure. Each theme has, I believe, considerable currency across a number of disciplinary boundaries and each is *centrally* present in all ethnomethodological studies.

The Agency/Structure Debate

A number of interlocking issues currently engage sociologists in a goodly amount of debate that is both theoretical and methodological.

In theory circles particularly, there is considerable energy being generated around old and new ways of characterizing the joint roles of human action and social structural arrangements. Several decades of functionalism (cf. Alexander and Colomy, this volume) gave way to a period of rather rigid varieties of structuralism, whether the American hybrid driven by the potential and limits of multivariate statistical manipulation or the European home-grown species of assorted Marxist theories followed by post-structuralism, neo-Marxism, and even post-Marxism. Now, from the far corners of the sociological map and beyond, there is a gathering of intuitive and innovative scholarship around the agency/structure issue, sometimes glossed as the micro-macro debate, or even as a qualitative-quantitative split (cf. Knorr-Cetina and Cicourel 1981; Collins 1981; Wilson 1982; Abrams 1982; Giddens 1984; Alexander et. al. 1987). These are, of course, not equivalent. But the underlying theoretical orientation of micro-level, qualitative analysis of actual human conduct has long been seen as servicing macro-level, quantitative studies of social systems, whether structural or functional. In an era that is largely post-positivist and recognizes the limits of natural science methods in the social domain, the results of this division of labor have come to trouble a growing number of theorists and, to a much lesser extent, empirical researchers.

The heart of this debate involves what Tourraine has characterized as the "return of the actor" (1985). Many metatheorists have long been routinely criticized for having action theories with no actors or structural frameworks with no room for anything but social puppets on fine, flexible wires dancing across stages not of their own making. From Marx to Parsons to Habermas and beyond, the social actor has been alienated or systematized or rationalized right out of the drama of society. Lately, however, there has been much creative effort to bring the agent back in, and virtually all of it has depended in a variety of ways on the work of interactional sociologists such as Becker, Goffman, and Garfinkel (cf. Ritzer 1985; Wiley 1988). It is not my intention to review these trends except to note that most theory moving beyond structuralism, Marxism, or Parsons has taken similar routes, starting with Giddens' pathbreaking *New Rules of Sociological Method* in 1976. Although not always explicitly acknowledged, the affinities, for example, of ethnomethodology and Giddens' structuration theory are considerable, from central concepts such as the duality of structure, recursivity, the intersection of action and structure, to the very process of *structuration* itself as developed most fully in *The Constitution of Society* (1984; *see* Cohen 1989). Similarly, Collins has expanded a primarily Goffmanian analysis of micro-macro linkages with more recent influences of ethnomethodology and conversation analysis (1981, 1987,

1988b). Most recently, Alexander (1988) has begun to inject notions of contingent action into his emerging neofunctionalist theory (*see also* Alexander and Colomy, this volume).

As we have already seen, the social actor and "the extraordinary organization of the ordinary" (Pollner 1987, xvii) are central to all ethnomethodological research. Members' methods and the basic notion of a knowledgeable agent are at the very heart of the matter. Although this is typically seen simply as a micro-analytic approach, the current debate over micro-macro linkages shows the implications of such an a priori theoretical position for all manner of sociological theorizing (*see* Ritzer, this volume). Actors are seen not only to act against a phenom-enological background of taken-for-granted assumptions but *accounta-bly*, which is to say that all social action is produced as an observable, describable, reasonable, responsible, and thereby *moral* matter (e.g., Pollner 1975; Heritage 1984a). Moreover, through their "accounts in action" (Heritage 1983) members discover not only what others mean by their actions (and accounts thereof) but what their *joint* actions *come* to mean as the observable product of their actual production. It is here that linguistic formulations tend to entrap the process they ac-tually seek to explicate, so let me attempt a clarification.

The *unfolding* properties of action and accounts of action are central to all ethnomethodological and conversation analytic work. A major argument of Garfinkel's and, in a variety of ways, of all practitioners (e.g., Zimmerman 1969; Maynard and Wilson 1980; Heritage 1984a) is that it is through language that members not only "explain" their actions or provide "excuses" (cf. Scott and Lyman 1968) but in the broadest sense make their actions transparent to others.[13] Social life is, moreover, characterized as a self-organizing and self-explicating system of action (Garfinkel [1967] 1984) in that *structures of action* locally shape immediate events, both redefining the past and consequentially prefiguring future action. Members' *ongoing* understanding and ac-counts provide meaning not only to current interaction, but to the realization of past relationships along a time trajectory extended into the future (*see* section on temporality, below). Everyday life is thus self-explicating in the sense that the shared accounts of participants provide a continuous updating of meaning and moment, and self-organizing in that the local details of actions actually constitute that dynamic matrix we can retrospectively see in organizational terms. In the same way as jurors' deliberations revealed the self-organizing nature of rational ac-tion (Garfinkel [1967] 1984, 104–115), so each ethnomethodological analysis can inform the current debate on the constitution of human agency. Conversation analysis, for instance, displays the highly specific ways in which the reflexive properties of agency and structure are "brought off" as contingent and constitutive events. The challenge remains to recognize the explanatory power of these ethnomethodological studies of active agency and to move beyond the notion that such findings are exclusively relevant to allegedly "micro" phenomena.

Reflexivity and the Embeddedness of Action

The ethnomethodological position can also enhance current interest in the analytic importance of "context" and "embeddedness," without recourse to some loosely conceived notion of "social construction." In perhaps one of the most cited and least fully read books of recent sociology, Berger and Luckmann (1966) unwittingly provided decades of sociologists with the perfect "residual" category of explanations; when the data don't fit the model, or the explained variance is low, we are told that the unexplained variance is due vaguely to socially constructed behavior (and, apparently, findings!). There is nothing wrong with the model, it is just that people refuse to act "rationally" or to produce behavior that "fits"; instead they apparently socially construct "irrational" lines of action or collectively construct a different version of the world than the one predicted by the theory.

Recently, the necessary role of "interrelatedness" of institutions or "embeddedness" of one in another has come to the fore. In a striking analysis, Granovetter (1986) has argued the limits of market-driven assumptions in economic models by demonstrating the essential embeddedness of the market in a larger social institutional matrix.[14] Rejecting utilitarian assumptions of "rational," self-interested behavior, Granovetter proposes that economic actions are so embedded in networks of social relations that they are guided as much by "sociability, approval, status, and power" (1986, 506) as by economic goals. This fact has led some economists and related proponents to adopt a naive psychological position as when Elster's often brilliant analyses lead him to resort to "magical thinking" (1988) as an explanation of what is missing in apparently non-rational economic behavior. What is missed, according to Granovetter on the other hand, is social structure. Drawing largely on a network analytic approach to social relations, he elegantly argues that the essentially cooperative relations observed within and between organizations can best be explained by the density of social networks that link and bind organizational members.

Yet it is also my sense that Granovetter misses the most important point. Those structurally defined social relations represented as nodes in matrices are much more than points of contact, nor is it simply a matter of frequency or intensity of connection, whether "strong" or "weak" (Granovetter 1973; *see also* Cohen 1989, 74–77). All of human history, as well as the best-kept diaries on Wall Street and Pennsylvania Avenue, repeatedly highlight the fact that infinitesimal shifts in social relations and in temporally and sequentially ordered events can have *huge* impacts on larger systems, just as recent work in physics shows the same holds true for physical systems.[15] Yet social systems—honestly observed—defy the parsimony of science. Granovetter rejects, for example, Williamson's "market and hierarchies" argument for the persistence of small firms within a system of vertical integration by proposing that it is the "dense structure of social relations [that overlays] the business relations connecting such firms and reduces pressures for integration" (1986, 507). In a study of top Fortune 500 corporations, Friedland and Palmer (1991) also find that interpersonal contact and interactional access consequentially shape these companies and their spatial arrangements. It remains, however, Garfinkel's enduring theoretical contribution to demonstrate just how those social relations—viewed in *detail*—really encapsulate and elaborate explicit sets of relationships in the live-through moments of people and organizations.

Of primary concern here—for both Granovetter and Garfinkel—is the so-called problem of relevance (Schutz 1962), namely how, why, when, and with what weighting do particular aspects of social structure come to be realized at particular moments, and in what specific and interactionally consequential ways? Structuralist rhetoric to the contrary, *all* of social structure does not weigh equally on the shoulders of actors all the time, nor do particular aspects—gender, for example—exert a constant force though they may always be consequential. It is just here that the typical insistence on natural science modeling of social data breaks down—hopelessly. In a world of language, meaning, and power, social science needs profoundly to recognize and analyze the problem of relevance. Laws of gravity may be depended upon to keep me attached to the earth's surface in highly specifiable ways, but no such set of equations or predictions can capture the complexity of conversational interaction nor which small firms in Granovetter's study will display which kinds of linkages at which points in time with what consequences, and so forth. Real advances in our understanding of the relatedness or embeddedness of one or other social group or institution will depend on a much elaborated study of these issues. One approach used in conversation analysis is to carefully observe and analyze the achievement of relevance as a local and interactional matter (Maynard and Zimmerman 1984; *see also* Schegloff 1987a, 1989a; Zimmerman and Boden 1990), but clearly any full study will depend on further conceptualization and appreciation of the basic issue. Both theoretical and empirical analysis of the embeddedness of social action will depend, for any degree of success, on being able to identify and explicate how *particular* aspects of "structure" or "history" or "power" come to be constituted at particular moments with particular actors (Molotch and Boden 1985). The issue is not, I think, one of collectivist versus individualist theories or analysis (cf. Alexander 1988), nor of structured versus socially constructed worlds, but rather it is one of articulating the individual with the collective, action within structure *and vice versa.*

Local Logic: Rationality in Action

A contemporaneous and not unrelated set of issues that have long engaged the attention of philosophers and sociologists revolves around the general nature and operation of rationality in modern society. Rationality and rationalization are typically tied to the development of formal logic within philosophy, the utilitarian tradition in political theory, and to the logic of scientific theory and method. Over the years, sociologists have sought to understand human action and emergent structure in terms of a singular logic, while economists and political scientists have assumed an ever-limiting range of reasonable behavior. That actual occasions of human events rarely approach, let alone match, either such abstract theorizing or models rarely deters anyone. Psychologists and cognitive scientists have furthered this unrevealing trend by offering a range of theories of cognition that characterize humans as either intense calculating machines constantly computing the marginal utility of their every move or as intelligent animals acting on and reacting to an elaborate environmental set of social bells and whistles. Economists have also combined impossible assumptions about a perfect market with the cognitive scripts and maps proposed by psychologists. Most recently, a number of sociologists (e.g., Friedman and Hechter, this volume) have actively engaged the approaches of economists and political scientists whose theories and models provide an apparently alternate set of ways of understanding rational choice, ambiguity, and rational action.

Ethnomethodology is, quite simply, the study of rational action, or, to hone the point, actual occasions of rationality-in-action. It has much to offer these apparently larger approaches in its ability to uncover the local logic of the world as it happens. One problem, for instance, is that of characterizing the domain of interest as "rationality," or "rationalization," or even "rational choice," as it implies that something is going on exclusively inside people's heads, whereas what is of empirical interest and availability is what people are *doing,* namely "rational action." Speaking of rationality in a singular and inclusive manner has the further problem that it is *one*, a single and presumed shared set of assumptions, intentions, motivations, and goals. An inclusive noun such as rationality has, moreover, a reifying and idealizing sort of inevitability such that its presumed universal and enduring properties exist outside of, beyond, and even despite any particular person or specific situation. Sociologists have typically dealt with unreasonable assumptions of, for example, organizational rationality by proposing an informal normative order (Blau 1973), but a close look at any organization reveals that it appears to be running on the informal *all* the time. How can this be so?

The ethnomethodological answer was derived as Garfinkel moved from Parsons' notion of purposive actors engaged in rule-governed behavior to a respecified understanding of social order as the local and contingent accomplishment of order. This is simply to propose that actors act and account for their actions in terms of a "local logic." That logic is, in turn, nested within and reflexively tied to past events and future outcomes, but it is irremediably and unavoidably local in that any and all larger "goals" or "rules" or even "laws" *must* be tailored to particular conditions, particular actors, specific times, definite places. Every soldier knows that, as does every air traffic controller, every law-enforcement official, every mother, every surgeon, every sociologist.

The world is built and rebuilt in and through the local logic of *moments* of people's lives, lives that just because we are human must be lived reasonably with others, but that reasonableness (or rationality) is *relevant* to those same particulars (or details) of action. This is not to say that the world is up for grabs at each succeeding moment but rather that it must, most elaborately, be brought off as a reasonable affair in the present, in the light of the past and with the horizon of the future. Thus what may appear as "irrational" or "unreasonable" from one or another vantage point has, locally and contingently, a fine and delicate immediacy on which later events will be based. When, as noted above, Garfinkel long ago studied the activities of jurors he found them profoundly engaged in and concerned with being able to later describe their actions as *reasonable* (Garfinkel [1967] 1984; *see also* Heritage 1984a). Succeeding studies in ethnomethodology have revealed over and over the way in which the world is a practical and accountable affair. Studies of conversation analysis have, moreover, demonstrated routinely the real-time realization of local logic, whether as the practical matter of locational formulations (Schegloff 1972), the coherence of telling a dirty joke (Sacks 1978), or, in more institutional settings, the contingent accomplishment of plea-bargaining decisions (Maynard 1984) or the split-second production of punctuality in network news interviews (Clayman 1989). Organizational rationality, so called, has these qualities, as do the rational actions of teachers, parents, bankers, politicians, and so too beggars, drug dealers, gang members, and the homeless. Rational action thus depends, first and finally, on the precise intersection of local knowledge and on its enactment as an intersubjectively available and accountable set of activities. Those actions are, as Heritage cogently suggests, computed in "the 'frame-by-frame' moments of interaction" (1984a, 64) and not as some externally located plan.

In ethnomethodological terms, actors are rarely "irrational" or "nonrational" but their logic is assuredly local and must be understood in terms of the concrete particulars of action rather than in terms of some overarching logic. Micromoments of local logic are, by the same token, accountable to that larger set of reasons of the collective which, in their turn, can only be realized at a local level.

Temporality: Time and Local Historicity

A final area in this discussion of ethnomethodology and current issues in social theory involves the constitution of social life in terms of temporal, sequential, and spatial relations, which is to say the "once through" and "no time out" qualities of lived experience (Garfinkel [1967] 1984). A flurry of recent social scientific theorizing has addressed issues of time and space (e.g., Foucault 1979; Giddens 1984, 1987, 1987b). Sociologists such as Zerubavel (1981, 1987) and Melbin (1978) have focused on issues of time and social organization, while a variety of human geographers and urban specialists have explored issues of social space from a variety of perspectives. In particular, Giddens (1981) has drawn time and space into the very center of the theoretical arena, spurring interest (e.g., Maines 1987; Friedland and Boden 1991; Boden, n.d.) and debate (e.g., Thrift 1986). Giddens' basic proposal is not that time or space should be studied directly (e.g., Zerubavel 1981) but incorporated as dynamic dimensions of social theorizing with such concepts as the time-space paths of individuals and the time-space distantiation capacities of modern organizations and nation-states (1984, 1987a).

Ethnomethodology has, by contrast, often been assumed to be ahistorical and atemporal. In developing his own "reflexive sociology," for example, Gouldner drew heavily on the ethnomethodological notion of reflexivity while simultaneously declaring the work of Garfinkel and Goffman and related sociologists to be studying phenomena "outside history" (1970, 444). Nothing could be further from the fact, though

Garfinkel assuredly does not address "history" in an undifferentiated manner as was the style of much Marxist and neo-Marxist work of the period. History too is seen as the local practical activities of real people and it is to the local historicity of action that Garfinkel has addressed himself, particularly in his later work on science and scientists (cf. Garfinkel et al. 1981; Lynch et al. 1983; Garfinkel et al. n.d.).

It is in the fine temporal organization of immediate action that the seeds of social change are to be found, what Braudel (1981) has called *"les poussières d'histoire"*—the fine dust of history. Across the *longue durée* of human events, the local *durée* of action transforms and literally writes its own story into the succeeding moments of history. To be sure, few would recognize Garfinkel's world to be at one with Tilly's or E. P. Thompson's, but what else might agency be, but the tiny meaningful actions of individual actors? Collins has, of course, made this argument most boldly in his microfoundations of macrosociology (1981) but both he (1987) and others (e.g., Fine 1987) have also noted the macrostructural influence on micro events. Garfinkel's concern, to be sure, is always with the local production of action, but it is also deeply preoccupied with the temporal structure of that action and with its sequential properties.

Thus, for Garfinkel, shared and joint activities are accountable, as noted earlier, *at each moment* of their production and are subject to a process of continuous updating (Heritage 1984a). Meaning is not so much "negotiated" as the symbolic interactionists would argue (*see* Fine, this volume). Instead structure is actualized in the interactional work of temporally and spatially located activities whose constitutive meaning is *discovered* in the lived-work of producing them. To students of "huge structures" and "large processes" (Tilly 1985) such an exchange is easily trivialized but it is through the fleeting yet durable structures of practical action that history is made and remade. Each succeeding moment of social action becomes the recognizable and intelligible and familiar condition for the next, and the next, and the next. The "work" of social action entails *discovering* and describing what we are doing *in fact*—that is, not some idealized or typified activity we might describe in the abstract, but what this activity has come to be in the actual production of it. Each moment of history thereby embeds the past not as some vast mantle of legitimacy or the crushing weight of unseen generations, but in terms of the local historicity of that moment, right there and then. That historicity *is* structure, but it is instantiated in our actions. When we "make" a decision, for example, it is a highly fragmented and incremental process in which the discrete points of tiny change and adjustment evaporate in our retrospective account of it. There is "an 'inner' temporal course of interpretation that displays an operational structure" (Garfinkel [1967] 1984, 31). Settings of interaction thereby contain and constitute social structure *from within*. They do so as a singularly temporal matter, once through, no going back, for "another next first time" (Garfinkel et al. n.d.).

WHITHER ETHNOMETHODOLOGY?

At this point in its short and provocative history a number of contemporaneous and immediate prospects for ethnomethodology seem clear. Studies *in* ethnomethodology and ethnomethodologically *informed* research in substantive areas of sociology continue along a solid front. Many of the latter, that is research using an essentially ethnomethodological framework, have tended—rightly—to be acknowledged more as studies in their own areas of science, education, medicine, law, gender, and so forth, rather than as ethnomethodology per se. The work of these scholars reflects a distinct engagement with issues in contemporary social theory and a flexibility of research metaphor and style. The result has been a variety of special journal issues[16] and the belated appearance of primary ethnomethodological and conversation analytic work in the mainstream American journals (e.g., Maynard 1985; Molotch and Boden 1985; Heritage and Greatbatch 1986; Clayman 1989).[17] A variety of studies have also branched out across disciplinary cleavages to address such issues as cognitive science (Coulter 1983, 1990; Suchman 1988), human-machine interaction (Suchman 1987), anthropological fieldwork (Liberman 1985), and so on. At the same time, Garfinkel's own core studies of science and the "work" of the discovering sciences, as noted earlier, have also advanced (e.g., Lynch et al. 1983; Garfinkel et al. 1981; Garfinkel 1986; Garfinkel et al. n.d.).

In theoretical terms, a number of developments merit mention. Conceptually, Garfinkel's own current and projected writings are using the respecification of what he is calling the "discovering" sciences as a vehicle for also reaffirming the essential ethnomethodological enterprise as being concerned with "immortal ordinary society" (Garfinkel 1988, 103). His powerful if often obfuscating insistence on precise and original terminology is being simultaneously extended and itself respecified. To be sure, these new linguistic turns will fully engage only the experienced explorer, but the reach of scholarship will, I am sure, intrigue and inform many more generations of scholarship. Moreover, the important and informal circulation of Harvey Sacks' lectures on conversation is soon to become more public, initially through the publication of early lectures in *Human Studies* in 1989, and through subsequent publication of related materials transcribed and edited by Gail Jefferson (Schegloff 1989).

At the same time, Heritage's (1984a) central interpretation of Garfinkel's intellectual roots and innovative early studies has opened this research to a whole new readership in ways that have yet to be assessed. Thus, in terms of Mullins' insightful model, the "intellectual materials" (1973, 26) of both ethnomethodology and conversation analysis have largely been amassed. For example, key thinkers within the field are also providing useful overviews of conversation analysis that locate its analytic arena firmly within the ethnomethodological purview (e.g., West and Zimmerman 1982; Heritage 1985; Zimmerman 1988; Boden 1990b) and provide a basis for assessing and advancing related research agendas. These position papers are essential at this stage of development and were generally lacking in the earlier decades when energies were absorbed defending ethnomethodology from the many attacks supported by major journals in the 1970s.

As outlined above, a considerable cross-section of European theorizing has by now felt obliged to engage both the theoretical stance and empirical findings of ethnomethodology and, increasingly, related work in conversation analysis. American theorists interested in European trends have also produced a number of key texts, both critical and evaluative (e.g., Lemert 1979) as well as several related review articles (e.g., Atkinson 1989). Moreover, as noted, a number of major American theorists have recently begun to incorporate substantial considerations of ethnomethodology into their own developing theories (e.g., Collins 1981, 1987, 1988b; Ritzer 1981; Wiley 1988; Alexander 1988).

Thus, the ideas of Garfinkel, Cicourel, Sacks, and with them, Goffman have enormous intuitive appeal. Rather than mistake them for micro studies or amusing anecdotes about the world, we would do well to recognize their systematic and highly theoretic orientation and merit (*see also* Giddens 1987b on Goffman; Rawls 1987). The considerable spread of ethnomethodology and conversation analysis internationally is less notable on home ground although all introductory texts include a garbled version of Garfinkel's early breaching experiments.[18] At the graduate level, most serious departments now include ethnomethodology in required theory courses and here the general readings are considerably better (e.g., Ritzer 1988; Collins 1988a). There are also an increasing number of texts by ethnomethodologists themselves (e.g., Leiter 1980; Handel 1982; Cuff et al. 1984; Benson and Hughes 1983; Silverman 1985; Sharrock and Anderson 1986; Livingston 1987) as well as Heritage's (1984a) *Garfinkel and Ethnomethodology*. No less than twenty-two graduate departments claim to offer subspecialties in ethnomethodology, according to the ASA *Guide to Graduate Departments*

(1988), and the subject is also well if not widely taught in Canada, Britain, and increasingly in France, Germany, Switzerland, and Holland (e.g., Widmer 1986; Coulon 1987).

Conversation analysis is also developing in a number of disciplines and promises to provide a further range of researchers and research agendas. Work in conversation analysis is proceeding along a number of intertwined strands, both in "basic" research into the mechanisms of conversational organization (e.g., Schegloff 1982, 1986, 1987, 1987b; Pomerantz 1984; Heritage 1984b; Button and Casey 1984; Jefferson 1984; Jefferson et al. 1986) and, as noted earlier, into a wide arena of institutional settings (e.g., Zimmerman 1984; Maynard, 1984, 1988a, 1989a; Whalen et al. 1988; Boden and Zimmerman 1990; Boden 1990a; Drew and Heritage 1991). Studies of mass media materials also promise a useful and theoretically provocative area (e.g., Heritage and Greatbatch 1986, 1990; Clayman 1989). Primary analysis of video materials generally is also bound to be taken up by more and more researchers following the pathbreaking work of Goodwin (1979, 1980, 1981) and Heath (1982, 1986). Used together, the joint concerns of ethnomethodology and conversation analysis work powerfully, as, for example, in Maynard's recent study of a clinic for developmentally disabled children. There, a primary concern for the *details* of interaction has revealed a pervasive "interactional substrate" to each stage of the process —from educational testing (Maynard and Marlaire 1987) to the delivery of diagnostic news by clinicians (Maynard 1990a, 1990b) to the general process of constituting the child as a "clinical object" (Maynard 1990a). The interwoven agendas of ethnomethodology and conversation analysis have far to go and much to offer to the sociological mainstream. At the same time, new generations of ethnomethodologists are also demonstrating their incorporation of current social theoretic issues in their own work and research repertoire.

So, ethnomethodology is here to stay. Under the surface of such a simple and, perhaps, pious claim lie several submerged yet critical issues of sociological import. These are, in turn, rooted in a bedrock concern for the fundamental nature of human experience, both immediate and *relevantly* structural and historical. The weight of dead generations does *not*, as Marx was wont to insist, simply burden the living in some undifferentiated and numbing sense. People are, and always have been, active agents in the constitution of their unfolding social worlds. That is, after all, the basic story of history. It is in its power to isolate and analyze the fine structure of human experience that ethnomethodology has an enduring, if challenging, agenda for sociology. Far from being "disaggregated" aberrations in the smooth flow of social research, concerted human actions are the very stuff of social inquiry.

The core of ethnomethodological and conversation analytic research to date has necessarily concentrated on exposing and mapping basic features of the patterned and persistent properties of human interaction. Current and future work will, as I have indicated, continue along a broad line of institutional issues, using the basic research findings of both fields to illuminate a variety of sociological areas. Through examination and understanding of the mundane features of the everyday world, always and everywhere bracketing social scientific labels of that world, ethnomethodologists may also broach new understandings of just those aspects of human behavior that currently defy effective analysis and thereby prediction. It is, I would contend, in a precise and detailed understanding of action that we may eventually be able to capture, in particular, those unintended consequences of action that are so resistant to social analysis.

NOTES

1. For an extended and excellent discussion on ethnomethodology, and Garfinkel, as well as an introduction to conversation analysis, there is no better source than Heritage (1984a).
2. Cf. Becker 1981 who provides a single equation for the family as an economic unit.
3. Notions such as "bad records for good organizational reasons" or "normal crimes" or the even more pervasive concept of taken-for-granted features of the social world have all simply been absorbed into the sociological mainstream.
4. For example, in education (Mehan 1979; McHoul 1982; Mehan et al. 1986), educational testing (Maynard and Marlaire 1987), gender (West and Zimmerman 1987; West and Garcia 1988), aging (Boden and Bielby 1986), medical settings (Frankel 1983; West 1984; Heath 1986), psychiatric settings (Hilbert 1977; Bergmann 1990), law (Atkinson and Drew 1979; Maynard 1984), law enforcement (Zimmerman 1984; Meehan 1986; Whalen and Zimmerman 1987), crisis management (Atkinson 1978; Whalen et al. 1988), politics (Atkinson 1984; Molotch and Boden 1985; Heritage and Greatbatch 1986; Bogen and Lynch, 1989), science (Lynch 1985, 1988; Mulkay 1985a; Livingston 1986; Law and Lynch 1988), computer science (Suchman 1987, 1988), mass media (Atkinson 1984; Heritage and Greatbatch 1986; Clayman 1988; Greatbatch 1988; Halkowski 1988), organizations (e.g., Anderson et al. 1987; Harper 1989; Boden 1990a), and so on.
5. The first generation of ethnomethodologists produced a series of studies that largely reshaped and redefined much understanding of organizational and interactional details, laying bare those seen-but-unnoticed, taken-for-granted features of social life on which human action and interaction depend (Garfinkel 1963, 1964, [1967] 1984, 1974; Cicourel 1964; Bittner 1965; Sudnow 1967; Zimmerman 1969; Wilson 1970; Zimmerman and Pollner 1970; Cicourel 1974; Wieder 1974; Smith 1975). Many of those early studies were drawn together in collections by Douglas (1970), Sudnow (1972), Wieder (1974), Turner (1974), and others. The publication of Mehan and Wood's (1975) *The Reality of Ethnomethodology* was, in many ways, a bench mark of that early period and the circle closed with the recent publication of Pollner's splendid dissertation as *Mundane Reason* (1987).

6. That is to say the sociologist is in no privileged position relative to members of society; this ethnomethodological claim moves beyond the mere negotiation of meaning recommended by symbolic interactionists and significantly anticipates recent social theoretic insistence that members are locally *knowledgeable* agents, and more, that structure does not work "behind the backs" of actors (cf. Abrams 1982; Giddens 1984; Sahlins 1985; see also Geertz 1983).

7. This is the concept that is at the heart of what Giddens calls the "double hermeneutic," namely that sociologists and their findings are continually spiraling in and out of the social worlds of which they are a part, reflexively changing those worlds in ways that affect subsequent analysis in ways very different from the work of the natural sciences (Giddens 1984; *see also* Cohen 1989, 202–205). While the concept of interpretive social science may be well developed and readily accepted today, it must be noted that writers such as Garfinkel were among the very first to, as it were, blow the whistle on positivism. Giddens' own work has been massively influenced by the ethnomethodologists since the early 1970s (e.g., 1976) and he continues to be a major advocate.

8. *See also* Garfinkel's (1988) discussion of topics of order in ethnomethodology.

9. Particularly Schutz's early discussion of rationality and the problem of relevance in everyday life (1962).

10. It is likely, for example, that in the 1990s artificial intelligence researchers will need to return to interactionally based approaches to solve the current impasse in human-machine communication. AI research is caught, for the moment, in a cognitive and psychologically oriented paradigm that largely bypasses the indexicality of human action (e.g., Suchman 1987, 1988; *see also* Collins 1986; Coulter 1983).

11. For a quite comprehensive review of the main work and publications, see Heritage (1985). Since that date Heritage has continued to maintain an active bibliography. Researchers working on Jeff Coulter's forthcoming edited collection, *Ethnomethodological Studies*, report compiling a bibliography of over 800 dissertations, articles, monographs, collections, and so forth, in ethnomethodology and conversation analysis generally.

12. Sadly, this ethnomethodological insistence on the details of action has led sociologists generally to trivialize the work and to assume a preoccupation with mere micro moments.

13. And, I suspect, to themselves (*see* Boden 1990b).

14. This work has caused quite a stir among methodologists and organization analysts as well as general sociologists, yet such basic ethnomethodological concepts as reflexivity and indexicality have long underlined the essential and irreducible embeddedness of *all* social action (Garfinkel [1967] 1984).

15. E.g., the so-called "Butterfly Effect" (*see*, for example, Sparrow 1982; Barnsley and Demko 1985).

16. E.g., *Sociology* 1978; *Sociological Inquiry* 1980; *Human Studies* 1986, 1989; *Social Psychology Quarterly* 1987; *Social Problems* 1988.

17. Although it is interesting to note that British journals have long published ethnomethodological work as a matter of routine.

18. In what are, almost without exception, utterly erroneous descriptions of the field based on little knowledge of any recent research. The exception to this claim is Anthony Giddens' forthcoming introductory text which may, in fact, contribute significantly to future generations of ethnomethodological scholarship by virtue of its inclusionary approach to the topic.

REFERENCES

Abrams, Philip. 1982. *Historical Sociology*. Shepton Mallet, U.K.: Open Court Publishing.

Alexander, Jeffrey. 1988. *Action and Its Environments: Toward a New Synthesis*. New York: Columbia University Press.

Alexander, Jeffrey et al., eds. 1987. *The Micro-Macro Link*. Berkeley: University of California Press.

Anderson, Robert, John Hughes, and Wesley Sharrock. 1987. "Executive Problem Finding: Some Material and Initial Observations." *Social Psychology Quarterly* 50:101–114.

Atkinson, J. Maxwell. 1978. *Discovering Suicide: Studies in the Social Organization of Sudden Death*. London: Macmillan.

Atkinson, J. Maxwell. 1984. *Our Masters' Voices: The Language and Body Language of Politics*. London: Methuen.

Atkinson, J. Maxwell, and Paul Drew. 1979. *Order in Court: The Organization of Verbal Interaction in Judicial Settings*. London: Macmillan.

Atkinson, J. Maxwell, and John C. Heritage, eds. 1984. *Structures of Social Action: Studies in Conversation Analysis*. Cambridge: Cambridge University Press.

Atkinson, Paul. 1988. "The Current Status of Ethnomethodology." *Annual Review of Sociology* 14:444–465.

Attewell, Paul. 1974. "Ethnomethodology since Garfinkel." *Theory and Society* 1:170–210.

Barnsley, Michael, and S. G. Demko, eds. 1985. *Chaotic Dynamics and Fractals*. New York: Academic Press.

Becker, Gary S. 1981. *A Treatise on the Family*. Cambridge, Mass.: Harvard University Press.

Benson, Douglas, and John A. Hughes, eds. 1983. *The Perspective of Ethnomethodology*. London: Longman.

Berger, Peter L., and Thomas Luckmann. 1966. *The Social Construction of Reality: A Treatise on the Sociology of Knowledge*. New York: Anchor.

Bergmann, Jorg. 1991. "Veiled Morality: Notes on Discretion in Psychiatry." In Drew and Heritage, eds., *Talk at Work*.

Besnier, Niko. 1989. "Information Withholding as a Manipulative and Collusive Strategy in Nukulaelae Gossip." *Language in Society* 18:315–341.

Bhaskar, Roy. 1979. *The Possibility of Naturalism*. Brighton, England: Harvester Publishers.

Bittner, Egon. 1965. "The Concept of Organization." *Social Research* 32:230–255.

Blau, Peter. 1973. *The Dynamics of Bureaucracy*. Chicago: University of Chicago Press.

Boden, Deirdre. 1983. "Talk International: Turn-Taking and Related Phenomena in Seven Indo-European Languages." Paper presented at the Annual Meetings of the American Sociological Association, Detroit.

Boden, Deirdre. 1990a. *The Business of Talk: Organizations in Action*. Cambridge: Polity Press.

Boden, Deirdre. 1990b. "People Are Talking: Conversation Analysis and Symbolic Interaction." In Howard S. Becker and Michal McCall, eds., *Symbolic Interaction and Cultural Studies*. Chicago: University of Chicago Press.

Boden, Deirdre, n.d. "Temporal Frames: Time, Talk, and Organization." Manuscript.

Boden, Deirdre, and Denise Bielby. 1986. "The Way It Was: Topical Organization in Elderly Conversation." *Language and Communication* 6:73–89.

Boden, Deirdre, and Don H. Zimmerman, eds. 1990. *Talk and Social Structure: Studies in Ethnomethodology and Conversation Analysis.* Cambridge: Polity Press.

Bogen, David, and Michael Lynch. 1989. "Taking Account of the Hostile Native: Plausible Deniability and the Production of Conventional History in the Iran-Contra Hearings." *Social Problems* 36:197–224.

Bourdieu, Pierre. 1982. *Le Sens Practique.* Paris: Editions Minuit.

Braudel, Fernand. 1981. *The Structures of Everyday Life: The Limits of the Possible.* Translated by Sian Reynolds. New York: Harper & Row.

Button, Graham, and Neil Casey. 1984. "Generating the Topic: The Use of Topic Initial Elicitors." In Atkinson and Heritage, eds., *Structures of Social Action: Studies in Conversation Analysis.*

Button, Graham, and John R. E. Lee, eds. 1987. *Talk and Social Organization.* Clevedon, England: Multi-Lingual Matters.

Callinicos, Alec. 1988. *Making History.* Cambridge: Polity Press.

Cicourel, Aaron. 1964. *Method and Measurement in Sociology.* New York: Free Press.

Cicourel, Aaron. 1974. *Cognitive Sociology: Language and Meaning in Social Interaction.* New York: Free Press.

Cicourel, Aaron. 1981. "The Role of Cognitive-Linguistic Concepts in Understanding Everyday Social Life." *Annual Review of Sociology* 7:87–106.

Clayman, Steven. 1988. "Displaying Neutrality in Television News Interviews." *Social Problems* 35:474–492.

Clayman, Steven. 1989. "The Production of Punctuality: Social Interaction, Temporal Organization, and Social Structure." *American Journal of Sociology.*

Cohen, Ira. 1988. "Structuration Theory and Social Praxis." In Anthony Giddens and Jonathan Turner, eds., *Social Theory Today.* Stanford: Stanford University Press.

Cohen, Ira. 1989. *Structuration Theory.* Basingstoke, England: Macmillan.

Collins, Randall. 1981. "On the Microfoundations of Macrosociology." *American Journal of Sociology* 86:984–1014.

Collins, Randall. 1984. "Statistics versus Words." *Sociological Theory* 1:329–362.

Collins, Randall. 1986. "Is 1980s Sociology in the Doldrums?" *American Journal of Sociology* 91:1336–1355.

Collins, Randall. 1987. "Interaction Ritual Chains, Power, and Property: The Micro-Macro Connection as an Empirically Based Theoretical Problem." In Jeffrey Alexander et al., eds., *The Micro-Macro Link.* Berkeley: University of California Press.

Collins, Randall. 1988a. *Theoretical Sociology.* San Diego: Harcourt Brace Jovanovich.

Collins, Randall. 1988b. "The Micro Contribution to Macro Sociology." *Sociological Theory* 6:242–253.

Coser, Lewis. 1975. "Two Methods in Search of a Substance." *American Sociological Review* 40:691–700.

Coulon, Alain. 1987. *L'Ethnomethodologie.* Paris: Presses Universitaires de France.

Coulter, Jeff. 1979. *The Social Construction of Mind: Studies in Ethnomethodology and Linguistic Philosophy.* New York: Rowman.

Coulter, Jeff. 1983. *Rethinking Cognitive Theory.* London: MacMillan.

Coulter, Jeff, ed. 1990. *Ethnomethodological Studies.* London: Edward Elgar.

Cuff, E. C., G. C. E. Payne, D. W. Francis, D. E. Hustler, and W. W. Sharrock. 1984. *Perspectives in Sociology.* 2d ed. London: George Allen and Unwin.

Denzin, Norman. 1970. "Symbolic Interactionism and Ethnomethodology." In Douglas, ed., *Understanding Everyday Life.*

Dingwall, Robert. 1981. "The Ethnomethodological Movement." In G. Payne, R. Dingwall, J. Payne and M. Carter, eds., *Sociology and Social Research*. London: Croome Helm.

Douglas, Jack D. 1970. *Understanding Everyday Life*. Chicago: Aldine.

Drew, Paul, and John C. Hentage, eds., 1990. *Talk at Work: Social Interaction in Institutional Settings*. Cambridge: Cambridge University Press.

Duncan, Otis Dudley. 1984. *Notes on Social Measurement: Historical and Critical*. New York: Russell Sage Foundation.

Elster, Jon. 1988. "Social Norms and Economic Theory." Paper presented at the Political Economy Seminar, Washington University, St. Louis.

Fine, Gary Alan. 1987. "On the Macrofoundations of Microsociology: Order, Meaning, and Comparative Context." Paper presented at the Stone-SSSI Symposium, Urbana, Illinois.

Foucault, Michel. 1979. *Discipline and Punish*. New York: Vintage.

Frankel, Richard. 1983. "The Laying on of Hands: Aspects of the Organization of Gaze, Touch, and Talk in a Medical Encounter." In Sue Fisher and Alexandra Todd, eds., *The Social Organization of Doctor-Patient Communication*. Washington, D.C.: Center for Applied Linguistics.

Friedland, Roger, and Donald Palmer. 1991. "Class, Corporation, and Space." In Friedland, Roger, and Deirdre Boden, eds., *Now/Here: Time, Space and Modernity*. Berkeley: University of California Press.

Garfinkel, Harold. 1963. "A Conception of, and Experiments with, 'Trust' as a Condition of Stable Concerted Actions." In O. J. Harvey, ed., *Motivation and Interaction*. New York: Rowland Press.

Garfinkel, Harold. 1964. "The Studies of the Routine Grounds of Everyday Activities." *Social Problems* 11:225–250.

Garfinkel, Harold. [1967] 1984. *Studies in Ethnomethodology*. Reprint. Cambridge: Polity Press.

Garfinkel, Harold. 1974. "On the Origins of the Term 'Ethnomethodology.' " In Turner, ed., *Ethnomethodology*.

Garfinkel, Harold, ed. 1986. *Ethnomethodological Studies of Work*. London: Routledge and Kegan Paul.

Garfinkel, Harold. 1988. "Evidence for Locally Produced, Naturally Accountable Phenomena of Order." *Sociological Theory* 6:103–109.

Garfinkel, Harold, Michael Lynch, and Eric Livingston. 1981. "The Work of a Discovering Science Construed with Materials from the Optically Discovered Pulsar." *Philosophy of the Social Sciences* 11:131–158.

Garfinkel, Harold et al. n.d. "Respecifying the Natural Sciences as Discovering Sciences of Practical Action." Manuscript.

Garfinkel, Harold, and Harvey Sacks. 1970. "The Formal Properties of Practical Actions." In J. C. McKinney and E. A. Tiryakian, eds., *Theoretical Sociology*. New York: Appleton-Century-Crofts.

Geertz, Clifford. 1983. *Local Knowledge*. New York: Basic Books.

Gellner, Ernest. 1975. "Ethnomethodology: The Re-Enchantment Industry of the California Way of Subjectivity." *Philosophy of the Social Sciences* 5:431–450.

Giddens, Anthony. 1976. *New Rules of Sociological Method*. London: Hutchinson.

Giddens, Anthony. 1979. *Central Problems in Social Theory*. Berkeley: University of California Press.

Giddens, Anthony. 1981. *A Contemporary Critique of Historical Materialism*. Berkeley: University of California Press.

Giddens, Anthony. 1984. *The Constitution of Society*. Cambridge: Polity Press.

Giddens, Anthony. 1987a. "Erving Goffman as a Systematic Social Theorist." In

Anthony Giddens, *Social Theory and Modern Sociology.* Stanford: Stanford University Press.

Giddens, Anthony. 1987b. "Time and Social Organization." In Anthony Giddens and Jonathan Turner, eds., *Social Theory and Modern Sociology.* Stanford: Stanford University Press.

Giddens, Anthony. 1989. *Sociology.* Cambridge: Polity Press.

Goodwin, Charles. 1979. "The Interactive Construction of a Sentence in Natural Conversation." In Psathas, ed., *Everyday Language: Studies in Ethnomethodology.*

Goodwin, Charles. 1980. "Restarts, Pauses, and the Achievement of Mutual Gaze at Turn Beginnings." *Sociological Inquiry.* 50:272–302.

Goodwin, Charles. 1981. *Conversational Organization: Interaction Between Speaker and Hearer.* New York: Academic Press.

Gouldner, Alvin W. 1965. *Enter Plato.* New York: Basic Books.

Gouldner, Alvin W. 1970. *The Coming Crisis in Western Sociology.* New York: Basic Books.

Gouldner, Alvin W. 1975. "Sociology and the Everyday Life," In Lewis A. Coser, ed., *The Idea of Social Structure.* New York: Harcourt Brace Jovanovich.

Granovetter, Mark. 1973. "The Strength of Weak Ties." *American Journal of Sociology* 78:1360–1380.

Granovetter, Mark. 1986. "Economic Action and Social Structure: The Problem of Embeddedness." *American Journal of Sociology* 91:481–510.

Greatbatch, David. 1988. "A Turn-Taking System for British News Interviews." *Language in Society* 17:401–430.

Gusfield, Joseph R. 1968. "The Study of Social Movements." In David L. Sills, ed., *International Encyclopedia of the Social Sciences.* New York: Macmillan.

Halkowski, Timothy. 1988. "The Interaction of Gaze and Talk in a Congressional Hearing: The Social Accomplishment of Answers." Manuscript.

Handel, Warren. 1982. *Ethnomethodology: How People Make Sense.* Englewood Cliffs, N.J.: Prentice-Hall.

Harper, Richard. 1989. "The Social Organization of Accounting." Ph.D. dissertation, University of Manchester.

Heap, James L., and Phillip Roth. 1973. "On Phenomenological Sociology." *American Sociological Review* 42:854–867.

Heath, Christian. 1982 "The Display of Recipiency: An Instance of a Sequential Relationship in Speech and Body Movement." *Semiotica* 42:147–167.

Heath, Christian. 1986. *Body Movement and Speech in Medical Interaction.* Cambridge: Cambridge University Press.

Heritage, John. 1983. "Accounts in Action." In G. N. Gilbert and P. Abell, eds., *Accounts and Action.* Farnborough, U.K.: Gower Press.

Heritage, John. 1984a. *Garfinkel and Ethnomethodology.* Cambridge: Polity Press.

Heritage, John. 1984b. "A Change-of-State Token and Aspects of its Sequential Placement." In Atkinson and Heritage, eds. *Structures of Social Action: Studies in Conversation Analysis.*

Heritage, John. 1985. "Recent Developments of Conversation Analysis." *Sociolinguistics* 5:1–19.

Heritage, John C., and David Greatbatch. 1986. "Generating Applause: A Study of Rhetoric and Response at Party Political Conferences." *American Journal of Sociology* 92(1):110–157.

Heritage, John C., and David Greatbatch. 1990. " On the Institutional Nature of Institutional Talk." In Boden and Zimmerman, eds., *Talk and Social Structure.*

Hilbert, Richard. 1977. "Approaching Reason's Edge: 'Nonsense' as the Final Solution to the Problem of Meaning." *Sociological Inquiry* 47:25–31.

Jefferson, Gail. 1973. "A Case of Precision Timing in Ordinary Conversation:

210 *Deirdre Boden*

Overlapped Tag-Position Address Terms in Closing Sequences." *Semiotica* 9:47–96.

Jefferson, Gail. 1984. "Notes on a Systematic Deployment of the Acknowledgement Tokens 'yeah' and 'mm hm.' " *Papers in Linguistics* 17:197–206.

Jefferson, Gail, Harvey Sacks, and Emanuel A. Schegloff. 1986. "Notes on Laughter in the Pursuit of Intimacy." In Button and Lee, eds., *Talk and Social Organization.*

Knorr-Cetina, Karin and Aaron Cicourel, eds. 1981. *Advances in Social Theory and Methodology: Toward an Integration of Micro- and Macro-Sociology.* London. Routledge and Kegan Paul.

Kuhn, Thomas S. 1970. *The Structure of Scientific Revolutions.* 2d ed. Chicago: University of Chicago Press.

Law, John, and Michael Lynch. 1988. "Lists, Field-Guides, and the Descriptive Organization of Seeing: Birdwatching as Exemplary Observational Activity." *Human Studies* 11:271–303.

Leiter, Kenneth. 1980. *A Primer on Ethnomethodology.* New York: Oxford University Press.

Lemert, Charles C. 1979. "De-Centered Analysis: Ethnomethodology and Structuralism." *Theory and Society* 7:307–318.

Liberman, Kenneth. 1985. *Understanding Interaction in Central Australia: An Ethnomethodological Study of Australian Aboriginal People.* London: Routledge and Kegan Paul.

Lieberson, Stanley. 1985. *Making it Count: The Improvement of Social Research and Theory.* Berkeley: University of California Press.

Livingston, Eric. 1986. *The Ethnomethodological Foundations of Mathematics.* London: Routledge and Kegan Paul.

Livingston, Eric. 1987. *Making Sense of Ethnomethodology.* London: Routledge and Kegan Paul.

Lynch, Michael. 1985. *Art and Artifact in Laboratory Science: A Study of Shop Work and Shop Talk in a Research Laboratory.* London: Routledge and Kegan Paul.

Lynch, Michael. 1988. "The Externalized Retina: Selection and Mathematization in the Visual Documentation of Objects in the Life Sciences." *Human Studies* 11:201–234.

Lynch, Michael, Eric Livingston, and Harold Garfinkel. 1983. "Temporal Order in Laboratory Work." In Karin Knorr-Cetina and Michael Mulkay, eds., *Science Observed: Perspectives on the Social Study of Science.* London and Beverly Hills: Sage.

McHoul, A. W. 1982. *Telling How Texts Talk: Essays on Reading and Ethnomethodology.* London: Routledge and Kegan Paul.

Maines, David R. 1987. "The Significance of Temporality for the Development of Sociological Theory." *Sociological Quarterly* 28:303–311.

Maynard, Douglas W. 1984. *Inside Plea Bargaining.* New York: Plenum Press.

Maynard, Douglas W. 1985. "On the Functions of Social Conflict Among Children, *American Sociological Review* 50:207–223.

Maynard, Douglas W. 1988a. "Language, Social Interaction, and Social Problems." *Social Problems* 35:311–334.

Maynard, Douglas W. 1988b. "Narratives and Narrative Structure in Plea Bargaining." *Law and Society Review* 22:449–481.

Maynard, Douglas W. 1989. "On the Ethnography and the Analysis of Talk in Institutional Settings." In James Holstein and Gale Miller, eds., *New Perspectives on Social Problems.* Greenwich, Conn: JAI Press.

Maynard, Douglas W. 1990a. "Perspective-Display Sequences and the Delivery and Receipt of Diagnostic News." In Boden and Zimmerman, eds., *Talk and Social Structure.*

Maynard, Douglas W. 1990b. "On Co-Implicating Recipients in the Delivery of Diagnostic News." In Drew and Heritage, eds, *Talk at Work*.

Maynard, Douglas W., and Thomas P. Wilson. 1980. "On the Reification of Social Structure." In Scott McNall, ed., *Current Perspectives in Social Theory*. Greenwich, Conn.: JAI Press.

Maynard, Douglas, and Courtney Marlaire. 1987. "The Interactional Substrate of Educational Testing." Paper presented at an Invited Session on Micro-Interactional Analysis in the Workplace, Annual Meetings of the American Anthropological Association, Chicago.

Maynard, Douglas, and Don H. Zimmerman. 1984. "Topical Talk, Ritual and the Social Organization of Relationships." *Social Psychology Quarterly* 47:301–316.

Meehan, Albert J. 1986. "Record-Keeping Practices in the Policing of Juveniles." *Urban Life* 15:70–102.

Mehan, Hugh. 1979. *Learning Lessons: Social Organization in the Classroom*. Cambridge, Mass: Harvard University Press.

Mehan, Hugh. 1990. "The Schools' Work in Sorting Out Students." In Boden and Zimmerman, eds., *Talk and Social Structure*.

Mehan, Hugh, Alma Hertweck, and J. Lee Meihls. 1986. *Handicapping the Handicapped: Decision-Making in Students' Educational Careers*. Stanford: Stanford University Press.

Mehan, Hugh, and Houston Wood. 1975. *The Reality of Ethnomethodology*. New York: Wiley.

Melbin, Murray. 1978. "Night as Frontier." *American Sociological Review* 43:3–22.

Moerman, Michael. 1977. "The Preference for Self-Correction in a Tai Conversational Corpus." *Language* 53/4:872–882.

Molotch, Harvey L., and Deirdre Boden. 1985. "Talking Social Structure: Discourse, Domination and the Watergate Hearings." *American Sociological Review* 50:273–288.

Mulkay, Michael. 1985a. *The Word and the World: Explorations in the Form of Sociological Analysis*. London: George Allen and Unwin.

Mulkay, Michael. 1985b. "Agreement and Disagreement in Conversations and Letters." *Text* 5:201–227.

Mullins, Nicholas. 1973. *Theories and Theory Groups in American Sociology*. New York: Harper & Row.

Pollner, Melvin. 1975. " 'The Very Coinage of Your Brain': The Anatomy of Reality Disjunctures." *Philosophy of the Social Sciences* 4:35–54.

Pollner, Melvin. 1987. *Mundane Reason: Reality in Everyday and Sociological Discourse*. Cambridge: Cambridge University Press.

Pomerantz, Anita. 1984. "Agreeing and Disagreeing with Assessments." In Atkinson and Heritage, eds., *Structures of Social Action: Studies in Conversation Analysis*.

Psathas, George, ed., *Everyday Language: Studies in Ethnomethodology*. New York: Irvington.

Rawls, Ann. 1987. "The Interaction Order Sui Generis: Goffman's Contribution to Social Theory." *Sociological Theory* 5:136–143.

Ritzer, George. 1980. *Sociology: A Multiple Paradigm Science*. Rev. ed. Boston: Allyn and Bacon.

Ritzer, George. 1981. *Toward an Integrated Sociological Paradigm: The Search for an Exemplar and an Image of the Subject Matter*. Boston: Allyn and Bacon.

Ritzer, George. 1985. "The Rise of Micro-Sociological Theory." *Sociological Theory* 3:88–98.

Ritzer, George. 1988. *Sociological Theory*. 2nd ed. New York: Random House.

Sacks, Harvey. 1963. "Sociological Description." *Berkeley Journal of Sociology* 8:1–17.

Sacks, Harvey. 1978. "Some Technical Considerations of a Dirty Joke." In Jim Schenkein, ed., *Studies in the Organization of Conversational Interaction.* New York: Academic Press.

Sacks, Harvey. 1984. "Methodological Remarks." In Atkinson and Heritage, eds., *Structures of Social Action.*

Sacks, Harvey. 1989. "Harvey Sacks' Lectures on Conversation: The 1964–65 Lectures." *Human Studies,* forthcoming.

Sacks, Harvey, Emanuel A. Schegloff, and Gail Jefferson. 1974. "A Simplest Systematics for the Organization of Turn-Taking in Conversation." *Language* 50:696–735.

Sahlins, Marshall. 1985. *Islands of History.* Chicago: Chicago University Press.

Schegloff, Emanuel A. 1968. "Sequencing in Conversational Openings," *American Anthropologist* 70:1075–1095.

Schegloff, Emanuel A. 1972. "Notes on Conversational Practice: Formulating Place." In David Sudnow, ed., *Studies in Social Interaction.* New York: Free Press.

Schegloff, Emanuel A. 1982. "Discourse as an Interactional Achievement: Some Uses of 'uhuh' and Other Things that Come Between Sentences." In Deborah Tannen, ed., *Analyzing Discourse, Text and Talk.* Georgetown Roundtable on Languages and Linguistics. Washington, D.C.: Georgetown University Press.

Schegloff, Emanuel A. 1986. "The Routine as Achievement." *Human Studies* 9:111–152.

Schegloff, Emanuel A. 1987a. "Between Micro and Macro: Context and Other Connections." In Jeffrey Alexander et al. eds., *The Micro-Macro Link.* Berkeley: University of California Press.

Schegloff, Emanuel A. 1987b. "Analyzing Single Episodes of Interaction: An Exercise in Conversation Analysis." *Social Psychology Quarterly* 50:101–114.

Schegloff, Emanuel A. 1990. "Reflections on Talk and Social Structure." In Boden and Zimmerman, eds., *Talk and Social Structure.*

Schegloff, Emanuel A. 1989 "Harvey Sacks' Lectures on Conversation: The 1964–65 Lectures: An Introduction/Memoir." *Human Studies,* forthcoming.

Schegloff, Emanuel A., and Harvey Sacks. 1973. "Opening Up Closings." *Semiotica* 7:289–327.

Schutz, Alfred. 1962. *Collected Papers II: The Problem of Social Reality.* Evanston, Ill.: Northwestern University Press.

Scott, Marvin B., and Stanford Lyman. 1968. "Accounts." *American Sociological Review* 33:46–52.

Sharrock, Wesley, and Robert Anderson. 1986. *The Ethnomethodologists.* New York: Metheun.

Silverman, David. 1986. *Qualitative Methodology and Sociology: Describing the Social World.* Aldershot, U.K.: Gower.

Smith, Dorothy. 1975. "Social Construction of Documentary Reality." *Sociological Inquiry* 44:257–267.

Sparrow, Colin. 1982. *The Lorenz Equations, Bifurcations, Chaos, and Strange Attractors.* Berlin: Springer-Verlag.

Suchman Lucy. 1987. *Plans and Situated Actions: The Problem of Human/Machine Communication.* Cambridge: Cambridge University Press.

Suchman, Lucy. 1988. "Representing Practice in Cognitive Science." *Human Studies* 11:305–325.

Sudnow, David. 1967. *Passing On: The Social Organization of Dying.* Englewood Cliffs, N.J.: Prentice-Hall.

Sudnow, David. 1972. *Studies in Social Interaction.* New York: Free Press.

Thrift, Nigel. 1986. "Bear and Mouse or Tree and Bear? Anthony Giddens's Reconstitution of Social Theory." *Sociology* 19:609–623.

Tilly, Charles. 1985. *Big Structures, Large Processes, Huge Comparison.* New York: Russell Sage Foundation.

Turner Roy, ed. *Ethnomethodology.* Harmondsworth, England: Penguin.

West, Candace. 1984. *Routine Complications: Troubles in Talk Between Doctors and Patients.* Bloomington: Indiana University Press.

West, Candace, and Richard Frankel. 1989. "Miscommunication in Medicine." In Nikolas Coupland, Howard Giles, and John Wiemann, eds., *The Handbook of Miscommunication and Problemmatic Talk.* Avon, U.K.: Multilingual Matters.

West, Candace, and Angela Garcia. 1988. "Conversational Shift Work: A Study of Topical Transitions Between Men and Women." *Social Problems* 35:551–575.

West, Candace, and Don H. Zimmerman. 1982. "Conversation Analysis." In Klaus R. Scherer and Paul Ekman, eds., *Handbook of Methods in Non-verbal Behavior Research.* Cambridge: Cambridge University Press.

West, Candace, and Don H. Zimmerman. 1987. "Doing Gender." *Gender and Society* 1:125–151.

Whalen, Jack, Don H. Zimmerman, and Marilyn L. Whalen. 1988. "When Words Fail: A Single Case Analysis." *Social Problems* 35:335–362.

Whalen, Marilyn, and Don H. Zimmerman. 1987. "Sequential and Institutional Contexts in Calls for Help." *Social Psychology Quarterly.* 30:172–185.

Widmer, Jean. 1986. *Langage et Action Sociale.* Fribourg: Editions Universitaires Fribourg Suisse.

Wieder, D. Lawrence. 1974. *Language and Social Reality.* The Hague: Mouton.

Wiley, Norbert. 1988. "The Micro-Macro Problem in Social Theory." *Sociological Theory* 6:242–253.

Wilson, Thomas P. 1970. "Conceptions of Interaction and Forms of Sociological Explanation." *American Sociological Review* 35:697–709.

Wilson, Thomas P. 1982. "Qualitative 'versus' Quantitative Methods in Social Research." Published in German in *Koelner Zeitschrift fur Soziologie und Sozialpsychologie* 34.

Wilson, Thomas P. 1990. "Social Structure and the Sequential Organization of Interaction." In Boden and Zimmerman, eds., *Talk and Social Structure.*

Zerubavel, Eviatar. 1981. *Hidden Rhythms: Schedules and Calendars in Social Life.* Chicago: University of Chicago Press.

Zerubavel, Eviatar. 1987. "The Language of Time: Toward a Semiotics of Temporality." *Sociological Quarterly* 28:343–356.

Zimmerman, Don H. 1969. "Record-Keeping and the Intake Process in a Public Welfare Agency." In Stanton Wheeler, ed., *On Record: Files and Dossiers in American Life.* New York: Russell Sage Foundation.

Zimmerman, Don H. 1984. "Talk and Its Occasion: The Case for Calling the Police." In Deborah Schiffrin, ed., *Meaning, Form and Use in Context: Linguistic Contexts.* Georgetown University Roundtable on Languages and Linguistics. Washington, D.C.: Georgetown University Press.

Zimmerman, Don H. 1988. "On Conversation." In James A. Anderson, ed., *Communication Handbook.* Newbury Park, Calif: Sage.

Zimmerman, Don H., and Deirdre Boden. 1990. "Structure in Action." In Boden and Zimmerman, eds., *Talk and Social Structure: Studies in Ethnomethodology and Conversation Analysis.*

Zimmerman, Don H., and Melvin Pollner. 1970. "The Everyday World as Phenomenon." In Jack Douglas, ed., *Understanding Everyday Life.* Chicago: Aldine.

Zimmerman, Don H., and D. Lawrence Wieder. 1970. "Ethnomethodology and the Problem of Social Order: Comment to Denzin." In Douglas, ed., *Understanding Everyday Life.*

8

The Comparative Advantages of Rational Choice Theory

❀

DEBRA FRIEDMAN AND MICHAEL HECHTER
Russell Sage Foundation
and University of Arizona

Social scientific theories are tools for research, not sacred texts to be pored over by scholars seeking to outdo one another with the ingeniousness of some new hermeneutic twist. Theories are necessarily incomplete and are bound to be supplanted by better ones. They are like lanterns that illuminate parts of the dark caves we explore in our research: they extend our understanding of the mysteries of social phenomena. We could all do without theories. We could scramble from fact to fact as a spelunker tries to discern the contours of the dark cavern on hands and knees. But as the spelunker's task is made easier with the lantern's aid, so the social researcher's task is made easier with the aid of a theory.

But which theory should we use? As this book shows, there are a great many different ones to choose among. What are the criteria by which theories should be selected? We could select on sentimental grounds, choosing the one we learned at father's knee, or in our dissertation supervisor's classroom. Alternatively, we could select on political grounds, choosing the one that seems to offer the promise of the best state of affairs for us, for our favorite group, or for the world as a whole. But since each of these selection criteria has more to do with the intrinsic properties of the *chooser* than with the intrinsic properties of the *theory*, we would have no assurance that the theory we have chosen is best equipped to cast the desired illumination.

Surely it makes sense to adopt some criterion for selection that deals with the intrinsic properties of the theory. One way is to rank theories on the basis of the light they cast on matters that otherwise would remain obscure, and then to select the one with the highest rank. We could also rank theories according to a ratio of their demonstrated explanatory power relative to their complexity, and then select the one with the highest rank. And, finally, theories might be compared on the basis of the number of counterintuitive (or nonintuitive) implications that they yield.

We are persuaded that rational choice fares relatively well by these criteria of theory choice. To demonstrate the explanatory power of rational choice as compared to that of its alternatives for any given empirical case requires more space than we have in this essay. However, we can provide some examples of the interesting empirical implications that have been generated from these theoretical premises.

The following is a list of twenty insights, each derived from a single theoretical perspective. The list contains some insights that might have remained obscure in the absence of this particular theory. It contains insights that are substantively diverse, but flow from relatively simple premises. And it contains some insights that are counterintuitive or nonintuitive. We will present each of these insights briefly, and then go on to describe the general theory from which they flow.

A GLIMPSE INTO THE CAVE: TWENTY INSIGHTS ABOUT DIVERSE SOCIAL PHENOMENA[1]

1. *American political parties that are self-consciously responsive to the preferences of a national constituency will produce vapid and relatively similar sets of policies.* Political parties in a two-party system that wish to garner the maximum number of votes will do so only by appealing to the center of the ideological spectrum (Downs 1957). Thus, each party will intentionally alter its platform to attract the median voter. As a result, the respective party platforms will become purposefully ambiguous.

2. *The preferences that are reflected in social outcomes can be more extreme than those held by the constituent individual actors.* Extreme residential segregation by race can occur even when the residents of a given neighborhood merely wish to live in a perfectly balanced neighborhood (50%–50% white/black), or in a neighborhood where they themselves do not constitute a minority (25%–75% white/black or black/white). The first outcome—a perfectly balanced neighborhood—is obviously unstable when there is any deviation from the 50–50 split; and the second outcome is almost impossible to reach, given the initial condition of a racially homogeneous neighborhood (Schelling 1978).

3. *In organized groups, successful collective action depends on mobilizing the disinterested.* In any given group, it is likely that some individuals will prefer to pursue one collective good, while others will

prefer to pursue another. Yet in many instances, the efforts of those who are least interested are as important to the attainment of the good as are the efforts of those who are most interested. All of the actors appreciate that successful collective action requires the contribution of a wide range of group members. The most interested need the least interested. But the least interested will contribute only if they get something in return. What they want is the contribution of the other actors to a good in which they have the greatest interest. Thus actors in an ongoing group will frequently be observed to exchange control and participation over collective goods (Coleman 1973).

4. *Social structural commonality alone is insufficient to produce collective action.* Collective action is oriented toward the attainment of public goods, and rational individuals will tend to consume them without contributing to their provision (Olson 1965). Hence, whenever individuals sharing some social structural commonality act in concert, this must be due to the presence of additional facilitating conditions.

5. *In unorganized groups, successful collective action depends on mobilizing potential beneficiaries.* The production of any collective good requires an initial investment by some critical number of individuals. Some kinds of collective goods can be provided by the contributions of a small critical mass, whereas the provision of other kinds requires a much larger number of initial contributors (Oliver, Marwell, and Teixeira 1985).

6. *Rewards and punishments do not follow commonsense expectations in motivating behavior oriented toward the attainment of a collective good.* Positive and negative sanctions have different implications for collective action: rewards are effective in motivating small numbers of participants, while punishments are effective only when the situation requires unanimous cooperation (Oliver 1980).

7. *Many structural categories are so broadly defined that they are inadequate to explain political outcomes.* The political behavior of peasants in certain regions of the same state differs markedly from their behavior in other regions despite their shared class locations (Brustein 1988).

8. *Dependence overcomes ideology.* The roll-call voting behavior of elected representatives is better predicted by their dependence on party leaders and constituents than by their personal ideologies (Hechter 1987).

9. *One cannot rely on wages alone to produce compliance.* Whereas agents are hired by principals to represent the principals' interests, they will do so only when they are sufficiently rewarded and constrained (Jensen and Meckling 1976). For example, this is why parents worry about the adequacy of their child care arrangements.

10. *Rulers with large amounts of discretionary resources at their behest will not enact economic policies that promote the collective welfare.* In England and France, both countries with ample resources during the Absolutist era, highly autonomous rulers enacted policies that hindered economic development (Kiser 1987).

11. *Even when facing death, people may not engage in collective action on their own behalf.* Jews in concentration camps did not revolt, not because of a lack of common interest or sufficient motivation to do so, but because the repression in those camps simply offered them no opportunities (Levi 1988).

12. *Collective outcomes that benefit the whole are difficult to achieve through individual actions.* Analyses of Prisoner's Dilemma games suggest that self-interested actors will find themselves choosing individual courses of action that lead to collectively sub-optimal outcomes (Luce and Raiffa 1957).

13. *Preferences do not solely determine actions.* Almost everyone in the Los Angeles basin would prefer to live in a smog-free environment, yet at the same time almost everyone contributes to the production of smog by driving an automobile.

14. *Individuals are sometimes responsible for perpetuating societal-level discriminatory practices.* In societies like Japan, where guidance and sponsorship are crucial for status attainment, educators and employers are motivated to sponsor individuals who are likely to remain committed employees. Due to family responsibilities, women are less likely to meet such a qualification than men. Understanding that employers engage in sex discrimination, parents invest differentially in sons and daughters. Both parents and employers unwittingly conspire to perpetuate gender stratification (Brinton 1988).

15. *The nuclear arms race is the product of a deterrent strategy.* The leaders of each superpower—and everyone else in the world—would prefer mutual disarmament. Yet because the most advantageous position for any one superpower to enjoy is to be armed when the other is disarmed, each will arm (Brams 1985).

16. *Certain kinds of collective goods (especially those involving moral hazard) can be provided only in the presence of institutions that enforce stringent controls.* Insurance offers protection against loss, but to the degree that insured persons are protected against loss, they have no incentive to guard against it. Unless individuals can be induced to behave responsibly, all insurers would go out of business. In order to provide insurance, stringent institutional controls designed to produce responsible behavior therefore are required (Heimer 1985).

17. *Stronger collective sanctions enhance incentives both for compliance and for revolt.* When a group is subjected to collective sanc-

tions, a variety of responses may be rational: the group may either create a secondary sanctioning system to enforce the agents's dictates, or it may revolt against the agent to destroy its sanctioning capacity (Heckathorn 1988).

18. *The rationality of the free rider and the rationality of the zealot arise under the same sort of social structural conditions.* In social organizations in which individuals have common—rather than conflicting or complementary—goals, the efforts of each person serve to satisfy his or her own interest and to reward others for their contributions to the corporate welfare (Coleman 1987).

19. *The solidarity of a group depends not on normative consensus, but on a combination of dependence and control mechanisms.* Because individuals join groups in order to receive collective goods, all groups are plagued by the free-rider problem. The free-rider problem can be solved only through control mechanisms. Thus, these are principally responsible for group survival (Hechter 1987).

20. *Regardless of initial endowments, children in classrooms with an average higher achievement level will perform better individually than those in classrooms with an average lower achievement level.* If teachers desire to enhance their own status within schools, they must strive to bring every student up to the mean performance level of the class, as well as to reward those students whose performance exceeds the mean. When the mean level is higher, poor students therefore will receive proportionally more teacher attention, and will perform at a higher level (de Vos 1989).

Granted that these insights are plausible—many of them even may be true—what does one have to do with the next? Some concern issues at the individual level, others concern those at the macro level of analysis; some are about formal organizations, others are about informal ones; some are about *gemeinschaft*, others are about *gesellschaft*; some are about structure, others are about process. What sort of theory might be able to provide explanations for such disparate social phenomena?

One answer is rational choice. In its most general and metatheoretical form, rational choice attempts to explain the emergence of *social outcomes* by the action of *purposive* agents who are subject to a variety of possible types of institutional and environmental *constraints*. Any event created by the interaction of two or more agents is a social outcome. Purposive agents have some particular set of preferences (that is, a utility schedule) that enable them to pursue goals (or ends) in a conscious and more or less efficient manner. (How efficient these choices are is a matter of continuing dispute.) The constraints that purposive agents face can arise either from their individual opportunity costs, or from existing institutional structures to which they are subjected (or in which they are embedded).

Two additional elements found in every rational choice explanation are, first, assumptions about the amount of *information* that agents have about the future consequences of their present actions (which is sometimes taken to be variable), and, second, assumptions about the mechanisms by which the individual preferences (or actions) of the agents are *aggregated* so as to yield the relevant social outcome.

While all rational choice theories, at least implicitly, include information and an aggregation mechanism, there are three separate paths to follow in charting a theoretical course from the actor to the social outcome. First are the arguments that rely on the preferences of actors to explain various social outcomes. Second are those arguments in which the outcomes are a function of opportunity costs. In the third kind of argument, different social outcomes are traced to variations in institutional constraints.

These turn out to correspond to the three major types of explanations found in rational choice theory. Insights 1 though 3 illustrate links between preferences and outcomes, insights 4 through 11 illustrate links between opportunity costs and outcomes, and insights 12 through 20 illustrate links between institutional constraints and outcomes. Despite their apparent diversity, on analytic grounds these insights can be parsed into three groups. In turn, these three groups are all derived from common first principles.

Elsewhere, we have written in detail about how rational choice theory yields empirical implications of this sort, and about the recent past of sociological rational choice (Friedman and Hechter 1988). There we argue that rational choice has been a highly efficacious lantern for exploring the cave comprised of macrosociological phenomena. Yet strong and clear as the light that this lantern casts is, significant portions of the cave's outlines remain impervious to its illumination.

In the remainder of this essay we try to say something about the future of sociological rational choice. Before beginning, however, we must make an important caveat. Speculating about the future of an academic field is among the riskiest of pursuits, and most wise prognosticators merely attempt to forecast by extrapolating present trends. In the case of rational choice, this kind of a forecast is relatively easy to perform, but, by the same token, it is correspondingly uninformative.

In our opinion rational choice is a highly productive way of explaining social outcomes, but it is also one that also suffers from some obvious flaws. In spite of these flaws, economists and political scientists have utilized rational choice to great effect in analyzing a variety of social phenomena. There is little doubt that sociologists can also follow suit, and, further, that they should do so. Yet, due to these flaws, there is a definite limit to the utility of rational choice models in social science. This limit can only be extended by addressing these flaws and by superseding them. The real future of rational choice—the interesting future that no one can predict with any confidence—will depend on finding solutions to these quandaries.

TOWARD A FUTURE RATIONAL CHOICE THEORY

Three possible subjects for fruitful investigation are introduced: 1) issues related to measuring key components of the theory; 2) approaches to the study of the genesis of institutions; and 3) possible ways to address the question of the preferences that individuals hold.

Contributions in the Area of Measurement

There are two major opportunities for theoretical contribution in the area of measurement. The first opportunity concerns the measurement of the rationality assumption itself. The second concerns alternative ways to aggregate individual choices and behavior so as to accurately derive social outcomes.

MEASUREMENT OPPORTUNITIES IN DECISION-MAKING PROCESSES

Does it matter whether individuals really are the rational actors depicted in rational choice theories? Sociologists have been particularly concerned with the assumption of individual rationality. They claim that the model's reliance on this assumption vitiates its utility in empirical research, since nearly anyone can think of a host of counter-examples to rational behavior. An argument can be made—and indeed, one has been made—that for theoretical purposes, the realism of the model's individual behavioral assumptions is unimportant. This argument typically assumes that since we are interested in social outcomes, and since these outcomes do not reflect the internal state of any one particular person, the mental and emotional idiosyncrasies of the constituent actors in effect cancel out, leaving only the hard central tendency of self-interest (Hechter 1987, 32; Stinchcombe 1968).

A somewhat different kind of answer to this question holds that whether actors behave rationally may be crucially important for psychology, but that it matters not a whit for economics and sociology

(Friedman 1953). If theories built on psychologically inadequate premises yield accurate empirical implications, and do better than their theoretical competitors, then such theories are to be preferred.

Yet even for those who subscribe to these kinds of arguments, the question of the realism of rational choice behavioral assumptions is a nagging one. The question is really not whether or not people are rational (in the technical sense that they have consistent and transitive preferences that are stable and independent of context)—most everyone would concur that this is an inadequate description of human beings—but whether better assumptions exist upon which to base a behavioral theory. To this end, a great deal of attention has been paid to laboratory research that has sought to measure actual decision-making processes (Dawes 1988). It is interesting to note that the work of psychologists Kahneman and Tversky (1979), showing systematic biases in perceptions of risk and in behavioral outcomes given different kinds of framing, has been widely discussed and debated among economists, political scientists, and other rational choice scholars (Schoemaker 1982).

While this kind of work will be carried on largely outside of the field of sociology, there is also room for sociological scholarship, some of it in the laboratory. If it were possible to measure normative motivations independently of the action they are said to inform, then we, too, could gain knowledge about the internal limits of rationality. Since the claim that behavior is normatively guided is both distinctly sociological and in direct contrast with the claim that it is rationally guided, research of this sort would have as many implications for rational choice theory as would the measurement of rationality itself.

There is a still more serious measurement problem regarding internal states and the development of behavioral theory. To claim, as rational choice scholars do, that agents maximize their utility leads to the question of what that utility looks like. Utility schedules are the great black box of rational choice scholarship, and we explore this issue more fully in a subsequent section.

MEASUREMENT OPPORTUNITIES IN AGGREGATION

Perhaps the most serious measurement problem facing rational choice theorists is the same problem that faces all theorists interested in explaining outcomes that occur at a different level of analysis than those of the postulated causal mechanism. Unlike the body of scholarship on the subjects of opportunity costs and utilities—which is highly theoretical, if not terribly empirical—there is not even much theoretical work on the aggregation problem (Markovsky 1988).[2]

There are, however, several strategies that might be pursued. The first strategy is well-illustrated by network analysis (Burt 1980), and by the experimental work in exchange theory (Cook et al. 1983). In these examples, the aggregation *becomes* the structure and the structure, in turn, implies the individuals who compose it. In one sense this is a neat solution: individual and structural levels of analysis are inextricably linked, and the network may be inferred thereby. The network is *defined* as the individual nodes that compose it. Then certain social outcomes—like collective action—are traced to particular network configurations.

But in order to use this strategy as a solution to the aggregation problem, rational choice theorists would want to know something about the origin of the network—that is, the reasons for individual cooperative production of network structures in the first place. (From the point of view of rational choice, networks are collective goods whose existence is therefore problematic.) On this issue network theorists, unfortunately, are mute.

Although it has not been conceived in this way, the accelerating and decelerating functions that are hypothesized to characterize the production of different sorts of collective goods (Oliver, Marwell, and Teixeira 1985) also can be seen as an aggregation process.[3] These production functions suggest that in predicting collective action, one should not assume that individuals will join the effort at a constant rate over time. Instead, it is likely that during a specified period of time, a given collective action will attract participants at a slower or a faster rate (due, in part, to the nature of the collective good to be produced). The slope of the production function is a prediction about the rate of joining over the period in question. The aggregation principle that applies, even though participants are certainly unaware of it, is: add participants at an inconstant rate, according to the slope of the production function.

The proper instructions for deriving macrosocial outcomes from individual actions can come only from a theory of aggregation. The demands on such a theory would be considerable. It would have to account for the frequent lack of resemblance between the preferences of individual actors and the preferences that are embodied in the results of their collective efforts. As the studies of voting rules so clearly demonstrate, there is no necessary relationship between the collective preference reflected in the social outcome and the preferences of the individuals who voted.

Further, it would have to take account of the complexities of interpersonal power. Only in rare cases are social outcomes the sum of equally weighted votes. More common are situations in which the uneven distribution of resources across individuals is reproduced in collective arrangements.

Finally, a theory of aggregation would have to include time as a key dimension. Some social outcomes—like American presidential elections—are decided nearly instantaneously. Yet others—like the French Revolution—occur over a long period of time. It is doubtful whether the process of revolt is linear. Thus, not only must such a theory include time, but it must do so in a nonlinear fashion.

The considerable effort that the formulation of this kind of theory would entail would be handsomely rewarded, we believe. A theory of aggregation is, after all, required for rational choice explanations, but it is also required for all explanations in which a macro outcome is derived from micro processes.

The Genesis of Social Institutions

As discussed above, one of the ways that rational choice has made its mark is by explaining social outcomes as a function of institutional constraints. At the most general level, social institutions—such as laws, rules, norms, and cultural values—produce observable collective behavioral regularities by constraining the individuals subject to them. In rational choice theory, institutions are conceived to be bundles of positive and negative incentives that raise the net benefit of engaging in certain behaviors, and lower the net benefit of engaging in others.[4]

Yet the standard assumption in analyses of these kinds that institutions are *given* begs a fundamental question from a rational choice perspective. Because institutions are themselves emergent phenomena, their very existence must be regarded as problematic in rational choice. This means that one of the major intellectual challenges facing rational choice analysts is to explain how rational egoists in a relatively *noninstitutional* environment can cooperate so as to produce institutions whose rationale is that they increase the collective welfare (these *cooperative institutions* can be distinguished from other kinds of institutions, such as *conventions* [*see* Hechter 1990a]).[5]

There have been two different kinds of new rational choice attempts to account for the emergence of institutions endogenously. By far the most attention has been paid to *invisible-hand* approaches to institutional genesis. Explanations of this kind view the emergence of institutions as a spontaneous byproduct of the voluntary actions of egoistic agents who share no common ends or values. Invisible-hand explanations of institutional genesis have been based on the theory of repeated games (Axelrod 1984 is the most popular example). Yet, for two reasons, repeated game theory offers no adequate solution to the emergence of cooperation among *n* players of a Prisoner's Dilemma supergame (Hechter 1990b). In the first place, there are multiple equilibria in the supergame, some of which are efficient and some inefficient. Yet under most conditions it is difficult to determine which of these multiple equilibria will be realized. In the second place, unique cooperative solutions to the supergame rest on a most unrealistic assumption— namely, that players are endowed with perfect monitoring capacity (Bendor and Mookherjee 1987). This assumption limits the application of game-theoretic solutions to the evolution of cooperative institutions to the smallest of groups.

The alternative rational choice approach to institutional genesis is *solidaristic* and depends on the existence of some common end among a given set of agents. In order to attain this common end, these agents must establish a set of obligations as well as an enforcement mechanism that enables them to count on the compliance of all to these obligations. From this solidaristic perspective institutions persist not because they constitute self-enforcing equilibria, but because they are supported by consciously designed controls.

Whereas it is clear that institutions can be imposed upon a given population by a conqueror or overlord, the major theoretical challenge is to understand how agents having roughly equal power can create institutions voluntarily. Hechter (1987, 1989) has begun to outline what one such solidaristic explanation of institutional genesis might look like. He sees cooperative institutions emerging as a function of (1) individuals' demands to provide themselves with jointly produced private goods, as well as on (2) these individuals' potential control capacity—that is, their opportunities either to dissuade each other from free riding, or to assure each other of their intent to cooperate.

The demand for cooperative institutions arises from agents' desire to consume private goods that cannot be obtained by following individual strategies. But the mere existence of demand for such institutions is insufficient to guarantee their production, on account of the free-rider problem. Whereas all of the given agents might desire some particular institution—say, a protective association to guard against the predation of invaders or bandits—it is generally not in the interest of these agents to help contribute to the establishment or maintenance of the institution. The agent tends to have such an interest only under one condition: if her consumption of the demanded private good (here, protection against loss and injury due to invaders) is directly contingent on her contribution to the establishment and maintenance of the protective association. This contingency, in turn, depends on the enactment of formal endogenously emergent controls.

The establishment of these formal controls may be seen as a series of solutions to a three-tier free-rider problem involving (1) the formulation of a joint plan to procure the demanded jointly produced good, (2) the establishment of an initial group constitution that permits these agents to reach collective decisions (Buchanan and Tullock 1962), and (3) the implementation of the agreed upon plan of action. An essential determinant of the rise of the necessary controls is the existence of *visibility* in both the production and consumption of joint goods. In relatively noninstitutionalized environments trust is a commodity that will be in short supply. Hence, the free-rider problem can be mitigated in such environments only when agents are fully visible to one another in their capacities both as producers and consumers.

In the state of nature, visibility will be at a maximum when joint goods are collected and dispersed from some central place. The collection and disbursement of killed meat among hunter-gatherers, the collection and disbursement of irrigated water among horticulturalists, the formation of partnerships to engage in long-distance trade, and the establishment of caravans on the American frontier—all examples of cooperative institutions that have emerged in relatively noninstitutional environments—satisfy this key requirement of visibility.

But this explanation is just a first step, and it will be the charge of further research on the rise of institutions to develop—and to formalize—both of these invisible-hand and solidaristic approaches to institutional genesis, to better understand the strengths and weaknesses of each, and to propose more comprehensive alternatives.

The Origin of Preferences

Another lacuna in rational choice—one that it shares with all other social scientific theories concerned with intentional action—stems from the standard practice of considering actors as maximizers of a unidimensional quiddity known as *utility*.[6] Just what this utility consists of, however, is a matter of considerable controversy.[7] Since neither preferences nor utility are directly measurable, rational choice theorists are continually vulnerable to charges that their explanations are either post-hoc or tautological. Some economists (Friedman 1953; Becker 1976) respond to this challenge by equating actors' utility with their wealth.

Yet it is evident that a great many individual behaviors, let alone social outcomes, are not the result of simple wealth maximization.[8] On the one hand, actors often are interested in goals other than those related to their own welfare. Whereas the incidence of altruism is far from universal, it is also far from negligible (Etzioni 1988)—even Gary Becker (1981) concedes this. On the other hand, preferences do not always appear to be stable. Individual responses to the vicissitudes of fashion provide all of us with ample impressionistic evidence to this effect. But there is also robust experimental evidence about preference reversals: the same agents in some contexts seek risk, but in other contexts become risk-averse (Kahneman and Tversky 1979).

Ultimately, these difficulties can only be allayed by a theory of preference formation. Such a theory would have payoffs at both the micro and macro levels. At the micro level, for instance, it would explain something that is otherwise counterintuitive—namely, the helping of others at grave personal risk. Why did some gentiles in the occupied territories of Europe during World War II shelter Jews from Nazis (Oliner and Oliner 1988)? Why did some witnesses called before the House Un-American Activities Committee refuse to testify? Why do people continue to join the Irish Republican Army, when a high proportion of this organization's membership ends up in jail or dead? And why did some young white northern Americans participate in Freedom Summer on behalf of black southerners who were strangers to them (McAdam 1988)?

Such a theory not only would enable us to understand individual differences in preferences, but it would also have implications for macrosociological phenomena, for social outcomes are affected—to a degree that is largely unknown—by individual preferences.[9] To some extent, social institutions undoubtedly reflect the preferences of the individuals who establish them, as well as affecting the preferences of those who are subject to them (Wildavsky 1987). Thus, it is not difficult to imagine that the preferences of the architects of the Scandinavian welfare states must have been different from those of the architects of apartheid in South Africa. Yet no adequate theory of preference formation exists in social science.

CONCLUSION

As the preceding section of this essay suggests, the future of research in rational choice is rich with questions and possibilities. While this new research will allow us to explore ever deeper into the currently obscure chambers of the cave that comprise the mysteries of unexplained social phenomena, these discoveries will be inextricably linked to our knowledge of those parts of the cave that are currently illuminated. Rapid accumulation of knowledge is one of the comparative advantages afforded by rational choice: since specific rational choice theories all are built on the same first principles, their implications are mutually informative.

Having a set of first principles allows scholars with a variety of substantive interests and areas of expertise to communicate with one another. The inclusiveness of rational choice theory produces a research community that is relatively large and diverse; it brings to bear on any given research question the expertise of sociologists, political scientists, economists, philosophers, and legal scholars. This inclusiveness distinguishes rational choice from most other (but clearly not all other) social scientific theories which tend to produce small, inbred research communities that are characterized by narrow linguistic and conceptual specialization. Such research communities tend to be less open to developments occuring in their own and other disciplines.

This, then, has been a brief case for the comparative advantages of rational choice theory. Its range of substantive applications and insights, its parsimony, its natural micro-macro orientation, its cumulative nature, and its inclusiveness of a broad range of social scientists all are arguments in its favor.

NOTES

1. A fuller discussion of most of these insights is found in Friedman and Hechter (1988). There is a certain degree of overlap between that essay and this. The emphasis of Friedman and Hechter (1988) is on the analytical structure of rational choice explanations in macrosociology, and on recent research in this genre. In contrast, the emphasis in this chapter is on the future of sociological rational choice. Hence, these two essays are complementary.

2. The work of Arrow and subsequent research on social choice is the principal exception to this statement.

3. We alone are responsible for this interpretation of production functions as a possible aggregation mechanism.

4. Deterrence theory in criminology offers a particularly clear example of how institutions—in this instance, legal institutions—are treated in a rational choice framework. It asserts that the greater the celerity, certainty, and magnitude of punishment for a specific behavior, the less its frequency. Hence, deterrence theorists argue, states that permit capital punishment will have fewer homicides than those that do not permit capital punishment. (Whether or not the proposition can be empirically supported is another question entirely, and one that is the subject of a large literature of its own.)

5. Of course, this is precisely the task that Thomas Hobbes took it upon himself to solve in *Leviathan*, but, as is by now well-appreciated, his solution was, in certain respects, inadequate (Hechter 1987, ch. 6).

6. A utility schedule is a ranking of all the individual's preferences over goods, both concrete and subtle, at a given point in time.

7. *See* Emerson (1982), Friedman (1987), and Etzioni (1988) for the harsh, but not wholly unreasonable, view that the economists' utility is conceptually empty.

8. Part of the problem may be that whatever preferences actors are conceived to be pursuing, they do not maximize them. Many choices seem to be made according to some decision rule other than maximization. Satisficing (Simon 1985) and meliorating (Herrnstein 1982) are two of the leading alternative decision rules in the

228   *Debra Friedman and Michael Hechter*

current literature. Unlike maximization, however, these alternative decision rules have seldom been employed to generate social outcomes.

9. As noted above, the effects of individual preferences on social outcomes are always mediated by the aggregation mechanism.

REFERENCES

Axelrod, Robert. 1984. *The Evolution of Cooperation.* New York: Basic Books.

Becker, Gary S. 1976. *The Economic Approach to Human Behavior.* Chicago: University of Chicago Press.

Becker, Gary. 1981. *A Treatise on the Family.* Cambridge, Mass.: Harvard University Press.

Bendor, Jonathan, and Dilip Mookherjee. 1987. "Institutional Structure and the Logic of Ongoing Collective Action." *American Political Science Review.* 81:129–154.

Brams, Steven. 1985. *Superpower Games.* New Haven: Yale University Press.

Brinton, Mary. 1988. "The Social-Institutional Bases of Gender Stratification: Japan as an Illustrative Case." *American Journal of Sociology* 94:330–334.

Brustein, William. 1988. *Social Origins of Political Regionalism: France 1849–1981.* Berkeley: University of California Press.

Buchanan, James S., and Gordon Tullock. 1962. *The Calculus of Consent.* Ann Arbor: University of Michigan Press.

Burt, Ronald S. 1980. "Models of Network Structure." *Annual Review of Sociology* 6:79–141.

Coleman, James S. 1973. *The Mathematics of Collective Action.* Chicago: Aldine.

Coleman, James S. 1987. "Free Riders and Zealots." In K.S. Cook, ed., *Social Exchange Theory.* Newbury Park, Cal: Sage.

Cook, Karen S., M. R. Gillmore, and T. Yamagishi. 1983. "The Distribution of Power in Exchange Networks: Theory and Experimental Results." *American Journal of Sociology* 89:275–305.

Dawes, Robyn. 1988. *Rational Choice in an Uncertain World.* Orlando, Fla.: Harcourt Brace Jovanovich.

de Vos, Henk. 1989. "A Rational-Choice Explanation of Composition Effects in Educational Research." *Rationality and Society* 1:220–239.

Downs, Anthony. 1957. *An Economic Theory of Democracy.* New York: Harper & Row.

Emerson, Richard M. 1982. "Social Exchange Theory." In M. Rosenberg and R. H. Turner, eds., *Social Psychology: Sociological Perspectives.* New York: Basic Books.

Etzioni, Amitai. 1988. *The Moral Dimension: Toward a New Economics.* New York: Free Press.

Friedman, Debra. 1987. "Notes on 'Toward a Theory of Value in Social Exchange.' " In K. S. Cook, ed., *Social Exchange Theory.* Newbury Park, Cal.: Sage.

Friedman, Debra, and Michael Hechter. 1988. "The Contribution of Rational Choice Theory to Macrosociological Research." *Sociological Theory,* 6:201–218.

Friedman, Milton. 1953. "The Methodology of Positive Economics." In Milton Friedman, *Essays in Positive Economics.* Chicago: University of Chicago Press.

Hechter, Michael. 1987. *Principles of Group Solidarity.* Berkeley: University of California Press.

Hechter, Michael. 1990a. "The Emergence of Cooperative Social Institutions." In M. Hechter, K. D. Opp, and R. Wippler, eds., *Social Institutions: Their Emergence, Maintenance and Effects.* New York: Aldine de Gruyter.

Hechter, Michael. 1990b. "On the Inadequacy of Game Theory for the Solution of Real-World Collective Action Problems." In K. S. Cook and M. Levi, eds., *The Limits of Rationality*. Chicago: University of Chicago Press.

Heckathorn, Douglas D. 1988. "Collective Sanctions and the Creation of Prisoner's Dilemma Norms." *American Journal of Sociology* 94:535–562.

Heimer, Carol A. 1985. *Reactive Risk and Rational Action: Managing Moral Hazard in Insurance Contracts*. Berkeley: University of California Press.

Herrnstein, Richard. 1982. "Melioration as Behavioral Dynamism." In M. L. Commons, R. J. Herrnstein, and H. Rachlin, eds., *Quantitative Analyses of Behavior: Vol. 2. Matching and Maximizing Accounts*. Cambridge, Mass.: Ballinger.

Jensen, Michael C., and William H. Meckling. 1976. "Theory of the Firm: Managerial Behavior, Agency Costs and Ownership Structure." *Journal of Financial Economics* 3:305–360.

Kahneman, Daniel, and Amos Tversky. 1979. "Prospect Theory: An Analysis of Decision Under Risk." *Econometrica* 21:263–291.

Kiser, Edgar. 1987. "Marx and Weber on the Role of Absolutist States in the Transition from Feudalism to Capitalism." Ph.D. dissertation, University of Arizona.

Levi, Primo. 1988. *Survival in Auschwitz*. New York: Macmillan.

Luce, R. Duncan, and Howard Raiffa. 1957. *Games and Decisions*. New York: Wiley.

McAdam, Doug. 1988. *Freedom Summer*. New York: Oxford University Press.

Markovsky, Barry. 1988. "From Expectation States to Macro Processes." In M. Webster, Jr. and M. Foschi, eds., *Status Generalization: New Theory and Research*. Stanford: Stanford University Press.

Oliner, Samuel P., and Pearl M. Oliner. 1988. *The Altruistic Personality*. New York: Free Press.

Oliver, Pamela, 1980. "Rewards and Punishments as Selective Incentives for Collective Action: Theoretical Investigations." *American Journal of Sociology* 85:1356–1375.

Oliver, Pamela, Gerald Marwell, and Ruy Teixeira. 1985. "A Theory of the Critical Mass. I. Interdependence, Group Heterogeneity and the Production of Collective Action." *American Journal of Sociology* 91:522–556.

Olson, Mancur. 1965. *The Logic of Collective Action*. Cambridge: Harvard University Press.

Schelling, Thomas C. 1978. *Micromotives and Macrobehavior*. New York: W. W. Norton.

Schoemaker, Paul J. H. 1982. "The Expected Utility Model: Its Variants, Purposes, Evidence and Limitations." *Journal of Economic Literature* 20:529–563.

Simon, Herbert A. 1985. "Human Nature in Politics: The Dialogue of Psychology with Political Science." *American Political Science Review* 79:293–304.

Stinchcombe, Arthur. 1968. *Constructing Social Theories*. New York: Harcourt Brace.

Wildavsky, Aaron. 1987. "Preferences by Constructing Institutions: A Cultural Theory of Preference Formation." *American Political Science Review* 81:3–21.

9

The Uses of French Structuralisms in Sociology

❀

CHARLES C. LEMERT
Wesleyan University

Todd Gitlin (1988, 1) has asked exactly the right question of postmodernism, the currently most popular installment of the French structuralisms: "Journals, conferences, galleries and coffee houses are spilling over with talk about postmodernism. What is this thing, where does it come from, and what is at stake?" The thing is very confusing. In its current form as an attack on modernist, enlightenment values, it comes mostly from recent French social theory. At stake are the most fundamental assumptions we make about knowledge. All these reasons explain, I think, why the French structuralisms are not at this point well understood or accepted in American sociology.

Still the question nags. Why has the single most popular intellectual fashion of the eighties been largely ignored in sociology? What is it about sociology, or the French ideas, that has permitted poststructuralism to revolutionize literary studies and make important contributions in anthropology, women's studies, social history, and philosophy, yet leave most sociologists cold? I believe the answer is that the structuralist line, from structuralism proper through postmodernism, involves very high stakes. It is a challenge to the nineteenth-century habits of thought out of which sociology arose and to which it is still wedded. The French structuralisms are, therefore, pretty much an all-or-nothing opportunity. They don't blend well with other intellectual viewpoints.

Nevertheless, I believe the French structuralisms offer something to sociology. But to discover that potential we must take recent French social theory seriously for what it is. One might grant that its language is confounding and its dismissal of modernity extreme, and many will not wish to bother with it for these reasons. But to understand and consider movements like post-structuralism and postmodernism one must be willing to deal with these two factors. Only then is it possible to determine their prospect of usefulness in sociology.

VARIETIES OF FRENCH STRUCTURALISM

Some years ago, Raymond Boudon, one of France's most distinguished sociologists, published a critique of structuralism with the title *a quoi sert la notion de "structure"*? in English the French title translates, "What use is the notion of structure?" However, the book's eventual English-language publishers, presumably afraid of killing their product with such a negative title, named the book *The Uses of Structuralism* (Boudon 1971). Boudon's book was indeed quite negative. He argued that French structuralism was not useful because it was little more than a reincarnation of all structural logics back to the Greeks. Writing in the sixties, when post-structuralism had not yet fully surfaced, Boudon saw only one side of the then very new movement. The uniquely different features of structuralism were invisible, hence useless, to him.

Most of the troubles American sociologists experience with recent French social thought are condensed in this reflection on Boudon and his title. The structuralist movement is a moving target. At first, as structuralism pure and simple, it appeared as a formalism that seemed to reduce the human sciences to pitiful abstractions—Lévi-Strauss's (1967) universal binary oppositions, Althusser's (1970) scientific Marx, Barthes's (1970) zero-degree writing and formalistic semiology. At a second moment, between roughly 1966 and 1970, post-structuralism burst on the scene, incorporating strange Nietszchean and psychoanalytic concepts. The target was different, yet it retained clear affinities with the structuralism it attacked. Then, a decade or so later in the seventies, postmodernism gathered force from numerous sources, presenting still another target both different from and continuous with the earlier structuralisms. It is difficult to take accurate interpretive aim at such a thing which is simultaneously different and the same.

To make matters even worse, the thing itself is intentionally obscure. It challenges what many of us believe to be true. Michel Foucault (1972, 210–211) understood quite well the problems his interpreters faced: "I understand the unease of all such people. They have probably found it difficult enough to recognize that their history, their economics, their social practices, the language *(langue)* they speak, the mythology of their ancestors, even the stories that they were told in their childhood, are governed by rules that are not all given to their consciousness." This is an important reason why no school of post-structuralist thought has developed in sociology.[1] It is too much an affront to our habits of thought. There being no such development, my discussion will necessarily confine itself to the prospects of a post-structuralist sociology, which can only be estimated from a solid grasp of what this thing is and whether or not the high stakes make it a good bet.

Structuralism, a movement in the fifties and early sixties, proposed a restructuring of the social and human sciences. Lévi-Strauss, the early Roland Barthes, and others used a formal theory of the structures of language, most importantly Saussure's *la langue*, to recast in more scientific terms anthropology and the study of culture and literature. Structuralism was a departure from the strong theories of the subject of which, in France, post-war existentialism and phenomenology were the dominant cases. In the introduction to *The Raw and the Cooked* Lévi-Strauss (1970, 44–45) says: "By pursuing conditions where systems of truth become mutually convertible and can therefore be simultaneously admissible for several subjects, the ensemble of these conditions acquires the character of an object endowed by a reality proper to itself and independent of any subject." At first reading, structuralism's attack on subjectivist thought seemed conveniently within the limits of modernism. Early structuralism had all the appearances of an objectivist swing against subjectivist extremes. There was, however, much more to the story.

Post-structuralism was born along with, and as a part of, structuralism. Derrida (1978, 278), speaking in 1966[2] at the first major international conference on structuralism, began with words that recognized the duality and duplicity of structuralism:

> Perhaps something has occurred in the history of the concept of structure that could be called an "event," if this word did not entail a meaning which it is precisely the function of structural—or structuralist—thought to reduce or to suspect. Let us speak of an "event" nevertheless and use quotation marks to serve as a precaution. What would this event be then? Its exterior form would be that of a *rupture* and a redoubling.

The words are opaque. They announce an event that ends events. They claim that the idea of structure had come to a point that would end both structure and event, yet they would remain in quotation marks, redoubled beyond this rupture.

For those not committed to its language and program, post-structuralism seemed (and seems) a stupid play with words. But from within it uses its language seriously, to liberate the play of words and ideas. Derrida announced a shift in Western thought. For this purpose he required the prior existence of structuralism, just as structuralism entailed, in Derrida's view, post-structuralism. The "post" in post-structuralism was a tactical joke, a playfully serious trick. Structure, Derrida went on to say, had served to limit and confine modern thought. "Event"—the concept structuralism sought to eliminate—was the false alternative, the artificial hope for emancipation from this confinement. Event was, after all, the code word of existentialism—and a cognate to other subjectivist ideals—the ideally free subject, consciousness, rational choice, subjectively intended meaning, the essential nature of "Man," and so on.[3]

Structuralism, in so far as it led to post-structuralism, was its own gravedigger. These two awkwardly bound perspectives attacked the formative conviction of modernist thought, that the world could be viewed through the lenses of the subject-object dichotomy. Structuralism, with all its first appearances of objectivism, was the beginning of the end for objectivism and subjectivism. At least this was the claim of Derrida and others who were central to the post-structuralist movement in the late sixties and through the seventies—Foucault, Lacan, Kristeva, Barthes, among others.

But this claim required a still subsequent movement, postmodernism. If October 21, 1966, the date of Derrida's talk to the Johns Hopkins conference, was the beginning of post-structuralism, then with equal daring one might accept Charles Jencks' (1977, 9) statement that postmodernism began with the death of modernist architecture at 3:32 P.M., July 15, 1972—the moment at which the Pruitt-Igoe housing project in St. Louis was destroyed. Both dates are of course symbolic, expressing only the unique feature of the departure. Thus, if Derrida's talk identified post-structuralism as the end of the structuring of thought in the human sciences, postmodernism extended that principle to the end of structure in modern culture, beginning with the point at which culture and the built environment intersect, architecture. "The post-modern world heralds the collapse and the unfeasability of the grand, centralized systems with which one once attempted to explain everything" (Portoghesi 1980, 106). Pruitt-Igoe, therefore, is a convenient symbol. This massive housing project in St. Louis represented modernist architecture's arrogant belief that by building the biggest and best public housing planners and architects could eradicate poverty and human misery. To have recognized, and destroyed, the symbol of that idea was to admit the failure of modernist architecture, and by implication modernity itself. If this is too oblique a symbol, social theorists may take 1979 as the better inaugural date for postmodernism, the year of publication of its two most frequently cited texts, Jean-Francois Lyotard's *The Postmodern Condition* and Richard Rorty's *Philosophy and the Mirror of Nature*.

Lyotard (1984, 3) began with a statement consistent with Derrida's in 1966. "Our working hypothesis is that the status of knowledge is altered as societies enter what is known as the postindustrial age and cultures enter what is known as the postmodern age." Rorty (1979, 7) states that the "therapeutic" aim of his book is "to undermine the reader's confidence . . . in 'knowledge' as something about which there ought to be a 'theory' and which has 'foundations.'" His view is comparable to Lyotard's that the conditions of knowledge have fundamentally changed because in the postmodern era knowledge, most especially "scientific knowledge, is a form of discourse" (Lyotard 1984, 3). These assertions built upon ideas that had developed in the preceding two decades. They were, therefore, consistent with Derrida's definition of the post-structuralist event within structuralism: "This was the moment," according to Derrida, "when language invaded the universal problematic, the moment when, in the absence of a center or origin, everything became discourse" (Derrida 1978, 280).

One way or another, everything in the three structuralisms comes back to language, or more accurately, to a specific commitment to the idea that language is now necessarily the central consideration in all attempts to know, act, and live. Though there are substantial disagreements within the structuralist line, all three movements—structuralism, post-structuralism, and postmodernism—intend to replace modernist principles of positive knowledge in the sciences, the social sciences, and philosophy with a new approach based on language. This conviction distinguishes this line of thought from others, like Habermas', that similarly accept the importance of language.[4] This is the stake in a prospective use of these ideas in sociology.

In another sense, language is an additional barrier to the reception of the structuralisms in American sociology. As the movement took each redoubled step, its language became more and more obscure. In the original structuralist phase the writings were difficult but not obscure. Levi-Strauss' "Structural Study of Myth" and Barthes' "Elements of Semiology," like much of Althusser in this period, were hard to read, but readable. But when post-structuralism emerged full blown in the late 1960s, the writings became more and more resistant to normal reading. One leaves many of these texts with a barely liminal comprehension—what Todd Gitlin (1988, 36) describes in reference to Lyotard as a "slapdash style, in the French mode" which insists rather than argues. One gets something, but one cannot be sure what. Gitlin admits he's not sure he understands Lyotard, yet with reasonable confidence goes on to characterize the argument. Critics frequently complain about this aspect of French social theoretical writings. It is important, however, to understand that it is an intended and, to the French, necessary experience of readers. The effect is sought, as a matter of principle.

I propose, as an example, the first phrase of Derrida's 1966 statement: *"Perhaps something has occurred in the history of concept structure."* The reader senses (though perhaps not consciously) that the first, surprisingly conditional word, "perhaps," serves a tactical purpose. It both brings Derrida's readers in and keeps them at bay. On the one hand, Derrida addressed his remarks to a largely American audience in Baltimore. The "perhaps" seeks out their relative unfamiliarity with his subject and the French style. It says, contrary to Gitlin's experience, I won't quite insist on the following. Yet, on the other hand, what follows is very much an insistence: an event has occurred in the history of the concept structure. Derrida is proclaiming prophetically, insisting. The juxtaposition of the "perhaps" opens a space between his utterance and his readers. He wants the event to proclaim itself. This, we learn a few paragraphs later on, is the space in which language can play out its effects and announce itself. This is why Gitlin and many others sense they don't quite understand or feel they can't quite "get" the line of argument.

Derrida's (1978, 280) argument is that this event was *"the moment when language invaded the universal problematic, . . . the moment when . . . [a] . . . everything became discourse . . . [b] . . . a system in which the central signified . . . [c] . . . is never absolutely present outside a system of differences."* The three ellipses (marked [a], [b], [c]) each contained significant qualifications. When the material is excluded, as above, the argument is relatively neat. But in each of these places Derrida's actual text presents material that strains the reading by introducing heavy qualifications which make a philosophical statement, namely:

[a] *"in the absence of a center or origin,"*
[b] *"provided we can agree on this word [discourse]—that is to say,"* and
[c] *"the original signifier."*

Each qualifying phrase contradicts a reader's attempt to understand the event Derrida announces as a positive, factual moment in history. The first, [a], and the third, [c], introduce philosophical claims that cannot be proven, and each is so sweeping as to be beyond argument. The absent center, for example, refers to the assumption that prior to poststructuralism all traditional thought, including modernism, relied on a restrictive, transcendent principle. This, of course, is less a point of fact than of interpretation. Even as a point of interpretation it would have been hard to argue convincingly in 1966 that this was the essential nature of modernist thought. It is hard enough to argue the point in 1990. The second qualification, [b], *"provided we can agree"* on the meaning of the term *"discourse,"* is both an acknowledgment of the strangeness of his idea to his readers and an expression of his now famous deconstructionist principle that we must use familiar language to express the totally unfamiliar.

The overall effect of the passage is to subject the reader to an insistence triply qualified, presented in the guise of an argument. It is not an argument that one can "follow" along a direct line of clear and distinct logical understanding. It is not a statement open to logical or empirical verification, but an invitation to enter a different, postmodern (that is, in 1966, post-structural) language within which one finds that everything is language. The argument which is not an argument is found only in a series of juxtaposed, different elements—conditional "perhaps"/proclamation, structuralism/end of structuralism, post-structuralism/continuity of structuralism, argument/insistence. One wants to ask, what does Derrida mean? To which he would reply, if he were to reply at all, I am playing, seriously. "Play is the disruption of presence," he says near the end of the text (Derrida 1978, 292). All attempts to be clear are based on the philosophical presumption that meaning and reality can be present to consciousness. To "make clear" is to reflect or, in Rorty's term, mirror nature. These are attempts to get around language which exists, so to speak, on its own terms.

Post-structuralism and postmodernism, though in different degrees and ways, each seek to destroy the ideal of pure, meaningful communication between subjects as a corollary to the disruption of the metaphysical distinction between subjects and objects. This is the way in which language invades the universal problematic. Language is assumed to be that one social thing which when it is made the center of things disrupts everything, including the possibility of a center of things. Language looks to the future. Thus Derrida (1978, 293) ends this essay with a hesitant, fearful anticipation of a liberating birth, cloaked in a language one understands, barely:

> I employ these words, I admit, with a glance toward operations of childbirth—but also a glance toward those who, in a society from which I do not exclude myself, turn their eyes away when faced by the as yet unnameable which is proclaiming itself and which can do so whenever a birth is in the offing, only under species of a non-species, in the formless, mute, infant, and terrifying form of monstrosity.

Any attempt to develop a post-structuralist, or postmodernist, sociology requires a willingness to face this monstrosity of language. According to such a perspective, when language is taken seriously for what it is, the social world is seen in a particular way. It is no longer possible to view the world as internally and necessarily coherent. To take language seriously, as the structuralisms do in their manner of writing as in their philosophy, is to decenter the world, to eviscerate it of grand organizing principles (God, natural law, truth, beauty, subjectivity, Man, etc.) that mask the most fundamental truth of human life, differences. Those who have followed recent developments in postmodernist feminist theory and literary theory realize that this conviction is filled with political intent.

> Aware that women writers inevitably engage a literary history and system of conventions shaped primarily by men, feminist critics now often strive to elucidate the acts of revision, appropriation and subversion that constitute a female text. (Abel 1980, 2)

> Scores of people are killed every day in the name of differences ascribed only to race. This slaughter demands the gesture in which the contributors to this volume are collectively engaged: to deconstruct, if you will, the ideas of difference inscribed in the trope of race, to explicate discourse itself in order to reveal the hidden relations of power and knowledge inherent in popular and academic usages of "race." (Gates 1985, 6)

Modernism is taken as the centered, hierarchical, Europeanized, dominant world against which the principle of difference is thrust to assert the realities of those whose daily lives are marked by the experience of difference—women, nonwhites, working class, the third world.

The question for sociology is what is it about language that permits such a long excursion from Lévi-Strauss' rediscovery of linguistics in the fifties to today's politics of difference? And what are the prospects in this for sociology?

POST-STRUCTURALISM AND SOCIOLOGY

Against philosophies of the Center, modernism in particular, post-structuralism introduced an intellectual politics based on the now famous concept of decentering. It is not always understood that decentering is less a philosophy, or a rival concept to those of modernism, than a practice. This is, in part, the point of post-structuralism's unsettling approach to writing.

From one point of view, decentering is a reasonably precise philosophical concept conveying Derrida's and Foucault's (1972) original attacks on centered philosophies, most especially phenomenology's extreme subjectivist philosophy of consciousness. This is the sense most accurately associated with the postmodernist rejection of Enlightenment theories of knowledge. From another point of view, decentering suggests a broad political opposition to all traditional and modern social forms, philosophy included, in which structures serve to inhibit social freedom. It is advisable, therefore, to think of post-structuralism and postmodernism as first and foremost a form of knowledge derived from a political practice. This attitude conveys not only post-structuralism's attempt to overcome philosophy for political purposes but also its claim that discourse and writing must be taken as the subject matter and means of intellectual work.

Such an interpretation of decentering makes a heavy demand on sociologists accustomed to viewing politics as something totally other than science, or, at most, that to which sociologists contribute expertise. Post-structuralism claims that intellectual work is political, and it does so with reference to concepts most sociologists would consider anything but political—text and discourse.

Roland Barthes defines the Text as "that *social* space that leaves no language safe or untouched, that allows no enunciative subject to hold the position of judge, teacher, analyst, confessor, or decoder. The theory of the Text can only coincide with the activity of writing" (Barthes 1979, 81, emphasis original). This statement is linked to the claim that decentering is an ongoing intellectual practice deriving from the theoretical decision to interpret the Text in relation to other texts, rather than in relation to its author. For Barthes this involves the distinction between the work and the Text:

> The work is concrete, occupying a portion of book-space (in a library, for example); the Text, on the other hand, is a methodological field. . . . This opposition recalls the distinction proposed by Lacan between "reality" and the "real"; the one is displayed, the other demonstrated. In the same way, the work can be seen in bookstores, in card catalogues, and on course lists, while the Text reveals itself, articulates itself according to and against certain rules. While the work is held in the hand, the text is held in language. (Barthes 1979, 74–75)

The work, therefore, is seen as the unit of modernist writing in which writing is a transitive activity—the production of literary objects by subjects, authors. Thus, the privileging of the Text over the work is another instance of the philosophical side of decentering, here the rejection of the purportedly modernist belief that the social world is inhabited by self-conscious subjects who project meaning into their works. It is a rejection of subjectivism as a cryptometaphysics.

This move replaces the original modernist couplet—*subject* (author)/*object* (work)—with something else which itself has the appearance of a couplet—*practices* (writing)/(intertextual) *field*. But the relationship of text to its intertextual field is active, creative, and practical. Practices/field has the form but not the substance of a conceptual dichotomy. It looks the same but is different—postdichotomous. Texts are products of intransitive writing, they are outside the subject-object dichotomy. "The Text cannot be thought of as a defined object" (Barthes 1979, 74.) It is, as noted, a methodological field, while the work is a concrete object. Texts are, therefore, play in a forever open and open-ended field which they produce and by which they are produced, and in which they must be interpreted.

The important thing to keep in mind is that post-structuralists view this reorientation as a general social theoretical move. Though they remain close to the language of text and discourse, post-structuralists situate their views with respect to a theory of society. The critique of the subject-author is an instance of opposition to all forms of social domination. Much of Foucault's writing on various topics, from *The Order of Things* to *The History of Sexuality*, is in opposition to dominations represented by the engendered, Europeanized humanism which, in another context, is characterized by the term patriarchy.[5] The link between a general social theory and the problem of the author is apparent in Foucault's "What Is an Author?" (Foucault 1979, 158–159).

> We are accustomed . . . to saying that the author is a general creator of a work in which he deposits with infinite wealth and generosity, an inexhaustible world of significations. We are used to thinking that the author is so different from other men, and so transcendent with regard to all languages, that as soon as he speaks meanings begin to proliferate. . . . The truth is quite contrary . . . the author does not precede the works, he is a certain fundamental principle by which, in our culture, one limits, excludes, and chooses. . . . The author is the ideological figure by which one marks the manner in which we fear the proliferation of meanings.

In this respect, post-structuralism is a social theory articulated within concrete studies of literary, historical, and philosophical questions.

Post-structuralism is very much a product of the political and social events leading to and ensuing from May 1968 in Paris. Foucault's (1978) sexual politics, Lacan's (1977) engendering of psychoanalysis, Kristeva and Irigaray's (*see* Moi 1987) feminist theories, Derrida's (1985) politics of difference, Deleuze and Guattari's (1977) schizoanalytic politics all are rooted, one way or another, in the late sixties revolutionary politics that challenged the world-centered ambitions of post-war Gaullism. If, at that same moment, left intellectuals in the United States sought a coherent New Left alternative to both Old Left Marxism and Johnson-Humphrey liberalism, French intellectuals searched for an alternative that rejected traditional communist and socialist party politics and was post-Marxist without being anti-Marxist. In the one joint programmatic statement of the post-structuralist movement, when Foucault, Barthes, Derrida, Sollers, and Kristeva allowed and caused their separate projects to be joined in an edition of *Tel Quel* titled "Théorie d'ensemble" (published not incidentally in the early autumn of 1968), these politics were quite explicit. The introduction stated that their joint project was, in part, "to articulate a politics logically bound to a dynamically non-representative writing, that is to say: analysis of the confusion created by this position, explicition of their social and economic character, construction of the relations of this writing with historical materialism and dialectical materialism" *(Tel Quel* 1968, 10). It would be an uncomfortable stretch to consider this a social theory in the usual sense, but that theory is there, however faintly. It is the basis for a positive connection with social theoretical work in sociology.

In more sociological terms, the implication of this attitude toward writing as an intellectual practice is that action is oriented to an open field of play that lacks inherent, limiting rules. Rules become resources in Giddens' sense; limits are social arbitraries serving only to define the possibilities of transgression in Foucault's sense; the field defines the conditions and terms of practices in Bourdieu's sense. The structured field is viewed as open, that is, characterized by differences, absence, play. Hence the various descriptive terms one associates with post-structuralist thinkers: discursive formation (Foucault), intertextuality (Barthes), *la langue* (Saussure), *champ* (Bourdieu). To these sometimes implicit visions of a field of play are juxtaposed the correlative notions that describe intransitive actions: practices, writing, speaking, habitus.[6]

On first examination, this would appear to be an interesting theoretical model in the form: *Think of social action as intransitive practices in a dynamically open field of play.* But this would not be a sufficient interpretation of post-structuralist thinking. Models, in its view, are modernist attempts to mirror the social world. Models depend on the assumption that the social (or natural) world can be represented, that is, "presented again" in the language of knowledge. Post-structuralism, implicitly, and postmodernism, explicitly, reject the Enlightenment ideas that knowledge is an autonomous and constituting feature of social life.

> The notion that our chief task is to mirror accurately, in our Glassy Essence, the universe around us is the complement to the notion, common to Democritus and Descartes, that the universe is made up of very simple, clearly and distinctly knowable things, knowledge of whose essences provides the master vocabulary which permits commensuration of discourses. (Rorty 1979, 357)

There are no post-structuralist models. "Let us wage a war on totality; let us be witnesses to the unpresentable; let us activate the differences and save the honor of the name" (Lyotard 1979, 82). Postmodernist knowledge, such as it is, is the consequence, not a representation, of action in a field of play.

Therefore, what is at stake in a possible post-structuralist sociology is a willingness to move sociology away from its historic role as a discipline, a social science, a type of knowledge, and toward a more politically self-conscious practice that is neither traditionally Marxist nor liberal. Postmodern knowledge entails a postmodern politics. Like the strange space Derrida sought to open and use in the first words of "Structure, Sign, and Play in the Human Sciences," a post-structuralist sociology would have to be willing to tolerate the idea of working in a confusing, different social space that is neither epistemological nor political, but both yet neither.

In a certain sense this is not an alien idea to sociology. We have been, from the beginning, the most artificial of disciplines and the clumsiest of sciences because sociology is, by its nature, a situated practice. It is only in recent years that sociologists have reincorporated ideas from ethnomethodology and other parasociological sources (including some of the post-structuralist literature) to recover the centrality of what Giddens (1984, xxxv) describes as the double hermeneutic, the fact that theories of society interpret that which they also help constitute, even while interpreting. Though post-structuralism makes a more radical claim than such indigenous sociological practices as ethnomethodology and Giddens' structuration theory, it bears this point of positive comparison with those aspects of sociology that forthrightly work within a recognition of the unique double nature of sociological knowledge. Ideas like the "double hermeneutic" and "writing as intransitive practice" are similarly comfortable with the uncomfortable social space in which knowledge is no longer the foundation of that which is, where instead language both is the universal problematic and, insofar as "knowledge" is concerned, is all that is.

Within post-structuralist perspectives, the generic name for this knowledge which is (nothing but) language is discourse. Discourse expresses, and is, the inherently transgressive quality of post-structuralist intellectual politics, as one can see in Hayden White's (1978, 4) definition:

> A discourse moves "to and fro" between received encodations of experience and the clutter of phenomena which refuses incorporation into conventionalized notions of "reality," "truth," or "possibility." . . . Discourse, in a word, is quintessentially a *mediative* enterprise. As such it is both interpretive and preinterpretive; it is always *about* the nature of interpretation itself as it is *about* the subject matter which is the manifest occasion of its own elaboration.

Post-structuralist social theory, whether avowedly sociological or not, is discursive in this sense of transgressing the subject matter it interprets by constantly reflecting on the necessity and nature of interpretation itself.[7]

Of course, there are problems with a proposal to make discourse both the subject matter and the medium of sociological analysis. A discursive sociology, as we have already seen, would require an uprooting of deeply ingrained convictions—belief in the subject-object dichotomy and other classical dualities; loyalty to the ideal of sociology as a well-founded, scientific source of knowledge; expectations that good work will produce identifiably worthwhile political and intellectual outcomes.

The far more serious problem with a discursive sociology in the post-structuralist tradition is that posed by taking discourse as an object of study. It is one thing to accept a discursive, transgressive method as the condition of sociological practice, another to deal with evident dilemmas in the discursive analysis of discourse. Sociologists and other intellectual practitioners can be discursive in the sense of appropriating the attitude of constant, as White puts it, to-ing and fro-ing with the real world. Social theory as reflective, intransitive action is thinkable even if objectionable to some. But what are the limits of discourse as an "object" of study? This question demonstrates the severity of the challenges posed by post-structuralism. One must bracket even the term "object." But what do the brackets mean? Does a discursive social theory mean there are no "objects," that is to say, no contents to intellectual practices? Is such a practice forever doomed to a world of talk about talk itself, of the interpretation of interpretation, of a program without performances? The problem is acute when one considers the question, Is there in the "real" world nondiscursive social action? It is one thing for a discursive intellectual work to treat other discursive materials of the same sort. This is what the post-structuralists mean by intertextuality in the strictest sense of the concept.

The success of post-structuralism in literary studies may rely considerably on the fact that, in this area, other texts are the proper subject matter. The most compelling successes, in my opinion, of applied post-structuralism have been among feminist, third world, and Afro-American critics who uncover the discursive power of hitherto silent, oppressed women, black, or third-world writers (Gates 1985, 1988; Carby 1987). In a case like Henry Louis Gates' (1988) discussion of the confluence between the African Esu-Elegbara and the Afro-American signifying monkey figures in two separated but historically bound cultural systems, the analyst is applying a discursive method to texts that are found to be surprisingly discursive themselves. Both figures served to contain and express the doubled cultural experience of those who are simultaneously African and in some fractured way American. The figures were discursive in that they mediate the divided social reality of people for whom colonial oppression and slavery was the decisive social attribute. This discovery of the discursive, and political consciousness of so-called nonliterate or otherwise excluded people is parallel to similar discoveries of the study of oppressed women, the working class, and other victims of colonial domination, and this literature—of which E. P. Thompson's *The Making of the English Working Class* is a locus classicus[8]—is familiar and assimilable to even normal sociological thought.

The greater difficulty concerns the hint strong within post-structuralist thought that everything social is discourse. Are there no events in the "real" world that lack this trangressive, mediative quality? This, of course, is a very familiar question, arrived at by a different route. What are we to make of the silence of oppressed people? Is their silence merely a latent discursivity, covered by false consciousness? It is one thing to say that certain slave narratives are discursive, and another to suggest that all which is said by or inscribed on behalf of slaves is discursive, and still another, by extension, to suggest that slavery is nothing but discourse. This is the question that separates a prospective sociological post-structuralism from the actual post-structuralist literary criticism. Sociologists should have little difficulty accepting the idea that there are hidden or underlying variables behind surface appearances. But they will have trouble with the suggestion that those variables are exclusively discursive. Is there nothing in the "real" world but texts and discursive talk? Literary theorists and others, including social historians, can plausibly study nothing but texts. Can sociologists? Or, better put, what does it mean to propose that sociology be the discursive study of nothing but discursive texts?

In a different guise this is the familiar problem of the presumption of a necessary difference between theory and concrete empirical data. Most sociologists could, if pressed, consider the proposition that theory is the discursive property of any sociological work. This would amount to little more than granting that in theory, whatever else we do, we state and describe both a statement about the "real" world and the rules by which we arrive at that interpretation. Usually, however, even in a radical version of this conviction, sociologists hold to the existence of a "real" world outside of the discursive sway of theory. The world's "reality" is taken, normally, as the source of concrete empirical data. This conviction, we can now see, would be treated with great skepticism by post-structuralism and postmodernism. The idea of a free-standing reality as the source of empirical data partakes of the modernist distinction between the knowing subject and the world of objects, and relies on a belief in attainable knowledge as the arbiter of that distinction. We might grant, therefore, that post-structuralism would have this particular philosophical attitude toward the division of theory and data. But, can we grant that sociology can get along without free-standing data, that is, without data from the world as the resource of theory? Viewed through the lens of a post-structuralist critique, we can see that the question need not be posed so narrowly. We can agree that data are necessary to even a post-structuralist sociology and *still* accept the proposition that those data are neither necessarily of an order different from theory nor nondiscursive.

This line of questioning requires a reconsideration of the status of our concept of reality; clearly postmodernism would abandon the notion altogether. But it seems possible, even if only for tactical purposes, that one can avoid the threats of such a course. Here is where the post-structuralist ideas of discourse and textuality offer considerable leverage even with their terrible philosophical troubles.

TEXTS, DISCURSIVE SOCIOLOGY AND VIETNAM: AN ILLUSTRATION

A post-structuralist or postmodernist approach to the concept of "reality" would be pragmatic. What do we intend by it? And can we get around it in order to enhance our ability to know and discuss? Can, therefore, the theory of Texts, including discursive texts, get us around the problems sociology, and other sciences, usually solve with reference to ideas like "empirical reality"?

The prospect of such an alternative depends on the plausibility of four assumptions already presented, explicitly or implicitly:

1. that theory is an inherently discursive activity;
2. that the empirical reality in relation to which theoretical texts are discursive is without exception textual;
3. that empirical texts depend on this relationship to theoretical texts for their intellectual or scientific value; and
4. that in certain, if not all, cases a discursive interpretation yields more, not less, adequate understanding.

Assumption #1 was stipulated in the above discussion. Assumptions #2 and #3 require further discussion. Assumption #4 is best considered with reference to a case study.

Theoretical statements mediate the "reality" contained in empirical texts—answers to questionnaires, performed rituals and observed behaviors (usually inscribed on film or tape or in notebooks), letters, corporate reports, transcripts, interviews, archives, census tracts. It is far from clear that there are any data "purer," that is, "more real," than these. And none of these is anything but textual in the two senses poststructuralism employs. First, they are literally inscribed on one medium or another and are never used for analysis without being thus written. Secondly, they are useful for knowledge only to the extent that they exist in an intertextual field—with other empirical texts of the same sort, without other empirical texts of a different kind, and, most of all, with the theoretical texts out of which sense is made of them. It hardly need be said that raw data, in whatever form, are useless until they are situated with respect to theoretical statements. Theoretical statements, regardless of the "school" or methodological style in which they are expressed (scientific, humanistic, qualitative, ethnographic, etc.), are never made without a relationship to empirical data or an empirical reference, however abstract. Parsons' most abstract theory of the AGIL paradigm requires a great number of assumptions about the reality of the social world, such as a willingness to believe that societies are patterned, that culture is an effective control over society, that societies need integrative mechanisms like laws. None of these beliefs, however arguable, is held without reference to a wealth of empirical references. These references when held by a reader are necessary to the sense of Parsons' theory. They arise from the many empirical texts—ranging from survey results to everyday life conversations and everything in between—that inform a reader's ability to read. Similarly, such texts are also written, whether consciously or not, as an intervention in the field of existing texts sociologists variously consider germane to their work. It is not at all clear why one needs the idea of an empirical reality existing beyond such an intertextual field.

Of the four assumptions, #4 is the sternest test of the prospects of a post-structuralist sociology. In the end, it is hardly worth the while to try something with so many inherent difficulties if there are no anticipated advantages over what we have now.

As I have indicated, some theoretical advantages are clear, and they have been reasonably well developed in other areas. The most significant of these is the articulation of the principle of difference as the substance of a decentering social theory. There is now an important body of work indebted to the post-structuralist idea that when the world is decentered the primacy of social differences becomes apparent (Abel 1980; Gates 1985; Marcus and Fischer 1986; Harding 1986). One of the most interesting is Sandra Harding's argument against all theories, including feminist standpoint theories, that would reduce social analysis to a totalizing principle. She proposes the concept of "fractured identities," explaining that one cannot account for and resolve the problems of sexism by reversing the gender principle because there is no such thing as an essential woman any more than there is an essential man. Rather, women must think of themselves (and they must act) in reference to identities fractured not only by gender but race, class, and world position as well. There is no abstract total woman, only black-African, or white-working class, wealthy American, . . . women.

> Once "woman" is deconstructed into "women," and "gender" is recognized to have no fixed referents, feminism itself dissolves as a theory that can reflect the voice of a naturalized or essentialized speaker. It does not dissolve as a fundamental part of our political identities, as a motivation for developing political solidarities—how could it in a world where we can now name the plethora of moral outrages designed exactly to contain us, to coerce us, within each of our culturally specific womanly activities? But because of the historical specificity of sexism's structures, this strain of feminist thought encourages us to cherish and defend our "hyphens"—those theoretical expressions of our multiple struggles. (Harding 1986, 246)

The value of the concept fractured identities is apparent. It is no coincidence that it arises at the very time when social theorists are reevaluating hitherto segregated categories such as race, class, and gender. This is one instance of a theoretical shift caused by the post-structuralist movement. Yet, as powerful as the idea of difference is, it is still not enough to suggest the advantages of a post-structuralist sociology.

I will conclude by proposing a case illustration that lends itself to post-structuralist analysis. Important as it is to recent American, and global, history the reality of Vietnam is far from certain. For the majority of persons who make any attempt to interpret it their most vivid impressions come not from direct experience but from a strange conglomeration of texts—the memorial on the Mall in Washington, films, firsthand accounts of speakers, friends, or relatives, novels, Neil Sheehan's *New Yorker* articles and prize-winning book, college and high school courses, rhetorical allusions by politicians, archives, microfilm and microfiche, and so on. Is it an accident that the most searing film account, if not the roulette scene in *The Deer Hunter*, is *Apocalypse Now*, a montage of craziness and dream-like irreality in which the viewer is made to feel that nothing real was there? Was Vietnam after all nothing more than a repetition of a classic Conradian narrative—a crazed voyage through an exotic jungle in search of an unattainable kingdom? One wants to argue that this is a fiction and that the reality is still there. Reviews of each serious Vietnam film center on the question, did this one, *Platoon* perhaps, finally capture the reality of the war?

It is possible that the search for the reality of social things is the true Conradian search. Where would one look for the reality of Vietnam? Are recollections of veterans or POWs more real than *Apocalypse Now!* Are the *Pentagon Papers!* Are Neil Sheehan's articles? Are Stanley Karnow's history and PBS documentary? Is that finer reality still buried in an archive somewhere? And cannot these questions be asked of most complex social historical events?

In pursuit of a post-structuralist sociology, what can then be said about the empirical reality of a series of events like the war in Vietnam? I propose that we ignore, for the moment, our sociological thirst for reality, and consider it simply and straightforwardly as though it were, for all intents and purposes, a huge, ugly but plausibly discursive text. In this respect we should have to entertain the proposition that the war itself was discursive, a global inscription in which the United States sought to mediate its own sense of the irreality of world history.[9]

In the years following the Second World War, the United States quickly encountered an intolerable set of contradictions. On the one hand, the United States emerged from the world war as the greatest military and industrial power in history. On the other hand, as early as 1947, the year of George Kennan's famous long telegram enunciating the policy of containment, the Soviet Union was taken seriously, as well it should have been, as a rival power. The United States suffered the contradiction of being the supreme world power, but one of two supreme powers, hence not supreme. The McCarthy blight, in the early fifties, was a flawed attempt to mediate this contradiction by turning inward with the unreal insistence that anyone and everyone could be communist, the cause of America's loss of world potency. In 1954 Joseph McCarthy was censured by the United States Senate. In the same year Dienbienphu fell. In 1955 Eisenhower approved direct military aid to the Saigon government, thus beginning the U.S. presence in Southeast Asia.

Was that presence, and the war which ensued, an attempt to resolve, discursively, the contradiction that McCarthyism failed to resolve? The answer lies in an analysis of the specific texts which articulate the theory that governed American war policy.

The decisive event which led to war was President Lyndon Johnson's decision in the first few days of February 1965 to escalate the bombing in the north. The previous summer, Johnson and his advisers invented an incident in the Gulf of Tonkin as cause to push through Congress the resolution that gave him virtually unchecked authority to engage in war. His defeat of Barry Goldwater in the November 1964 election added substantially to his mandate both for foreign policy leadership and the pursuit of his plans of a Great Society at home. In 1965 Johnson submitted sixty-three pieces of social legislation, a domestic program that exceeded even Roosevelt's for its ambition and commitment to America's disadvantaged. Few, if any, American presidents possessed so extensive a social vision. Yet that vision is easily forgotten because it was held along with a view of America's world position that led to Vietnam.

On February 5, 1965, the Vietcong attacked an American installation at Pleiku, killing nine, and wounding a hundred American advisers. Johnson responded immediately by authorizing "Operation Flaming Dart," air raids against the north carefully selected because Soviet Prime Minister Aleksi Kosygin was then visiting Hanoi. The question before Johnson was, shall the air strikes be expanded and the American engagement enlarged?

At the same time, on February 6 and 7, Johnson's adviser McGeorge Bundy, en route home from Vietnam, completed the draft of a memorandum that confirmed an earlier (January 27) report that the situation in Vietnam was deteriorating. Bundy's February 7 memorandum coined the ironic, and highly discursive phrase, "sustained reprisal." This evidently duplicitous phrase came to justify and be the name for Johnson's evolving war policy. The memorandum argued that a policy of reprisals against the north would eventually "improve the situation in the South" by demonstrating to Hanoi the military resolve of the United States. The policy decision came quickly. On February 24, 1965, Johnson ordered Operation Rolling Thunder, sustained air raids on the north which by year's end totaled 55,000 sorties.

Like George Kennan's famous long telegram twenty years earlier which invented the equally discursive concept of containment, Bundy's sustained reprisal memorandum defined Johnson's fatal policy. By December 1965, 200,000 troops had replaced the 20,000 or so advisers in Vietnam at the beginning of the year. And by 1968 Johnson's presidency and his Great Society program would be in ruins, and the direction of American foreign and domestic policies would be, it now seems, irreversibly altered.

Bundy's February 7 memorandum did not cause the war. Texts don't cause anything in the traditional sense. They are practices in an intertextual field. Their significance relies on their relationship to that field. It is easy to see both the discursive nature of the Bundy text and its crucial place in an intertextual field that included Johnson's own statements, the preceding generation's dilemma over America's contradictory world position, and subsequent interpretations of the war itself.

As Godfrey Hodgson (1976, 229) points out, Bundy's phrase, sustained reprisal, is a subtly double-sided notion that suits a former dean of Harvard College. Operation Rolling Thunder and all that went with it was surely "sustained" but in the dramatic escalation that followed the very meaning of "reprisal" was subverted. The supposed reprisal for Pleiku (and more remotely the nonexistent Tonkin incident) became initiative. The restraint suggested by the term reprisal was confounded by the reality of devastation that came to pass. Though the Pentagon wanted even more, the reality of over 500,000 troops and countless air sorties in the north and south altered, as we now know, the map of Southeast Asia, just as it altered the terrain of American political and moral conscience. In some very specific sense, "sustained reprisal" literally rewrote the reality of American life as it rewrote the geopolitical boundaries of Asia.

Again, one must resist the temptation to say that Bundy's memo caused all this. It was, rather, a crucial discursive text that provided the theory which encouraged American desires to have it all—to be supreme aboard, while being a Great Society at home. The text's meaning is lodged in this more complex field, and its discursive value was that it both revealed and masked (to-ed and fro-ed so to speak) the reality of the policy's appeal to the best and brightest who advised Johnson and to Johnson himself. Johnson's famous complex about his Harvardian advisers did not prevent him from sharing their theory. He could not use the language of a Harvard dean, but he could understand it. His own public statement announcing Flaming Dart used quite a different, and richer, metaphor: "We have kept our guns over the mantel and our shells in the cupboard for a long time. . . . I can't ask our American soldiers out there to fight with one hand tied behind their backs" (Kearns 1976, 261). This Alamo metaphor from Johnson's Texas frontier background conveyed the same meaning as did "sustained reprisal." It lacked only the (to him) noxious qualities of a more Harvardian abstraction. He saw himself, as Doris Kearns' (1976) biography shows, as a tough, virile man of peace, defending America against an aggressor. "Rolling Thunder," to Johnson, was an act of peace, an instance of what William Gibson (1986) rightly calls doublethink. But as discourse it has the same attributes as "sustained reprisal"—a play with words that plays with reality, simultaneously constituting and deconstituting the reality of the words and the world. And both figures of speech take their place alongside the war's most famous expression of double think, "We had to destroy the village in order to save it."

Doublethink is the discursive form required when there is no plausible reality on the ground to support the actions taken in the air of a contradictory theory of the world. This is not to say that nothing happened on the ground of Vietnam, that no one died. It does say, however, that we have no interpretive access to that reality, in large part because those who lived and died in the jungles did so because of the real irreality of a series of highly theoretical texts. The war was whatever reality it was because of a theoretical field in which sustained reprisal and Johnson's Alamo figure stood side by side, without prejudice to all the contradictions they contained.

This intertextual field in which the war in Vietnam was constituted stretches along several axes—horizontally across the differences of language between Johnson and Bundy, and vertically from their gross theory of the world to the irreality experienced by men and women on the ground. Bundy's abstract theory was not of a different order from the accounts of combatants. Hundreds of firsthand accounts by veterans describe the bizarre incongruence between hours spent when nothing happened, a fleeting and often unseen enemy, and eerie nothingness punctuated by death—of buddies, of the enemy, of people who looked like but were not enemy, of old women and children, and eventually of fragged soldiers. Foot soldiers lost all sense of the reality of normal distinctions—between war and just walking around, between enemy and ally, between combatant and civilian. "We knew," said Specialist Fourth Class Charles Strong, "where the North Vietnamese were, but we knew that if we got into it, they would probably have wiped a big portion of the company out. We were really dropped there to find the North Vietnamese, and here we was hiding from them. Running because we was hungry. We were so far up in the hills that the place was so thick you didn't have to pull guard at night" (Terry 1984, 55). This collapse of reality on the ground is perfectly well explained by the irreality of the theoretical policy that invoked the war. Some might think this destroys the material reality of jungles, death, and Vietnam. But does it? Is it not certain that our men would never find the enemy, or recognize them when they found them, when the war itself had little to do with anything real? After all, Bundy and Johnson could have learned from Dienbienphu that this was to be a war with enemies that could not be found. They ignored this lesson because they were creating another, textual reality having more to do with the Alamo and postwar fear of communism than anything actually on the ground in Vietnam.

From Hamburger Hill to Johnson's situation room the reality of Vietnam was created, then breached, then recreated in countless texts. What after all truly went on there? Where was there? And what is the meaningful distinction among the realities written in journals of American and Vietcong combatants, Johnson's memoirs, Bundy's memorandum, the Pentagon Papers, *Apocalypse Now*, the heartwrenching V-shaped memorial on the Mall, deaths which rewrote family histories, defoliation which rewrote the ecology of Southeast Asia, a military failure that rewrote the boundaries of Vietnam? How could there be a study, including a sociological study, of Vietnam based on anything but these texts? Nothing else is out there, not now, and in an eerie sense not then.

It is certainly not by chance that the single most successful piece of post-structuralist sociology is about Vietnam. William Gibson's *The Perfect War* argues in the terms of a Focauldian semiotics that Vietnam was an extensive elaboration of the codes contained in late liberal technocracy of which the Johnson administration was the epiphany. He demonstrates, to take one example, that the bombing around which the war was built was nothing more than an elaborate code for communications with Hanoi. The message was: "We want peace. We are resolved. You stop and we will too." Yet the message had no receiver to whom it made sense. In fact, the air raids on Hanoi's oil storage facilities were based on a certifiable denial of reality. The manifest purpose of these bombings was, Gibson shows, to communicate American resolve by destroying the bulk of Hanoi's oil reserves supporting infiltration of the south. By July 1965, when sorties reached more than 10,000 a month, almost seventy percent of the north's oil reserves had, in fact, been destroyed. Yet the actual daily need for petroleum fuel in the south was an amount that could be carried in fifteen pickup trucks. The thirty percent reserve not destroyed was more than enough. This reality was knowable by the simplest of intelligence reports. But the bombing continued, directed in part by Secretary of Defense Robert McNamara who, as a younger man, had directed a study demonstrating that allied bombing missions in World War Two had similarly little effect on the course of that war. What did the bombings mean? Their sense had nothing at all to do with an external reality. They were the necessary utterance dictated by a theoretical war policy code.

Gibson ends his book with a statement in which he means every word in a strict post-structuralist sense. He says, referring to the irrelevance of a distinction between his sociological text on the war and the fated experiences of men and women who lived the war's irreality: "In this *corpus* men and women live and die; the stories of their lives and their deaths have their truths beyond incorporation in any theoretical arguments" (Gibson 1986, 476). In a world where reality is constituted in and by means of texts, everything is theoretical in some sense, because everything is discursive and, in situations where this is the case, what other reality is there?

What then are the prospects for a post-structuralist sociology? One answer might be found in the fact, reported by Russell Jacoby (1987), that between 1959 and 1969, the crucial years of the war, the three leading political science journals published 924 pieces of which exactly one concerned Vietnam. Sociology did not do much better. In the forty-six years between 1936 and 1982, the *American Sociological Review* published 2,559 articles, of which a scant five percent concerned political and social issues of any kind. This does not speak well for social science's grasp of reality.

Quite possibly a post-structuralist sociology would do better, however high the stakes. It would not be difficult to do as well.

NOTES

1. A number of writers have proposed a revision of sociology along post-structuralist lines. Richard Harvey Brown (1987) has made the most sustained effort. *See also* Rossi (1983) and Lemert (1979a). It is also true that the work of Pierre Bourdieu (e.g., 1977) and Anthony Giddens (e.g., 1984) bear obvious theoretical affinities to post-structuralism. Yet, neither could be said to be post-structuralists strictly speaking and neither has yet engendered a school.

2. The lecture was given in October 1966 at the Johns Hopkins University conference, the proceedings of which were edited by Richard Macksey and Eugenio Donato, *The Structuralist Controversy* (Baltimore: Johns Hopkins University Press, 1970). The essay also appears in Derrida 1978.

3. The French attacks on the subject are well known and perhaps most explicitly put in Foucault's (1972) *Archaeology of Knowledge. See also* recent writings of Habermas on the centrality of subjectivity to modernity, "Psychic Thermidor and the Rebirth of Rebellious Subjectivity," pp. 67–77 in Bernstein (1985).

4. *See* Rorty, "Habermas and Lyotard on Postmodernity," pp. 161–176 in Bernstein (1985). *See also* Fredric Jameson's (1984) preface to Lyotard's *Postmodern Condition.*

5. Foucault's attacks on the logocentric and anthropocentric basis of modernism are explicit, though sometimes overlooked, in this regard. See Lemert 1979b.

6. In reference to the concepts presented in this paragraph see Giddens (1984), Foucault (1972), Bourdieu (1977), and Barthes (1970, 1979).

7. Compare Giddens' idea of discursive consciousness (Giddens 1984, 41–45).

8. Cultural studies, a movement with strong ties to sociology and to post-structuralism, expressly takes Thompson's work as among its classical references (*see* Hall et al. 1980).

9. Sources for following section are: the Pentagon Papers (Gravel 1971), Kearns (1976), Gibson (1986), Hodgson (1976), Karnow (1983). One should also not forget that though this is stated with reference to the American discursive dilemma the same analysis can, and should, be applied to the people of Southeast Asia.

REFERENCES

Abel, Elizabeth, ed. 1980. *Writing and Sexual Difference.* Chicago: University of Chicago Press.

Althusser, Louis. 1970. *For Marx.* New York: Vintage.

Barthes, Roland. 1970. *Writing Degree Zero and Elements of Semiology.* Boston: Beacon Press.

Barthes, Roland. 1979. "From Work to Text." In Josue Hariri, ed., *Textual Strategies: Perspectives in Poststructuralist Criticism*. Ithaca: Cornell University Press.

Bernstein, Richard. 1985. *Habermas and Modernity*. Cambridge: MIT Press.

Boudon, Raymond. 1971. *The Uses of Structuralism*. London: Heinemann.

Bourdieu, Pierre. 1977. *Outline of a Theory of Practice*. Cambridge: Cambridge University Press.

Brown, Richard Harvey. 1987. *Society as Text*. Chicago: University of Chicago Press.

Carby, Hazel. 1987. *Reconstructing Womanhood: The Emergence of the Afro-American Woman Novelist*. New York: Oxford University Press.

Deleuze, Gilles, and Felix Guattari. 1977. *Anti-Oedipus: Capitalism and Schizophrenia*. New York: Viking Press.

Derrida, Jacques. 1978. "Structure, Sign and Play in the Discourse of the Human Sciences." In Jacques Derrida, *Writing and Difference*. Chicago: University of Chicago Press.

Derrida, Jacques. 1985. "Racism's Last Word." In Gates, ed., *"Race," Writing and Difference*.

Foucault, Michel. 1972. *The Archaeology of Knowledge*. New York: Pantheon.

Foucault, Michel. 1978. *Hisorty of Sexuality*. Vol. I. New York: Pantheon.

Foucault. Michel. 1979. "What Is an Author?" In Josue V. Hariri, ed., *Textual Strategies: Perspectives in Post-Structuralist Criticism*. Ithaca: Cornell University Press.

Gates, Henry Louis, 1985. *"Race," Writing and Difference*. Chicago: University of Chicago Press.

Gates, Henry Louis. 1988. *The Signifying Monkey: A Theory of Afro-American Literary Criticism*. New York: Oxford University Press.

Gibson, William. 1986. *The Perfect War*. Boston: Atlantic Monthly Press.

Giddens, Anthony. 1984. *The Constitution of Society*. Berkeley: University of California Press.

Gitlin, Todd. 1988. "Hip-Deep in Post-Modernism." *New York Times Book Review*, November 7.

Gravel, Mike, ed. 1971. *The Pentagon Papers*. Vols. I–IV. Boston: Beacon Press.

Hall, Stuart, et al. 1980. *Culture, Media, and Language: Working Papers in Cultural Studies, 1972–79*. London: Hutchinson.

Harding, Sandra. 1986. *The Science Question in Feminism*. Ithaca: Cornell University Press.

Hodgson, Godfrey. 1976. *America in Our Time*. New York: Vintage.

Jacoby, Russell. 1987. *The Last Intellectuals*. New York: Basic Books.

Jameson, Fredric. 1984. "Foreword." In Lyotard, *The Postmodern Condition*.

Jencks, Charles. 1977. *The Language of Post-Modern Architecture*. New York: Rizzoli.

Karnow, Stanley. 1983. *Vietnam: A History*. New York: Penguin.

Kearns, Doris. 1976. *Lyndon Johnson and the American Dream*. New York: Harper and Row.

Kristeva, Julia. 1974. *La révolution du language póetique*. Paris: Editions du Seuil.

Lacan, Jacques. 1968. *The Language of the Self*. New York: Delta.

Lacan, Jacques. 1977. *Ecrits: A Selection*. New York: Norton.

Lemert, Charles. 1979a. "Language, Structure, and Measurement: Structuralist Semiotics and Sociology." *American Journal of Sociology* 84:929–957.

Lemert, Charles. 1979b. *Sociology and the Twilight of Man: Homocentrism and Discourse in Sociological Theory*. Carbondale: Southern Illinois University Press.

Lemert, Charles. 1982. *Michel Foucault: Social Theory and Transgression*. New York: Columbia University Press.

Lévi-Strauss, Claude. 1967. "The Structural Study of Myth." In Claude Lévi-Strauss, *Structural Anthropology*. New York: Anchor.

Lévi-Strauss, Claude. 1970. "Overture to *le Cru et le cuit*." In Jacques Ehrmann, ed., *Structuralism*. New York: Anchor.

Lyotard, Jean-Francois. 1984. *The Postmodern Condition: A Report on Knowledge*. Minneapolis: University of Minnesota Press.

Marcus, George, and Michael M. J. Fischer. 1986. *Anthropology as Cultural Critique*. Chicago: University of Chicago Press.

Moi, Toril, ed. 1987. *French Feminist Thought: Politics, Patriarchy, and Sexual Difference*. New York: Basil Blackwell.

Portoghesi, Paolo. 1980. *After Modern Architecture*. New York: Rizzoli.

Rorty, Richard. 1979. *Philosophy and the Mirror of Nature*. Princeton: Princeton University Press.

Rorty, Richard. 1985. "Habermas and Lyotard on Postmodernity." In Bernstein, ed., *Habermas and Modernity*.

Rossi, Ino. 1983. *From the Sociology of Symbols to the Sociology of Signs*. New York: Columbia University Press.

Tel Quel. 1968. "Theorie d'ensemble." Paris: Editions du Seuil.

Terry, Wallace. 1984. *Bloods*. New York: Ballantine Books.

White, Hayden. 1978. *Tropics of Discourse*. Baltimore: Johns Hopkins University Press.

10

The Postmodern Turn: Positions, Problems, and Prospects

❊

DOUGLAS KELLNER
University of Texas

During the 1980s, debates over postmodernism entered the domain of social theory and both a new postmodern social theory and sociological attempts to define the multi-faceted aspects of postmodernity emerged.[1] Advocates of the postmodern turn aggressively attacked traditional social theory, and social theorists responded either by ignoring the new challenger, by attacking it in return, or by attempting to come to terms with and appropriate the new wave. Assimilating postmodernism to social theory was and is extremely difficult both because of the intrinsic difficulty of the work of those associated with it (Baudrillard, Lyotard, Deleuze and Guattari, Foucault, and others) and because the radicality of the postmodern critique of social theory puts the very concepts of society, representation, and social theory into question. In addition, there has been no real agreement as to what constitutes postmodernity and its correlate, postmodern theory. Conceptualizing postmodernity is complicated by the fact that its discourses have emerged in several different fields (art and cultural theory, philosophy, social theory, etc.) and because within these fields there are fierce debates as to what constitutes the postmodern and how it differs from the modern.

In this essay, I shall discuss the ramifications of the postmodern debates for social theory but will draw on some of the philosophical debates because the postmodern critique of traditional social theory was initiated by post-structuralist criticisms of the basic premises of

A previous attempt to analyze postmodern social theory appeared in *Theory, Culture, and Society* 5:239–270 (1988) and I am grateful to Mike Featherstone for soliciting the article and for discussions which helped in development of this new study, some of which I first presented at a 1988 Global Futures Conference which Featherstone and his associates organized. For helpful criticism and suggestions of the present study, I am also indebted to Robert Antonio, Stephen Bronner, George Ritzer, and especially to Steve Best for incisive criticism and editing of many versions of the study and for sustained discussion of the issues involved.

philosophy and social theory, a critique influenced by such diverse figures as Nietzsche, Saussure, Heidegger, Bataille, and Derrida. Nietzsche's attack on concepts of the subject, representation, truth, and value, combined with Heidegger's critique of metaphysics, led post-structuralists to question the very framework and deep assumptions of philosophy and social theory (Derrida 1976; Dews 1987). In addition, Saussure's reflections on language, Bataille's alternative conception of economy based on excess and expenditure, and Lacan's reconstruction of Freud promoted new views of language, theory, and social reality (Jameson 1972; Coward-Ellis 1977; Kellner 1989b).

The postmodern social theories of such French figures as Baudrillard, Lyotard, Deleuze and Guattari, and others were also influenced by theoretical developments in France such as Roland Barthes' (1962) explorations of mythologies and popular culture, Henri Lefebvre's (1971) critical dissections of everyday life, Guy Debord's (1976) critiques of "the society of the spectacle," and developments in literary and cultural criticism which advanced new conceptions of writing, theory, and discourse (Derrida, Foucault, *Tel Quel*, the later Barthes, etc.). The 1960s and 1970s in France were a period of intense theoretical and political debates which produced a fascinating diversity of new theoretical trends. By the late 1970s, new postmodern social theories began appearing which drew on these developments. Jean Baudrillard (1983a, 1983b) describes a postmodern society in which "radical semiurgy," the constantly accelerating proliferation of signs, produces simulations and simulacra that create new forms of society, culture, experience, and subjectivity. Jean-Francois Lyotard (1984) describes a "postmodern condition" that marks the end of the grand hopes of modernity and the impossibility of continuing with the totalizing social theories and revolutionary politics of the past. Gilles Deleuze and Felix Guattari (1977) propose developing micro analyses of desire, a "schizo-analysis" which will trace the trajectories and inscriptions of desire in cultural texts and everyday life and seek possible "lines of escape" from repressive social and psychological structures. Attempting to preserve Marxism against the postmodern critique, Fredric Jameson (1984) argues that postmodernism should be interpreted as the "cultural logic of late capitalism," thus promoting totalizing Marxian theories as the grand narratives—or the most inclusive social theories—of the present age, while locating postmodernism itself as a mere cultural logic within a new stage of capitalism. Arthur Kroker and his colleagues (1986, 1989) describe contemporary society as a new fin-de-millennium "panic" scene which eludes the categories and social theories of the past, and which requires new theorizing. Other social theorists like Habermas

(1981, 1987), by contrast, are skeptical of claims for a postmodern break in history and attack postmodernism as a form of irrationalist ideology.

In view of these disputes, it is time to investigate the genesis and developments of postmodern social theory and to distinguish its central positions, insights, and limitations. Before beginning, it should be pointed out that there is nothing like a unified "postmodern social theory." Rather one is struck by the diversities among theories often lumped together as "postmodern." Instead of defining characteristics and traits which would distinguish a postmodern social theory, there are rather a plurality of different postmodern theories and positions. One is also struck by the inadequate and undertheorized notion of the "postmodern" in the theories which adopt, or are identified in, such terms. Consequently, I shall begin by attempting to sort out the various notions of the postmodern operative in various discourses and fields and shall trace the genealogy of the concept of the postmodern as a designation for a new historical epoch requiring new theories and categories.

GENEALOGIES OF THE POSTMODERN

To avoid confusion between the various discourses of the postmodern, it is useful to distinguish between members of the family of concepts related to the distinction between the modern and the postmodern. Following Featherstone (1988), we might therefore distinguish between "modernity" conceptualized as the modern age and "postmodernity" as a descriptive, epochal term for describing the period which follows modernity. Modernity, as theorized by Marx, Weber, and others (Berman 1982), refers to the epoch of industrial capitalism which follows the Middle Ages or feudalism. One might also describe the processes by which modernity produced a new industrial and colonial world as "modernization" and the new processes producing the current world as those of an as yet relatively untheorized "postmodernization." Modernity is opposed to tradition and is characterized by innovation, novelty, and dynamism and one might describe the experiences of this era of constant change by the French term *modernité* (Frisby 1985) while the experiences of postmodernity could be described as *postmodernité*. "Modernism," finally, could be used to describe the art movements of the modern age (art for art's sake, the avant-garde, expressionism, surrealism, etc.) while "postmodernism" can describe those diverse aesthetic forms and practices which come after modernism.

In all cases, the term "post" describes a break or rupture between the modern and the postmodern. It also functions as a sequential concept, describing that which follows and comes after the modern. The term thus functions in a periodizing discourse which marks historical distinctions. Yet there is also an ambiguity inherent in this particular set of "post" terms which is exploited by various adherents of the postmodern. For the term "post" describes a "not" modern that can be read as an active term of negation which attempts to move beyond the era and practices of modernity. This negation can be interpreted positively as a liberation from old constraining and oppressive conditions and as an affirmation of new developments, a moving into new terrains, a forging of new discourses and ideas (Lyotard 1984). Or the movement can be interpreted negatively, as a deplorable regression, as a loss of traditional values, certainties, stabilities, and so on (Toynbee 1954; Bell 1976).

The "post" in postmodern also signifies, however, a dependence on and a continuity with that which it follows, leading some to conceptualize the postmodern as merely an intensification of the modern, as a hypermodernity (Merquior 1986; During 1987), or a new "face of modernity" (Calinescu 1987). Yet most theorists of postmodernity deploy the term—as it was introduced by Toynbee—to characterize a dramatic rupture or break in Western history. What all of these conceptions of the "postmodern" have in common, then, is the assumption of a radical break or rupture with the past. The discourse of the postmodern therefore presupposes a sense of an ending, the sense of something new, and the sense that we must develop new categories, theories, and methods to explore and conceptualize this novum, this novel social and cultural situation. Such a conception of a radical rupture within history presupposes global and epochal historical periodization, and not surprisingly some of the first conceptions of the postmodern appeared in historians like Arnold Toynbee and Geoffrey Barraclough, or historically oriented sociologists like C. Wright Mills and Daniel Bell.

After the Second World War notions began emerging concerning both a new postmodern age which succeeded the modern age and new postmodern art which succeeded modernism (Calinescu 1987). In the later volumes of his monumental *A Study of History*, Toynbee (1947–1954) argued that Western civilization had entered a new transitional period beginning around 1875 which he termed the "postmodern age." This period constituted a dramatic mutation and rupture from the previous "modern age" and was characterized by wars, social turmoil, and revolution. Toynbee described the age as one of "anarchy" and "total relativism." He characterized the previous period as a middle-class, bourgeois era marked by social stability, rationalism, and progress. The postmodern age, by contrast, is a "Time of Troubles" marked by the collapse of rationalism and the ethos of the Enlightenment.

This scenario is reminiscent of Nietzsche's *Will to Power* and Spengler's *Decline of the West* with their diagnoses of social and cultural regression in the present age. A somewhat similar notion of a "postmodern age" emerges in C. Wright Mills *The Sociological Imagination* (1959). Mills claims that "we are at the ending of what is called The Modern Age. Just as Antiquity was followed by several centuries of Oriental ascendancy, which Westerners provincially call The Dark Ages, so now The Modern Age is being succeeded by a post-modern period" (Mills 1959, 165–166). Mills believed that "our basic definitions of society and of self are being overtaken by new realities" and that it is necessary to struggle to conceptualize the changes taking place and to "grasp the outline of the new epoch we suppose ourselves to be entering" (Mills 1959, 165–166). In conceptualizing transformations of the present, he believed, many previous expectations and images, and standard categories of thought and of feeling, are no longer of use in characterizing the present situation. In particular, he believed that Marxism and liberalism are no longer convincing because both take up the Enlightenment belief in the inner connection between reason and freedom, which holds that increased rationality would produce increased freedom. By contrast, Mills claims that in the present one can no longer assume this.

In an analysis close to that of the Frankfurt School, Mills charts out some of the ways that increased societal rationalization is diminishing freedom and paints the specter of a society of "cheerful robots" who might well desire, or cheerfully submit to, increased servitude.[2] A much more systematic and detailed notion of the postmodern age than is found in the work of Toynbee and Mills is present in Geoffrey Barraclough's *An Introduction to Contemporary History* (1964). Barraclough opens his explorations of the nature of contemporary history by claiming that the world in which we live today is "different, in almost all its basic preconditions, from the world in which Bismarck lived and died" (Barraclough 1964, 9). Barraclough claims that analysis of the underlying structural changes between the "old world" and the "new world" requires "a new framework and new terms of reference" (Barraclough 1964, 9). Against theories which emphasize continuity in history, Barraclough argues: "What we should look out for as significant are the differences rather than the similarities, the elements of discontinuity rather than the elements of continuity. In short, contemporary history should be considered as a distinct period of time, with characteristics of its own which mark it off from the preceding period, in much the same way as what we call 'medieval history' is marked off . . . from modern history" (Barraclough 1964, 12).

After discussing some of the contours of the "new era," Barraclough rejects various attempts to characterize the current historical situation and then proposes the term "post-modern" to describe the period which follows "modern" history (Barraclough 1964, 23). He describes the "new age" as being constituted by revolutionary developments in science and technology, by a new imperialism meeting resistance in Third World revolutionary movements, by the transition from individualism to mass society, and by a "new outlook on the world" and new forms of culture.

Amitai Etzioni also introduced the notion of a postmodern society in his book *The Active Society* (1968). For Etzioni, the Second World War was a turning point in history; he argued that the post-war introduction of new modes of communication, information, and energy inaugurated a new postmodern period. He hypothesized that either relentless technological development would itself destroy all previous values, or would make possible the use of technology to better human life and to solve all social problems. Etzioni championed this "active society" in which normative values would guide technological developments and human beings would utilize and control technology for the benefit of humanity. This "activist" normative ideal was one of the few positive visions of a postmodern future, though Etzioni was also aware of the dangers.

In the mid-1970s more books appeared in the United States which used the term postmodern to designate a new era in history. Frederick Ferré's *Shaping the Future: Resources for the Post-Modern World* projected a new set of values and institutions for a "post-modern consciousness" and new future (1976). His emphasis was positive and took the form of quasi-religious prophecy and advocacy of primarily religious values to guide the new age. In *The Cultural Contradictions of Capitalism* (1976), Daniel Bell also took up the theme that the modern era was coming to an end and that humanity now faced fundamental choices for the future, writing: "We are coming to a watershed in Western society: we are witnessing the end of the bourgeois idea—that view of human action and of social relations, particularly of economic exchange—which has molded the modern era for the last 200 years" (Bell 1976, 7). He interprets the "post-modern" age much as Toynbee; it represents for him the unleashing of instinct, impulse, and will, though he tends to identify it with the 1960s counterculture (Bell 1976, 51). For Bell, the postmodern age exhibits an extension of the rebellious, anti-bourgeois, antinomic, and hedonistic impulses which he sees as the legacies of the modernist movements in the arts and their bohemian subcultures. He claims that cultural modernism perpetuates hedonism, the lack of social identification and obedience, narcissism, and the withdrawal from status and achievement competition. The postmodern age is thus a product of the application of modernist revolts to everyday life, the extension and living out of a rebellious, hyperindividualist, and hedonist life-style.

Bell interprets contemporary society as a radical disjunction and fragmentation into the spheres of the economy, polity, and culture, all of which are structured according to different principles and which come into inexorable conflict with each other (Bell 1976). He sees contemporary postmodern culture as a radical assault on tradition connected with an aggressive narcissism which is in profound contradiction with the bureaucratic, technocratic, and organizational imperatives of the capitalist economy and democratic polity. This development signifies for him the end of the bourgeois world view with its rationality, sobriety, and moral and religious values (Bell 1976, 53). In response to the corrosive force of postmodernism on traditional values, Bell calls for a revivification of religious values.

Yet as Habermas has argued (1981, 14), Bell tends to blame culture for the ills of the economy and polity, as when he refers to "cultural crises which beset bourgeois societies and which, in the longer run, devitalize a country, confuse the motivations of individuals, instill a sense of *carpe diem*, and undercut its civic will. The problems are less those of the adequacy of institutions than of the kinds of meanings that sustain a society" (Habermas 1981, 28). In passages like this, Bell obscures the extent to which the development of the consumer society itself with its emphasis on consumption, instant gratification, easy credit, and hedonism is responsible for the undermining of traditional values and culture and the production of what he calls the "cultural contradictions of capitalism." Bell sees the latter as a result of the disjunction of the economy and culture rather than as a production of the capitalist system itself. Thus while Mills' (1959) early critique of a postmodern society of cheerful robots derived from a progressive concern with diminution of the ability to shape, control, and change the conditions of society and one's life, Bells' critique derived from fear of the collapse of the bourgeois world view and its value system.

In any case, the discourse of the postmodern has a negative valence for Toynbee, Mills, Belh, and others and describes what they see as a crisis of Western civilization and a dramatic rupture with modernity. This apocalyptic outlook is shared by French theorists of postmodernity such as Baudrillard who claims that the previous era of industrial modernity is over—an event which he announces in characteristically dramatic terms:

> The end of labor. The end of production. The end of political economy.
> The end of the dialectic signifier/signified which permitted an accumulation of knowledge and of meaning, and of a linear syntagam of cumulative discourse. The end simultaneously of the dialectic of ex-

change value/use value which alone previously made possible capital accumulation and social production. The end of linear discourse. The end of linear merchandising. The end of the classic era of the sign. The end of the era of production. (Baudrillard 1988, 127–128; translation modified)

Baudrillard's narrative concerns the end of a "modernity" dominated by production and industrial capitalism, and the advent of a new postindustrial "postmodernity," constituted by "simulations," "hyperreality," and "implosion" which are instantiated in new forms of technology, culture, and society (Baudrillard 1983a; *see* Kellner 1988, 1989b). For Baudrillard, modernity was characterized by the explosion of commodification, mechanization, technology, exchange, and the market, while postmodern society is the site of an *implosion*, a collapsing, of all boundaries, regions, and distinctions between high and low culture, appearance and reality, and just about every other binary opposition maintained by traditional philosophy and social theory. For Baudrillard, in the postmodern world the boundary between image or simulation and reality implodes and with this the very experience and ground of "the real" disappears. This process of "postmodernization" signifies the end of all the positivities, grand referents, and finalities of previous social theory: the real, meaning, power, revolution, history, the subject, and even the social itself (Baudrillard 1983a, 1983b). Thus while modernity could be characterized as a process of increasing differentiation of spheres of life (Max Weber as interpreted by Habermas 1981, 1984) with attendant social fragmentation and alienation, postmodernity could be interpreted as a process of de-differentiation (Lash 1988) and attendant implosion.

Postmodernity is characterized by Baudrillard as the "catastrophe" of modernity, in the sense of current scientific theories which posit a catastrophe as "a radical, qualitative change in an entire system" (Baudrillard 1984, 18). Jean-Francois Lyotard (1984, 15) criticizes Baudrillard's somewhat apocalyptic vision of "the end of the social" but agrees with Baudrillard that "the postmodern condition" refers to a social order organized around information, knowledge, and the computerization of society (1984, 7). Although Lyotard uses the term "postmodern condition" which also, like Baudrillard's conception, signifies a fundamental break or rupture, he focuses on analyzing what he calls postmodern knowledge, which, in effect, provides a new epistemology for postmodern social theory, a theme that I shall take up in the next section.

In Baudrillard's perspectives, postmodern society is characterized by a process of "radical semiurgy" whereby "simulations" produce a new social order in which models precede "the real" and come to constitute society as a "hyperreality" (Baudrillard 1983a). Closely following Baudrillard, Arthur Kroker and David Cook (1986) develop a theory of "the postmodern scene" as the catastrophe of modernity and in *Panic Ency-clopedia* (1989), they and others provide a "(panic) reader's guide to the fin-de-millennium." For Kroker and Cook postmodernity constitutes a fundamental "rupture in Western experience" that requires a complete reworking of modern theoretical categories and political projects. Baudrillard is taken as the theoretical "password" to this new universe and Kroker and Cook attempt to out-Baudrillard Baudrillard, using his major categories as the key constituents of the postmodern scene while raising some of his more marginal notions—dead power, excremental culture, panic, and so on—to fundamental categories of a new postmodern social theory. They develop the Baudrillardian theme of an all-powerful cybernetic system consisting of the "fantastic perfection" of schemes of control and in reducing individuals to "vacant nodes on a relational power grid" (Kroker and Cook 1986, 259), and thus erase categories of subjectivity, praxis, and struggle from radical social theory, a theme to which I shall return.

Within these varying attempts to theorize postmodernity, however, a variety of postmodern positions emerges concerning epistemology, the tasks of social theory, and politics, and it is to discussing some of these issues that I shall now turn.

POSTMODERN POSITIONS

In his book *The Postmodern Condition*, Jean-Francois Lyotard (1984) attempts to develop a postmodern epistemology which will replace the philosophical perspectives dominated by Western rationalism and instrumentalism.[3] Subtitled *A Report on Knowledge*, the text was commissioned by a Canadian government agency to study new developments in knowledge and information in the most highly developed societies. "I have decided to use the word *postmodern* to describe that condition. The word is in current use on the American continent among sociologists and critics; it designates the state of our culture following the transformations which, since the end of the nineteenth century, have altered the game rules for science, literature, and the arts" (Lyotard 1984, xxiii). For Lyotard, the "postmodern" concerns developing a new epistemology responding to new conditions of knowledge, and he attempts to explicate the differences between the grand narratives of traditional philosophy and social theory, the practice and legitimation of contemporary science, and what he calls "postmodern science" which he defends as a preferable form of knowledge to traditional and currently hegemonic philosophical and scientific forms.

This epistemological focus influences his definition of terms and emphasis on modern and postmodern forms of knowledge rather than society and culture (as with Baudrillard, Jameson, Kroker and Cook, and others). Lyotard by contrast writes: "I will use the term *modern* to designate any science that legitimates itself with reference to a meta-discourse . . . making an explicit appeal to some grand narrative, such as the dialectics of Spirit, the hermeneutics of meaning, the emancipation of the rational or working subject, or the creation of wealth" (Lyotard 1984, xxiii). From this perspective the *"postmodern"* is defined "as incredulity toward metanarratives," the rejection of metaphysical philosophy, philosophies of history, and any form of totalizing thought—be it Hegelianism, liberalism, Marxism, or whatever. Postmodern knowledge, by contrast, "refines our sensitivity to differences and reinforces our ability to tolerate the incommensurable. Its principle is not the expert's homology, but the inventor's paralogy" (Lyotard 1984, xxv).

Lyotard thus valorizes differences, incommensurability, heterogeneity, paradox, and paralogies which disrupt or challenge existing forms of knowledge over unities, totalities, systems, and foundations of knowledge. His postmodern epistemology therefore specifically attacks macro social theory and metatheories. Uncritically reproducing a cliché of late 1970s French thought initiated by the so-called "new philosophers," Lyotard suggests that totalizing narratives are connected with totalitarian and terroristic politics. This point is highlighted in the conclusion to a 1982 article published as an appendix to the English version of *The Postmodern Condition:*

> Finally, it must be clear that it is our business not to supply reality but to invent allusions to the conceivable which cannot be presented. And it is not to be expected that this task will effect the last reconciliation between language games (which, under the name of faculties, Kant knew to be separated by a chasm), and that only the transcendental illusion (that of Hegel) can hope to totalize them into a real unity. But Kant also knew that the price to pay for such an illusion is terror. The nineteenth and twentieth centuries have given us as much terror as we can take. We have paid a high enough price for the nostalgia of the whole and the one, for the reconciliation of the concept and the sensible, of the transparent and the communicable experience. Under the general demand for slackening or for appeasement, we can hear the mutterings of the desire for a return of terror, for the realization of the fantasy to seize reality. The answer is: Let us wage a war on totality; let us be witness to the unpresentable; let us activate the differences and save the honour of the name. (Lyotard 1984, 82)

This passage—often cited but rarely interpreted—is highly revealing. Lyotard seems to privilege here art (supplying allusions) over theory while valorizing nonrepresentational attempts to present that "which cannot be presented." This position is congruent with his earlier privileging of figure over discourse, avant-garde art over theory (*see* Lyotard 1971). Moreover, Lyotard equates totalizing social theory with terror and nostalgia for totality, for reconciliation, and for a unity which for him constitutes the danger of suppression of differences and particularity. Lyotard rejects such theories, which he describes as master narratives, as being intolerably reductionist, simplistic, and even "terroristic" (i.e., providing legitimations for totalitarian terror, and suppressing differences in unifying schemes). Consequently, Lyotard joins at this juncture the so-called "new philosopher" who attempted to associate totalizing thought with totalitarianism *tout court*, replaying an ideologically loaded argument about the theoretical-historical route from Hegel and Marx to the Gulag. This renunciation of programs of radical social change also places him, as Peter Dews (1986, 6) has suggested, in the "end of ideology" camp which draws similar associations between grand schemes of social change, like Marxism, and many catastrophes of the twentieth century.

Lyotard's polemic contains as well an attack against the position that discourse aims at consensus, associated with Jurgen Habermas (Lyotard 1984, xxv, 65). He adopts a language games approach to knowledge, proposing that we conceive of various discourses as types of games with their own rules, structure, and moves.[4] Different language games are governed by different criteria and rules, and none are to be privileged: "All we can do is gaze in wonderment at the diversity of discursive species, just as we do at the diversity of plant or animal species. Lamenting the 'loss of meaning' in postmodernity boils down to mourning the fact that knowledge is no longer principally narrative" (Lyotard 1984, 26). Yet Lyotard wants to privilege and proliferate precisely this plurality of language games, and rejects all modes of philosophical discourse which would legislate between the various validity claims, values, positions, etc., affirmed in the proliferation of discourses which circulate through society. Rather than engaging in totalizing macro social theory and critique, Lyotard wants more localized, heterogeneous microanalysis with "little narratives" (Lyotard 1984, 60). "A recognition of the heteromorphous nature of language games is a first step. . . . The second step is the principle that any consensus on the rules defining a game and the 'moves' playable within it *must* be local, in other words, agreed on by its present players and subject to eventual cancellation" (Lyotard 1984, 66).

Yet participation in language games involves struggle and conflict for Lyotard; he claims that "the first principle underlying our method as a whole" is that "to speak is to fight, in the sense of playing, and speech acts fall within the domain of a general agonistics" (Lyotard 1984, 10). His model of a postmodern society posits individuals in struggle within various language games in an unforced consensus. Furthermore, postmodern knowledge for Lyotard involves knowledge of local terrains, and tolerance of a variety and diversity of different language games.

Lyotard assumes that all attempts at consensus involve some sort of terroristic imposition of uniformity and oppression. Thus for Lyotard there is something intrinsically repressive about traditional social theory and its concern for truth, universality, totality, and emancipation.[5] While Lyotard criticizes Habermas' alleged desire for a unitary ground for consensus and a universal ground for social theory, both Lyotard and Habermas accept Kant's division of reason into the spheres of theoretical, practical and aesthetic judgments, and both defend the sort of cultural differentiation analyzed by Max Weber. Both concretize the Kantian distinctions in terms of contrasting communicative practices and both thus take something of a "speech acts" and "pragmatic" approach to communication which both believe to be the "social bond" which constitutes societies (though here a difference emerges as Lyotard emphasizes the primacy and desirability of agonistic competition while Habermas attempts to formulate the grounds for consensus). In addition, their aesthetics take two opposing Kantian poles, with Lyotard unambiguously advocating an aesthetics of the sublime while Habermas has at least some propensities for an aesthetics of the beautiful. They also differ as Lyotard defends a more incommensurable division of different language games while Habermas wants more dialogue and consensus among the various spheres of life. In contrast to Baudrillard, however, their similar Kantian proclivities are rather striking. Other postmodern social theorists, like Baudrillard (1983b), posit the end of the social and the end of history.

In a text first published in 1978, "In the Shadow of the Silent Majorities," Baudrillard puts in question fundamental presuppositions of previous social theories, including the concepts of the social, class, and class conflict, arguing that these categories have imploded and lost their significance and reference in the society of simulations. Baudrillard, in effect, interprets "the social" in terms of "masses" and proliferates a series of metaphors to capture the nature of the masses who he describes as that "spongy referent, that opaque but equally translucent reality, that nothingness"; "a statistical crystal ball . . . 'swirling with currents and flows,' in the image of matter and the natural elements,"; an "inertia," "silence," "figure of implosion," "social void," and— what is probably his favorite metaphor—an "opaque nebula whose growing density absorbs all the surrounding energy and light rays, to collapse finally under its own weight. A black hole which engulfs the social" (Baudrillard 1983b, 1–4). This "black hole" of the masses absorbs all meaning, information, communication, messages, and so on, and renders them all meaningless through refusing to accept and produce "meaning." Thus, for Baudrillard, the masses—indifferent and apathetic in the face of the messages which bombard them and which they refuse—absorb "the social" which disappears in a black hole of indifference, apathy, and cynicism.

Baudrillard also postulates "the end of history" (1988), claiming that in a media-saturated society no event attains historical consequences any longer beyond the present moment, both because change is so rapid and intense that no events can have a decisive impact, and because the society is so saturated with information that it has reached the point of inertia, where all events and ideas are simply absorbed into the cynical and oversaturated mediascape. Baudrillard's analysis implies as well that traditional social theory, which posits causality and social determination from stable structures like the economy or political institutions, is obsolete, for he questions whether social theory can any longer be said to be able to "represent" society at all, or to posit clear lines of causal determination.[6] Kroker and Cook (1986) also take up the theme of the impossibility of delineating social causality in a society marked by implosion, fragmentation, rapid change, and metamorphosis. Instead, postmodern society is described as a flat, one-dimensional, "fantastic and grisly implosion of experience as Western culture itself runs under the signs of passive and suicidal nihilism" (Kroker and Cook 1986, 8).

For these social theories, it is no longer possible to discern a "depth dimension," an underlying reality, essence, or structure as when Marx discovered class interests behind ideology, or Freud discovered unconscious complexes between texts or actions of individuals. The erasure of history also flattens out experience, for lost in a postmodern present, one is cut off from those sedimented traditions, those continuities, those historical memories which nurtured historical consciousness and provided for a rich, textured, multidimensional present. Some postmodernists, like Baudrillard, in this situation postulate a radical presentism, a self-conscious erasure of history which eschews diachronic, historical analysis and contextualization in favor of synchronic description of the present moment. Jameson, by contrast, attempts to historicize and contextualize his analyses of postmodernism, though he too fears a loss of history in contemporary postmodern society.

Most postmodern social theory also exhibits a certain anti-utopianism, a certain political pessimism and renunciation of hopes for radical political change. For Lyotard, "there is sorrow in the Zeitgeist" (1984,

x), while Baudrillard claims that "melancholy" is the appropriate response to the disappearence of previous eras of history and theoretical-
political constructions (1988). Much postmodern social theory is motivated by disillusionment with liberal ideals of progress and radical
hopes for emancipation. Its political matrix is disappointment over
failures of the radical movements of the 1960s to produce the desired
results, followed by despair over conservative hegemony (or in France,
the failure of the French socialists) in the 1980s. These disappoint-
ments have led postmodern theorists to either scale down their political projects and ambitions (as with Lyotard, Foucault, and Deleuze and
Guattari) in order to focus on micro-politics, more local concerns and
struggles, or with Baudrillard to abandon radical politics altogether
(Kellner 1989b).

Furthermore, there is a certain ideological kinship and (mostly unar-
ticulated) lines of continuity with theories of the post-industrial society. In a sense, current postmodern social theory replays many of the
themes and positions of so-called "post-industrial society" and share, I
would argue, their characteristic limitations and distortions. Both exhibit a form of technological determinism, with theorists of the post-
industrial society such as Bell claiming that information and knowledge are the new "axial," or organizing, principles of society (Bell 1973,
1976), while postmodern theorists ascribe a variety of forms of extreme
power to new technologies.[7] Baudrillard, for example, reproduces Mc-
Luhan's technological determinism in his media theory by claiming
that "the Medium is the Message," and thus reducing media to their
formal effects while erasing content, possibilities of emancipatory or
progressive uses, and alternative media from the purview of his theory
(Kellner 1989b). Baudrillard assigns a primary role in constituting postmodern society to simulations, codes, models, and new technologies
and completely erases political economy from his theory, claiming that
"TV and information in general are a kind of catastrophe in Rene
Thom's formal, topological sense: a radical, qualitative change in an
entire system" (Baudrillard 1984, 18). Such theories posit an "autonomous technology" (*see* Winner 1977) which, as with theories of post-
industrial society, is taken as the fundamental organizing principle of
contemporary society.

Both postmodern theories and those of the post-industrial society
thus make technological development the motor of social change and
occlude the extent to which economic imperatives, or a dialectic between technology and the mode of production, continue to structure
contemporary societies. Both erase human subjects and social classes
as agents of social change and both explicitly renounce hope for radical
social change. Both—despite the postmodern critique of totality—to-

talize and project a rupture or break within history that, as I shall argue, exaggerates the novelty of the contemporary moment and occludes continuities with the past. They take trends as constitutive facts, and developmental possibilities as finalities, and both assume that a possible future is already present. From this perspective, postmodern social theory can be seen as a continuation of theories of the post-industrial society in a new context and with new theoretical instruments. These "post" theories can thus be read as two successive attempts to identify new social conditions, to provide new theoretical paradigms, and to yield new sources of cultural capital during an era when undeniable change was forcing conscientious individuals to question old paradigms and theories.

Consequently, I would argue that many criticisms of earlier theories of the post-industrial society are relevant to debates over postmodern social theory, which shares some of the presuppositions and weaknesses of its predecessor (*see* Frankel 1987; Poster 1990 for critiques of theories of the post-industrial society). In some ways, however, postmodern theories might be seen as an advance over theories of post-industrial society by more adequately theorizing the role of culture in the constitution of contemporary societies, though some versions might be interpreted as a regression due to their excessive rhetoric, hyperbole, and lack of sustained empirical analysis (I am thinking here of Baudrillard).

Furthermore, theorists of the post-industrial society tended to subscribe to Enlightenment values of rationality, autonomy, and progress, often with a deep faith in science and technology. Postmodern theorists, by contrast, tend to be sharply critical of the Enlightenment and to affirm opposing values. Indeed, defenders of the postmodern turn in social theory argue that it is precisely the emphasis on notions of difference or pluralism that distinguishes postmodern theory and that constitutes its significance for contemporary social theory. Charles Lemert (1990), for instance, argues that the concept of difference championed by postmodern theorists demands that social theory attend to cultural, racial, gender, and other differences. On this view, postmodern theory is distinguished by refusal of a cultural imperialism that imposes the views of one's group on other groups or cultures, and that respects differences and discontinuities which are not absorbed into a homogenizing universal or general theory.

Wolfgang Welsch (1988) argues that the pluralistic perspectives of postmodern theory constitute an important contribution which has both theoretical and political implications. Welsch argues that the postmodern refusal to privilege a single discourse undermines the dogmatism and reductionism which infects much contemporary social theory. Further, he believes that pluralist perspectives are also valuable for a postmodern politics which refuses to privilege one political subject or focus, instead championing a multiplicity of issues and movements. Critics of postmodern theory and politics complain in turn of a fetishism of difference in postmodern theory, or uncritical celebration of single-issue interest group politics, which fail to articulate common issues and universal political values (*see* Bronner 1990).

In the following section, I shall argue for more dialectical perspectives in social theory and politics which advocate differences and pluralism, as well as more global modes of thought and Marxist and feminist political perspectives. I shall argue that postmodern thought tends to be excessively one-sided in significant cases and suffers from a series of aporia which undermine key theoretical positions.

POSTMODERN APORIA

Some postmodern social theory privileges fragmentation as a key feature of texts, experience, and society itself in the postmodern era. Lyotard (1984) describes and celebrates a plurality of language games while attacking unitary concepts of reason and subjectivity. Jameson describes a schizophrenic fragmentation of experience as central to postmodern culture and claims that both postmodern subjectivity and texts are marked by lack of depth, fragmentation, and schizoid intensities alternating with an absence of affect (Jameson 1983, 119; 1984a, 71). Postmodern space too is fragmented, dispersed, and disorienting, requiring new modes of perception and cognitive mapping. Lyotard calls for a further pluralization and fragmentation of knowledge and politics on the grounds that totalities, systems, and consensus produces "terroristic oppression." And for Baudrillard, postmodernism itself can be described as a playing with the fragments and vestiges of past cultures, art forms, theories, etc. (Kellner 1989a).

From the standpoint of developments in contemporary capitalist society, postmodern social theory thus can be read as articulating social processes toward fragmentation and heterogeneity, and one of their contributions is to illuminate these trends. Yet there are also arguably trends towards increased centralization, new totalizations, and new forms of social organization as well (Kellner 1989a). For example, although there is an ever-proliferating product differentiation and market fragmentation in a capitalist consumer economy, there are also trends toward economic concentration, the extension of a world market system, and growing commodification as capitalism penetrates every sphere of everyday life and the totality of the globe from Peking to Topeka.

While there are new emphases on cultural differentiation and autonomy, a homogeneous mass consumer and media society is also working
to standardize tastes, wants, and practices. Bureaucratization and administration also continue to be major trends of contemporary society
and postmodern social theory tends to obscure these fundamental aspects of our everyday life and social experience.

In effect, postmodern social theory is highly one-sided, articulating
tendencies toward fragmentation (Lyotard) or implosion (Baudrillard)
while neglecting to properly conceptualize counter-tendencies. Likewise, in both the theoretical and political spheres it is sometimes
valuable to stress differences, plurality, and heterogeneity while in
other contexts it may be preferable to seek generalities, unity, and
consensus. While in some contexts in which consensus is produced it
may be forced and oppressive, it does not seem accurate to characterize
all attempts at consensus as "terroristic" or oppressive. Likewise, in
regard to Lyotard's championing paralogy over consensus, there seem
to be at least some situations in which consensus might be preferable
to paralogy, just as there might be some contexts in which attempts to
capture universality and commonality might be preferable to articulating differences and dissent. Mobilizing progressive forces against reactionary programs like aid for the Nicaraguan contras, or conservative
attempts to curtail abortion rights, requires producing consensus that
some actions (i.e., covert actions against democratically elected govern-
ments) are wrong while other rights (i.e., women's control of their own
bodies) are legitimate. In a discussion of the relation between postmodernism and feminism, Fraser and Nicholson (1988) argue that one needs
totalizing narratives that cut across the lines of race, gender, and class
if one wants to engage in radical social theory and politics. They argue
that Lyotard's "justice of multiplicities" "precludes one familiar, and
arguably essential, version of normative political theory: identification
and critique of macrostructures of inequality and injustice which cut
across the boundaries separating relatively discrete practices and institutions. There is no place in Lyotard's universe for critique of pervasive
axes of stratification, for critique of broad-based relations of dominance
and subordination along lines like gender, race and class" (Fraser and
Nicholson 1988, 377–378).

Consequently, while it is sometimes appropriate in theory and politics to valorize differences, in other contexts it is better, even necessary, to valorize macrostructures and consensus. Lyotard's epistemology, by contrast, makes a (positive) fetish out of difference and paralogy
while stigmatizing such things as totality, grand narratives, consensus,
and universality. Curiously, he does not, however, differentiate between different types of totality, instead completely rejecting any and

all totalizing modes of thought. Against this one-sided and terroristic epistemology, certain contemporary theorists (i.e., Rorty) operate with a more contextual epistemology which derives epistemological criteria from specific tasks, goals, and topics. Such a "conceptual pragmatism" is consistent with the spirit of Lyotard's emphasis on a plurality of language games but cuts against his proscriptions against certain kinds of social theory.

Consequently, against Lyotard one could argue that in some contexts it is necessary and desirable to use totalizing modes of thought to grasp certain empirical trends, to make connections between various realms of experience to contextualize events and institutions, and to target centers of oppression and domination. Yet due to Lyotard's polemic against totality and grand narratives, it is impossible—or undesirable—in principle to conceptualize totalizing social trends because of his ban on macrotheory. Yet this epistemological position disables social theory and raises questions concerning the legitimacy and effects of such a position. I would argue that just because some "narratives of legitimation" are highly dubious, politically suspect, and not very convincing does not entail that we should reject *all* grand narratives—that is, all of traditional philosophy and social theory which has systematic and comprehensive aims (see Kellner 1989a and Best 1989). Consequently, I propose that critical social theory today should conceptualize both totalities and differences, centralizing and decentralizing trends and institutions. Similarly, in political theory and practice it is sometimes preferable to stress plurality and the preservation of differences while in other contexts it is preferable to produce alliances and to articulate common interests.

In fact, Lyotard's absolutizing polemic against grand narratives points to a major aporia in certain French postmodern theories. For theories of a "postmodern condition" presuppose a very dramatic break from modernity. Consequently, the very concept of postmodernity, or a postmodern condition, presupposes a master narrative, a totalizing perspective, which envisages the transition from a previous stage of society to a new one. Such theorizing presupposes *both* a concept of a period of modernity *and* a presupposition of a radical break, or rupture, within history that leads to a totally new condition which justifies the term *post*modern. Thus, the very concept "postmodern" seems to presuppose both a master narrative and some notion of totality, or some notion of a periodizing and totalizing thought—precisely the sort of epistemological operation and theoretical hubris which Lyotard and others oppose and want to do away with!

Against Lyotard, we might want to distinguish between metanarratives that tell a (say Cartesian, or Lockean) story about the foundation of knowledge contrasted to the narratives of macro social theory that attempt to conceptualize and interpret a complex diversity of phenomena within a global or totalizing context. We might also distinguish between synchronic narratives that tell a story about a given society at a given point in history, and diachronic narratives that analyze historical change, discontinuities, and ruptures, thus suggesting that narrative and discontinuity are not opposed concepts. Lyotard, by contrast, tends to lump all "grand narratives" together and thus does violence to the diversity of theoretical narratives in our culture. Rejecting totalizing theories, I believe, simply covers over the problem of providing a theoretical analysis of the contemporary historical situation and points to the undertheorized nature of Lyotard's theory of the postmodern condition, which would require at least some sort of rather large narrative of the transition to postmodernity—a rather big and exciting story, one would think. There is also an inconsistency in Lyotard's call for a plurality and heterogeneity of language games juxtaposed to his exclusion from his kingdom of discourse of those grand narratives which he suggests have illicitly monopolized the discussion and proffered illegitimate claims in favor of their privilege.

In addition, when one does not specify and explicate the specific sort of narrative of contemporary society involved in one's theoretical gaming, there is a tendency to make use of the established narratives at one's disposal. For example, in the absence of an alternative theory of contemporary society, Lyotard uncritically accepts theories of "postindustrial society" and "postmodern culture" as accounts of the present age (1984, 3, 7, 37). Yet this move presupposes the validity of these narratives without defending his model and without an adequate social theory which would delineate the transformation suggested by the "post" in "post-industrial' or "postmodern." Indeed, Lyotard (inadvertently?) places himself within the camp of post-industrial theory by failing to more closely and critically examine this rather grand narrative which he himself makes use of.

Furthermore, it seems like a more promising venture to critically discuss, take apart, and perhaps reconstruct and rewrite the grand narratives of social theory rather than to just prohibit them from the terrain of social theory. It is likely—as Jameson argues—that narrative is a fundamental human way of organizing and making sense of our experience and that the narratives of social theory will continue to operate in our social analysis in any case (Jameson 1984b, xi). If this is so, it would seem preferable to bring to light the narratives of social theory so as to critically examine and dissect them rather than forcing them underground to escape censure by a Lyotardian Thought Police on the lookout for illicit narratives. And in general it seems better to highlight and develop the narrative component of social theory and to be aware of the extent to which narrative is an important and arguably indispensable aspect of historiography and social theory (see Ricoeur 1984).

In fact, if Lyotard was consistent with his epistemology, he wouldn't play the "post" game at all, for the terminology of "post" imbricates one in a historical, sequential discourse that implies a master narrative, totalizing periodizations, and historical, sequential thinking—all modes of "modern" thought which Lyotard attacks. Occasionally, he takes note of this dilemma and attempts to extricate himself by trying to provide a different sense to the "post" in postmodern. In the highly convoluted appendix to the English translation of *The Postmodern Condition*, Lyotard defines the postmodern as that which "puts forward the unpresentable in presentation itself," that which works without rules and establishes new rules or models. From this perspective, *"Post modern* would have to be understood according to the paradox of the future *(post)* anterior *(modo)"* (Lyotard 1984, 81). In other words, postmodernism is merely a species of modernism that, like modernism, is radically innovative, produces its own rules and norms, and is in constant flux. Yet here Lyotard puts himself in the position of being for artistic modernism while against modern epistemology.

In other texts from the period, Lyotard concedes that " 'postmodern' is probably a very bad term because it conveys the idea of a historical 'periodization.' 'Periodizing,' however is still a 'classic' or 'modern' ideal. 'Postmodern' simply indicates a mood, or better a state of mind" (Lyotard 1986–1987, 209). Yet here too Lyotard is merely engaging in a verbal subterfuge and seems to both want to exploit the prestige of the "postmodern" (which he, after all, helped to promote) while extricating himself from some of the theoretical commitments of "post" discourse and from justifying one's use of the discourse.

Furthermore, it seems wrong to operate with unitary notions of a postmodern "condition," "scene," or whatever, for it would seem to be more in the spirit of postmodern thought (and more accurate!) to talk of postmodern scenes, trends, and texts which are themselves plural, multiple, heterogeneous, and often contradictory. One could also argue that postmodern social theory greatly exaggerates the alleged break or rupture in history from which it gains its currency and prestige. Indeed, neither Baudrillard nor Lyotard nor any other postmodern theorist has adequately theorized what is involved in a break or rupture between the modern and the postmodern. Baudrillard and Kroker and Cook dramatically proclaim a fundamental break in history with the advent of a new postmodern era without providing a clear account of the transition to postmodernity and without seeing or specifying the continuities between the previous era and the allegedly new one. Jameson gives a fairly precise periodization of postmodern culture and a detailed account of its differences from the culture of high modernism, yet while he is prepared to postulate the existence of a new stage of society in terms of important new developments within capitalism, he does not provide a detailed narrative of the transition from the stages of capitalism described by Marx, Lenin, and earlier Marxists, relying on a rather brief synopsis of Mandel instead of providing a more detailed analysis. And Lyotard in principle is prohibited from producing a postmodern social theory of this kind by his postmodern epistemology which explicitly renounces grand narratives and macro social theory.

Rather than simply positing a radical break in history, we should grasp the differences between the old and the new stages of society (or art, philosophy, etc.), *and* the continuities between the previous and new stages—a continuity constituted precisely by the ongoing primacy of capitalist relations of production in the current organization of society (Kellner 1989a). Thus, against postmodernists who celebrate the radically "new"—and rupture, discontinuity, and difference—I would argue that we need to characterize both the continuities and the discontinuities in the historical process and that this involves both pointing to ruptures and breaks in recent history as well as continuities (*see also* Barraclough 1964; Foucault 1970; Derrida 1981, 24; Jameson 1983, 123; Hall 1986, 46).

Raymond Williams' (1977) distinctions between "residual," "dominant," and "emergent" cultures might help with this task. Williams proposes that rather than speaking of "stages" or "variations" within culture, we should recognize "the internal dynamic relations of any actual process. We have certainly still to speak of the 'dominant' and the 'effective,' and in these senses of the hegemonic. But we find that we have also to speak, and indeed with further differentiation of each, of the 'residual' and the 'emergent,' which in any real process, and at any moment in the process are significant both in themselves and in what they reveal of the characteristics of the 'dominant' " (Williams 1977, 121–122).

Using Williams' distinctions we might want to speak of postmodernity as an emergent tendency within a still dominant modernity which is haunted as well by various forms of residual, traditional cultures. Our present moment, in this view, is thus a contradictory transitional and borderline situation which does not yet allow any unambiguous affirmations concerning an alleged leap into full-blown postmodernity. At this point it appears premature to claim that we are fully in a new postmodern scene, though one might, using Williams' terminology, see postmodernity as an important new emergent tendency. Consequently, while postmodern social theory has attempted to cross the borderline and to chart out the terrain of the new, its claims for an absolute break between modernity and postmodernity are not always convincing. Although we may be living within a borderline, or transitional space, between the modern and the postmodern, and may be entering a terrain where old modes of thought and language are not always useful, it seems that in many ways postmodern social theory exaggerates the break or rupture in history and thus covers over the extent to which the contemporary situation continues to be constituted by capitalism, patriarchy, bureaucracy, and other aspects of the past.

THEORIZING POSTMODERNITY: CONTRIBUTIONS, LIMITATIONS, AND FUTURE PROSPECTS

Although there has been both a faddish embrace of the new postmodern theories, and an equally fervent rejection of these theories—frequently predicated, I suspect, on reluctance to spend the time reading some difficult theoretical works which may subvert one's previous theoretical positions—I imagine that the postmodern debates will be with us for a long time to come. There is a sense in many disciplines of the end of an era and there are equally compelling searches for new paradigms, new politics, and new theories (see Jameson 1984a, 53; Baynes et al. 1987). The debates over the postmodern pose in a dramatic way the issue of competing paradigms for social theory and the need to choose paradigms that are most theoretically and practically applicable to social conditions in the present era. The debate also highlights the importance of social theory for a wide variety of discussion within the arts, philosophy, politics, and everyday life. Although one wing of postmodern theory wants to jettison, or dramatically revise, social theory, on the whole I think that the postmodernity debate highlights precisely the importance of social theory for a variety of disciplines and problems.

Indeed, I believe that the postmodernity debate points to the need for *better* and *more* social theory. Interestingly, social theory has gained a certain amount of prestige and currency in that much contemporary literary and cultural studies, philosophy, anthropology, and other disciplines are informed by critical social theory. The postmodern crossing of disciplinary boundaries sanctions and encourages such moves and the postmodern emphasis on the social construction of reality, language, theory, and human life requires that all disciplines concerned with these phenomena theorize the social dimensions of texts, practices, discourses, and institutions. On the other hand, postmodern boundary subversion points to the need for social theory to draw on the most advanced currents of philosophy, cultural theory, political economy, history, and other disciplines.

In addition, the postmodern challenge forces social theory to clarify and strengthen its presuppositions, to develop its methodology to respond to postmodern critiques of representation, macro theory, and theories of social change. From this perspective, one of the positive challenges and developments in postmodern social theory is its exploding of boundaries between previous academic disciplines and its putting in question the very field of social theory. Postmodernists, like critical theorists, tend to subvert boundaries between disciplines and draw upon a sometimes bewildering variety of academic fields, discourses, and positions. Such an approach contributes to the development of a multidisciplinary social theory which could provide a richer, more comprehensive critical social theory of the present age by drawing on the latest developments in philosophy, anthropology, political economy, and the other human and social sciences. Such a multidimensional social theory could well be preferable to the more abstract disciplinary enterprises which would limit social theory to the domain of academic sociology, cut off from developments in other fields.

And yet the most radical postmodern theory rejects social theory altogether. Baudrillard, for example, argues that the social has vanished in the black hole of the masses. It is impossible to claim any longer that social theory represents social reality in a society of simulations, implosion, and hyperreality where it is no longer possible to distinguish between simulations and the real, illusion and reality (1983a, 1983b). Against such postmodern epistemological skepticism, Stuart Hall strenuously asserts that postmodern notions of the collapse or implosion of the real, the end of history, and the loss of meaning are highly exaggerated, and against these claims argues for the continuing importance of the problematics of representation, ideological critique, and political struggle. Hall argues that "there is all the difference in the world between the assertion that there is no one, final absolute meaning—no ultimate signified, only the endlessly sliding chain of signification, and, on the other hand, the assertion that meaning does not exist" (1986, 49).

As noted, Lyotard argues that we should abandon the project of developing a theory of society which inevitably involves the construction of a grand narrative. In contrast to traditional social theory, he offers a new paradigm for the practice of theory: just gaming (Lyotard and Thebaud, 1985). He argues that in opposition to the ambitious systematic social theories of the past, social theorists should intervene in a wide variety of different sorts of language games, making moves in a plurality of debates while opposing the moves and positions of other players. Against the systematic theories of justice and notions of a just society in traditional social theory and politics, Lyotard and Thebaud argue for a "justice of multiplicities" and more modest and pragmatic notions of social and political change.

Certain postmodern theorists like Baudrillard also reject completely the problematic of radical politics, while Lyotard, Deleuze and Guattari, and others attempt to develop a micropolitics of desire, accompanied by proposals for a postmodern politics of differences (Foucault), margins (Derrida), and new social movements (Laclau and Mouffe).[9] As I have suggested, some of the theoretical commitments of postmodern theory, however, create obstacles to produce a politics of alliances, a macropolitics, or more traditional theories of radical social change. In addition to postmodern rejections of macrotheory, their rejections of concepts of the subject and rather impoverished theory of subjectivity provide real limitations to producing a postmodern politics. Theories of political change require theories of agency and the postmodern rejection of the subject and categories of agency raises the question of how one can develop political theories without theories of agency, of praxis and action.

Hall particularly objects to Baudrillard and other postmodern theorists' conception of the masses as a passive, sullen, "silent majority," and their political cynicism and nihilism which he relates to

> the collapse of the critical French intelligentsia during the Mitterand era. What raises my political hackles is the comfortable way in which French intellectuals now take it upon themselves to declare when and for whom history ends, how the masses can or cannot be represented, when they are or are not a real historical force, when they can or cannot be mythically invoked in the French revolutionary tradition, etc. French intellectuals always had a tendency to use "the masses" in the abstract to fuel or underpin their own intellectual positions. Now that the intellectuals have renounced critical thought, they feel no inhibition in renouncing it on behalf of the masses—whose destinies they have only shared abstractly. . . . I think that Baudrillard needs to join the masses for a while, to be silent for two thirds of a century, just to see what it feels like. (1986, 51–53)

Other British cultural Marxists find postmodern theory to be equally debilitating in its political implications. Dick Hebdige recognizes the contributions in Baudrillard's theory but also articulates "suspicions that the kind of will motivating his work seems to be poisonous . . . there's not much future in it . . . he . . . seems to promote its other:

heresy, sorcery, *irrationality*" (1987, 70). Those allied with British cultural studies tend to be most concerned with what they see as the nefarious political effects of postmodern social theory, with Iain Chambers criticizing its dark, pessimistic vision (1986, 100; see also McRobbie 1986, 110), Hebdige its "cynicism/nihilism" and "fatalism" (1986, 92, 95), and John Fiske and Jon Watts attacking its lack of "respect" for social groups and its contempt for "the masses" (1986, 106). As opposed to Baudrillardian monolithic categories of the "masses," British cultural studies attempt to analyze society in terms of different classes, groups, and subcultures with their own unique patterns of experience, cultural styles, modes of resistance, etc., in a neo-Gramscian analysis which attempts to specify the concrete forces of hegemony and counterhegemonic forces and struggles in a specific sociohistorical conjuncture.

Jürgen Habermas is also worried about the political and theoretical implications of postmodern social theory. Habermas has been arguing (1981, 1987) that the new postmodern social theories are irrationalist ideologies which constitute a regressive development in contemporary social theory. For example, in an article on "Das Moderne—ein unvollendes Projekt" (translated as "Modernity versus Postmodernity"), Habermas (1981) argued that the various theories of postmodernism are a form of attack on modernity and have their ideological precursors in various irrationalist and counter-Enlightenment theories. In a series of succeeding *Lectures on the Philosophical Discourse of Modernity*, Habermas (1987) continued to attack the (primarily French) theories of postmodernity. He used standard methods of ideology critique and suggested that the French theories of postmodernity which had their roots in Nietzsche and Heidegger were aligned with the counter-Enlightenment, and exhibited a disturbing kinship with fascism. Against theories of postmodernity, Habermas defended "the project of modernity" which he believed was "an unfinished project" containing unfulfilled emancipatory potential.

Postmodernists by contrast see modernity, the Enlightenment, and its political projects as themselves flawed and containing the seeds of social domination. Against these critiques, Habermas and his colleagues have responded with critiques of the postmodern attacks on reason, enlightenment, universality, and so on by New French Theorists such as Foucault, Derrida, and Lyotard (Benhabib 1984; Honneth 1985; Frank 1983). The latter discussion has for the most part focused on postmodern theory, or forms of knowledge, and its allegedly irrationalist proclivities. With the exception of Habermas who takes on a broad panorama of postmodern theory, the critical theory response has focused on critiques of Lyotard's *The Postmodern Condition* (1984), and on defenses of reason, universality, consensus, and normativity against the postmodern attack (*see* the discussion in Kellner 1989a).

These debates, I believe, have forced social theorists of different positions to define their fundamental presuppositions and to rethink what assumptions are involved in critical social theory and radical politics. Thus despite its limitations, postmodern social theory poses a provocative challenge to other traditions of social theory and theories of political change. Consequently, if contemporary social theorists want to continue to be relevant to the theoretical and political concerns of the present age, they must address the issues advanced by the postmodern challenge. This means that critical social theory today must attempt to theorize the new social conditions and phenomena analyzed by the postmodernists, and must demonstrate that categories and theories developed earlier continue to be applicable and illuminating in theorizing the new social conditions. This requires rethinking such enterprises as the Enlightenment, Marxism, critical theory, structuralism, feminism, and so on in terms of the new issues posed and the new challenges advanced by the current configurations of the media, consumer, and information societies; by cybernetics and design; by the restructuring of labor and production; by the new configurations of class; and by the new modes of the colonization of everyday life.[10]

For instance, in light of the continued vitality and hegemony of capitalism, I would prefer to situate and analyze contemporary culture and social conditions in terms of a theory of techno-capitalism that would present the current social order in the capitalist countries as a synthesis of new technologies and capitalism that is characterized by new technical, social, and cultural forms combining with capitalist relations of production to create the social matrix of our times (Kellner 1989a). This move points to continuities with the social theories of the past (i.e., Marxism) and the need to revive, update, expand, and develop previous theories in the light of contemporary conditions. Analyzing the new configurations of capitalism and technology would allow emphasis on the new role of information, media, consumerism, the implosion of aesthetics and commodification, and other themes stressed by postmodernists while situating these developments within a larger socio-historical context (Kellner 1989a, 1990).

It is my view that postmodern social theorists like Baudrillard, Lyotard, Foucault, and Kroker and Cook have made a serious theoretical and political mistake in severing their work from the Marxian critique of capitalism precisely at a point when the logic of capital accumulation has been playing an increasingly important role in structuring the new stage of society which I conceptualize as a new technological restructuring in a techno-capital society. Indeed, I would argue that

Marxian categories are of central importance precisely in analyzing the phenomena focused on by postmodern social theory: the consumer society, the media, information, computers, etc. Although theorists of both the post-industrial society and postmodern society posit the primacy of knowledge and information as new principles of social organization, it is arguably capitalism that is determining what sort of media, information, computers, etc. are being produced and distributed according to its logic and interests. That is, in techno-capitalist societies, information, as Herbert Schiller (1981, 1984) and others have shown, is being more and more commodified, accessible only to those who can pay for it. Education itself is becoming more and more commodified as computers become essential to the process of education, and while more domains of knowledge and information themselves are commodified and transmitted through computers (I'm thinking both of computer learning programs which force consumers to buy programs to learn typing, math, history, foreign languages, etc., as well as modem-programs and data bases which provide access to an abundance of information, entertainment, networking, etc. via computer for those who can afford to pay its per minute information prices).

Interestingly, in a recent article, Lyotard himself has made this point, arguing: "The major development of the last twenty years, expressed in the most vapid terms of political economy and historical periodization, has been the transformation of language into a productive commodity: phrases considered as messages to encode, decode, transmit, and order (by the bundle) to reproduce, conserve, and keep available (memories), to combine and conclude (calculations), and to oppose (games, conflicts, cybernetics); and the establishment of a unit of measure that is also a price unit, in other words, information. The effects of the penetration of capitalism into language are just beginning to be felt" (Lyotard 1986–1987, 217).

Yet against Lyotard and others who reject macrotheory, the category of totality, or meta-narratives, I would argue that it is precisely now that we need such totalizing theories to capture the new totalizations being undertaken by capitalism in the realm of consumption, the media, information, etc. From this perspective one needs totalizing theories to conceptualize, describe, and interpret totalizing social processes (Kellner 1989a), just as one needs political theories to articulate common or general interests that cut across divisions of gender, race, and class (Fraser and Nicholson 1988; Bronner 1990). Without such macrotheories that attempt to cognitively map the new forms of social development and the relationships between spheres like the economy, culture, education, politics, we are condemned to live among the fragments without clear indications of what impact new technologies and

Concl.

social developments are having on the various domains of our social life. "Cognitive mapping" is therefore necessary to provide theoretical and political orientation as we move into a new and confusing social terrain (Jameson 1988).

NOTES

1. These distinctions are made by Mike Featherstone (1988) in the introduction to a special issue of *Theory, Culture, and Society* dedicated to postmodernism and social theory. Other special journal issues devoted to postmodernism include *Journal of Communication Inquiry* 10(2), Summer 1986; *Cultural Critique* 5, 1986–1987; and *Social Text* 18, Winter 1987/88; on postmodern social theory, see also Denzin 1987 and Dickens and Fontana 1990.

2. Habermas also projected the possibility of a postmodern social organization in *Legitimation Crisis* (1975): "The interest behind the examination of crisis tendencies in late- and post-capitalist class societies is in exploring the possibilities of a 'post-modern' society—that is, a historically new principle of organization and not a different name for the surprising vigor of an aged capitalism" (17). Yet Habermas has never really undertaken an inquiry into what might follow modernity and has generally treated postmodern theories as irrationalist ideologies—a point that I shall take up later.

3. Lyotard's earlier work *Discours, Figure* (1971) (*see* Lash [1988]) and later *Just Gaming* (with Theabaud 1985) and *Le Differend* (1989) could also be taken as prototypical postmodern texts.

4. Rejecting the structuralist, semiological, and formalist theories of language previously dominant in France, Lyotard adopts the pragmatic approach to language which would analyze its uses, rules, and practices as moves in a language game—an approach developed by Wittgenstein, Austin, Searle, and others. Interestingly enough, his opponent Habermas adopts a similar approach.

5. Benhabib (1984) points out a contradiction in Lyotard's program in which Lyotard seems unable to decide if he wishes to maintain a relativist and pluralist heterogeneity of language games or develop an epistemological standpoint from which he can criticize "grand narratives" or the "performativity" legitimation practices of the sciences: "The choice is still between an uncritical polytheism and a self-conscious recognition of the need for criteria of validity, and the attempt to reflexively ground them" (Benhabib 1984, 111). Benhabib suggests that Lyotard doesn't seem to be able to make the choice, though he seems to tend toward the pluralism and relativism pole, which would mean that he does not really have a standpoint from which he can criticize competing positions. Habermas, by contrast, has exerted much theoretical labor in attempting to develop a critical standpoint for critical theory today.

6. For a debate over the ways that postmodernism problematicizes social theory and puts in question established theory, *see* the exchanges between Denzin (1986, 1987) and Bogard (1987).

7. Lyotard, as noted, explicitly characterizes postmodern society as the computerization of society, thus replaying a central theme of the "post-industrial society" and the "information society" that knowledge and information are fundamental organizing principles of society. He differs, however, by sometimes insisting that capitalism continues to be a fundamental organizing principle (Lyotard 1984, 1986–1987, 215). These gestures, however, point to inadequacies in his own theory which has never developed analyses of the relationships between captialism and technol-

ogy. In the most curious assimilation of social theory and human beings to ma-chines, in *Anti-Oedipus*, Deleuze and Guattari (1977) use the concept of "desiring machines" to describe human beings and use the mechanistic concept of flows and intensities of desire as the basis for their revolutionary theory.

8. *See* Foucault 1970. For a provocative discussion of rupture in history and the categories needed to conceptualize both continuity and discontinuity, *see* Foucault 1972.

9. For a critical review of some of these positions, *see* Ryan 1988 and Best and Keller 1990.

10. Several important works on feminism and postmodernism were published while my text was going to press. They include Kipnis 1988; Lovibond 1989; Flax 1990; Nicholson 1990.

REFERENCES

Barraclough, Geoffrey. 1964. *An Introduction to Contemporary History.* Balti-more: Penguin.

Barthes, Roland. 1962. *Mythologies.* New York: Hill and Wang.

Baudrillard, Jean. 1983a. *Simulations.* New York: Semiotext (e).

Baudrillard, Jean. 1983b. *In the Shadows of the Silent Majorities.* New York: Semiotext (e).

Baudrillard, Jean. 1984. *The Evil Demon of Images.* Annandale, Australia: Power Institute.

Baudrillard, Jean. 1988. "The Year 2000 Has Already Happened," In Arthur Kroker and Marlouise Kroker, eds., *Body Invaders: Panic Sex in America.* Montreal: New World Perspectives.

Baudrillard, Jean. 1988. *Jean Baudrillard: Selected Writings.* Edited by Mark Poster. Cambridge and Stanford: Polity and Stanford University Press.

Baynes, Kenneth, James Bohman, and Thomas McCarthy, eds. 1987. *After Philos-ophy. End or Transformation?* Cambridge: MIT Press.

Bell, Daniel. 1973. *The Coming of Post-Industrial Society.* New York: Basic Books.

Bell, Daniel. 1976. *The Cultural Contradictions of Capitalism.* New York: Basic Books.

Benhabib, Seyla. 1984. "Epistemologies of Postmodernism." *New German Cri-tique* 33:103–127.

Berman, Marshall. 1982. *All That is Solid Melts Into Air.* New York: Simon and Schuster.

Berman, Russell. 1984. "Modern Art and Desublimation." *Telos* 62:31–58.

Bernstein, Richard. 1985. *Philosophical Profiles: Essays in a Pragmatic Mode.* Cambridge: Polity Press.

Best, Steven. 1989. "Jameson, Totality and the Post-Structuralist Critique." in Douglas Kellner, ed., *Postmodernism/Jameson/Critique.* Washington, D.C.: Maison-neuve.

Best, Steven, and Douglas Kellner. 1990. *Postmodern Theory. An Introduction and Critique.* London: Macmillan.

Bogard, William. 1987. "Reply to Denzin." *Sociological Theory* 5:206–209.

Bronner, Stephen Eric. 1990. *Socialism Unbound.* New York: Routledge.

Burger, Peter. 1984. *Theory of the Avant-Garde.* Minneapolis: University of Min-nesota Press.

Calinescu, Matei. 1987. *Five Faces of Modernity.* Durham: Duke University Press.

284 *Douglas Kellner*

Chambers, Iain. 1986. "Waiting on the End of the World?" *Journal of Communication Inquiry* 10:99–103.

Chen, Kuan-Hsing. 1989. " 'IF I'M NOT ME, WHO ARE YOU?,' or Collapsing the War Zone between Postmodernism and Cultural Studies." Manuscript.

Coward, Rosalind, and John Ellis, 1977. *Language and Materialism*. London: Routledge and Kegan Paul.

Debord, Guy. 1976. *The Society of the Spectacle*. Detroit: Black and Red.

Deleuze, Gilles, and Felix Guattari. 1977. *Anti-Oedipus*. New York: Viking.

Denzin, Norman K. 1986. "Postmodern Social Theory." *Sociological Theory* 4:194–204.

Denzin, Norman K. 1987. "Reply to Bogard." *Sociological Theory* 5:209–211.

Derrida, Jacques. 1976. *Of Grammatology*. Baltimore: Johns Hopkins University Press.

Derrida, Jacques. 1981. *Positions*. Chicago: University of Chicago Press.

Dews, Peter, ed. 1986. *Habermas. Autonomy and Solidarity*. London: Verso.

Dews, Peter. 1987. *Logics of Disintegration*. London: Verso.

Dickens, David, and Andrea Fontana, eds. 1990. *Postmodernism and Social Inquiry*. Chicago: University of Chicago Press.

During, Simon. 1987. "Postmodernism or Post-Colonialism Today." *Textual Practice* 1:32–47.

Etzioni, Amitai. 1968. *The Active Society*. New York: Free Press.

Featherstone, Mike. 1988. "In Pursuit of the Postmodern." *Theory, Culture and Society* 5:195–216.

Ferre, Frederick. 1976. *Shaping the Future: Resources for the Post-Modern World*. New York: Harper and Row.

Fiske, John, and Jon Watts. 1986. "An Articulating Culture." *Journal of Communication Inquiry* 10:104–107.

Flax, Jane. 1990. *Thinking Fragments*. Berkeley: University of California Press.

Foster, Hal, ed. 1983. *The Anti-Aesthetic: Essays on Postmodern Culture*. Port Townsend, Wash.: Bay Press.

Foucault, Michel. 1970. *The Order of Things*. New York: Random House.

Foucault, Michel. 1972. *The Archaeology of Knowledge*. New York: Harper and Row.

Frank, Manfred. 1983. *Was ist Neostrukturalismus?* Frankfurt: Suhrkamp.

Frankel, Boris. 1987. *The Post-Industrial Utopians*. Cambridge: Polity Press.

Fraser, Nancy, and Linda Nicholson. 1988. "Social Criticism Without Philosophy: An Encounter between Feminism and Postmodernism." *Theory, Culture and Society* 5:373–394.

Grossberg, Larry. 1986. "History, Politics and Postmodernism." *Journal of Communication Inquiry* 10:61–77.

Habermas, Jürgen. 1975. *Legitimation Crisis*. Boston: Beacon Press.

Habermas, Jürgen. 1981. "Modernity versus Postmodernity." *New German Critique* 22:3–14.

Habermas, Jürgen. 1984. *Theory of Communicative Action*. Vol. 1. Boston: Beacon Press.

Habermas, Jürgen. 1987. *Lectures on the Philosophical Discourse of Modernity*. Cambridge, Mass.: MIT Press.

Hall, Stuart. 1986. "On Postmodernism and Articulation: An Interview." *Journal of Communication Inquiry* 10:45–60.

Hebdige, Dick. 1986. "Postmodernism and 'The Other Side.' " *Journal of Communication Inquiry* 10:78–98.

Hebdige, Dick. 1987. "Hiding in the Light." *Art and Text* 26:64–79.

Honneth, Axel. 1985. "An Aversion Against the Universal." *Theory, Culture and Society* 2:147–157.

Jameson, Fredric. 1972. *The Prison House of Language*. Princeton: Princeton University Press.

Jameson, Fredric. 1983. "Postmodernism and the Consumer Society." In Foster, ed., *The Anti-Aesthetic*.

Jameson, Fredric. 1984a. "Postmodernism, or the Cultural Logic of Late Capitalism." *New Left Review* 146:53–93.

Jameson, Fredric. 1984b. "Foreword." In Lyotard, *The Postmodern Condition*.

Jameson, Fredric. 1988. "Cognitive Mapping." In L. Grossberg and C. Nelson, eds., *Marxism and the Interpretation of Culture*. Urbana: University of Illinois Press.

Kellner, Douglas. 1988. "Postmodernism as Social Theory: Some Problems and Challenges." *Theory, Culture and Society* 5(2–3):239–270.

Kellner, Douglas. 1989a. *Critical Theory, Marxism, and Modernity*. Cambridge and Baltimore: Polity Press and Johns Hopkins University Press.

Kellner, Douglas. 1989b. *Jean Baudrillard: From Marxism to Postmodernism and Beyond*. Cambridge: Polity Press.

Kellner, Douglas. 1989c. "Jameson, Marxism, and Postmodernism." In Douglas Kellner, ed., *Postmodernism/Jameson/Critique*. Washington, D.C.: Maisonneuve.

Kellner, Douglas. 1990. *Television and the Crises of Democracy*. Boulder, Colo.: Westview.

Kipnis, Laura. 1988. "Feminism: The Political Conscience of Postmodernism?" In Andrew Ross, ed., *Universal Abandon?* Minneapolis: University of Minnesota Press.

Kroker, Arthur, and David Cook. 1986. *The Postmodern Scene*. New York: St. Martin's.

Kroker, Arthur, Marilouise Kroker, and David Cook. 1989. *Panic Encyclopedia*. New York: St. Martin's.

Lash, Scott. 1988. "Discourse or Figure? Toward a Postmodern Semiotics." *Theory, Culture and Society* 5:311–336.

Lefebvre, Henri. 1971. *Everyday Life in the Modern World*. New York: Harper and Row.

Lemert, Charles. 1990. "General Social Theory, Irony, Postmodernism." In S. Seidman and D. Wagner, eds., *Social Theory and Its Critiques*. New York: Basil Blackwell.

Lovibond, Sabina. 1989. "Feminism and Postmodernism." *New Left Review* 178:5–28.

Lyotard, Jean-Francois. 1971. *Discours, Figure*. Paris: Klincksieck.

Lyotard, Jean-Francois. 1984. *The Postmodern Condition*. Minneapolis: University of Minnesota Press.

Lyotard, Jean-Francois. 1986–1987. "Rules and Paradoxes and Svelte Paradox." *Cultural Critique* 5:209–219.

Lyotard, Jean-Francois. 1988. "An Interview." *Theory, Culture and Society* 5:277–310.

Lyotard, Jean-Francois. 1989. *Le Differend*. Minneapolis: University of Minnesota Press.

Lyotard, Jean-Francois, and Jean-Loup Theabaud. 1985. *Just Gaming*. Minneapolis: University of Minnesota Press.

McRobbie, Angela. 1986. "Postmodernism and Popular Culture." *Journal of Communication Inquiry* 10:108–116.

Mandel, Ernest. 1975. *Late Capitalism*. London: New Left Books.

Merquior, J. G. 1986. "Spider and Bee." In *Postmodernism*. London: ICA Documents 4 and 5.

Mills, C. Wright. 1959. *The Sociological Imagination*. New York: Oxford University Press.

Nicholson, Linda J., ed. 1990. *Feminism/Postmodernism*. New York: Routledge.

286 *Douglas Kellner*

Poster, Mark. 1990. *Mode of Information.* Cambridge: Polity Press.

Ricoeur, Paul. 1984. *Time and Narrative.* Vol. 1. Chicago: University of Chicago Press.

Rorty, Richard. 1979. *Philosophy and the Mirror of Nature.* Princeton: Princeton University Press.

Ryan, Michael. 1988. "Postmodern Politics." *Theory, Culture and Society* 5:559–576.

Schiller, Herbert. 1981. *Who Knows: Information in the Age of the Fortune 500.* Norwood, N.J.: Ablex.

Schiller, Herbert. 1984. *Information and the Crisis Economy.* Norwood, N.J.: Ablex.

Toynbee, Arnold. 1934–1954. *A Study of History.* Vols. I–XI. London: Oxford University Press.

Wellmer, Albrecht. 1985. "On the Dialectic of Modernism and Postmodernism." *Praxis International* 4:337–362.

Welsch, Wolfgang. 1988. *Unsere postmoderne Moderne.* Weinheim: VCH, Acta Humaniora.

Williams, Raymond. 1977. *Marxism and Literature.* New York: Oxford University Press.

Winner, Langon. 1977. *Autonomous Technology.* Cambridge, Mass.: MIT Press.

Wolin, Richard. 1984. "Modernism versus Postmodernism." *Telos* 62:9–30.

11

Betwixt and Between: Recent Cultural Sociology in Europe and the United States

❀

MICHÈLE LAMONT AND ROBERT WUTHNOW
Princeton University

In the last twenty years, the social theory landscape has been significantly reshaped by a set of theories dealing in various ways with symbols, symbolic codes, and culture. Many of the most significant theoretical developments in conflict theory, poststructuralism, symbolic interactionism, and important criticisms of rational choice theories have come from the quarters of culture theorists, such as Peter Berger, Pierre Bourdieu, Mary Douglas, Michel Foucault, and Clifford Geertz. Yet, considered together, these theorists transcend each of the more traditional labels—conflict theory, symbolic interactionism, and so forth—that sociologists have devised to classify their theoretical world; they produced a literature which has a distinct dynamic and addresses issues of importance for understanding society. Hence, their contribution deserves to be considered as one of this world's strands.

Two topics central to this cluster of works are symbolic codes and culture-mediated power relations.[1] Studies of symbolic codes focus on the description and analysis of cultural classification systems, while work on culture-mediated power relations is concerned with the ways in which inequality is shaped by cultural signals, and shapes them in turn. While symbolic codes have created much interest on both sides of the Atlantic, it is only recently that interest in culture-mediated power relations has spread in American sociology.

In general, there is much overlap between the American and European literatures on culture, and at this point the two traditions have borrowed a great deal from one another. Nevertheless, significant cross-Atlantic differences can be identified. The purpose of the present paper is to discuss some of these differences. The European concern with symbolic codes and classification systems is contrasted with the American focus on the role of experience and action in grounding cultural

287

categories and meaning. While this difference in perspective is not deep, more significantly distinct are the American and European sociological approaches to culture-mediated power relations. The first section deals with symbolic codes; the second section is concerned with culture-mediated power relations.

Thematic bifurcations between European and American theories of culture are undoubtedly linked to their context of elaboration: European and American authors are not necessarily dealing with the same object, the same "culture." Indeed, their relation with high culture, their everyday life experience, as well as the inarticulate social definitions of culture permeating their environment differ, and affect in different ways what "culture" they talk about, and how they talk about it. Recognizing the importance of sociologizing theoretical analysis of culture, the last section of this paper endeavors to analyze how some of the continental differences in theorizing about culture relate to the social and cultural contexts in which theories are produced. Factors such as differences in the social position and prestige of academics are considered. It is argued that with their interest in rationalism and symbolic codes, European theories often propose a top-down approach to symbolic life which parallels the relationship that intellectuals have with culture and society as a whole. American theories of culture often express the instrumental role bequeathed to knowledge and academics in American society metaphorically, a role subordinate to the imperatives of the profit motive and other practical pursuits.

Cultural differences in political and organizational culture, and specific organizational features of academic life in Europe and the United States, account for cross-Atlantic differences in theoretical approaches to culture-mediated power relations. We focus on the French case because it is from there that most of the European theories dealing with this topic have emerged. Evidence suggests that the French perceive a broader set of relationships as power relations than do Americans. We argue that this has influenced the types of theory of culture to which the two national settings have given birth.

SYMBOLIC CODES AND/IN ACTION

Studies of symbolic codes have a long tradition on both sides of the Atlantic. They focus squarely on the description and analysis of cultural classification systems. The analyst seeks to know how symbolic elements are put together to form systems; whether and to what degree these systems are internally coherent; how they express content both explicitly and implicitly; and what are the underlying rules involved in their formation. Questions of this kind may be asked of a wide variety of symbolic codes, ranging from myths, religio-moral creeds, scientific dialogue, political rhetoric, plot structure in novels, to the conversations of lovers.[2]

The Durkheimian tradition, especially that of *The Elementary Forms of the Religious Life* and the work of Marcel Mauss, provides an early example of anthropological work concerned with classification systems and the internal patterning of symbols. This legacy has, of course, been carried on in the work of Claude Lévi-Strauss, Michel Foucault, Mary Douglas, Kai Erikson, and others, and has been a continuing emphasis in American anthropology. The Weberian tradition inspired a rich legacy of inquiry into the nature of rationality among religious codes and some secular cultural expressions, such as music. Both of these traditions played important roles in the development of American sociology, especially through the efforts of Talcott Parsons, for whom cultural systems comprised a central element in the study of social action.

There has been, however, a more distinctly American approach to the study of cultural codes as well, which over the past few decades has differed significantly in theoretical origin and empirical focus from its European counterpart. This approach is indebted to American pragmatism, symbolic interactionism, the social construction of reality approach, the social psychology of attitudes, and ethnographic research. From pragmatism it has inherited the epistemological assumption that *experience* is the basis of knowledge and that knowledge should be useful in practice. From symbolic interactionism it has inherited the assumption that meaning (and indeed the ability to reflect about meaning) cannot be separated from the social interaction situations in which meaning arises (e.g., Fine 1979; Hall 1988). And the social psychology of attitudes and ethnography have reinforced the connection between human agency and the production of symbolic codes. It has also been influenced by the work of Berger and Luckmann (1966), who drew heavily from the phenomenology of Schutz (1971; Schutz and Luckmann 1973), and indirectly from Heidegger (1962). In Berger and Luckmann's formulation, knowledge was primarily rooted in the subject's experience of everyday life. Symbolic codes, therefore, consisted of primordial categories for making sense of everyday experience and of secondary and tertiary codes that helped to legitimate experience by placing it in broader frameworks of meaning (*see also* Hunter and Ainlay 1986; Wuthnow et al. 1984). This emphasis was compatible with the more purely American theoretical tradition of symbolic interactionism and was reinforced by participant-observation methods in sociology and ethnographic emphases in anthropology (Joas 1987).

These assumptions differ most sharply from European assumptions that place emphasis on the *rationality* of symbolic codes, and that locate codes within *formal systems of knowledge*, rather than relating them to the *lived experience* of the individual. They also differ in point of departure from European approaches that attempt to "de-center" the agency of code production and focus more directly on codes themselves. These approaches, such as deconstructionism, define themselves against the "logocentrism" of the Western humanist tradition. Their own textual strategy makes no room for human experience, practice, and interaction, all so central in American approaches to culture.

The European *cognitive* focus can be best seen in structuralist theories that treat symbolic codes largely as classification systems. In these theories, codes are "flat," consisting primarily of cognitive categories or boxes in which elements of reality are located. Here, the important questions are: what categories exist, what gets located in the various categories, and how are their boundaries delineated? The categories are assumed, or known, and their origin and relation to experience is not problematic. But the major brand of structuralism posits a dual layer of investigation: signifiers and the signified. At the surface level, symbolic codes look much like they do in the unidimensional approach, consisting of categories and boundaries between categories. There is in addition, however, another level, a subsurface of meaning or "deep structure," that interacts with the manifest content of the symbolic code. One must pay attention to both, looking not only at classification systems but also at what is implied, what is not spoken, what is "really meant," as in the work of Lévi-Strauss (1963). The work of Barthes (1968, 1972) also provides a number of examples of this orientation.

The European cognitive focus is reflected in the place of rationality in European cultural analysis: cognitive dimensions, whether they be rational discourse or formal categories, are often posited either as more essential or more "advanced" cultural forms, which contrasts with the American pragmatic tradition where culture is in some ways subordinated to, instrumental to, or generated by experience. Habermas serves as a leading example of the European concern with rationality: in his view, validity claims, warrants, and the rules regulating rational discourse in the public sphere need to be understood. Moreover, the pursuit of rationality is rooted in a broad evolutionary perspective that relegates myth and religion to the past, regards science and technical reason as the dominant cultural codes of the present, and envisions a future in which the limitations of technical reason are transcended by a rational understanding of language itself.

In contrast, the thrust of cultural studies in the United States tends to be more skeptical of this quest for ever-increasing rationality. Alexander (1988) states, for example, that "action and its environments are indelibly interpenetrated by the nonrational," and goes on to argue that Habermas' and Weber's conceptions of rationalization need rethinking. Similarly, Swidler's (1986) conception of culture emphasizes that the symbolic repertoire of any given group is not likely to be unified or consistent, nor even particularly self-aware, but will contain diverse, contradictory capacities that individuals draw on largely for purposes of expedience. And Wuthnow (1987), along with Meyer and Rowan (1977), while perceiving a great deal of rationality in modern culture, suggests that rationality itself is a ceremonial code that may serve nonrational ends.

This is not to say, however, that European theories of culture have simply exhibited greater faith in the prospects of rationality than their American counterparts have shown. To say this would be to underemphasize the importance of European theories that have reacted strongly against rationalism. The work of such theories as Lyotard, Derrida, and Foucault illustrates this reaction. Unlike Habermas, these writers do not envision possibilities of a rationally derived consensus about societal values; rather, they emphasize the power relations inherent in cultural codes. They also advance a radical view of the subconscious and unspoken elements of language—a view that if taken to its logical conclusion suggests the final impossibility of purely rational discourse. Nevertheless, even within the anti-rational vision of a Lyotard or Derrida (or Feyerabend 1978), there is a commitment to rational theory that often seems lacking in the American context.

At present, sociologists in the United States are demonstrating a great deal of interest in the study of symbolic codes defined broadly (for an overview, see Wuthnow and Witten 1988). Much interest has emerged in studies of public discourse. These range from studies of specific issues, such as public discourse about abortion (e.g., Luker 1984) or drunken driving (Gusfield 1981), to general inquiries into the nature of communication about public values (Hart 1984) or the role of narrative in public argument (Fisher 1984). Recent work has continued to focus on symbolic codes expressed in art, music, and literature. DiMaggio (1987) has written a provocative essay that analyzes artistic classification systems along the dimensions of differentiation, hierarchy, universality, and boundary strength, and has suggested hypotheses relating these dimensions to variations in social structure. A number of empirical indices for comparing the complexity of musical codes have been developed by Cerulo (1985, 1988, 1989), who also suggests ways in which these indices may vary with societal differences. Literary codes, including variations in genre and plot structure, have been examined in several recent studies (*see* especially Griswold 1983, 1986, 1987).

Studies of religious codes also continue to attract interest. Using quite different methods, Hunter (1987) and Harding (1987) have generated insightful analyses of the structure and functioning of evangelical Protestant discourse. Witten (1988) has extended this work by examining narrative cohesiveness in fundamentalist sermons. The internal logic of religious codes has also been emphasized in recent studies of the development of teachings about purgatory (LeGoff 1984), the language of African revivalism (Fields 1985), and patterns of Catholic heresy (Kurtz 1986). Overlapping with these studies have been an increasing number of inquiries concerned with moral codes as cultural systems. Tipton's (1982) examination of moral meaning in three quasi-religious movements of the 1960s stands as an exemplar of ethnographic research brought together with sophisticated analysis of ethical reasoning. Another study has suggested the importance of identifying the symbolic boundaries along which moral codes are internally organized and of examining the impact of social change on these boundaries (Wuthnow 1987).

In fields closely associated with sociology, the study of political ideology has remained an important area in which symbolic codes have been a prominent focus as well. A recent study of the American presidency, for example, has traced the origins of rhetorical interpretation as a style of leadership (Tulis 1987). Using in-depth interviews, Hochschild (1981) has examined the ways in which political discourse about distributive justice is expressed and understood. Drawing from quite different sources, Pocock (1987) and others have shown how political events themselves become textualized historically to form ideological themes. Following this approach, Ashcraft (1986) has produced a detailed study of the origins and shaping of Lockean democratic theory.

Much discussion within American sociology continues to focus on broader cultural patterns that seem to rest on underlying codes, such as the codes of individualism and rationality. Bellah and his associates (1985) have provided a widely read examination of the extent to which individualistic themes govern middle-class Americans in their commitments to themselves and to family, work, religion, and politics. Gans (1988) has pursued many of the same questions in a recent book. Still influential in these discussions are the studies of cultural narcissism that appeared in the 1970s, especially those of Sennett (1976) and Lasch (1979). At a more abstract level, Wuthnow (1987) has presented a conception of individualism and rationality as dynamic systems of interrelated elements that adapt differentially to heterogeneous environments. Zerubavel (1988), Lamont (1989), and Gusfield (1966) are concerned with cultural codes and symbolic boundaries.

The European and American literature are not always sharply contrasted because there has been an increasing amount of cross-continental borrowing of the theoretical approaches that shape the study of cultural systems. Work in the United States has benefited, at least in gaining greater legitimacy, from theoretical developments in European social science which have given prominence to cultural codes. DiMaggio's work on art classification has borrowed ideas from Bourdieu (1977, 1984), as has Lamont and Lareau's (1988) work on cultural capital. Kurtz's study of Catholic heresy has drawn inspiration from Douglas' (1966, 1970) work on symbolic boundaries and grid-group distinctions. Harding has looked to Bakhtin (1981) for thoughts about textual dialogue in her study of evangelical discourse. Alexander (1988, 153–174) relies not only on Parsons but also on Durkheim and Evans-Pritchard in developing three models of the relations between cultural systems and social structure, which he illustrates with evidence from the Watergate hearings. Swidler's (1986) discussion of culture as "toolkit" is similar to Lacan's (1977) earlier usage of the same metaphor, and to Bourdieu's (1977) concept of habitus.

More recent borrowings from European theorists of culture have placed less emphasis on experience and greater emphasis on the internal structure of cultural codes themselves. Legitimation for this perspective has come especially from Michel Foucault (1977), who attempted to achieve a radical "de-centering" of texts from their authors. Other cues have been taken from Jacques Derrida (1973, 1976, 1980), from the communicative semiotics of Umberto Eco (1979), and of course from the structuralism of Claude Lévi-Strauss (1963). With the influence of Paul Ricoeur and Victor Turner still prominent, with Jurgen Habermas' recent rediscovery of the life-world, with Pierre Bourdieu's work on "habitus" as sets of dispositions shaped by former conditions of existence and experiences, and with current empirical work drawing heavily on participant-observation and depth-interviewing techniques, however, it appears doubtful that a complete bifurcation of codes and experience will be maintained (e.g., *see* Turner and Bruner 1986).

It should be noted also that both the European and American contributions are as divided internally as they are from one another. This is clear in the case of discussions of rationality, for instance. In Habermas (1984, 1987), one sees a fundamental emphasis on the possibilities of rationality for the reconstruction of modern social life, whereas in Gadamer (1976) a greater emphasis on the nonrational dimensions of tradition is present; Ricoeur (1976) stresses the hermeneutic act of intepretation often involved in cultural studies; and Luhmann (1985) attaches importance to the paradoxical limitations inherent in all concepts of rationally ordered social systems. Among theorists in the United States, similar differences in emphasis are evident. For example, Alexander (1988) stresses the value of retaining subjectivity as a component of cultural systems, while Wuthnow (1987) argues for an analytic distinction between subjective and structural approaches to culture. Swidler (1986, 1987) emphasizes the ways in which cultural codes are put into practice in everyday behavior, while Griswold (1986) and Lamont (1987a) are more concerned with cultural codes, and theories as objects, and therefore seek to understand the social conditions shaping these objects.

As the foregoing suggested, the study of symbolic codes has witnessed much borrowing between Europe and the United States over the years, and might be at present divided more deeply by theoretical traditions than it is by nationality or geography. Consequently, comparisons of the influences leading to different styles or emphases in European and American cultural sociology are at best risky. Any assertion about general tendencies and their social sources is likely to evoke counter-examples and exceptions. With this caveat in mind, it is fair to say that the continental literature has given a privileged role to symbolic codes. In contrast, the American work has been more concerned with the role of experience in grounding meanings.

POWER AND CULTURE

Differences between the American and the continental treatments of culture-mediated power relations are again differences in emphasis. Indeed, American sociologists have a narrower view of the ways by which power relations shape cultural codes, centering mostly on control and the division of labor in cultural industries (for a review, *see* Lamont 1989). In contrast, the most influential European writings on culture focus more squarely on the relationships between culture, inequality, and power. European analysts seek to know how cultural signals affect people's position in stratification systems; how institutions (such as the state), groups, and resources affect social definitions of reality; and how these definitions exclude people from access to resources. Concretely, they study class cultures, discourses, ideologies, styles, and rebel subcultures. In America, these European theorists have been most influential outside sociology, in popular culture studies, symbolic anthropology, cultural history, literary criticism, and women's studies (*see*, for instance, Mukerji and Schudson 1986).

With important qualifications, the European literature can be read as refining Marx and Engels' dominant ideology thesis which centers on the role of ideology in cementing relations of domination by camouflaging exploitation and differences in class interest. However, contrary to Marx and Engels, recent authors have been more concerned with classification systems than with representations of the social world itself, i.e., with how representations of social relationships, the state, religion, and capitalism contribute to the reproduction of colonial, gender, or class domination. Building on the work of Gramsci (1971), they have made inroads in analyzing the subjective process of consolidation of class domination, focusing on the shaping of the categories through which the world is perceived. The control of subjectivity in *everyday life* through the shaping of common sense and the naturalization of social relations became a focus of attention in the work of Louis Althusser, Roland Barthes, Pierre Bourdieu, Norbert Elias, Michel Foucault, Henri Lefebvre, and Raymond Williams, to name only a few.

A broader view of power seems to be shared by many of the foremost European theorists of culture: implicitly or explicitly, they define power as the capacity to impose a specific definition of reality which is disadvantageous to others (e.g., Bourdieu's "symbolic violence"), or as the capacity to structure the situation of others so as to limit their autonomy and life-chances (e.g., Foucault's "régime"). They are concerned with "the power to frame alternatives and contain opportunities, to win and shape consent, so that the granting of legitimacy to the dominant classes appears not only spontaneous but natural and normal" (Hall 1984, 38). They are also concerned with the structural effects of culture, i.e., how culture, whether it be cultural signals (cultural capital) or ideology, affects people's positioning in the stratification system. In such an approach, power is ubiquitous in social life, operating in micro-level face-to-face relationships and at the macro levels of social reality, and as an unintended effect of most actions. The exercise of power is not measured by the occurrence of unwilling compliance, and is not limited to affecting others' *behavior*. Influencing their *situation*, or position in the social structure, in a disadvantageous way is conceived as a more pervasive and important way of exercising power. Such a conception of power has received labels as varied as three-dimensional power, meta-power, relational power, and more often, hegemony (Benton 1981; Clegg 1979; Giddens 1984; Lukes 1974).

A first important, and primarily British, strand of work is built on the early Frankfurt School's view that cultural products, particularly mass culture, misrepresent relations of domination, and prevent political mobilization by providing escapist entertainment and by diffusing passive attitudes (Horkheimer and Adorno 1944). Recent theorists (*see* Wolff 1984, 51) have attempted to specify this relationship, looking at the link between cultural products and their context of production (i.e., the mode of production, system of production, distribution and consumption, or the class situation of producers). Eagleton's (1976) study of the world-view of the Brontë sisters, and T. J. Clark's (1973) work on Le Courbet are illustrative of this trend. Again, inspired by studies such as Adorno (1949/1973) on music, and Goldman (1964) on writers as spokespeople of groups, these discussions have mostly spread outside sociology, especially in art history, cultural history, and literary criticism.

A second European strand of thought, also inspired by the Frankfurt School, has developed around Habermas and focuses more squarely on cultural changes in advanced industrial societies, and on the growing influence of instrumental and technical rationality. Adopting a neo-Platonist position which, again, confers great power on rationality and on intellectuals as a group, Habermas conceives a hermeneutic solution to alienation and the politics of unreason, a solution which would be viable in the context of capitalist society, although reserved for a small group of enlightened minds communicating under ideal conditions.

The French developments have been more Durkheimian in influence, and are concerned with the making of cultural codes themselves. With Foucault and Bourdieu, analyses of subjectivity shift away from capitalism, class relations, and the state, which had been a center of interest for Althusser, Goldman, Lefebvre, and others, to focus on classification systems and how they *structure* reality. Foucault's writings reconstruct how discourse shapes and frames subjectivity, and has been institutionalized from the classical age on. He follows Lévi-Strauss' (1963) concern with what culture hides, with the unthinkable and the unconscious; however, he adds a political twist to Lévi-Strauss' concerns and deals with discourse's role in producing a "Kafkaesque" system which constrains and frames human potentialities. He analyzes knowledge and truth as bases for the institutionalization of mechanisms of control, and as resources for excluding deviants and framing the context and terrain of social life. For instance, the institutionalization of clinical medicine provided definitions of symptoms and sickness, and designated who can make judgments and prescribe remedies. His perspective is that "in a society such as ours, but basically in any society, there are manifold relations of power which permeate, characterise and constitute the social body, and these relations of power cannot themselves be established, consolidated nor implemented without the production, accumulation, circulation and functioning of a discourse" (Foucault 1980, 93). For Foucault, social control is mostly "positive" (in the Marxian sense of the term), i.e., linked to the framing of people's lives and to the organization of social life, rather than "negative," exercised through coercion; this positive character of power appeared in the classical age, and differentiates modern society from the Middle Ages. Foucault denounces this increasingly powerful and insidious exercise of domination through positive means.

Bourdieu and his colleagues' work on cultural reproduction is akin to theories of hegemony and discourse, in that it is also concerned with how the dominated groups contribute to their own subordination. Bourdieu's distinctive focus is on class-differentiated mental structures, or habitus, i.e., on class-differentiated dispositions and categories of perception shaped by conditions of existence:[3] the dominant symbolic system made of binary oppositions (rare/common, interested/disinterested, vulgar/noble) values the experiences and attributes of the dominant class broadly defined (i.e., including most professionals and managers). These categories of perception and thought are internalized by the middle and lower class, and used as standards by this educational system.

For Foucault and Bourdieu, cultural codes also structure social relations by defining boundaries between groups, therefore *excluding* groups from access to resources and positions. This is Foucault's concern in *Madness and Civilization* (1965) where he documents the processes by which deviants come to be excluded from society; Bourdieu and his colleagues also address this issue in their work on the educational system (Bourdieu and Passeron 1977), and on class culture (Bourdieu 1984). Like Douglas and Isherwood (1979), and Barthes (1983), Bourdieu looks at the classifying effects of cultural practices. However, he is more specifically concerned with the political aspect of this process, such as how these effects reproduce the social structure by influencing access to high status groups and resources. Contrary to status attainment research, which also looks at life-chances, the French work takes the position that the limitation of one's life-chances is a form of domination (Lamont and Lareau 1988).

In Great Britain, the Birmingham School has provided a complement to Boudieu's work by focusing on how groups develop spheres of cultural autonomy by expressing their cultural differences in their own particular subculture, and therefore challenging and resisting the system: dress, speech, and leisure activities are manipulated as domains of cultural autonomy and resistance to construct group identity (Marcus and Fischer 1986, 152; *see* Hebdige 1979; Willis 1977).[4] In just a few years, journals concerned with related issues, such as *Theory, Culture, and Society*, have gained an important following.

The work of the Birmingham School has inspired new developments among American symbolic anthropologists and students of popular culture concerned with modes of resistance, and with "discovering the variety of modes of accommodation and resistance by individuals and groups to their shared social order [and] . . . the diversity in what appears to be an ever more homogeneous world" (Marcus and Fischer 1986, 133). Journals such as *Social Text* and *Culture Critique* have become important in diffusing the Birmingham School's perspective. This school has not had as strong an influence on American sociology because writings by its members are often regarded as insufficiently theoretically grounded.

Mary Douglas' work stands apart in the European literature. Her vision of the micro-politics of everyday life is narrower than that of most European culture theorists. Indeed, in *Purity and Danger* (1966), she is concerned with the order-producing, meaning-making, and form-giving functions of classification systems, and in the role of rituals and restriction in dramatizing and creating boundaries grounded in fears and beliefs. In *Natural Symbols* (1970) and in her other essays concerned with grids and groups, she argues that the publicly shared character of classification systems affect forms of *social control* and the degree of personal autonomy left to individuals, but she does not seem to conceive control as part of a general decentered enterprise of social control of the dominated groups, the way Bourdieu or Foucault does.

The World of Goods (1979) is a point of departure from her previous work as she and Isherwood are concerned not only with control but also with exclusion which forces people "into a position of minimum choice and maximum isolation" (43). This marks a transition to a broader conception of power, also characteristic of the work of the Frankfurt School, Foucault, and Bourdieu, a conception that views a broader range of relations as power relations, where power is not only exercised when there is coercion and unwilling compliance, but also when people's position is structured in a disadvantageous way. Nevertheless, overall Douglas is more concerned with order and control than with domination.[5]

This picture contrasts with the recent research conducted by American sociologists of culture. A first category of sociologists identified with the production-of-culture approach focus on cultural industries (*see* Peterson 1979). These authors are concerned with power to the extent that they study control and coercion in cultural industries, analyzing issues such as the division of labor and the control of resources in art worlds (Becker 1982; Crane 1987; White and White 1965; for a recent review *see* Blau 1988), and decision-making processes in the publishing industry (Coser, Kadushin, and Powell 1982; for a critique of this perspective *see* Tuchman 1983). A second category includes authors such as Cantor (1980), Schudson (1984), and Tuchman (1978) who explore topics related to the social and political control of the content of popular culture, or to how cultural resources (i.e., already existing constructs) are mobilized to define reality. Although these authors conceive social construction as an integral part of the control process, they do not seem to focus primarily on how people's position in the stratification system affects their capacity to influence the definition of the world; the system of control is implicitly conceived by these authors as less powerful or total than it is in Foucault's writings, for instance. Finally, a third important group of American sociologists of culture, strongly influenced by the work of Antonio Gramsci, looks at the constitution of hegemony through American popular culture (Gitlin 1980; Aronowitz 1981; Jameson 1981; Long 1986). Even if much borrowing occurs between American and European sociologies of culture, overall the majority of American sociologists of culture seem to hold a narrower view of power as control, while the broader European approach is more popular in American disciplines other than sociology.

The restricted view of power is also shared by most American researchers concerned with cultural codes. Important cultural analysts such as Clifford Geertz, Peter Berger, and Erving Goffman have paid very little attention to class-differentiated resources and to the politics of culture, the way Bourdieu or Foucault does. For instance, Geertz's symbolic anthropology looks at symbols as vehicles for meaning and culture; his approach being mostly actor-centered, he does not analyze how they relate to broader macro-sociological power relations. While he (1973) analyzes the Balinese cockfight as providing an *"éducation sentimentale"* about power relations in a community, he does not draw theoretical conclusions concerning the interplay of power and culture. In his later work, *Negara* (1980, 134) in particular, he attempts to draw more general conclusions, but his view of the interplay of power and culture remains narrower than Foucault's and Bourdieu's, to the extent that Geertz does not propose a variant of the hegemony thesis. The same can be said about Berger and Luckman's (1966) view of the institutionalization process. In *The Social Construction of Reality* they suggest briefly that "the confrontation of alternative symbolic universes implies a problem of power—which of the conflicting definitions of reality will be made to stick to the society" (1966, 108), and that "power in society includes the power to determine decisive socialization processes, and therefore, the power to produce reality" (119). Nevertheless, they do not provide a full-fledged analysis of this process the way Foucault does. Along the same lines, Goffman, while mostly concerned with the cognitive order, and the constraints imposed on it by past actions, does not draw conclusions pertaining to the effect of the cognitive order on the maintenance of a structure of domination. Past frames are important resources transposed on new situations (Gonos 1977; *see also* Fine 1988), but other types of resources are not considered central (Collins 1981). While *Asylums* (1961) suggests obvious conclusions for analyzing how definitions of reality are affected by power relations, Goffman does not draw those conclusions. The same observation holds for Becker's (1963) labeling theory of deviance.

The above characterization also applies to the more recent American literature on culture. For instance, in their innovative work on the process of the institutionalization of cultural accounts of individual actions, Thomas and his colleagues (Thomas et al. 1987) do not consider how groups and resources participate in the institutionalizing of these accounts as do European students of ideology. They are mostly concerned with cultural outcomes; they point to the role of the state in the institutionalization process, but social groups and classes are absent. Similarly, Swidler (1986) does not discuss how people's position in stratification systems affects the type of cultural "tool-kit" available to them.

The differences between the American and European literatures are highlighted when comparing the work on cultural capital which analyze the role of class culture and credentials in the creation of status groups and the monopolization of privileges. While the French literature on cultural capital considers exclusion to be one of the main forms of power, and has proposed a sophisticated theoretical framework for distinguishing among forms of exclusion, by and large the American literature has not considered the micro-political aspect of cultural exclusion and instead considers cultural capital as one variable in the status attainment process, as in DiMaggio and colleagues' important work (DiMaggio and Mohr 1985; *see* Lamont and Lareau 1988). An important exception to this might be the influential work of neo-Weberians who remain concerned with forms of domination (e.g., Collins 1975).

The key propositions of the broader approach to power present obvious problems of operationalization: if actors do not perceive their class interests or are unconscious of being dominated, how can it be demonstrated that specific definitions of situations are detrimental to them (on this *see* Benton 1981; Bradshaw 1976; Gaventa 1980; Lears 1985; Wrong 1979)? Are these operationalization problems sufficient grounds for dismissing theories of indirect power altogether? For European researchers, documenting and describing power in all its subtle forms is a valuable enterprise per se, even if it does not produce falsifiable theories.

Even if the situation is rapidly changing, American sociologists who adopt the broader conception of indirect power in their cultural analysis continue to be a minority. Again, only a few researchers are concerned with how culture mediates power relations, with culture's role in reproducing the social system, or with symbolic conflicts over the definition of reality. Those who do (e.g., Gottdiener 1985; Gitlin 1979, 1980; Long 1968; Sennett and Cobb 1972), borrow profusely from Gramsci, Raymond Williams, and the more recent French work. Again, the bulk of the literature inspired by European theories of culture diffused less in sociology than in literary criticism, symbolic anthropology, and cultural history (Lamont and Witten 1988). American cultural anthropologists and historians who draw on European work are more concerned with the constraining nature of culture on action. As noted by Ortner (1984), their focus has recently shifted from "what culture allows and enables people to see, feel and do to what it restricts and inhibits them from seeing, feeling and doing" (152). They are also concerned with the system's "configuration and why and how it excludes alternative possible configurations" (153). However, again, a growing number of American cultural sociologists are increasingly reading outside their discipline, and are becoming more influenced by the interdisciplinary current in which European cultural theorists play a central role.

We saw that that the American and the European literatures have noticeable differences in their treatment of both culture and experience, and of the effect of power on cultural codes. In both cases, we need to understand the sources of the theoretical differences, and we need to treat those differences themselves as cultural objects. While continental differences in approach with respect to power are related to the imperative of empirical support in American sociology, they may have more to do with how researchers experience power on a daily basis, and with the extent to which power is perceived as shaping personal experience and access to resources. The last section will suggest that these lived definitions of the situation are likely to affect what makes sense theoretically for American and European sociologists.

EXPLAINING THE DIFFERENCES

The place attributed to formal knowledge codes and rationality in American and European cultural sociology parallels the influence of intellectuals and high culture in the two societies. European theories of culture provide culture with a greater autonomy from experience: their newest questions are post-Kantian ones. They are concerned with issues such as whether a theory of culture can press entirely toward rational communication, or whether it must be deconstructed to disclose the expressivity of the unspoken. In the American context, neither the likelihood of pure rationality nor the sophistication associated with aesthetic discourse are as likely to be raised because the referent for cultural studies remains more deeply pragmatic. Culture consists of discourse, cues, and symbolic gestures oriented toward achieving some practical objective: the discourse of therapy, sermons, religious cults, romance, corporate cultures, and the like. Intellectuals do not dominate these realms of symbolic expression; rather, it is the practical, everyday speech of actors in the world at large that more often gives American sociologists of culture their topics of inquiry.

These continental differences in orientation have to be related to the *status* enjoyed by *intellectuals* in Europe and the United States: a top-down vision of culture is more likely in societies where intellectuals are influential as cultural producers. This appears to be the case in several European societies, despite the loss of influence suffered by intellectuals since World War II (Gagnon 1987). The French case provides an illustration of this. Many researchers have noted that the French intellectual elite enjoys high social status.[6] The historical role of French philosophers and social thinkers in the development of Western thought as well as the early institutionalization of the French educational system under Napoleon has contributed to making academics a part of the French national grandeur. Left-of-center parties have sustained this influence by providing intellectuals with an organizational arena around which they could develop a subculture and a group identity (Debray 1981; Lamont 1987b; Ross 1988; Verdès-Leroux 1983).

In contrast, elements of American culture such as anti-intellectualism, pragmatism, materialism, populism, and the role of the mass media in producing mass culture have contributed to limiting the influence of intellectuals as cultural producers (Hofstadter 1963). These elements have also shaped the role of academics, who have tended to view themselves as experts without special political or symbolic missions (Jacoby 1987; Janowitz 1972). Universities have become centers of professional training which do not always foster the growth of a strong intellectual subculture. Also, private and public universities are dependent on private donations, which reinforces, at least symbolically, a greater dependency of knowledge and culture on the business sector. In contrast, in Europe the public sector is generally the sole source of support for research and education, which provides scholars greater independence from the profit motive. This certainly affects their view of their place in society, as well as their vision of knowledge as a transcendental activity. They attribute much *molding* power to culture and to culture producers like themselves, as illustrated by Foucault's and Habermas' writings, for instance.

Closely associated with differences in the role attributed to rationality is a lingering emphasis on positivism in the American context, compared with a fuller appreciation of the hermeneutic approach in European studies of culture. While sociologists in both settings might well acknowledge the general validity of the hermeneutic perspective, Americans appear more often to adopt what might be called an inductive or *ad hoc* form of positivism in their practical orientation toward research. Legitimate and useful knowledge is assumed to be possible by observing the social world, even if some interpretation is required; thus, studies abound in which theoretical conclusions are derived and defended primarily on the basis of empirical induction, whereas European studies of culture seem to place greater faith in the capacity of theoretical deduction itself to generate useful knowledge. The inductive approach minimizes the importance of cultural categories, assuming the transparency of the world, whereas hermeneutics posits as a principle the necessary role of discussion by enlightened minds in the learning process. This role is more likely to be valued in national cultures where *notables* have a long-lasting tradition of collectively defining the nature of the surrounding world. In Europe, the relatively homogeneous social recruitment of national intellectual elites until the expansion of the educational system certainly sustained beliefs in the adjudicative role of intellectuals as cultural arbiters. In the United States, before and after World War II, circles of mostly second-generation East Coast intellectuals were able to sustain the same belief, as revealed by the relative numerical importance of intellectual magazines in this period (Lamont 1987b; Kadushin, 1974).

Parallel to the greater focus on rationality and formal knowledge codes in Europe, we find a lesser interest in religious studies, theological discourse, popular religion, and popular culture among European theorists, which is also symptomatic of how cultural environments shape research interests. Nearly all the established theorists of culture in the United States have devoted serious attention to religion (e.g., Bellah, Berger, Geertz, Parsons), and many of those who are currently contributing work to this field have at one point or another focused on religion or popular culture, whereas European theorists who have written systematically about religion are the exception (e.g., Luhmann) rather than the rule. Also, leading European theologians (e.g., Pannenberg 1983) have borrowed heavily from social theorists, such as Habermas and Althusser, whereas American scholarship demonstrates a greater influence of theology and popular religion on sociologists of culture. This difference is certainly a result of the greater degree of secularization of intellectual life in Europe over the past century, and particularly of the influence of atheist-leftist parties among intellectuals. Some of the difference must also be attributed to the fact that religious belief and practice is simply a more prominent characteristic of American society at large than it is of most European societies (Wuthnow 1988a, 17).

Differences in topics and style between Europe and the United States are related to the *immediate conditions* in which research is conducted. The paucity of research funding in Europe has undoubtedly encouraged sociologists to do theoretical work, and to neglect more empirically based work. In this context qualitative areas, such as cultural analysis, have become very popular in Europe, as illustrated by the fact that *all* major European theoreticians deal with culture, and that important research groups have developed in Great Britain (the Birmingham School), in France (Centre de Sociologie Européenne), and in various places in West Germany. In contrast, the American sociology of culture has been known as a poor cousin. Few jobs and insufficient research funds were available to culture specialists, who often had to pose as organization specialists to obtain research money. Consequently, the study of culture in the United States has partly focused on corporate cultures and cultural industries. Also, studies of religious discourse have been promoted by the availability of large research sums from private foundations and by an enthusiastic audience among denominational leaders. As a result, new theoretical ideas have penetrated the discipline via empirical research rather than via grand theory; studies of communication codes or organizational settings have often shaped the perspective of sociologists of culture to an even greater extent than the abstract theoretical contributions of leading theorists.

Differences between American and European work is also related to cross-national differences in *how people experience power,* and in the frames of reference they use to interpret their experience. The broader definition of culture-mediated power relations characteristic of European work seems to spring in part from differences in the theoreticians' experience of the social world.

European organizational theorists provide information on cross-national differences in management styles and in how people experience power. They have found that French managers are much *less likely* to perceive power relations as *legitimate* in contrast with American managers. For instance, Laurent (1983) compared managers from a number of industrial societies and found that the French were significantly more likely to believe that "managers are motivated by gains of power —rather than by achieving objectives" (France: 56%; United States: 36%). Inzerilli and Laurent (1983) demonstrated that American managers have an instrumental conception of organizational structures where people perform tasks defined in roles—a conception which incidentally parallels Parsons' (1967) definition of power as "the ability to mobilize others in the pursuit of collective goals." The authors argue that this conception depersonalizes and rationalizes authority relations. In contrast, Crozier (1964) argued that in French organizations authority is seen as absolute and arbitrary rather than specific, rational, and functionally bound (*see also* Shonfeld 1976). French managers attach more importance to subordination (i.e., loyalty and dependency) than do their American counterparts (Inzerilli and Laurent 1983, 112). This evidence suggests that in contrast to the Americans the French perceive a wider range of relationships as relations of domination, and the French are less likely to confer legitimacy to authority.[7]

In contrast, in the American *Weltanschauung*, the victim is to be blamed because structural discrimination is not understood as a form of indirect power (Ryan 1972). The encompassing and negative view of power relations predominating in France and the more restricted and legitimate view of power predominating in American society are likely to mold problems that sociologists are concerned with as well as their assumptions about everyday life.[8]

Finally, theoretical differences between American and European cultural theorists in their approach to power can also be related to the immediate settings in which researchers work. In the United States, despite important tensions within the academic community, mechanisms of distribution of professional rewards seem to sustain a more legitimate view of society in general, and of professional life in particular. In sociology, for instance, the competitive allocation of research funding as well as the anonymous reviewing of journal articles legitimizes reward distribution and standardizes the prestige associated with various types of accomplishments, while reinforcing normative control within the field (Lamont 1984). The greater resources and jobs available also supports stronger normative control within the profession. Finally, the greater horizontal and vertical mobility of American academia seems to foster a conception of the competition process as open rather than zero-sum. In contrast, in France, the scarcity of research funds and of professional resources in general has probably weakened professional normative control (Montlibert 1982). In sociology, anonymous journal refereeing is not widely institutionalized and journals are often controlled by cliques. Book publishing is more highly regarded, but the assessment of books depends on cultural media such as the *Nouvel Observateur*, and on journalists rather than peers. Finally, the system is one in which *grand patrons* have considerable control over the fate of their protégés, whether they be students or senior researchers, which leaves much room for individual arbitrariness and delegitimizes the system. Considered together, these factors most certainly sustain a representation of power as arbitrary, of the social system as unfair, and of power relations as ubiquitous, expressed not only through coercion, but through omnipresent zero-sum relations.[9] It is interesting to note that in the United States, European culture theorists are more widely received in the humanities disciplines which have less resources and weaker normative control (Lamont and Witten 1988). More specific empirically based analyses of the diffusion of European cultural theories could document under what conditions specific subcultural disciplinary niches come to favor more encompassing views of power relationships.

CONCLUSION

Our conclusions about the nature and sources of differences in cultural sociology between Europe and America are, of course, to a considerable degree conjectural. We have tried to interpret some of the points of emphasis that separate the two traditions and suggest some of the contextual and intellectual influences that may lie beneath these divergences. But these interpretations also reflect our own training and experience within these differing contexts.

We have argued that students of symbolic codes in European sociology have focused more on formalized and rational systems of culture, while their counterparts in American sociology have emphasized the grounding of such codes in practical everyday experience. We have also argued that European sociology of culture stresses the importance of power relations—and its manifestations both in class differences and modes of exclusion—to a greater extent than most American contributions to the study of culture. Some of the influences enforcing these differences include: the greater cultural influence of European intellectuals, the legacy of pragmatism in the American case, and differences in primary sources of funding for sociological research.

What confounds any sharp conclusions about continental differences in cultural sociology is the high degree of borrowing—and the equally high degree of internal diversity—that characterizes work in both locations. As American cultural sociology has begun to flourish again in recent years, it has been increasingly influenced by the work of scholars such as Foucault, Habermas, Douglas, and Bourdieu. Finding a more responsive audience for their ideas among American sociologists, some of these theorists have also begun to incorporate the results of empirical research on this side of the Atlantic into their own perspectives.

The importance of tradition and context, however, is signaled by the fact that this borrowing has necessitated a considerable degree of selective reading—selectivity that has often altered the terms of debate, changed the meanings of concepts, and increased the level of theoretical ambiguity. As we have suggested, even such basic concepts as symbolic codes, power, and knowledge have different connotations in the various theoretical traditions. For many decades, American sociologists have wrestled with questions of what Weber or Durkheim or Marx really meant, realizing arguments had often been framed in terms unfamiliar to the American context. The current borrowings from European cultural theorists are likely to require long years of interpretation and debate as well.

What of the future? At the present juncture, cultural sociology holds considerable promise for creative and productive work. On the European side, valuable opportunities remain for borrowing insights from empirical studies, both within sociology and in related disciplines such as anthropology and history, and for new syntheses based on a broader array of theoretical perspectives. The continuing integration of Geertzian perspectives into the Annales school would be an example of the former; Habermas' efforts to incorporate the work of George Herbert Mead into his own theoretical framework provides an illustration of the latter. On the American side, cultural sociologists are likely to continue to reflect on the legacy of the European classics, particularly Marx, Weber, and Durkheim. Continued borrowing from contemporary theorists also seems likely, especially as American cultural sociologists dialogue with members of neighboring disciplines that deal with culture. But our efforts are likely to be vacuous unless accompanied by attempts to *make sense of empirical evidence,* to frame the study of culture in terms of its usefulness for understanding *larger questions of human experience and power relations,* and to determine through this process which theoretical refinements have operational and heuristic value.

If cultural sociology is currently a growth area, as many perceive it to be, chances also remain high that it will show an increasing tendency in the next few years to divide into competing sub-schools, organized around different theoretical, epistemologial, and substantive orientations. Lines of demarcation within the field are likely to appear between those who are looking for answers in the classical texts, and those who take a more eclectic and inductive approach, arguing that innovation should come from substantive studies and wide borrowing from the work of cultural interpreters in a number of disciplines. Another important line of demarcation in the immediate future seems to be emerging around the division between institutional and ethnographic approaches. On the institutional side, work is likely to emphasize formal cultural production, such as the creation of literary texts, political speeches, art and music, and religious creeds. On the ethnographic side, work is more likely to emphasize the implicit and latent cultural byproducts of social interaction, such as the everyday forms of resistance that may be evident among oppressed minorities. Finally, a fourth line of demarcation is emerging between those concerned with style and aesthetics and those concerned with conditions of cultural production. But one can only hope that the present vitality of the field will not be drawn off by petty boundary-maintaining games and intellectual posturing for the sake of protecting and arrogating academic turf. Cultural sociology is presently beset with sufficient intellectual challenges that there remains much room for complementary academic contributions.

In our opinion, a number of topics using the broader conception of power will need to be examined with greater care in the future: 1) the issue of how—and to what extent—symbolic codes interact with social experience where greater clarity is needed concerning the manner in which experience is constituted by discourse and the extent to which discourse textualizes and transforms experience; 2) the manner in which unequal distributions of authority influence the production of culture; 3) the ways in which discourse itself textualizes and dramatizes authority, i.e., the ways in which speech genres make room for and close down opportunities for multiple voices to engage in dialogue; and 4) the ways in which cultural codes qua cultural capital structure people's positioning in the stratification system. Also, as this essay has implicitly argued, cultural sociology is in need of greater reflexivity: an analysis of the conditions under which cultural sociology is produced and of how these conditions fashion our questions and answers might be the condition for the growth of a substantively rich and dynamic field that nourishes little unproductive theoretical infighting.

NOTES

1. Other issues include the organization of cultural industries and the composition of audiences for art forms (e.g., Radway 1984; Long 1986; Zolberg 1988).

2. The term "symbolic code" is often used interchangeably with "culture" in the American literature, although the latter is sometimes distinguished as the broader set of values and assumptions, or rules, from which specific symbolic codes emanate.

3. Bourdieu defines habitus in these terms: "the durable installed, generative principle of regulated improvisation produces practices which tend to reproduce the regularities immanent in the objective conditions of the production of their generative principle, while adjusting to the demands inscribed as objective potentialities in the situation as defined by the cognitive and motivating structure making up the habitus" (Bourdieu 1977). In other words, dispositions are determined by their conditions of existence and reproduce them, which reminds one of the *Theses on Feuerbach*.

4. The Birmingham School is explicitly concerned with how dominated agents try to negotiate relationships through "the informal culture of the workplace, attempts to exercise day-to-day control over the work process" (Clarke et al. 1977, 41) and "win space," building a "*répertoire* of resistance" or a "line of defense." (*See also* De Certeau 1984.)

5. This paper focuses on the works that have been most influential in American sociology. Space limitations prevent consideration of the European work on cultural imperialism (Katz and Wedell 1978; Mattelart 1979), the political economy of cultural industries (Garnham 1986; Murdoch and Golding 1974), the role of culture in political mobilization (Adorno 1973; Bloch et al. 1977), and postmodernism (Baudrillard 1968; Foster 1983; Kellner 1988).

6. Clark (1979, 1987) has shown, using cultural indicators, that 1) compared to the American literary elite, the French literary elite is better supported, both financially and culturally, by the governmental and traditional elites; 2) one finds in France more symbols of recognition of the importance of intellectuals; and 3) intellectuals' activity is more widely covered by the media in France than in the United States.

7. More research is needed to estimate precisely how this conception extends to other European countries. The existence of strong anarchist, "autogestionnaire," and leftist traditions in most western European societies suggests that these populations also confer less legitimacy to the prevailing distribution of power than Americans do.

8. It is interesting to note in this context that the foremost critics of major American theories of power (Dahl 1968; Bachrach and Baratz 1962) are Europeans (*see also* Benton 1981; Birnbaum 1976; Lukes 1974; Chazel 1983).

9. This is shown for instance in Bourdieu's (1983) analysis of the intellectual field, where positions are defined relationally. This is a direct reflection of the small intricate circles in which Parisian researchers have to operate (*see* Lemert 1981).

REFERENCES

Adorno, Theodor. [1949] 1973. *Philosophy of Modern Music*. Reprint. London: Sheed and Ward.

Alexander, Jeffrey C. 1988. *Action and Its Environments: Toward a New Synthesis*. New York: Columbia University Press.

Althusser, Louis. 1971. "Ideology and the Ideological State Apparatuses." In Louis Althusser, *Lenin and Philosophy*. New York: Monthly Review Press.

Aronowitz, Stanley. 1981. "Culture and Politics." In Stanley Aronowitz, *The Crisis of Historical Materialism*. New York: Praeger.

Ashcraft, Richard. 1986. *Revolutionary Politics and Locke's Two Treatises of Government*. Princeton: Princeton University Press.

Bachrach, P., and M. Baratz. 1962. "The Two Faces of Power." *American Political Science Review* 56:947–952.

Bakhtin, M. M. 1981. *The Dialogic Imagination*. Austin: University of Texas Press.

Barthes, Roland. 1968. *Elements of Semiology*. New York: Hill and Wang.

Barthes, Roland. 1972. *Mythologies*. New York: Hill and Wang.

Barthes, Roland. 1983. *The Fashion System*. New York: Hill and Wang.

Baudrillard, Jean. 1968. *Le système des objects. La consomation des signes*. Paris: Gallimard.

Becker, Howard. 1963. *Outsiders. Studies in the Sociology of Deviance*. New York: Free Press.

Becker, Howard. 1982. *Art Worlds.* Berkeley: University of California Press.

Bellah, R. N., R. Madsen, W. M. Sullivan, A. Swidler, and S. Tipton. 1985. *Habits of the Heart.* Berkeley: University of California Press.

Benton, T. 1981. "Objective Interests and the Sociology of Power." *Sociology* 15:161–184.

Berger, Peter L., and Thomas Luckmann. 1966. *The Social Construction of Reality.* Garden City, N.Y.: Anchor.

Birnbaum, Pierre. 1976. "Power Divorced from Its Sources: A Critique of Exchange Theory of Power." In B. Barry, ed., *Power and Political Theory: Some European Perspectives.* London: Wiley.

Blau, Judith. 1988. "The Study of the Arts: A Reappraisal." *Annual Review of Sociology* 14:269–292.

Bloch, Ernst et al. 1977. *Aesthetics and Politics.* London: New Left Books.

Bourdieu, Pierre. 1977. *Outline of a Theory of Practice.* Cambridge: Cambridge University Press.

Bourdieu, Pierre. 1983. "The Field of Cultural Production, or: The Economic World Reversed." *Poetics* 12:311–356.

Bourdieu, Pierre. 1984. *Distinction.* Cambridge, Mass.: Harvard University Press.

Bourdieu, Pierre, and J.-C. Passeron. 1977. *Reproduction: In Culture, Education, Society.* Beverly Hills, Cal.: Sage.

Bradshaw, A. 1976. "A Critic of Steven Lukes's 'Power: A Radical View.' " *Sociology* 10:121–127.

Cantor, Muriel. 1980. *Prime-Time Television: Content and Control.* Beverly Hills, Cal.: Sage.

Cerulo, Karen A. 1985. "Music as Symbolic Communiation: The Case of the National Anthem." Ph.D. dissertation, Princeton University.

Cerulo, Karen A. 1988. "Analyzing Cultural Products: A New Method of Measurement." *Social Science Research* 17:317–352.

Cerulo, Karen A. 1989. "Socio-Political Control and the Structure of National Symbols: An Empirical Analysis of National Anthems." *Social Forces*, forthcoming.

Chazel, Francois. 1983. "Pouvoir, Structure et Domination." *Revue Française de Sociologie* 24:369–394.

Clark, P. P. 1979. "Literary Culture in France and the United States." *American Journal of Sociology* 84:1057–1076.

Clark, P. P. 1987. *Literary France. The Making of a Culture.* Chicago: University of Chicago Press.

Clark, T. J. 1973. *Image of the People: Gustave Courbet and the 1848 Revolution.* London: Thomas and Hudson.

Clarke, J., S. Hall, T. Jefferson, and B. Roberts. 1977. "Subcultures, Cultures and Class." In S. Hall and T. Jefferson, eds., *Resistance through Rituals.* London: Hutchison.

Clegg, Stewart. 1979. *The Theory of Power and Organization.* London: Routledge and Kegan Paul.

Collins, Randall. 1975. *Conflict Sociology.* New York: Academic Press.

Collins, Randall, 1981. "Three Stages of Erving Goffman." In Randall Collins, *Sociology Since Midcentury: Essays in Theory Cumulation.* New York: Academic Press.

Coser, Lewis, Charles Kadushin, and Walter Powell. 1982. *Books: The Culture and Commerce of Publishing.* New York: Basic.

Crane, Diana. 1987. *The Transformation of the Avant-Garde. The New York Art World, 1940–1985.* Chicago: University of Chicago Press.

Crozier, Michel. 1964. *The Bureaucratic Phenomenon.* Berkeley: University of California Press.

Dahl, Robert. 1968. "Power." *International Encyclopedia of the Social Sciences* 12:205–214.

Debray, Regis. 1981. *Teachers, Writers and Celebrities. The Intellectuals of Modern France.* London: Verso.

De Certeau, Michel. 1984. *The Practice of Everyday Life.* Berkeley: University of California Press.

Derrida, Jacques. 1973. *Speech and Phenomena.* Evanston, Ill.: Northwestern University Press.

Derrida, Jacques. 1976. *Of Grammatology.* Baltimore: Johns Hopkins University Press.

Derrida, Jacques. 1980. *Writing and Difference.* Chicago: University of Chicago Press.

DiMaggio, Paul. 1987. "Classification in Art." *American Sociological Review* 52:440–455.

DiMaggio, Paul, and John Mohr. 1985. "Cultural Capital, Educational Attainment, and Marital Selection." *American Journal of Sociology* 90:1231–1261.

Douglas, Mary. 1966. *Purity and Danger.* London: Penguin.

Douglas, Mary. 1970. *Natural Symbols.* New York: Vintage.

Douglas, Mary. 1986. *How Institutions Think.* Syracuse: Syracuse University Press.

Douglas, Mary, and Baron Isherwood. 1979. *The World of Goods: Towards an Anthropology of Consumption.* New York: W. W. Norton.

Durkheim, Emile. 1961. *The Elementary Forms of Religious Life.* New York: Collier.

Eagleton, Terry. 1976. *Criticism and Ideology.* London: Verso.

Eco, Umberto. 1979. *The Role of the Reader.* Bloomington: Indiana University Press.

Elias, Norbert. 1978. *The History of Manners.* New York: Pantheon.

Feyerabend, Paul. 1978. *Against Method.* London: Verso.

Fields, Karen E. 1985. *Revival and Rebellion in Colonial Central Africa.* Princeton: Princeton University Press.

Fine, Gary Alan. 1979. "Small Groups and Culture Creation." *American Sociological Review* 44:733–745.

Fine, Gary Alan. 1988. "On the Macrofoundations of Microsociology: Constraint and the Exterior Reality of Structure." Manuscript.

Fisher, Walter R. 1984. "Narration as a Human Communication Paradigm: The Case of Public Moral Argument." *Communication Monographs* 51:1–21.

Foster, Hal, ed. 1983. *The Anti-Aesthetic: Essays on Postmodern Culture.* Port Townsend, Wash.: Bay Press.

Foucault, Michel. 1965. *Madness and Civilization: A History of Insanity in the Age of Reason.* New York: Random House.

Foucault, Michel. 1972. *The Archeology of Knowledge.* New York: Pantheon.

Foucault, Michel. 1977. *Discipline and Punish.* New York: Vintage.

Foucault, Michel. 1980. *Power-Knowledge.* New York: Pantheon.

Gadamer, Hans-Georg. 1976. *Philosophical Hermeneutics.* Berkeley: University of California Press.

Gagnon, A. G., ed. 1987. *Intellectuals in Liberal Democracies: Political Influence and Social Involvement.* New York: Praeger.

Gans, Herbert J. 1988. *Middle American Individualism: The Future of Liberal Democracy.* New York: Free Press.

Garnham, Nicholas. 1986. "Contribution to a Political Economy of Mass Communications." In Richard Collins et al., eds. *Media, Culture and Society: A Critical Reader.* Beverly Hills: Sage.

Gaventa, John. 1980. *Power and Powerlessness: Quiescence and Rebellion in an Appalachian Valley.* Oxford: Clarendon Press.

Geertz, Clifford. 1973. *The Interpretation of Culture.* New York: Basic.

Geertz, Clifford. 1980. *Negara, The Theatre State in Nineteenth-Century Bali.* Princeton: Princeton University Press.

Giddens, Anthony. 1984. *The Constitution of Society.* Berkeley: University of California Press.

Gitlin, Todd. 1979. "Prime-Time Ideology: The Hegemonic Process in Television Entertainment." *Social Problems* 26:251–266.

Gitlin, Todd. 1980. *The Whole World is Watching.* Berkeley: University of California Press.

Goffman, Erving. 1961. *Asylums.* New York: Doubleday.

Goldman, Lucien. 1964. *The Hidden God.* London: Routledge and Kegan Paul.

Gonos, Georges. 1977. " 'Situation' versus 'Frame': The 'Interactionist' and the 'Structuralist' Analysis of Everyday Life." *American Sociological Review* 42:854–867.

Gottdiener, Marc. 1985. "Hegemony and Mass Culture: A Semiotic Approach." *American Journal of Sociology* 90:979–1001.

Gramsci, Antonio. 1971. *Selections from the Prisons Notebooks.* London: Lawrence and Wishart.

Griswold, Wendy. 1983. "The Devil's Techniques: Cultural Legitimation and Social Change." *American Sociological Review* 48:668–680.

Griswold, Wendy. 1986. *Renaissance Revivals: City Comedy and Revenge Tragedy in the London Theatre, 1576–1980.* Chicago: University of Chicago Press.

Griswold, Wendy. 1987. "The Fabrication of Meaning: Literary Interpretation in the United States, Great Britain, and the West Indies." *American Journal of Sociology* 92:1077–1177.

Gusfield, Joseph R. 1966. *Symbolic Crusade.* Urbana: University of Illinois Press.

Gusfield, Joseph R. 1981. *The Culture of Public Problems: Drinking-Driving and the Symbolic Order.* Chicago: University of Chicago Press.

Habermas, Jürgen. 1984. *The Theory of Communicative Action. Vol. I: Reason and the Rationalization of Society.* Boston: Beacon.

Habermas, Jürgen. 1987. *The Theory of Communicative Action. Vol. II: Lifeworld and System: A Critique of Functionalist Reason.* Boston: Beacon.

Hall, John R. 1988. "Social Interaction, Culture and Historical Studies." Paper presented at the Stone Symposium of the Society for the Study of Symbolic Interaction, Chicago.

Hall, S. 1984. "Cultural Studies at the Center: Some Problematics and Problems." In S. Hall, Dorothy Hobson, Andrew Lowe, and Paul Willis, eds., *Culture, Media, Language.* London: Hutchison.

Harding, Susan F. 1987. "Convicted by the Holy Spirit: The Rhetoric of Fundamental Baptist Conversion." *American Ethnologist* 35:167–181.

Hart, Roderick P. 1984. "The Functions of Human Communication in the Maintenance of Public Values." In Carroll C. Arnold and John Waite Bowers, eds., *Handbook of Rhetorical and Communication Theory.* Boston: Allyn and Bacon.

Hebdige, Dick. 1979. *Subculture: The Meaning of Style.* London: Methuen.

Heidegger, Martin. 1962. *Being and Time.* New York: Harper and Row.

Hochschild, Jennifer L. 1981. *What's Fair? American Beliefs about Distributive Justice.* Cambridge, Mass.: Harvard University Press.

Hofstader, R. 1963. *Anti-Intellectualism in American Life.* New York: Vintage Books.

Horkheimer, M., and T. Adorno. 1944. "The Culture Industry: Enlightenment of

Mass Deception." In M. Harkheimer and T. Adorno, *Dialectic of Enlightenment*. New York: Seabury Press.

Hunter, James Davison. 1987. *Evangelicalism: The Coming Generation*. Chicago: University of Chicago Press.

Hunter, James Davison, and Stephen C. Ainlay, eds. 1986. *Making Sense of Modern Times: Peter L. Berger and the Vision of Interpretive Sociology*. London: Routledge and Kegan Paul.

Inzerilli, Giorgio, and André Laurent. 1983. "Managerial Views of Organizational Structure in France and the U.S.A." *International Studies of Management and Organization* 13:97–118.

Jacoby, R. 1987. *The Last Intellectuals: American Culture in the Age of Academe*. New York: Basic.

Jameson, Frederic. 1981. *The Political Unconscious: Narrative as a Socially Symbolic Act*. Ithaca: Cornell University Press.

Janowitz, M. 1972. "Professionalization of Sociology." *American Journal of Sociology* 78:105–135.

Joas, Hans. 1987. "Symbolic Interactionism." In A. Giddens and J. H. Turner, eds., *Social Theory Today*. Cambridge: Polity Press.

Kadushin, Charles. 1974. *The American Intellectual Elite*. Boston: Little, Brown.

Katz, Elihu, and George Wedell. 1978. *Broadcasting in the Third World: Premise and Performance*. London: Macmillan.

Kellner, Douglas. 1988. "Postmodernism as Social Theory: Some Challenges and Problems." *Theory, Culture, and Society* 5:239–270.

Kurtz, Lester R. 1986. *The Politics of Heresy*. Berkeley and Los Angeles: University of California Press.

Lacan, Jacques. 1977. *Ecrits: A Selection*. New York: Norton.

Lamont, Michèle. 1984. "Institutional and Intellectual Differences Between French and American Sociology." In B. Crousse and M. Th. Greven, eds., *Political Science and Science Policy in an Age of Uncertainty*. Frankfurt: Campus Verlag.

Lamont, Michèle. 1987a. "How to Become a Dominant French Philosopher: The Case of Jacques Derrida." *American Journal of Sociology* 93: 584–622.

Lamont, Michèle. 1987b. "The Production of Culture in France and the United States Since World War II." In A. Gagnon, ed., *The Role of Intellectuals in Liberal Democracies*. New York: Praeger.

Lamont, Michèle. 1989. "The Power-Culture Link in a Comparative Perspective." In C. Calhoun, ed., *Comparative Social Research*. Vol. 11. Greenwich, Conn.: JAI Press.

Lamont, Michèle, and Annette Lareau. 1988. "Cultural Capital: Allusions, Gaps and Glissandos in Recent Theoretical Developments." *Sociological Theory* 6:153–168.

Lamont, Michèle, and Marsha Witten. 1988. "Surveying the Continental Drift: The Diffusion of French Social and Literary Theory in the United States." *French Politics and Society* 6:17–23.

Lasch, Christopher. 1979. *The Culture of Narcissism*. New York: Norton.

Laurent, André. 1983. "The Cultural Diversity of Western Conceptions of Management." *International Studies of Management and Organization* 13:75–96.

Lears, T. J. Jackson. 1985. "The Concept of Cultural Hegemony: Problems and Possibilities." *American Historical Review* 85:567–593.

Lefebvre, Henri. 1968. *La Vie Quotidienne dans le Monde Moderne*. Paris: Gallimard.

LeGoff, Jacques. 1984. *The Birth of Purgatory*. Chicago: University of Chicago Press.

Lemert, Charles, ed. 1981. *French Sociology: Rupture and Renewal Since 1968.* New York: Columbia University Press.

Lévi-Strauss, Claude. 1963. *Structural Anthropology.* New York: Basic Books.

Long, Elizabeth. 1986. "Women, Reading and Cultural Authority: Some Implications of the Audience Perspective in Cultural Studies." *American Quarterly* 38:591–612.

Luhmann, Niklas. 1985. "Society, Meaning, Religion—Based on Self-Reference." *Sociological Analysis* 46:5–20.

Luker, Kristin. 1984. *Abortion and the Politics of Motherhood.* Berkeley: University of California Press.

Lukes, Steven. 1974. *Power: A Radical View.* New York: Wiley.

Lyotard, Jean-Francois. 1984. *The Postmodern Condition: A Report on Knowledge.* Minneapolis: University of Minnesota Press.

Marcus, G. E., and M. J. Fischer. 1986. *Anthropology as Cultural Critique.* Chicago: University of Chicago Press.

Marx, K., and F. Engels. 1979. *The German Ideology.* London: Lawrence and Wishart.

Mattelart, Armand. 1979. *Multinational Corporations and the Control of Culture.* Sussex: Harcester.

Meyer, John W., and Brian Rowan. 1977. "Institutionalized Organizations: Formal Structure as Myth and Ceremony." *American Journal of Sociology* 83:340–363.

Montlibert, C. de. 1982. "La professionalisation de la sociologie et ses limites." *Revue Française de Sociologie* 23:37–53.

Mukerji, C., and M. Schudson. 1986. "Popular Culture." *Annual Review of Sociology* 12:47–66.

Murdoch, Graham, and Peter Golding. 1974. "For a Political Economy of Mass Communication." *Socialist Register 1973.* London: Merlin.

Ortner, Sherry B. 1984. "Theory in Anthropology since the Sixties." *Comparative Studies in Society and History* 26:126–166.

Pannenberg, Wolfhart. 1983. *Christian Spirituality.* Philadelphia: Westminster.

Parsons, T. 1967. "On the Concept of Political Power." In T. Parsons, *Sociological Theory and Modern Society.* New York: Free Press.

Peterson, Richard A. 1979. "Revitalizing the Culture Concept." *Annual Review of Sociology* 5:137–166.

Pocock, J. G. A. 1987. "Texts as Events: Reflections on the History of Political Thought." In Kevin Sharpe and Steven N. Zwicker, eds., *Politics of Discourse.* Berkeley: University of California Press.

Radway, Janice A. 1984. *Reading the Romance: Women, Patriarchy and Popular Literature.* Chapel Hill: University of North Carolina Press.

Ricoeur, Paul. 1976. *Interpretation Theory.* Fort Worth: Texas Christian University Press.

Ross, George. 1988. "Mastersigners, Artisans, Youth: The Sociology and Politics of Intellectuals in France." Paper presented at the conference "In Search of the New France," Brandeis University.

Ryan, William. 1972. *Blaming the Victim.* New York: Vintage.

Schudson, Michael. 1984. *Advertising, the Uneasy Persuasion: Its Dubious Impact on American Society.* New York: Basic Books.

Schutz, Alfred. 1971. *Collected Papers, Vol. I: The Problem of Social Reality.* The Hague: Martinus Nijhoff.

Schutz, Alfred, and Thomas Luckmann. 1973. *Structures of the Life-World.* Evanston, Ill.: Northwestern University Press.

Sennett, Richard. 1976. *The Fall of Public Man.* New York: Random House.

Sennett, Richard, and Jonathan Cobb. 1972. *The Hidden Injuries of Class.* New York: Random House.

Shonfeld, W. K. 1976. *Obedience and Revolt: French Behavior Toward Authority.* Beverly Hills, Cal.: Sage.

Swidler, Ann. 1986. "Culture in Action: Symbols and Strategies." *American Sociological Review* 51:273–286.

Swidler, Ann. 1987. "The Uses of Culture in Historical Explanation." Paper presented at the annual meeting of the American Sociological Association, Chicago.

Thomas, George M., John W. Meyer, Francisco O. Ramirez, and John Boli. 1987. *Institutional Structure; Constituting State, Society and the Individual.* Beverly Hills, Cal.: Sage.

Tipton, Steven M. 1982. *Geting Saved from the Sixties: Moral Meaning in Conversion and Cultural Change.* Berkeley: University of California Press.

Tuchman, Gaye. 1978. *Making News: A Study on the Construction of Reality.* New York: Free Press.

Tuchman, Gaye. 1983. "Consciousness Industries and the Production of Culture." *Journal of Communication* 33:330–341.

Tulis, Jeffrey K. 1987. *The Rhetorical Presidency.* Princeton: Princeton University Press.

Turner, Victor W., and Edward M. Bruner, eds. 1986. *The Anthropology of Experience.* Urbana: University of Illinois Press.

Verdès-Leroux, Jeanine. 1983. *Au Service du Parti.* Paris: Fayard.

White, Harrison, and Cynthia White. 1965. *Canvases and Career.* New York: Wiley.

Williams, Raymond. 1977. *Marxism and Literature.* Oxford: Oxford University Press.

Willis, Paul. 1977. *Learning to Labor.* New York: Columbia University Press.

Witten, Marsha. 1988. "The Structure of Symbolic Codes and the Restriction of Meaning: Devices of Disambiguation in a Fundamentalist Christian Church." Manuscript.

Wolff, Janet. 1984. *The Social Production of Arts.* New York: New York University Press.

Wrong, Dennis H. 1979. *Power: Its Forms, Bases and Uses.* Oxford: Blackwell.

Wuthnow, Robert. 1987. *Meaning and Moral Order: Explorations in Cultural Analysis.* Berkeley: University of California Press.

Wuthnow, Robert. 1988a. *The Restructuring of American Religion. Society and Faith since World War II.* Princeton: Princeton University Press.

Wuthnow, Robert. 1988b. "Infrastructure and Superstructure: Revisions in Marxist Sociology of Culture." Paper presented at the annual meeting of the American Sociological Association, Atlanta.

Wuthnow, Robert, James Davison Hunter, Albert Bergesen, and Edith Kurzweil. 1984. *Cultural Analysis.* London: Routledge and Kegan Paul.

Wuthnow, Robert, and Marsha Witten. 1988. "New Directions in the Study of Culture." *Annual Review of Sociology* 14:49–67.

Zerubavel, Eviatar. 1988. "The Fine Line: Boundaries and the Construction of Social Reality." Paper presented at the Department of Sociology, Princeton University.

Zolberg, Vera L. 1988. "New York Cultural Institutions: Ascendant or Subsistent?" Paper prepared for SSRC Comittee on New York City, New School for Social Research.

12

Feminist Sociological Theory: The Near-Future Prospects

❀

PATRICIA M. LENGERMANN
George Washington University
and

JILL NIEBRUGGE-BRANTLEY
Northern Virginia Community College
and George Washington University

In contemporary discourse about sociological theory, feminist sociological theory is a new and relatively unfamiliar contender for the attention of social theorists. This paper opens with a definition of "feminist sociological theory." The body of the paper is then devoted to one of the focal questions of this volume: *what are the near-future prospects for a feminist sociological theory?* This focal discussion concentrates on the following five themes: (1) the organizational prospects for incorporation of this approach into sociology; (2) the model of social structure that comes from feminist sociological theory's confrontation with the issue of difference; (3) the implications of a feminist epistemology for sociological practice; (4) feminism's inherent challenge to mainstream sociology's dualistic rhetoric; and (5) the establishment of a new basis for sociological critique in feminism's definition of power.[1]

DEFINITION OF FEMINIST SOCIOLOGICAL THEORY

Feminist sociological theory attempts a systematic and critical reevaluation of sociology's core assumptions in the light of discoveries being made within another community of discourse—the community of those creating feminist theory. Before turning to some of the dimensions of sociological theory being reworked through the lens of feminist theory, we focus on the lens itself, offering a working definition of feminist theory (Smith 1979, 1987; Jaggar 1983; Lengermann and Niebrugge-Brantley 1988).[2]

316

In the past two decades women's social and political mobilization reached one of its historic high points both in the United States and globally. This so-called "second wave" of the women's movement has been marked by an unprecedented volume of research about women's lives, labeled variously "Women's Studies," "the new scholarship on women," or in Jessie Bernard's phrase, "the Feminist Enlightenment."

Feminist theory is that part of this new scholarship on women that implicitly or formally presents a generalized, wide-ranging system of ideas about the world from a *woman-centered perspective.* Feminist theory arrives at a general statement about social life and human experience by being "woman-centered" in *three* distinct ways. *First,* in all feminist scholarship, woman is the primary object of study. For over twenty years the basic question of feminist scholarship has been *"and what about the women?"* In other words, where are the women in any situation being studied by any scholar in any discipline? If they are not present, why not? If they are present, in what capacity? Persistent asking of this question has led to the important discovery that women along with men actively produce the world—be it economy, science, art, religion, settlement of new territories, etc.

This recognition of a whole new set of actors calls for a reworking of our description and explanation of every social situation. Moreover, the discovery itself prompts further questioning: Why have people in general and the scholarly community in particular been so blind for so long to women's presence? By what processes have women been rendered invisible? Theoretical conclusions from these questions raise further questions about the organization of the social world, especially about the working of its hierarchies of domination.

Second, feminist theory is woman-centered in that it makes women the central subject, the guiding subjectivity, from which the world is viewed. Feminist scholars seek not only to locate women in social life but to discover how that life appears to women. In terms of epistemology, the consequences of this effort are as revolutionary for twentieth-century social science as Marx's discovery of the views of the working class were for nineteenth-century political economy. In each case, knowledge of the world once taken for granted as absolute now is seen as the relativized ideology of a particular group. In the case of feminist theory, it is the discovery that from the vantage point of women this "absolute knowledge" is really a particularistic account developed largely by males and always in circles of discourse dominated by men who have generalized on the basis of their own gender and power experiences.

Third, feminist theory is woman-centered in that it is critical and activist on behalf of women. Feminists ask, "How can we change and improve the world in ways that are more just and humane not only for women, but for humankind?" Within sociology, only Marxian and neo-Marxian theories have this intense interest in critique and change, and the emergence of feminist sociological theory becomes an important addition to the configuration of critical theories in sociology.

In light of feminism's claim that sociological theory, like other knowledge systems, may be particularistically biased in the direction of male experience of the world, every sociological concept and thesis, as well as the overall patterning of these concepts and theses, is potentially open for reconsideration. Accepted social science knowledge should be reevaluated to take account of all the actors or relations involved in the multidimensional production of social life. Feminist theory suggests we seek out essential workers rendered invisible by prevailing ideological/knowledge systems and that we understand that much though not all production occurs in intimate relations of inequality. The classic sociological distinctions between macro and micro theory may disappear in a feminist depiction in which social reality is seen instead as an interweaving of levels of activities. The social world is made visible, enacted and reproduced in intimate, often unequal interactions of social production, relationships embedded in, constrained, and patterned by large-scale socio-historical structures about which the actors may know little or nothing. Working out the details of this process is one of the major tasks of a feminist sociological theory and will require a new vocabulary not yet in place.[3] Feminism's conscious centering on women as objects *and* subjects should lead to a reintrojecton into sociology of a deep central concern with verstehen procedures, extended by feminist theory to include a reflexive monitoring of the sociologist's subjectivity and an assumption that tensions in the subjects' knowledge may provide a basis for critique and change. With the emergence of feminist sociological theory, the critical emphases in sociology are strengthened by an insistence that sociological work be critical and change-oriented, not only towards society, as the Marxians too suggest, but also, as critical theorists argue, in an intensely reflexive way towards sociology itself.

PROSPECTS FOR INCORPORATION

Three factors affect the degree to which feminist sociological theory may be incorporated into general sociology: (1) the organization of sociology as a profession (Collins 1985; Stacey and Thorne 1985; Ritzer 1988); (2) the relationship of feminist sociological theory to feminism

(Jaggar 1983; Donovan 1985; Bernard 1987, 1989); and (3) the issue of differences in vocabulary and tone between sociology and feminism (Smith 1979, 1987; Bernard 1987; de Vault 1988; and as illustrations, Rich 1976; Daly 1978; Lorde 1984).

The possibility of full incorporation into sociology is tempered by the organization of sociology itself. Sociology can be seen as a "balkanized" region in academia, an aggregation of sub-specialties, each working in a fairly self-contained way, with occasional aggressive forays into or border incidents with other specialty communities. Full integration of feminist theory would mean the reworking of prevailing viewpoints in each of sociology's specialties—work to be undertaken by the membership of each of the subspecialties. The organization of the profession makes it unlikely that incorporation in any particular sub-specialty, even the sub-community of social theorists, will generate rapid reworking of all the other areas of sociological work.

What has so far happened is that the first question of feminist theory —"and what about the women?"—has made an impact on sociological sub-specialties. Gender has itself become a sub-specialty within the profession, accorded sections at annual meetings, producing its own journal *(Gender and Society)*, and having its own parallel organization (Sociologists for Women in Society). Gender as a social category is now being included in nearly all other sub-specialty work—organizations, health, race and ethnicity, social stratification, education, etc. Further, the shape of the profession has been changed by the impact of feminist thinking with the addition of such sub-specialties as the "sociology of the emotions."

But with rare exceptions, the other aspects of feminist theory—the radical revisioning of the world and redefinition of social structure it implies—have not really been incorporated into the profession. The inclusion of gender as a social category does not equal incorporation of feminist sociological *theory* into the basic practice of sociology. Thus, despite proliferation of gender work in the past few years, we stand with Stacey and Thorne (1985) in arguing that there has been no systematic feminist reworking of sociology.

Nor can we expect that the incorporation of feminist sociological theory into sociological theory will significantly alter this situation. For while theorists would like to see themselves as the pivotal point in the profession, it is more realistic to see sociologial theory as only another sub-specialty, itself divided among theoretical schools. In this paper, then, the question of integrating feminist sociological theory becomes more narrowly the question of incorporating this theory into sociology's community of theoretical discourse in the next five to ten years, an incorporation affected both by feminist sociological theory's relation to feminism and by sociological theory's ability to accommodate to a feminist vocabulary and tone.

Feminist sociological theorists are members of two communities, the sociological profession and the world of feminist scholarship. From the latter world feminist sociological theorists gain most of their inspiration and the theoretical/critical basis for a reworking of sociology. Feminist sociological theorists divide their attention between two socio-political groups and ultimately have more loyalty to the world of feminism, because it is in this world where they participate in pure theoretical creativity, the products of which they must then try to transpose to sociology. The analogy for this kind of divided loyalty in sociology is Marxian sociology, practitioners of which also have to maintain a primary relationship with the interdisciplinary community of Marxian scholarship. This divided loyalty poses a problem for full incorporation into sociology. Feminist sociological theorists cannot allow themselves to be assimilated, even if their ideas are, since such assimilation would separate them from their source of ideas. Further, other sociologists may view feminist sociological theory with understandable suspicion as a theory which calls for a radical reworking of sociology, but one whose proponents come with suspect credentials as "half-sociologists" or even "non-sociologists," and as members of a community, feminism, whose active political commitment seems to cast doubt on the academic/scientific merits of its viewpoint.

The distinction between traditional sociological theory and feminist sociological theory is illustrated in the vocabulary and tone of feminist sociological theory which originates in a multidisciplinary community of discourse and aims at a critique of sociology's present vocabulary.

Feminists argue that male dominance through control of language has shaped all areas of human perception. Feminist sociologists bring this awareness to their attempt to reshape the discipline. On the one hand, they ask, as Dorothy E. Smith (1979, 1987) has, can we practice feminist sociology using a language devised by a male-dominated profession? On the other hand, they confront the problem that a discipline is its concepts and at some point a reworking of vocabulary can create such a transformation that one must ponder, "Is the practice taking place here any longer 'sociology'?"

This question of vocabulary is not a superficial political one but a fundamental epistemological issue (returned to below). Smith (1979, 137–138) reasons,

> as members of an intelligentsia, [women] had learned . . . to work inside a discourse which we did not have part in making, which was not "ours" as women. The discourse expresses, describes, and provides the working concepts and vocabulary for a landscape in which women are strangers.

That strangeness is an integral part of the socially organized practices which constitute it. In a short story, Doris Lessing tells of a girl growing up in Africa whose consciousness has been wholly transformed by traditional British literary culture. Her landscape, her cosmology, her moral relations, her botany, are those of English novels, poetry, and stories. Her own immediate landscape, with its life forms, the character of her everyday world, the actuality of Africa, do not fully penetrate and occupy her consciousness. They are not named. This is paradigmatic of the same rupture in consciousness—the line of fault from which this inquiry begins.

By "line of fault," Smith means the gap between an actor's actual lived experience and the way s/he is taught to think about that experience—especially if s/he is a member of a subordinate group.

Experiencing this line of fault, feminist sociological theorists are increasingly drawn to answer Smith's question, can we do feminist sociology using a male-fashioned vocabulary, in the negative. But this answer lays upon feminist sociological theorists the burdens of providing a new vocabulary, adding to the existing vocabulary of sociological theory, or enforcing a change in standard definitions so that feminist conceptions of key terms are at least include among possible meanings. Some indications of these efforts are to be found in the remainder of this paper.

An additional problem in the development of an appropriate vocabulary arises from feminist theory's creation in a multidisciplinary community. This origin gives an element of "strange-ness" to both basic feminist terms and to the tone in which feminist sociological theory may be phrased—strangeness, that is, if the audience is one of mainstream sociologists. Examples of this strangeness include: "patriarchy," "a woman-centered perspective," "bifurcated vision," "invisible actors," "master-servant relations," "inter-viewing" and "eros as power." In tone, feminist discourse draws together viewpoints not only from the natural and social sciences, but also from the humanities and the creative arts. From the rational sociological viewpoint much of feminist theory will appear to be infused with a tone both visionary and poetic, and feminist accounts deliberately weave formal analytic modes with procedures that appeal to intuitive, personal, aesthetic, and even revelatory modes of knowing. To a non-feminist sociologist this tone may make all feminist theory suspect as something other than science. To feminist theorists this tone is deeply satisfying, for they claim that it is necessary to bring together art and science, indeed all truth-seeking strategies, if one hopes to escape the restricted disciplinary vision which may be one instrument of domination.

Whatever the degree of incorporation, the future importance of feminist sociological theory for sociology in the next five years will be in the exploration of the substantive issues of difference, epistemology, rhetoric, and power—to which we now turn.

DIFFERENCE

Feminist sociological theory's model of societal organization derives from feminist theory's exploration of issues of difference. This exploration of difference can be seen as having three overlapping phases or dialectically interacting moments. In the first phase, feminist scholars following de Beauvoir's classic framing in *The Second Sex* (1957) began the work of discovering that "other" or "marginal" or "invisible" constituency, "women." Women's typical life experiences, psyche and mental processes, place in history, society, and culture were extensively described by feminists in all disciplines, including sociology, a work of discovery that continues to the present (for example on women's life experiences, Bernard 1981, 1987; on their mental processes, Gilligan 1982; in history, Boulding 1976; in society, Rich 1976; in science, Keller 1983; in religion, Daly 1968; and in art, Greer 1979).

This work of discovery is anchored in the assumptions that: (1) women may be treated as a generic social category or type by virtue of their common experience of inequality/subordination/oppression (the term varies by school of feminist theory), and (2) much of what is distinctive about women, including their subordination, is a social construction, not "a natural fact." This first phase of work focuses on the difference between women and men but is primarily devoted to trying to describe women's experience—so excluded have women been from male discourse about humankind. But as this work of exploration and discovery has proceeded, feminist scholars have developed two new themes about difference (Eisenstein 1985).

In the second phase, women became not only objects of inquiry but also subjects, *the subjectivities from which the world could be viewed.* The world feminist scholars viewed from a woman-centered perspective was still one created by dominant males. But now these males became "other," the stranger no longer taken for granted, whose ways of being and social creations were not seen as universal and natural but as socio-historically specific. From this perspective, feminist scholars began a critique of the male-made world in terms of values significant to women (as revealed by phase one's research). This second phase led to a major shift in feminist goals. In the first phase, the goals had been primarily *liberal*, women seeking "equal opportunity" to join and compete in a male-made world. In the second phase, the goals became primarily *radical/critical*, women seeking to identify and change those elements of the male-made world they found life-threatening or life-diminishing (Dinnerstein 1976; MacKinnon 1982; Hartsock 1983; Benjamin 1985; Keller 1985; Smith 1987).

As these first and second phases evolved, feminist scholarship entered a third phase, exploration of *differences among women*. Partly as the women's movement drew in a more diverse population of women, but also significantly as part of feminist theory's practice of reflexively scrutinizing its own activities, questions were raised about differences among women. Especially challenged was the assumption that all women were alike in and because of their experience of subordination. One of the most intense debates in contemporary feminism is about differences among women—by age, ethnicity, class, sexual preference, age, nationality, and culture. In this debate a work of discovery is again underway as the lives, psyches, histories and socio-cultural activities of different types of women are explored and described—a task that has only just begun (Rich 1980; Hooks 1984; Lorde 1984; Eisenstein and Jardine 1985; Bernard 1987). At the same time, feminist theory is using this discovery of differences among women as a way of viewing the world from multiple vantage points.

Transposing this exploration of difference from feminist theory, feminist sociological theory has created a distinctive view of social organization, a view anchored in two premises: that gender is not a role but a pervasive system of stratification; and that the universality of this system of stratification can be explained by the concept of *social production*, a concept to which feminist sociological theory gives a very wide definition. Social production, in feminist sociological theory, is expanded beyond the production of social goods, as depicted in Marxian theory, to the production of social life. This view of social production brings into focus such activities as child bearing and rearing; household maintenance; sexual and emotional work; the creation and maintenance of health, personality, prestige, and meaning; as well as the production of economic commodities and of structures of social control. The multidimensional process of social production is seen by feminist sociological theory to be organized in each of its zones into a hierarchy of master/order-giver/surplus value-appropriator and servant/producer/exploited laborer (Smith 1979; Ehrenreich and Fuentes 1987; Hartsock 1983; Rollins 1985). Gender, like class, is a social structure within a universal system of stratification based on the organization of social production and sustained by ideology. Extensive study of the complex differences between women and men and of the social reproduction of these differences—including the application of psychoanalytic theory to social processes—has shown ideology's centrality in sustaining domination and the intricacy of the ideological patterning of social life.

Feminist sociological theory's model of societal organization is currently anchored in these five ideas: (1) that gender, like class, is a pervasive system of stratification; (2) that stratification in any society arises from the organization of social production; (3) that social production has to be broadly construed as a multifaceted, hierarchically organized process that reproduces and maintains social life; (4) that analyzing this process effectively requires suspension of the convention of categorizing phenomena as micro- or macro-social, and the creation of a vocabulary to describe the fluidity of the relation between interactional and structural arrangements; and (5) that ideology masks the reality of social production while reproducing stratification in the intricacies of personality and social interaction. Ideology explains women's invisibility in both public and academic knowledge systems, their historic failure to alter their situation, and their even more pervasive compliance with this subordination. This explanation leads feminist sociological theory to call for a constant reflexive critique of both public and academic knowledge production.

In developing this model, feminist sociological theory has interpreted the data of feminist scholarship by drawing widely and innovatively on Marxist, critical, interpretive, psychoanalytic, phenomenological, and hermeneutic theory while focusing persistently on the sociological problematics of social inequality and of the relations between macro and micro social life. This model is still emergent in feminist sociological theory. In the next five to ten years, we can expect the following elaborations of feminism's model of societal organization, elaborations growing out of feminism's continuing discovery of the significance of difference.

There should be *an intense scrutiny of the interface among major patterns of social stratification, including race, class, and global stratification within the world system.* This scrutiny will be a descriptive effort, an extension of feminism's exploration of women's worlds and of differences among women. This description should serve to incorporate into sociology knowledge about the life experiences and vantage points of heretofore invisible groups and about how multiple stratification systems intersect in the biographies, psyches, and relational experiences of individuals. This analysis will in turn lead to *a greater emphasis on the global system as the ultimate unit of analysis.* Feminist sociological theory will bring to existing world systems theory its distinctive concept of social production and its persistent interest in the interface among structures, relational experience, and subjectivity. From this formulation, feminist sociological theory can *broaden its focus on inequality to include not only that experienced by women in all their variety but also the experience of non-privileged men,* that is, the vast majority of men. This effort will have to explore the dialectic between commonalities in minority experience and the persistent fact of gender stratification (Ehrenreich and Fuentes 1987; Hooks 1984; Seager and Olson 1986; Bernard 1987; Smith, in progress).

EPISTEMOLOGY

Within feminist theory, the issue of what constitutes "certain" or "adequate" knowledge of social reality—that is, the issue of epistemology—has produced a rapidly growing literature (Cook and Fonow 1986; Farganis 1986; Keller 1985; Harding 1986; Smith 1987; Lorber 1988; Haraway 1988). Amidst intense debate in this literature, there is also growing consensus. This section describes feminist sociological theory's engagement with feminist epistemology. What we trace here is an emergent epistemology, a pattern still taking shape. Our expectation is that within the next five years, feminist sociological theorists will create an epistemological protocol for feminist sociologial research analogous to that produced by Merton for functionalism in 1949.

Like its model of societal organization, feminist sociological theory's epistemology derives from feminism's exploration of difference. Two fundamental concepts issue from that exploration: *we construct our knowledge of the world from the accounts of differently situated social actors; and that construction involves the (re)searcher in a series of dialectical acts.* Inherent in these two assumptions are questions central to the development of feminist sociological epistemology:

1. What is the relationship among the "we," the "differently situated actors" and their "accounts"?
2. What constitutes an act of "construction"?
3. By what criteria is the truth of "knowledge of the world" to be measured?

1. What is the relationship among the "we," the "differently situated actors," and their "accounts"?
The answer to this question has both an empirical and a normative component. Further, the answer must be understood within the context of the balkanization of sociology itself. Femininst sociological theory's interest in the subjectivity of invisible actors, most particularly of women, means that feminist epistemology is intensely oriented towards the creation of a verstehen sociological method. Central to this orientation is a rejection of rational, positivistic scientific procedure. Fem-

inists argue that objectivity is not a transcendent truth-seeking principle, but derives from the particularistic experiences of dominant males in capitalist society. In developing this critique of positivism, feminist epistemology adds a distinctive and radical voice to the growing sociological literature critical of positivist practice. But these criticisms are developed within *sociological* theory's discourse about method; the discussion about the theory of method within *methodology* or within other sub-specialties tends still to hold to the ideals of a value-free, researcher vs. subject, objective practice (see for example any past issue of the *ASR*). And we would argue that even when sociologists acknowledge the impossibility of attaining objectivity, they do not substitute the feminist ideal of identification with the research subject as another human being rather than a means to their research ends.

A basic feminist principle is that the researcher does not, cannot, and ought not to stand separate from the subject of research. Developing this epistemological point from the perspective of the natural sciences, mathematical microbiologist Evelyn Fox Keller writes in *Reflections on Gender and Science:*

> My argument is not simply that the dream of a completely objective science is in principle unrealizable, but that it contains precisely what it rejects: the vivid traces of a reflected self-image. The objectivist delusion reflects back an image of self as autonomous and objectified: an image of individuals unto themselves, severed from the outside world of other objects . . . and simultaneously from their own subjectivity. It is the investment in impersonality, the claim to have escaped the influence of desires, wishes, and beliefs . . . that constitutes the special arrogance . . . of modern man, and at the same time reveals his peculiar subjectivity. (1985, 70)

The subjectivity that makes this extraordinary investment in objectivity is a subjectivity that is deeply afraid of the loss of its own individuation. Yet identity for any individual requires some recognition by "other," that is, some relationship with "other" (Mead 1934; Schutz and Luckmann 1973; Benjamin, 1985). Faced with the dilemma of seeking both individuation and recognition, a subjectivity may choose domination as a way of relating. The subjectivity making that choice "reasons" that only by controlling and subduing "other" can it "safely" achieve both recognition and individuation. This theme of domination, and its effects on selfhood, is more fully explored below. But the theme is important to epistemology because it is the unease about the intertwining of objectivity and domination that fuels feminism's normative critique of dominant male-created science.

To the already existent critique of dominant science, feminism contributes a radically new alternative. Feminist epistemology argues that the normatively and empirically correct relationship between researcher and subject is one of "mutuality of recognition" (Reinharz 1983; Mies 1983). This mutuality of recognition begins in the idea of a "we" as the constructor of knowledge. Within the research act, "we" must come to include both the researcher and the subject as socially located actors.

Several corollaries flow from this general position. The researcher is obliged to recognize and reflexively monitor her/himself as a socially located actor engaged in a project. This project is not a separate, "objective" research undertaking but an activity socially located in the researcher's interests and meanings. The researcher must recognize that that project involves other human beings who have their own projects similarly socially located within personal interests and meanings. Therefore, the researcher cannot treat the subject as a mechanism within her/his research design but must instead orient to the subject as an equal. The research process becomes one in which all actors participate in activities that facilitate each other's projects and in so doing engage in a mutual process of discovery—a process Ann Oakley (1981) has described as "inter-viewing." Within this process of discovery, the researcher and subject relate as vulnerable equals over a range wider than the research project. Knowledge of the world emerges through this process of interrelating projects and accounts. In this process, the feminist sociologist confronts a crucial dialectic between the world as text (i.e., "subject's account") and the world as obdurate reality (i.e., the subject her/himself). This confrontation leads feminist epistemology to the uneasy but accurate middle ground between a simple positivism and the radical relativism of postmodernism.

2. What constitutes the act of construction?

The feminist sociologist confronts three acts of translation in constructing knowledge: (1) the task of enabling subjects to translate their lived experiences into texts which can be shared; (2) the task of translating these texts into the symbol system of sociology; and (3) the task of translating personal, historically specific texts into general statements without losing the individuality of the original accounts.

The first task requires that the subject "speaks authentically," that is, that the subject gives an account of projects, interests, and meanings as s/he most fully understands them. The two most common barriers to speaking authentically are lacking the language to do so and having projects, meanings, and interests one does not wish to reveal.

The problem of lacking a language is more frequently encountered by the disempowered because part of their disempowerment lies in being forced to speak in the vocabulary of dominants. Feminist research consistently shows women's lack of vocabulary for naming their own experiences—of their own bodies, their sexuality, their work both in-side and outside the wage sector, their mothering, their friendships (Glazer 1976; Rubin 1976; Rich 1976, 1980; Hochschild 1983; Snitow et al. 1982). This problem is exacerbated because subjects often have to move beyond the dominants' ideological patterning of experience in order to know their own lived actualities.

A central work of feminist practice is to help women discover the power of naming their experiences as they have lived them. The opera-tive word in feminist method here is "discover." The feminist re-searcher does not provide vocabulary for the subject but rather a setting and a responsiveness that may allow the subject to find expression for problems and experiences that heretofore have had "no name" (Friedan 1963). Feminist researchers use a variety of techniques to help subjects empower themselves: conversations which are in-depth, unstructured, and egalitarian in that the subject participates equally in setting the agenda, time, and space; a research stance in which the subject is approached as "expert" and the researcher enters as "initiate"; collec-tive creation in which women produce dramas and other art to embody their lived experience; "consciousness-raising groups" that deconstruct ideology by allowing women to voice and have reinforced interpreta-tions of reality heretofore felt as "taboo" or "crazily idiosyncratic" (Reinharz 1983; Kasper 1988; Mies 1983; MacKinnon 1982).

The problem of dealing with the inauthentic research subject is one to which feminism has paid less attention. Presumably inauthenticity may be brought to the surface in several ways: sustained conversation between subject and researcher with the researcher calling attention to apparent contradictions in the subject's statements; group discussions involving variously socially situated actors in an egalitarian setting; film records of the subject in action and discussion of the film with the subject; and "triangulation" in which various account-gathering tech-niques are used as checks on each other (Cook and Fonow 1986). In seeking authenticity of accounts, the feminist researcher is not seeking agreement with feminist goals. For example, male accounts of money, sex, and power may be accurate statements of how a certain elite does indeed experience these goods (Hartsock 1983). When inauthenticity cannot be overcome, the researcher may choose to call attention to this very fact (Brownmiller 1975; Barry 1979; Scully 1980, 1986).

Having achieved what researcher and subject concur to be an authen-tic account (or being faced with an apparently inauthentic account), the feminist sociologist then confronts the problem of translating this ac-count into "sociology." The feminist sociologist repeatedly finds her/himself struggling for expression in a discourse inappropriate to the experience s/he seeks to describe: the experience and language of the disempowered must be translated into a disciplinary form crafted by dominants. This problem, treated at length below can be illustrated by the standard sociological model of the actor as a rational, goal-pursuing agent, a model which contrasts with women's reports of themselves as responders to the demands and needs of others and to incidents beyond their own attempts at control and rational self-direction (Smith 1979, 1987; Rich 1976).

The final task in constructing sociological knowledge is to move from individual accounts to some form of generalization. This movement, a requirement not only of sociology but also of feminist theory as a basis for social critique, is nevertheless difficult for the feminist theorist and probably constitutes the major problem in the construction of knowledge. The difficulty arises from feminist theory's intense concern with respect for the subject and for the individual differences among subjects. The feminist sociologist is in a sense "caught" in the dialectic between the need for generalization as one basis for critique and the need for individual visibility as the goal toward which that critique aims.

It is this dialectic that underlies debates about quantitative accounts vs. qualitative and micro level vs. macro analyses. Many feminist sociologists regard the existing body of quantified research findings about the world as so alienated from social actors' experience of that world and so permeated at every stage of the research process with the biases of a dominant male-based science as to be worthless as a source of knowledge about the world. Feminist social scientists trained in quantitative research procedure argue that a quantified study designed to be sensitive to feminist value concerns can produce useful knowledge and be part of a multidimensional research design. They reason that such an account at least deserves equal consideration with other situated accounts; that is, the quantitative researcher should be allowed to explain the interests and meanings that the account has for her/him. At present the debate between these two groups continues (Reinharz 1983; Jayaratne 1983; Spalter-Roth 1986).

Within the macro-micro form of this debate, the challenge for feminist theorists is to move from a data base focused primarily on the subjective and micro social situation of specific individuals and groups to a comprehensive understanding of societal organization and trends. Several strategies for this movement suggest themselves. One is the obvious strategy of aggregation, bringing together the vast number of situated accounts being researched by feminist scholars. Another is the only slightly less obvious strategy of using these situated accounts as a means of testing feminist theories already in place about the macro order. Third is the strategy of researcher orientation: the researcher takes as a project, shared with the research subject, to know both the particular situation and the nature of the macro order impinging on and being enacted within it. A fourth is to focus on the seeming separation between micro subjective experience and macro structures and ideology, and to try to make visible the exact points and moments of interface.

Examples of the successful working through of this dialectic tension between the need to respect the individual and the equally compelling need to generalize are steadily emerging in feminist sociology. For instance, Dorothy E. Smith's various studies of nurses, psychiatric health care, schools, and social workers have shown—from subjects' accounts—the growing demand for document and record production and the reduced emphasis on service within those sectors (1987). Smith has used these data to describe much more massive corporate trends in the late industrial capitalist world system. Similarly, Arlie Hochschild's researches (1982) on a specific group of women workers— flight attendants—has revealed the commercial packaging of human emotions as an exchange commodity in the present world system. Most recently, Rajan and Pathak (1989) have deconstructed political bureaucratic discourse among collective actors—the Indian Supreme Court, the Indian National Congress, the Islamic Fundamentalist League, and Indian feminists—to show how that discourse has obscured the micro tragedy of a seventy-three-year-old Muslim woman whose divorce precipitated the very discourse that obscured her. Rajan and Pathak (1989) ask what remains the critical issue for feminist theory: "Where, in all these discursive displacements, is Shabbano the woman? Has the discourse on the Muslim woman, torn away from its existential moorings, sucked her in and swallowed her up?" In studies such as these, feminist sociologists are struggling with the need for a vocabulary to describe the interface between individual lived experience and social organization.

3. *By what criteria is "knowledge of the world" to be judged as true?*

Feminist sociological theory advances three standards for measuring the truth of a proposition or knowledge construct: (1) evidential base; (2) theoretical congruity; and (3) practical effectiveness in addressing problems viewed as central by the theoretical community. These three standards are in form the same applied by all sociological theory, the distinctions lying in the content.

The evidential base that feminist sociological theory ultimately looks to is the lived experience of individual actors. Whatever knowledge construct is presented—whether in qualitative or quantitative terms, whether micro or macro, and regardless of level of generality—that construct must be traceable to the lives of individual subjects who have been involved as equals in the research process. Or, at least, this is the highest ideal for evidence in feminist research. In evaluating evidence, feminists seek not only to assess the authenticity of the individual accounts but also the relationship the researcher has established among competing accounts. Depending on circumstance, a researcher may choose to give equal weight to all accounts, to "privilege" certain accounts, or to seek points of tension or intersection among accounts. In the case of competing accounts by dominants and subordinates, even the equal weighting of those accounts by the feminist researcher is a kind of privileging of the subordinate account since it is obscured in usual channels of discourse (Bernard 1987). Feminist practice more typically tends to privilege the accounts of the disempowered by focusing almost exclusively on what they reveal. The theoretical justification for this privileging is that as the researcher moves through the layers of social production to reach the least visible but indispensable producer, the researcher gains a more detailed and therefore a new, more authentic picture of the entire organization of society (Hartsock 1983; Farganis 1986; Smith 1987; Haraway 1988).

Evaluating a knowledge construct for theoretical congruity, feminist sociological theory asks how well this construct addresses one or more of five basic elements in feminist sociology's current model of society: (1) the pervasiveness of gender stratification; (2) the origins of stratification in the organization of social production; (3) the hierarchical, multifaceted nature of social production; (4) the significance of ideology in masking the reality of social production, and (5) the fluidity of the relation between micro and macro production.

Examining the knowledge construct as a guide for practice, feminist theorists assess how that knowledge addresses what feminism sees as its central goal: to eliminate domination and to achieve the equal empowerment of differently situated actors. The argument for evaluation along value lines is at odds with the ideology of sociology as objective science but in keeping with Marxian and neo-Marxian method. And it is an established point in the philosophy of science that the worth of a paradigm is measured by how effectively it treats the problem at hand for the paradigmic community (Kuhn 1962). As Keller (1985) has said, the appeal of the physical sciences, in part, is that they do produce knowledge "that works." Feminism's stated ends are social transformation to a more just and humane world, and therefore feminist research can be assessed on the criterion of whether it produces knowledge that works to that end.

THE CRITIQUE OF SOCIOLOGICAL RHETORIC

Feminist sociological theorists are beginning to examine closely "textual strategies in sociology" as part of feminist theory's critique of male-engendered language (Stanton 1985; de Vault 1988). This critique goes beyond issues of vocabulary to encompass "rhetoric," in the Aristotelian sense of the art of organizing material to present truth effectively by an appeal to the intellect rather than the emotions. Rhetoric as part of the construction of disciplinary knowledge is not simply a way of presenting truth but of shaping its discovery.

One rhetorical principle for Westerners generally and the Western intelligentsia in particular is dualism, or some cognitive process anchored in dualistic thinking. This rhetorical mode has had important consequences for sociological description and has become a particular focus of feminist critique. By "dualistic rhetoric," we mean that Westerners think in terms of distinctive, relatively impermeable, and contrasting categories and that they see, cognitively organize their relationships to, and often experience the world in terms of such categories. But sometimes experiences of the world do not slip easily into preexisting dualistic categories. This is the experiential anomaly that, in a Kuhnian (1962) sense, makes one pause occasionally to look reflexively at this categorical mode of thinking. This anomaly is one instance of what Smith (1979, 1987) calls "the line of fault." This reflexive pause is particularly noticeable in the circle of feminist theorists who have made it their project to rediscover the world through the eyes of subordinated and often publicly invisible social actors. The accounts of these actors show a pattern of experiencing that does not flow easily into mutually exclusive analytical categories or dualisms (Ruddick 1980; Bernard 1981; Gilligan 1982; Hooks 1984).

What does this anomaly—the tensions between categorical thinking and human experiences which on occasion elude, permeate, flow through, or interface these categories—suggest theoretically? Not that the categories are an illusion or a collective self-deception, but that they are a knowledge construction, an ideology. It suggests further that since the accounts of subordinates are most unamenable to dualistic thinking, that such dualisms may better mirror the experience and interests of dominants. (Reasons for the appeal of dualistic thinking to dominants have already been suggested in our discussion of objectivity as ideology above and will be further explored below in an analysis of power.) The presence of this anomaly also suggests that academic disciplines, including sociology, are actors in this discourse, unwittingly legitimizing in the name of scholarship one particular mode of perceiving reality.

And finally this anomaly suggests that social theorists might better understand the organization of social reality if they trace the consequences of this ideology, and bracket it to see what we can discover about the world when we cease to look at it through this dualistic lens.

Feminists argue that one of the deepest dualistic structures in Western thought is that centering on gender, on the categories male and female. The ideological attributes associated with those two categories have ramifications for a complex of other dualisms: self and other, man and nature, mind and body, spirit and flesh, reason and emotion, sacred and profane, science and poetics, logic and intuition, strong and weak, active and passive, hard and soft. There are other crucial dualistic structures such as light and dark, good and evil, and virtue and vice, which have links both to gender and to the Western orientation to race. But the workings out of gender-associated traits suggest that gender is not merely a role arrangement in society or even a stratification structure, but a complex and pervasive categorical system patterning all of Western thought—that we live in a deeply gendered culture (Warner 1976; Griffin 1978; Stimpson 1979; Spender 1981; Keller 1985; Kristeva 1986).

Sociology is both a product of and an active contributor to this categorical, dualistic, gender-permeated culture. The discipline is rich in dualistic concepts: organic and mechanical solidarity, gemeinschaft and gesellschaft, rational and traditional, primary and secondary groups, capitalist and proletariat, achievement and ascription, universalistic and particularistic, micro and macro—and constant reference in the discipline to hard and soft methodology. In the next five to ten years feminist sociological theorists will pursue the task of systematically working through this whole system. As de Vault (1988, 1) notes, "Social scientists have become increasingly self-conscious about their writings as constructed texts, and have begun to analyze their own representational work. One aspect of this new project must involve asking how gender matters." Here we illustrate the sociological implications of this reworking by thinking through one of sociology's gender-associated dualistic categories, that of public vs. private.

The categories public and private permeate the thought of ordinary people, policymakers, and sociologists (Durkheim, Tonnies, Parsons, Berger) in Western societies. Public vs. private is a mapping of the psychological, social, and physical space of people's lives. The baseline for this mapping process is our sense of "the private," a concept which, like the Western concept of woman, is used both to idealize and disempower.

Private space centers on the area regarded as home, the place where one is safe; where the world endures; where relationships are guaranteed, close, intimate; where personalities are shaped, nurtured, expressed, renewed. Private space is sacred space, and women belong in it and are the stewards and keepers of this place.

In contrast, public space is profane. It is the space distant from home, a world of strangers with whom the actor must be on guard and where one must constantly prove oneself. Public space is the domain of economic, political, educational, and other bureaucratized services. It is the zone in which one earns money, power, and the applause of strangers. It is a world associated with men; it is their birthright.

So deeply are members of Western society imbued with this construct that even when they question the detail of women's access to public space, they find it nearly impossible to think past it, to a general social space in which humans move, where the demarcations "public" and "private" are only loose and permeable territorial markings. But feminist sociology attempts to offer an alternative view: a view of social reality as occurring in unified social space. This view, when juxtaposed with the conceptual and behavioral implications of the public vs. private ideology, raises several interesting possibilities.

First, feminist sociologists ask what the functions of this ideology might be. It idealizes the space in which a subordinate group, women, have traditionally been placed and is ambivalent towards the area in which dominants move and from which they derive their society-wide power—even over the home or private space. Clearly the ideology serves to legitimize the different locations of dominants and subordinates, as well as to mask the actual rewards of participation in public space and the realities of dependency and disempowerment experienced by those confined to private space. It may also serve to legitimize the claims to privileged treatment exercised by dominants when they enter private space, after their "travail" in the "wilderness" of the public world (Glennon 1979; Bernard 1981; Lengermann and Wallace 1985).

Second, feminist sociologists ask how these two domains, socially defined as separate, are linked. This question leads to some of the invisible work of women, whose daily schedules help to tie home to markets and public services, and whose continuous relational juggling coordinates the schedules of school, adult earners' job requirements, and the rhythms of home and family life. Third, feminist sociologists ask how this ideology of male and female placement in social space blinds us to the location of either gender in the space which is ideologically inappropriate to it. It is this question that has led feminist scholars to a focus on the history of women's wage work, and to their contributions to politics, science, art, religion, and academia. Feminist sociologists suggest too that we begin to look for men's work in maintaining private space—male friendships, male parenting, male emotional work. Fourth, feminist sociologists look for spillover activities from one sphere to another: women as domestic workers, i.e., as a paid labor force in the household; the economic value of unpaid housework; the emotional work which becomes part of so many women's jobs in the wage sector; the *intimate* nature of so many public-sphere relations of hierarchy and production (Berch 1982; Matthaei 1982; Rollins 1985; Smith and Griffith 1985; Ehrenreich 1986).

Fifth, and most importantly, feminist sociologists explore how factors hitherto trivialized or screened from scrutiny as natural qualities of the private sphere may in fact be complex and major dynamics in society as a whole, intricately interwoven with political economy and ideology. Some of these factors include mothering, childhood, the body and its functions, emotions, and sexuality—all those private, "natural" things which are assumed to be so wholesome, obvious, and straightforward (or at least protected by the mantle of private behavior) that sociological theorists often fail to explore their significance for social organization as a whole (Rich 1976; Chodorow 1978; Hochschild 1982; Snitow et al. 1982).

This brief critique of the ideology of public vs. private reveals the theoretical and practical usefulness of "seeing through" dualistic thought, an activity feminist sociological theorists will in the near future expand as part of their overall reexamination of the rhetoric of sociological theory.

THE CONCEPT OF POWER

Feminists generally agree that any feminist theory must do four things: (1) describe what is in place, (2) explain what is in place, (3) envision change, and (4) develop strategies for implementing that change (Harding 1986; Palmer 1988). Central to feminist sociological theory's accomplishment of these tasks is a reworking of the concept of power.

Contemporary sociological theories vary widely in the attention they give to power. It is central to conflict, critical, and post-structuralist sociologies; a muted and second-tier concept for functionalism and exchange theory; and peripheral for symbolic interaction and phenomenology, in the sense that it only occasionally impinges on explanation. But regardless of emphasis, most theorists begin with Weber's (1979, 38) working definition of power *(Macht):* "the probability that one actor within a social relationship will be in a position to carry out his own will despite resistance, regardless of the basis on which this probability rests." The basic image here is one actor subduing another —an image carried to its logical extreme in Gerhard Lenski's argument "that survival is the chief goal of the great majority of men. If this is so, then it follows that the ability to take life is the most effective form of power" (Lenski 1966; in Collins 1985, 99). Weber's qualifying phrase "regardless of the basis on which this probability rests" is the basis for the further sociological division of power into types. Sociologists typically identify five power resources: physical force, the basis for *coercion*; control of necessary material resources, the basis for *domination*; the strength of the better argument, the basis for *influence*; the capacity to deliberately misrepresent, the basis for *manipulation*; and advantageous location within a system of meanings, the basis for *authority*.

So taken for granted is this conception of power in both life and sociology that it seems to require neither explanation nor critique. But beginning with just this work of explanation and critique, feminist sociological theory posits that this concept of power is another case in which the experiences of a male-elite group have been accepted as "universal." Feminist sociological theory consolidates these various descriptions of power and its types under the general concept, *domination*. Domination in feminist theory is understood as the "desire or capacity to master or rule another." Any form of power is subsumable under domination when the actors seek to rework the will of the subordinate with the goal of making the subordinate an instrument of his/her will—whether the dominant puts a gun to the subordinate's head, withholds money, argues, plays with emotions, or uses the advantages accorded by social location (Smith 1979; Hartsock 1983; Jaggar 1983; Benjamin 1985; French 1985).

Although domination taps only one part of the range of possibilities for the experience of power, sociological theory has focused so exclusively on domination that it has failed to developed a vocabulary for what Elizabeth Janeway (1980) calls "the powers of the weak." This absence of vocabulary reproduces in the social world a sense of the nonexistence of forms that are unnamed, but nevertheless real, such as acts of nurturing life, creating use or beauty, maintaining one's own will and projects against the will of dominants, witnessing to injustice, and so on. Thus, sociology's failure to explore the power exercised by subordinate peoples means that sociology helps legitimize as universal the experience of the dominant elite.

Further, the presentation of power given by sociology becomes another projection on the world of the selfhood of this dominant elite. Since this selfhood too is assumed to be universal rather than sociohistorically specific, sociology has failed to critique and expand its own theories of the self.

Feminist sociological theory links its explanation and critique of domination to an expanded theory of the development of the self. This theory, drawing on a feminist reworking of the object-relations school of psychoanalytic theory, develops the insight of both Mead (1934) and Schutz (1973) that the evolution of the self lies in the relationship to significant others from whom one learns role-taking and the experience of being held responsible for one's actions. But Mead and Schutz focus exclusively on the self rather than the dynamics of interaction between the self and others as interrelated independent subjectivities. Feminists see that non-neurotic development of self requires a dialectic between "the need to establish autonomous will and the need to be recognized by another" (Benjamin 1985, 42). The establishment of autonomous will requires differentiation of self from others and environment. The establishment of social identity requires recognition by others. The achievement of the healthy self requires recognition from an other who is experienced as an independent, functioning subjectivity. This dialectic between differentiation and recognition always occurs in a historically specific context. Within the context of Western patriarchal capitalism this dialectic is distorted, overemphasizing differentiation and undervaluing recognition for the male self. The male child's first intense relational experiences are typically with a female caregiver, usually his mother. But the male child receives signals from all actors in the cultural script, including the mother, that the way to selfhood is radical differentiation from the woman-mother—that is, the way to count in the cultural script is not to be a woman. This separation from the mother in an effort to preserve male power occurs when the boy is still so young (between six and eight) that his emotional mechanisms for doing this are primitive. He separates by radically rejecting the mother.

> This repudiation of the mother by men has also meant that she is not recognized as an independent person, another subject, but as something Other: as nature, as an instrument or object, as less-than-human. A male child's independence is bought at the price of saying: I am nothing like she who serves and cares for me! I am the recognized and nurtured one, not the recognizer and nurturer. (Benjamin 1985, 44)

This male as an adult will relate to others via domination, that is, he will satisfy his need "to separate without being alone . . . by possessing or controlling the other" (Benjamin 1985, 47). Conversely, the female child, who will become the mother, is taught to overvalue recognition by other and undervalue the differentiation that leads to autonomous will. She thus is "perfectly" socialized to reproduce the capitalist patriarchal male, having been reduced to seeing herself as an other, a dependent subjectivity. In male-elite discourse communities like sociology, the concept of power reflects this male selfhood; power is understood only as domination (Mitchell 1975; Dinnerstein 1976; Chodorow 1978; Benjamin 1985; Keller 1985).

Feminism's alternative vision begins in a new definition of power: *power is the ability to set and execute projects; social power is the ability to set and execute projects involving other people.* Within this conception, the actor need not control or conquer any other subjectivities; instead the actor must be able to align actions with others, cooperate in undertakings, help others to achieve goals, be able to wait her/his turn, allow others social space that s/he may be allowed space also. One form of this empowerment is described by Heilbrun (1988, 18): "Power is the ability to take one's place in whatever discourse is essential to action and the right to have one's part matter." The actor must perform a host of complex actions for which sociology lacks vocabulary because they are not acts of domination; they are actions that may be performed by the subordinate as well as by the dominant.

From this perspective, the full experience of power lies in both the setting and executing of projects. When an actor is denied one of these experiences, s/he will feel alienated. The alienation of the worker so long described in Marxian theory is reiterated here: the worker experiences alienation because s/he must use her/his body to perform actions leading ultimately to the fulfillment of another's projects. The feminist perspective also allows sociologists to explore the dangers of the alienation of the master. The master who understands power only as the ability to set projects, ordering others to execute, is left forever longing because s/he also is only partially empowered. The danger is that in seeking to satisfy this longing for power, the master increasingly enacts the experience of order-giving.

For feminists, the experience of power is the satisfying of *eros*. The concept of *eros* has been so distorted in Western patriarchal capitalist society, limited to that small corner of the world called "sexuality," that feminist theorists must work to reclaim it. Understood in its most basic meaning, *eros is the longing for completeness, for wholeness:*

> The erotic is a measure between the beginnings of our sense of self and the chaos of our strongest feelings. It is an internal sense of satisfaction to which, once we have experienced it, we know we can aspire. For having experienced the fullness of this depth of feeling and recognizing its power, in honor and self respect we can require no less of ourselves. . . . For the erotic is not a question only of what we do; it is a question of how acutely and fully we can feel in the doing. Once we know the extent to which we are capable of feeling that sense of satisfaction and completion, we can then observe which of our various life endeavors brings us closest to that fullness. (Lorde 1984, 54–55)

The erotic occurs in those moments when people are fully consumed in executing projects they have freely set.

Patriarchy and capitalism seek to limit erotic experience, excluding it from the world of work and encompassing it in distorted form in the area of sexuality (an area permeated by the imagery of domination). That limitation is imposed because eros comes only through a unity of project-setting and project-executing which threatens the basis of class distinction and hierarchy in all areas of social production. From the Greeks onward, eros has been discredited as dangerous, operating without any check save one's own feelings which have been defined a priori as unreliable (Hartsock 1983).

But two points contradict the direction of this argument. First, as Lorde (1984, 56) says, "the male world . . . values this . . . feeling enough to keep women . . . to exercise it in the service of men, but . . . fear this same [feeling] too much to examine the possibilities of it within themselves." This picture is similar to that painted by Keller (1985) in describing the self that projects an objective science as a self deeply afraid of its own feelings, its own needs for connectedness. In valuing but fearing the depth of feeling that is eros, men maintain women "at a distant-inferior position to be psychically milked, much the way ants maintain colonies of aphids to provide a life-giving substance for their masters" (Lorde 1984, 57). Women are used to meet the erotic need but are not allowed fully to assert it by setting and executing their own projects. Such assertion would undermine the structures of domination by which the male-elite protects itself as unchallenged, individuated subjectivities. This protection is a necessary construct of patriarchy and capitalism, which demand of their key actors a life lived in fealty to the ethic of competitive individualism.

Second, the argument that feeling is the enemy of reason, that "it feels right" is always logically in opposition to "it is right," is another example of dualistic thinking. For the erotic has its own self-corrective power: "We have been raised to fear the *yes* within ourselves, our deepest craving. But once recognized, those which do not enhance our future lose their power and can be altered" (Lorde 1984, 57). The individual in the dual action of setting and carrying out projects can discover what truly satisfies—and in a feminist vision that true satisfaction will be found in acts that "enhance the future," that nurture life.

Finally, a feminist sociological theory of power must offer some strategies for change. Those strategies applied to feminist practice in sociology would include: (1) the development of a stance toward the research subject in which the researcher recognizes the subject as an equal with projects and shares the research project with the subject; (2)

the development of a vocabulary to describe all types of power in social production; and (3) the organization of professional activities to be inclusionary, cooperative, and non-authoritarian rather than exclusionary, competitive, and authoritarian. But this reworking of power has implications not only for sociological practice. More generally, it provides a basis for feminist social critique; ultimately action must be judged by whether it fosters domination or empowerment.

CONCLUSION

The present and near-future work of feminist sociologists focuses on a critical reworking of the foundations of sociology: its model of society, its investigative procedures, its modes of conceptualization, and its relationship to the task of societal transformation. Perhaps at some more distant point in time feminist sociologists will begin to chart their interface with and linkages to the prevailing traditions in sociology. But presently, feminist sociological theory is still running with the excitement of the feminist discovery described by philosopher Sandra Harding (1986, 251): "I don't think that in our wildest dreams we ever imagined that we would have to reinvent both science and theorizing itself in order to make sense of women's social experience."

NOTES

1. Feminist sociologists are reworking most of the established fields of sociology, e.g., the history of the discipline (Deegan 1988), complex organizations (Kanter 1977), the family (Thorne and Yalom 1982). They are also contributing to the interest in new fields in the profession, e.g., the sociology of the emotions (Chodorow 1978; Hochschild 1983). Instead of exploring some of these developments, we select the five themes listed in this paragraph because they address the foundations of a feminist sociological theory: the politics that will affect this theory's acceptance into the discipline, and the fundamental issues of the theory's model of society, its methodological stance, its vocabulary, and the value base from which it practices its work of critique.

2. An extensive bibliography on feminism and feminist sociology is to be found in Lengermann and Niebrugge-Brantley 1988. Our referencing strategy for this paper has four parts: 1) brief listings of exemplary statements on issues covered by this paper, as for example the list of statements on feminist theory preceding the indication of note 2; 2) obviously, acknowledgment of works quoted or closely paraphrased; 3) occasional reference to very recent, "state-of-the-art work" published since the bibliography in Lengermann and Niebrugge-Brantley 1988; and 4) a general recommendation that readers interested in a fuller reference structure consult that bibliograhy.

3. While we hold to the theoretical stance advanced here that feminist sociological theory in substance and at its best transcends the macro-micro split, we ac-

knowledge that we are limited by the lack of an alternative vocabulary for describing the interface between lived experience and societal organization. At times in this paper we therefore are forced back to a vocabulary based on macro-micro analysis in order to approximate a rough description of social life.

REFERENCES

Barry, Kathleen. 1979. *Female Sexual Slavery.* Englewood Cliffs, N.J.: Prentice-Hall.

Benjamin, Jessica. 1985. "The Bonds of Love: Rational Violence and Erotic Domination." In Eisenstein and Jardine, eds., *The Future of Difference.*

Berch, Bettina. 1982. *The Endless Day: The Political Economy of Women and Work.* New York: Harcourt Brace Jovanovich.

Bernard, Jessie. 1981. *The Female World.* New York: Free Press.

Bernard, Jessie. 1987. *The Female World in a Global Perspective.* Bloomington: Indiana University Press.

Bernard, Jessie. 1989. "The Feminist Enlightenment." Manuscript.

Boulding, Elise. 1976. *The Underside of History.* Boulder, Colo.: Westview Press.

Brownmiller, Susan. 1975. *Against Our Will: Men, Women and Rape.* New York: Simon and Schuster.

Chodorow, Nancy. 1978. *The Reproduction of Mothering: Psychoanalysis and Sociology of Gender.* Berkeley: University of California Press.

Collins, Randall. 1985a "Sociology as Oz." *The Insurgent Sociologist* 10:33–57.

Collins, Randall. 1985b. *Three Sociological Traditions: A Book of Readings.* New York: Oxford University Press.

Cook, Judith, and Mary Margaret Fonow. "Knowledge and Women's Interests." *Sociological Inquiry* 56:2–29.

Daly, Mary. 1968. *The Church and the Second Sex.* New York: Harper and Row.

Daly, Mary. 1978. *Gyn/Ecology: The Meta Ethics of Radical Feminism.* Boston: Beacon Press.

Deegan, Mary Jo. 1988. *Jane Addams and the Men of the Chicago School, 1889–1918.* Rutgers, N.J.: Transaction Books.

de Beauvoir, Simone. 1957. *The Second Sex.* New York: Vintage.

de Vault, Marjorie. 1988. "Writing for Women: Textual Strategies in Sociology." Paper presented at the meetings of the Mid-Atlantic National Women's Studies Association.

Dinnerstein, Dorothy. 1976. *The Mermaid and the Minotaur.* New York: Harper and Row.

Donovan, Josephine. 1985. *Feminist Theory: The Intellectual Traditions of American Feminism.* New York: Unger.

Ehrenreich, Barbara. 1986. *The Hearts of Men.* New York: Harper and Row.

Ehrenreich, Barbara, and Annette Fuentes. 1987. "The Global Assembly Line." In Paul J. Baker and Lewis E. Anderson, eds., *Social Problems: A Critical Thinking Approach.* Belmont, Cal.: Wadsworth.

Eisenstein, Hester. 1985. "Introduction." In Eisenstein and Jardine, eds., *The Future of Difference.*

Eisenstein, Hester, and Alice Jardine, eds. *The Future of Difference.* New Brunswick, N.J.: Rutgers University Press.

Farganis, Sondra. 1986. "Social Theory and Feminist Theory: The Need for Dialogue." *Sociological Inquiry* 56:50–68.

French, Marilyn. 1985. *Beyond Power: On Women, Men, and Morals.* New York: Summit.

Friedan, Betty. 1963. *The Feminine Mystique.* New York: Dell.
Gilligan, Carol. 1982. *In a Different Voice: Psychological Theory and Women's Development.* Cambridge, Mass.: Harvard University Press.
Glazer, Nona. 1976. "Housework." *Signs* 1:905–922.
Glennon, Lynda M. 1979. *Women and Dualism.* New York: Longman.
Greer, Germaine. 1979. *The Obstacle Race: The Fortunes of Women Painters and Their Work.* New York: Farrar, Straus and Giroux.
Griffin, Susan. 1978. *Women and Nature: The Roaring Within Her.* New York: Harper and Row.
Haraway, Donna. 1988. "Situated Knowledges: The Science Question in Feminism and the Privilege of Partial Perspective." *Feminist Studies* 14:575–600.
Harding, Sandra. 1986. *The Science Question in Feminism.* Ithaca, N.Y.: Cornell University Press.
Hartsock, Nancy. 1983. *Money, Sex and Power: Towards a Feminist Historical Materialism.* New York: Longman.
Heilbrun, Carolyn. 1988. *Writing a Woman's Life.* New York: Norton.
Hochschild, Arlie. 1982. *The Managed Heart: Commercialization of Human Feeling.* Berkeley: University of California Press.
Hochschild, Arlie. 1983. "Attending to, Codifying and Managing Feelings: Sex Differences in Love." In Laurel Richardson and Verta Taylor, eds., *Feminist Frontiers: Rethinking Sex, Gender and Society.* New York: Random House.
Hooks, Bell. 1984. *Feminist Theory: From Margin to Center.* Boston: South End Press.
Hooks, Bell. 1989. *Talking Back: Thinking Feminist, Thinking Black.* Boston: South End Press.
Jaggar, Alison M. 1983. *Feminist Politics and Human Nature.* Totowa, N.J.: Rowman and Allenheld.
Janeway, Elizabeth. 1980. *The Powers of the Weak.* New York: Morrow Quill Paperbacks.
Jayaratne, Toby Epstein. 1983. "The Value of Quantitative Methodology for Feminist Research." In Gloria Bowles and Renate Duelli Klein, eds., *Theories of Women's Studies.* London: Routledge and Kegan Paul.
Kanter, Rosabeth Moss. 1977. *Men and Women of the Corporation.* New York: Basic Books.
Kasper, Anne. 1988. "Women with Breast Cancer: A Feminist Analysis." Ph.D. dissertation, George Washington University.
Keller, Evelyn Fox. 1983. *A Feeling for the Organism: The Life and Work of Barbara McClintock.* New York: Freeman.
Keller, Evelyn Fox. 1985. *Reflections on Gender and Science.* New Haven: Yale University Press.
Kristeva, Julia. 1986. *The Kristeva Reader.* Edited by Toril Moi. New York: Columbia University Press.
Kuhn, Thomas. 1962. *The Structure of Scientific Revolutions.* Chicago: University of Chicago Press.
Lengermann, Patricia M., and Jill Niebrugge-Brantley. 1988. "Contemporary Feminist Theory." In George Ritzer, *Sociological Theory.* 2d ed. New York: Knopf.
Lengermann, Patricia M., and Ruth A. Wallace. 1985. *Gender in America: Social Control and Social Change.* Englewood Cliffs, N.J.: Prentice-Hall.
Lenski, Gerhard. 1966. *Power and Privilege: The Theory of Social Stratification.* New York: McGraw-Hill.
Lorber, Judith. 1988. "From the Editor." *Gender and Society* 2:5–8.
Lorde, Audre. 1984. *Sister Outsider.* Trumansburg, N.Y.: Crossings Press.
MacKinnon, Catherine. 1982. "Feminism, Marxism, Method and the State: An

Agenda for Theory." In Nammerl D. Keohane et al., eds., *Feminist Theory: A Critique of Ideology*. Chicago: University of Chicago Press.

Matthaei, Julie A. 1982. *An Economic History of Women in America: Women's Work, the Sexual Division of Labor, and the Development of Capitalism*. New York: Schocken.

Mead, George H. 1934. *Mind, Self and Society*. Chicago: University of Chicago Press.

Merton, Robert K. 1957. "On Manifest and Latent Functions." In Robert Merton, *Social Theory and Social Structure*. New York: Free Press.

Mies, Maria. 1983. "Towards a Methodology for Feminist Research." In Gloria Bowles and Renate Duelli Klein, eds., *Theories of Women's Studies*. London: Routledge and Kegan Paul.

Mitchell, Juliet. 1975. *Psychoanalysis and Feminism*. New York: Vintage.

Oakley, Ann. 1981. "Interviewing Women: A Contradiction in Terms." In H. Roberts, ed., *Doing Feminist Research*. London: Routledge and Kegan Paul.

Palmer, Phyllis. 1988. "Syllabus for Feminist Theory." George Washington University.

Rajan, Rajeswari Sunder, and Zakia Pathak. 1989. "Shabano." *Signs*, forthcoming.

Reinharz, Shulamit. 1983. "Experiential Analysis: A Contribution to Feminist Research." In Gloria Bowles and Renate Duelli Klein, eds., *Theories of Women's Studies*. London: Routledge and Kegan Paul.

Rich, Adrienne. 1976. *Of Woman Born: Motherhood as Experience and Institution*. New York: Bantam.

Rich, Adrienne. 1980. "Compulsory Heterosexuality and Lesbian Existence." In Catherine Stimpson and Ethel Spector Person, eds., *Women, Sex, and Sexuality*. Chicago: University of Chicago Press.

Ritzer, George. 1988. "Appendix: Metatheory and a Metatheoretical Schema for Analyzing Sociological Theories." In George Ritzer, *Sociological Theory*. 2d ed. New York: Knopf.

Rollins, Judith. 1985. *Between Women: Domestics and their Employers*. Philadelphia: Temple University Press.

Rubin, Lillian. 1976. *Worlds of Pain*. New York: Basic Books.

Ruddick, Sara. 1980. "Maternal Thinking." *Feminist Studies* 6:342–367.

Schutz, Alfred. 1967. *The Phenomenology of the Social World*. Evanston, Ill.: Northwestern University Press.

Schutz, Alfred, and Thomas Luckmann. 1973. *The Structure of the Life World*. Evanston, Ill.: Northwestern University Press.

Scully, Diana. 1980. *Men Who Control Women's Health: The Miseducation of Obstetrician-Gynecologists*. Boston: Houghton-Mifflin.

Scully, Diana. 1986. Presentation at the Feminist Roundtable in Honor of Dorothy E. Smith, George Mason University, Fairfax, Va.

Seager, Joni, and Ann Olson. 1986. *Women in the World*. New York: Simon and Schuster.

Smith, Barbara. 1983. "Notes for Yet Another Paper on Black Feminism, or Will the Real Enemy Please Stand Up." In Laurel Richardson and Verta Taylor, eds., *Feminist Frontiers: Rethinking Sex, Gender and Society*. New York: Random House.

Smith, Dorothy E. 1979. "A Sociology for Women." In Julia Sherman and Evelyn Torton-Beck, eds., *The Prism of Sex: Essays in the Sociology of Knowledge*. Madison: University of Wisconsin Press.

Smith, Dorothy E. 1987. *The Everyday World as Problematic*. Boston: Northeastern University Press.

Smith, Dorothy E. Research in progress on the interface of gender, class, and race stratification.

Smith, Dorothy E., and Alison Griffith. 1985. "Coordinating the Uncoordinated:

344 Patricia M. Lengermann and Jill Niebrugge-Brantley

How Women Manage the School Day." Paper presented at the Annual Meetings of the American Sociological Association, Washington, D.C.

Snitow, Ann et al. 1982. *Powers of Desire: The Politics of Sexuality.* New York: Monthly Review Press.

Spalter-Roth, Roberta. 1986. Presentation at the Feminist Roundtable in Honor of Dorothy E. Smith, George Mason University, Fairfax, Va.

Spender, Dale, ed. 1981. *Men's Studies Modified: The Impact of Feminism on Academic Disciplines.* New York: Pergamon Press.

Stacey, Judith, and Barrie Thorne. 1985. "The Missing Feminist Revolution in Sociology." *Social Problems* 32:301–316.

Stanton, Donna. 1985. "Language and Revolution: The Franco-American Disconnection." In Eisenstein and Jardine, eds., *The Future of Differences.*

Stimpson, Catherine. 1979. "The Power to Name: Some Reflections on the Avant-Garde." In Julia Sherman and Evelyn Torton-Beck, eds., *The Prism of Sex: Essays in the Sociology of Knowledge.* Madison: University of Wisconsin Press.

Thorne, Barrie, and Marilyn Yalom, eds. 1982. *Rethinking the Family: Some Feminist Questions.* New York: Longman.

Warner, Marina. 1976. *Alone of All Her Sex.* New York: Random House.

Weber, Max. 1979. *Selections in Translation.* Edited by W. C. Runciman; translated by Eric Matthews. Cambridge: Cambridge University Press.

III

OVERVIEWS OF
SOCIAL AND
SOCIOLOGICAL THEORY

❁

13

Micro-Macro Linkage in Sociological Theory: Applying a Metatheoretical Tool

❄

GEORGE RITZER
University of Maryland

In a recent essay (Ritzer 1988) I sought to delineate the parameters of one broad type of metatheorizing (the systematic study of the underlying structure of sociological theory) which seeks to attain a deeper understanding of sociological theory.[1] The goal of the present paper is to illustrate what this type of metatheorizing, or at least one of its subtypes (internal-intellectual),[2] has to offer in terms of understanding developments, problems, and prospects in sociological theory. The internal-intellectual type leads one to look within sociology itself and to focus on cognitive factors within the field. There are a number of varieties of internal-intellectual metatheory (e.g., looking for the basic paradigms within sociology), but the one employed in this paper will examine recent developments in sociological theory utilizing one of the basic internal-intellectual metatheoretical "tools"[3]—the micro-macro continuum.[4]

Metatheoretical tools provide us with the means to make sense of a wide range of seemingly disparate theoretical developments. For example, Parsons (1937) did this implicitly when he used "voluntarism"[5] as a tool to ferret out of the diverse and wide-ranging bodies of work produced by Marshall, Weber, Durkheim, and Pareto convergence on a theory of action.[6] Similarly, utilization of the micro-macro instrument will allow us to examine a wide range of contemporary theories and to see, among other things, that after decades of micro-macro theoretical extremism, there has been a dramatic rebirth of concern with micro-macro linkages.[7] In some cases the theorists explicitly utilize the micro-macro terminology, in others the theorists use very different terms, and in still others the theorists vehemently oppose the use of such

I would like to thank Shanyang Zhao, Sherry Reiriz, and especially Ken Kammeyer for helpful comments on earlier drafts of this paper.

terms and of such an orientation. One of the things that this paper will show is that whether they use micro-macro terminology, other terminology, or even appear to oppose the use of such terms (and apparently oppose such an orientation), a wide range of theorists *are* converging on the micro-macro linkage issue.[8]

However, the main interest in this paper will not be to simply describe this situation, but rather to use the micro-macro instrument to analyze these developments and to show that there has already emerged major new threats to theoretical progress on the linkage issue. The fundamental assumption behind this evaluative work is that an integrative theory must give reasonably equal weight to micro and macro phenomena. Theories will be criticized, even if their intent is integrative, if they overemphasize either end of the continuum. The paper will also offer some ideas on what needs to be done in the future in theoretical work on the micro-macro linkage.

I am *not* implying that *all* theories must give rough equivalence to micro and macro phenomena. There is certainly a role for macro and micro theories; indeed sociology has been dominated by such theories. However, there is *also* a place for theories that deal in a truly integrated manner with the two ends of the continuum. There is great lure in the micro and macro extremes and theories seeking integration must be wary of them lest they degenerate into simple variants of micro or macro theories.

A review of the corpus of sociological theory reveals that the micro-macro tool encompasses two only partially related components. On the one hand, one can set about integrating micro (e.g., symbolic interactionism) and macro (e.g., structural functionalism) *theories*. On the other, one can develop a theory that deals in an integrated manner with micro (e.g., personality) and macro (e.g., society) *levels of social analysis*. We will encounter both types of works in this paper as well as those which attempt to do both things simultaneously.

Among those sociologists who focus on levels of social analysis,[9] there is a broadly accepted tendency to equate the micro level with the empirical reality of the individual in everyday life and the macro with social reality or the social world. This is the *sociological conception* of the micro-macro continuum and, even though we will see later that there are problems with its looseness, we will use it to orient this paper, at least at the beginning.

There is also a very attractive, *general conception*[10] that argues that micro and macro do not describe empirical realities, but are rather analytic concepts that can be used to analyze any empirical reality. Alexander (1987, 290–291) (and neo-Parsonians in general) is a strong advocate of this position: "There can be no empirical referents for micro or macro as such. They are analytical contrasts, suggesting emergent levels within empirical units themselves. . . . The terms 'micro' and 'macro' are completely relativistic. What is macro at one level will be micro at another." While it is certainly useful to employ the terms "micro" and "macro" analytically, the fact is that most sociologists use these terms empirically.

This is not the first effort to use the micro-macro tool to analyze sociological theory. For example, in the mid-1960s Helmut Wagner (1964) dealt with the relationship between small-scale and large-scale theories. At the end of the decade Walter Wallace (1969) utilized the micro-macro continuum, but it occupied a secondary role in his analysis and was included as merely one of the "complications" of his basic taxonomy of sociological theory. In the mid-1970s Kemeny (1976) called for greater attention to the micro-macro distinction as well as to the ways in which micro and macro relate to one another. Kemeny (1976, 731) concluded at the time that so "little attention is given to this distinction that the terms 'micro' and 'macro' are not commonly even indexed in sociological works."

However, in the 1980s we have witnessed a growth in metatheoretical work on the micro-macro linkage issue. Collins (1986, 1350) has argued that work on this topic "promises to be a significant area of theoretical advance for some time to come."[11] In their introduction to a two-volume set of books, one devoted to macro theory (Eisenstadt and Helle 1985a) and the other to micro theory (Helle and Eisenstadt 1985), Eisenstadt and Helle (1985b, 3) conclude that "the confrontation between micro- and macro-theory belong[s] to the past."[12] Similarly, Munch and Smelser (1987, 385), in their conclusion to the anthology *The Micro-Macro Link* (Alexander et al.1987), assert that "those who have argued polemically that one level is more fundamental than the other . . . must be regarded as in error. Virtually every contributor to this volume has correctly insisted on the mutual interrelations between micro and macro levels."

Things have changed dramatically in the last decade not only in metatheory, but also in theory where a great deal of attention has been devoted, explicitly and implicitly, to the micro-macro issue. We will shortly turn to an interpretation of theoretical work in the 1980s from a micro-macro perspective, but first we need to provide a brief historical backdrop for these recent developments.

Although it is possible to interpret (and many have) the classic sociological theorists (e.g., Marx, Weber, Durkheim, Simmel, Mead, etc.) as either macro or micro extremists, the most defensible perspective, or at least the one that will orient this paper, is that they were most generally concerned with the micro-macro linkage. If we accept this characterization, then it appears that the half-century of sociological theory ending about 1980 involved a loss of a concern for this linkage[13] and the dominance of macro and micro extremists. Among the most notable of the twentieth-century macro extremists are the later Parsons (1966), his "cultural determinism,"[14] and the structural functionalism he helped institutionalize; Dahrendorf's (1959) conflict theory which aligned itself with structural functionalism as a macro extremist position;[15] and Peter Blau's (1977, x) macrostructuralism epitomized by his proud announcement, "I am a structural determinist." Macro structural extremism comes from other sources as well (Rubinstein 1986) including network theorists like White, Boorman, and Breiger (1976), ecologists like Duncan and Schnore (1959), and structuralists like Mayhew (1980).[16] Few are more extreme than Mayhew (1980, 349) who says such things as: "In structural sociology the unit of analysis is always the social network, *never the individual.*"

On the micro extreme side we can point to a good portion of symbolic interactionism and the work of Blumer (1969) who often seemed to have structural functionalism in mind as he positioned symbolic interactionism as a sociological theory single-mindedly concerned with micro-level phenomena. An even clearer case of micro extremism is exchange theory and George Homans (1974) who sought an alternative to structural functionalism and found it in the extreme micro orientation of Skinnerian behaviorism. Then there is ethnomethodology and its concern for the everyday practices of actors. Garfinkel (1967) was put off by the macro foci of structural functionalism and its tendency to turn actors into "judgmental dopes."

While micro-macro extremism has characterized much of twentieth-century sociological theory, it has been possible in the 1980s to discern a movement away from micro-macro extremism and toward a broad consensus that *the* focus instead should be on *the integration (or linkage) of micro and macro theories and/or levels of social analysis.*[17] It could be argued that at least in this sense sociological theorists have rediscovered the theoretical project of the early masters.

The efforts at micro-macro integration have a broad base of support and stem from a wide variety of theoretical directions.[18] This wide and deep base of support is important because it, like the relative youthfulness of most of its advocates, bodes well for the future of such theoretical efforts. Had they been derived from a single source, or a limited number of sources, one would be much less sanguine about their future chances of success.

On the other hand, even though they are seeking to overcome it, these efforts at integration have been shaped and distorted by the history of twentieth-century micro-macro extremism. Most sociologists working toward integration come at it from bases in either extreme micro or macro theories and these bases often serve as straitjackets that limit integrative efforts. Although this is a serious problem, there are some signs that it is being overcome.

While many of the works in the body of contemporary micro-macro theoretical work do not explicitly address this linkage, the use of the micro-macro tool allows us to see the commonality in their work. From the micro theoretical end there is Hechter's (1983a, 1983b, 1987; Friedman and Hechter 1988; see also Wippler and Lindenberg 1987) effort based on rational choice theory; Collins' (1981a, 1987a, 1987b) attempt which focuses on "interactional ritual chains"; the largely social psychological efforts of the participants at the 1979 Symposium on Consciousness, Human Action and Structure (Secord 1982); the micro side of the 1983 Symposia on Macro and Micro Sociological Analysis (Helle and Eisenstadt 1985), Coleman's (1986, 1987) effort to move toward the system level from an action base, Boudon's (1979, 1987; see also Wippler and Lindenberg 1987) "methodological individualism" which, in spite of its name, does try to integrate actors and systems;[19] efforts (e.g., by Kurzweil 1987; Smelser 1987) to build toward the macro level from a Freudian base; Schegloff's (1987) work on an ethnomethodological/conversational analysis base as well as similar work by Knorr-Cetina (1981) and Cicourel (1981); and Emerson's (1981) integrative work stemming from an exchange theory orientation.[20] Coming more from the macro theoretical end are Habermas' (1984, 1987) attempt, strongly influenced at least originally, by Marxian dialectical theory; Alexander's (1982, 1987, 1988) multidimensional work stemming from a structural functional base as well as Munch's (1987) neo-Parsonian effort; the macro side of the 1983 Symposia on Macro and Micro Sociological Analysis (Eisenstadt and Helle, 1985a); Luhmann's (1987) systems theory approach; and Burt's (1982) integrative effort rooted in macro-oriented network theory. There are also overtly integrative works without an apparent prior commitment to the macro or micro end of the continuum. Included in this latter category are Giddens' (1984) "structuration" theory, Bourdieu's (1977) work on "habitus," Ritzer's (1981) "integrated sociological paradigm," Hindess' (1986) effort to deal with actors and social relations and, in the process, to avoid the extremes of "theoretical humanism" and "structuralism," and Fararo and Skvoretz's (1986) attempt to integrate network theory and the social-psychological expectation states theory. Thus, efforts are coming from both macro and micro directions and from a variety of theoretical positions within and between each. In general, we can say that whether they start with a macro or a micro base, or with an integrative orientation, many sociological theorists seem to be converging in their efforts to develop an integrated theory. As we begin the 1990s, there is now enough work on the micro-macro linkage to begin to take stock of where we stand in this body of work and where we ought to be headed in the near future.

TAKING STOCK OF WORK ON
MICRO-MACRO INTEGRATION

One of the major difficulties to this point on micro-macro integration is a fundamental (and dimly understood) split among those working on the issue. Some focus on integrating macro and micro *theories*,[21] while others see it as a problem of developing a theory that deals with the linkage between micro and macro existential *levels* (Edel 1959; Alford and Friedland 1985; Wiley 1988; Ritzer 1989) of social analysis. Earlier in this paper, for example, we quoted Eisenstadt and Helle (1985b, 3) who concluded that the confrontation between micro and macro *theories* was behind us, while in contrast Munch and Smelser (1987, 385) came to a similar conclusion about the need to choose between emphasizing either micro or macro *levels*. There are important differences between trying to integrate macro (e.g., structural functionalism) and micro (e.g., symbolic interactionism) theories and attempting to develop a theory that can deal with the relationship between macro (e.g., social structure) and micro (e.g., personality) levels of social analysis. There is a tendency to slip back and forth between these two types of work and to encompass them under the broad heading of micro-macro integration. At the minimum we should be aware that these involve different kinds of work and that the relationship between them needs to be specified.

Among those who define it, at least in part, as a problem of integrating theories are Burt (1982), Fararo and Skvoretz (1986), Hechter (1983b), Hindess (1986), and Smelser (1987). On the other side are those who define the task primarily in terms of developing a theory that focuses on integrating micro and macro levels of existential analysis, including Alexander (1982), Boudon (1979, 1987), Coleman (1986), Collins (1981a), Giddens (1984), Munch (1987), Wiley (1988), and Ritzer (1981). Gerstein (1987, 86) offers a good example of the latter approach when he distinguishes between the two basic levels of analysis and then argues for the need "to create theoretical concepts that translate or map variables at the individual level into variables characterizing social systems, and vice versa." A pressing need in the work on macro-micro integration is a delineation of the relationship between these two literatures.

In addition, there are substantial differences within the groups working toward theoretical integration and integration of levels of social analysis. Among those seeking to integrate micro and macro theories there are important differences depending on which specific theories are being integrated. For example, Hindess (1986) sought to avoid the extremes of "theoretical humanism" and "structuralism"; Hechter (1983b) pitted rational choice theory against normative and structural theories; Burt (1982) tried to bridge the schism between atomistic and normative orientations; Fararo and Skvoretz (1986) endeavored to integrate structural theory and expectation states theory; and Smelser (1987) sought to synthesize psychoanalytic and sociological perspectives. Two major questions need to be dealt with by those working in this area. First, how do efforts at integrating very different pairs of theories relate to one another? Second, how does each of these theoretical efforts contribute to our understanding of the linkages between levels of social analysis?

There are similar differences among the theorists seeking to deal with the relationship between micro and macro levels of social analysis. For example, are they seeking to integrate micro and macro structures, micro and macro processes, or more specific aspects of the micro and macro levels of social analysis? More specifically, differences in levels are reflected in Giddens' (1984, 25) structuration theory which focuses on "the structural properties of social systems [as] both medium and outcome of the practices they recursively organize"; Alexander's (1982, 65) multidimensional sociology involving an "alternation of freedom and constraint" in both action and order; Ritzer's (1981) integrated paradigm focusing on the dialectical interrelationship of macro objectivity and subjectivity and micro objectivity and subjectivity; Wiley's (1988) effort to deal with the relationships among four "levels" —self, interaction, social structure, and culture; Collins' (1981) focus on "interaction ritual chains"; Coleman's (1986) interest in the relationship between action and system, Boudon's (1981) *homo sociologicus* which integrates intentional agent and structural context; and Munch's (1987, 320) work on the "interrelation between microinteraction and macrostructures." How do these efforts at dealing with very different elements of the social world relate to one another and contribute to our broader understanding of macro-micro integration in the social world? In addition, what is the relationship between this kind of work and the previously discussed attempts at theoretical integration?

While there is a tendency for theorists to focus on either integrating theories *or* levels of analysis, a major exception (and a potential model for those who seek to do both) is Jürgen Habermas (1984, 343) who has devoted at least some of his attention to the theoretical problem of "integrating action theory and systems theory." In the process of working on theoretical integration he has differentiated existentially between the life world (a more micro-level world where "participants in communication come to an understanding with one another about something" [Habermas 1984, 337]) and the social system and its subsystems.[22] This distinction between life world and social system must be made, and the two examined independently, otherwise theoretical integration "can lead, as it did with Parsons, to a systems-theoretic absorption of action theory" (Habermas 1984, 343). Obviously, Habermas does not want macro-level systems theory to overwhelm action theory and, as a result, develops an approach which seeks to integrate the two. Habermas (1987, 1) does even more theoretical integration in his recent examination of the work of "Mead with his communication-theoretic foundation of sociology" and "Durkheim with a theory of social solidarity connecting social integration and system integration."

The task of empirical integration is made even more difficult because there are great differences among sociologists in terms of what they define as the micro and macro levels (Munch and Smelser 1987). Depending on who is offering the definition, the micro level can range from psychological phenomena, to individuals, to interaction patterns among individuals. The macro level ranges from positions, to population, to society and its structures, to world systems. Thus, seemingly similar views about integrating micro and macro levels are, in fact, quite dissimilar because they are integrating very different social phenomena. As a basic requisite, theorists working with the terms micro and macro should clearly define what they mean by each.

Furthermore, even though like-sounding terms may be used by sociologists at the micro level (psychological characteristics, action, behavior, practices, intentional agent, micro objectivity and subjectivity, interaction, life world, etc.) and the macro level (structural context, system, population, positions, macro objectivity and subjectivity, structural properties of social systems, society, culture), there are in fact often substantial differences among these phenomena. For example, at the micro level, those who see behavior as produced by rewards and costs tend to have a very different sense of the social world than those who are concerned with action produced by intentional agents. Similarly, there are substantial differences between those who work at the macro level with population structures and those who focus on culture. Thus, we need to do more than simply carefully define our terms; we also need to spell out the theoretical implications of the kinds of terms we use at both levels.

Perhaps the major problem in the body of work devoted to the micro-macro issue stems from the fact that given the history of micro-macro extremism, most theorists working on the linkage question start at either the micro or macro end and work toward integration. Starting at one end or the other, the theorist often does not do full justice to the entire micro-macro continuum.

Kemeny (1976) labeled one stance on the micro-macro issue the cumulative position in which one begins at the micro end and builds up from there. Hechter takes this position theoretically by arguing *for* (micro) rational choice theory and *against* macro theories. Coleman's (1986) work, given its action theory roots, seems much stronger on the micro levels. Furthermore, Coleman (1987) expresses a highly limited interest in the "micro-to-macro" problem, but does not express a parallel interest in the "macro-to-micro" problem. Emerson seeks to move to the macro levels, but he is hampered by the micro concerns of his base in exchange theory. Boudon's "methodological individualism" seems aptly named since it does emphasize the importance of the actor. As he recently put it, "explaining any phenomenon . . . amounts to showing that it is the outcome of actions" (Boudon 1987, 55). Wippler and Lindenberg (1987) adopt a similar point of view in according theoretical primacy to the individual. Haferkamp (1987) begins with complex meaningful action and builds toward the intentional and unintentional creation of macro structures.

Many integrationists who begin their efforts at the micro level tend to overemphasize that domain rather than giving equal weight to the macro levels, even though they claim to be seeking integration. A notable example of this is Collins who, although he claims to be dealing with the micro-macro connection, sees macrostructures as nothing more than repeated microencounters. Collins labels his approach "radical microsociology" and seeks to show how "all macro-phenomena" can be translated "into combinations of micro-events" (Collins 1981a, 985). In other words, Collins (1981b, 82) wants to "reconstitute macrosociology upon radically empirical micro-foundations." In a later essay Collins (1987a, 195) argues, "Macrostructure consists of nothing more than large numbers of microencounters, repeated (or sometimes changing) over time and across space." He concludes, unashamedly: "This may sound as if I am giving a great deal of prominence to the micro. That is true" (Collins 1987a, 195). However, in his most recent work on the issue, Collins (1988) seems to be moving toward a conception that gives the macro level greater significance. I will return to this work later in the chapter.

Another microextremist is Schegloff (1987, 229). Writing from an ethnomethodological, and specifically conversational analysis (CA), perspective, Schegloff (1987, 229) implies that sociology "takes the understanding of human action as its goal." He seems dubious about the macro level and micro-macro linkage: "It is not clear how the kind of microanalysis CA does (if it *is* microanalysis) is to be related to macro-level theorizing or whether it should be" (Schegloff 1987, 209).

The other major current integrative approach is to start at the macro levels and build down. The best example is Alexander (1982, 1987; *see also* many of the essays in Eisenstadt and Helle 1985a). Alexander (1987, 295) believes that according privilege to the micro level is "a theoretical mistake." He is highly critical of all theories (e.g., symbolic interactionism) that begin at the micro levels with non-rational voluntary agency and build toward the macro levels. From his point of view, the problem with these theories is that while retaining notions of individual freedom and voluntarism, they are unable to deal with the unique (sui generis) character of collective phenomena. He is also critical of theories (e.g., exchange theory) that begin with rational action and link it to material structures like the economy. On the macro side, Alexander criticizes "collectivist, rationalist," materialist theories (e.g., economic and structural determinism) that emphasize coercive order and eliminate individual freedom.

While he expresses an interest in the relationship among all four levels (individualist–non-rational; individualist-rational; collectivist-rationalist; collectivist–non-rationalist [normative]), Alexander's priority (not surprisingly given his Parsonian and structural-functional sympathies) lies with the "collectivist, normative" position. As he puts it, "The hope for combining collective order and individual voluntarism lies within the normative, rather than the rationalist tradition" (Alexander 1982, 108). Central to this is the view (the faith?) that because the sources of order are internal rather than external, voluntarism is maintained along with order. In addition, Alexander (1985, 27) argues that an individualist perspective ends up with "randomness and complete unpredictability" rather than order. Again, Alexander (1985, 28, italics added) is quite explicit about this: "The general framework for social theory can be derived *only* from a collectivist perspective." To him, social theorists must choose either a collectivist or an individualist perspective. If they choose a collectivist theory, they can incorporate a "relatively small" element of individual negotiation. If, however, they choose an individualist theory, they are doomed to the "individualist dilemma" of trying to sneak into their theory supraindividual phenomena to deal with the randomness inherent in their theory. This dilemma can only be resolved "if the formal adherence to individualism is abandoned" (Alexander 1985, 27).

In spite of a number of promising leads, Alexander gives inordinate significance to macro (subjective) phenomena, and as a result his contribution to the development of a theory of micro-macro integration is highly limited. (However, it should be said that in his more recent work Alexander [1987], like Collins, has expressed a more balanced integrative perspective and I will have more to say about it shortly. The movement toward greater balance by prominent macro and micro extremists augurs well for the future of micro-macro integration.)

While not directly addressing Alexander's work, Giddens (1984) comes to the conclusion that *all* work derived from the Parsonian distinction between action and order inevitably ends up weak at the micro level, especially on "the knowledgeability of social actors, as constitutive in part of social practices. I [Giddens] do not think that *any* standpoint which is heavily indebted to Parsons can cope satisfactorily with this issue at the very core of social theory" (Giddens 1984, xxxvii).

While efforts emanating from one end of the micro-macro continuum or the other (and most efforts discussed in this paper have done just that) are useful beginnings and not to be rejected out of hand, a commitment to start theorizing at either end limits our understanding of integration and tends to lead toward a repetition of sociological extremism of one kind or the other. Alexander (1987, 314) implies a similar criticism: "I believe theorists falsely generalize from a single variable to the immediate reconstruction of the whole." While we might welcome all efforts at micro-macro integration, it would appear that a starting point different from either the micro or the macro end would likely be more successful. I will discuss this type of work later in this chapter.

COPING WITH THE STRAINS TOWARD THE MACRO OR MICRO EXTREMES

As we have seen, perhaps the most troubling issue now facing advances in our understanding of the micro-macro linkage is the fact that major tensions have already surfaced among those oriented to the development of an integrated approach. Given the fact that most people working on this issue have been shaped by the history of micro-macro extremism in sociology, some integrationists are tugging in a micro direction while others are pulling the other way. Thus they threaten to undermine the nascent effort at integration and to repeat *within* the integrative approach the largely unnecessary tension between micro and macro orientations that has dominated sociological theory in the twentieth century. In this section we will look at some ways of avoiding this problem.

One less than wholly satisfactory solution is for macro-oriented theorists to focus on micro-level issues and micro-oriented theorists to work at the macro levels. Three good examples of this are Alexander's (1987) focus (coming from macro-level neofunctionalism) on such micro-level processes as typification, strategization, and invention; Fine's (1988) effort to delineate (from a micro-level symbolic interactionist perspective) the "obdurate reality" of the built environment, institutional linkages, tradition, and beliefs in organizational primacy; and Collins' (1988) attempt to give greater weight to macro-level phenomena.[23] It is highly beneficial to the development of an integrated micro-macro approach for theorists to focus on the empirical realities that are on the opposite end of the continuum from their theoretical orientations. The major problem is the tendency for theorists to allow their theoretical biases to affect their work at the other end of the social continuum.

More promising are efforts at integrating macro and micro theories by those who are not apparently predisposed to one or the other (e.g., Hindess, Fararo and Skvoretz). While a lack of commitment (Mitroff 1974) may make such works more evenhanded, they may suffer from theorists' lack of intimate knowledge of, and devotion to, the theoretical perspectives they are working with.

Another possibility would involve starting at neither the micro nor the macro levels, but rather somewhere in the middle of the social continuum, on what has been termed the "meso level" in the study of formal organizations (Hage 1980) and the study of negotiated order by symbolic interactionists (Maines 1982). There are problems involved in meso-level perspectives. If one focuses at the meso level (formal organizations, negotiated order) can one adequately get at, and deal effectively with, macro-level phenomena? At the same time, it can also be asked whether such a meso-level focus allows one to be sufficiently microscopic? Meso-level analyses have yet to demonstrate the ability to be satisfactorily integrative.

A promising direction involves focusing on ongoing relationships between the micro and macro levels. Munch and Smelser (1987) have offered some useful beginnings here, but since their ideas are drawn from work influenced by micro-macro extremism, it shows again how easily we can move in either an extreme micro or macro direction. The useful part of their essay involves a discussion of the linkages between micro and macro; the focus is on relationships rather than the micro or macro extreme. Among these relationships they discuss aggregation; externalization; creating, sustaining, reproducing the macro; conformity; internalization and limit setting. A focus on these relational processes helps us move away from micro-macro extremism and is inherently integrative. However, Munch and Smelser divide these processes into micro-to-macro and macro-to-micro categories thereby tending, once again, to reflect the strain toward micro-macro extremism.

A much more promising alternative is to reject a focus on *any* level (micro, meso, macro) of analysis and adopt instead an inherently integrative, dialectical approach. Despite my criticisms above of Alexander's collectivistic bias, there are signs in his recent work of the development of such an inherently integrative position, one that defines macro and micro in terms of one another. Here is the way Alexander (1987, 303) expresses this perspective: "The collective environments of action simultaneously inspire and confine it. If I have conceptualized action correctly, these environments will be seen as its products; if I can conceptualize the environments correctly, action will be seen as their result." I think that Alexander is moving toward a much more complex, dialectical sense of the micro-macro nexus. Similarly, Collins (1988, 244), although he still gives inordinate significance to the micro level,[24] has developed a more balanced approach in his most recent work: "The micro-macro translation shows that everything macro is composed out of micro. Conversely, anything micro is part of the composition of macro; it exists in a macro context . . . it is possible to pursue the micro-macro connection fruitfully in either direction."

However, the most promising efforts thus far at developing a dialectical approach to micro-macro integration are Giddens' (1984) "structuration theory,"[25] and Bourdieu's focus on "habitus."[26] Giddens (1984, 2) defines structuration theory in inherently integrative terms: "The basic domain of the study of the social sciences, according to the theory of structuration, is neither the experience of the individual actor, nor the existence of any form of societal totality, but social practices ordered across time and space." Structuration is premised on the idea that "the constitution of agents and structures are not two independently given sets of phenomena, a dualism, but represent a duality . . . the structural properties of social systems are both medium and outcome of the practices they recursively organize"; or "the moment of the production of action is also one of reproduction in the contexts of the day-to-day enactment of social life" (Giddens 1984, 25, 26). Structure is not external to the actor, it exists in both memory traces and social practices. Moving away from the Durkheimian sense of structure as constraining, Giddens (1984, 25, italics added) makes the crucial point that structure "is *always* both constraining and enabling." However, actors can lose control over the "structured properties of social systems" as they stretch away in time and space, but such a loss of control is not inevitable.

Similarly, Bourdieu (1977, 3) seeks to avoid the extremes of objectivism and subjectivism in his effort to develop "a science of the *dialectical* relations between the objective structures . . . and the structured dispositions within which those structures are actualized and which tend to reproduce them," or the *"dialectic of the internalization of externality and the externalization of internality."* At the heart of this dialectic is habitus which is neither objectively determined nor the product of subjective intentionality. Habitus is defined as "systems of durable, transposable *dispositions"* (Bourdieu 1977, 72) that are produced by objective structures and conditions, but are capable of producing and reproducing those structures. "As an acquired system of generative schemes objectively adjusted to the particular conditions in which it is constituted, the habitus engenders all the thoughts, all the perceptions, and all the actions consistent with those conditions, and no others" (Bourdieu 1977, 95). Thus, Bourdieu's notion of habitus avoids the deterministic and free will extremes and offers us a dialectical sense of the relationship between micro and macro levels of social reality.

What Giddens and Bourdieu have done (and Alexander and Collins have begun to do), and I think must be done if we are to avoid a repeat of micro-macro extremism, is to redefine the linkage issue and focus on it relationally and dialectically rather than dichotomously. The focus of integrationists should be on the relationship and not on the micro or macro ends of the social continuum. Given the macro or micro biases of extant theories, this means that we are going to need to create new theories (perhaps by combining parts of a number of existing theories) and that is precisely what Giddens and Bourdieu appear to be doing.

Giddens' inclusion of the time factor in his analysis brings us to another continuing issue in the work on micro-macro integration—the effort to make it dynamic rather than static; interested in social change rather than ahistorical structure. The key point here is that work on micro-macro integration can easily degenerate into static descriptions of unchanging, ahistorical realities. However, Giddens and Collins, among others, have explicitly sought to add a time dimension to the analysis of micro-macro linkages. Like Giddens, Collins is interested in time in addition to spatial issues. As Collins (1981, 987) puts it: "Micro and macro are relative terms in both time and space." Given the difficulties in defining macro, micro, and their interrelationship, it is clear that adding a time dimension complicates enormously what is already a daunting problem. Nevertheless, it seems clear that the future development of micro-macro theory depends on its ability to work with both temporal and spatial variables.

MICRO-MACRO INTEGRATION: WORK TO BE DONE

While the various forms of micro and macro extremism are far from dead, and even likely to enjoy periodic resurgences, it is safe to say that integrative micro-macro work is now well established in sociology and likely to remain an attractive alternative into the foreseeable future. In fact, it is likely to attract more adherents in the future because it is being advanced by some of the best young theorists in the field, it is stemming from a wide variety of theoretical directions, it represents a rediscovery of an orientation that lay at the base of the work of the discipline's classic theorists,[27] and because it is a vast and complex area that offers many challenges to sociological theorists.

A decade ago Kemeny (1976, 747) argued that "[w]hat is first needed is increasing awareness of the problem of scope so that positions are not taken unwittingly and implicitly." Given recent developments, it is doubtful that present and future sociologists will be able to operate without a sense of the issue of scope in their work. In other words, it is now unlikely that sociologists will ignore scale or unwittingly take a position on this issue.

In spite of this emerging consensus there is much to be done. First, much of the work that is needed on the micro-macro linkage has to do with specifying in much greater detail the nature of what is at the moment only a very general orientation. Many of those working on this general issue are, in fact, focusing on very different things. They have different senses of what they mean by micro phenomena, macro phenomena, and the linkages between them. Careful definitions are required and theorists need to address conceptual differences between their work on this issue and that of others. Much more work is needed of the type undertaken by Markovsky (1987) in specifying the conditions that affect the relative significance of micro- and macro-level phenomena.

Second, while there is obviously great need to continue to extend work on the micro-macro linkage, additional work is also needed *within* the micro and macro domains. That is, there is still a need for sociologists to focus their attention on micro or macro issues, thereby extending knowledge of those domains. The emergence of a focal concern with the micro-macro linkage does not preclude work on a given level. Even the keenest advocates of a focus on micro-macro linkages do not see it as becoming the sole focus of sociology. In fact, advances in our knowledge of the micro and macro levels can serve to enrich work on micro-macro integration.

Third, while there is need for further work within the micro and macro domains, care must taken to ensure that the still immature effort at micro-macro integration is not overwhelmed by reinvigorated supporters of micro and/or macro extremism. There are, at the same time as there is an increasing focus on micro-macro integration, some very powerful theoretical forces pulling sociology away from this central problem and in the direction of micro or macro extremism. Concomitant with the emergence of a theoretical consensus is the existence and emergence of theoretical perspectives which are threatening that consensus before it is even solidified. In this category are either extreme micro-oriented theories that deny or downplay the existence and significance of macro-level phenomena as well as extreme macro-level theories that deny or minimize the role of micro-level phenomena. There are also some very powerful sociologists overtly arguing *against* the possibility of micro-macro integration. One such voice is that of Peter Blau (1987b, 87) who, by his own admission, has changed his mind on this issue since the publication of his (1964) integrative effort within exchange theory:

> An important issue in constructing macrosociological theory is the linkage with microsociological theory. One approach is to start with microsociological principles and use these as the foundation for building macrosociological theory. The alternative approach rests on the assumption that different perspectives and conceptual frameworks are necessary for micro and macro theories, primarily because the major terms of macrosociological theories refer to emergent properties of population structures that have no equivalent in microsociological analysis. *I have come to the conclusion that the second approach is the only viable one, at least at this stage of sociological development.* (italics added)

Thus, while we have made the case for a growing focus in sociology on micro-macro integration, it is clear that such an orientation is far from universal and has some very powerful opponents.

Fourth, perhaps a greater danger lies in the extremists *within* the group working on micro-macro integration. We have in mind here macro-end extremists like Alexander (at least in his earlier work) and micro-end extremists like Collins (although he, too, seems to be moving toward a more balanced perspective). They threaten to tear apart this intellectual movement before it has a chance to develop fully. We must be wary of recreating extremism within the micro-macro camp.

Fifth, there is great need to clarify the relationship between efforts at integrating micro and macro theories and those aimed at developing a theory that deals with the integration of micro and macro levels of social analysis. Our thinking on this relationship is most likely to be advanced by more efforts that seek to bring together theoretical and empirical efforts.

Sixth, additional work is needed on the relationship between the micro-macro continuum and the various other continua (e.g., methodological individualism-holism) that have been used to analyze the social world. Particularly promising are those efforts at integrating the micro-macro and objective-subjective continua. Also worth doing is an analysis of the relationship between micro-macro and agency-structure. Throughout this paper I have subsumed work on agency-structure (e.g., by Giddens) under the micro-macro heading, but the fact is that there are significant differences between these conceptualizations. Agency is usually micro, but may be macro. Structure is usually macro, but may be micro. Micro usually indicates agency, but may include mindless behavior. Macro usually means structure, but may refer to culture.

Seventh, this highly abstract metatheoretical work needs to be translated into terms and approaches that are accessible to sociologists interested in concrete empirical and theoretical questions. In other words, it needs to be transformed into ideas, concepts, tools, theories, and methods that can be used by sociologists in their professional activities. A welcome recent example of this is Calhoun's (1988) effort to use Habermas' distinction between social system and life world to analyze political efforts at democratization.

Finally, there is a need for more methodologists and empirical researchers to address the micro-macro issue which to this time has been largely dominated by theorists. Some welcome signs in these areas are Bailey's (1987) work on macro-micro methods, Markovsky's (1987) experimental efforts, and Marini's (1987, 45) criticism of gender research for studying macro-level phenomena with micro-level data.

As we move into the 1990s it is likely that there will be a subtle, yet crucially important, shift in work on micro-macro integration. Up to this point, given the micro and macro extremism of much of twentieth-century sociology, those who have dealt with the issue have come at it from either the micro or the macro end of the continuum. As micro-macro integration becomes widely accepted as a central theoretical problem, the focus will shift to more inherently integrative orientations. Among the promising directions are the works that integrate micro and macro theories without being predisposed to either, the focus on the micro level from a macro theoretical orientation (and vice versa), work at the meso level, interest in the ongoing relationships between macro and micro, and most promising of all the work (e.g., Giddens, Bourdieu, Alexander's and Collins' later statements) that defines micro and macro in terms of one another, thereby focusing on an ongoing dialectic (Ritzer 1981). These types of work, especially the latter, promise to move thinking on micro-macro integration to a new level, a level in which the emphasis will be on *integration* or *synthesis*, rather than on the macro or micro poles of the social continuum. This is in line with the view expressed by Alexander and Giesen (1987, 37) who argue for the need for "establishing a radically different starting point" in order to make "a genuinely inclusive micro-macro link." Since virtually all extant theories are primarily either macro or micro perspectives, such a shift in emphasis will lead to the need for the creation of new theories (or new combinations of several old theories) primarily attuned to such integrative concerns. Most generally, we are likely to move away from a concern for micro and macro levels and/or theories and in the direction of more synthetic existential interests and theoretical efforts.

NOTES

1. I label this type *metatheorizing as an effort to achieve a deeper understanding of theory*. It, like the other two main types, is defined by its end product, in this case a deeper understanding of theory. The second type, *metatheorizing as a prelude to theory development*, seeks to create new sociological theory. The third type, *metatheorizing in order to create an overarching theoretical perspective*, is aimed at the production of an orientation that transcends sociological theory.

2. The other three types are internal-social, external-intellectual, and external-social.

3. Other tools are "levels of analysis," "action-order," "objective-subjective," etc.

4. While the use of the terms micro and macro sometimes appears as if we are dealing with a dichotomy, we are always aware of the fact that there is a *continuum* ranging from the micro to the macro end.

5. As well as "positivism" and "idealism," although negatively.

6. Parsons' work also shows the danger of this kind of metatheoretical endeavor since he is often accused of distorting the work of the masters in order to demonstrate convergence on *his* theoretical orientation. Metatheoretical tools can, and should, be used to understand theory without distorting it.

7. This is clearly evidenced by the fact that two sessions at the 1988 American Sociological Association meetings were devoted to this theme and, most importantly, micro-macro integration was *the* theme of the 1989 ASA meetings.

8. While this paper will focus on the micro-macro linkage issue in sociological theory, it should be made clear that there is much more to all of these theories than a concern for this relationship. Thus, while it will be shown later that a broad consensus emerged in the 1980s on the focus on micro-macro linkage, this similar concern far from exhausts the similarities (and differences) of these theories. There are clearly many substantive differences (and similarities) and the use of other metatheoretical tools (e.g., objective-subjective) would show a wide array of additional similarities and differences.

9. An interesting metatheoretical concern is the relationship between the more

broadly defined issue of "levels of analysis" (e.g., Ritzer 1981; Wiley 1988; Ritzer 1989) and the more specific micro-macro issue.

10. This conception is not only usable by sociologists, but also by those in a wide range of fields.

11. Collins devotes only a few lines to the issue in the context of a broader discussion of current trends in sociology.

12. However, by creating separate macro and micro volumes, Eisenstadt and Helle have done more to heighten the split than to develop an integrated approach.

13. Coleman (1986, 1313) argues that a similar loss occurred in empirical research with the shift toward micro-oriented survey research. This raises the issue of the need for a paper parallel to this one dealing with methods and whether a similar trend in the 1980s toward macro-micro integration is occurring there as well.

14. Even as sympathetic an observer as Alexander (1987, 296) admits Parsons' "own collectivist bias"; *see also* Coleman (1986, 1310). However, while Parsons' greatest influence was in collectivistic theory, it is also possible to find within his work a strong micro-macro integrative theory.

15. Coleman (1986, 1312) also makes this point: "Subsequent challenges to functionalism (the principal one being 'conflict theory') have acquiesced in remaining at the collective or systemic level, thus failing to provide a theory grounded in the purposive action of individuals." I would, however, disagree with Coleman in his characterization of conflict theory as the principal challenge to structural functionalism. Conflict theory and structural functionalism are best seen as paradigmatic partners and the principal discipline-wide challenges to functionalism have long come from the micro-theories (e.g., symbolic interactionism, ethnomethodology, exchange theory) associated with other paradigms (Ritzer 1975, 1980).

16. Interestingly, Rubenstein (1986, 87) argues that even structural extremists end up with an integrated perspective because "elements of culture and consciousness are theoretically excluded and then smuggled back in through substantive concepts."

17. This is slightly stronger than the position taken by Alexander and Giesen (1987, 1) who argue that the micro-macro problem "has emerged as *a* key issue in contemporary sociological theory" (italics added).

18. We will focus only on the major works on the macro-micro linkage in this discussion, but many others can be subsumed under this heading: Rossi's (1983) "dialectical conception of structure and subjectivity"; Shalin's (1986) dialectical sense of symbolic interactionism; Thomason's (1982, 161) effort within the context of an analysis of Schutzian theory to develop a conception of reification based on a "positive bridging of the constructionist/realist divide"; Markovsky's (1985) multi-level justice theory and his effort to deal with the macro-micro link experimentally (Markovsky 1987); Swidler's (1986) analysis of culture as a "tool kit" of habits, etc., out of which actors construct strategies for dealing with social reality; Hilbert's (1986, 15) effort to integrate Durkheim's macro-level theory of anomie with the "reality construction tradition, particularly ethnomethodology"; Haines' (1985, 70) effort to reorient ecology (inspired by the integrative work of Giddens, Collins, and Burt) away from a macro-level orientation and toward "a relational methodology which views social phenomena as both causes and consequences of individual phenomena"; Hayes', (1985) attempt to integrate "causal and interpretive analyses"; Hekman's (1983, 14) analysis of Weber's ideal-type methodology in which she sees him as having "effected a synthesis between the analysis of subjective meaning and the analysis of structural forms"; Podgorecki and Los' (1979) "multi-dimensional sociology"; Kreps' (1985, 50) effort to use the Alexander-inspired "dialectical relationship between social action and social order"; and a similarly oriented paper by Bosworth and Kreps (1986).

19. Coleman (1986) also sees himself as a methodological individualist endeavoring to build a more integrated theory.

20. Cook (1987a) says of Emerson's approach: "it can provide one coherent, systematic basis for building a theory of social structure and structural change that is not devoid of actors and the microprocesses that generate and modify these structures."

21. Yet to be dealt with adequately is the issue of whether at least some of these theories are incommensurable and therefore impossible to integrate. There are some (Gergen and Gergen 1982; Bhaskar 1982, 285) who argue against the possibility of theoretical integration and their position needs to be considered by those who are working on such integration.

22. We do not want to go too far here in our praise for Habermas' two-pronged effort. On the existential side, it is clear that his micro (lifeworld) and macro (social system) levels are highly abstract and theoretical. In spite of his effort to be both theoretical and empirical, it could easily be argued that Habermas is not nearly empirical enough. Given his philosophical orientation, this would not be a difficult argument to defend.

23. Still another example is Friedman and Hechter's (1988) effort to deal with macro-level phenomena from a base in micro-level rational choice theory.

24. For example, he still sees the "big challenge" in showing "how micro affects macro" (Collins 1988, 244).

25. Giddens (1984, 139) directly addresses the micro-macro issue and explains why he does not use those more familiar terms rather than ideas like "social and system integration." First, he feels that macro and micro are often pitted against one another and he does not believe "that there can be any question of either having priority over the other" (Giddens 1984, 139). Second, even when there is no conflict, "an unhappy division of labour tends to come into being between them" (Giddens 1984, 139). That is, theories like symbolic interactionism tend to focus on the activities of free actors while theories like structural functionalism devote their attention to structural constraint. In the end, Giddens (1984, 141, italics added) concludes that "the micro/macro *distinction* is not a particularly useful one." The key point here is that a rigid distinction between micro and macro is *not* useful, but their integration *is*, as Giddens himself demonstrates. The view in this chapter is that we need not jettison macro-micro terminology since rigid distinctions between them, and between theories that deal with them, are *not* inherent in the use of the terminology.

26. My own work (Ritzer 1979, 1981) on an integrated sociological paradigm is also of this genre; *see also* Wiley (1988).

27. It is also likely that we will witness a rethinking of the work of the master theorists in light of these developments. It is likely that that there will be much more emphasis on the integrative character of their work.

REFERENCES

Alexander, Jeffrey C. 1982. *Theoretical Logic in Sociology. Volume I. Positivism, Presuppositions, and Current Controversies.* Berkeley: University of California Press.

Alexander, Jeffrey C. 1985. "The 'Individualist Dilemma' in Phenomenology and Interactionism." In Eisenstadt and Helle, eds., *Macro-Sociological Theory.*

Alexander, Jeffrey C. 1987. "Action and Its Environments." In Alexander et al., eds., *The Micro-Macro Link.*

Alexander, Jeffrey C. 1988. *Action and Its Environments: Toward a New Synthesis.* New York: Columbia University Press.

Alexander, Jeffrey C., and Bernhard Giesen. 1987. "From Reduction to Linkage: The Long View of the Micro-Macro Link." In Alexander et al., eds., *The Micro-Macro Link.*

Alexander, Jeffrey C. et al., eds. 1987. *The Micro-Macro Link.* Berkeley: University of California Press.

Alford, Robert R., and Roger Friedland. 1985. *Powers of Theory: Capitalism, the State, and Democracy.* Cambridge: Cambridge University Press.

Bailey, Kenneth D. 1987. "Globals, Mutables, and Immutables: An Alternative Approach to Micro/Macro Analysis." Paper presented at the meetings of the American Sociological Association, Chicago.

Bealer, Robert C. 1979. "Ontology in American Sociology: Whence and Whither?" In William E. Snizek, Ellsworth R. Fuhrman, and Michael K. Miller, eds., *Contemporary Issues in Theory and Research.* Westport, Conn.: Greenwood Press.

Bhaskar, Roy. 1982. "Emergence, Explanation, and Emancipation." In Secord, ed., *Explaining Human Behavior.*

Blau, Peter. 1964. *Exchange and Power in Social Life.* New York: Wiley.

Blau, Peter. 1977. *Inequality and Heterogeneity: A Primitive Theory of Social Structure.* New York: Free Press.

Blau, Peter. 1987a. "Contrasting Theoretical Perspectives." In Alexander et al., eds., *The Micro-Macro Link.*

Blau, Peter. 1987b. "Microprocess and Macrostructure." In Cook, ed., *Social Exchange Theory.*

Blumer, Herbert. 1969. *Symbolic Interaction: Perspective and Method.* Englewood Cliffs, N.J.: Prentice-Hall.

Bosworth, Susan Lovegren, and Gary A. Kreps. 1986. "Structure as Process: Organization and Role." *American Sociological Review* 51:699–716.

Boudon, Raymond. 1979. *The Logic of Social Action: Introduction to Sociological Analysis.* London: Routledge and Kegan Paul.

Boudon, Raymond. 1987. "The Individualistic Tradition in Sociology." In Alexander et al., eds., *The Micro-Macro Link.*

Bourdieu, Pierre. 1977. *Outline of a Theory of Practice.* Cambridge: Cambridge University Press.

Burt, Ronald. 1982. *Toward a Structural Theory of Action: Network Models of Social Structure.* New York: Academic Press.

Calhoun, Craig. 1988. "Populist Politics, Communications Media and Large Scale Societal Integration." *Sociological Theory* 6:219–241.

Cicourel, Aaron. 1981. "Notes on the Integration of Micro- and Macro-Levels of Analysis." In Knorr-Cetina and Cicourel, eds., *Advances in Social Theory and Methodology.*

Coleman, James. 1986. "Social Theory, Social Research, and a Theory of Action." *American Journal of Sociology* 91:1309–1335.

Coleman, James. 1987. "Microfoundations and Macrosocial Behavior." In Alexander et al., eds., *The Micro-Macro Link.*

Collins, Randall. 1981a. "On the Microfoundations of Macrosociology." *American Journal of Sociology* 86:925–942.

Collins, Randall. 1981b. "Micro-Translation as a Theory-Building Strategy." In Knorr-Cetina and Cicourel, eds., *Advances in Social Theory and Methodology.*

Collins, Randall. 1986. "Is 1980s Sociology in the Doldrums?" *American Journal of Sociology* 91:1336–1355.

Collins, Randall. 1987a. "Interaction Ritual Chains, Power and Property: The Micro-Macro Connection as an Empirically Based Theoretical Problem." In Alexander et al., eds., *The Micro-Macro Link.*

Collins, Randall, 1987b. "A Micro-Macro Theory of Intellectual Creativity: The Case of German Idealistic Philosophy." *Sociological Theory* 5:47–69.

Collins, Randall. 1988. "The Micro Contribution to Macro Sociology." *Sociological Theory* 6:242–253.

Cook, Karen S. 1987a. "Emerson's Contributions to Social Exchange Theory." In Cook, ed., *Social Exchange Theory.*

Cook, Karen S., ed. 1987b. *Social Exchange Theory.* Beverly Hills, Cal.: Sage.

Dahrendorf, Ralph. 1959. *Class and Class Conflict in Industrial Society.* Stanford, Cal.: Stanford University Press.

Duncan, O. D., and L. F. Schnore. 1959. "Cultural, Behavioral and Ecological Perspectives in the Study of Social Organization." *American Journal of Sociology* 65:132–146.

Edel, Abraham. 1959. "The Concept of Levels in Sociological Theory." In L. Gross, ed., *Symposium on Sociological Theory.* Evanston, Ill.: Row Peterson.

Eisenstadt, S. N., and H. J. Helle, eds. 1985a. *Macro-Sociological Theory: Perspectives on Sociological Theory.* Vol. 1. London: Sage.

Eisenstadt, S. N., and H. J. Helle. 1985b. "General Introduction to Perspectives on Sociological Theory." In Eisenstadt and Helle, eds., *Macro-Soiological Theory.*

Emerson, Richard. 1981. "Social Exchange Theory." In Morris Rosenberg and Ralph H. Turner, eds., *Social Psychology: Sociological Perspectives.* New York: Basic Books.

Fararo, Thomas J., and John Skvoretz. 1986. "E-State Structuralism: A Theoretical Method." *American Sociological Review* 51:591–602.

Fine, Gary Alan. 1988. "On the Macrofoundations of Microsociology: Meaning, Order, and Comparative Context." Paper presented at the meetings of the American Sociological Association, Atlanta.

Friedman, Debra, and Michael Hechter. 1988. "The Contribution of Rational Choice Theory to Macrosociological Research." *Sociological Theory* 6:201–218.

Garfinkel, Harold. 1967. *Studies in Ethnomethodology.* Englewood Cliffs, N.J.: Prentice-Hall.

Gergen, Kenneth J., and Mary M. Gergen. 1982. "Explaining Human Conduct: Form and Function." In Secord, ed., *Explaining Human Behavior.*

Gerstein, Dean. 1987. "To Unpack Micro and Macro: Link Small with Large and Part with Whole." In Alexander et al., eds., *The Micro-Macro Link.*

Giddens, Anthony. 1984. *The Constitution of Society: Outline of the Theory of Structuration.* Berkeley: University of California Press.

Habermas, Jürgen. 1984. *The Theory of Communicative Action. Vol. 1. Reason and the Rationalization of Society.* Boston: Beacon Press.

Habermas, Jürgen. 1987. *The Theory of Communicative Action. Vol. 2. Lifeworld and System: A Critique of Functionalist Reason.* Boston: Beacon Press.

Haferkamp, Hans. 1987. "Complexity and Behavior Structure, Planned Associations, and Creation of Structure." In Alexander et al., eds., *The Micro-Macro Link.*

Hage, Jerald. 1980. *Theories of Organization.* New York: Wiley.

Haines, Valerie. 1985. "From Organicist to Relational Human Ecology." *Sociological Theory* 3:65–74.

Hayes, Adrian. 1985. "Causal and Interpretive Analysis in Sociology." *Sociological Theory* 3:1–10.

Hechter, Michael. 1983a. "Introduction." In Michael Hechter, ed., *The Microfoundations of Macrosociology.* Philadelphia: Temple University Press.

Hechter, Michael. 1983b. "A Theory of Group Solidarity." In Michael Hechter, ed., *The Microfoundations of Macrosociology.* Philadelphia: Temple University Press.

Hechter, Michael. 1987. *Principles of Group Solidarity.* Berkeley: University of California Press.

Hekman, Susan. 1983. *Weber, the Ideal Type, and Contemporary Social Theory.* South Bend, Ind.: University of Notre Dame Press.

Helle, H. J., and S. H. Eisenstadt, eds. 1985. *Micro-Sociological Theory: Perspectives on Sociological Theory.* Vol. 2. London: Sage.

Hilbert, Richard A. 1986. "Anomie and Moral Regulation of Reality: The Durkheimian Tradition in Modern Relief." *Sociological Theory* 4:1–19.

Hindess, Barry. 1986. "Actors and Social Relations." In Mark L. Wardell and Stephen P. Turner, eds., *Sociological Theory in Transition.* Boston: Allen and Unwin.

Homans, George. 1974. *Social Behavior: Its Elementary Forms.* Rev. ed. New York: Harcourt Brace Jovanovich.

Kemeny, Jim. 1976. "Perspectives on the Micro-Macro Distinction." *Sociological Review* 24:731–752.

Knorr-Cetina, Karen D. 1981. "Introduction: The Micro-Sociological Challenge of Macro-Sociology: Towards a Reconstruction of Social Theory and Methodology." In Knorr-Cetina and Cicourel, eds., *Advances in Social Theory and Methodology.*

Knorr-Cetina, Karen D., and Aaron Cicourel, eds. 1981. *Advances in Social Theory and Methodology.* New York: Methuen.

Kreps, Gary A. 1985. "Disaster and the Social Order." *Sociological Theory* 3:49–64.

Kurzweil, Edith. 1987. "Psychoanalysis as the Macro-Micro Link." In Alexander et al., eds., *The Micro-Macro Link.*

Luhmann, Niklas. 1987. "The Evolutionary Differentiation between Society and Interaction." In Alexander et al., eds., *The Micro-Macro Link.*

Maines, David. 1982. "In Search of Mesostructure: Studies in the Negotiated Order." *Urban Life* 11:267–279.

Marini, Margaret M. 1987. "Sex and Gender." In Edgar F. Borgatta and Karen S. Cook, eds., *The Future of Sociology.* Beverly Hills, Cal.: Sage.

Markovsky, Barry. 1985. "Multilevel Justice Theory." *American Sociological Review* 50:822–839.

Markovsky, Barry. 1987. "Toward Multilevel Sociological Theories: Simulations of Actor and Network Effects." *Sociological Theory* 5:101–117.

Mayhew, Bruce H. 1980. "Structuralism versus Individualism: Part I. Shadowboxing in the Dark." *Social Forces* 59:335–375.

Mitroff, Ian. 1974. "Norms and Counter-Norms in a Select Group of Apollo Moon Scientists: A Case Study of the Ambivalence of Scientists." *American Sociological Review* 39:579–595.

Munch, Richard, 1987. "The Interpenetration of Microinteraction and Macro-structures in a Complex and Contingent Institutional Order." In Alexander et al., eds., *The Micro-Macro Link.*

Munch, Richard, and Neil Smelser. 1987. "Relating the Micro and Macro." In Alexander et al., eds., *The Micro-Macro Link.*

Parsons, Talcott. 1937. *The Structure of Social Action.* New York: Free Press.

Parsons, Talcott. 1966. *Societies.* Englewood Cliffs, N.J.: Prentice-Hall.

Podgorecki, Adam, and Maria Los. 1979. *Multi-Dimensional Sociology.* London: Routledge and Kegan Paul.

Ritzer, George. 1975. *Sociology: A Multiple Paradigm Science.* Boston: Allyn and Bacon.

Ritzer, George. 1979. "Toward an Integrated Sociological Paradigm." In William Snizek, Ellsworth R. Fuhrman, and Michael K. Miller, eds., *Contemporary Issues in Theory and Research.* Westport, Conn.: Greenwood Press.

Ritzer, George. 1980. *Sociology: A Multiple Paradigm Science.* Rev. ed. Boston: Allyn and Bacon.

Ritzer, George. 1981. *Toward an Integrated Paradigm: The Search for an Exemplar and an Image of the Subject Matter.* Boston: Allyn and Bacon.

Ritzer, George. 1988. "Sociological Metatheory: Defending a Subfield by Delineating Its Parameters." *Sociological Theory* 6:187–200.

Ritzer, George. 1989. "Of Levels and 'Intellectual Amnesia.' " *Sociological Theory*, forthcoming.

Rossi, Ino. 1983. *From the Sociology of Symbols to the Sociology of Signs.* New York: Columbia University Press.

Rubinstein, David. 1986. "The Concept of Structure in Sociology." In Mark L. Wardell and Stephen P. Turner, eds., *Sociological Theory in Transition.* Boston: Allen and Unwin.

Schegloff, Emanuel. 1987. "Between Macro and Micro: Contexts and Other Connections." In Alexander et al., eds., *The Micro-Macro Link.*

Secord, Paul F., ed. 1982. *Explaining Human Behavior: Consciousness, Human Action and Social Structure.* Beverly Hills, Cal.: Sage.

Shalin, Dmitri. 1986. "Pragmatism and Social Interactionism." *American Sociological Review* 51:9–29.

Smelser, Neil. 1987. "Depth Psychology and the Social Order." In Alexander et al., eds., *The Micro-Macro Link.*

Swidler, Ann. 1986. "Culture in Action: Symbols and Strategies." *American Sociological Review* 51:273–286.

Thomason, Burke C. 1982. *Making Sense of Reification: Alfred Schutz and Constructionist Theory.* Atlantic Highlands, N.J.: Humanities Press.

Wagner, Helmut. 1964. "Displacement of Scope: A Problem of the Relationship Between Small-Scale and Large-Scale Sociological Theories." *American Journal of Sociology* 69:571–584.

Wallace, Walter. 1969. "Overview of Contemporary Sociological Theory." In Walter Wallace, ed., *Sociological Theory.* Chicago: University of Chicago Press.

White, H. C., S. A. Boorman, and R. L. Breiger. 1976. "Social Structure from Multiple Networks: Parts 1 and 2." *American Journal of Sociology* 81:730–780; 1384–1446.

Wiley, Norbert. 1988. "The Micro-Macro Problem in Social Theory." *Sociological Theory* 6:254–261.

Wippler, Reinhard, and Siegwart Lindenberg. 1987. "Collective Phenomena and Rational Choice." In Alexander et al., eds., *The Micro-Macro Link.*

14

The Past, Present, and Future of Theory in American Sociology

❊

JONATHAN H. TURNER
University of California at Riverside

What is the current state and future prospects of sociological theory in America? To answer such a question requires a criterion for evaluation, a yardstick by which to measure present work and to assess future prospects. My yardstick is science, or the currently unfashionable presumption that sociology can develop universal abstract laws and assess these laws through systematic empirical tests. In using this particular yardstick, I immediately fall "out of step" with many currents in sociological theory today and, sadly, in the future. Yet, even though much of what passes for "theory" has no, or very little, relevance to science and to the cumulation of knowledge, there is some basis for optimism, not for theory in general but for that small group of theorists who presume that sociology can be a natural science.

Not only do we require a yardstick of evaluation, but it is also desirable to have the perspective of time. To appreciate the current state and future prospects of theory, then, I think it wise to have a sense of where theory began in America and what it has been doing for the nine decades of this century. We will see that, in a very real sense, sociological theory has increasingly abandoned its early faith in scientific sociology.

EARLY THEORY: 1890–1920

Early American sociologists were decidedly Comtean in their beliefs (Comte 1830–1842). There was a perceived consensus that a science of society, to borrow Radcliffe-Brown's (1948) phrase, was possible and desirable. Moreover, there was a presumption that discovery of the laws of human organization could be used for the progressive betterment of

371

society. To some extent, as had been the case for Comte, this position was taken as a tack for legitimating sociology in a hostile intellectual environment, but much more was involved. For despite their many differences, sociologists *really believed* that sociology could emulate the natural sciences; and as a result, there was considerable intellectual integration during sociology's early period, from 1890 through World War I. And the basis of this integration was the development of general laws about basic social processes. As Roscoe Hinkle (1980, 267) notes:

> It was, indeed, general theory which was believed to confer academic respectability on the discipline and to prevent the field from "degenerating" into mere practical amelioration of social problems. General theory . . . sought to discover the first principles, causes, and laws of the origin, structure, and change of human association, human society, or social phenomena generically and irrespective of variant, particular, idiosyncratic, or unique forms. . . . All special (or specialized sociology or sociologists) were assumed to begin from, contribute, and eventually return to general sociology or general theory.

What, then, was the nature of such general theory? The most decisive influence was Herbert Spencer, a scholar scarcely read today in comparison with the holy European trio of Marx, Weber, and Durkheim. These later giants of the modern era were hardly noticed by early American theorists whose work represents a blending of Comte's positivism with Spencer's organicism and individualism in a uniquely American combination.

While continental European sociologists became skeptical of Comte's and Spencer's advocacy of the development of laws about the social universe, American sociologists embraced the idea that patterns of social organization could be studied scientifically. They wanted sociology to be a respectable science; and they devoted considerable space in their texts arguing for Comte's position. To be a Comtean, however, posed a very severe problem: Comte did not have a theory of human organization, save for a few rather imprecise analogies between organisms and society (e.g., "society is like an organism" and can be analyzed in terms of the contribution of parts to the "body social"). Early American sociologists were thus drawn to Herbert Spencer and, to a lesser extent, the German Albert Schaeffle. Spencer was particularly appealing for several reasons. First, Spencer adopted the Comtean view that the goal of sociology, indeed of philosophy in general, was the discovery of abstract laws and principles. Second, Spencer fine-tuned Comte's organismic analogizing and converted it into a much more precise analysis of basic processes that "functioned" to meet the needs of the social organism (Schaeffle took this line of argument to the extreme, seeking exact analogies of biological functions of bodies in the "social body"). Third, Spencer was an evolutionary thinker, although not of the crude unilineal and ethnocentric variety (i.e., society is progressing toward the Anglo-Saxon ideal) that proliferated in the latter half of the nineteenth century. But, since evolutionary thinking was so prominent in biology, it was a useful legitimating strategy to conceptualize societies in evolutionary terms—population density, struggle and competition, and "speciation" or "specialization" into differentiated systems. At the same time, this Darwinian image of speciation was reconciled with organicism—functional integration of differentiated parts into a coherent whole, or "body social." Thus, the borrowing of ideas from biology, via Spencer and his monumental *The Principles of Biology* (1864–1867) and *The Principles of Sociology* (1874–1896), occurred at two levels: the ecological/demographic level where populations, environments, and niches were of central concern; and the organismic level where the mechanisms and processes for integrating, coordinating, regulating, and controlling system wholes were of concern. Fourth, in his moral philosophy, Spencer (1892–1898, 1850) was an individualist, arguing for the rights of individuals to do as they please as long as they do not harm others. Such liberalism and individualism—what might be called "libertarian" today—were highly appealing to American sociologists who, from the beginning, were interested in the behaviors of individuals as an essential ingredient of sociological analysis. While this micro focus was to stand in contrast and contradiction to the macro evolutionism and organicism of much early American theory, it posed no great problem for early theorists, just as it had not created undue agonizing for Spencer.

What emerges in early American sociology, then, is a commitment to science that seeks to develop abstract general theory and, at the same time, to reconcile individualism and mentalism with evolutionism, organicism, and implicit functionalism. Yet the seeds of controversy were evident in these early theories, creating a situation where American theory began to differentiate into three distinctive strains. One is the continuation of Spencer's evolutionary approach in the work of William Graham Sumner and later Albert Keller. Their four volume *The Science of Society* (Sumner and Keller 1927) represents the culmination of this tradition (we should note that Sumner's [1907] famous *Folkways* was originally intended to be part of *The Science of Society*, but Sumner got carried away and published it as a separate book). *The Science of Society* was initiated in 1899, but Sumner's declining health forced him to take on his former student, Albert Keller, to complete the project. Owing to this early beginning and to Sumner's commitment to many Spencerian ideas, *The Science* looks very much like

Spencer's *The Principles of Sociology*. It is filled with ethnographic and historical data; it explores both primitive and advanced patterns of social organization; and it covers almost every conceivable topic as it traces the unfolding (what today we would call "differentiation") of ever more complex forms of social organization.

A second prominent approach of early American sociological theory is best personified by Charles Horton Cooley (1909, 263), who admitted that "nearly all of us who took up sociology between 1870, say and 1890, did so at the instigation of Spencer." But Cooley (1909, 266) was quick to add that Spencer's major flaw was his "defect of sympathy" and his tendency to conceptualize "the structure of human life . . . (as) phenomena almost wholly by analogy." For Cooley (1909, 269) "the organic wholes of the social order are mental facts of much the same nature as personality, and much the same kind of sympathetic imagination is needed to grasp them." Social organization must be conceptualized, therefore, in terms of the mental processes that allow actors to create a "sense of common sympathy" or a "common spirit" from their face-to-face interactions (Cooley 1909). Cooley's ideas were, of course, to be extended considerably by George Herbert Mead and modern interactionism, but the key point is that within Spencer's broad evolutionary and organismic view, a much more mentalistic and, in general, micro sociology was being spawned in America.

Between the more macro evolutionary approach of Sumner and Keller on the one side, and the micro sociology of Cooley on the other, were a variety of intermediate approaches which accepted the organismic view of social structure and, at the same time, stressed the importance of interpersonal sympathy and consciousness as crucial dynamics by which organic wholes are sustained. This more intermediate position is best represented by the work of Franklin Giddings. For example, Giddings' *Readings in Descriptive and Historical Sociology* (1906) best captures the duality of his approach. Much of the early part of the book describes in macro evolutionary terms various societies; it shifts to a more analytical discussion of population, patterns of group organization, and processes of homogeneity and differentiation of groups; next, "the social mind" is explored for several hundred pages; and finally, the book closes with a return to more macrostructural analysis of "social organization." But some twenty years later, Giddings had begun to conceptualize social phenomena in far less grandiose terms, signaling not only a change in his own thought, but that of the profession as well. *The Scientific Study of Human Society* (Giddings 1924) best illustrates this shift; for now Giddings examines "societal patterns" as "societal variables" and the methods for classifying, sampling, and assessing cause among phenomena denoted by variables are blended with older appeals for using knowledge for "social telesis." But such telesis is constrained by fortuitous and evolutionary forces. Indeed, Giddings (1924, 142) argues that "the study of societal phenomena by statistical methods has now, for those who understand them, terminated controversy over this hoary question of societal self-determination by demonstrating that the societal process is telic as well as fortuitously and physically evolutionistic." This shift in emphasis in Giddings' thought was not abrupt, however, for his very first work also revealed a heavily individualistic and mentalistic bent, sandwiched between Spencerian evolutionism and organicism. For example, in the conclusion to his *The Principles of Sociology* (1896, 400), Giddings emphasized that "since society is essentially a psychical phenomenon that is conditioned by a physical process, the strictly sociological laws are, first, laws of the psychical processes, and, second, laws of the limitation of the psychical by the physical process."

In Giddings' and Cooley's early work, this mentalism was macro, in much the way that Durkheim's ([1893] 1933) early work conceptualized the "collective conscience" in macro terms. But increasingly, this concern with the "psychical" became micro and social psychological. This change was highly compatible with statistical analysis, especially survey research where people are asked questions about their attitudes, opinions, and orientations. Indeed, statistics prospered in American sociology primarily because of this early mentalistic thrust of all theory, even its more organismic, macro, and evolutionary versions. But there were also more institutional reasons for the rise of quantitative methods; and these were perhaps even more decisive. Before WW I, municipal surveys had begun to involve sociologists (Turner and Turner 1990), and later, as private foundations, such as that initiated by John D. Rockefeller, came to fund work in social science, emphasis was on the use of statistics. The monies from the Rockefeller Foundation to sociology in the early 1920s, especially at Chicago, increasingly encouraged quantification. And in many of the social sciences, attitude scales became a convenient way to reconceptualize and measure more macro mentalisms in quantitative terms. Macro-level variables did not lend themselves to such quantification, although Albert Keller's student, George Murdock, was to initiate an effort along these lines, culminating in the HRAF files. Moreover, the unit of analysis in American sociology shifted to the "community," primarily under the impact of the survey movement. Money for sociology came from public and private organizations that wanted surveys on community institutions, and American sociologists were quick to respond.

Thus, partly for intellectual reasons and substantially for funding concerns, American sociology increasingly emphasized mental processes at the individual level. At about the same time, Durkheim (Durkheim and Mauss 1903; Durkheim 1912) in France was supplementing his macro evolutionary and organismic work of the 1890s (Durkheim [1893] 1933) with an interest in the cognitive and mental underpinnings of social structure, and Max Weber ([1922] 1968) was writing the early verstehen and action arguments for his major work on *Economy and Society*. In France, Durkheim's shift was to evolve into "structuralism," whereas in Germany Weber's orientation was to become more phenomenological (e.g., Schutz 1932). In America, this cognitive thrust was to encourage a concern with research on social action and the use of interviews, questionnaires, and statistical analyses of "attitudes," "definitions," and "orientations" of individual actors in concrete empirical settings. The reason for the European concern with the micro level was intellectual: scholars wanted to understand the linkage between micro and macro processes. But as noted above, the reorientation in America was the consequence of the funding sources of sociology. For as the organizations of the Rockefeller Foundation, such as the Social Science Research Council, increasingly funded social science research in the post-WW I period, the community became the locus of research. As a result, the macro evolutionary concerns of early sociology receded and sociology became topic-oriented—family, poverty, immigration, delinquency, deviance, church, school, etc. Each topic could be the subject of an empirical study, increasingly quantitative, and each could be a domain of theory—what Robert Merton (1958) was later to praise as "theories of the middle range."

BETWEEN THE WARS: 1920—1945

The early part of the period between World Wars I and II was dominated by the Chicago School, although Franklin Giddings' influence from Columbia was to become evident as his students assumed leadership of not only the Chicago department, but other midwestern departments as well. The Chicago School is, of course, famous for its pioneering work using case study methods—participant observation and ethnographic narratives on a subpopulation in urban areas. Indeed, there is a sense of romanticism about these "glory years," despite the fact that few of these "classic" case studies are ever read today.

Whatever its nature, the growing emphasis on empirical research, per se, created a theoretical vacuum in American sociology. Grand theory virtually disappeared, with a few exceptions (e.g., Sorokin 1937); and in its place much narrower "theories of (some substantive topic)" emerged. This narrowing of theory coincided with the rise of firsthand empirical research. American sociologists now wanted to integrate the two and believed that theory should inform firsthand research, and vice versa. The grand theorizing of the pre-WWI years disappeared.

The term, "grand theory," is of more recent vintage (Mills 1959), but if we were to typify theory in the pre-WWI years it was indeed grand. It was macro and micro; and at the same time, it was historical in the sense of following the evolutionary paradigm. One of the first significant events in precipitating the rise of narrower theories was the demise of evolutionism in anthropology and sociology. Comte, Spencer, Marx, and Durkheim all employed an evolutionary framework; and as Robert Nisbet (1969) stressed, this evolutionism was simply one incarnation of the metaphor of progress. Except for Sorokin, who was European in temperament and style, American sociology became concerned with "social change" rather than evolution; and even such important works as William F. Ogburn's Social Change (1922) and Stuart Chapin's Cultural Change (1928) do not reveal even the modest evolutionary character of the work of their mentor, Franklin Giddings. Rarely does one see during this period the truly ambitious evolutionism of Sumner and Keller's monumental treatise on The Science of Society.

Probably more fundamental to the transformation of theory was the growing debate over, and use of, quantitative methodology. As Roscoe Hinkle (1980, 302) notes:

> The considerable interest generated in the debate over the nature of science and appropriate methodology had fundamentally negative consequences for general, comprehensive, or macro-theory as it had been envisaged in the years before 1915. Generally, such theory was attacked and (often) abandoned because it was held to be abstract, conjectural-speculative, obtuse, deductive, subjective, unreliable, and was based on indirectly acquired (or secondary) data.

Yet general theory could still be found, not just in transplanted Europeans, such as Sorokin, but also in the work of one of the core figures of the Chicago School, Robert Park. For example, Park and Burgess' Introduction to the Science of Sociology (1924) contains a general theory of social organization that retains many Spencerian elements. The social world is viewed as a biotic order of population in territories and in interaction; such interaction often involves competition leading to conflict and a resulting pattern of dominance and succession; out of such competition various forces of social control are set into motion, including accommodation and assimilation. Many of Park's students continued to develop such ideas, although on an increasingly less macro scale. Lewis Wirth (1938), for example, was to take these ideas and create the human ecology school which, if anything, was a more micro version of Spencerian sociology (although it is not clear whether or not Wirth recognized the Spencerian sources of these ideas). Despite these broader approaches, however, Park's students are identified with narrow empirical studies, most often on roles, interactions, natural groups (such as criminal/youth "gangs"), and specific subcultures within urban communities. As with all American theorists, Park stressed that societies are ultimately "composed of individuals who act independently of one another, who compete and struggle with one another for mere existence, and treat one another, as far as possible, as utilities." Such statements are far more individualistic than anything ever uttered by Spencer in his formal sociology, and they helped shift analytical (and empirical) attention to the behavior of individuals in specific settings. But in the above passage from Park, the very next sentence argues that "on the other hand, it is quite as true that men and women are bound together by affections and common purposes . . . and they maintain, in spite of natural impulse to the contrary, a discipline and a moral order that enables them to transcend what we originally call nature, and through their collective action, recreate the world in the image of their collective aspirations and their common will." Durkheim could not have said it better; and this blending of individualism and collectivism tended to produce studies of *particular* groups as they adapted and adjusted to competitive existence through the creation of structure and shared culture.

Thus, even when theory was general, it was micro, despite using much of the vocabulary of the older and much grander macro evolutionism of the pre-war years. And while we might see some of Park's students as macro theorists—Lewis Wirth and Howard Becker, for example—their theories were, at best, "meso." More importantly, the vast majority of other students were decidedly micro in their concerns.

Norbet Wiley (1986) has argued that the critical battle in early American sociology was the separation of sociology from its biological roots, especially biological notions of instincts as driving human interaction and organization. In Wiley's view, Park's colleagues, W. I. Thomas and Florian Znaniecki, were critical figures in making this separation. Their famous book, *The Polish Peasant* (1918), was a critical landmark because it was "sociology's most effective and decisive break with biology and enunciation of a disciplinary point of view" (Wiley 1986, 23). This emancipation occurred through the elevation of the concepts of "attitude" and "value" which highlighted the importance of the symbols and cultural order, moving concern with culture to the theoretical center. Such a concept could, in Wiley's argument, contradict the presumption that social interaction and organization could be explained by instincts.

I do not fully agree with Wiley's account of the reasons behind the growing emphasis on mental processes. American sociology did not seek to liberate itself so much from notions of instinct as from evolutionism and organicism which, from the very inception, posed a potential conflict with the individualism and micro mentalism of early American theorists. The concept of attitude, in my view, was simply an acknowledgement of what some American theorists had always emphasized: the "psychical" or "mental" processes among individuals.

In contrast to Wiley's provocative argument, then, I entertain an alternative hypothesis: the emergence of the concepts of "attitude" and "value" in Thomas and Znaniecki's work enabled them, and many others using similar concepts, to be more precise in discussing mental processes; moreover, this conceptualization encouraged measurement at first with interview/observational procedures, and then, increasingly with "attitude-scales" and other quantitative techniques. Thus, sociology's real crisis was not presenting a tenable alternative to instinct theories in biology, but rather trying to construct a discipline in the wake of the collapse of its main biological props: evolutionism, and to a lesser extent, extreme organicism. As these became less fashionable metaphors for organizing sociological theory, the individualistic part of early theory emerged, if only by default. This emergence was, as noted earlier, encouraged by the sources of funding for sociology during the 1920s and early 1930s: private foundations granting monies for quantitative survey research. Thus, the movement to social psychology involved more than default; it was demanded by sociology's patrons.

This concern with how individuals orient themselves to, and define, situations was butressed by the uniquely American philosophical doctrine of pragmatism, especially as it was incorporated into George Herbert Mead's (1934) "social behaviorism." At the core of Mead's behaviorism is the assertion that mind and self are behaviors which facilitate adaptation to the social environment (note, again, that biology is not rejected but used to buttress sociological claims). The concept of "role-taking" becomes the crucial link in Mead's scheme, because it is the mechanism behind the process of interpersonal cooperation, the emergence of self, and the assumption of the perspective of the "generalized other" or the "community of attitudes" (Mead 1934). Yet Mead's ideas were not a full-fledged theory in the 1920s; it was only later that they became the theoretical base for several modern theoretical perspectives.

In fact, if we ask ourselves what general theories endure today from this period, the answer is: Spencerian sociology as it was transformed by Park and later Wirth, Hawley (1950), and others into human ecology; and Median pragmatism as it provided the conceptual core for interactionism, role theory, dramaturgy, and other related perspectives. Very little theory from other prominent scholars of this time endures, except perhaps certain classic phrases like "looking glass self," "the primary group," "differential association," and "definition of the situation." What most sociologists perceive about this period, then, is not great theoretical unity or sophistication, but rather a sense of middle-range theories on various processes—from delinquency and crime to urbanization and ethnic conflict—and a feeling that theory and research were somehow tied together. But was there a general metatheory undergirding our retrospective perceptions of this period?

Talcott Parsons' *The Structure of Social Action* (1937) perhaps illustrates this implicit metatheory. Indeed, the title of the book describes this metatheory, but its contents reinvigorate and legitimate it by the reintroduction of continental European scholars into discussions of theory. Parsons begins with the famous quote, "Who now reads Spencer?" and then engages in a rather long and detailed review of converging thought—mostly European—with respect to the "analytical elements" of unit acts. Stripped of their European context, these "unit acts" turn out to be very American-sounding concepts: individuals' orientations to goals, means, values, and situational constraints. In my view, Parsons' work did not represent so much a radically new conceptualization, as some have argued, but a reaffirmation of what American theory had always possessed—a concern with the goal-directed orientations of individuals. Parsons' contribution was to insert European thought into the social psychological thrust of American theory. Indeed, in reading Parsons' account of Marx, Weber, Durkheim, Pareto, Marshall, and others, one would never guess that some of these early figures employed organismic analogies or spoke in evolutionary terms. Parsons did not so much "Parsonize" these figures, as some contend, as Americanize them and convert them to social psychologists. For what is offered by Parsons at this stage is a framework for social psychology—especially those cultural orientations that influence decisions over courses of action. Thomas, Znaniecki, Thurstone, and others who helped bring a "cognitive" thrust to sociology and psychology would hardly find any new metatheory in Parsons' account.

Among the many ironies of work during this period is Parsons' reemergence in the 1950s and 1960s as the ultimate Spencerian, theorizing in a heavily functional mode that was replete with implicit analogies to organisms. As many have argued, Parsons abandoned social psychology, or at least converted it to a more Freudian model, and became a modern-day Spencerian. Of course, the seeds of Parsons' shift to macrostructural and cultural processes can be seen in the last pages of *The Structure of Social Action*, but the early Parsons was a product of his times, joining in the concern for analysis of mental orientations and decision-making processes. Hinkle (1980, 312) has termed this later phase between the wars as the epoch of "social action theory"; and his listing of its tenets is a reasonable summary of the 1930s and early 1940s: 1) human action and interaction are mediated by consciousness; 2) human action is social in that people are aware of themselves and others; 3) human action is "rational" in the broadest sense of making decisions over means to ends; 4) human action is purposive or teleological in that it is directed by intentions, purposes, and goals; 5) human action is constrained by conditions (biological, physical, ecological); and 6) human action is constrained by moral codes, rules, norms, and values.

Such concerns were highly compatible with the methodological individualism which was emerging during this period; that is, with the position that individual responses to interviews, questionnaires, and other instruments could be statistically aggregated and analyzed to inform sociologists about social and cultural phenomena. Yet at the very time that "action" theory began to dominate and legitimate the quantitative revolution, older organismic themes were beginning to reemerge in the form of functionalism. As Durkheim was reintroduced to American audiences, and as anthropologists such as Bronislaw Malinowski and A. R. Radcliffe-Brown began to use functional analysis, sociologists took notice, especially at Harvard which was finally beginning to acknowledge sociology. Indeed, one senses that as concern with measurement of attitudes and other cognitive processes amenable to questionnaire methodologies came to dominate much sociological inquiry, some sociologists began to crave something a little more grand, macro, and inclusive. Such was certainly the case at Harvard, where Sorokin had kept macro theory alive during the 1930s and where Parsons was later to assemble his "school" with monies from the Carnegie Foundation. As a result of the intellectual craving and the favored financial position of Parsons, who could buy students and colleagues, ideas very reminiscent of Spencer were once again entertained, even though most converts now conformed to Parsons' observation on the opening page of *The Structure of Social Action* and no longer read Spencer. Hence, they often did not know from whom their functionalism sprang.

Thus, action theories helped legitimate firsthand research, but they created a conceptual appetite for a more grand theory which, in the end, was to split theory and research irrevocably in American sociology and which, in the overreaction to functionalism, was to fragment theory in America and elsewhere in the world.

Such fragmentation, however, was clearly evident in the underlying structure of American sociology before the contemporary period. When the foundation monies dried up during the Depression, partly because of economic hard times but also because of Rockefeller's disgust with the work produced by sociologists, a crisis of funding emerged. In turn, this crisis created an intellectual problem over what sociology should be: applied-pure; empirical-theoretical; quantitative-qualitative; value neutral-reformist; and so on. Moreover, the professional organization of the field reflected these emerging intellectual divisions. For example, the American Sociological Society membership dropped to about 1000 in the 1930s, and yet all of the major regional and subregional associations emerged at this time, signaling an interest in sociology but not that advocated by the elite of ASS. Additionally, the elite of sociology —as personified by the "invitation only" club of 100 in the Sociological Research Organization—split themselves from the rank and file. This "club" was perhaps a desperation move to impose a common view of the profession; and it was certainly a sign that the power of the elite universities was declining, as is illustrated by the fact that in 1918 Chicago and Columbia produced 74 percent of all sociology Ph.D.s, whereas in 1928 this figure had dropped to 32 percent. As a result, it was no longer possible for Chicago and Columbia to dictate, as they once had, the intellectual content of the field. Sociology was quietly growing, but outside the ASS and the Chicago-Columbia axis. This growth occurred in a period with little theoretical coherence and few agreed upon standards—except among the small elite of the Sociological Research Organization who pushed quantitative sociology. Sociology was thus a field in need of integration, intellectually and professionally. The tragedy of the modern period was the ultimate failure to achieve either.

CONTEMPORARY THEORY

The social action approach of the 1930s and early 1940s was not a unified theoretical orientation. Rather, it was more of a sensitizing framework which called attention to the importance of self, thought, decision-making, and symbolic constraints within micro groups and subcultures. While there were some creative attempts to link this framework to larger, macro structures, especially in the introductory textbooks of this period, there was little integrated theory that cut across micro and macro phenomena. There were many "theories of" just about any substantive topic—delinquency, crime, urbanization, family, professions, organizations, and so on. But there was little in the way of a theory that could integrate these proliferating "theories of."

Ironically, it was Merton, as a graduate student and part-time instructor in the newly created sociology department at Harvard in the early 1930s, who inadvertently initiated the "grand theory" which he was later to attack. He did not generate such theory himself, but his introduction of functionalism to graduate students, such as Kingsley Davis and Wilbert Moore, and to a new instructor in the department of economics, Talcott Parsons, was to spawn the rise of functional theorizing in American sociology. Indeed, the early post-WW II period can be typified by the rise of grand theory in the form of functionalism on the one side, and the growing emphasis on narrow theories on a wide variety of empirical topics on the other. And while Merton's eloquent pleas for "theories of the middle range" sought to integrate the two, such was not to be the case. For even after the grand functionalism of Parsons' was replaced by a splintering of theoretical sociology into a variety of camps, orientations, and perspectives, empirical research and theory were never to be systematically coupled again.

It is difficult to know exactly why these functional ideas were taken over by a generation of scholars who, in the post-WWII period, were to carry the banner of functionalism, but it is reasonable to assume that the appeal of functionalism was its emphasis on systemic wholes. In functional analysis, structures and processes are explained by reference to their "functions" or "consequences" for meeting the basic survival needs or requisites of the social whole.

The war curtailed, or at least delayed, the introduction of the functional orientation into mainstream sociology, but its debut occurred in 1945 when two Harvard students, Kingsley Davis and Wilbert Moore, published the first modern functional analysis in sociology—their famous (or infamous) "Some Principles of Stratification" (Malinowski's 1944 synthesis was of the prewar years and more anthropological than sociological).

Soon, others of this Harvard group were postulating lists of functional needs for all societies—a tack very similar to Malinowski's earlier effort (1944). For example, David Aberle and several faculty-student collaborators (1950) were confidently constructing lists of "the functional requisites of a society." This analysis had been preceded by Kingsley Davis' introductory text, *Human Societies* (1948). Others from this Harvard group also began to publish functional analyses, one of the most notable and influential being Marion J. Levy's *The Structure of Society* (1952).

Curiously, during the very instigation of all this, Robert K. Merton published a critique of functional analysis in 1949. His famous "Manifest and Latent Functions" chapter in his *Social Theory and Social Structure* (Merton 1958) attacked "straw man" representations of

Malinowski and Radcliffe-Brown, but his main line of attack was the analytical thrust of the emerging functional orientation. Merton's criticisms were, of course, to be echoed many times in the succeeding decades, but he set the tone of the empiricist critique of functionalism as it was then emerging: the failure to descend from the analytical clouds to concrete empirical settings. Merton's and others' criticisms were to become more shrill as the functional approach of Talcott Parsons came to dominate not just functional theory but sociological theory in general, especially as Parsons could use his Carnegie monies and the considerable resources of Harvard to create his functional school of thought. By the 1960s, Parsonian "action theory" (which was and still is a misnomer reflecting Parsons' early conceptual work in the 1930s where social psychology was prominent) had become the dominant theoretical perspective in American sociology. It came close to the same hegemonic status of Spencerian-inspired organicism-evolutionism (with some social psychology thrown in) of the pre-WW I era. Its only rivals in America were Herbert Blumer's (1969) adoption of Meadian ideas in symbolic interactionism, various other adoptions of Mead in such narrow approaches as role theory and dramaturgy, and Marxian analysis which, because of the repression of the McCarthy era, was just reemerging from the closets and attics of academia.

But even as early as the late 1950s, the conflict theoretic critique of Parsonian theory was initiated, primarily by Europeans (Lockwood 1956; Dahrendorf 1958) along with a few American Marxists (e.g., Mills 1959). These criticisms became a familiar theme in the 1960s; and as the 1960s progressed, this conflict critique was joined by other substantive and logical criticisms (*see* J. Turner 1986; Turner and Maryanski 1979, 1988 for a review). Parsonian functionalism then began to fall from favor; as functionalism declined, older perspectives, such as Marxian conflict analysis and Meadian interactionism, became more prominent and themselves began to split off in varying directions. In addition, a wide variety of new theoretical perspectives emerged, or were transported to America from Europe. The end result was that, in the wake of functionalism's brief moment of domination, a period of eclecticism, diversity, debate, and acrimony came to typify American theory, and theory in other parts of the world. Moreover, a general questioning of the possibility for scientific theory began to erode the early optimism of American theorists. As the criterion of science was abandoned, any abstract set of ideas could be "theoretical."

The rise and fall of Parsonian functionalism corresponds to the period in which sociology grew dramatically. This growth reflected several interrelated forces: the dramatic increase in federal government funding in the post-Sputnik era; the capacity to fund increased numbers of graduate students; the use of funding the student demand to expand the number of graduate programs in sociology to over 200; the entrance of baby-boom children into the university system in the mid-1960s during the height of the Vietnam protest era, thereby increasing sociology enrollments from 10,000 or so in 1960 to about 34,000 in 1972; and the use of these increased enrollments to justify faculty hiring and expansion of graduate programs. Thus, the expanded resource base—federal monies and students—allowed sociology to grow. But this growth occurred in an organizationally fragmented field and in an intellectual climate where the major integrating forces—functional theory and quantitative methods—were about to lose their hegemonic status. The result was further fragmentation into specialized subfields, associations, journals, sections of the ASA, and regional associations. Under these structural conditions, there was no organizational force to constrain theory; and with the collapse of functionalism, there was no intellectual force either.

Theoretical sociology has moved in several directions over the last three decades. One direction revolves around the continued proliferation of specialty theories, or what I (Turner 1984) call "theories of (pick your favorite substantive topics)." These are theories about some structure, process, or phenomenon—crime, delinquency, sex roles, urban ecology, attitude change, group dynamics, demographic transitions, personality, economic growth, world system dynamics, societal revolutions, the rise and fall of empires, ethnic relations, class relations, political elites, organizational growth, emotions, and so on, for virtually all substantive subfields in sociology.

Another direction has been the development of more general integrative theories that cut across substantive topics. These theories make claims for being inclusive; in fact, these claims are often excessive, as theorists assert that their approach explains all of reality and is *the* only appropriate theoretical strategy. For example, to list just some of these perspectives, we have: old and neofunctionalism; varieties of symbolic interactionism; role theory; dramaturgy; behavioral, utilitarian, and structural versions of exchange theory; neo-Marxist, neo-Weberian, Simmelian conflict theories; various structural theories, including network analysis, mathematical models, macrostructuralism, microstructuralism, and systems theory; types of structuralist analysis such as structuration theory and structuralist mentalism; types of phenomenology and ethnomethodology; and so on. Since the very existence of multiple orientations suggests that it will be difficult to achieve theoretical integration, proponents of various orientations often view each other with suspicion, if not acrimony. Moreover, practitioners *within* orientations frequently lob insults and criticisms at each other.

For example, symbolic interactionists frequently disagree; various sub-camps within ethnomethodology are always fighting; conflict sociologists carry such diverse philosophical baggage (from positivism to revolutionary advocacy) as well as diverse mentors (Marx, Simmel, and Weber, to name the most prominent) that they rarely agree; exchange theorists are perhaps more unified, although there are disagreements over how to deal with emergent social structures (some are blatant reductionists, others attempt to conceptualize emergent social structures); and structural sociology is simply a name for very different approaches which have little in common, and whose advocates frequently attack one another. Since each of these and other general approaches has aggressive advocates and a substantial following, none can dominate, as functionalism once did (and even then, the domination was far from complete). Thus, it is unlikely that these various orientations can intellectually unify American, or world, sociology.

Yet another recent direction is metatheory. Here, scholars analyze existing theories, seeking to sort out their presuppositions, epistemologies, ontologies, and metaphysics. This metatheorizing can also involve attempts to create a general set of guidelines for all theory. In a sense, metatheory recognizes the fractured and diverse nature of current theories, and it tries to do something about the situation. But their advice is often rather vague and general, often of the nature: study acts and interaction, structure and culture, or action and order. As a result, metatheorists talk primarily to each other, and no one else. Thus, as an integrating effort, metatheorizing has failed miserably.

Yet another direction has been an effort to expand existing theoretical orientations, or to create new ones, which are more eclectic and pull together elements of other theoretical orientations into a synthesis. For example, the British social theorist Anthony Giddens (1984) has a much more receptive audience in America than Europe because his "structuration theory" pulls together what are often considered incomparable approaches—structuralism, phenomenology and ethnomethodology, dramaturgy, Marxism, and psychoanalytic theory. But even these eclectic theories create camps, as in the case for Giddens' approach, which antagonizes all positivists as well as prominent theorists from whom he borrows. Similar fates have awaited others who have sought to be synthetic; they manage to antagonize some ad hoc coalition of very strange bedfellows who are offended by some inappropriate use of "their" and their idols' ideas.

Thus, while these recent synthetic theories and the present popularity of metatheorizing signal a thirst for some kind of conceptual unity, these efforts have not been successful. And even when they win converts, they are usually members of the theoretical community—a rather small group of 500 to 600 in America and perhaps that many in the rest of the world. The result is that most American sociologists, especially research-oriented sociologists, do not pay much attention to what are seen as vague, excessively abstract, and arcane pronouncements from general theorists. Researchers feel much happier with narrow "theories of" than the more integrative efforts of general theorists. Indeed, the proliferation of "theories of" various institutional contexts, world system dynamics, organizational structures, stratification processes, urban structure, forms of deviance, collective behavior, and specific processes in social psychology is by far the most prominent conceptual activity in sociology.

The post-Parsonian period thus reveals a growing split between "theorists' theory" and "researchers' theory." Moreover, there appears to be an expanding series of partitions within theory itself. These partitions not only reflect varying substantive commitments, but also strategic and philosophical commitments. Some believe that laws of human organization can be developed; others view the very nature of human organization as changeable by human agency, and hence not subject to invariant laws. Some argue for metatheory, others for deductive systems of propositions, still others for discursive analyses, and yet another group for formal models. Some argue that theory must begin with micro processes, others just the reverse. And so it goes. It is perhaps not surprising, therefore, that researchers simply throw up their hands at theorists and get on with the process of collecting data.

These intellectual trends are supported by the structure of American sociology. The American Sociological Association has adopted a cooptive strategy, offering all types of thinking a home, even a section, for the price of membership. Hence, any kind of thought is now professionally acceptable. Specialty associations have also proliferated—numbering well over 60 (Turner and Turner 1990)—and provide a home for different stripes of sociologists. The number of sociologically inclined journals published in America is now well over 200 (Turner and Turner 1990), thereby providing a publishing outlet for most kinds of work. The regional associations are not allied with the ASS and ASA, as they once were, and now split memberships in sociology on a regional basis. And the gap between researchers and teachers remains large, with the former having very different institutional affiliations, interests, and needs than the latter. Moreover, the sources of funding for sociological work have decreased dramatically over the last decade with the result that local sources of support are as important as "big grants" for supporting research; and as the "big grant" elite declines, scholars at many diverse locations can fund and produce research equal to that of the old elite. This kind of structural base for sociology hardly encourages consensus over its mission; and it does not encourage a unified vision of theory.

WHAT OF THE FUTURE?

On the one hand, I am very pessimistic about the future of theoretical sociology in general, while on the other, I am very optimistic about what the small positivist wing of theory will accomplish in the next two decades. For theory in general, we will see more of the current trend: theorizing about any topic in any way that someone wants. The reason for this situation is that there are few shared intellectual commitments among theorists over subject matter, philosophical assumptions, theory-building strategies, or methodologies. This intellectual diversity is compounded by the organizational structure of American sociology.

The overall result is that sociologists can pretty much go their own way and find a network of like-minded thinkers, a cluster of journals, specialty associations, a section of a national association, and a departmental clique (students and fellow faculty), all of whom will embrace any line of thinking. Thus, sociologists can "do their own thing" which, whatever other values this capacity might personify, prevents the discipline from becoming intellectually integrated. And if theorists cannot integrate the field—indeed, they are considered largely irrelevant by most practicing sociologists—the field cannot achieve much coherence. The future, then, is for sociology in general to be an amorphous, loosely structured, intellectually eclectic, and not a very respected discipline.

Among the small camp of those who are more positivistically oriented, however, there is reason for optimism. There is very creative and synthetic work currently being done at both the micro and macro level, as well as in efforts to link these. Most of this work builds on the early masters, employs formalisms, and states propositions that are testable. Moreover, I sense that positivistic sociology is on the verge of developing laws and models that are the equivalent of those in the natural sciences and that will bring us closer to Comte's original dream.

Without being unduly modest, some of my own work falls into this category, but there are many others who are even more creative and representative of this positivistic promise. For example, Randall Collins' theory of "interaction ritual chains"; Ralph Turner's role theory; Harrison White's efforts to explain structural equivalence and markets; Joseph Berger's and various colleagues', such as Morris Zelditch's and David Wagner's, status characteristics approach; Peter Blau's macrostructuralism; Ron A. Burt's effort to develop a general theory of action in networks; David Willer's, Karen Cook's, and others' efforts to develop structural network theories; Michael Hechter's and James Coleman's work on a rational choice theory that takes account of and tries to explain social structure, and so on for perhaps two more pages (my apologies to those I did not list here).

One possible scenario is that these more positivistic theorists will simply leave mainstream theory which, at present and into the foreseeable future, will have too many inhibitions and reservations about the prospects for scientific sociology. For increasingly, positivistic work simply ignores the way much theory is currently practiced in American sociology. The relativistic, solipsistic, particularistic, anti-positivistic, and meta-istic (to invent a word) character of theory is no longer a challenge to debate. Increasingly, it is something to be ignored. Efforts at metatheory cannot help, because these often become philosophical treatises in their own right, and hence of less interest to positivistic theorists and researchers than might otherwise be the case.

Thus, the future will bring about a clearer differentiation of these theorists who believe, as Comte, Spencer, and most early American sociologists did, that there are fundamental and invariant properties of the social universe, that sociologists can develop abstract laws and models of these properties, that these laws and models can be tested, and that knowledge about human organization can be cumulative. Comte's original dream is alive and well, but I doubt if most sociologists who view themselves as "theorists" care. My only hope is that, in the very distant future when the bankruptcy of much current "theory" is recognized, the creative work of this relatively small group—fifty or sixty thinkers at most—will be recognized for what it was: the realization of Comte's original vision for a "social physics."

REFERENCES

Aberle, David F. et al. 1950. "The Functional Requisites of a Society." *Ethics* 55:100–111.

Blumer, Herbert. 1969. *Symbolic Interaction: Perspective and Method.* Englewood Cliffs, N.J.: Prentice-Hall.

Chapin, Stuart. 1928. *Cultural Change.* New York: Century.

Comte, Auguste. 1830–1842. *A System of Positive Philosophy.* 3 vols. London: George Bell.

Cooley, Charles Horton. 1902. *Human Nature and the Social Order.* New York: Scribners.

Cooley, Charles Horton. 1909. *Social Organization.* New York: Scribners.

Dahrendorf, Ralf. 1958. "Out of Utopia Toward a Reorientation of Sociological Analysis." *American Journal of Sociology* 74:115–127.

Davis, Kingsley. 1948. *Human Societies*. New York: Macmillan.

Davis, Kingsley, and Wilbert Moore. 1945. "Some Principles of Stratification." *American Sociological Review* 10:242–249.

Durkheim, Émile. [1893] 1933. *The Division of Labor in Society*. Reprint. New York: Macmillan.

Durkheim, Émile. 1912. *Elementary Forms of Religious Life*. New York: Macmillan.

Durkheim, Émile, and Marcel Mauss. 1903. *Primitive Classification*. London: Cohen and West.

Giddens, Anthony. 1984. *The Constitution of Society*. Cambridge: Polity.

Giddings, Franklin H. 1896. *The Principles of Sociology*. New York: Macmillan.

Giddings, Franklin H. 1906. *Readings in Descriptive and Historical Sociology*. New York: Macmillan.

Giddings, Franklin H. 1924. *The Scientific Study of Human Society*. Chapel Hill: University of North Carolina Press.

Hawley, Amos. 1950. *Human Ecology*. New York: Ronald Press.

Hinkle, Roscoe. 1980. *Founding Theory of American Sociology: 1881–1915*. Boston: Routledge and Kegan Paul.

Levy, Marion J. 1952. *The Structure of Society*. New Haven: Yale University Press.

Lockwood, David. 1956. "Some Remarks on 'The Social System.'" *British Journal of Sociology* 7:134–146.

Malinowski, Bronislaw. 1944. *A Scientific Theory of Culture*. Chapel Hill: University of North Carolina Press.

Mead, George Herbert. 1934. *Mind, Self, and Society*. Chicago: University of Chicago Press.

Merton, Robert K. 1958. *Social Theory and Social Structure*. New York: Free Press.

Mills, C. Wright. 1959. *The Sociological Imagination*. New York: Oxford University Press.

Nisbet, Robert A. 1969. *Social Change and History*. New York: Oxford University Press.

Ogburn, William F. 1922. *Social Change*. New York: B. W. Huebsch.

Park, Robert E. and Ernest W. Burgess. 1924. *Introduction to the Science of Sociology*. Chicago: University of Chicago Press.

Parsons, Talcott. 1937. *The Structure of Social Action*. New York: McGraw-Hill.

Radcliffe-Brown, A. R. 1948. *A Natural Science of Society*. Glencoe, Ill.: Free Press.

Schutz, Alfred. 1932. *The Phenomenology of the Social World*. Evanston, Ill., Northwestern University Press.

Sorokin, Pitirim A. 1937. *Social and Cultural Dynamics*, 4 vols. New York: American Book Co.

Spencer, Herbert. 1892–1898. *Principles of Ethics*. New York: D. Appleton.

Spencer, Herbert. 1850. *Social Statics*. New York: D. Appleton.

Spencer, Herbert. 1864–1867. *Principles of Biology*. 3 vols. New York: D. Appleton.

Spencer, Herbert. 1874–1896. *The Principles of Sociology*. 3 vols. New York: D. Appleton.

Sumner, William Graham. 1907. *Folkways*. New York: Ginn.

Sumner, William Graham, and Albert Galloway Keller. 1927. *The Science of Society*. 4 vols. New Haven: Yale University Press.

Thomas, W. I. and Florian Znaniecki. 1918. *The Polish Peasant in Europe and America*. 5 Vols. Chicago: University of Chicago Press.

Turner, Jonathan H. 1984. *Societal Stratification: A Theoretical Analysis*. New York: Columbia University Press.

Turner, Jonathan H. 1986. *The Structure of Sociological Theory*. 4th ed. Chicago: Dorsey Press.

Turner, Jonathan H., and Alexandra Maryanski. 1979. *Functionalism*. Menlo Park: Benjamin Cummings.

Turner, Jonathan H., and Alexandra Maryanski. 1988. "Is Neofunctionalism Really Functional?" *Sociological Theory* 6:110–121.

Turner, Stephen P., and Jonathan H. Turner. 1990. *The Impossible Science: An Institutional Analysis of American Sociology*. Newbury Park, Cal.: Sage.

Weber, Max. [1922] 1968. *Economy and Society: An Outline of Interpretive Sociology*. Edited by G. Roth and C. Wittich. Berkeley: University of California Press.

Wiley, Norbert. 1986. "Early American Sociology and the Polish Peasant." *Sociological Theory* 4:20–40.

Wirth, Lewis. 1938. "Urbanism as a Way of Life." *American Journal of Sociology* 1:46–63.

15

The History and Politics of Recent Sociological Theory

❈

NORBERT WILEY
University of Illinois

The essays in this volume reflect major tendencies in social theory today. They are open, pluralistic, innovative, and full of energy. There is no dominating orthodoxy or even a hint of one—no hegemonic theory, no mandatory method, no ideological straitjacket, and no ruling clique. This pluralism has its own historical causes, but quite apart from its origins, I think it is a healthy condition for social theory. In this respect, my view is closer to Ritzer's than to Turner's (both in this volume), although the latter's position, given its premises, is certainly well-argued.

Before considering the essays in this volume, both in relation to the past and in relation to each other, I will first discuss the historical trends that led to the present situation in theory. Next, the advantages of the present pluralism will be considered. And finally I will look briefly at the near future, examining the possibilities of some new hegemony against the alternative possibility of a continued multiplicity of language games.

THE PRESENT AS HISTORY

To get a sense of tendency in theory it is useful to take a systematic look at the past. I have previously described the history of American sociology as the rise and fall of two dominating points of view: that of the Chicago School in the 1920s and early 1930s and that of Parsons-Merton, Harvard-Columbia functionalists, in and around the 1950s. The periods before, between, and after these two hegemonies are "interregnums," during which there were no hegemonic points of view (Wiley 1979, 1985, 1986). The three interregnums are interesting in their own right. According to Thomas Kuhn's theory of scientific history, a paradigm falls because it is replaced by a new one (Kuhn 1970). That scheme does not allow interregnums. Admitting that sociology has not had the well-developed paradigms of the natural sciences, this field's interregnums—and, for that matter, those of the other social sciences as well—are decidedly un-Kuhnian. This will be discussed later.

The first interregnum, or "pre-regnum," extended from the formal beginnings of American sociology in the 1880s until around World War I. During this early period American sociology was in formation in two senses: the birth of the field—the definition and legitimation of the discipline—was still being established; in addition, the first quasi-paradigm, that of the Chicago School, was being readied to fill the niche.

In my view, W. I. Thomas and Florian Znaniecki's *The Polish Peasant in Europe and America* (1918–1920) completed both tasks, the "founding" and the "filling."[1] For these authors, the entry concept was meaning, or the symbol, both as it exists in the human subject ("attitudes") and in the social or cultural structure ("values"). This founding contrasts with Durkheim's earlier creation of the discipline around the notion of "structure," itself rather similar to Thomas and Znaniecki's value realm. Both contrast with Simmel's founding around the concept of interaction (Levine 1989). The relations among these three, and possibly other, foundings have not been looked at in social theory, despite Durkheim's call for examining the origins of institutions.

Thomas and Znaniecki attempted to fill the newly legitimized disciplinary niche with a particular vision of how attitudes and values (or "agency" and "structure") are mutually causal. This attempt was not completely successful, although the current theory of "structuration" —found in Anthony Giddens (1984), Pierre Bourdieu (1989), and Roy Bhaskar (1979), among others—is rather similar to the argument of *The Polish Peasant.*

The distinction between niche and occupant, space and content, foundings and fillings is another problem for Kuhn's theory of science, since this distinction, like the concept of interregnum, has no place in his scheme.

The second interregnum, extending from the mid-1930s until the rise of the functionalists after World War II, had a different, less originary quality than the first. The disciplinary niche was already present, so there was no need to again construct the discipline out of nothing. The genesis of the second quasi-paradigm was more ontogeny than phylogeny, the former, as Durkheim pointed out, decidedly not "recapitulating" the latter. The move toward the new paradigm was not virginal, but was a response to the fall of the old: to its anomalies, its loss of elective affinity with the times, and its decline in control of the means of intellectual production (mainly jobs, research monies, publication media, and the teaching curriculum). The second interregnum involved a lot of "dirty hands," if only because power was now being lost and gained. This process was zero-sum and conflict was unavoidable.

When the functionalists declined in the late 1960s, the third interregnum began. This one too has unique qualities, particularly its longevity and lack of movement toward a new, and third hegemonic, paradigm. Instead there has been continued diversity and theoretical competition, without any of the theoretical fish getting big enough to begin swallowing the others. The essays in this volume reflect the peculiarities of this current interregnum.

If we date the present interregnum from the late 1960s until the present, twenty years is a long time for a discipline to be without any dominating "center." It is not easy to analyze these twenty years historically, since we are so close to them, but in a tentative and exploratory spirit, I will propose three stages, so far, in the present interregnum: 1) the fall of functionalism; 2) the positivist bid for hegemony; and 3) the resurgence of European social theory.

The Fall of Functionalism

The decline of the functionalists was a complex process, its effects extending over a number of years. This decline had already begun by the mid-sixties, thus producing some overlap in the rough periodization I am working with. I will focus on intellectual attacks, although historical changes in American and world society were also important factors. History produced three reversals for the functionalists, all weakening their fitness for or elective affinity with the times. These were 1) social protest in the 1960s, 2) the rise of feminism and women's interests by the end of the decade, and 3) the decline in the capitalist world economy, including the American leadership of that economy, in the early 1970s. All three of these events were difficult to explain in the functional style, i.e., by way of needs and the nested attitudes-norms-values that fill the needs. The functionalists had used the concept of "strain" to explain protest and conflict (for example, Smelser 1962), but there was simply too much strain, and the times called for a totally different theory.

The intellectual attacks were to some extent based on the three historical anomalies, but in and of themselves they constituted a separate problem for the functionalists. The most noticeable group of attacks on the functionalists was from the macro conflict positions, themselves quite diversified, but all gaining from the flow of the times. They included Marxists of various kinds, conflict-oriented and left Weberians, the semi-institutionalized conflict position of Ralf Dahrendorf, and the functional conflict position of Lewis Coser. If the conflict people had won the fight and become the new hegemony, they would have had a difficult time deciding which conflict position was to lead.

A second group of attackers were the qualitative, micro-based positions. These included symbolic interactionism, phenomenological sociology, and ethnomethodology. This grouping too would have had trouble deciding what they were had they won. Some of these qualitative micros were using recent ideas, foreshadowing the much more recent resurgence of European theory, although at the time—the mid-sixties to early seventies—these micro positions were weak, disunited among themselves, and without strong European backing.

A small number of thinkers criticized the functionalists on both macro and micro grounds, thus having a foot in each of the critical groupings already mentioned. Leading representatives of this position were Randall Collins and Anthony Giddens.

There was yet a third segment of opposition. Some of the the leading quantitative positivists were originally allied—loosely—with the functionalists. This interrelationship was symbolized and led by two particular alliances: that of Samuel Stouffer with Parsons at Harvard and that of Paul Lazarsfeld with Merton at Columbia. During the functionalist hegemony, the positivists, subordinate to the functionalists, supplied the nuts and bolts of method along with much of the empirical research. But the positivists slowly and quietly uncoupled from this alliance, doubtless emboldened by the advent of the computer among other things, and they eventually became a third point of attack on the functionalists.

This attack was primarily based on the philosophy of science and the logic of explanation, for the "functional explanation" of the functionalists and the "causal explanation" of the positivists were never really compatible in the first place (though *see* Stinchcombe 1968, 80–101). Once the working alliance stopped working, it was easy, particularly for logicians, to point out this incompatibility. Perhaps Ernest Nagel's critique of Merton's "Manifest and Latent Functions" paper (Nagel 1956), given, ironically, at the request of Merton and Lazarsfeld, was the earliest move in this direction. Nagel's paper, originally presented in 1953, showed that functional explanation could be reduced to the causal, without significant remainder (*see also* Hempel 1959; Bernstein 1976, 27–28). I am not sure the functionalists ever understood the force of the logician's critique. As recently as 1977 Merton was to remark, informally, that "the Nagel formulation in particular only reinforced the heuristic value of functional analysis. The claim is that functional analysis leads heuristically to hypotheses which do not emerge from an exclusively causal perspective. Subsequent reciprocal translatability is all to the good, doing away with a make-believe dualism" (personal letter from Merton to Wiley). But some people thought the translatability was only one-way: positivism could explain functionalism but functionalism could not explain positivism. The logical critique of functionalism would gradually give the positivists the issue they needed to uncouple from the alliance.

Finally there was the attack from George Homans and exchange theory. This was a micro position, but it was not qualitative and certainly not kindred with the micro critiques previously mentioned. It was closer to the Nagel-Hempel critique, though it was not positivist in the same way. It was a second form, based on positivist action theory, and it would never quite assimilate with the classic positivism of the natural science analogy. The divisions within positivism would later become more significant and troublesome.

The first stage of the current interregnum ended with the functionalists settling into a decline, but with no clear replacement. All of the attacking positions gained something, but none gained hegemony itself. The winner was neither the conflict grouping, even though it had the best explanation for the times. Nor was it the insistent micro positions. The closest thing to a winner was the former allies, the positivists themselves.

The Positivist Bid for Hegemony

While the functionalists were declining the positivists were gaining, partly—but by no means completely—at the expense of the functionalists. The most dramatic gains were in the means of production: university positions, government monies for research, control of graduate school curricula, and space in key journals. The positivists also began to send out feelers, especially through the influential writings of H. M. Blalock (1968, 1969, 1979), toward declaring themselves the new dominant theory, by arguing that method can replace theory.

In the early seventies, overlapping with the first stage of this interregnum, the positivists seemed to achieve a near-hegemony. In other words, the new situation looked like a hegemony to some, but it turned out not to be. Their dominance was noticeably uneven, much stronger in empirical research then in theory itself. The great power base was in the means of production, which gave this grouping an increasingly dominating presence in empirical research. Theoretical ideas were much harder to attain, for the philosophy of science to which the positivists were committed was incompatible with the construction of general ideas.

During the period of positivist partial reign, there began a variety of new attacks, now on the positivists themselves. These critiques were reminiscent of those directed at the functionalists, for it was again the "outs versus the ins." In addition, the attacks came largely from the groupings that had attacked the functionalists, but gained only slightly from their fall: the conflict positions and the qualitative micros. There was a certain tactical ease in criticizing the positivists, for they had invested so heavily in methodology. In contrast to the largely theoretical critiques of functionalism the new round of attacks could be trained parsimoniously on method.

The method employed by the positivists required pluralities of events, preferably in large numbers. Infrequent events were hard to approach, and one-of-a-kind happenings completely elusive. Accordingly, the macro conflict positions, often drawing on the historicism of Max Weber, argued that positivism could not explain the major events and turning points of history. To get enough cases for statistical analysis—enough revolutions, for example—it was necessary to water down the concept and include minor cases. The central tendency of the enlarged sample would be different from that of the major events themselves. In addition, the temporally embedded, "world-historical" (Skocpol 1979, 19–24) process would be lost in the trivialization and detemporalization of the sample.

A second criticism came from the Marxist end of conflict theory. Change, and therefore causation, was not mechanical, it was argued, but praxis-based and dialectical. Praxis and dialectic, in fact, supplied the appropriate logical model—as opposed to statistical analysis—for the explanation of one-of-a-kind cases.

In contrast, the qualitative micro positions concentrated their criticisms at the levels of self and interaction. Positivism, it was argued, could not reach the subjective fact as it is intensive, intentional (in Husserl's sense), and reflexive. To treat the meaningful contents of self and interaction as linear magnitudes, comparable to length and breadth, was an obvious fallacy to these people.

Even the recently demoted functionalists, including the neofunctionalists, were critical of their former allies. Jeffrey Alexander (1982, 30–33) spoke for this position in extolling the advantages of postpositivism; the "post" in this expression refers to all the recent and telling critiques of positivism, launched from the philosophy and history of science.

During their heyday in the 1970s, the positivists also encountered tensions and problems from within. One problem was the lack of convincing statistical findings. The coefficients of correlation and the combinations and derivations thereof were very low. Too much went unexplained. The positivist method did not deliver the empirical explanation it promised. Status attainment research was the major empirical failure of positivism, for despite dozens of studies and generous financial support from the federal government, the problem was left pretty much as it was found. Status attainment, formerly and less tendentiously called social mobility, was due to a complex mixture of both merit and "ascriptive" causes, and the method did not deliver a noticeably better picture of the mix than was already available. In addition, a profound and historically embedded concept from Max Weber was reduced to a demographic variable. Finally, with the economic doldrums of the 1970s and 1980s, people lost interest in status attainment as such—more serious problems had arisen—and the research dribbled off inconclusively.

A second internal problem was the development of several distinct kinds of positivism. At one level all varieties of positivism seem to be alike, but at a level somewhat closer to practice there are several versions (Parsons 1937, 70–81, distinguished four). I will give my impressions of the current splits within positivism, basing this not only on differences in method but also on the theory groupings that underlie these differences.

It was statistical positivism, based on the notion of samples, that produced the status attainment research. Then there is an action theoretical variety—action theory in James Coleman's, not Talcott Parsons', sense—based on the notion of a rationalizing, hedonistic actor. The latter falls easily into methodological individualism; the former does not. The statistical approach could be called epistemological positivism, akin to the Vienna Circle's principle of verification. The action theoretical approach might be called practical or praxiological positivism, for here the interest is not in the blind relation of cause and effect, but in the conscious directing of means to ends.

Both versions use a natural-science analogy, and both are "scientistic." Statistics uses physics as a model, whereas action theory uses biology, specifically evolutionary biology, where evolution is nature-as-maximizer. This metaphor was used in both classical and neoclassical economics and in behavioristic psychology, two disciplines which acted as models for the use of the metaphor in sociology. Within social theory, exchange theory and rational choice—two somewhat competing approaches—were pursuing a distinctive version of positivism. Throughout the 1970s the praxiologists were gaining on the statisticians, the latter slowed down by the status attainment boondoggle, creating a certain imbalance within positivism as a whole.

A related split opened between statistics and network or structural mathematics. Again, these are both forms of positivism but they go in different directions. Perhaps the most clearly disputed problem in the statistics-network split was over the nature of contemporary capitalism. The statistical approach has a cognitive affinity with the structure of a non-oligopolistic market economy. Oligopoly is the same kind of methodological threat as revolution, i.e., both are one-of-a-kind, qualitative-historical events, inaccessible to statistical treatment. Not only status attainment but the economy as such tended to be viewed as a market. In contrast, the network approach had the mathematical tools for analyzing small numbers of cases, including oligopolies. In addition, the network people could study a single case, finding the relations among its parts, in ways the statisticians could not.

The three-part split—statistics, action theory, and networks—did not go unnoticed by the critics, for a separate and distinct line of attack was soon mounted against each of the three branches of positivism. [2]

By the end of the 1970s, which concluded the second stage of the interregnum, the positivists were losing the appearance of hegemony, both from external attacks and internal difficulties. Most of the material base—jobs, curricular control, and access to key journals—remained, but research monies, due to the poor economy, were diminishing. What was more noticeable was that the spirit was gone. The attacks could not be adequately refuted, the product (those coefficients of correlation, etc.) was embarrassingly modest, the splits were getting worse, and the money itself—the oil that made the machine run—was getting scarce.

In my opinion, the main thing that stopped positivism from gaining hegemony was the inability to create theory. If theory without research tends to be "empty," research without theory tends to be decidedly "blind." In particular, the measurement implications of positivism have opposite effects for theory and empirical research, easily facilitating a version of the latter, but constituting an epistemological obstacle to reaching the former.

By the 1980s the positivists had lost their bid for hegemony. They were settling into a series of specialties, united only by a quite generic philosophy of science. Though they were certainly not dismantled, as the functionalists had been, neither did the attacking positions gain much ground. Instead something rather unexpected happened to sociology in the 1980s, as the current interregnum realigned itself into still a third stage.

The Resurgence of European Social Theory

In the early eighties ideas started wafting in from Europe, particularly from the continent. Paris, Frankfurt, and Oxford/Cambridge were becoming the newest centers for social theory, first slowly and then with a growing pace. Not only had American positivism become uninteresting from the standpoint of world sociology, the critics of positivism had become uninteresting. In fact, the whole American system of sociology and social theory became uninteresting, under the burden of being slightly old-fashioned. The excitement and the "action" simply began to go elsewhere, and the Americans, of whatever stripe, were increasingly viewed as provincial and unimaginative.[3] I am not suggesting that European ideas have a hegemony in sociology, or even in social theory. Rather this approach is beginning to be the most noticeable beneficiary of positivism's theoretical failure, somewhat as positivism itself gained when functional theory declined.

The role of British social theory is important in this latest stage of the interregnum, for these theorists received the continental ideas first —often in the original language—and acted as brokers of these ideas to the Americans. Anthony Giddens' *New Rules of Sociological Method* (1976) and *Central Problems in Social Theory* (1979), for example, rendered the new ideas into terms that Americans could understand.

But the British also supplied ideas of their own. The left cultural studies of Stuart Hall, the structuration theory of Anthony Giddens, the conflict theory of Perry Anderson and Michael Mann, and the linguistic ideas of the Wittgensteinians had an impact that was distinct from the continental turn. The British were becoming a new force in sociology, both as original thinkers and as links to the continent. During the earlier functionalist period the British had been following American styles, including conflict theory, as well as functionalism and positivism. When they broke from American influence in the 1970s, their orientation shifted largely to the continent. At the 1985 American Sociological Association convention Jennifer Platt, then on leave from England, told me, "When I first came here in the fifties, I was one of many. Now I'm still turned American because of my research, but I am among the few. Most are turning to the Continent."

The British influence on American social theory is, if anything, increasing, as British sociologists, largely for logistic reasons, have taken jobs in the United States. In very recent years this list includes Stephen Lukes (Columbia), John Heritage (UCLA), Perry Anderson (the New School), Gianfranco Poggi (Virginia), John Hall (Harvard), Michael Mann (UCLA), and Anthony Giddens (Santa Barbara), among others.

Another way the European, and especially continental, influence is noticeable in the eighties is in neighboring disciplines in American universities. Literary criticism has been quite taken with continental theory, including phenomenology, critical theory, hermeneutics, and especially French structuralism, post-structuralism, and later spin-offs. In a major university literary criticism in turn affects several departments, such as English, classics, comparative literature, French, Slavic languages, Spanish, Italian, and Portuguese, linguistics, and speech communication. Continental theory is also now important in anthropology, of growing importance in philosophy and women's studies, and even making inroads into history and political science. Sociology departments have now been encircled, almost administratively, for universities are bustling with European theory, even though sociology itself has been slow to recognize these ideas.

I have now brought the historical sketch up to the present. Before continuing, let us consider some interim conclusions.

1. The history of American social theory has moved, stepwise, from an emphasis on interaction (the Chicago School) to social structure (functionalism) to culture (the continental turn). Each of these three is a distinct and important sui generis level in human life, but they are also interconnected. As we shall see, the theoretical integration of these levels is both a problem and an opportunity for current social theory.

2. Kuhn's theory of science does not work for the history of sociology. His approach cannot explain our paradigm space, paradigms, or interregnums. There is also a unique kind of "anomaly" in sociology's history; for Kuhn, anomalies were systematic empirical or theoretical problems that a given theory could not solve. But in addition to these systematic problems, sociology has had one-of-a-kind historical problems that come out of the blue to defeat theories. The Great Depression was such a problem for the Chicago School, itself too centered on interaction to be able to theorize this collapse in social structure. Unrest in the 1960s and economic stagflation in the 1970s were similar historical anomalies for the functionalists. The vagaries of history have a tendency to betray social theories, periodically giving them at best a hegemony of ten to twenty years. The social sciences need to understand the dynamics of their own histories, and for this to happen they need a separate historiography.

3. Lacking this historiography, it still seems plausible to say sociology will not have another dominating school of thought, either in the United States of worldwide, for the indefinite future. The theoretical stalemate of the last twenty years suggests this prediction, although I will return to this question in the last section of this paper.

Perhaps as long as world capitalism remains unstable and, so to speak, downwardly mobile, none of the social sciences will have clear hegemonies. In particular, the field of economics will probably not settle, theoretically, until world capitalism falls into a clearer pattern, whether for better or worse. Sociology does not depend directly on economic theory very much, and in some respects this field has always defined itself in opposition to economics. But this very opposition is important to sociology's self-definition. In addition, economic theory tends of formalize state policy, and sociology must work within the parameters of this policy.

4. Finally, the present situation in social theory—a kind of rolling and dynamic pluralism—has been around for enough years to show some signs of institutionalization. University departments are beginning to adjust to this principle to some extent. In addition, a sort of balance-of-power process is setting in, whereby any group or coalition of groups that starts moving ahead is met by a newly formed coalition of "outs," who resist the move.

THE ESSAYS AS HISTORICAL

These essays come right out of the historical flow. They group into waves, which themselves have causes and meanings, as I have tried to show in the first part of this essay. The wave of "former glory" carries two riders: the symbolic interactionists, who draw selectively on the Chicago School theory, and the neofunctionalists, who draw similarly on 1950s functionalism. Old paradigms don't die in sociology (another problem for Kuhn); they just drop their weakest concepts, readjust their alliances, slim down, and keep fighting. As Ritzer notes in this volume, both symbolic interactionism and neofunctionalism are feisty, upbeat, and surprisingly successful comebacks from old paradigms.

The protests of the 1960s launched another historical wave. The essays on feminism and Marxism are the most "sixties-ish" papers, although both show the continuous development of these positions right up to the present. Ethnomethodology is in some ways also a product of the 1960s, although Garfinkel's major theoretical innovation preceded that decade. Still, the unmasking theme in Garfinkel fit the sixties mood. Conflict theory is also a great unmasker and a product of the 1960s. Marxism criticizes capitalism, but conflict theory—at least in Collins' version—criticizes all positions (all the "grand narratives").

A third wave is that of positivism, pictured as weak and barely hanging on in Turner's essay, but obviously alive, well, and expansive. This wave contains about three and a half essays. Those on exchange theory, rational choice, and Turner's own history are squarely positivist, although in different ways. The one on conflict theory by Collins is about half positivist. Collins often tries to use the positivist style on problems that have been considered inaccessible to positivism. In particular he has attempted to decompose ritual processes—drawing on Durkheim and Goffman—into positivist, cause-and-effect underpinnings. I think he actually departs from positivist logic and slides into other modes of explanation in these interesting forays, and that is why I score him only half.

Then there is the European wave, solidly represented in several essays and full of its own newness. Kellner on postmodernism and Lemert on post-structuralism—each creative in its own way—are thoroughly European. Antonio on Marxism is in this wave too, for the Marxism Antonio is tracking is highly responsive to the European intellectual climate. The essay on culture, by Wuthnow and Lamont, is partly concerned with French thought, but a less "continental," more nearly empirical variety.

The paper on feminism by Lengermann and Niebragge-Brantley is not very concerned with continental thought, although feminist scholarship itself is. This paper, however, lays out a great challenge to continental theories of culture in its provocative discussion of gender and epistemology.

Boden's essay on ethnomethodology also belongs in this batch. In retrospect, Garfinkel was a "scout" for the current European invasion, the ideas of which are a later version of what Garfinkel was importing from Europe in the fifties. Boden makes this point by showing how the central themes of ethnomethodology have resonance with similar themes in continental thought.

Finally there is Ritzer's essay on the micro-macro issue, connecting them all. Why is this issue so important right now? This question used to be considered meta-sociological and quasi-philosophical, but it is now clearly open to empirical investigation as well. Theories that are confined to one level, e.g., micro or macro, are reaching for the other levels. This can be done by stretching concepts across levels or trying for syntheses with theories at the unavailable levels. A sought-after prize in these essays is network theory, for both Collins on conflict theory and Cook, O'Brien, and Kollock on exchange are trying to coalesce with it.

More generally, some of the cross-level moves in social theory are attempts to reduce one level to another, constituting a kind of "levels imperialism." This creates backlash. For example, both Althusser and, in a less self-conscious way, Parsons tended to dissolve the individual in the social structure, thus creating an imperialism of structure over "agency" (DiTomaso 1982). The same sort of imperialism is present in post-structuralism and postmodernism, although here it is the culture that dissolves the individual.

Perhaps an underlying reason for the currency of the micro-macro issue is the economic malaise of the last twenty years. The world economy, both capitalist and communist, is experiencing downward mobility. This condition has a delegitimizing effect on all of the political ideologies, right, left, and center, for they are all based on the promise of material progress. To maintain legitimacy in the face of stalled and declining living standards, states have a strong temptation to "colonize" the micro world, i.e., the ordinary beliefs of the "natural attitude." The political purpose of this colonization is to make populations think they are better off materially than they actually are. At least this is how I interpret Habermas' critique of contemporary capitalism, and it gives another reason why the levels question is a hot issue. In this case the reason is "self" defense and resistance to the iron cage.

MOVES TOWARD SYNTHESIS IN THE ESSAYS

Shifting now from history to systematics, some of these essays fall into clusters or local syntheses, as Ritzer points out in his introductory comments. These syntheses are still in process and not yet clearly successful, although they do represent an important tendency in the volume. The two strongest attempts are among the positivist and the European-influenced essays.

The Positivist Synthesis

Earlier I spoke of splits within positivism, distinguishing statistical, praxiological, and network branches. The two praxiological or "action" essays in this collection are those on exchange and rational choice. The former derives partly from behavioristic theory in psychology and partly from the rational actor of economics; the latter derives solely from economics. Both of these positions are primarily micro and both are trying to establish more presence at the macro level. The exchange essay makes contact with network's macro theory, and the rational choice essay of Friedman and Hechter attempts to picture the macro level as itself a rational structure.

Both moves to macro are expansive for these theories, but there are associated problems. For one, there is the awkwardness of the partial overlap between exchange and rational choice. Why two theories? One could say that there is a lot of synthesis between the two, but one could also ask why there need be two in the first place, since they cover much the same ground with similar premises. A second problem is that network theory is in large part critical of economics, both in the rational actor and the market. If exchange theory connects itself to this macro position, it will weaken its increasingly economic micro position. This problem would be even greater in a synthesis of rational choice and network.

Turner's provocative history of American sociology is also part of the positivist synthesis, or attempt at synthesis, in this volume. Turner's position encompasses both statistical and praxiological positivism, the former being largely a macro structuralism and the latter a micro interactionism. His structuralism, however, is not the network structuralism that exchange theory is eyeing. His, like Blau's, is based on populations and their distributions, whereas network theory is based on the relations among "nodes." The plurality of approaches to structuralism among the positivists creates troubles for their synthesis.

Collins' semi-positivism does not fit the positivist synthesis well either. He wants to connect his version of macro conflict theory—which is neither network theory nor the Turner-Blau population structuralism—with a micro theory. But Collins' choice of micro is neither rational choice nor exchange. Instead it is the semi-positivist semiotic or ritualism which he has created on his own.

What we have here are five positions—exchange, rational choice, Turner's positivism, network structuralism, and Collins' semi-positivism—all maneuvering to get as much as they can of the positivistic intellectual space. The result is a strong effort at synthesis, but given the clashes and contradictions, there is also something of a centrifugal, dissipating effect, continuous with the positivists' earlier, unsuccessful bid for hegemony.

The European Synthesis

As mentioned earlier, this grouping includes the essays on postmodernism and post-structuralism, and to some extent those on Marxism, feminism, and culture. The lodestone of this cluster is recent French thought, especially structuralism (e.g., Saussure and Levi-Strauss), post-structuralism (e.g., Lacan, Althusser, Foucault, Barthes, and Derrida), and postmodernism (e.g., Baudrillard and Lyotard). Other kinds of recent trends in European though have tended to get caught up in debates with the French. This is true of critical theory, including Habermas' version, forms of phenomenology that survived Levi-Strauss' attack on Sartre, various kinds of hermeneutics and the closely associated semiotics, and Wittgensteinian linguistic theory.

This bundle of ideas has given us what I called stage three of the current interregnum. If there is a single theme cutting across these ideas it is that of the linguistic model, both in the strong form—that social reality is basically linguistic—and in the weaker, more analogical form—that social reality is structured "like" a language.

This cluster is full of novelty for social theory. Number, the great model of the positivists, is pretty much demoted. Instead language is the preferred epistemological model. And, as positivism has always resonated with the physical sciences in universities, this cluster has increasing resonance with the humanities.

One weakness of this cluster, however, is the emphasis on culture to the neglect of the social structure, including the class system. Some of the new European thinkers—especially Bourdieu, Foucault, and Althusser among the French—are quite concerned with social structure and conflict, but this is not the dominant position. The essays by Kellner and Antonio are at great pains to try to bring the continental discussion back to considerations of social structure, especially the class system. This seems a useful corrective to the continent's heavy emphasis on culture.

Another weakness of this cluster is that its central concepts have not yet settled down into clear, examinable premises. Its key ideas have all the flux and ambiguity of the too-new. For example, let us look at two terms, decentering and narrative.

The French have used the term "decentering" in many—perhaps too many—senses. It started with Sartre's "Transcendence of the Ego" paper ([1936–1937] 1957), where he did a kind of decentering of Husserl's concept of the ego, showing it to be "nothing" at its core. Levi-Strauss introduced a second kind of decentering in separating mythical and other structures from selves, although allowing for a collective, unconscious self. Foucault, Barthes, and Althusser pushed Levi-Strauss still farther by historicizing the self—i.e., by showing how it allegedly came to be from historical causes—and by eliminating the collective self. Derrida went in still another direction by arguing that all sets of meanings are without logical "centers," and that texts should be decentered from their authors. Finally Lacan, returning to Sartre's focus, gave another internal decentering of the self, although this time the argument was based on linguistics, not phenomenology.

This is a rather diverse batch of meanings to place on the word "decentering." I think it is entirely possible to systematize and clarify this concept, although it would not be in the spirit in which the concept has grown, and in any case this systematization is yet to be done.

"Narrative" is another term that has come fast, at least in sociology, and in several guises. The term was made popular by Lyotard in his *The Postmodern Condition: A Report on Knowledge* (1984), in which he argues against the continuing viability of the "grand narratives." He defines these narratives primarily by enumeration as Hegelianism, hermeneutics, critical theory, Marxism, and neoclassical economics (xxiii). In contrast, Lyotard advocated little or first-order narratives, which he identified with Wittgenstein's language games. These are not the same as Merton's middle range theories, for in principle Merton allowed the possibility of a grand theory that would unite them all. But Lyotard introduces so many qualifiers to the game analogy that the result is a less than clear concept.

Before Lyotard introduced this term, it was already being used in other disciplines, especially history and literary criticism. The historical discussion, which began in the early twentieth century with Croce, heated up in the 1960s (Thompson 1984, 207). Here the term is a humanistic one (e.g., against Hempel 1942), used to interpret the historical enterprise in an anti-positivist way. History as story or narrative was depicted as including the human subject, not only as topic but also as author and audience.

In literary theory the term was used by various kinds of structuralists, their purpose often being anti-humanist and anti-subject. For example, Levi-Strauss' analysis of myths depicts them as narratives which lack both authors and subjects, except for the collective subject. The dominant position in the field of "narratology" portrays discourse of all kinds as lacking an author and existing independently of human subjects (Mitchell 1981; *Modern Fiction Studies* 1987).

The use of the term narrative in the present essays, drawing on Lyotard, but also on the two somewhat contradictory scholarly traditions, has too many overtones for precise theoretical usage. In particular the term has not yet been systematically contrasted to more conventional terms such as "theory" and "ideology."

Nevertheless, Lyotard's essay has been extremely influential, and there is a sense in which the grand narratives are indeed in disrepute in social theory, the current lengthy interregnum being characterized by precisely that fact. Like the positivist cluster, the European grouping has its share of weak spots, and only time will tell how much is style and how much substance.

Ethnomethodology and Symbolic Interactionism

In principle, both of these lines of qualitative, micro theory are open and kindred to the European wave, Garfinkel, in fact, having paved the way for it. It is striking that ethnomethodology did not wither away, despite a relatively inhospitable response from the rest of sociology. Spin-offs from Garfinkel, as in the works of Aaron Cicourel, Harvey Sacks, and John Heritage, have also become a force of their own. While American support for ethnomethodology has been modest, European support has been much stronger. Ethnomethodology has also established links with other disciplines, such as linguistics, artificial intelligence, and cognitive theory in psychology.

Symbolic interactionism too, as Fine's essay shows, has had a noticeable persistence in the theoretical competition. I think this is partly because the ideas of classical American pragmatism and early interactionism are such a strong patrimony. The symbolic interactionists have leaned heavily on George Herbert Mead, despite conflicts of interpretation. But pragmatism still has unexploited resources in the works of James, Dewey, Baldwin, Cooley, and Peirce, among others. The overall social theory, or family of theories, embedded in pragmatism has never been worked out, and the symbolic interactionists could deepen their position by looking more closely at their patrimony.

Such an examination could also strengthen the symbolic interactionists' connection to the European wave, for pragmatism was one of the early sources for this wave. In particular, Husserl borrowed heavily from William James, Lacan appears to have done the same from Baldwin, and contemporary European semiotics draws heavily on Peirce. Symbolic interactionism could deepen its articulation to the present by better mining its past.

Neofunctionalism

This grouping has inherited the earlier critics of Parsons-Merton functionalism. Those criticisms had come from exchange theory, the qualitative micro positions, the macro conflict positions, and the logical wing of positivism. The neofunctionalists in the United States, in contrast to the increasingly influential Niklas Luhmann in Germany, have downplayed the concept of "function" (Turner and Maryanski 1988), thus evading some of the criticisms. But the neofunctionalists have, if anything, leaned more heavily on the notion of moral causation, via norms and values.

This shift in emphasis creates two problems. For one, social theory at large has moved away from the moral toward the cognitive, linguistic, and meaningful. This gives the neofunctionalists a somewhat out-of-date aura. In addition, it is difficult to ground morality without functions. If morality is based on functional need, it has a clear, causal foundation. If functions are discarded, morality becomes relativistic and loses much of its explanatory force. If morality is not based on function, then one cannot but ask about its cognitive and meaningful foundations. The neofunctionalists might have to choose: either to return to function as the basis of morality (toward Luhmann), or to soften the emphasis on morality and turn in a more semiotic direction (toward continental theory).

Nevertheless, the neofunctionalists are making an important impact on contemporary theory. They are exploring connections with neighboring positions, including those of the earlier critics. In addition, they are producing a large number of important works, especially in cultural sociology. Jeffrey Alexander, in particular, has become established as a major social theorist and a highly competent group leader.

THE ADVANTAGES OF PLURALISM

Contemporary sociology has differentiated itself into a number of points of view, both empirical and theoretical. So far I have been talking about the history and systematics of this pluralism. Now let me shift to its possibilities for theoretical progress.

1. *Competition.* Pluralism implies competition, and without being a tunnel-vision capitalist, one can say competition has its strengths. During sociology's take-off period, from the late nineteenth century until World War I, theoretical competition prevailed, not only in the United States, but more importantly in Europe. The competition was to some extent expressed as nationalistic rivalry, leading toward World War I, but still it was productive for theory. The great patrimony of social theory dates from that period. This includes not only the works of Durkheim and Weber, but also those of Marx and the Marxists, a little earlier, and John Maynard Keynes (Wiley 1983) a little later. In addition, the great American contribution to micro theory, extending from Peirce and James to Mead and Cooley came from that period. If sociology had been centered, worldwide, around a dominant point of view during that time, there would not have been the creative flowering that issued from such competition.

Early sociology was trying to understand the great transformation into capitalism, urbanism, and democracy. Today we are at the other end of modernization, trying to understand and theorize what appears to be another transformation, into a new institutional and cultural pattern.

It seems to me that the worst imaginable way of trying to theorize the contemporary experience is to narrow the intellectual options. In particular, a changing system requires wide-open qualitative analysis, preferably from many points of view. If there is a problem here with the present pluralism, it is in the inadequate attention paid to the "hard" social structure. In this paper the term "structuralism" has come up in about a half dozen different ways, but too many of these are not getting at the historically embedded structure of armies, economies, and nations. The essays most concerned with the new transformation are those by Collins, Antonio, and Kellner.

2. *Cause and Meaning.* Another strength of the present pluralism is that social theory has a better chance of providing adequate and comprehensive explanations. Both Weber and Durkheim respected the broad positivistic goal of causal analysis, but they also thought explanation required something more. Weber was quite explicit about wanting both cause and meaning. Durkheim was a little fuzzier about what he would add to cause. In the *Rules of Sociological Method* he added function, but in the *Elementary Forms of Religious Life* he moved closer to the Weberian formula, that of cause and meaning.

The present diversity in theory is well adapted to pursuing the Weber-Durkheim formula for adequate explanation. The causal side has been deepened by the computer, new statistical developments, and the energy of the positivist groupings. The meaningful side has been strengthened by semiotic and linguistic models, by new theories of meaning, and by a variety of other European innovations.

At present, these two approaches to explanation are operating independently and in relative isolation from each other, but there are little signs that this may be changing (e.g., Giddens 1984; Jasso 1988; Fararo 1989). Theorists are beginning to try to integrate the two aspects of explanation, some signs of which appear in the present collection.

3. *Mediating the Natural Sciences and the Humanities.* Social theory's capacity for combining causal and meaningful explanation is related to its strategic, mediating position between the natural sciences and the humanities.

Human beings are at the crossroads of the material and non-material worlds, for they combine physical bodies with selves. The natural sciences can study the bodies and the humanities can study the selves and their cultural products. These two approaches find aspects of the truth, but they also tend to pull the problem apart, for they split human nature into two unintegrated parts. The social sciences, despite the historical vagaries of their origins, have always had the strategic opportunity of studying human nature and the social as totalities. Causal explanation tends to be based on the body and meaningful explanation on the self. A complete theory of human life requires both kinds of explanation together, as Weber and Durkheim sensed. Such an explanation fulfills sociology's potential as mediator between the natural sciences and humanities, a crucial role for integrating universities as well as bodies of knowledge.

4. *Theoretical Diversity and Ideological Freedom.* Social theorists are always engaged in ideological disputes with each other, even if only implicitly. Ideological closure, always the bane of social theory, ends the competition and creativity. Hitler and Stalin were examples of this closure, although there are plenty of less dramatic examples.

There is no way to decree ideological tolerance in social theory, although the general principle of intellectual respect seems to help. At present there is a relatively healthy state of tolerance in theory, a circumstance conducive to pluralism and diversity. Creativity is partly the result of the clash of ideologies, as the beginnings of sociology illustrate, and pluralism fosters this sort of clash. I do not think a theoretical hegemony is necessarily an ideological straightjacket, but it is nevertheless easier for states to impose ideologies under these circumstances. In fact, states decree scientific hegemonies—as Hitler and Stalin did—to facilitate ideological uniformity.

I have listed a series of advantages to the present diversity in social theory. These work together toward creative and comprehensive explanation. The present period in world history seems especially ripe for theoretical progress, for there is an elective affinity between this relatively open, reconstitutive period in time and the similarly open situation in theory.

POSSIBLE FUTURES FOR SOCIAL THEORY

It goes without saying that the future of social theory depends on what happens in world history. World war or a sharp ideological change in world politics would have massive effects, and the near-future of the world economy, including the American role therein, is an obvious contextual force. Even such a specific factor as which political party holds the American presidency affects theory. In particular, the continental turn in the humanities seems to be unpopular with recent Republican administrations, and given the federal control over the means of intellectual production, this could eventually affect the growth of these ideas. But if we suspend these elective affinity questions,[4] the best prediction is probably to extrapolate the present into the future, i.e., to expect continued pluralism, despite continual bids for hegemony.

Let me approach this by a process of elimination. I see three alternative scenarios to continued pluralism: 1) a methodological hegemony, either all-positivist or all-interpretive; 2) a break-up of sociology into two separate disciplines; or 3) a new hegemony, which combines both causal and meaningful explanation.

A methodological hegemony seems most unlikely, even though some of the essays in this collection seem to favor such an outcome. The historical precedent argues against this, at least in the United States. Both previous hegemonies—those of the Chicago school and functionalism—were methodological hybrids, combining quantitative and qualitative elements. In addition, these overarching, methodological terms are little more than ritualistic labels. Both the quantitative and qualitative wings are internally divided into sharply competing approaches, and I do not think either one could ever find enough internal unity to "rule." Finally there is an epistemological "blind spot" in both methods, requiring each to seek out the other.

The second option—the internal break-up of sociology into two "differentiated" disciplines—also seems unlikely, if only for reasons of material security and logistical survival in universities. Such an eventuality would not strengthen sociology but would seem more likely to mark its resorption into the same neighboring disciplines from which it emerged in the first place.

The more likely option would seem to be a new hybrid hegemony, based on some creative merger of positivist and interpretive ingredients. I have been examining this scenario throughout the paper, however, and it simply does not look like a serious, near-term possibility, either historically or systematically. There *are* little signs of this possibility in the essays; for example, exchange theory's interest in symbolic interaction or ethnomethodology's interest in artificial intelligence, but they are just too little—hardly more than glints in the essayists' eyes.

I return, then, to my prediction of a continuation of present trends. This condition not only has the advantages listed earlier; it is also consonant with the postmodernist argument—overstated as it is—that the grand narratives are dead and middle-level language games are the discourse of the future (I would add "for the time being"). Coalitions will be explored and hegemonies will be sought after, but the strength of social theory today lies in the multiplicity of its tools and perspectives.

The essays in this collection, and the highly successful conference on which they are based, were intended to capture the main trends in each theoretical field. I think they do so with amazing fidelity, and I can think of no better place in which to look for finding out what is going on right now in social theory.

NOTES

1. Jonathan Turner in the present volume argues that *The Polish Peasant* was not so much based on the replacement of instinct, as I have argued (1986), as on the replacement of evolution and organicism in general. He further argues that *The Polish Peasant* opened the way for the more precise measurement of mental processes, specifically attitudes. I am unconvinced on both counts.

By the time of *The Polish Peasant*, the macro theory of evolution, as a competitive process among and within species, had already been considerably moderated and softened in sociology. What remained as an obstacle to sociology's disciplinary emergence was the micro notion that individuals were biologically determined— that the physiological processes alone produced thought and affect. It is significant that the theory of instinct, as an explanation of individual behavior, was by then the argument of the discipline of psychology, not biology. As Znaniecki put it, retrospectively in 1950, the purpose of the concept of attitude was to eliminate "naturalistic explanations of individual conduct in terms of biological 'instinct,' innate 'drives,' etc."

The subsequent move toward the measurement of attitudes, initiated by Thurstone (1928), deflected Thomas and Znaniecki's project away from its phenomenological orientation. The deflection was not back to instincts again, but nevertheless to another kind of positivism.

In this paper I cannot go into the difference between the theory of *The Polish Peasant* and that of the 1920s Chicago School, the two being similar but not the same.

2. Some varieties of systems theory, including the influential version of Niklas Luhmann, could be considered a fourth kind of positivism. The nature, causes, and consequences of the splits in positivism have never been adequately looked into, despite Parsons' promising beginning in *The Structure of Social Action* (1937, 70–81).

3. I deliberately emphasize the novel aspects of European social theory. In addition, the Europeans are pursuing some more conventional lines, including the development of ideas from Mead, Goffman, ethnomethodology, and Parsons.

4. Obviously you cannot really "suspend" these questions. They are too big, and they give a fundamental "uncertainty," in the Keynesian sense, to sociology's future. As Keynes put it:

> By "uncertain" knowledge, let me explain, I do not mean merely to distinguish what is known for certain from what is only probable. The game of roulette is not subject, in this sense, to uncertainty; nor is the prospect of a Victory bond being drawn. Or, again, the expectation of life is only slightly uncertain. Even the weather is only moderately uncertain. The sense in which I am using this term is that in which the prospect of a European war is uncertain, or the price of copper and the rate of interest twenty years hence, or the obsolescence of a new invention, or the position of private wealth-owners in the social system in 1970. About these matters there is no scientific basis on which to form any calculable probability whatever. We simply do not know. (Keynes 1937, 213–214)

REFERENCES

Alexander, Jeffrey C. 1982. *Positivism, Presuppositions, and Current Controversies.* Berkeley: University of California Press.

Bernstein, Richard J. 1976. *The Restructuring of Social and Political Theory.* New York: Harcourt Brace Jovanovich.

Bhaskar, Roy. 1979. *The Possibility of Naturalism.* Atlantic Highlands, N.J.: Humanities Press.

Blalock, H. M. 1968. "The Measurement Problem: A Gap between the Languages of Theory and Research." In H. M. Blalock and Ann B. Blalock, eds., *Methodology in Social Research.* New York: McGraw-Hill.

Blalock, H. M. 1969. *Theory Construction: From Verbal to Mathematical Formulations.* Englewood Cliffs, N.J.: Prentice-Hall.

Blalock, H. M. 1979. "Dilemmas and Strategies in Theory Construction." In William E. Snizek, Ellsworth F. Fuhrman, and Michael K. Miller, eds., *Contemporary Issues in Theory and Research: A Metasociological Perspective.* Westport, Conn.: Greenwood Press.

Bourdieu, Pierre. 1989. "Social Space and Symbolic Power." *Sociological Theory* 7:14–25

DiTomaso, Nancy. 1982. "Sociological Reductionism from Parsons to Althusser." *American Sociological Review* 47:14–28.

Fararo, Thomas J. 1989. "The Spirit of Unification in Sociological Theory." *Sociological Theory* 7:175–190.

Giddens, Anthony. 1976. *New Rules of Sociological Method.* New York: Basic Books.

Giddens, Anthony. 1979. *Central Problems in Social Theory.* Berkeley: University of California Press.

Giddens, Anthony. 1984. *The Constitution of Society.* Berkeley: University of California Press.

Hempel, Carl G. 1942. "The Function of General Laws in History." *Journal of Philosophy* 39:35–48.

Hempel, Carl G. 1959. "The Logic of Functional Analysis." In Llewellyn Gross, ed., *Symposium on Sociological Analysis.* Evanston, Ill.: Row Peterson.

Jasso, Guillermina. 1988. "Principles of Theoretical Analysis." *Sociological Theory* 6:1–20.

Keynes, John Maynard. 1937. "The General Theory of Employment." *Quarterly Journal of Economics* 51:209–223.

Kuhn, Thomas S. 1970. *The Structure of Scientific Revolutions,* 2d ed. Chicago: University of Chicago Press.

Levine, Donald N. 1989. "Parsons' Structure (and Simmel) Revisited." *Sociological Theory* 7:161–174.

Lyotard, Jean-Francois. 1984. *The Postmodern Condition: A Report on Knowledge.* Minneapolis: University of Minnesota Press.

Mitchell, W. J. T., ed. 1981. *On Narrative.* Chicago: University of Chicago Press.

Modern Fiction Studies. 1987. "Narrative Theory." Special Issue. Vol. 33, no. 3.

Nagel, Ernest. 1956. "A Formalization of Functionalism." In Ernest Nagel, *Logic Without Metaphysics.* Glencoe, Ill.: The Free Press.

Parsons, Talcott. 1937. *The Structure of Social Action.* New York: McGraw-Hill.

Sartre, Jean-Paul. [1936–1937] 1957. *The Transcendence of the Ego.* Reprint. New York: Farrar, Straus and Giroux.

Skocpol, Theda. 1979. *States and Social Revolutions.* Cambridge: Cambridge University Press.

Smelser, Neil J. 1962. *Theory of Collective Behavior.* New York: The Free Press.

Stinchcombe, Arthur L. 1968. *Constructing Social Theories.* New York: Harcourt, Brace and World.

Thomas, William I., and Florian Znaniecki. 1918–1920. *The Polish Peasant in Europe and America.* 5 vols. Boston: Richard G. Badger. (Vols. 1 and 2 originally published by the University of Chicago Press, 1918.)

Thompson, John B. 1984. *Studies in the Theory of Ideology.* Berkeley: University of California Press.

Thurstone, L. L. 1928. "Attitudes can be Measured." *American Journal of Sociology* 33:529–554.

Turner, Jonathan H., and A. R. Maryanski. 1988. "Is 'Neofunctionalism' Really Functional?" *Sociological Theory* 6:110–121.

Wiley, Norbert. 1979. "The Rise and Fall of Dominating Theories in American Sociology." In William E. Snizek, Ellsworth F. Fuhrman, and Michael K. Miller, eds., *Contemporary Issues in Theory and Research: A Metasociological Perspective.* Westport, Conn.: Greenwood Press.

Wiley, Norbert. 1983. "The Congruence of Weber and Keynes." *Sociological Theory* 1:30–57.

Wiley, Norbert. 1985. "The Current Interregnum in American Sociology." *Social Research* 52:179–207.

Wiley, Norbert. 1986. "Early American Sociology and the *Polish Peasant.*" *Sociological Theory* 4:20–40.

Znaniecki, Florian. 1950. " 'Comment' on John L. Thomas's 'Marriage Prediction in the Polish Peasant.' " *American Journal of Sociology* 55:577–578.

NAME INDEX

Abel, Elizabeth, 237, 245, 252
Aberle, David, 383, 389
Abrams, Philip, 189, 193, 206
Acker, Joan, 63
Adorno, T., 7, 111, 113, 295–96, 309
Ainlay, Stephen, 289, 313
Alexander, Jeffrey, 4, 5, 6, 14, 19, 21, 22,
    24, 33–34, 38, 40–41, 44–48, 53, 56,
    137, 148, 171, 177, 186–89, 191, 193,
    194–97, 202, 206, 290–91, 293–94,
    309n, 349, 351–53, 356, 357–59, 360,
    362, 364n, 365–67, 397, 409, 414
Alford, Robert, 352, 367
Althusser, Louis, 57, 97–98, 111, 231,
    234, 252n, 295–96, 303, 309n, 403,
    405–6
Anderson, Perry, 69, 84–85, 88, 104–5,
    111, 400
Anderson, Robert, 10, 167, 181, 202, 203
Antonio, Robert, 4, 8, 14, 21, 90, 99–
    111, 403, 406, 410
Archer, Margaret S., 38, 40, 53, 60
Aristotle, 108
Aronowitz, Stanley, 88, 105, 110–11,
    299, 309
Aronson, Ronald, 89, 111
Ashcraft, Richard, 292, 309
Ashley, David, 120, 143, 148
Atkinson, Maxwell, 10, 202, 206
Attewell, Paul, 186, 206
Axelrod, Robert, 223, 228

Bachrach, P., 309
Bailey, Kenneth, 363, 367
Bakhtin, M. N., 293
Baldwin, John, 120–21, 143–44, 148
Bales, Robert Freed, 117, 142, 148
Baraclough, Geoffrey, 258–60, 275, 283
Baratz, M., 309
Barnett, B., 142, 155
Barry, Kathleen, 328, 341
Barth, F., 162, 177
Barthes, Roland, 231, 233–34, 238–40,
    252n, 256, 283n, 290, 295, 297, 309n,
    405–6
Baudrillard, Jean, 3, 14, 104–5, 112, 114,
    255–56, 261–64, 266–71, 274, 277–
    78, 283n, 309–10, 405
Bauer, Otto, 57
Baum, R. C., 63
Bauman, Zygmunt, 111
Baynes, Kenneth, 276, 283
Bealer, Robert, 367
Beardon, James, 17
Becker, Gary, 158, 163, 177, 193, 206,
    225, 228
Becker, Howard, 37, 60n, 121, 127–28,
    130, 146n, 148, 298–99, 310, 378
Beeker, Caroline, 16
Bell, Daniel, 111, 258, 260, 261, 283
Bellah, R. N., 40, 45, 50, 58n, 60n, 292,
    303, 310
Bendor, Jonathan, 224, 228

417

Benhabib, Seyla, 96, 100, 111, 279, 282n, 283

Benjamin, Jessica, 7, 323, 326, 336–37, 341

Ben-Porath, Y., 163, 170, 177

Bennett, H., 128, 148

Bensman, Joseph, 147, 157

Benson, Douglas, 202, 206

Benton, T., 7, 24, 295, 300, 309–10

Berch, Bettina, 335, 341

Berger, Joseph, 52, 67, 389

Berger, Peter, 11, 14, 18, 24, 139, 148, 195, 206, 287, 289, 299, 303, 310, 333

Bergesen, Albert, 8

Berman, Marshall, 111

Berman, Russell, 257, 283

Bernard, Jessie, 317, 319, 323, 325, 331–32, 334, 341

Bernstein, Charles, 111

Bernstein, Eduard, 57

Bernstein, Richard, 252–53, 283n, 395, 414

Berscheid, E., 161, 177, 179

Besnier, Niko, 190, 206

Best, Steven, 272, 283

Bhaskar, Roy, 367, 393, 414

Bielby, Denise, 207

Birnbaum, Pierre, 309–10

Bittner, Egon, 206

Black, Max, 45

Blalock, H. M., 396, 414

Blau, Judith, 298, 310

Blau, Peter, 9, 16, 17, 24, 37, 60n, 159–60, 164, 168–69, 172–73, 176–77, 198, 206, 350, 362, 367, 389, 405

Bloch, Ernst, 309–10

Blum, Terry C., 16, 25

Blumer, Herbert, 8, 9, 19, 37, 47, 117–21, 124–28, 132, 137, 140, 143–44, 146–48, 350, 367, 384, 389

Boden, Deirdre, 11, 22, 23, 37, 63, 129, 138, 148, 153, 185, 213, 403

Bogard, William, 282, 283

Bogen, David, 207

Boli-Bennett, John, 85, 87

Bonford, Robert D., 155

Boorman, S. A., 350

Boswell, Terry, 8, 25

Bosworth, Susan, 365, 367

Bottomore, Tom, 7, 25

Boudon, Raymond, 231, 252n, 351–54, 367

Boulding, Elise, 322, 341

Bourdieu, Pierre, 3, 14, 25, 57, 82, 85–86, 187, 189, 207, 240, 252–53, 287, 293, 295–99, 306, 308n, 209–10

Bowles, Samuel, 8, 25, 102–3, 111

Bradshaw, A., 300, 310

Brams, Steven, 217, 228

Braudel, Fernand, 81, 86, 207

Breiger, R. L., 350

Brennan, Geoffrey, 177

Brezhnev, Leonid, 94

Brinton, Mary, 217, 228

Bronner, Stephen E., 270, 281, 283

Brown, Richard H., 19, 25, 145, 148, 252–53

Brownmiller, Susan, 328, 341

Brulin, Goran, 12, 29

Bruner, Edward, 293

Brustein, William, 216, 228

Buchanan, James, 225, 228

Bucher, Rue, 155

Bulmer, Martin, 25

Burawoy, Michael, 136, 143, 148

Burger, John S., 144, 148–49

Burke, Kenneth, 124, 130, 132, 145, 149

Burt, Ronald S., 17, 25, 81, 86, 167, 177, 225, 228, 351–53, 365n, 367

Button, Graham, 203, 207

Cahill, Spencer, 134, 149

Calhoun, Craig, 37, 60n, 79, 86, 363, 367

Calinescu, Matei, 258, 283

Callinicos, Alex, 105, 111, 189, 207

Camic, Charles, 35, 60

Cantor, Muriel, 298, 310

Carby, Hazel, 242, 253

Carley, K. M., 169, 177

Carling, Alan, 101, 111

Carrillo, Santiago, 95

Casey, Neil, 202

Castoriadis, Cornelius, 96

Cerreto, M., 180

Cerulo, Karen, 291, 310

Chafetz, Janet Saltzman, 15, 25

Chambers, Iain, 279, 283

Champagne, Duane, 53, 60

Chapin, Stuart, 377, 389
Chazel, Francois, 309, 310
Chen, Kuan-Hsing, 105, 111, 283
Chirico, JoAnn, 54, 65
Chodrow, Nancy, 15, 25, 335, 338, 340–41
Christenson, A., 179
Cicourel, Aaron, 37, 63, 186, 188, 189, 193, 202, 207, 351, 367, 408
Clark, Candace, 134, 149
Clark, M. S., 161, 177, 180
Clark, P. P., 309–10
Clark, T. J., 296, 310
Clarke, J., 309, 310
Clawson, Dan, 17, 25
Clayman, Steven, 199, 201, 202, 207
Clegg, Stewart, 295, 310
Clifford, James, 131–32, 149
Clough, Patricia, 120, 127, 145, 147n, 149
Cobb, Jonathan, 301
Cohen, G. A., 101, 111
Cohen, Ira, 188, 193, 196, 207
Cohen, N. D., 135, 147
Coleman, James S., 5, 9, 12, 19, 25, 37, 60n, 159–60, 162–65, 167–71, 173, 176–78, 216, 218, 282n, 351–53, 355, 365n, 367, 389, 398
Collins, Randall, 3, 4, 6, 7, 8, 9, 17, 22, 25, 26, 35–36, 38–39, 60n, 70, 72, 77–81, 83, 86, 124, 138, 141–42, 149, 172, 178, 186, 189, 191, 192, 193, 200, 202, 207, 300, 310, 316, 336, 341, 349, 351–52, 355, 357–60, 362–63, 365–68, 388, 395, 401–3, 405, 410
Colomy, Paul, 4, 5, 6, 19, 22, 26, 40–41, 47–48, 53, 55, 58n, 60–61, 137, 148, 193–94, 207
Comte, Auguste, 371–72, 377, 388–89
Conrad, Peter, 130, 147
Cook, David, 104, 114, 262–64, 267, 274, 280
Cook, Gary A., 144, 149
Cook, Judith, 325, 341
Cook, Karen, 4, 10, 17, 22, 23, 26, 78, 86, 161, 165–67, 169–70, 173–74, 178, 222, 228, 365n, 368
Cooley, Charles H., 119, 122, 124, 134, 138, 146n, 149, 374, 389, 408–9
Corsaro, Lillian, 129, 138, 149

Coser, Lewis, 3, 61, 70, 86, 186, 188, 207, 298, 310, 395
Cottrell, Leonard, 143, 149
Couch, Carl J., 119, 149
Coulon, Alain, 203, 207
Coutler, Jeff, 201, 207
Coutu, Walter, 122, 149
Coward, Rosalind, 256, 283
Crane, Diana, 298, 310
Creelan, Paul, 138, 142, 149
Cuff, E. C., 202, 207
Cullenberg, Stephen, 107, 115

Dahl, Robert, 309–11
Dahrendorf, Ralf, 36, 71, 86, 350, 368, 384, 390, 395
Dalton, Melville, 135, 149
Daly, Mary, 319, 341
Darnton, Robert, 37, 61
Darwin, Charles, 117, 373
Davis, Kingsley, 383, 390
Davis, Murray, 140, 149
Dawes, Robyn, 221, 228
de Beauvoir, Simone, 322, 341
Debord, Guy, 256, 283
Debray, Regis, 302, 311
DeCerteau, Michel, 309, 311
Deegan, Mary Jo, 144, 148–49, 340–41
Deleuze, Gilles, 104, 111–12, 239, 253, 255–56, 268, 278, 282n, 283
Della Fave, L. Richard, 165, 178
DeMan, Paul, 104
de Montilbert, C., 305
Denzin, Abraham, 3, 26, 112
Denzin, Norman, 120, 135, 139, 145, 149, 188, 207, 282, 284
Derrida, Jacques, 104, 111–12, 145, 231, 234–37, 239, 241, 252–53, 256, 275, 279, 283n, 291, 311, 405, 406
Deutsch, M., 161, 178
Deutschberger, Paul, 122, 156
deVault, Marjorie, 319, 332–33, 341
Devereaux, Edward C., 45, 61
deVos, Henk, 218, 228
Dewey, John, 118, 144, 408
Dews, Peter, 104–5, 112, 256, 265, 284
Dickens, David, 282, 284
Diderot, Denis, 124
DiMaggio, Paul, 127, 149, 291, 293, 300, 311

Dingwall, Robert, 188, 208
Dinnerstein, Dorothy, 323, 338, 341
DiTomaso, Nancy, 404, 414
Ditton, Jason, 124, 150
Donato, Eugenio, 252
Donovan, Josephine, 319, 341
Douglas, Jack, 132, 150
Douglas, Mary, 14, 287, 289, 293, 297–98, 306, 311
Downing, Brian, 78, 86
Downs, Anthony, 215, 228
Dubiel, Helmut, 96, 112
Duncan, O. D., 350, 368
During, Simon, 258, 284
Durkheim, Emile, 3, 21, 38, 49–51, 57n, 124, 130, 137, 142–44, 150, 289, 293, 296, 307, 311, 333, 347, 349, 354, 359, 365n, 372, 375–78, 380–81, 390, 392, 403, 409–11
Duval, Raymond, 30

Eagleton, Terry, 112, 295, 311
Eco, Umberto, 311
Edel, Abraham, 19, 26, 352, 368
Eder, Klaus, 53, 61
Edles, Laura D., 55, 58n, 61
Edwards, Richard 94, 112
Ehrenreich, Barbara, 323, 325, 335, 341
Ehrlich, D., 155
Eisenstadt, S. N., 26, 38, 40, 45, 50, 53, 61, 349, 351, 356, 365n, 368
Eisenstein, Hester, 322–23, 341
Ekeh, P. P., 176, 178
Elias, Norbert, 3, 295, 311
Ellis, John, 133–34, 256, 283
Elster, Jon, 3, 7, 26, 95, 101, 112, 208
Emerson, Richard M., 10, 17, 26, 86, 159–61, 165, 167–70, 172–74, 176, 178–79, 181, 227–28, 351, 355, 365n, 368
Engels, Friedrich, 57, 68, 71, 86, 89–92, 109n, 111, 115, 294–95, 314
Erikson, Kai, 130, 133, 150, 289
Etzioni, Amitai, 26, 225, 227–28, 260, 284

Faia, Michael H., 137, 150
Fararo, Thomas, 169, 179, 351–53, 358, 368, 410, 414
Farberman, Harvey, 135, 140, 142, 150, 155

Farganis, Sondra, 15, 26, 325, 331, 341
Faulkner, Robert R., 128, 135, 150
Featherstone, Mike, 257, 282n, 284
Ferre, Frederick, 284
Feyeraband, Paul, 291, 311
Fields, Karen, 292, 311
Fine, Gary A., 4, 8, 9, 21, 22, 26, 37, 61, 118, 120, 125–26, 128–30, 132–33, 135, 140, 142–44, 147n, 150, 152, 200, 208, 289, 299, 311, 358, 368, 408
Finegold, Kenneth, 37, 66
Fireman, Bruce, 126, 151
Fischer, C. S., 166, 179
Fischer, Ernest, 127, 146n, 150
Fischer, Michael, 245, 297–98, 314
Fisher, Bernice, 150
Fisher, Walter, 291, 311
Fisk, Milton, 112
Fiske, John, 284
Fitzpatrick, Kevin, 16
Fonow, Mary M., 325, 328, 341
Fontana, Andrea, 11, 26, 282n, 283
Foote, Nelson W., 134, 150
Foucault, Michel, 3, 13, 14, 26, 38, 57n, 61, 104–5, 111, 112, 199, 208, 231, 233, 237, 239–40, 251, 252n, 253, 255–56, 268, 275, 278–80, 283n, 284, 287, 289, 293, 295–99, 302, 306, 316, 405–6
Frank, Arthur, 120, 140, 150
Frank, Manfred, 279, 284
Franke, Boris, 269
Fraser, Nancy, 271, 281, 284
Frazer, Sir James, 162, 179
French, Marilyn, 336, 341
Freud, Sigmund, 7, 50, 143, 256, 267, 351
Frey, B., 165, 181
Friedan, Betty, 328, 342
Friedland, Roger, 196, 199, 209, 352, 367
Friedman, Debra, 1, 12, 13, 22, 26, 197, 209, 214, 219, 225, 227–28, 351, 366n, 268, 404
Friedman, Jonathan, 112
Friedman, Lisa, 63
Friedman, Milton, 221, 228
Friedman, Ray, 1, 12, 27
Friedrichs, Robert, 36, 61
Fuentes, Annette, 323, 325, 341
Fuller, Lon, 51

Gadamer, Hans-Georg, 145, 293, 311
Gagnon, A. G., 302, 311
Galaskiewicz, J., 166, 179
Gallant, Mary, 139, 150
Gamson, Lillian, 126, 151
Gans, Herbert, 147, 151, 292, 311
Garfinkel, Harold, 36, 51, 73, 138, 185, 191, 193, 194, 196, 198, 199, 200, 201, 202, 208, 350, 368, 402–3
Garnham, Nicholas, 309, 312
Gates, Henry L., 237, 242, 245, 253
Gecas, Viktor, 122–23, 153
Geertz, Clifford, 40, 42, 61, 133, 208, 287, 299, 303, 307, 312
Gellner, Ernest, 187, 188, 208
Geras, Norman, 103, 112
Gergen, Kenneth, 366, 368
Gergen, Mary, 366, 368
Gerstein, Dean, 5, 19, 26, 352, 368
Geuss, Raymond, 100, 112
Gibson, William, 249, 251, 252n, 253
Giddens, Anthony, 3, 21, 26, 35–36, 38, 61, 124, 151, 186, 189, 193, 199, 202, 208, 240–41, 245, 252–53, 295, 312, 351–53, 357, 359–60, 363, 365–66, 368, 390, 395, 400, 410, 414
Giddings, Franklin, 364, 365–66
Giesen, Bernhard, 40, 58n, 60n, 62, 171, 177, 364, 365–66
Gill, Sandra, 54, 62
Gilligan, Carol, 322, 332, 342
Gillmore, Mary R., 86, 165, 174, 178–79, 228
Gilmore, Samuel, 128, 151
Gilpin, Robert, 77, 86
Gintis, Herbert, 8, 102–3, 111
Gitlin, Todd, 230, 234, 299, 301, 312
Glaser, Barney, 118, 133, 140, 151
Glazer, Nona, 328, 342
Glennon, Lynda, 334, 342
Gluckman, Max, 126, 151
Goff, Tom W., 143, 151
Goffman, Erving, 9, 13, 14, 36–37, 51, 62, 72, 73, 118–21, 123–24, 126, 129, 132, 138–40, 142, 146–47, 151, 193, 194, 202, 299–300, 312, 403, 413
Golding, Peter, 309, 314
Goldman, Lucien, 127, 151, 296
Goldstone, Jack A., 78, 84, 86
Gonos, George, 9, 26, 147n, 151, 299, 312

Goode, Lillian, 37, 62
Goodwin, Charles, 203, 208
Gorbachev, Mikhail, 107
Gordon, David M., 94, 112
Gordon, Steven, 134, 151
Gorz, Andre, 96
Gottdiener, Marc, 301, 312
Gould, Mark, 46–49, 51, 62
Gouldner, Alvin, 18, 26, 90, 92, 112, 118, 130, 151, 163–64, 179, 188, 199, 209
Gove, Walter, 46–49, 51, 62
Gramsci, A., 57, 93, 112, 279, 295, 299, 301, 312
Granovetter, Mark, 17, 26, 27, 195, 196, 209
Graventa, John, 312
Greatbatch, David, 11, 27, 37, 62, 201, 203, 209
Greer, Germaine, 322, 342
Griffin, Susan, 33, 342
Griswold, Wendy, 291, 294, 312
Gross, Edward, 125, 147n, 151
Grossberg, Larry, 284
Guattari, Felix, 104, 111, 239, 253, 255–56, 268, 278, 283
Gurvitch, G., 175, 179
Gusfield, Joseph, 88, 125, 130, 151, 209, 291–92, 312

Haas, Jack, 9, 27
Habermas, Jürgen, 5, 7, 14, 21, 27, 34, 38–39, 47, 51, 55, 58n, 62, 99–100, 106, 109, 112–13, 142–43, 145, 151, 186, 193, 234, 252n, 256, 261–62, 265–66, 279, 282n, 284, 290–91, 293, 296, 302–3, 306–7, 312, 351, 353–54, 363, 366n, 368, 404–5
Haferkamp, Hans, 355, 368
Hage, Jerald, 358, 368
Haines, Valerie, 365, 368
Halkowski, Timothy, 209
Hall, John, 289, 312, 400
Hall, Peter, 146, 151
Hall, Stuart, 253, 275, 277–78, 284, 295, 312, 400
Handel, Warren, 209
Haraway, Donna, 325, 331, 342
Harding, Sandra, 245–46, 253, 284
Harding, Susan, 292, 312, 325, 335, 340n, 342

Harper, Richard, 209
Hart, Roderick, 291, 312
Hartsock, Nancy, 15, 27, 323, 328, 331, 336, 339, 342
Harvey, J. H., 179
Harvey, Lee, 18, 27
Hassan, Ihab, 104, 113
Hatfield, E., 161, 179
Hauser, Philip M., 127, 148
Hawley, Amos, 379, 390
Hay, J., 179
Hayes, Adrienne, 365, 368
Heap, James, 186, 209
Heath, Anthony, 163–64, 168, 176, 179
Heath, Christian, 203, 209
Hebdige, Dick, 278, 284, 297, 312
Hechter, Michael, 12, 13, 22, 27, 162, 179, 197, 214, 216, 218–20, 223–24, 227n, 228–29, 351–53, 355–56, 365n, 389, 404
Heckathorn, Douglas, 218, 229
Hekman, Susan, 365, 368
Hegel, Georg, 51, 264–65
Hegtvedt, Karen, 165, 178
Heidegger, Martin, 139, 255, 289, 312
Heilbrun, Carolyn, 338, 342
Heimer, Carol, 217, 229
Held, David, 96, 112
Helle, H. J., 26, 140, 151–52, 349, 351, 356, 365n, 368, 369
Hempel, Carl, 395–96, 407, 414
Heritage, John, 10, 11, 27, 37, 62, 400, 408
Herrnstein, Richard, 227, 229
Hewitt, John, 122, 124
Hilbert, Richard, 3, 27, 369
Himmelstrand, Ulf, 12, 29
Hindess, Barry, 35–53, 101, 113, 358, 369
Hinkle, Gisela, 120
Hinkle, Roscoe, 372, 377, 381, 390
Hirsch, Paul, 1, 12, 27, 56, 113, 127, 152
Hobbes, Thomas, 124, 227
Hochschild, Arlie, 132, 134, 152, 328, 330, 335, 340n, 342
Hochschild, Jennifer, 292, 312
Hodgson, Godfrey, 95, 113, 248, 252–53, 284
Hofstadter, R., 302, 312
Holton, Robert J., 39, 49–50, 58n, 62

Homans, George, 9, 27, 36, 138, 146n, 159–60, 169, 176, 179, 350, 369, 396
Hondrich, Karl Otto, 53, 62
Honneth, Axel, 279, 284
Hooks, Bell, 323, 325, 332, 342
Horkheimer, A., 113, 295, 313
House, James, 166, 179
Huaco, George, 5, 27
Huber, Joan, 118, 152
Hughes, Everett, 119, 124, 128, 140, 146n, 152
Hughes, John, 202, 206
Hunter, James, 289, 292, 312
Husserl, Edmund, 11, 57n, 139, 397, 406, 408
Huston, T. L., 179
Huyssen, Andreas, 113

Ingram, David, 105, 113
Inzerelli, Giorgio, 304–5, 313
Irigaray, Luce, 239
Isherwood, Baron, 297–98
Israel, Joachim, 113

Jacoby, Russell, 93, 113, 251, 253, 302, 313
Jaggar, Alison, 316, 319, 336, 342
James, William, 118, 122, 134, 144, 152, 408–9
Jameson, Fredric, 14, 105, 106, 109n, 113, 252–53, 256, 264, 267, 270, 273, 275–76, 282n, 284, 299, 313
Janeway, Elizabeth, 336, 342
Janovitz, M., 302, 313
Jardine, Alice, 323, 341
Jasso, Guillermina, 411, 414
Jay, Martin, 90, 92, 99, 105, 113
Jayaratne, Toby, 329, 342
Jefferson, Gail, 128, 147n, 190, 202, 203, 209
Jencks, Charles, 233, 253
Jensen, Michael C., 216, 229
Joas, Hans, 117, 144, 152, 313
Johnson, G. David, 144, 152
Johnson, Harry, 45, 62
Johnson, John, 132, 152
Johnson, Len, 94, 114
Johnson, Miriam, 54, 62–63, 66
Jones, Robert, 142, 152

Kadushin, Charles, 298, 303, 313
Kahne, M. J., 135, 153
Kahneman, Daniel, 168, 179, 221, 226, 229
Kalab, Kathleen A., 125, 152
Kamens, David H., 135, 152
Kant, Immanuel, 264, 266, 301
Kanter, Rosabeth Moss, 340, 342
Karnow, Stanley, 245, 252–53
Kasper, Anne, 328, 342
Katovich, Michael A., 149
Katz, Elihu, 309, 313
Kautsky, Karl, 57
Kealy, Edward, 128, 152
Kearns, Doris, 247, 252n, 253
Keller, Albert, 373–75
Keller, Evelyn, 322–23, 325–26, 331, 333, 338–39, 342
Kellner, Douglas, 3, 4, 14, 22, 27, 97, 105, 110–11, 114, 255–86, 309, 313, 403, 406, 410
Kelly, H. H., 159, 161, 179
Kemeny, Jim, 27, 349, 355, 361, 369
Kemper, Theodore, 134, 147n, 152
Kennedy, Paul, 77, 86
Keynes, John M., 51, 409, 413n, 414
Khruschev, Nikita, 94
Killian, Lewis, 126, 156
Kilmann, Ralph, 135, 153
Kitahara, Michio, 9, 27
Kitsuse, John I., 130, 155
Kleinman, Sherryl, 118, 120, 132, 135, 139, 143–44, 150, 152
Kloppenberg, James T., 109, 114
Knoke, David, 79, 86
Knorr-Cetina, Karen, 193, 210, 351, 369
Kollock, Peter, 10, 23, 169, 179
Korsch, Karl, 57, 93, 114
Kosik, Karel, 114
Kotarba, Joseph A., 11, 27
Kreps, Gary, 365, 367, 369
Kristeva, Julia, 145, 233, 239, 253, 333, 342
Kroker, Arthur, 104–5, 114, 256, 262–64, 267, 274, 280
Kroker, Marilouise, 256, 262–64, 267, 274, 280
Kuhn, Manfred H., 119, 152
Kuhn, Thomas, 18, 19, 27, 186, 210, 331–32, 342, 393, 401–2, 414

Kurtz, Lester, 292–93, 313
Kurzweil, Edith, 13, 28, 351, 369

Labov, William, 129, 152
Labriola, A., 7
Lacan, Jacques, 164, 233, 237–39, 253, 256, 293, 313, 405–6, 408
Laclaw, Ernesto, 102–3, 114
Lakatos, Imre, 19
Lamont, Michéle, 4, 14, 20, 22, 23, 287, 315, 403
Lareau, Annette, 293, 297, 300, 313
Lasch, Christopher, 292
Lash, Scott, 262, 282n, 285, 313
Laumann, Edward N., 79, 86, 167, 180
Laurent, Andre, 304–5, 313
Law, John, 210
Lazarsfeld, Paul, 395
Lears, T. J., 300, 313
LeBon, Gustave, 126
Lechner, Frank, 58, 63, 65
LeFebvre, Henri, 86, 256, 285, 295–96, 313
Lefort, Claude, 96
LeGoff, Jacques, 292, 313
Lehman, Edward W., 55, 63
Leitner, Kenneth, 202, 210
Lemert, Charles, 13, 14, 202, 210, 230–52, 253, 269, 285, 309, 314, 403
Lengermann, Patricia, 4, 15, 16, 20, 21, 28, 316–44, 403
Lenin, Vladimir Ilyich, 57
Lenski, Gerhard, 335–36
Lessing, Doris, 321
Levi, Primo, 217, 229
Levine, Andrew, 114
Levine, Donald, 393, 414
Lévi-Strauss, Claude, 14, 97, 159, 176, 180, 231, 234, 253, 289–90, 293, 296, 314, 405–7
Levy, Marion, 383, 390
Lewis, David J., 37, 63, 117, 144, 152
Liderman, Kenneth, 201, 210
Lidz, Victor, 46, 50, 63
Lieberson, Stanley, 131, 152, 191, 192, 210
Liebow, Elliott, 147, 152
Lindenberg, S., 37, 67, 162, 181, 351, 355
Livingston, Eric, 202, 210

Lockwood, David, 36, 72, 384, 390
Lofland, John, 125, 130, 133, 152
Long, Elizabeth, 299, 301, 308n, 314
Lorber, Judith, 325, 342
Lorde, Audre, 319, 323, 338–39, 342
Los, Maria, 365
Loseke, Donileen, 130, 153
Lotringer, Sylvere, 114
Loubser, J. J., 46, 63
Luce, R. Duncan, 217, 229
Luckmann, Thomas, 11, 28, 139, 148, 195, 206, 289, 299, 310, 326
Luhmann, Niklas, 5, 47, 53, 58n, 63, 293, 303, 314, 351, 369, 408–9, 413
Lukacs, Georg, 57, 93, 114
Luker, Kristin, 291, 314
Lukes, Steven, 295, 309n, 314, 400
Luttwak, Edward O., 77, 86
Lyman, Stanford, 19, 30, 124, 146n, 153, 155, 194
Lynch, Michael, 200, 201, 207, 210
Lyon, Eleanor, 128, 153
Lyotard, Jean-Francois, 3, 14, 38, 57n, 63, 89, 104, 114, 233–34, 241, 252–53, 255–56, 258, 262–63, 265–68, 270–75, 277, 279, 281, 285, 291, 314, 405, 407, 414

McAdam, Doug, 226, 229
McCarthy, John D., 79, 86
MacDonald, M. G., 180
Machiarelli, Niccolo, 134
Machina, Mark J., 168, 180
McHoul, A. W., 210
MacKinnon, Catherine, 323, 328, 342
McMahon, A. M., 17, 28
Macneil, Ian R., 162, 180
McPartland, Thomas S., 199, 152
McPhail, Clark, 117, 126, 143, 153
McRobbie, Angela, 279, 285
Macsey, Richard, 252
Maines, David, 120, 135, 147n, 153, 199, 210, 358, 369
Malinowski, Bronislaw, 158–59, 162, 176, 180, 381, 383–84, 390
Mandel, Ernest, 95, 106, 114, 285
Mann, Michael, 6, 7, 28, 73–76, 84, 85n, 86, 400
Mannheim, Karl, 57
Manning, Peter, 120, 130, 132, 153
March, J. G., 135, 149

Marcus, George, 131–32, 149, 245, 253, 297–98, 314
Marcuse, Herbert, 93, 96–97, 99, 114
Marin, B., 166–67, 180
Marini, Margaret, 363, 369
Markovic, Mihako, 114
Markovsky, Barry, 167, 173–74, 180, 221, 229, 361, 363, 369
Marlaire, Courtney, 203, 211
Marolla, Joseph, 125, 155
Marsden, Peter, 167–68, 173, 180
Marshall, Alfred, 21, 357, 380
Marske, Charles E., 3, 28
Martin, Bill, 8, 30
Marwell, Gerald, 78, 87, 216, 222, 229
Marx, Karl, 9, 21, 34, 49–51, 57n, 68–69, 71, 86, 89–94, 97, 99–104, 107, 114–15, 143, 144, 193, 203, 210, 231, 257, 265, 267, 275, 294, 296, 307, 314, 316, 349, 372, 377, 380, 384, 386, 395, 403, 409
Maryanski, Alexandra, 5, 35, 67, 384, 408, 415
Mattelart, Armand, 309, 314
Matthaei, Julie, 335, 343
Mauss, Marcel, 57, 159, 162, 176, 180, 289, 376
Mayhew, Bruce, 350, 369
Mayhew, Leon, 48, 53, 63
Maynard, Douglas, 194, 196, 198, 201, 203, 210
Mead, George H., 3, 8, 21, 37, 51, 99–100, 117–19, 121–24, 128, 139–45, 146n, 153, 307, 326, 337, 343, 344, 354, 374, 379, 384, 390, 408–9, 413
Meckling, William H., 216, 229
Meehan, Albert, 211
Meeker, B. F., 163, 180
Mehan, Hugh, 186, 211
Melbin, Murray, 211
Merquoir, J. G., 115, 258, 285
Merton, Robert, 1, 3, 28, 43, 163–64, 325, 343, 376, 383–84, 390, 392, 396–97, 407
Messenger, Sheldon E., 124, 153
Messner, Steven F., 17, 28
Meszaros, Istvan, 115
Meyer, John, 37, 63, 291, 314
Michaels, Stuart, 1, 12, 27
Michels, Robert, 68, 71, 141
Mies, Maria, 327–28, 343

Miller, David, 126, 143, 153
Miller, Gale, 135, 153
Mills, C. W., 58–59, 72, 124, 153, 261, 285, 377, 384, 390
Mills, J., 161, 177, 180
Mitchell, Juliet, 338, 343, 407
Mitchell, W. J. T., 407, 414
Mitroff, Ian, 358, 369
Mizruchi, Mark S., 17, 28
Moerman, Michael, 190, 211
Mohr, John, 300, 311
Moi, Toril, 239, 253
Molm, Linda D., 167, 174, 180
Molotch, Harvey, 37, 63, 129, 138, 153, 197, 201, 211
Monk, Richard, 28
Mookherjee, Dilip, 224, 228
Moore, Barrington, 37, 64
Moore, Wilbert, 5, 28, 84, 175, 179, 383
Mosca, Gaetano, 68
Mouffe, Chantel, 102–3
Mouzelis, Nicos, 103, 115
Mujeski, Stephen J., 169, 180
Mukerji, C., 128, 147n, 153, 294
Mullins, Nicolas, 19, 28, 185, 202, 211
Munch, Richard, 5, 28, 34, 47–48, 51, 53, 58, 64, 175, 179, 349, 351–52, 354, 358–59, 369
Murdoch, Graham, 309, 314
Murdock, George, 375
Murphy, Raymond, 80, 87
Murstein, B. I., 161, 180

Naffziger, Claudeen, 63
Nagel, Ernest, 395–96, 414
Natanson, Maurice, 143, 153
Neustadtl, Alan, 17
Nicholson, Linda, 115, 271, 281
Niebrugge-Brantley, Jill, 4, 15, 16, 20, 21, 316–44, 403
Nietszche, Friedrich, 104, 115, 231, 256, 259
Nisbet, Robert, 377, 390

Oakley, Ann, 327, 343
O'Brien, Jodi, 4, 10, 22, 163, 169, 178, 180
O'Connell, L., 161, 180
O'Connor, James, 69, 87
Ogburn, Williams, 377, 390
Oliner, Pearl, 226, 229

Oliner, Samuel, 226, 229
Oliver, Pamela, 79, 87, 216, 222, 229
Ollman, Bertell, 115
Olsen, J. P., 135, 149
Olson, Ann, 325, 343
Olson, Mancur, 165, 181, 216, 229
Opp, K. D., 228
Orru, Marco, 34–35, 64
Ortner, Sherry, 301, 314
Ouchi, William G., 135, 153, 163, 181

Page, Charles, 34, 64
Paine, Robert, 126, 154
Palmer, Phyllis, 196, 335, 343
Pannenberg, Wolfhart, 303, 314
Pappi, Franz W., 167, 180
Pareto, Vilfredo, 21, 71, 347, 380
Park, Robert, 119, 140, 146n, 377–79, 390
Parkin, Frank, 80, 87
Parsons, Talcott, 3, 4, 5, 6, 9, 14, 21, 28, 33, 35–36, 39–40, 43–49, 50–51, 54, 56–58, 64, 120, 137, 146, 154, 186, 193, 245, 289, 303–4, 314, 333, 349, 351, 354, 356–57, 365, 369, 380–81, 383, 392, 395, 398, 403, 413n, 414
Passeron, J.-C., 82, 86, 297, 314
Pathak, Zakia, 330
Patterson, Orlando, 85
Patton, Travis, 180
Peirce, Charles, 51, 118, 144
Perinbanayagam, Robert S., 8, 28, 139, 154
Peters, John D., 55, 64
Peters, Robert, 9
Peterson, Richard, 127, 154, 298, 310, 314
Pettigrew, Andrew M., 135, 154
Peyrot, Mark, 135, 154
Pfeffer, Jeffrey, 135, 154
Piaget, Jean, 50–51
Picou, J. Steven, 144
Plato, 118, 124
Platt, Jennifer, 400
Pocock, J. G. A., 292, 314
Podgorecki, Adam, 365, 369
Poggi, Gianfranco, 400
Pollner, Melvin, 190, 194, 211
Pomerantz, Anita, 203, 211
Portoghesi, Paolo, 233, 252
Poulantzas, Nicos, 98, 115

Powell, Walter, 298
Prager, Jeffrey, 37, 54, 64
Przeworski, Adam, 101–2, 115
Psathas, George, 138, 154, 211

Rabinow, Paul, 132, 154
Radcliffe-Brown, A. R., 371, 381, 384, 390
Radway, Janice, 308, 314
Raiffa, Howard, 217, 229
Rajan, Rajeswari, 330, 343
Rambo, Eric, 55, 58n, 64
Ramirez, Francisco O., 85, 87
Raulet, Gerard, 105, 115
Rawls, Ann Warfield, 9, 28, 154, 202, 211
Ray, Melvin C., 125, 154
Relhorick, David Allan, 11, 28
Reich, Michael, 94, 112
Reinharz, Shulamit, 327–29, 343
Rex, John, 36, 72
Rexroat, Cynthia, 117, 145, 153
Rhoades, Gary, 40, 53, 55, 61, 64
Rich, Adrienne, 15, 28, 319, 322–23, 328–29, 335, 343
Ricoeur, Paul, 274, 285, 293, 314
Ritzer, George, 3, 6, 8, 10, 19, 20, 22, 23, 28, 29, 35–36, 56, 64, 120, 141, 154, 186, 191, 194, 202, 211, 318, 343, 347–70, 392, 402–4
Robertson, Roland, 40, 48, 54, 64–65
Rochberg-Halton, Eugene, 120, 144, 154
Rock, Paul, 147, 154
Rockford, E. Burke, Jr., 155
Roemer, John, 7, 29, 101, 115
Rollins, Judith, 323, 335, 343
Rorty, Richard, 233, 236, 240, 252, 254, 271, 285
Rose, Gillian, 13, 29
Rosen, Sherwin, 173, 181
Rosenberg, Morris, 119, 122–23, 154
Rosenblum, Barbara, 128, 154
Rosnow, Ralph, 126, 154
Ross, George, 302, 314
Rossi, Ino, 252, 254, 365n, 70
Roth, Phillip, 186
Rothbart, Mary K., 63
Rothenbuhler, Eric W., 55, 64–65
Rousseau, Jean Jacques, 124
Rowan, Brian, 291, 314
Roy, Donald, 135, 154

Royce, Josiah, 118
Rubin, Lillian, 328, 343
Rubinstein, David, 350, 365n, 370
Ruddick, Sara, 332, 343
Ryan, Michael, 283, 285
Ryan, William, 305, 314
Rytina, Steven, 126, 151

Sabshin, M., 155
Sacks, Harvey, 73, 128, 147n, 154, 190, 191, 198, 201, 202, 212, 408
Sahlins, Marshall, 162, 181, 189, 212
Sampson, Harold, 153
Samuel, Raphael, 93, 115
Sapir, Edward, 129, 154
Sartre, Jean-Paul, 11, 57n, 93, 115, 406, 414
Saussure, Ferdinand de, 140, 256, 405
Saxton, Stanley L., 149
Schachter, Stanley, 134, 154
Schaeffle, Albert, 372
Schaff, Adam, 115
Schatzman, Leonard, 155
Schegloff, Emanuel, 29, 37, 65, 73, 128, 147n, 154, 190, 196, 201, 203, 212, 251, 355–56, 370
Schelling, Thomas C., 79, 87, 215, 229
Schiller, Herbert, 281, 285
Schmidt, Emerson, 117
Schnore, L. F., 350
Schoemaker, Paul J. H., 221, 229
Schroyer, Trent, 115
Schudson, M., 294, 298, 314
Schumpeter, Joseph A., 81, 87, 138
Schutz, Alfred, 11, 51, 124, 139, 189, 196, 212, 289, 314, 326, 337, 343, 365n, 376, 390
Schwartz, Barry, 120, 135, 142, 155
Schweider, Joseph W., 130, 149
Sciulli, David, 4–9, 29, 51, 53, 65–66, 137, 147n, 158
Scott, Marvin, 124, 155, 194, 212
Scott, W. Richard, 37, 63
Scully, Diana, 125, 155, 328, 343
Seager, Joni, 325, 343
Secord, Paul, 370
Sennett, Richard, 292, 301, 314
Sewell, William, Jr., 37, 66
Shaffir, William, 9
Shalin, Dmitri, 8, 19, 29, 118, 144, 155, 365, 370

Shapiro, S. P., 162–63, 181
Sharrock, Wesley, 10, 29, 202, 206, 212
Shibutani, Tamotsu, 125–26, 155
Shils, Edward, 19, 29
Shonfeld, W. K., 305, 315
Shott, Susan, 155
Silverman, David, 212
Simmel, Georg, 9, 77, 84, 87, 124, 137, 140–41, 144, 147, 155, 349, 386, 393
Simon, Herbert A., 227, 229
Simons, Ronald L., 125, 154
Skinner, B. F., 350
Skocpol, Theda, 36–37, 66, 77, 84, 87, 397, 414
Skvoretz, John, 169, 179, 351–53, 358, 368
Smelser, Neil, 5, 28–29, 39–40, 45, 50, 53, 66, 175, 180, 349, 351–52, 354, 358–59, 370, 394, 414
Smith, Adam, 124, 138, 158
Smith, Dorothy, 15, 29, 312, 316, 320–21, 323, 325, 329–32, 335–36, 343
Smith, Richard L., 152
Smith, Robert, 37, 63
Smith, Victoria, 117, 136, 143–44, 155
Snitow, Ann, 328, 335, 343
Snow, David A., 9, 12, 29, 126, 155
Sober, Elliot, 114
Sorokin, Pitirim, 376–77, 381, 390
Spalter-Roth, Roberta, 329, 343
Spector, Malcolm, 130, 155
Spencer, Herbert, 57, 372–74, 377–78, 380–81, 389–90
Spender, Dale, 333, 343
Sprecher, S., 179
Stacey, Judith, 318–19, 343
Stanton, Donna, 332, 343
Stearns, Peter N., 134, 155
Stephanson, Anders, 105, 115
Stimpson, Catherine, 333, 343
Stinchcombe, Arthur, 1, 29, 163, 180, 220, 229, 395, 414
Stockard, Jean, 54, 62–63, 66
Stokes, Randall, 124, 152
Stolte, John, 165, 181
Stone, Gregory, 125, 132, 140, 142, 151, 155
Stouffer, Samuel, 395
Strauss, Ansel M., 118, 124, 133, 135, 140, 146*n*, 150–51, 155
Stroebe, W., 165, 181

Stryker, Sheldon, 37, 66, 118–19, 122–23, 138–39, 144, 155–56
Suchman, Lucy, 201, 212
Sudnow, David, 212
Sumner, William G., 373–74, 390
Surace, Samuel, 53, 66
Swedberg, Richard, 12, 29
Swidler, Ann, 38, 291, 293–94, 300, 315, 365, 370
Syzmanski, Albert, 46, 66
Szwed, John F., 126, 156

Tarde, Gabriel, 142
Tausig, Mark, 53, 61
Teggart, Frederick, 146
Teixeira, Ruy, 216, 222, 229
Tejera, V., 143, 157
Terry, Wallace, 254
Therborn, Goren, 115
Thibaut, J. W., 161, 179
Thomas, George, 300, 315
Thomas, W. I., 119, 146*n*, 378–80, 390, 392, 413, 414
Thomason, Burke, 365, 370
Thompson, E. P., 57, 200, 243
Thompson, John, 407, 414
Thorne, Barrie, 318–19, 340*n*, 343
Thrift, Nigel, 199, 212
Thucydides, 68
Thurstone, L. L., 413, 415
Tilly, Charles, 79, 84, 87, 200, 212
Tipton, Steven, 292, 315
Tiryakian, Edward, 18, 19, 29, 53, 66
Toennies, Ferdinand, 333
Touraine, Alan, 193
Towne, Robert D., 153
Toynbee, Arnold, 258–61, 285
Traugott, Mark, 79, 87
Traupman, J., 161, 179
Truzzi, Marcello, 120, 141, 156
Tuchman, Gaye, 298, 315
Tucker, Charles, 120, 147*n*, 156
Tulis, Jeffrey, 292, 315
Tullock, Gordon, 225, 228
Turner, Bryan, 57, 62, 66–67
Turner, Jonathan, 3, 4, 5, 20, 21, 29, 30, 35, 40, 49–50, 57*n*, 61, 67, 119, 122, 146, 157, 158, 162, 164, 167, 172–73, 176, 181, 371–91, 392, 402–3, 405, 408, 413, 415
Turner, Ralph, 123, 125, 156, 388

Turner, Roy, 212
Turner, Stephen, 138, 156, 375, 387, 391
Turner, Victor, 293, 315
Tversky, Amos, 168, 179, 221, 226, 229

Unruh, David, 119, 156
Utne, M., 179

Van Maanen, John, 132, 152
Verdès-Leroux, Jeannine, 302, 315
Vester, Heinz-Gunter, 120, 140, 156
Vico, Giovanni Battista, 57
Vidich, Arthur J., 19, 30, 147, 156
Von Wiese, Leopold, 57

Wagner, David, 18, 30, 52, 67, 389
Wagner, Helmut, 30, 349, 370
Walczak, David, 6
Wallace, Ruth, 334, 342
Wallace, Walter, 30, 349, 370
Wallerstein, Immanuel, 8, 30, 69, 75, 77, 84, 87
Warner, Marina, 333, 343
Watson, John, 117
Weber, Max, 4, 8, 21, 49–51, 57n, 68–69, 71, 74, 80–81, 85, 87, 96, 99–100, 109, 137–38, 141, 144, 257, 262, 266, 289, 291, 300, 307, 335–36, 343, 347, 349, 365, 372, 376, 380, 386, 395, 397–98, 409–11
Wedell, George, 309, 313
Weider, Lawrence, 186, 213
Weinstein, Eugene A., 122, 156
Weldes, Jetta, 30
Welk, Karl, 135, 156
Wellman, Barry, 17, 30
Wellman, David, 120, 147n, 156
Wellmer, Albrecht, 115, 282, 285
Welsch, Wolfgang, 269, 285
West, Candace, 129, 138, 156–57, 212, 213
West, James, 147, 156
Whalen, Jack, 213
Whalen, Marilyn, 213
White, Cynthia, 298, 315
White, Hayden, 24–42, 254
White, Harrison, 81–82, 87, 298, 315, 388

Whorf, Benjamin, 129, 156
Whyte, William Foote, 147, 156
Widmer, Jean, 201, 213
Wildavsky, Aaron, 226, 229
Wiley, Norbert, 4, 18, 19, 30, 191, 193, 202, 213, 352–53, 364n, 366, 370, 378–79, 390, 396, 415
Wilkens, Alan L., 135, 153
Willer, David, 79, 87, 167, 180–81, 389
Williams, Raymond, 275, 285, 295, 301
Williams, Robin, 45, 62, 67
Williamson, O. E., 163, 181
Willis, Paul, 297, 315
Wilson, Thomas, 190, 194, 213
Winner, Langon, 268, 286
Winship, Christopher, 173, 181
Wippler, R., 37, 67, 162, 181, 228, 351, 355
Wirth, Lewis, 377–79, 390
Witten, Marsha, 291–92, 301, 306, 315
Wittgenstein, Ludwig, 139, 282n, 406–7
Wolf, Charlotte, 120, 143, 156
Wolff, Janet, 295, 315
Wolin, Richard, 96, 105, 115–16, 285
Wood, Ellen Melksins, 103–4, 116
Worden, Steven K., 155
Wright, Eric Olin, 8, 30, 36, 101, 114, 116
Wrong, Dennis, 300, 315
Wuthnow, Robert, 4, 13, 14, 20, 22, 23, 30, 38, 67, 287–315, 403

Yalom, Marilyn, 340, 343
Yamagishi, T., 86, 165, 167, 173–74, 178, 181, 228

Zald, Mayer, 79, 86, 176, 181
Zelditch, Morris, 389
Zerubavel, Eviatar, 120, 140, 142, 155–57, 199, 213, 292, 315
Zimmerman, Don, 129, 139, 157, 186, 189, 190, 194, 196, 202, 207, 213
Znaniecki, Florian, 146, 378–80, 391–92, 414–15
Zolberg, Vera, 308, 315
Zurcher, Louis A., 9, 30, 119, 122–23, 157

SUBJECT INDEX

Accountability, 194
Accounting systems, 161
"Accounts in action," 194
Action/system integration, 353
Action theory, 4, 9, 141, 347, 354–55, 376, 381, 384, 397–98, 404
Agency/structure, 3, 11, 21, 143, 192–95, 356, 359, 363, 393, 403–4
Agents, 218, 219, 224, 278, 329, 354, 356, 359, 387, 404
Aggregation, 221–23, 227, 358
AGIL, 285
Alienation, 97, 110n, 338; between theorists and empiricists, 73
American Journal of Sociology, 2, 33, 173
American sociological theory, *see* Sociology: American theory
Analysis: levels of, 350, 354; meso-level of, 358; multiple levels of, 2, 19, 159, 172, 174; qualitative-quantitative, 193, 329; *see also* Micro-macro analysis
Anomie, 365
Anthropology, 289, 307, 401; cognitive, 169; functional, 158; philosophical, 12; symbolic, 299, 301
Archaeology of knowledge, 3, 13
Artificial intelligence, 169
ASA Guide to Graduate Departments, 202
Authority, 305
Automatic system of machinery, 92

Base/superstructure, 99
Behavioral psychology, 158
Behavioral theory, 221
Behaviorism, 350, 398, 404
Birmingham School, 297, 304, 309

Capitalism, 91, 339, 409; corporate, 94
Capitalist, 91, 333
Chicago School, 376–77, 382, 392–93, 401–2, 412
Class conflict, 72
Classification systems, 287, 290; cultural, 288, 291, 293–94, 297
Cognitive anthropology, *see* Anthropology: cognitive
Cognitive maps, 106, 281
Collective action, 215–17, 222
Collective conscience, 375
Collective irrationalities, 171
Collectivist theory, 356, 365, 378
Columbia University, 376, 382, 392, 395
Commodification, 262, 280
Commodity fetishism, 96
Communicative democracy, 99
Communicative rationality, 99
Conflict theory, 3, 5, 21–22, 33, 158, 287, 335, 365, 384–86, 395, 397, 400, 402–3; and capitalism, 69; and commonalities with Marxism, 69; future prospects of, 84–85; macro-historical, 74–76; and its scope, 70–73; and socialism, 68–69

Consciousness, 236–37, 321, 374, 381;
  false, 243
Constitution of Society, The (Giddens),
  193
Constructionist approach, 186
"Context," 195
Critical theory, 7, 14, 17, 21, 37, 99–
  100, 317, 324, 335, 401, 405, 407
"Cult of the individual," 3
Cultural capital, 293–94, 300, 308
Cultural codes, 292–93, 296–97, 308
Cultural determinism, *see* Determin-
  ism: cultural
Cultural imperialism, 269, 309
Cultural narcissism, 292
Cultural politics, 106
Cultural rationalization, 100
Cultural sociology, *see* Sociology: cultural
Cultural system, 288, 306; and subjectivity, 294
Culture, 291, 354, 401, 404–6; corporate, 304; and ethnography, 289; and
  industries, 298, 304, 309; organizational, 288; and power, 294–301; and
  pragmatism, 289, 306; and production, 298, 302, 308; and social construction of reality, 289; and social
  psychology of attitudes, 289; and the
  social system, 301; and symbolic interactionism, 289; top-down vision of,
  302
Culture-mediated power relations, 287–
  88, 294–301, 304

Decentering, 245, 406
Decision-making process, 298
Decision theory, 168–69
Deconstruction, 236, 290
De-differentiation, 262
Determinism, 360; cultural, 350; eco-
  nomic, 356; micro, 12; structural,
  250, 356; technological, 268
Diachrony, 267; narrative, 272
Dialectic, 261, 351, 353, 359–60, 397; of
  enlightenment, 96; and feminist the-
  ory, 325, 327, 329–30, 337
Dialectical materialism, 240
Differentiation, 6, 39, 48
Discourse, 234–35, 238–39, 241–43,

  249, 255–58, 261–62, 264–65, 269,
  276, 290–92, 294, 296–97, 302, 308;
  feminist, 316, 320, 326, 330–31; and
  metadiscourse, 264
Disempowerment, 334
"Disenchantment," 100
Division of labor, 294, 298
Domination, 300, 305, 338; definition
  of, 335
Double hermeneutic, 241
Doublethink, 249
Dramaturgy, 380, 384, 386
Dualism, 316, 332–33, 335, 339, 359

Economic determinism, *see* Determin-
  ism: economic
Economics, 398, 407; neo-classical, 101;
  theory, 402; utilitarian, 158
Emancipatory modernity, 92, 96, 103
Emancipatory theory, 108
"Embeddedness," 195
Empirical integration, 354
Empowerment, 338, 340
Enlightenment, 240, 258–59, 268, 269
Epistemology, 104, 241, 263, 289, 398,
  406, 412; feminist, 316–17, 320–21,
  325–31, 403; postmodern, 264, 271–
  72, 274–75
Ethnography, 292, 307; new, 140
Ethnomethodology, 241, 350–51, 355,
  365, 385–86, 395, 402–3, 408, 413; as
  absorbed into mainstream sociology,
  187; and conversational analysis, 4,
  10, 194, 203, 351, 355–56; dense and
  technical style of, 186; and Garfinkel,
  202; as "incommensurably alternate
  sociology," 186; and indifference, 191;
  reality of, 204n; studies in, 205n
European social theory, *see* Social theory: resurgence of European
Evolutionary dogmatism, 108
Evolutionary perspective, 273–74, 290,
  377, 379, 384
Exchange commodity, 330
Exchange theory, 4, 9–10, 33, 37, 72,
  158–81, 335, 350–51, 356, 365, 385–
  86, 396, 398, 402–5
Exchange value, 261
Existential sociology, *see* Sociology: existential

Expectation states theory, 351–52
Extensiveness: of networks, 74

Feminism, 320, 402–3, 405
Feminist social theory, *see* Social theory: feminist
Feudalism, 90
Figurational sociology, *see* Sociology: figurational
"Fractured identities," 246
Frankfurt School, 7, 96–97, 110*n*, 259, 277, 280, 295–96, 298
Free rider, 218, 225
French social theory, *see* Social theory: French
Functional anthropology, *see* Anthropology: functional
Functionalism, 141, 325, 335, 365, 373, 381, 383–86, 393–94, 397, 401–2, 408, 412; decline of, 394–96; structural, 2–5, 17, 21, 33, 348, 350–52, 356, 365

Game theory, 223–24; and Marxism, 7, 12, 101
Gemeinschaft, 218, 333
Gender, 319, 333–34; as social structure, 321; as stratification system, 324–25, 331; *see also* Feminism; Social theory: feminist
Gender and Society, 15
"Genealogy of power," 3, 13
General equilibrium theory, 101
Geopolitics, 73–78, 85
Gesellschaft, 49, 218, 233

Habitus, 3, 240, 293, 308–9, 351, 359; definition of, 360
Hegelianism, 264, 407
Hegemony, 102, 268, 275, 280, 295–97, 299, 384–85, 392, 394, 396–99, 402, 412
Hermeneutics, 8, 264, 293, 303, 324, 401, 406–7
Historical holism, 8, 89, 100, 103, 107, 109*n*
Historical materialism, 90, 101, 240
Historical sociology, *see* Sociology: historical
Homo sociologicus, 353
Human Studies, 10, 201, 205*n*

Humanism: theoretical, 351–52
Hyperreality, 262, 277

Ideology, 323–24, 331, 407; and ideological freedom, 411; and ideological systems, 318
Inequality and Heterogeneity (Blau), 164
Individualism, 292
Individualist theory, 356
Institutionalization, 300, 302
Integrated paradigm, 351, 353, 363, 366
Integrative theory, 348; theoretical, 7
"Intellectual deviance," 188
Intensiveness: of networks, 74
Interaction: "frame-by-frame" moments of, 199; rituals, 72
Interaction Durkheimians, 142–43
"Interaction Order, The" (Goffman), 142
Interactional ritual chains, 350, 353, 388
"Interactional substrate," 203
Interpretive theories, 324
Inter-viewing, 327

Knowledge, 307; codes, 301, 303; construction, 327, 329–30, 332; feminist theory of absolute, 317; production, 324; systems, 290, 318

Labeling theory, 300
Labor markets: split, 80
Legitimation crisis, 39
Linguistics, 237, 401, 406

Macro theories, 9, 21, 33, 49, 51, 72
Macrostructuralism, 350, 385, 389
Marxian sociology, *see* Sociology: Marxian
Marxist theory, 241, 264–65, 270, 275, 280, 324, 351, 384; and British cultural Marxists, 278; critical, 90; post-Marxists and, 239; structural, 7; *see also* Neo-Marxian theory; Sociology: Marxian
Materialist emancipatory modernism, 8
Mathematical modeling, 101
Mentalism, 373, 375, 379
Metasociology, 403
Metatheory, 73, 193, 380, 386–87; of culture, 40; and micro-macro tools,

Metatheory (*Continued*)
  347–49; M$_O$, 18; M$_P$, 18, 21–22; M$_U$,
  18, 22, 347
Methodological individualism, 12, 101,
  110*n*, 351, 355–56, 365, 372–73,
  378–79, 381, 398; and holism,
  363
Micro determinism, *see* Determinism:
  micro
Micro-macro analysis, 330, 351, 377;
  and feminist theory, 329–30, 340
Micro-macro continuum, 347–48, 355,
  357, 363
Micro-macro extremism, 347–51, 355,
  357–60, 362, 363
Micro-macro linkage, 2–4, 10, 13, 17–
  19, 22, 37, 40, 55, 171–72, 175, 193–
  94, 347–70, 382, 385, 388, 403; in ra-
  tional choice theory, 227, 351; work
  to be done on, 361–64
Micro-macro methods, 363
Micro-macro processes, 353, 376
Micro-macro structures, 353
Micro-macro terminology, 347, 349
Microstructuralism, 385
Modernity, 230, 235, 237–38, 243, 257–
  58, 262, 274, 276
Modernization, 46
Monopoly capitalism, 91
Multivariate statistical manipulation,
  193

Narrative, 291, 406; grand, 89–90, 92–
  94, 96, 98, 100–2, 107, 110*n*, 256, 264,
  271, 273, 275, 282, 402, 407; master,
  265, 272; meta-, 264, 272, 281; synchronic, 273
Negotiated order, 358
Neofunctionalism, 4–5, 21–22, 33, 35,
  358, 385, 397, 402, 408–9; and generalized discourse, 45–52; and Parsons'
  new relevance, 35, 39–41; research
  programs in, 52–55
Neo-Marxian theory, 2, 4, 7, 33
Network theory, 10, 16–17, 21–22, 222,
  350–51, 385, 389, 398, 403–5; and
  analysis, 165; cultural/ideological, 82;
  and economics, 80–82; geopolitical,
  77–78; political, 78–80; social, 17,
  167

Objectivity/subjectivity, 354, 360
Organicism, 372–76, 379, 381, 384
Organizations, formal: study of, 358

Paradigm analysis, 19, 276–77, 293–94,
  401
Participant observation, 289
Patriarchy, 339
Periodization, 258, 274, 281, 394
Phenomenology, 8–9, 11, 13, 17, 33,
  141, 232, 289, 324, 335, 376, 385–86,
  395, 400–1, 406
Philosophical anthropology, *see* Anthro-
  pology: philosophical
Pluralism, 409–12
Political sociology, *see* Sociology: politi-
  cal
Political Systems of Empires, The (Eisenstadt), 45
Positivism, 303, 327, 386, 388, 395,
  397–98, 406, 412; statistical, 405; and
  synthesis, 404–5, 412
Postcapitalism, 92
Postdichotomy, 238–39
Post-feminism, 145
Post-industrial society, 268, 269, 281–
  82
Post-Marxism, 89, 193
Postmodernism, 2–4, 7, 14, 21–22, 89,
  99, 104–5, 108–9, 145, 230–38, 240–
  45, 252, 258, 285–86, 309, 327, 403–5,
  412; and anthropology, 277; condition
  of, 272; critique of, 255, 261; culture
  of, 261, 270, 274; definition of, 274; as
  emergent, 275; and feminism, 271; future of, 260, 276–82; and knowledge,
  264; and science, 263; and social theory, 255, 257, 266, 268–70, 275, 279–
  80; and society, 260–61, 265, 267; and
  subjectivity, 270
Post-structuralism, 2, 4, 7, 13–14, 145,
  193, 230–36, 238–45, 247, 251, 255–
  56, 287, 335, 401, 403–5; and anthropology, 230
Power, 307; and culture, 294–301; definition of, 295, 304, 338; -dependence/
  exchange principles, 166; feminist definition of, 316, 335–340; indirect,
  300; and metapower, 295; relations,
  295; resources, 336

Pragmatism, 272, 306, 379, 408
Praxis, 278, 397, 404–5
Preference formation: and individual preference, 226, 228; theory of, 225–26
Prisoner's Dilemma, 217, 224
Problem of relevance, 196
Production: mode of, 268, 295; system of, 295
Proletariat, 91, 333
Protestant Reformation, 83
Psychoanalysis, 231, 353, 386; and feminist theory, 323–24, 337
"Purposive-rationalization," 100

Radical democracy, 101
Radical microsociology, 355
Rational action, 197, 356, 404–5
Rational behavior, 220
Rational choice theory, 4, 7, 10, 12, 22, 101, 169, 197, 214–29, 287, 352, 355, 365, 398, 403–5; and aggregation, 221–23, 227; and decision-making process, 220–21, 227, 381; and economics, 219–21, 225–26; and empirical implications, 219; future of, 220–26; and ideology, 216; and laboratory research, 221; and law, 226; and meta-theoretical form, 218; and micro processes, 222; and philosophy, 226; and political science, 219, 221, 226; and psychology, 220, 226; and rationality, 218; and sanctions, 216–17; twenty insights of, 215–20
Rationalism, 258, 263, 269, 287, 293–98, 301, 303, 398
Rationalization theory, 99
Reductionism, 265, 269, 386
"Reflexive sociology," *see* Sociology: "reflexive"
Reification, 96–97
Resource mobilization theory, 79
"Return of the actor," 193
Revolution: theory of, 77
Rhetoric, 292, 296; critique of, 332–35; dualistic, 332; feminist, 316, 322, 335
Role taking, 379
Role theory, 382, 384–85

Sacred and profane, dichotomy of, 334
Science, philosophy of, 18

Secularization: of Protestant values, 100
Semiotics, 281–82, 405–6, 408–9
Signifier/signified, 235, 261, 290
Signs, 15
Social behaviorism, 379
Social conflict, 102
Social definition paradigm, 141
Social facts, 142
Social institutions: definition of, 223; emergent, 223; genesis of, 223–25
Social integration, 354, 366
Social movement theory, 73
Social outcome, 218; institutional constraints on, 219 macro level of, 222; opportunity costs of, 219; and preference of actors, 219
Social power: sources of, 73
Social problems, 205n
Social production, 323–24, 340
Social Psychology Quarterly, 205n
Social reality: levels of, 348–49, 352–53, 360
Social telesis, 374
Social theory: feminist, 3–4, 15, 316–44, 394; French, 230, 234; future of, 411–13; present, 33; resurgence of European, 400–2
Sociologists for Women in Society, 15
Sociology, 205n; contemporary, 33, 269, 382–88, 409; cultural, 3–4, 14–15, 37, 287–315; of education, 73; existential, 8, 11, 17; figurational, 3; general, 318, 372; historical, 37, 73; Marxian, 256, 317, 320, 331, 338, 402, 405–6; political, 73; of professions, 73; "reflexive," 199; theoretical logic in, 33
Solidarity: mechanical and organic, 333; social, 354
Statistical positivism, *see* Positivism: statistical
Structural determinism, *see* Determinism: structural
Structural functionalism, *see* Functionalism: structural
Structural Marxism, *see* Marxist theory: structural
Structuralism, 4, 13, 16, 98, 141, 193, 280, 290, 293, 351–52, 375, 385–86, 410; French, 230–254, 401, 405
Structuration theory (Giddens), 3, 241, 351, 353, 386, 393, 400

Structure-in-action, 189
Symbolic anthropology, *see* Anthropology: symbolic
Symbolic boundaries, 292, 293
Symbolic codes, 287–94, 306–8; and action, 288–94; "deep structure" of, 290
Symbolic expression, 302; gestures and, 302
Symbolic interaction, 2, 4–5, 8–10, 17, 32, 33, 37, 287, 335, 348, 350, 352, 355, 358, 365, 380, 384–86, 395, 401–2, 408; and Chicago vs. Iowa schools, 119; contributions of, 121–31; diversity of, 120–21; methodology of, 131–33; in post-Blumerian age, 120; premises of, 118; and self vs. situation, 119
Symbolism: macro construction of, 143
Synthesis: grand, 2; new, 2, 14, 18, 20–21, 33, 36, 39–40, 45
Systems theory, 36, 351, 354, 385, 412

Tautology, 225
Technological determinism, *see* Determinism: technological
Teleology, 381
Text, 239, 243–52, 267, 270, 276; definition of, 238

Theoretical humanism, *see* Humanism: theoretical
Theoretical integration, *see* Integrative theory: theoretical
Theory: general, 372, 377; grand, 1, 376–77, 381, 383, 407
Theory, Culture and Society, 3
Theory and Society, 2
Typification, 358

Urbanism, 409
Use value, 261
Utility, 225, 227; maximization of, 221, 227–28
Utopian cultural radicalism, 97

Vietnam, 244–52
Verstehen, 141, 318, 325, 375
Voluntarism, 347, 356

Weltanschauung, 305
Women's movement, 317, 322; *see also* Feminism
World market, 91
World systems theory, 8, 75, 77, 159, 324